La Palabra Justa

A Glossary of
Academic Vocabulary for
Bilingual Teaching & Learning

La Palabra Justa

ENGLISH-SPANISH / ESPAÑOL-INGLÉS

A GLOSSARY OF
ACADEMIC VOCABULARY FOR
BILINGUAL TEACHING & LEARNING

EDITED BY

SHARON ADELMAN REYES
SALVADOR GABALDÓN
JOSÉ SEVERO MOREJÓN

WITH CONTRIBUTIONS BY

JAMES CRAWFORD • ZAHYLIS FERRO
SUZANNE KAPLAN • ALISA LECKIE
JEILYN MOREJÓN JIMÉNEZ • J. ANDRÉS RAMÍREZ
REGINA SURIEL • SARA TOLBERT

DiversityLearningK12

PORTLAND, OREGON

For permission to reprint, send email to:
info@diversitylearningk12.com
Or send postal mail to:
DiversityLearningK12
P. O. Box 19790
Portland, OR 97280

ISBN 978-0-9847317-2-5
Library of Congress Control Number: 2014906236

Library of Congress Subject Headings:
1. Education, bilingual—Study and teaching
2. Second language acquisition—Study and teaching
3. English language —Dictionaries—Spanish
4. Spanish language—Dictionaries—English

Book design and typography by James Crawford
Printed in the United States of America
First edition
10 9 8 7 6 5 4 3 2 1

CONTENTS

ENGLISH-SPANISH

ESPAÑOL-INGLÉS

Contents

Preface

By Sharon Adelman Reyes

Like many teachers of my generation, I was assigned to a bilingual classroom merely because of my Spanish surname. So, at the age of twenty-four, I found myself facing a classroom that I was largely unqualified to teach. My Spanish language ability was only at a conversational level. Not expecting to be a bilingual teacher, I had never taken a single university class that would prepare me to teach in two languages. My predicament was hardly unusual at that time in the Chicago Public Schools.

Nonetheless, I took my responsibility to the children seriously, returning to the university for advanced Spanish classes and working with a Spanish-language tutor. I also attended professional workshops on teaching bilingually and later earned a doctoral degree in curriculum design with a specialization in bilingual/bicultural teaching and learning.

It was an unexpected path to discovering my vocation. But I count myself very fortunate. My professional misplacement of long ago introduced me to a field that would become my passion. As a university professor, I was put in charge of developing and implementing a teacher preparation program in Spanish-English bilingual education. Students who chose this major were required to take courses in the foundations and methodology of bilingual education, along with advanced-level courses in the Spanish language. I thought I had all the important bases covered — until my students let me know otherwise.

As they began their clinical experiences, many asked for help in learning the specialized vocabulary needed to teach language arts, math, science, and social studies in Spanish. These requests came just as frequently from native speakers of Spanish born in the United States as from speakers of Spanish as a second language. Because Chicago was home to Spanish-speaking children and youth who came from all over Latin America, speaking a wide variety of regional dialects, my students were also concerned about variations in content area vocabulary

Although I immediately recognized the problem, the university offered no easy solution. The Department of Modern Languages had not been created to serve K–12 bilingual education majors, after all, either in Spanish or in other languages represented in my classes, such as Korean, Polish, Urdu, and Vietnamese, to name a few. It seemed to me that a comprehensive glossary for bilingual teachers would have been invaluable, especially for those entering the profession. Yet what I was looking for did not exist. The commercially available resources at that time, advertised as "Spanish for Special Purposes," consisted of specialized dictionaries for the medical and legal professions. Hardly what my university students needed as they prepared to teach math, science, social studies, and language arts.

Even primary-grade bilingual teachers are frequently challenged to use appropriate content-area vocabulary. For example, the multiple ways of signifying "addition" — with words such as *sum, add, plus,* and *combine* — can cause confusion for beginners in arithmetic. Not uncommonly, when facing such obstacles, teachers revert to English to provide the appropriate explanation. Aside from the well-known problems created by code-mixing during a lesson, such practices can also give students the false impression that Spanish lacks the sophistication of English in articulating academic material.

Several studies in recent years have confirmed that, all too often, bilingual teachers are poorly prepared to teach across the curriculum in Spanish.* Most often the cause is a lack of academic vocabulary in Spanish that is needed to access content in math, science, social studies, and even lan-

*See, e.g., Michael D. Guerrero, "Acquiring and Participating in the Use of Academic Spanish: Four Novice Latina Bilingual Education Teachers' Stories," *Journal of Latinos and Education* 2 (2003): 159–81; and Howard L. Fleischman & Paul J. Hopstock, *Descriptive Study of Services to Limited English Proficient Students,* Vol. 2: *Survey Results* (Washington DC: U.S. Department of Education, 1993).

guage arts. Such gaps are found even among otherwise fluent speakers of the language.

Of course, some bilingual teachers do develop academic vocabulary in Spanish through their reading of academic texts in Spanish. This approach, whenever feasible, is the ideal. Research shows that *academic language* is acquired much in the same way as *conversational language:* through understanding messages in that language, except that the "comprehensible input" is primarily written rather than spoken. Direct instruction in vocabulary — through flash-cards, repetition, and memorization — has proven far less effective. Instead, the most promising avenues are "extensive self-selected reading for pleasure, which provides the linguistic and conceptual background that makes academic reading more comprehensible, [and] selective reading of a large number of academic texts, in an area of great personal interest to the reader."[†] We wholeheartedly recommend these routes to competence in academic Spanish.

Yet we also recognize that educators' time and access to Spanish-language texts are often limited, while the everyday pressures of schooling are immediate. Classroom teachers must be able to identify *la palabra justa* — the right word — instantaneously when preparing a lesson, in order to provide both content instruction and second-language input at the same time. Academic language must be of high quality for bilingual education to be effective. In this situation, an English-Spanish/Español-Inglés glossary becomes an essential tool.

After searching in vain for such a volume, I discussed with one of my colleagues at Loyola University Chicago the idea of creating one. But to no avail. It was frustrating that we lacked the resources and institutional support to undertake a project of this magnitude. Finally, a decade later, I saw an opportunity to make it happen. As Program Director of DIVERSITYLEARN-INGK12, I now have the privilege of working with an impressive team of bilingual education specialists in the areas of literacy, math, science, social studies, technology, and the arts. By pooling our expertise, we have produced a comprehensive glossary tailored to the needs of Spanish-English bilingual practitioners, whether experienced teachers or novices.

[†]Stephen Krashen, "Comment," *Reading Research Quarterly,* 47(2012): 233.

LET ME INTRODUCE MY COEDITORS, who have brought a wealth of diverse experience to this project. **Salvador Gabaldón,** Director of Culturally Responsive Pedagogy for the Tucson Unified School District, also came to the field by chance. While teaching high-school English, he was recruited by the district's Bilingual Education and Hispanic Studies Department to promote the use of Mexican American literature.

In his subsequent career as a bilingual teacher, whether speaking Spanish with students or parents, Sal recalls many instances of struggling to find the right word for English terms such as *acquisition, budget, graph, metaphor, provide, semicolon,* or *waiver,* among many others. Although his Spanish vocabulary was extensive in the context of home and family, his schooling in Mexico had lasted just one year. As a result, he had developed virtually no academic vocabulary.

Whenever Sal reached for a word and came up empty, he had three ways of responding. Sometimes he would awkwardly substitute a term that didn't quite fit but helped to get the idea across — perhaps *dinero* for *budget.* Or he would take a wild guess that the Spanish was similar to the English, often leading to embarrassing "pochismos," such as *curriculo* for *curriculum* (instead of *plan de estudios*). Finally, he might simply use the English word, apologizing for his poor Spanish, and lamely asking listeners whether they understood. Invariably, students and parents would respond helpfully, but he could see the question in their eyes. Was this semi-bilingual teacher going to provide the quality of instruction that students deserved? Ultimately, Sal became fully proficient in academic Spanish, but he had to acquire it gradually through reading and through tedious trial and error in the classroom.

His experience was far from unique. In interactions with bilingual teachers, whether collaborating with colleagues, observing lessons, or attending parent meetings, he has often noticed hesitations and awkward phrasings as speakers struggle to find Spanish versions of words they know in English. Consider the difficulties of a bilingual teacher who began discussing a tragic incident with students in her high-school classroom, but was unfamiliar with the Spanish for *coroner* and *autopsy.* Substituting explanatory phrases for specific terms, she did admirably under the circumstances (*"el oficial que examina los cuerpos de las víctimas de un accidente para descubrir precísamente como murieron"*). But the process was unnecessarily taxing and painfully slow. Significantly, none of the Spanish-dominant students knew the Spanish terms either: *el médico forense* and *autopsia*, respectively.

This embarrassing episode could have been avoided if the teacher or her students had had ready access to a bilingual glossary covering high-school subject matter. It also illustrates that, while the social language learned at home is important, there are other types of vocabulary that are developed primarily in school. Sal has learned that it's necessary for teachers to explain this distinction to parents, who often wonder why their children should continue learning in Spanish after becoming proficient in English. At home, the student might learn that a frog has a hearing organ but no ears *("no tiene orejas pero sí tiene oídos")*. But in science class she will encounter more specific vocabulary *("no tiene pabellones auditivos, diferenciándose únicamente una membrana timpánica superficial.")* To be effective, of course, teachers must have a firm command of academic vocabulary themselves.

* * *

GLOSSARY COEDITOR **José Severo Morejón** contributes yet another perspective. As an English professor at the Pedagogical University "Rafael María de Mendive" in Pinar del Río, Cuba, he has taught English for more than forty years. For the last thirty, he has prepared English language teachers for the elementary, secondary, and preuniversity levels, as well as for adult language schools throughout the province. In addition, his department oversees the teaching of English for specific purposes, including careers in mathematics, technical sciences, computing, and social sciences. Lacking specialized texts and glossaries designed to cover these subjects, José and his colleagues have had to rely on general English dictionaries. This has been especially problematic in teacher education.

Earlier in his career, when José taught English to students of music and plastic arts, he encountered the same problem in those fields. As a result, his students often had difficulty with simple terms such as *artwork, brush, clay, fresco, easel, bass clef,* and *choir.* Later he taught prospective teachers of English, using the arts — especially music, painting, and film — to help develop their communicative competence. Once again, the lack of glossaries related to these fields made teaching more difficult. It required the students to learn specialized terms exclusively from their professor, José recalls, and also hindered them in completing independent work assignments. While online dictionaries now exist, many of the students lived in remote areas where Internet service was unavailable.

Students in other Latin American countries, such as Guyana and Venezuela, face similar challenges. General dictionaries can be helpful in some cases, but can be confusing and time-consuming to use when seeking specialized terms. So José was enthusiastic about joining a project to create a glossary targeted to the specific needs of language teachers, both English and Spanish. He notes that, while dialect differences exist between countries in the Caribbean and South and Central America, these apply mainly to everyday vocabulary. For academic terms there is much more standardization.

* * *

OUR EDITORIAL TEAM ALSO INCLUDES the following teachers, teacher educators, and other bilingual professionals who contributed sections of the glossary and reviewed them for accuracy: **Alisa Leckie, Ph.D.,** Assistant Professor of Teaching & Learning, Georgia Southern University; **Suzanne Kaplan, Ph.D.,** Adjunct Assistant Professor of Education, University of Arizona, and Curriculum Specialist for the Arizona School Transformation Group; **J. Andrés Ramirez, Ph.D.,** Assistant Professor of Curriculum, Culture, and Educational Inquiry, Florida Atlantic University; **Regina Suriel, Ph.D.,** Assistant Professor of Education, Valdosta State University; **Sara Tolbert, Ph.D.,** Assistant Professor of Teaching, Learning, and Sociocultural Studies, University of Arizona; **Zahylis Ferro,** a former bilingual teacher in the Miami-Dade County Public Schools; **Jeilyn Morejon Jiménez,** a graduate student in language education at the University of British Columbia; and **Nelda Reyes,** an actress, musician, and translator in Portland, Oregon. In addition, **James Crawford,** President of DIVERSITYLEARNINGK12 LLC, served as production editor, book designer, and typographer.

• •

Finally, we gratefully acknowledge the valuable assistance provided by **Dr. Mary Carol Combs,** of the University of Arizona; **Dr. Victor R. Ferro,** of La Universidad Autónoma de Madrid; **Dr. Jaume Gelabert,** of Arcadia University; and by the following colleagues at La Universidad de Ciencias Pedagógicas "Rafael María de Mendive" in Pinar del Río, Cuba: **Lic. Eida Aguiar Hernández, MSc. María Carolina Mora Herryman, MSc. Teresa Iglesias Hernández, Dr. C. Jesús Miranda, Dra. C. Débora Mainegra Fernández,** and **MSc. Odalys Estrada Molina.**

How to Use This Glossary

....

*L*A PALABRA JUSTA was compiled by and for Spanish-English bilingual educators, covering key terms in literacy, the arts, technology, and academic content areas. It is not meant to be used as an introductory phrase book for school personnel, nor as a list of key words to be explicitly taught. Rather, it is a reference tool specifically designed to meet the needs of language teachers and learners.

The glossary includes no guides to grammar or pronunciation. A basic knowledge of both languages is assumed. To keep the volume concise and easy to use, we have focused on specialized academic vocabulary, grouped separately by discipline. A mathematics teacher, for example, can go directly to the *Arithmetic & Algebra/Aritmética y Algebra* subsection to find the Spanish word for *power* or the English word for *potencia*. Because entries are translated in a specific context, unlike dictionary definitions, there is no need to sort through numerous possible meanings (e.g., *poder, capacidad, facultad, autoridad, potestad, fuerza, influencia, impacto, energía, electricidad*) to find the one that is relevant for a math lesson. We have included synonyms or variations where appropriate, while avoiding lengthy definitions.

For the sake of clarity and simplicity, language mechanics are kept to a minimum. Parts of speech are identified in italics for each boldfaced entry, which may include masculine and feminine forms, followed by a translation and by italicized gender markings for Spanish nouns. In addition, alternate uses of a word or phrase are noted in abbreviated form, as follows:

> **power** *n.* (exponent) potencia *f.;* **p. of**
>   **ten** potencia de diez
> **predict** *v.* predecir
> **prediction** *n.* predicción *f.*
> **prime** *adj.* primo, -ma; **p. factorization** *n.* factori-
>   zación de primos *f.,* descomposición en factores
>   primos *f.;* **p. number** número primo *m.*

A final note: Because this volume is tailored to the needs of bilingual teachers in the United States, it gives preference to the varieties of Spanish spoken by their students — that is, to the Spanish of Latin America and the Caribbean.

ENGLISH-SPANISH

LANGUAGE ARTS

Grammar & Composition

A

abbreviation *n.* abreviatura *f.*

abridge *v.* abreviar

abstract *n.* resumen *m.,* sinopsis *f.*
  accent *n.* acento *m.;* **a. mark** tilde
  f., acento ortográfico *m.;* **acute a.**
  acento agudo

acronym *n.* acrónimo *m.*

action verb *n.* verbo de acción *m.*

active voice *n.* voz activa *f.*

adjective *n.* adjetivo *m.;* **a. phrase**
  frase adjetiva *f.;* **comparative a.**
  adjetivo comparativo; **compound
  a.** adjetivo compuesto; **indefinite
  a.** adjetivo indefinido; **predicate
  a.** adjetivo predicativo; **superlative a.** adjetivo superlativo

adverb *n.* adverbio *m.*

affirmative *adj.* afirmativo, -va

affix *n.* afijo *m.*

alphabet *n.* alfabeto *m.*

ampersand *n.* signo et *m.,* símbolo
  & *m.,* ampersand *m.*

antecedent *n.* antecedente *m.*

antonym *n.* antónimo *m.*

apostrophe *n.* apóstrofo *m.,* virguilla *f.*

append *v.* anexar

appositive *n.* apositivo *m.*

archaic *adj.* arcaico, -ca

argumentation *n.* argumento *m.*

article *n.* artículo *m.;* **definite a.**
  artículo definido; **indefinite a.**
  artículo indefinido

asterisk *n.* asterisco *m.*

attribution *n.* atribución *f.*

auxiliary verb *n.* verbo auxiliar *m.*

awkward construction *n.* construcción inadecuada *f.*

B

begging the question *n.* petición
  de principio *m.*

bibliography *n.* bibliografía *f.*

blend *n.* mezcla *f.*

blend *v.* mezclar

body *n.* cuerpo *m.*

boldface *n.* negrita *f.*

LANGUAGE ARTS

brackets *n.* corchetes *m.pl.*

brainstorm *v.* hacer lluvia de ideas

brainstorming *n.* lluvia de ideas *f.,* puesta en común *f.*

C

calligraphy *n.* caligrafía *f.*

capital letter *n.* mayúscula *f.*

capitalization *n.* uso de mayúsculas *m.*

capitalize *v.* escribir con mayúscula

card catalog *n.* tarjeta de catálogo *f.*

case *n.* caso *m.;* **objective c.** caso objetivo; **subjective c.** caso nominativo, primer caso

character *n.* (letter) carácter *m.*

chart *n.* tabla *f.,* grafica *f.,* gráfico *m.*

chronological *adj.* cronológico, -ca; **c. order** *n.* orden cronológico *m.*

circular reasoning *n.* razonamiento circular *m.*

circumlocution *n.* circunlocución *f.*

citation *n.* citación *f.*

clarity *n.* claridad *f.*

clause *n.* oración *f.,* cláusula *f.;* **conditional c.** oración condicional, cláusula condicional; **dependent c.** oración dependiente, cláusula dependiente; **independent c.** oración principal, cláusula independiente; **relative c.** oración relativa, cláusula de relativo; **subordinate c.** oración subordinada, cláusula subordinada

cliché *n.* cliché *m.*

closing *n.* (letter) despedida *f.*

cognate *n.* cognado *m.,* palabra afín

f.; **false c.** cognado falso

coherence *n.* coherencia *f.*

collaborate *v.* colaborar

collaboration *n.* colaboración *f.*

collaborative *adj.* colaborativo, -va; **c. writing** *n.* escritura colaborativa *f.*

colloquial *adj.* coloquial

colloquialism *n.* coloquialismo *m.*

colon *n.* dos puntos *m.pl.*

column *n.* columna *f.*

comma *n.* coma *f.*

command *n.* comando *m.,* orden *f.*

command *v.* comandar, ordenar

communication *n.* comunicación *f.*

comparative adjective *n.* adjetivo comparativo *m.*

comparison *n.* comparación *f.*

compile *v.* compilar, recopilar

complement *n.* complemento *m.*

complete sentence *n.* oración completa *f.*

complex *adj.* complejo, -ja; **c. sentence** *n.* oración compleja *f.*

compose *v.* componer, redactar

composition *n.* composición *f.,* redacción *f.*

compound *adj.* compuesto, -ta; **c. adjective** *n.* adjetivo compuesto *m.;* **c. sentence** oración compuesta *f.;* **c. verb** verbo compuesto *m.;* **c. word** palabra compuesta *f.*

compound-complex sentence *n.* oración compuesta compleja *f.*

comprehension *n.* comprensión *f.*

concept *n.* concepto *m.*

● ●

concise *adj.* conciso, -sa

concrete *adj.* concreto, -ta

condense *v.* abreviar, resumir, compendiar

conditional *adj.* condicional; **c. clause** *n.* oración condicional *f.*, cláusula condicional *f.*

conjunction *n.* conjunción *f.;* **coordinating c.** conjunción coordinante; **correlative c.** conjunción correlativa; **subordinating c.** conjunción subordinada

connotation *n.* connotación *f.*

consecutive *adj.* consecutivo, -va

consonant *n.* consonante *f.;* **beginning c.** consonante inicial; **c. blend** grupo consonántico *m.;* **c. substitution** sustitución de consonante *f.;* **ending c.** consonante final

constructive criticism *n.* crítica constructiva *f.*

content *n.* contenido *m.*

contraction *n.* contracción *f.*

contradiction *n.* contradicción *f.*

contrast *n.* contraste *m.*

coordinating conjunction *n.* conjunción coordinativa *f.*

correct *adj.* correcto, -ta

correct *v.* corregir

correlation as causation *n.* correlación como causalidad *f.*

correlative conjunction *n.* conjunción correlativa *f.*

creative writing *n.* escritura creativa *f.*

cross-reference *n.* referencia cruzada *f.*

cursive *adj.* cursivo, -va; **c. writing** *n.* letra cursiva *f.*

D

dash *n.* raya *f.*

debate *n.* debate *m.*

declarative sentence *n.* oración declarativa *f.*, declaración *f.*

decode *v.* decodificar

decoding strategies *n.pl.* estrategias para decodificar *f.*

deductive reasoning *n.* razonamiento deductivo *m.*

definite article *n.* artículo definido *m.*

definition *n.* definición *f.*

delete *v.* borrar

demonstrative pronoun *n.* pronombre demostrativo *m.*

denotation *n.* denotación *f.*, significado *m.*

dependent clause *n.* oración dependiente *f.*, cláusula dependiente *f.*

details *n.pl.* detalles *m.;* **relevant supporting d.** información relevante *f.*, detalles que fortalecen el argumento *m.pl.*

diacritical marks *n.pl.* signos diacríticos *m.*

dictionary *n.* diccionario *m.;* **d. entry** entrada del diccionario *f.;* **geographic d.** diccionario geográfico; **picture d.** diccionario ilustrado; **rhyming d.** diccionario de rima; **surname d.** diccionario de apellidos

LANGUAGE ARTS

diminutive *adj.* diminutivo, -va

diphthong *n.* diptongo *m.*

direct object *n.* objeto directo *m.*, complemento directo *m.*

directions *n.pl.* instrucciones *f.*

discussion *n.* discusión *f.*

documentation *n.* documentación *f.*

double negative *n.* negación doble *f.*

draft *n.* borrador *m.*

draft *v.* redactar, hacer un borrador de

E

edit *v.* editar, corregir

ellipsis *n.* elipsis *f.*, puntos suspensivos *m.pl.*

elliptical *adj.* elíptico, -ca

encyclopedia *n.* enciclopedia *f.*

endnote *n.* nota al final *f.*

entry *n.* entrada *f.*, anotación *f.*

enumeration *n.* enumeración *f.*

enunciate *v.* enunciar

enunciation *n.* enunciación *f.*

epithet *n.* epíteto *m.*

etymology *n.* etimología *f.*

evidence *n.* evidencia *f.*, prueba *f.*

exclamation mark *n.* signo de exclamación, signo de admiración *m.*

exclamatory sentence *n.* oración exclamativa *f.*

explanatory note *n.* nota explicativa *f.*

exposition *n.* exposición *f.*

expository *adj.* expositivo, -va; **e. text** *n.* texto expositivo *m.*; **e. writing** escritura expositiva *f.*

F

fact *n.* hecho *m.*

feedback *n.* retroalimentación *f.*

figure of speech *n.* figura del discurso *f.*

first person *n.* primera persona *f.*

footnote *n.* nota al pie de página *f.*

foreign word *n.* palabra extranjera *f.*

format *n.* formato *m.*

fragment *n.* fragmento *m.*

future *adj.* futuro, -ra

future tense *n.* futuro *m.*; **f. perfect tense** futuro perfecto

G

gender *n.* género *m.*

generality *n.* generalidad *f.*

generalization *n.* generalización *f.*

generalize *v.* generalizar

gerund *n.* gerundio *m.*

glossary *n.* glosario *m.*

grammar *n.* gramática *f.*

grammatical *adj.* gramatical; **g. form** *n.* forma gramatical *f.*; **g. rule** regla gramatical *f.*

graph *n.* gráfico, -ca *m.f.*

grapheme *n.* grafema *m.*

graphic organizer *n.* organizador gráfico *m.*

greeting *n.* (letter) saludo *m.*

H

handwriting *n.* escritura a mano *f.*

heading *n.* encabezamiento *m.*, título *m.*

headline *n.* titular *m.*, encabezado *m.*

homograph *n.* homógrafo *m.*

· ·

homonym *n.* homónimo *m.*

homophone *n.* homófono *m.*

hyphen *n.* guión *m.*

hyphenation *n.* separación silábica *f.*

I

idiom *n.* expresión idiomática *f.*

idiomatic *adj.* idiomático, -ca

imperative *adj.* imperativo, -va; **i. mood** *n.* modo imperativo *m.;* **i. sentence** *n.* oración imperativa *f.*

indefinite *adj.* indefinido, -da; **i. adjective** *n.* adjetivo indefinido *m.;* **i. article** artículo indefinido *m.;* **i. pronoun** pronombre indefinido *m.*

indentation *n.* sangría *f.*

indent *v.* sangrar, poner sangría

indented *adj.* sangrado, -da

independent clause *n.* cláusula independiente *f.,* oración principal *f.*

indicative *adj.* indicativo, -va; **i. mood** *n.* modo indicativo *m.*

indirect object *n.* objeto indirecto *m.,* complemento indirecto *m.*

inductive reasoning *n.* razonamiento inducido *m.*

infinitive *n.* infinitivo *m.;* **split i.** infinitivo dividido

inflection *n.* inflexión *f.*

interjection *n.* interjección *f.*

interrogative *adj.* interrogativo, -va; **i. pronoun** *n.* pronombre interrogativo *m.;* **i. sentence** oración interrogativa *f.*

interview *n.* entrevista *f.*

intransitive verb *n.* verbo intransitivo *m.*

irregular verb *n.* verbo irregular *m.*

italicize *v.* poner in bastardilla, poner in cursiva

italicized *adj.* bastardilla; cursivo, -va

italics *n.pl.* bastardilla *f.,* cursiva *f.,* itálicas *f.*

J

jargon *n.* jerga *f.*

jingle *n.* cancioncilla *f.*

juxtaposition *n.* yuxtaposición *f.*

L

language *n.* idioma *m.,* lengua *f.;* **l. acquisition** adquisición del idioma *f.;* **target l.** idioma de llegada, idioma de destino

legend *n.* (map) leyenda *f.*

legible *adj.* legible

letter *n.* (writing) carta *f.;* (type) letra *f.;* **business l.** carta de negocio

letter-sound relationship *n.* relación grafofonética *f.*

lexicon *n.* léxico *m.*

libel *n.* libelo *m.*

library *n.* biblioteca *f.;* **l. catalog** catálogo bibliográfico *m.*

linguistics *n.* lingüística *f.*

linking verb *n.* verbo atributivo, verbo copulativo *m.*

literal *adj.* literal; **l. translation** *n.* traducción literal *f.*

log *n.* registro *m.,* diario *m.,* bitácora *f.*

logic *n.* lógica *f.*

LANGUAGE ARTS

7

LANGUAGE ARTS

logical *adj.* lógico, -ca
long vowel *n.* vocal larga *f.*
lower case *adj.* minúsculo, -la; **l. c. letter** *n.* letra minúscula *f.*

M
main idea *n.* idea principal *f.*
map *n.* mapa *m.*
margin *n.* margen *m.*
mass media *n.pl.* medios de difusión, medios de comunicación *m.*
memo *n.* nota *f.*
misprint *n.* error tipográfico *m.*
misspell *v.* escribir incorrectamente, deletrear mal
misspelling *n.* error de ortografía *m.*
mnemonic device *n.* recurso mnemotécnico *m.*
mood *n.* modo *m.;* **imperative m.** modo imperativo; **indicative m.** modo indicativo; **subjunctive m.** modo subjuntivo
morphology *n.* morfología *f.*

N
name *n.* nombre *m.;* **first n., given n.** nombre de pila; **last n.** apellido; **maiden n.** nombre de soltera; **middle n.** segundo nombre
negative *adj.* negativo, -va
neologism *n.* neologismo *m.*
newsletter *n.* boletín informativo *m.*
newspaper *n.* periódico *m.*
nickname *n.* apodo *m.,* nombrete *m.*
nonverbal *adj.* no verbal
notes *n.pl.* apuntes *m.*
noun *n.* sustantivo *m.,* nombre *m.;*

proper n. nombre propio
nuance *n.* matiz *m.*
number *n.* número *m.*

O
object *n.* objeto *m.,* complemento *m.;* **direct o.** objeto directo, complemento directo; **indirect o.** objeto indirecto, complemento indirecto; **o. of the preposition** objeto de la preposición, objeto preposicional, complemento de la preposición
objective *adj.* objetivo -va; **o. case** *n.* caso objetivo *m.*
obscene *adj.* obseno, -na
obsolete *adj.* obsoleto, -ta
opinion *n.* opinión *f.*
oral *adj.* oral; **o. presentation** *n.* presentación oral *f.;* **o. report** reporte oral *m.*
organizational patterns *n.pl.* patrones de organización *m.*
outline *n.* esbozo *m.,* boceto *m.*
overgeneralization *n.* sobregeneralización *f.*
overstatement *n.* exageración *f.*

P
page *n.* página *f.*
paragraph *n.* párrafo *m.*
parallel structure *n.* estructura paralela *f.*
parallelism *n.* paralelismo *m.*
paraphrase *n.* paráfrasis *f.*
paraphrase *v.* parafrasear
parenthesis *n.* paréntesis *m.*

• •

part of speech *n.* categoría gramatical *f.*

participle *n.* participio *m.*

passive voice *n.* voz pasiva *f.*

past *adj.* pasado, -da; **p. participle** *n.* pasado participio *m.*

past tense *n.* pasado *m.;* **p. perfect tense** pasado perfecto

patronymic *n.* patronímico *m.*

period *n.* punto *m.*

person *n.* persona *f.;* **first p.** primera persona; **second p.** segunda persona; **third p.** tercera persona

personal *adj.* personal; **p. attack** *n.* ataque personal *m.;* **p. connections** *n.pl.* conecciones personales *f.;* **p. narrative** narración personal *f.*

phoneme *n.* fonema *m.*

phrase *n.* frase *f.*

picture dictionary *n.* diccionario ilustrado *m.*

plagiarism *n.* plagio *m.*

plural *adj. & n.* plural *m.*

portfolio *n.* portafolio *m.*

possessive *adj.* posesivo, -va

predicate *adj.* predicativo, -va

predicate *n.* predicado *m.;* **p. adjective** adjetivo predicativo *m.;* **p. nominative** predicado nominal

prefix *n.* prefijo *m.*

preposition *n.* preposición *f.*

prepositional phrase *n.* frase preposicional *f.*

present *adj.* presente; **p. participle** *n.* presente participio *m.*

present tense *n.* presente *m.;* **p.**

perfect tense presente perfecto

prewriting *n.* plan de escritura *m.,* proceso previo a la escritura *m.*

primary source *n.* fuente primaria, fuente principal *f.*

print *n.* letra *f.*

print *v.* imprimir

printer *n.* impresor, -ora *m.f.*

problem *n.* problema *m.,* dificultad *f.*

pronoun *n.* pronombre *m.;* **indefinite p.** pronombre indefinido; **reflexive p.** pronombre reflexivo; **relative p.** pronombre relativo

pronunciation *n.* pronunciación *f.*

proofread *v.* corregir

proper noun *n.* nombre propio *m.*

punctuation *n.* puntuación *f.*

Q

question *n.* pregunta *f.;* **begging the q.** petición de principio *f.;* **q. mark** signo de interrogación *m.*

question *v.* preguntar

quotation *n.* cita *f.;* **direct q.** cita directa; **divided q.** cita dividida; **q. dictionary** diccionario de citas *m.;* **q. marks** comillas *f.pl.*

R

read-aloud *n.* lectura en voz alta *f.*

reading *n.* lectura *f.;* **r. log** registro de lectura *m.,* diario de lectura *m.*

reasoning *n.* razonamiento *m.;* **circular r.** razonamiento circular; **deductive r.** razonamiento deductivo; **inductive r.** razonamiento inductivo

redraft *v.* reescribir, redactar de nuevo

redundancy *n.* redundancia *f.*

redundant *adj.* redundante

reference materials *n.pl.* materiales de referencia *f.*

reflection *n.* reflexión *f.*

reflexive pronoun *n.* pronombre reflexivo *m.*

regular verb *n.* verbo regular *m.*

relative *adj.* relativo, -va; **r. clause** *n.* oración relativa *f.*, cláusula de relativo *f.;* **r. pronoun** pronombre relativo *m.*

relevant *adj.* relevante

repeat *v.* repetir

report *n.* reporte *m.*, informe *m.*, reportaje *m.*

research paper *n.* trabajo de investigación *m.*

résumé *n.* curriculum vitae *m.*, hoja de vida *f.*

revise *v.* revisar, corregir

revised *adj.* revisado, -da

revision *n.* revisión *f.*, corrección *f.*

rewrite *v.* reescribir

rewritten *adj.* reescrito, -ta

rhyme *n.* rima *f.*

rhyming dictionary *n.* diccionario de rimas *m.*

Roman type *n.* romana *f.*

root word *n.* raíz de la palabra *f.*

rubric *n.* rúbrica *f.*

run-on sentence *n.* oración inconexa, oración seguida *f.*

S

salutation *n.* saludo *m.*

script *n.* (writing) caligrafía *f.*

second person *n.* segunda persona *f.*

secondary source *n.* fuente secundaria *f.*

semantics *n.* semántica *f.*

semicolon *n.* punto y coma *m.*

sentence *n.* oración *f.;* **complete s.** oración completa; complete s. oración compleja; **compound-complex s.** oración compuesta compleja; **declarative s.** oración declarativa; **exclamatory s.** oración exclamativa; **imperative s.** oración imperativa; **interrogative s.** oración interrogativa; **run-on s.** oración inconexa; **s. combining** combinación de oraciones *f.;* **s. fragment** fragmento de oración; **s. structure** estructura de la oración *f.;* **simple s.** oración simple; **topic s.** oración principal

shared *adj.* compartido, -da; **s. reading** *n.* lectura compartida *f.;* **s. writing** escritura compartida *f.*

short vowel *n.* vocal corta *f.*

sight word *n.* palabra a simple vista *f.*

signature *n.* firma *f.*

singular *adj. & n.* singular *m.*

skim *v.* hojear, examinar superficialmente

slang *n.* jerga *f.*

slogan *n.* eslogan *m.*

Socratic seminar *n.* seminario socrático *m.*

source *n.* fuente *f.*

space *n.* espacio *m.*

speech *n.* discurso *m.*

spell *v.* deletrear

spelling *n.* ortografía *f.,* deletreo *m.*

split infinitive *n.* infinitivo dividido *m.*

standard English *n.* inglés estándar *m.*

stress *n.* (syllable) acento *m.*

style manual *n.* manual de estilo *m.*

subhead *n.* subtítulo *m.*

subject *n.* (grammar) sujeto *m.,* (topic) tema *m.,* (plot) asunto *m.*

subjective *adj.* subjetivo, -va; **s. case** *n.* caso nominativo, primer caso *m.*

subject-verb agreement *n.* concordancia entre sujeto y verbo *f.*

subjunctive *adj.* subjuntivo, -va

subordinate clause *n.* oración subordinada *f.,* cláusula subordinada *f.*

subordinating conjunction *n.* conjunción subordinada *f.*

substitution *n.* sustitución *f.;* **consonant s.** sustitución de consonante

suffix *n.* sufijo *m.*

summarize *v.* resumir

summary *n.* resumen *m.*

superlative adjective *n.* adjectivo superlativo *m.*

surname *n.* apellido *m.;* **s. diction-**ary diccionario de apellidos *m.*

syllabication *n.* silabeo *m.*

syllable *n.* sílaba *m.*

synonym *n.* sinónimo *m.*

synopsis *n.* sinopsis *f.*

syntax *n.* sintaxis *f.*

T

table *n.* (text) tabla *f.,* cuadro *m.*

target language *n.* idioma de llegada, idioma de destino *m.*

tense *n.* tiempo *m.;* **t. shift** cambio de tiempo *m.*

tension *n.* tensión *f.*

thesaurus *n.* tesauro *m.,* diccionario de ideas afines *m.*

third person *n.* tercera persona *f.*

topic *n.* tema *m.,* asunto *m.,* argumento *m.;* **t. sentence** oración principal *f.*

train of thought *n.* secuencia de pensamiento *f.*

transition *n.* transición *f.*

transitive verb *n.* verbo transitivo *m.*

translate *v.* traducir

translation *n.* traducción *f.;* **literal t.** traducción literal; **simultaneous t.** traducción simultánea

typeface *n.* letra de imprenta *f.*

typographical error *n.* error tipográfico *m.*

U

upper case *adj.* mayúsculo, -la; **u. c. letter** *n.* mayúscula *f.*

usage *n.* uso *m.*

LANGUAGE ARTS

11

LANGUAGE ARTS

V

valid *adj.* válido, -da
validity *n.* validez *f.*
variant *n.* variante *f.*
verb *n.* verbo *m.;* **action v.** verbo de acción; **auxiliary v.** verbo auxiliar; **compound v.** verbo compuesto; **intransitive v.** verbo intransitivo; **irregular v.** verbo irregular; **linking v.** verbo atributivo, verbo copulativo; **regular v.** verbo regular; **transitive v.** verbo transitivo; **v. phrase** frase verbal *f.*
verbal *adj.* verbal
vocabulary *n.* vocabulario *m.*
voice *n.* voz *f.;* **active v.** voz activa; **passive v.** voz pasiva
vowel *n.* vocal *f.;* **long v.** vocal larga; **short v.** vocal corta; **v. combination** combinación de vocales *f.;* **v. sound** sonido de vocal *m.*
vulgar *adj.* vulgar
vulgarity *n.* vulgaridad *f.*, vulgarismo *m.*

W

word *n.* palabra *f.;* **compound w.** palabra compuesta; **foreign w.** palabra extranjera; **sight w.** palabra a golpe de vista; **w. processing** procesamiento de texto *m.*
works cited *n.pl.* obras citadas *f.*
write *v.* escribir
writing escritura *f.*, redacción *f.;* **expository w.** escritura expositiva
written *adj.* escrito, -ta

Literature

A

abridged *adj.* abreviado, -da
abstract *adj.* abstracto, -ta
acknowledgments *n.pl.* agradecimientos *m.*
action *n.* acción *f.;* **falling a.** acción descendente; **rising a.** acción ascendente
adaptation *n.* adaptación *f.*
adapted *adj.* adaptado, -da
aesthetic *adj.* estético, -ca; **a. purpose** *n.* propósito estético *m.;* **a. quality** calidad estética *f.*

allegory *n.* alegoría *f.*
alliteration *n.* aliteración *f.*
allusion *n.* alusión *f.*
almanac *n.* calendario *m.*, almanaque *m.*
ambience *n.* ambiente *m.*
ambiguity *n.* ambigüedad *f.*
analogy *n.* analogía *f.*
analysis *n.* análisis *m.;* **structural a.** análisis estructural
anecdote *n.* anécdota *f.*
annotated bibliography *n.* bibliografía comentada *f.*

anonymous *adj.* anónimo, -ma
antagonist *n.* antagonista *m.f.*
anthology *n.* antología *f.*
anticlimax *n.* anticlímax *f.,* decepción *f.*
antihero *n.* antihéroe *m.*
apocryphal *adj.* apócrifo, -fa
appeal to authority *n.* apelación a la autoridad *f.*
appendix *n.* apéndice *f.*
archetype *n.* arquetipo *m.*
article *n.* artículo *m.*
articulation *n.* articulación *f.*
artifact *n.* artefacto *m.,* objeto de arte *m.*
assonance *n.* asonancia *f.*
audience *n.* audiencia *f.,* público *m.,* auditorio *m.*
author *n.* autor, -ora *m.f.;* **a.'s purpose** propósito del autor *m.;* **a.'s bias** influencia del autor *f.*
autobiography *n.* autobiografía *f.*
autograph *n.* autógrafo *m.*
avant-garde *adj.* de vanguardia
avant-garde *n.* vanguardia *f.*

B

background *n.* trasfondo *m.,* antecedentes *m.pl.*
ballad *n.* balada *f.*
bard *n.* poeta *m.f.,* bardo *m.*
belief system *n.* sistema de creencias *m.*
bias *n.* influencia *m.*
bibliography *n.* bibliografía *f.;* **annotated b.** bibliografía comentada
biography *n.* biografía *f.*

blank verse *n.* verso libre *m.*
book *n.* libro *m.;* **chapter b.** libro de capítulos; **picture b.** libro ilustrado; **wordless b.** libro sin texto
bookstore *n.* librería *f.*
brochure *n.* folleto *m.*

C

cadence *n.* cadencia *f.*
canon *n.* (literature) canon *m.*
cast of characters *n.* reparto de personajes *m.*
causation *n.* causalidad *f.*
cause and effect *n.* causa y efecto *f.*
censor *v.* censurar
censorship *n.* censura *f.*
chapter *n.* capítulo *m.;* **c. book** libro de capítulos
character *n.* personaje *m.,* carácter *m.;* **c. development** desarrollo del personaje *m.;* **c. trait** rasgo del carácter de personaje *m.;* **flat c.** personaje plano; **main c.** personaje principal; **minor c.** personaje secundario; **round c.** personaje redondo; **static c.** personaje estático
characterization *n.* caracterización *f.*
choral reading *n.* lectura en coro *f.*
chorus *n.* coro *m.*
chronicles *n.pl.* crónicas *f.*
chronology *n.* cronología *f.*
classical *adj.* clásico, -ca; **c. text** *n.* texto clásico *m.*
classics *n.pl.* clásicos *m.*
cliffhanger *n.* suspenso *m.*
climax *n.* clímax *m.*
clincher *n.* argumento decisivo, ar-

LANGUAGE ARTS

gumento final *m.*

clue *n.* pista *f.*

coauthor *n.* coautor, -ora *m.f.*

collection *n.* colección *f.;* **c. of stories** colección de historias, colección de cuentos

comedy *n.* comedia *f.*

compare and contrast *v.* comparar y contrastar

conclusion *n.* conclusión *f.,* fin *m.;* **draw c.** *v.* sacar conclusión

condensed *adj.* condensado, -da; **c. version** *n.* versión condensada *f.*

conflict *n.* conflicto *m.;* **c. resolution** solución del conflicto *f.;* **external c.** conflicto externo; **internal c.** conflicto interno; **interpersonal c.** conflicto interpersonal

consonance *n.* consonancia *f.*

contemporary text *n.* texto contemporáneo *m.*

context *n.* contexto *m.;* **c. clue** clave de contexto *f.*

convention *n.* convención *f.*

copyright *n.* derechos de autor *m.pl.*

couplet *n.* copla *f.*

cover *n.* (book) portada *f.;* **back c.** contraportada *f.;* **front c.** cubierta *f.*

credibility *n.* credibilidad *f.*

credible *adj.* creíble

crime novel *n.* novela policiaca *f.*

criteria *n.pl.* criterios *m.*

critical analysis *n.* análisis crítico *m.*

criticism *n.,* **critique** *n.* crítica *f.*

culture *n.* cultura *f.*

D

dedication *n.* dedicatoria *f.*

denouement *n.* desenlace *m.*

description *n.* descripción *f.;* **physical d.** descripción física

descriptive language *n.* lenguaje descriptivo *m.*

detective story *n.* novela policiaca *f.*

device *n.* recurso *m.*

dialect *n.* dialecto *m.*

dialogue *n.* diálogo *m.*

diarist *n.* diarista *m.f.*

diary *n.* diario *m.*

diction *n.* dicción *f.*

direct address *n.* discurso directo *m.*

discourse *n.* discurso *m.,* disertación *f.*

drama *n.* drama *m.*

drama-documentary *n.* docudrama *m.*

dramatic *adj.* dramático, -ca; **d. dialogue** *n.* diálogo dramático *m.*

E

edition *n.* edición *m.f.*

editor *n.* editor, -ora *m.;* redactor, -ora *m.f.*

editorial *n.* editorial *f.*

elaboration *n.* elaboración *f.*

elegy *n.* elegía *f.*

emotional appeal *n.* apelación emocional *f.*

emphasis *n.* énfasis *m.*

ending *n.* fin *m.,* final *m.;* **open e.** final abierto

epic *adj.* épico, -ca; **e. poem** *n.* poema épico *m.,* epopeya *f.*

epigraph *n.* epígrafe *m.*

episode *n.* episodio *m.*

episodic *adj.* episódico, -ca

essay *n.* ensayo *m.*

essence *n.* esencia *f.*

euphemism *n.* eufemismo *m.*

evocative *adj.* evocador, -ora; evocativo, -va

evoke *v.* evocar

excerpt *n.* extracto *m.*, segmento *m.*

explicit *adj.* explícito, -ta; **e. theme** *n.* tema explícito *m.*

expressive *adj.* expresivo, -va; **e. writing** *n.* escritura expresiva *f.*

F

fable *n.* fábula *f.*

fairy tale *n.* cuento de hadas *m.*

fallacious *adj.* engañoso, -sa; falaz

fallacy *n.* falacia *f.*

falling action *n.* acción descendente *f.*

fantasy *n.* fantasía *f.*

farce *n.* farsa *f.*

feature story *n.* reportaje principal *m.*

fiction *n.* ficción *f.*, novela *f.*; **science f.** ciencia ficción

fictional narrative *n.* narración de ficción *f.*

figurative *adj.* figurativo, -va; **f. language** *n.* lenguaje figurativo *m.*

figure of speech *n.* figura retórica *f.*

film review *n.* reseña de cine *f.*

flashback *n.* escena retrospectiva *f.*

fluency *n.* fluidez *f.*

folktale *n.* cuento tradicional *m.*

foreshadow *v.* presagiar, anunciar

foreword *n.* prólogo *m.*

free verse *n.* verso libre *m.*

G

genre *n.* género *m.*

ghost story *n.* cuento de fantasmas *m.*

ghost writer *n.* escritor (-ora) fantasma *m.f.*

gist *n.* esencia *f.*

Gothic *adj.* gótico, -ca

guided reading *n.* lectura guiada *f.*

guilt by association *n.* culpabilidad por asociación *f.*

H

hackneyed *adj.* trillado, -da; manido, -da

haiku *n.* haiku *m.*

hardcover *n.* cubierta dura *f.*

hero *n.* héroe *m.*

heroine *n.* heroína *f.*

hierarchic structure *n.* estructura jerárquica *f.*

historical *adj.* histórico, -ca; **h. fiction** *n.* ficción histórica *f.*; **h. narrative** narración histórica *f.*

hostile audience *n.* auditorio hostil *m.*, público hostil *m.*

humor *n.* humor *m.*

hyperbole *n.* hipérbole *f.*

hypothesis *n.* hipótesis *f.*

I

iambic pentameter *n.* pentámetro yámbico *m.*

LANGUAGE ARTS

illustrate *v.* ilustrar

illustration *n.* ilustración *f.*

imagery *n.* imágenes *f.pl.*, imaginería *f.*

implicit *adj.* implícito, -ta; **i. theme** *n.* tema implícito *m.*

incongruity *n.* incongruencia *f.*

index *n.* índice *m.*

inference *n.* inferencia *f.*

inferential *adj.* inferencial

informational text *n.* texto informativo *m.*

interior monologue *n.* monólogo interior *m.*

interpretation *n.* interpretación *f.*

intonation *n.* entonación *f.*

introduction *n.* introducción *f.*

irony *n.* ironía *f.*

J

journal *n.* diario *m.*, revista *f.*

journalist *n.* periodista *m.f.*

K

key word *n.* palabra clave *f.*

L

language *n.* lengua *f.*, lenguaje *m.*, idioma *m.;* **descriptive l.** lenguaje descriptivo; **figurative l.** lenguaje figurado; **formal l.** lenguaje formal; **informal l.** lenguaje informal; **l. pattern** patrón del lenguaje *m.;* **source l.** lengua de origen

lecture *n.* conferencia *f.*

legend *n.* leyenda *f.*

lexicon *n.* léxico *m.*, vocabulario *m.*

limerick *n.* limerick *f.*

literary *adj.* literario, -ria; **l. criticism** *n.* crítica literaria *f.;* **l. device** recurso literario *m.;* **l. elements** *pl.* elementos literarios *m.;* **l. works** *pl.* obras literarias *f.*

literature *n.* literatura *f.*

love story *n.* novela romántica, novela rosa *f.*

lyric poem *n.* poema lírico *m.*

lyrical *adj.* lírico, -ca

M

magazine *n.* revista *f.*

manuscript *n.* manuscrito *m.*

meaning *n.* significado *m.;* **multiple m.** *pl.* significados múltiples

melodrama *n.* melodrama *m.*

memoir *n.* memoria *f.*

metacognition *n.* metacognición *f.*

metaphor *n.* metáfora *f.*

meter *n.* metro *m.*

metonymy *n.* metonimia *f.*

misquotation *n.* error de cita *m.*

modernism *n.* modernismo *m.*

monologue *n.* monólogo *m.*

moral *n.* (story) moraleja *f.*

motif *n.* tema *f.*, asunto *m.*

motive *n.* motivo *m.*

mystery *n.* misterio *m.;* **m. writer** escritor de misterio *m.*

myth *n.* mito *m.*

mythology *n.* mitología *f.*

N

narration *n.* narración *f.*

narrative *adj.* narrativo, -va

● ●

narrative *n.* narración *f.;* **fictional n.** narración de ficción; **historical n.** narración histórica; **n. text** texto narrativo *m.*

narrator *n.* narrador, -ora *m.f.;* **limited n.** narrador (-ora) limitado (-da); **omniscient n.** narrador (-ora) omnisciente

naturalism *n.* naturalismo *m.*

neoclassic literature *n.* literatura neoclásica *f.*

newspaper *n.* periódico *m.,* diario *m.*

nom de plume *n.* nombre artístico *m.,* seudónimo *m.*

nonfiction *n.* literatura factual, literatura no ficcional *f.*

novel *n.* novela *f.;* **crime n.** novela policiaca, novela detectivesca; **utopian n.** novela utópica

novelist *n.* novelista *m.f.*

novella *n.* novela corta *f.*

nuance *n.* tonalidad *f.,* matiz *m.*

nursery rhyme *n.* canción infantil, canción de cuna *f.*

O

ode *n.* oda *f.*

omniscient *adj.* omnisciente; **limited o.** omnisciente limitado

onomatopoeia *n.* onomatopeya *f.*

onset *n.* comienzo *m.*

oral tradition *n.* tradición oral *f.*

oration *n.* oración *f.,* discurso *m.*

oratory *n.* oratoria *f.*

oxymoron *n.* oxímoron *m.*

P

palindrome *n.* palíndromo *m.*

pamphlet *n.* panfleto *m.*

paperback *n.* libro en rústica, libro en edición de bolsillo *m.*

parable *n.* parábola *f.*

paradox *n.* paradoja *f.*

parody *n.* parodia *f.*

passage *n.* pasaje *m.*

pastiche *n.* pastiche *m.,* imitación *f.*

pastoral *adj.* pastoral

pathos *n.* pathos *m.*

periodical *n.* publicación periódica *f.*

personification *n.* personificación *m.*

perspective *n.* perspectiva *f.,* punto de vista *m.*

persuasive *adj.* persuasivo, -va; **p. devices** *n.pl.* recursos persuasivos *m.;* **p. text** texto persuasivo *m.*

picture book *n.* libro ilustrado *m.*

plot *n.* argumento *m.;* **p. development** desarrollo del argumento *m.*

poem *n.* poema *m.;* **epic p.** poema épico; **lyric p.** poema lírico

poet *n.* poeta *m.f.,* bardo *m.*

poetry *n.* poesía *f.*

point of view *n.* punto de vista *m.;* **limited p. o. v.** punto de vista limitado

potboiler *n.* libraco *m.*

prediction *n.* predicción *f.*

preface *n.* prefacio *m.*

premise *n.* premisa *f.*

prologue *n.* prólogo *m.,* introducción *f.*

propaganda *n.* propaganda *f.*

prose *n.* prosa *f.*

LANGUAGE ARTS

prosody *n.* prosodia *f.*
protagonist *n.* protagonista *m.f.*
proverb *n.* proverbio *m.*
pseudonym *n.* seudónimo *m.*
publication *n.* publicación *f.*
publish *v.* publicar, editar
published *adj.* impreso, -sa
publisher *n.* editor, -ora *m.f.;* publicador (-ora) *m.f.;* (company) editorial *f.*
pun *n.* juego de palabras *m.*
purpose *n.* propósito *m.*

R

read *v.* leer; **r. aloud** leer en voz alta
reader *n.* lector, -ora *m.f.*
realism *n.* realismo *m.;* **magical r.** realismo mágico
recurring theme *n.* tema recurrente *m.*
refrain *n.* estribillo *m.,* coro *m.*
relevant *adj.* relevante
repeated *adj.* repetido, -da
repetition *n.* repetición *f.*
reporter *n.* reportero, -ra *m.f.;* periodista *m.f.*
reread *v.* releer, leer de nuevo
resolution *n.* resolución *f.,* propósito *m.*
retell *v.* recontar, volver a contar
rhetoric *n.* retórica *f.*
rhetorical *adj.* retórico, -ca; **r. device** recurso retórico *m.;* **r. question** pregunta retórica *f.*
rhythm *n.* ritmo *m.*
riddle *n.* adivinanza *f.*
rising action *n.* acción ascendente *f.*

Romantic *adj.* romántico, -ca; **R. period literature** *n.* período literario romántico *m.*
romanticism *n.* romanticismo *m.*

S

saga *n.* saga *f.*
sarcasm *n.* sarcasmo *m.*
satire *n.* sátira *f.*
scan *v.* (verse) escandir
scene *n.* escena *f.*
science fiction *n.* ciencia ficción *f.*
semantics *n.* semántica *f.*
sensory *adj.* sensorio, -ria; sensorial; **s. details** *n.pl.* detalles sensorios *m.;* **s. image** imagen sensorial *f.*
sequence *n.* secuencia *f.*
serial *n.* serial *m.*
sermon *n.* sermón *m.*
setting *n.* escenario *m.*
short story *n.* cuento corto *m.*
simile *n.* simil *m.*
slanted *adj.* sesgado, -da
slippery slope *n.* pendiente resbaladiza *f.*
soliloquy *n.* soliloquio *m.*
solution *n.* solución *f.*
sonnet *n.* soneto *m.*
source language *n.* lengua de origen *f.*
spine *n.* (book) lomo *m.*
stanza *n.* estanza *f.*
stereotype *n.* estereotipo *m.*
stereotypical *adj.* estereotípico, -ca
story *n.* cuento *m.,* historia *f.;* **detective s.** cuento policiaca, cuento

detectivesca; **feature s.** cuento largo; **ghost s.** cuento de fantasmas; **horror s.** cuento de horror; **love s.** cuento de amor romántico; **short s.** cuento corto; **s. line** argumento *m.;* **s. structure** estructura del cuento *f.*

straw man *n.* falacia del hombre de paja *f.*

stream of consciousness *n.* flujo de conciencia *m.,* monólogo interior *m.*

structural analysis *n.* análisis estructural *m.*

structured poetry *n.* poesía estructurada *f.*

style *n.* estilo *m.*

stylized *adj.* estilizado, -da

subplot *n.* argumento secundario *m.*

suggestion *n.* sugerencia *f.*

supernatural tale *n.* cuento sobrenatural *m.*

supporting details *n.pl.* detalles secundarios, detalles de apoyo *m.;* **relevant s. d.** detalles relacionados que lo apoyen *m.*

surrealism *n.* surrealismo *m.*

surrealist *adj. & n.* surrealista *m.f.*

suspense *n.* suspenso *m.*

symbol *n.* símbolo *m.*

symbolism *n.* simbolismo *m.*

synthesis *n.* síntesis *m.*

T

table of contents *n.* índice *m.,* tabla de contenidos *f.*

tale *n.* cuento *m.,* relato *m.;* **fairy t.** cuento de hadas; **tall t.** cuento fantastico, relato absurdo

Teutonic *adj.* teutónico, -ca

text *n.* texto *m.;* **classical t.** texto clásico; **popular t.** texto popular; **t. feature** característica del texto *f.;* **t. structure** estructura del texto *f.*

textbook *n.* texto, libro de texto *m.*

theme *n.* tema *m.;* **primary t.** tema principal; **recurring t.** tema recurrente

thesis *n.* tesis *f.*

thriller *n.* novela de suspenso *f.*

time lapse *n.* lapso de tiempo *m.*

title *n.* título *m.;* **t. page** portada *f.,* página de presentación *f.*

tome *n.* tomo *m.,* volumen *m.*

tone *n.* tono *m.*

tongue-twister *n.* trabalenguas *m.*

tragedy *n.* tragedia *f.*

tragicomedy *n.* tragicomedia *f.*

trait *n.* rasgo *m.;* **character t.** rasgo del carácter

treatise *n.* tradado *m.*

trickster tale *n.* cuento picaresco, cuento de travesuras *m.*

trite *adj.* manido, -da; trillado, -da

turning point *n.* momento crucial *m.*

U

understatement *n.* subestimación *f.*

universal theme *n.* tema universal *m.*

unpublished *adj.* inedito, -ta

utopia *n.* utopía *f.*

utopian *adj.* utópico, -ca; **u. novel** *n.* novela utópica *f.*

V

verbose *adj.* verboso, -sa
verisimilitude *n.* verosimilitud *f.*
vernacular *adj.* vernáculo, -la
vernacular *n.* lengua vernácula *f.*
verse *n.* verso *m.;* **blank v., free v.** verso libre
version *n.* versión *f.*
Victorian *adj.* victoriano, -na; **V. novel** novela victoriana *f.*
viewpoint *n.* punto de vista *m.*
vignette *n.* bosquejo corto *m.*

villain *n.* villano *m.*
volume *n.* volumen *m.*

W

word play *n.* juego de palabras *m.*
wordless book *n.* libro sin texto *m.*
wordsmith *n.* artífice de la palabra *m.f.*
work *n.* (literary) obra, obra literaria *f.*
writer *n.* escritor, -ora *m.f.*

Languages

Amharic *n.* amárico *m.*, amhárico *m.*
Apache *n.* apache *m.*
Arabic *n.* árabe *m.*
Armenian *n.* armenio *m.*
Aymara *n.* aymará *m.*
Basque *n.* vasco *m.*
Bengali *n.* bengalí *m.*
Cambodian *n.* camboyano *m.*
Cantonese *n.* cantonés *m.*
Castilian *n.* castellano *m.*
Catalan *n.* catalán *m.*
Cherokee *n.* cheroqui *m.*
Cheyenne *n.* cheyenne *m.*
Choctaw *n.* choctaw *m.*
Crow *n.* crow *m.*
Czech *n.* checo *m.*
Danish *n.* danés *m.*
Dutch *n.* holandés *m.*, neerlandés *m.*
English *n.* inglés *m.;* **Old E.** inglés

antiguo
Eritrean *n.* eritreo *m.*
Farsi (Persian) *n.* persa *m.*
Finnish *n.* finés *m.*, finlandés *m.*
French *n.* francés *m.;* **F. Creole** criollo francés
Gaelic *n.* gaélico *m.*
Galician *n.* gallego *m.*
German *n.* alemán *m.*
Greek *n.* griego *m.*
Guarani *n.* guaraní *m.*
Gujarati *n.* gujarati *m.*
Haitian Creole *n.* criollo haitiano *m.*
Hawaiian *n.* hawaiano *m.*
Hebrew *n.* hebreo *m.*
Hindi *n.* hindú *m.*
Hmong *n.* hmong *m.*
Hopi *n.* hopi *m.*
Hungarian *n.* húngaro *m.*

Ilocano *n.* ilocano *m.*

Indonesian *n.* indonesio *m.*

Inupiak *n.* iñupiaq *m.*

Italian *n.* italiano *m.*

Japanese *n.* japonés *m.*

Keres *n.* keres *m.*

Korean *n.* coreano *m.*

Kurdish *n.* kurdo *m.*

Ladino *n.* ladino *m.*

Lakota *n.* lakota *m.*

Laotian *n.* lao *m.*

Latin *n.* latín *m.*

Malay *n.* malayo *m.*

Mandarin *n.* mandarín *m.*

Maori *n.* maorí *m.*

Maya *n.* maya *m.*

Mixtec *n.* mixteco *m.*

Nahuatl *n.* náhuatl *m.*

Navajo *n.* navajo *m.*

Norwegian *n.* noruego *m.*

Ojibwa *n.* ojibwa *m.*

Otomi *n.* otomí *m.*

Papago *n.* papago *m.*

Pima *n.* pima *m.*

Polish *n.* polaco *m.*

Portuguese *n.* portugués *m.*

Punjabi *n.* punjabí *m.*

Quechua *n.* quechua *m.*

Romanian *n.* rumano *m.*

Russian *n.* ruso *m.*

Samoan *n.* samoano *m.*

Serbo-Croatian *n.* serbocroata *m.*

Somali *n.* somalí *m.*

Spanish *n.* español *m.*

Sudanese *n.* sudanés *m.*

Swedish *n.* sueco *m.*

Tagalog *n.* tagalo *m.*

Tamil *n.* tamil *m.*

Tewa *n.* tewa *m.*

Thai *n.* tailandés *m.*

Turkish *n.* turco *m.*

Tzeltal *n.* tzeltal *m.*

Ukrainian *n.* ucraniano *m.*

Urdu *n.* urdú *m.*

Vietnamese *n.* vietnamita *m.*

Xhosa *n.* xhosa *m.*

Yiddish *n.* yídish *m.*

Yup'ik *n.* yupik *m.*

Zapotec *n.* zapoteco *m.*

Zulu *n.* zulú *m.*

Zuni *n.* zuñi *m.*

LANGUAGE ARTS

MATHEMATICS

Arithmetic & Algebra

A

above *adv. & prep.* por encima de

abscissa *n.* abscisa *f.*

absolute value *n.* valor absoluto *m.*

accurate *adj.* exacto, -ta; preciso, -sa

add *v.* sumar

addend *n.* sumando *m.*

addition *n.* adición *f.*, suma *f.;* **a. and subtraction** sumas y restas *pl.;* **a. fact** hecho aditivo *m.;* **a. sign** signo de adición, signo de suma *m.*

additive *adj.* aditivo, -va; **a. identity** *n.* identidad aditiva *f.;* **a. inverse** inverso aditivo *m.*

after *adv. & prep.* después de

algebra *n.* álgebra *f.*

algebraic *adj.* algebraico, -ca; **a. equation** *n.* ecuación algebraica *f.;* **a. expression** expresión algebraica *f.*

algorithm *n.* algoritmo *m.*

alike *adj.* semejante

all *adj.* todo, -da

almost *adv.* casi

answer *n.* solución *f.*, respuesta *f.*

applications *n.pl.* aplicaciones *f.*

apply *v.* aplicar

approximate *adj.* aproximado, -da

approximate *v.* aproximarse, acercarse

approximately *adv.* aproximadamente

Arabic numeral *n.* número árabe *m.*

arithmetic *n.* aritmética *f.;* **a. sequence** progresión aritmética *f.;* **a. series** serie aritmética *f.*

arrange *v.* organizar

array *n.* matriz *f.*, orden *m.*, arreglo *m.*

as many as *adv.* tantos como

associative property *n.* propiedad asociativa *f.*

at least *adv.* al menos

at most *adv.* como máximo

average *n.* media *f.*, promedio *m.*

axis *n.* eje *m.;* **horizontal a.** eje horizontal; **vertical a.** eje vertical; **x-axis** eje x; **y-axis** eje y

B

balance *n.* balance *m.*, balanza *f.*, saldo *m.*

base *n.* base *f.;* **b. of a power** base de una potencia; **b. ten** base diez

before *adv. & prep* antes de

below *adv. & prep.* debajo de

benchmark number *n.* número de referencia *m.*

between *adv. & prep.* entre

binomial *n.* binomio *m.*

border *n.* borde *m.*

bottom *n.* pie *m.*, fondo *m.*, parte inferior *f.*

C

calculate *v.* calcular

calculator *n.* calculadora *f.*

calendar *n.* calendario *m.*

cardinal number *n.* número cardinal *m.*

Cartesian coordinate *n.* coordenada cartesiana *f.*

category *n.* categoría *f.*

certain *adj.* certero, -ra; cierto, -ta

certainty *n.* certeza *f.*

change *n.* (money) cambio *m.*

chart *v.* graficar

check *n.* (money) cheque *m.*

check *v.* verificar

choose *v.* escoger

classify *v.* clasificar

cluster *n.* grupo *m.*

coefficient *n.* coeficiente *m.*

coin *n.* moneda *f.*

column *n.* columna *f.*

combination *n.* combinación *f.*

combine *v.* combinar

common *adj.* común; **c. denominator** *n.* denominador común *m.;* **c. factor** factor común *m.;* **c. multiple** múltiplo común *m.*

communicative property *n.* propiedad conmutativa *f.*

compare *v.* comparar

composite number *n.* número compuesto *m.*

compound interest *n.* interés compuesto *m.*

conclusion *n.* conclusión *f.*

conditional statement *n.* enunciado condicional *m.*

conjecture *n.* conjetura *f.*

connection *n.* conexión *f.*

consecutive *adj.* consecutivo, -va

consecutively *adv.* consecutivamente

constant *adj. & n.* constante *f.*

constraints *n.pl.* restricciones *f.*

construction *n.* construcción *f.*

coordinate *n.* coordenada *f.;* **c. grid** cuadrícula de coordenadas *f.;* **c. plane** plano coordenado *m.*

corner *n.* esquina *f.*

correlation *n.* correlación *f.*

cosine (cos) *n.* coseno *m.;* **c. ratio** proporción del coseno *f.*

cotangent (cot) *n.* cotangente *f.*

count *v.* contar

cross multiply *v.* multiplicar en cruz

cross product *n.* producto cruzado *m.*

currency *n.* moneda corriente *f.*

cycle *n.* ciclo *m.*

MATHEMATICS

MATHEMATICS

D

decimal *adj. & n.* decimal *m.;* **d. number** número decimal *m.;* **d. point** punto decimal *m.,* coma decimal *f.;* **mixed d.** decimal mixto; **repeating d.** punto periódico *m.;* **terminating d.** decimal finito

denominator *n.* denominador *m.;* **common d.** denominador común

determine *v.* determinar

difference *n.* diferencia *f.*

different *adj.* diferente

digit *n.* dígito *m.;* **significant d.** dígito significativo

discount *n.* descuento *m.*

distributive property *n.* propiedad distributiva *f.*

divide *v.* dividir

dividend *n.* dividendo *m.*

divisible *adj.* divisible

division *n.* división *f.;* **d. fact** hecho de división *m.;* **d. sign** signo de división *m.*

divisor *n.* divisor *m.*

domain *n.* dominio *m.*

double *adj. & n.* doble *m.*

double *v.* doblar

dozen *n.* docena *f.*

E

each *adj.* cada

elasped time *n.* tiempo transcurrido *m.*

element *n.* elemento *m.*

eliminate *v.* eliminar

elimination method *n.* método de eliminación *m.*

empty *adj.* vacío, -cía

enough *adj.* suficiente

enough *adv.* bastante

equal *adj.* igual

equal *v.* igualar

equality *n.* igualdad *f.*

equation *n.* ecuación *f.*

equivalent *adj. & n.* equivalente *m.*

estimate *v.* estimar

estimation *n.* estimación *f.;* **front-end e.** estimación por la izquierda, estimación frontal

evaluate *v.* evaluar

even *adj.* par; **e. number** *n.* número par *m.*

exactly *adv.* exactamente

examine *v.* examinar

excercises *n.pl.* ejercicios *m.*

expanded form *n.* forma desarrollada *f.*

explain *v.* explicar

explanation *n.* explicación *f.*

exponent *n.* exponente *m.*

exponential *adj.* exponencial; **e. factor** *n.* factor exponencial *m.;* **e. growth** crecimiento exponencial *m.*

express *v.* expresar

expression *n.* expresión *f.*

F

fact family *n.* familia de hechos *f.*

factor *n.* factor *m.;* **f. tree** árbol de factores *m.*

factorial *adj.* factorial

false *adj.* falso, -sa

far *adj.* lejano, -na

. . . .

farther *adj.* más lejano (-na)

farthest *adj.* el más lejano, la más lejana

few *adj. & n.* pocos, -cas *m.f.pl.*

fewer *adj.* menos; **f. than** *adv.* menos que

fewest *adj. & n.* menos *m.f.*, menor número de *m.*, mínima cantidad de *f.*

Fibonacci sequence *n.* secuencia de Fibonacci *f.*

find *v.* hallar, encontrar

finite *adj.* finito, -ta

first *adj.* primero, -ra

first *n.* primer *m.*

formula *n.* fórmula *f.*

fraction *n.* fracción *f.*

full *adj.* completo, -ta; lleno, -na

function *n.* función *f.*; **f. table** tabla de funciones *f.*

fundamental counting principle *n.* principio fundamental de conteo *m.*

G

gap *n.* intervalo *m.*, distancia *f.*, diferencia *f.*, espacio *m.*

gather *v.* recopilar, compilar

general *adj.* general

generalization *n.* generalización *f.*

generalize *v.* generalizar

generate *v.* generar

goal *n.* objetivo *m.*, meta *f.*

golden ratio *n.* número áureo *m.*

gradual *adj.* gradual

graph *n.* gráfica *f.*, gráfico *m.*

greater *adj.* mayor; **g. than** *adj. & adv.* mayor que; **no g. than** no mayor que

greatest common factor *n.* máximo común divisor *m.*, factor común mayor *m.*

group *n.* grupo *m.*

grow *v.* crecer

growing *adj.* creciente

growth *n.* crecimiento *m.*; **g. factor** factor de crecimiento *m.*

guess *n.* suposición *f.*, conjetura *f.*

guess *v.* suponer; **g. correctly** acertar, atinar

guess and check *n.* estimación y verificación *f.*

H

half *adj.* medio, -dia

half *adj. & n.* mitad *f.*

heavier *adj.* más pesado (-da)

heaviest *adj.* el más pesado, la más pesada

heavy *adj.* pesado, -da

high *adj.* alto, -ta

higher *adj.* más alto (-ta)

highest *adj.* el más alto, la más alta

horizontal *adj.* horizontal; **h. axis** *n.* eje horizontal *m.*

How many? *adv.* ¿Cuántos?; **How many more?** ¿Cuántos más?

hundredth *n.* (series) centésimo *m.*, centavo *m.*; (proportion) centésima parte *f.*

I

imaginary number *n.* número imaginario *m.*

impossible *adj.* imposible

MATHEMATICS

improper fraction *n.* fracción impropia *f.*

inequality *n.* desigualdad *f.*

infinite *adj.* infinito, -ta

input *n.* entrada *f.*

inside *adv. & prep.* dentro de, adentro

integer *n.* entero *m.;* **negative i.** entero negativo; **positive i.** entero positivo

integral *adj.* integral

interest *n.* interés *m.;* **compound i.** interés compuesto

inverse *adj.* inverso, -sa; **i. operation** *n.* operación inversa *f.;* **i. square** cuadrado inverso *m.*

inverse *n.* inverso *m.;* **additive i.** inverso aditivo; **multiplicative i.** inverso multiplicativo

irrational number *n.* número irracional *m.*

isolate *v.* separar, aislar

J
join *v.* juntar, unir

K
key *n.* clave *f.*

L
large *adj.* grande

larger *adj.* más grande

largest *adj.* el más grande, la más grande

last *adj.* último, -ma

least *adj.* mínimo, -ma; menos, menor

least *adv. & n.* lo mínimo *m.;* **at l.**

adv. por lo menos; **l. common denominator** *n.* mínimo común denominador *m.;* **l. common multiple** mínimo común múltiplo *m.*

less *adj. & adv.* menos; **l. than** menor que, menos que; **no l. than** no menos que, no menor que

light *adj.* liviano, -na

linear *adj.* lineal, linear; **l. equation** *n.* ecuación lineal *f.;* **l. function** función lineal *f.*

list *n.* lista *f.*

list *v.* listar

locate *v.* localizar

logarithm *n.* logaritmo *m.*

look for *v.* buscar

low *adj.* bajo, -ja

lower *adj.* más bajo (-ja)

lowest *adj.* el más bajo, la más baja

M
mathematics *n.pl.* matemáticas *f.*

matrix *n.* matriz *f.*

maximum *adj.* máximo, -ma

maximum *n.* máximo *m.*

method *n.* método *m.*

middle *adj.* medio, -dia

minimum *adj.* mínimo, -ma

minimum *n.* mínimo *m.*

minus *adj. & prep.* menos; **m. sign** *n.* signo de menos, signo de sustracción *m.*

missing *adj.* faltante

mix *v.* mezclar

mixed *adj.* mixto, -ta; **m. decimal** *n.* decimal mixto *m.;* **m. fractions**

• •

fracciones mixtas *f.pl.;* **m. num-**
ber número mixto *m.*

monomial *n.* monomio *m.*

more *adj. & adv.* más; **m. than** *adv.*
más que, mayor que; **no m. than**
no más que

most *adj. & n.* mayoría de *f.,* mayor
número de *m.,* mayor parte de *f.*

most *adv.* el más, la más; **at m.** como
máximo, como mucho, a lo sumo

multiple *n.* múltiplo *m.*

multiplication *n.* multiplicación *f.;*
m. fact hecho de multiplicación
m.; **m. sign** signo de multiplicación *m.*

multiplicative *adj.* multiplicativo,
-va; **m. identity** *n.* identidad multiplicativa *f.;* **m. inverse** inverso
multiplicativo *m.*

multiplier *n.* multiplicador *m.*

multiply *v.* multiplicar

N

natural numbers *n.pl.* números naturales *m.*

near *adj.* cercano, -na

nearer *adj.* más cercano (-na)

nearest *adj.* el más cercano, la más
cercana

negative *adj.* negativo, -va; **n. expo-**
nent *n.* exponente negativo *m.;* **n.**
integer entero negativo *m.;* **n.**
number número negativo *m.*

no less than *adv.* no menos que, no
menor que

no more than *adv.* no más que, no
mayor que

none *pron.* ninguno

nonlinear *adj.* no lineal

nothing *pron.* nada

number *n.* número *m.;* **cardinal n.**
número cardinal; **even n.** número
par; **imaginary n.** número imaginario; **n. fact** hecho numérico *m.;*
n. line línea numérica *f.;* **n. se-**
quence secuencia de números *f.;*
odd n. número impar; **ordinal n.**
número ordinal; **prime n.** número
primo; **rational n.** número racional; **real n.** número real; **whole n.**
número entero

numeral *n.* número *m.;* **Arabic n.**
número árabe; **Roman n.** número
romano

numerator *n.* numerador *m.*

numerical *adj.* numérico, -ca

O

odd *adj.* impar; **o. number** *n.*
número impar *m.*

ones *n.pl.* unidades *f.*

opposite *adj.* opuesto, -ta

order *n.* (command) orden *f.,* (sequence) orden *m.;* **o. of opera-**
tions orden de operaciones *m.;* **o.**
property (addition, multiplication) propiedad de orden *f.*

order *v.* ordenar

ordinal number *n.* número ordinal *m.*

origin *n.* orígen *m.*

output *n.* salida *f.*

outside *adv. & prep.* afuera de

over *prep.* sobre

MATHEMATICS

P

pair *n.* par *m.;* **coordinated p.** par coordenado; **ordered p.** par ordenado; **zero p.** par nulo

parabola *n.* parábola *f.*

part *n.* parte *f.*

pattern *n.* patrón *m.*

percent *adv.* por ciento

percent *n.* centésimo *m.*

percentile *n.* percentil *m.*

percentage *n.* porcentaje *m.*

perfect *adj.* perfecto, -ta; **p. cube** *n.* cubo perfecto *m.;* **p. square** cuadrado perfecto *m.*

piece *n.* parte *f.,* porción *f.*

place value *n.* valor posicional *m.*

plan *n.* plan *m.*

plan *v.* planificar

plus *adv.* más; **p. sign** *n.* signo de adición, signo de suma *m.*

polynomial *n.* polinomio *m.*

positive *adj.* positivo, -va; **p. exponent** *n.* exponente positivo *m.;* **p. integer** entero positivo *m.*

power *n.* (exponent) potencia *f.;* **p. of ten** potencia de diez

practice *v.* practicar

precise *adj.* preciso, -sa

precision *n.* precisión *f.*

predict *v.* predecir

prediction *n.* predicción *f.*

prime *adj.* primo, -ma; **p. factorization** *n.* factorización en primos *f.,* descomposición en factores primos *f.;* **p. number** número primo *m.*

problem *n.* problema *m.*

product *n.* producto *m.;* **partial p.** producto parcial

progression *n.* progresión *f.;* **arithmetic p.** progresión aritmética; **geometric p.** progresión geométrica

proportion *n.* proporción *f.*

Q

quadrant *n.* cuadrante *m.*

quadratic *adj.* cuadrático, -ca; **q. q. equation** *n.* ecuación cuadrática *f.* **formula** fórmula cuadrática *f.;* **q. function** función cuadrática *f.*

quarter *adj. & n.* cuarto, -ta *m.f.*

quotient *n.* cociente *m.*

R

radical *adj. & n.* radical *m.;* **r. sign** signo radical *m.*

rate *n.* tasa *f.;* **r. of change** tasa de cambio *f.*

ratio *n.* proporción *f.*

rational number *n.* número racional *m.*

real number *n.* número real *m.*

reasonable *adj.* razonable

reasoning *n.* razonamiento *m.*

reciprocal *n.* recíproca *f.*

recursive *adj.* recursivo, -va; **r. rule** *n.* regla recursiva *f.*

reduced form *n.* forma reducida *f.*

regroup *v.* reagrupar

relation *n.* relación *f.*

remainder *n.* resto *m.,* residuo *m.,* restante *m.*

repeating decimal *n.* decimal periódico *m.*

replace *v.* reemplazar

represent *v.* representar

results *n.pl.* resultados *m.*

right *adj.* correcto, -ta

rise *n.* distancia vertical *f.*

Roman numeral *n.* número romano *m.*

root *n.* raíz *f.*

round *v.* redondear

row *n.* fila *f.*

run *n.* distancia horizontal *f.*

S

sale price *n.* precio de oferta *m.*

sales tax *n.* impuesto sobre las ventas *m.*

same *adj.* mismo, -ma; **s. as** *adv.* el mismo que, la misma que

scale *n.* escala *f.;* **s. drawing** dibujo a escala *m.;* **s. factor** factor de escala *m.;* **s. model** modelo a escala *m.*

schedule *n.* cronograma *m.,* horario *m.*

scientific notation *n.* notación científica *f.*

score *n.* puntaje *m.*

separate *adj.* separado, -da

sequence *n.* secuencia *f.;* **arithmetic s.** progresión aritmética *f.;* **Fibonacci s.** secuencia de Fibonacci; **number s.** secuencia de números

set *n.* conjunto *m.*

show *v.* demostrar

significant digits *n.pl.* dígitos significativos *m.*

simple interest *n.* interés simple *m.*

simplest form *n.* forma más simple *f.;* **s. f. of a fraction** expresión mínima de una fracción *f.*

simplify *v.* simplificar

simulation *n.* simulación *f.*

sine (sin) *n.* seno *m.;* **s. ratio** proporción seno *f.*

single *adj.* único, -ca

skip-count *n.* cuenta salteada *f.*

slope *n.* pendiente *f.;* **s. intercept** forma pendiente-intercepto *f.*

small *adj.* pequeño, -ña

smaller *adj.* más pequeño (-ña)

smallest *adj.* el más pequeño, la más pequeña

solution *n.* solución *f.*

solve *v.* resolver

sort *v.* ordenar, clasificar

space *n.* espacio *m.*

span *n.* lapso *m.*

square *n.* cuadrado *m.,* segunda potencia *f.;* **s. root** raíz cuadrada *f.*

square *v.* cuadrar

standard *adj.* estándar; **s. form** *n.* forma estándar *f.;* **s. notation** notación estándar *f.*

step *n.* paso *m.*

story problem *n.* problema narrativo *m.*

straight *adj.* derecho, -cha

subsitute *v.* sustituir

subsitution method *n.* método de sustitución *m.*

subtract *v.* restar, sustraer

subtraction *n.* resta *f.,* sustracción *f.;* **s. fact** hecho de resta, hecho de

MATHEMATICS

sustracción *m.;* **s. sign** signo de resta, signo de sustracción *m.*

sum *n.* suma *f.*

summation *n.* sumatoria *f.;* **s. notation** notación sumatoria, notación de sumatoria *f.*

symbol *n.* símbolo *m.*

system *n.* sistema *m.;* **metric s.** sistema métrico; **s. of equations** sistema de ecuaciones; **s. of linear inequalities** sistema de desigualdades lineales

T

table *n.* tabla *f.*

tangent (tan) *n.* tangente *f.*

tens *n.pl.* decenas *f.*

tenth *n.* (series) décimo *m.;* (proportion) décima parte *f.*

term *n.* término *m.*

thermometer *n.* termómetro *m.*

thousandth *n.* (series) milésimo *m.;* (proportion) milésima parte *f.*

timeline *n.* línea de tiempo *f.*

times *prep.* por, multiplicado por

timetable *n.* cronograma *m.,* horario *m.*

top *n.* tope *m.,* parte superior *f.*

total *n.* total *m.*

trade *n.* intercambio *m.*

trend *n.* tendencia *f.*

trigonometry *n.* trigonometría *f.*

trinomial *adj.* trinomio, -ma

trinomial *n.* trinomio *m.*

triple *adj.* triple

triple *v.* triplicar

true *adj.* verdadero, -ra

U

under *adv.* debajo de, abajo de

unit *n.* unidad *f.;* **u. price** precio unitario *m.;* **u. rate** tasa unitaria *f.*

unequal *adj.* desigual

unlike *adj.* desigual, disímil; **u. fractions** *n.pl.* fracciones con denominadores distintos *f.;* **u. terms** términos no semejantes *m.*

unlikely *adv.* improbable

unreasonable *adj.* no razonable

V

value *n.* valor *m.*

variable *adj. & n.* variable *f.*

Venn Diagram *n.* diagrama de Venn *m.*

verify *v.* verificar

W

wedge *n.* forma de cuña *f.*

whole number *n.* número entero *m.*

X

x-axis *n.* eje x *m.*

x-coordinate *n.* coordenada x *f.*

x-intercept *n.* intercepto en x *m.*

Y

y-axis *n.* eje y *m.*

y-coordinate *n.* coordenada y *f.*

y-intercept *n.* intercepto en y *m.*

Z

zero pair *n.* par nulo *m.*

Geometry

A

acute *adj.* agudo, -da; **a. angle** *n.* ángulo agudo *m.;* **a. triangle** triángulo agudo *m.*

adjacent *adj.* adyacente; **a. angle** *n.* ángulo adyacente *m.*

alternate *adj.* alterno, -na; **a. angles** *n.pl.* ángulos alternos *m.;* **a. exterior angles** ángulos externos alternos; **a. interior angles** ángulos internos alternos

altitude *n.* altitud *f.*

angle *n.* ángulo *m.;* **a. bisector** bisectriz del ángulo *f.;* **a. of rotation** ángulo de rotación; **central a.** ángulo central; **complementary a.** *pl.* ángulos complementarios; **corresponding a.** *pl.* ángulos correspondientes; **degree of an a.** grado de un ángulo *m.;* **exterior a.** ángulo exterior; **opposite a.** *pl.* ángulos opuestos; **straight a.** ángulo llano; **supplementary a.** ángulo suplementario; **vertical a.** ángulo verticale

arc *n.* arco *m.;* **major a.** arco mayor; **minor a.** arco menor

area *n.* área *f.*

axiom *n.* axioma *m.*

B

base *n.* base *f.*

bisect *v.* bisecar

bisector *adj. & n.* bisectriz *f.*

C

capacity *n.* capacidad *f.*

center *n.* centro *m.*

chord *n.* cuerda *f.*

circle *n.* círculo *m.;* **c. graph** gráfica circular *f.*

circular *adj.* circular

circumference *n.* circunferencia *f.*

classify *v.* clasificar

clock *n.* reloj *m.*

clockwise *adj. & adv.* en sentido de las agujas del reloj

compare *v.* comparar

compass *n.* compás *m.*

concave *adj.* cóncavo, -va

cone *n.* cono *m.*

congruent *adj.* congruente

construct *v.* construir

convex *adj.* convexo, -xa

corresponding *adj.* correspondiente; **c. parts** *n.pl.* partes correspondientes *f.;* **c. sides** lados correspondientes *m.*

counterclockwise *adj. & adv.* en sentido contrario a las agujas del reloj

cube *n.* cubo *m.;* **c. root** raíz cúbica *f.*

cube *v.* cubicar

cubic *adj.* cúbico, -ca; **c. unit** unidad cúbica *f.*

curve *n.* curva *f.*

curved *adj.* curvo, -va

MATHEMATICS

MATHEMATICS

customary system *n.* sistema anglosajón de unidades *m.*
cylinder *n.* cilindro *m.*

D

dart board *n.* tablero de dardos *m.*
decagon *n.* decágono *m.*
degree *n.* grado *m.;* **d. of an angle** grado de un ángulo
density *n.* densidad *f.*
depth *n.* profundidad *f.*
describe *v.* describir
design *n.* diseño *m.*
diagonal *adj.* diagonal
diameter *n.* diámetro *m.*
dilation *n.* dilatación *f.*
dimension *n.* dimensión *f.*
distance *n.* distancia *f.*
draw *v.* dibujar, diseñar
drawing *n.* dibujo *m.*

E

edge *n.* borde *m.,* (prism) arista *f.*
ellipse *n.* elipse *m.*
elliptical *adj.* elíptico, -ca
endpoints *n.pl.* extremos *m.*
equilateral triangle *n.* triángulo equilátero *m.*
estimate *v.* estimar
exterior angle *n.* ángulo exterior *m.*

F

face *n.* cara *f.*
figure *n.* figura *f.;* **closed f.** figura cerrada; **open f.** figura abierta; **plane f.** figura plana; **similar f.** figura semejante; **solid f.** figura sólida
flip *v.* invertir
front *n.* frente *m.;* **in f.** *adj. & adv.* al frente
full *adj.* completo, -ta; lleno, -na

G

geometric *adj.* geométrico, -ca; **g. series** *n.* serie geométrica *f.;* **g. solids** *pl.* sólidos geométricos *m.*
geometry *n.* geometría *f.;* **Euclidean g.** geometría euclidea
glide reflection *n.* reflexión con desplazamiento y traslación *f.*
grid *n.* cuadrícula *f.,* partición *f.*

H

height *n.* altura *f.;* **h. of a triangle** altura de un triángulo
hemisphere *n.* hemisferio *m.*
heptagon *n.* heptágono *m.*
hexagon *n.* hexágono *m.*
hyperbola *n.* hipérbola *f.*
hypotenuse *n.* hipotenusa *f.*

I

identify *v.* identificar
interior angle *n.* ángulo interno *m.*
intersect *v.* intersectar
irregular *adj.* irregular; **i. polygon** *n.* polígono irregular *m.*
isosceles *adj.* isósceles; **i. trapezoid** *n.* trapezoide isósceles *m.;* **i. triangle** triángulo isósceles *m.*

L

leg *n.* (right triangle) cateto *m.*

● ●

length *n.* longitud *f.*

line *n.* línea *f.;* **l. of symmetry** línea de simetría; **l. segment** segmento de línea *m.;* **secant l.** línea secante

linear symmetry *n.* simetría lineal *f.*

long *adj.* largo, -ga; **How l. is ... ?** ¿Qué tan largo (-ga) es ... ?

longer *adj.* más largo (-ga)

longest *adj.* el más largo, la más larga

M

mass *n.* masa *f.*

measure *v.* medir

measurement *n.* medida *f.*

metric *adj.* métrico, -ca; **m. system** *n.* sistema métrico *m.*

midpoint *n.* punto medio *m.*

mirror image *n.* imagen en espejo *f.*

model *n.* modelo *m.;* **scale m.** modelo a escala

model *v.* modelar

N

net *n.* red *f.*

O

obtuse *adj.* obtuso, -sa; **o. angle** *n.* ángulo obtuso *m.;* **o. triangle** triángulo obtuso *m.*

octagon *n.* octágono *m.*

one-dimensional *adj.* unidimensional

open figure *n.* figura abierta *f.*

opposite angles *n.pl.* ángulos opuestos *m.*

P

parallel *adj.* paralelo, -la; **p. lines** *n.pl.* líneas paralelas, líneas rectas *f.*

parallelogram *n.* paralelogramo *m.*

Pascal's triangle *n.* triángulo de Pascal *m.*

pentagon *n.* pentágono *m.*

perimeter *n.* perímetro *m.*

perpendicular *adj.* perpendicular; **p. bisector** *n.* bisectriz perpendicular *f.;* **p. lines** *pl.* líneas perpendiculares *f.*

pi *n.* pi *m.*

plane figure *n.* figura plana *f.*

point *n.* punto *m.;* **p. of rotation** punto de rotación

polygon *n.* polígono *m.;* **regular p.** póligono regular; **similar p.** póligono semejante

polyhedron *n.* poliedro *m.*

postulate *n.* postulado *m.*

prism *n.* prisma *m.;* **rectangular p.** prisma rectangular; **triangular p.** prisma triangular

proof *n.* prueba *f.*

prove *v.* demostrar, comprobar

protractor *n.* transportador *m.*

pyramid *n.* pirámide *f.*

Pythagorean Theorem *n.* teorema de Pitágoras *m.;* **P. triple** trío pitagórico *m.*

Q

quadrilateral *adj.* cuadrilátero, -ra

quadrilateral *n.* cuadrilátero *m.*

quadrant *n.* cuadrante *m.*

MATHEMATICS

R

radius *n.* radio *m.*
ray *n.* rayo *m.*
rectangle *n.* rectángulo *m.*
rectangular *adj.* rectangular
reflection *n.* reflejo *m.*
rhombus *n.* rombo *m.*
right *adj.* recto, -ta; **r. angle** *n.* ángulo recto *m.;* **r. trapezoid** trapecio recto *m.;* **r. triangle** triángulo recto *m.*
rotation *n.* rotación *f.*
rotational symmetry *n.* simetría rotacional *f.*
ruler *n.* regla *f.*

S

scalene triangle *n.* triángulo escaleno *m.*
secant line *n.* línea secante *f.*
sector *n.* sector *m.*
segment *n.* segmento *m.*
semicircle *n.* semicírculo *m.*
shaded *adj.* sombreado, -da
shape *n.* forma *f.*
short *adj.* corto, -ta
shorter *adj.* más corto (-ta)
shortest *adj.* el más corto, la más corta
side *n.* lado *m.;* **left s.** lado izquierdo; **right s.** lado derecho
similar *adj.* similar, semejante; **s. figure** *n.* figura semejante *f.;* **s. polygon** polígono semejante *m.*
size *n.* tamaño *m.*
sketch *n.* boceto *m.,* dibujo *m.*
slant height *n.* apotema lateral *f.;* **s.**

h. of a regular pyramid apotema lateral de una pirámide regular
slide *n.* traslación *f.,* deslizamiento *m.*
slope *n.* pendiente *f.*
solid *adj.* sólido, -da; **s. figure** *n.* figura sólida *f.*
solid *n.* sólido *m.,* cuerpo geométrico *m.*
sphere *n.* esfera *f.*
square *adj.* cuadrado, -da; **s. unit** *n.* unidad cuadrada *f.*
square *n.* cuadrado *m.*
surface *n.* superficie *f.;* **s. area** área de superficie *f.*
symmetry *n.* simetría *f.*

T

tall *adj.* alto, -ta
taller *adj.* más alto (-ta)
tallest *adj.* el más alto, la más alta
tangent *n.* tangente *f.*
tangram *n.* rompecabezas chino *m.*
tape measure *n.* cinta métrica *f.*
tessellate *v.* teselar
tessellation *n.* teselado *m.,* teselación *f.*
tetrahedron *n.* tetraedro *m.*
theorem *n.* teorema *m.*
three-dimensional *adj.* tridimensional
trace *v.* trazar
transformation *n.* transformación *f.*
transversal *adj. & n.* transversal *f.*
trapezoid *n.* trapecio *m.,* trapezoide *m.*
triangle *n.* triángulo *m.;* **acute t.** triángulo agudo; **equilateral t.**

MATHEMATICS

triángulo equilátero; **isosceles t.** triángulo isósceles; **obtuse t.** triángulo obtuso; **Pascal's t.** triángulo de Pascal; **right t.** triángulo recto, triángulo rectángulo; **scalene t.** triángulo escaleno

triangular *adj.* triangular

tube *n.* tubo *m.*

turn *n.* giro *m.*

turn *v.* girar, voltear

two-dimensional *adj.* bidimensional

U

unit *n.* unidad *f.;* **cubic u.** unidad cúbica; **square u.** unidad cuadrada

unshaded *adj.* sin sombra

V

vertex *n.* vértice *m.*

vertical *adj.* vertical; **v. angle** *n.* ángulo vertical *m.;* **v. axis** eje vertical *m.*

volume *n.* volumen *m.*

W

weight *n.* peso *m.;* **gross w.** peso bruto

wide *adj.* ancho, -cha

Probability & Data Analysis

A

analyze *v.* analizar

arrow *n.* flecha *f.*

B

bar graph *n.* gráfica de barras *f.*

biased question *n.* pregunta sesgada, pregunta capciosa *f.;* **b. sample** muestra sesgada *f.*

box and whiskers plot *n.* diagrama de caja y bigotes *m.*

C

causality *m.* causalidad *f.*

chance *n.* oportunidad *f.*, riesgo *m.*

compound event *n.* suceso compuesto *m.*

control group *n.* grupo de control *m.*

convenience sample *n.* muestra de conveniencia *f.*

correlation *n.* correlación *f.;* **negative c.** correlación negativa; **positive c.** correlación positiva

D

data *n.pl.* datos *m.;* **d. analysis** análisis de datos *m.;* **produce d.** *v.* arrojar datos

dependent *adj.* dependiente; **d. events** *n.pl.* eventos dependientes *m.;* **d. variable** variable dependiente *f.*

diagram *n.* diagrama *m.*

MATHEMATICS

35

MATHEMATICS

E

error *n.* error *m.;* **greatest possible e.** máximo error posible

event *n.* evento *m.*

experiment *n.* experimento *m.*

experimental *adj.* experimental; **e. probability** *n.* probabilidad experimental *f.*

extreme *adj.* extremo, -ma

extreme *n.* extremo *m.;* **lower e.** extremo inferior; **upper e.** extremo superior

F

frequency table *n.* tabla de frecuencias *f.*

G

graph *n.* gráfico, -ca *m.f.;* **bar g.** gráfica de barras; **line g.** gráfica de líneas

graph *v.* graficar

H

histogram *n.* histograma *m.*

I

independent *adj.* independiente; **i. events** *n.pl.* eventos independientes *m.;* **i. variable** variable independiente *f.*

interval *n.* intervalo *m.*

L

label *n.* rótulo *m.,* etiqueta *f.*

label *v.* rotular, nombrar, etiquetar

likely *adj.* probable; **equally l.**

igualmente probable

line *n.* línea *f.;* **l. graph** gráfica de líneas *f.;* **l. of best fit** línea de ajuste; **l. plot** diagrama de líneas *m.*

M

margin of error *n.* margen de error *m.*

maximum *adj.* máximo, -ma

maximum *n.* máximo *m.*

mean *adj.* medio, -dia

mean *n.* media *f.,* promedio *m.*

measure of central tendency *n.* medida de tendencia central *f.*

median *adj.* mediano, -na

median *n.* mediana *f.*

minimum *adj.* mínimo, -ma

minimum *n.* mínimo *m.*

mode *n.* modo *m.*

mutually exclusive events *n.pl.* sucesos mutuamente excluyentes *m.*

O

outcome *n.* resultado *m.,* consecuencia *f.*

outlier *n.* valor atípico *m.*

P

permutation *n.* permutación *f.*

pictograph *n.* pictografía *f.*

pie chart *n.* gráfica circular *f.*

population *n.* población *f.*

possibility *n.* posibilidad *f.*

possible *adj.* posible

probability *n.* probabilidad *f.;* **experimental p.** probabilidad experimental; **theoretical p.** probabilidad teórica

Q

quartile *n.* cuartil *m.;* **lower q.** cuartil inferior; **upper q.** cuartil superior

R

random *adj.* aleatorio, -ria; **r. sample** *n.* muestra aleatoria *f.*
randomly *adv.* aleatoriamente
range *n.* rango *m.,* alcance *m.*

S

sample *n.* muestra *f.,* muestreo *m.;* **biased s.** muestra sesgada; **convenience s.** muestra intencional, muestra de conveniencia; **random s.** muestra aleatoria
scatter plot *n.* diagrama de dispersión, diagrama de puntos *m.*
skew lines *n.pl.* líneas alabeadas *f.*
skewed distribution *n.* distribución asimétrica *f.*
standard deviation *n.* desviación estándar, desviación típica *f.*
statistics *n.* estadística *f.*
stem and leaf plot *n.* diagrama de tallo y hojas *m.*
survey *n.* encuesta *f.*

T

tally mark *n.* marca de conteo *f.*

Numbers & Measures

NUMERALS

	Cardinal	Ordinal
0	cero	
1	uno, -na	primero, -ra
2	dos	segundo, -da
3	tres	tercero, -ra
4	cuatro	cuarto, -ta
5	cinco	quinto, -ta
6	seis	sexto, -ta
7	siete	séptimo, -ma
8	ocho	octavo, -va
9	nueve	noveno, -na
10	diez	décimo, -ma

MATHEMATICS

	Cardinal	**Ordinal**
11	once	undécimo, -ma; onceavo, -va
12	doce	duodécimo, -ma
13	trece	decimotercero, -ra
14	catorce	decimocuarto, -ta
15	quince	decimoquinto, -ta
16	dieciséis	decimosexto, -ta
17	diecisiete	decimoséptimo, -ta
18	dieciocho	decimoctavo, -va
19	diecinueve	decimonoveno, -va
20	veinte	vigésimo, -ma
21	veintiuno, -na	vigésimo (-ma) primero (-ra)
30	treinta	trigésimo, -ma
31	treinta y uno	trigésimo (-ma) primero (-ra)
40	cuarenta	cuadragésimo, -ma
50	cincuenta	quincuagésimo, -ma
60	sesenta	sexagésimo, -ma
70	setenta	septuagésimo, -ma
80	ochenta	octogésimo, -ma
90	noventa	nonagésimo, -ma
100	cien, ciento	centésimo, -ma; centavo, -va
101	ciento uno, -na	centésimo (-ma) primero (-ra)
200	doscientos, -tas	ducentésimo, -ma
300	trescientos, -tas	tricentésimo, -ma
400	cuatrocientos, -tas	cuadringentésimo, -ma
500	quinientos, -tas	quingentésimo, -ma
600	seiscientos, -tas	sexcentésimo, -ma
700	setecientos, -tas	septingentésimo, -ma
800	ochocientos, -tas	octingentésimo, -ma
900	novecientos, -tas	noningentésimo, -ma
1,000	mil	milésimo, -ma
1,001	mil uno	milésimo (-ma) primero (-ra)
1,000,000	un millón	millonésimo, -ma
1,000,000,000	mil millones	mil millonésimo, -ma
1,000,000,000,000	un billón	billonésimo, -ma

MATHEMATICS

38

LENGTHS

inch *n.* pulgada *f.*
foot *n.* pie *m.*
yard *n.* yarda *f.*
mile *n.* milla *f.*

millimeter *n.* milímetro *m.*
centimeter *n.* centímetro *m.*
meter *n.* metro *m.*
kilometer *n.* kilómetro *m.*

AREAS

square inch *n.* pulgada cuadrada *f.*
square foot *n.* pie cuadrado *m.*
square yard *n.* yarda cuadrada *f.*
square mile *n.* milla cuadrada *f.*
acre *n.* acre *m.*

square centimeter *n.* centímetro cuadrado *m.*
square meter *n.* metro cuadrado *m.*
square kilometer *n.* kilómetro cuadrado *m.*

VOLUMES

teaspoon *n.* cucharadita *f.*
tablespoon *n.* cucharada *f.*
cup *n.* taza *f.*
pint *n.* pinta *f.*
quart *n.* cuarto de galón *m.*

gallon *n.* galón *m.*
milliliter *n.* mililitro *m.*
deciliter *n.* decilitro *m.*
liter *n.* litro *m.*
kiloliter *n.* kilolitro *m.*

WEIGHTS

ounce *n.* onza *f.*
pound *n.* libra *f.*
ton *n.* tonelada *f.*

milligram *n.* miligramo *m.*
gram *n.* gramo *m.*
kilogram *n.* kilogramo *m.*

TIME

second *n.* segundo *m.*
minute *n.* minuto *m.*
hour *n.* hora *f.*
minute hand *n.* minutero *m.*
hour hand *n.* horario, manecilla de las horas *f.*
second hand *n.* segundero *m.*

quarter hour *n.* cuarto de hora *m.*
half hour *n.* media hora *f.*
day *n.* día *m.*
week *n.* semana *f.*
month *n.* mes *m.*
year *n.* año *m.*
decade *n.* década *f.*

MATHEMATICS

• •

MONEY

penny *n.* centavo *m.*, penique *m.*
nickel *n.* níquel *m.*
dime *n.* diez centavos *m.pl.*

dollar *n.* dólar *m.*

quarter *n.* veinticinco centavos *m.pl.*
half dollar *n.* medio dólar *m.*

POWER

ampere *n.* amperio *m.*
milliampere *n.* miliamperio *m.*
hertz *n.* hertz *m.*
megahertz *n.* megahertz *m.*
joule *n.* julio *m.*

volt *n.* voltio *m.*
watt *n.* vatio *m.*
kilowatt *n.* kilovatio *m.*
megawatt *n.* megavatio *m.*
gigawatt *n.* gigavatio *m.*

MATHEMATICS

SCIENCE

Earth Sciences

A

abrasion *n.* abrasión *f.*

acid soil *n.* suelo ácido *m.*

aftershock *n.* réplica de terremoto *f.*

age *n.* edad *f.;* **absolute a.** edad absoluta; **relative a.** edad relativa

air *n.* aire *m.;* **a. mass** masa del aire *f.;* **a. movement** movimiento del aire *m.;* **a. pollution** contaminación atmosférica *f.;* **a. pressure** presión atmosférica *f.;* **a. quality** calidad del aire *f.*

alluvial fan *n.* abanico alubial *m.*

alpine *adj.* alpino, -na; alpestre

anenometer *n.* anemómetro *m.*

animal remains *n.pl.* restos animales *m.*

anticline *n.* plegamiento anticlinal *m.*

anticyclone *n.* anticiclón *m.*

aquatic *adj.* acuático, -ca

aquifer *n.* acuífero m.

arctic tundra *n.* tundra ártica *f.*

arid *adj.* árido, -da

ash *n.* ceniza *f.*

atmosphere *n.* atmósfera *f.*

atmospheric *adj.* atmosférico, -ca; **a. gases** *n.pl.* gases atmosféricos *m.;* **a. water** agua atmosférica *f.*

aurora *n.* aurora *f.;* **a. borealis** aurora boreal

autum *n.* otoño *m.*

autumnal equinox *n.* equinoccio de otoño *m.*

avalanche *n.* avalancha *f.*

B

barometer *n.* barómetro *m.;* **aneroid b.** barómetro aneroide

barometric pressure *n.* presión barométrica *f.*

barrier *n.* barrera *f.*

basin *n.* cuenca *f.*

batholith *n.* batolito *m.*

beach *n.* playa *f.*

bedrock *n.* lecho de roca *m.*

blizzard *n.* ventisca *f.,* tormenta de nieve *f.*

body of water *n.* cuerpo de agua *m.*

boreal forest *n.* bosque boreal *m.,* taiga *f.*

SCIENCE

boulder *n.* roca *f.,* peñasco *m.,* canto rodado *m.*
brackish water *n.* agua salobre *f.*
brick *n.* ladrillo *m.,* bloque *m.*

C

calcite *n.* calcita *f.*
caldera *n.* caldera volcánica *f.*
Cambrian Period *n.* Período Cámbrico, Período Cambriano *m.*
canyon *n.* cañón *m.*
cape *n.* cabo *m.*
cave *n.* cueva *f.*
cementation *n.* cementación *f.*
Cenozoic Era *n.* Cenozoico *m.,* Era Cenozoica *f.*
chemical *adj.* químico, -ca; **c. rock** roca química *f.;* **c. weathering** desgaste químico *m.*
chronological *adj.* cronológico, -ca
cinder cone *n.* cono de ceniza *m.*
cirrus *n.* cirro *m.*
clastic rock *n.* roca clástica *f.*
clay *n.* arcilla *f.,* barro *m.*
cliff *n.* acantilado *m.,* peñasco *m.*
climate *n.* clima *m.*
cloud *n.* nube *f.;* **c. forest** bosque nuboso *m.;* **storm c.** nubarrón *m.;* **stratus c.** nube estrato *f.*
cloudy *adj.* nublado, -da; **partly c.** parcialmente nublado
coal *n.* carbón mineral *m.*
coarse *adj.* grueso, -sa
cold front *n.* frente frío *m.*
compaction *n.* compactación *f.*
composite volcano *n.* volcán compuesto *m.*

compression *n.* compresión *f.*
conglomerate *n.* conglomerado *m.*
conifer *n.* conífera *f.*
conservation *n.* conservación *f.;* **c. plowing** arado de conservación *m.*
conserve *v.* conservar
contaminant *n.* contaminante *m.*
continental *adj.* continental; **c. drift** *n.* deriva continental *f.;* **c. slope** talud continental *m.*
contour *n.* contorno *m.;* **c. interval** intervalo de contorno *m.;* **c. line** curva de nivel *f.;* **c. plowing** arado de contorno *m.*
convection *n.* convección *f.;* **c. current** corriente de convección *f.*
convergent boundary *n.* frontera convergente *f.*
coral reef *n.* arrecife de coral *m.*
core *n.* núcleo *m.*
crater *n.* cráter *m.*
Cretaceous Period *n.* Período Cretácico, Período Cretáceo *m.*
Cryptic Era *n.* Era Críptica *f.*
crystal *n.* cristal *m.*
crystallization *n.* cristalización *f.*
cumulus *n.* cúmulo *m.*
current *n.* corriente *f.*
cycle *n.* ciclo *m.*

D

dam *n.* presa *f.,* represa *f.*
deciduous forest *n.* bosque caducifolio, bosque deciduo *m.*
decomposer *n.* descomponedor *m.*
decomposition *n.* descomposición *f.,* putrefacción *f.*

deep-ocean trench *n.* fosa oceánica profunda *f.*

deflation *n.* deflación *f.*

deforestation *n.* deforestación *f.*

deglaciation *n.* deshielo *m.*

degree *n.* grado *m.*

delta *n.* delta *m.*

density *n.* densidad *f.*

deposit *n.* yacimiento *m.*

deposition *n.* sedimentación *f.*

depth *n.* profundidad *f.*

desert *n.* desierto *m.*

dew *n.* rocío *m.;* **d. point** punto de condensación *m.*

dewdrop *n.* gota de rocío *f.*

diamond *n.* diamante *m.*

diverge *v.* divergir, bifurcar(se)

divergent *adj.* divergente; **d. boundary** *n.* borde divergente *m.;* **d. zone** zona de divergencia, zona divergente *f.*

dormant *adj.* inactivo, -va

drainage basin *n.* cuenca hidrográfica *f.*

drizzle *n.* llovizna *f.*

drought *n.* sequía *f.*

dune *n.* duna *f.*

dust *n.* polvo *m.;* **d. bowl** cuenca de polvo *f.;* **d. storm** tormenta de polvo *f.*

dyke *n.* dique *m.*

E

earth *n.* tierra *f.*

earth's crust *n.* corteza terrestre *f.*

earthquake *n.* temblor de tierra *m.,* sismo *m.,* seísmo *m.,* terremoto *m.*

ecological *adj.* ecológico, -ca

ecology *n.* ecología *f.*

El Niño *n.* El Niño *m.*

element *n.* elemento *m.*

elevation *n.* elevación *f.*

emerald *n.* esmeralda *f.*

energy *n.* energía *f.*

environment *n.* medio ambiente *m.*

Eocene Epoch *n.* Eoceno *m.,* Época del Eoceno *f.*

epicenter *n.* epicentro *m.*

epoch *n.* época *f.*

equator *n.* ecuador *m.*

equinox *n.* equinoccio *m.;* **autumnal e.** equinoccio de otoño; **vernal e.** equinoccio de primavera

erosion *n.* erosión *f.*

erupt *v.* hacer erupción, entrar en erupción

eruption *n.* erupción *f.*

evolution *n.* evolución *f.*

expansion *n.* expansión *f.*

explosion *n.* explosión *f.*

exposure *n.* exposición *f.*

extrusion *n.* extrusión *f.*

extrusive rock *n.* roca extrusiva *f.*

F

fall *n.* otoño *m.*

fault *n.* falla *f.;* **normal f.** falla normal; **reverse f.** falla inversa; **strike-slip f.** falla transcurrente, falla de rumbo

feldspar *n.* feldespato *m.*

fire *n.* fuego *m.,* incendio *m.;* **forest f.** incendio forestal

fissure *n.* fisura *f.*

SCIENCE

43

SCIENCE

flood *n.* inundación *f.;* **f. plain** llanura aluvial *f.*

fluorite *n.* fluorita *f.*

focus *n.* foco *m.*

fog *n.* niebla *f.*

foggy *adj.* neblinoso, -sa; brumoso, -sa; lleno de niebla

fold *n.* pliegue *m.*

foliated *adj.* foliado, -da

footwall *n.* bloque yacente *m.*

forecast *n.* pronóstico *m.*

forest *n.* bosque

formation *n.* formación *f.*

fossil *adj. & n.* fósil *m.;* **f. fuels** *pl.* combustibles fósiles *m.;* **f. record** registro fósil *m.;* **petrified f.** fósil petrificado; **trace f.** vestigio fósil *m.*

fracture *n.* fractura *f.,* rotura *f.*

freezing *adj.* helado, -da

freezing *n.* congelación *f.;* **f. point** punto de congelación *m.*

freshwater *n.* agua dulce *f.*

friction *n.* fricción *f.*

front *n.* frente *m.;* **cold f.** frente frío; **warm f.** frente cálido

frost *n.* escarcha *f.*

fuel *n.* combustible *m.*

G

gem, gemstone *n.* gema *f.,* piedra preciosa *f.*

geocentric *adj.* geocéntrico, -ca

geode *n.* geoda *f.*

geographical *adj.* geográfico, -ca; **g. feature** *n.* accidente geográfico *m.*

geological *adj.* geológico, -ca; **g. time** *n.* tiempo geológico *m.;* **g. time scale** escala geocronológica *f.*

geothermal activity *n.* actividad geotérmica *f.*

geyser *n.* géiser *m.*

glacial *adj.* glacial; **g. lake** *n.* lago glacial *m.;* **g. movement** movimiento glacial *m.;* **g. till** caja glacial *f.*

glacier *n.* glaciar *m.*

global *adj.* global; **g. positioning system (G.P.S.)** *n.* sistema de posicionamiento global *m.;* **g. warming** calentamiento global *m.*

globe *n.* (map) globo terráqueo *m.*

gorge *n.* cañón *m.,* desfiladero *m.*

gradient *n.* gradiente *m.*

granite *n.* granito *m.*

graphite *n.* grafito *m.*

grassland *n.* pradera *f.,* pastizal *m.*

gravel *n.* grava *f.,* gravilla *f.*

greenhouse *n.* invernadero *m.;* **g. effect** efecto invernadero *m.;* **g. gas** gas invernadero *m.*

ground *n.* suelo *m.,* terreno *m.,* tierra *f.;* **g. water** agua subterránea *f.,* aguas freáticas *f.pl.*

gully *n.* barranco *m.*

gypsum *n.* yeso *m.*

H

hail *n.* granizo *m.*

hail *v.* granizar

halo *n.* halo *m.*

hanging wall *n.* bloque colgante *m.*

hardness *n.* dureza *f.;* **h. scale** escala de dureza *f.*

• •

headland *n.* promontorio *m.,* cabo *m.*

heating *n.* calefacción *f.*

hemisphere *n.* hemisferio *m.*

high *adj.* alto, -ta; **h. pressure** *n.* alta presión *f.;* **h. tide** marea alta *f.,* pleamar *f.;* **h. wind** viento fuerte *m.*

hill *n.* colina *f.*

hilly *adj.* montañoso, -sa

hollow *adj.* hueco, -ca

Holocene Epoch *n.* Holoceno *m.,* Época del Holoceno *f.*

hot *adj.* caliente; **h. spot** *n.* punto caliente *m.;* **h. spring** agua termal *f.,* manantial termal *m.*

humidity *n.* humedad *f.;* **relative h.** humedad relativa

hurricane *n.* huracán *m.*

hydrometer *n.* hidrómetro *m.*

hydrosphere *n.* hidrósfera *f.,* hidrosfera *f.*

hygrometer *n.* higrómetro *m.*

I

ice *n.* hielo *m.;* **i. age** edad de hielo *f.,* era glacial *f.;* **i. cap** casquete de hielo *m.;* **i. sheet** capa de hielo *f.;* **i. wedging** cuña de hielo *f.*

iceberg *n.* iceberg *m.*

igneous rock *n.* roca ígnea *f.*

impact *n.* impacto *m.*

index contour *n.* curva de nivel índice *f.*

inner core *n.* núcleo interno *m.*

inorganic *adj.* inorgánico, -ca

intertidal zone *n.* zona intermareal *f.*

intrusion *n.* intrusión *f.*

intrusive rock *n.* roca intrusiva *f.*

invasion *n.* invasión *f.*

iron *n.* hierro *m.,* fierro *m.*

island *n.* isla *f.;* **i. arc** arco de islas *m.*

isobar *n.* isobara *f.*

isotherm *n.* isoterma *f.*

ivory *n.* marfil *m.*

J

jet stream *n.* corriente en chorro *f.*

Jurassic Period *n.* Período Jurásico *m.*

K

kettle *n.* marmita de gigante *f.*

L

lagoon *n.* laguna *f.*

lake *n.* lago *m.*

land *n.* tierra *f.;* **l. breeze** brisa terrestre *f.;* **l. mass** masa terrestre *f.*

landfill *n.* vertedero de basura *m.*

landscape *n.* paisaje *m.*

landslide *n.* deslave *m.,* desprendimiento de tierras *m.,* derrumbe *m.*

latitude *n.* latitud *f.*

lava *n.* lava *f.;* **l. flow** corriente de lava *f.,* colada de lava *f.*

law of superposition *n.* ley de la superposición *f.*

layer *n.* capa *f.;* **l. of the Earth** *pl.* capas profundas de la tierra, capas interiores de la tierra

leeward *adj.* de sotavento

levee *n.* dique *m.*

lightning *n.* rayo *m.,* relámpago *m.*

limestone *n.* caliza *f.,* piedra caliza *f.*

liquefaction *n.* licuefacción *f.*

SCIENCE

45

lithosphere *n.* litósfera *f.*, litosfera *f.*
litter *n.* basura *f.*
littoral zone *n.* zona litoral *f.*
load *n.* carga *f.*
loam *n.* marga *f.*
loess *n.* loess *m.*
longitude *n.* longitud *f.*
longshore drift *n.* deriva litoral *f.*
low *adj.* baja; **l. pressure** *n.* baja presión *f.;* **l. tide** marea baja *f.*
luminous *adj.* luminoso, -sa
luster *n.* lustre *m.*, brillo *m.*

M

magma *n.* magma *m.;* **m. chamber** cámara magmática *f.*
magnitude *n.* magnitud *f.*
mantle *n.* manto *m.*
map *n.* mapa *m.;* **m. en relieve** relief map; **m. projection** proyección cartográfica *f.*
marble *n.* mármol *m.*
marine *adj.* marino, -na
maritime air mass *n.* masa de aire marítima *f.*
marsh *n.* pantano *m.*, ciénaga *f.*
marshland *n.* pantanal *m.*
mass extinction *n.* extinción en masa, extinción masiva *f.*
massive *adj.* masivo, -va
meander *n.* meandro *m.*
meander *v.* (river) serpentear
mechanical weathering *n.* desgaste mecánico *m.*
Mercalli scale *n.* escala de Mercalli *f.*
meridian *n.* meridiano *m.*
mesosphere *n.* mesosfera *f.*

Mesozoic Era *n.* Mesozoico *m.*, Era Mesozoica *f.*
metallic *adj.* metálico, -ca
metamorphic rock *n.* roca metamórfica *f.*
meteorologist *n.* meteorólogo, -ga *m.f.*
mica *n.* mica *f.*
mid-ocean ridge *n.* dorsal centrooceánica *f.*
mineral *n.* mineral *m.;* **m. water** agua mineral *f.*
Mohs hardness scale *n.* escala de dureza de Mohs *f.*
moisture *n.* humedad *f.*, vaho *m.*
mold *n.* molde *m.*
moment magnitude scale *n.* escala de magnitud de momento *f.*
monsoon *n.* monzón *m.*
moraine *n.* morrena glaciar *f.*
motion *n.* movimiento *m.*
mountain *n.* montaña *f.;* **m. range** cordillera *f.*
mountainous *adj.* montañoso, -sa
mud *n.* lodo *m.*

N

natural *adj.* natural; **n. disaster** *n.* catástrofe natural *f.;* **n. gas** gas natural *m.;* **n. process** proceso natural *m.;* **n. resources** *pl.* recursos naturales *m.*
nimbus *n.* nimbo *m.*
North Pole *n.* Polo Norte *m.*

O

obsidian *n.* obsidiana *f.*

• •

ocean *n.* océano *m.*, mar *m.*

oil *n.* (crude) petróleo *m.*

ore *n.* mena *f.;* **o. mineral** mineral metalífero *m.*

organic rock *n.* roca orgánica *f.*

origin *n.* origen *m.*

overpopulation *n.* sobrepoblación *f.*, superpoblación *f.*

oxbow lake *n.* lago oxbow, lago de meandro *m.*

ozone *n.* ozono *f.;* **o. depletion** disminución del ozono *f.*, agotamiento de la capa de ozono *m.;* **o. layer** capa de ozono *f.*

P

P-wave *n.* onda P *f.*

pahoehoe *n.* lava cordada *f.*

Paleocene Epoch *n.* Paleoceno *m.*, Época del Paleoceno *f.*

Paleozoic Era *n.* Paleozoico *m.*, Era Paleozoica *f.*

Pangaea *n.* Pangea *f.*

pebble *n.* guijarro *m.*

pelagic zone *n.* zona pelágica *f.*

península *n.* península *f.*

period *n.* período, periodo *m.*

permeable *adj.* permeable

Permian Period *n.* Período Pérmico *m.*

petrified fossil *n.* fósil petrificado *m.*

physical process *n.* proceso físico *m.*

pipe *n.* tubería *f.*, chimenea volcánica *f.*

plain *n.* llanura *f.*

plant remains *n.pl.* restos de plantas *m.*

plate *n.* placa *f.;* **p. tectonics** placas tectónicas *pl.*, tectónica de placas *f.*

plateau *n.* meseta *f.*

Pleistocene Epoch *n.* Pleistoceno *m.*, Época del Pleistoceno *f.*

plucking *n.* extracción glaciar *f.*

polar zones *n.pl.* zonas polares *f.*

pole *n.* polo *m.;* **North P.** Polo Norte; **South P.** Polo Sur

pollutant *n.* contaminante *m.*

pollution *n.* contaminación *f.*

pond *n.* charca *f.*, estanque *m.*

precipitation *n.* precipitación *f.*

prehistoric *adj.* prehistórico, -ca

pressure *n.* presión *f.*

prime meridian *n.* meridiano cero, meridiano de Greenwich *m.*

pyrite (fool's gold) *n.* pirita *f.*

pyroclastic flow *n.* flujo piroclástico *m.*, corriente piroclástica *f.*

Q

quartz *n.* cuarzo *m.*

Quaternary Period *n.* Período Cuaternario *m.*

R

radiation *n.* radiación *f.*

radioactive *adj.* radiactivo, -va; **r. dating** *n.* datación radiactiva *f.;* **r. decay** descomposición radiactiva *f.*

radioactivity *n.* radiactividad *f.*, radioactividad *f.*

rain *n.* lluvia *f.;* **heavy r.** lluvia fuerte; **r. gauge** pluviómetro *m.*

rainforest *n.* bosque lluvioso *m.*, selva *f.*, jungla *f.;* **tropical r.** selva

SCIENCE

SCIENCE

tropical

recycle *v.* reciclar

refinery *n.* refinería *f.*

relative *adj.* relativo, -va; **r. age** *n.* edad relativa *f.;* **r. dating** datación relativa *f.;* **r. humidity** humedad relativa *f.*

resource *n.* recurso *m.;* **limited r.** recurso limitado; **renewable r.** recurso renovable

reuse *v.* reutilizar

Richter scale *n.* escala de Richter *f.*

rift valley *n.* valle del rift *m.*

rill *n.* arroyuelo *m.,* riachuelo *m.*

Ring of Fire Cinturón de Fuego *m.,* Anillo de Fuego *m.*

rip current *n.* corriente de resaca *f.*

rise *v.* (sun) salir, (tide) subir, (river) crecer

river *n.* río *m.*

rock *n.* piedra *f.,* roca *f.;* **chemical r.** roca química, roca de precipitación química; **clastic r.** roca clástica; **extrusive r.** roca extrusiva; **igneous r.** roca ígnea; **intrusive r.** roca intrusiva; **metamorphic r.** roca metamórfica; **organic r.** roca orgánica; **r. cycle** ciclo de la roca *m.;* **sedimentary r.** roca sedimentaria

runoff *n.* escurrimiento *m.*

S

S-wave *n.* onda S *f.*

salinity *n.* salinidad *f.*

salt *n.* sal *f.;* **s. marsh** marisma *f.*

saltwater *n.* agua salada *f.*

sand *n.* arena *f.;* **s. dune** duna de arena *f.;* **s. storm** tormenta de arena *f.*

sandstone *n.* arenisca *f.*

savanna *n.* sabana *f.*

scale *n.* escala *f.*

sea *n.* mar *m.;* **s. breeze** *n.* brisa marina *f.;* **s. level** nivel del mar *m.*

sea-floor spreading *n.* expansión del piso marino *f.*

season *n.* estación *f.,* temporada *f.*

sedimentary rock *n.* roca sedimentaria *f.*

sediments *n.pl.* sedimentos *m.*

seismic wave *n.* onda sísmica *f.*

seismogram *n.* sismograma *m.*

seismograph *n.* sismógrafo *m.*

severe weather *n.* inclemencia climática *f.,* tiempo severo *m.*

shale *n.* esquisto *m.*

shearing *n.* cizallamiento *m.,* deslizamiento *m.*

shield volcano *n.* volcán en escudo *m.*

shoal *n.* banco de arena *m.*

shore *n.* orilla *f.*

sill *n.* umbral submarino *m.*

silt *n.* sedimento *m.*

sky *n.* cielo *m.*

slate *n.* pizarra *f.*

sleet *n.* aguanieve *f.,* cellisca *f.*

slope *n.* pendiente *f.*

smelting *n.* fundición *f.*

smog *n.* niebla tóxica *f.,* esmog *m.*

smoke *n.* humo *m.*

snow *n.* nieve *f.*

snow *v.* nevar

sod *n.* tepe *m.*

soil *n.* suelo *m.,* tierra *f.;* **s. composition** composición del suelo *f.,* estructura de la tierra *f.;* **s. conservation** conservación del suelo *f.;* **s. horizon** horizonte del suelo *m.;* **s. texture** textura del suelo *f.*

solar power *n.* energía solar *f.*

solstice *n.* solsticio *m.;* **summer s.** solsticio de verano; **winter s.** solsticio de invierno

spit of land *n.* lengua de tierra *f.*

spring *n.* primavera *f.;* **s. tide** marea viva *f.*

stalactite *n.* estalactita *f.*

stalagmite *n.* estalagmita *f.*

station model *n.* modelo meteorológico, modelo de estación *m.*

steppe *n.* estapa *f.*

storm *n.* tormenta *f.;* **s. cloud** nubarrón *m.*

stratosphere *n.* estratósfera *f.,* estratosfera *f.*

stratus cloud *n.* nube estrato *f.*

streak *n.* veta *f.,* racha *f.*

stream *n.* arroyo *m.,* riachuelo *m.*

stress *n.* fuerza *f.,* esfuerzo *m.*

strike-slip fault *n.* falla transcurrente, falla de rumbo *f.*

subduction *n.* subducción *f.*

subsoil *n.* subsuelo *m.*

summer *n.* verano *m.*

sunny *adj.* soleado, -da

supply *n.* suministro *m.*

surface *n.* superficie *f.;* **s. water** agua superficial *f.;* **s. wave** onda superficial *f.*

survey *n.,* **surveying** *n.* agrimensura *f.*

syncline *adj. & n.* sinclinal *m.*

T

taiga *n.* bosque boreal *m.*

talc *n.* talco *m.*

temperate *adj.* templado, -da; **t. forest** bosque templado *m.;* **t. grassland** pastizal templado *m.;* **t. rainforest** bosque pluvial templado; **t. zone** zona de clima templado *f.*

temperature *n.* temperatura *f.*

tension *n.* tensión *f.*

texture *n.* textura *f.*

thawing *n.* derretimiento *m.,* descongelación *f.*

thermometer *n.* termómetro *m.*

thunder *n.* truenos *m.pl.*

thunderstorm *n.* tormenta eléctrica *f.*

tidal wave *n.* maremoto *m.,* tsunami *m.*

tide *n.* marea *f.;* **t. pool** poza de marea *f.*

time zone *n.* huso horario *m.*

topaz *n.* topacio *m.*

topographic map *n.* mapa topográfico *m.*

topography *n.* topografía *f.*

topsoil *n.* capa superior del suelo *f.*

tornado *n.* tornado *m.*

trade winds *n.pl.* vientos alisios *m.*

transform boundary *n.* borde de transformación *m.*

tremor *n.* temblor *m.*

Triassic Period *n.* Período Triásico *m.*

SCIENCE

tributary *n.* afluente *m.*

tropics *n.pl.* trópicos *m.*

troposphere *n.* tropósfera *f.*, troposfera *f.*

tsunami *n.* tsunami *m.*

tundra *n.* tundra *f.*

turbulence *n.* turbulencia *f.*

typhoon *n.* tifón *m.*

U

undertow *n.* resaca *f.*

V

valley *n.* valle *m.;* **rift v.** valle del rift; **v. glacier** glaciar de valle, glaciar alpino *m.*

vein *n.* vena *f.*

vent *n.* boca *f.*

vernal equinox *n.* equinoccio de primavera *m.*

viscosity *n.* viscosidad *f.*

volcanic *adj.* volcánico, -ca; **composite v.** volcán compuesto; **v. neck** *n.* cuello volcánico *m.;* **v. pipe** chimenea volcánica *f.*

volcano *n.* volcán *m.;* **shield v.** volcán en escudo

W

warm front *n.* frente caliente *m.*

warming *n.* calentamiento *m.*

water *n.* agua *f.;* **w. source** fuente de agua *f.;* **w. vapor** vapor de agua *m.*

waterfall *n.* cascada *f.*

watershed *n.* cuenca hidrográfica *f.*

wave *n.* (water) ola *f.*, (physics) onda *f.;* **seismic w.** onda sísmica

weather *n.* tiempo *m.;* **severe w.** inclemencia climática *f.*, tiempo severo; **w. conditions** condiciones meteorológicas *f.pl.;* **w. forecast** pronóstico del tiempo *m.;* **w. map** mapa meteorológico *m.;* **w. pattern** patrón meteorológico *m.*

weathering *n.* erosión *f.*, desgaste *m.;* **chemical w.** desgaste químico; **mechanical w.** desgaste mecánico

wetlands *n.pl.* tierras pantanosas *f.*, humedales *m.*

whirlpool *n.* remolino *m.*

wind *n.* viento *m.*, aire *m.;* **high w.** viento fuerte; **w. chill factor** factor de enfriamiento del viento *m.;* **w. direction** dirección del viento, dirección del aire *f.;* **w. speed** velocidad del viento *f.;* **w. storm** tormenta de viento *f.;* **w. vane** veleta *f.*

windward *adj.* de barlovento

windy *adj.* ventoso, -sa

winter *n.* invierno *m.*

Z

zone *n.* zona *f.;* **divergent z.** zona de divergencia; **intertidal z.** zona intermareal; **littoral z.** zona litoral; **pelagic z.** zona pelágica; **polar z.** *pl.* zonas polares; **temperate z.** zona de clima templado; **time z.** huso horario *m.*, zona horaria *f.*

Life Sciences

A

abdomen *n.* abdomen *m.*

absorption *n.* absorción *f.*

active *adj.* activo, -va; **a. transport** *n.* transporte activo *m.;* **a. virus** virus activo *m.*

adaptation *n.* adaptación *f.*

adult *adj. & n.* adulto, -ta *m.f.*

algae *n.pl.* algas *f.*

algal bloom *n.* floración de algas *f.*

alive *adj.* viviente

allele *n.* alelo *m.;* **dominant a.** alelo dominante; **multiple a.** *pl.* alelos múltiples; **recessive a.** alelo recesivo

amino acids *n.pl.* aminoácidos *m.*

amoeba *n.* ameba *f.*

amphibian *n.* anfibio *m.*

ankle *n.* tobillo *m.*

antlers *n.pl.* cuernos *m.*, cornamenta *f.*

aquatic *adj.* acuático, -ca

arachnid *n.* arácnido *m.*

arm *n.* brazo *m.*

asexual reproduction *n.* reproducción asexual *f.*

autotroph *n.* autótrofo *m.*

auxin *n.* auxina *f.*

B

baby teeth *n.pl.* dientes de leche *m.*

backbone *n.* columna vertebral *f.*, espina dorsal *f.*

bacteria *n.* bacteria *f.*

bacteriophage *n.* bacteriófago *m.*

bark *n.* corteza *f.*

beak, bill *n.* pico *m.;* **curved b.** pico encorvado; **hooked b.** pico ganchudo; **straight b.** pico recto

behavior *n.* comportamiento *m.*

belly *n.* barriga *f.*, panza *f.*

biceps *n.pl.* bíceps *m.*

binary fission *n.* fisión binaria *f.*

binomial nomenclature *n.* nomenclatura binomial *f.*

biodegradable *adj.* biodegradable

biodiversity *n.* biodiversidad *f.*

biomagnification *n.* biomagnificación *f.*

biosphere *n.* biosfera *f.*

bird *n.* ave *f.*, pájaro *m.*

birth *n.* nacimiento *m.*

bladder *n.* vejiga *f.*

blood *n.* sangre *f.;* **b. cell** glóbulo *m.;* **red b. cell** glóbulo rojo; **white b. cell** glóbulo blanco

bone *n.* hueso *m.;* **compact b.** hueso compacto; **spongy b.** hueso esponjoso

brain *n.* cerebro *m.*

branch *n.* rama *f.*

break down *v.* descomponer

buttocks *n.pl.* nalgas *f.*

C

camouflage *n.* camuflaje *m.*

cancer *n.* cáncer *m.*

SCIENCE

canines *n.pl.* (teeth) caninos *m.*

canopy *n.* manto *m.*

capillary *n.* capilar *m.*

carbohydrate *n.* carbohidrato *m.*

carbon *n.* carbono *m.;* **c. dioxide** dióxido de carbono *m.;* **c. monoxide** monóxido de carbono *m.*

carcinogen *n.* carcinógeno *m.*

cardiovascular system *n.* sistema cardiovascular *m.*

carnivore *n.* carnívoro *m.*

carpel *n.* carpelo *m.*

carrier *n.* portador, -ora *m.f.*

cartilage *n.* cartílago *m.*

cell *n.* célula *f.;* **c. cycle** ciclo celular *m.;* **c. division** división celular *f.;* **c. growth** crecimiento celular *m.;* **c. membrane** membrana celular *f.;* **c. theory** teoría celular *f.;* **c. wall** pared celular *f.;* **guard c.** *pl.* células guardianas

cellular *adj.* celular

cellulose *n.* celulosa *f.*

central nervous system *n.* sistema nervioso central *m.*

cerebellum *n.* cerebelo *m.*

cerebrum *n.* cerebro *m.*

characteristic *n.* característica *f.*

cheek *n.* mejilla *f.*

chest *n.* pecho *m.*

chlorophyll *n.* clorofila *f.*

chloroplast *n.* cloroplasto *m.*

cholesterol *n.* colesterol *m.*

chromosome *n.* cromosoma *m.*

chrysalis *n.* crisálida *f.*

cilia *n.pl.* cilios *m.*

circulate *v.* circular

circulatory system *n.* sistema circulatorio *m.*

class *n.* (taxonomy) clase *f.*

classification *n.* clasificación *f.*

clavicle *n.* clavícula *f.*

claw *n.* garra *f.*

clone *n.* clon *m.*

cochlea *n.* cóclea *f.*

cocoon *n.* capullo *m.*

codominance *n.* codominancia *f.*

cold-blooded *adj.* de sangre fría

colon *n.* colon *m.*

commensalism *n.* comensalismo *m.*

competition *n.* competencia *f.*, competición *f.*

concussion *n.* contusión *f.*

conjugation *n.* conjugación *f.*

connective tissue *n.* tejido conectivo *m.*

contraception *n.* anticoncepción *f.*

control *v.* controlar

cornea *n.* córnea *f.*

corolla *n.* corola *f.*

coronary artery *n.* arteria coronaria *f.*

cytokinesis *n.* citocinesis *f.*

cytoplasm *n.* citoplasma *m.*

D

dead *adj. & n.* muerto, -ta *m.f.*

death *n.* muerte *f.*

decay *n.* descomposición *f.*

decomposer *n.* organismo descomponedor *m.*

decomposition *n.* descomposición *f.*

decrease *v.* disminuir

dendrite *n.* dendrita *f.*

deoxyribonucleic acid (D.N.A.) *n.* ácido desoxirribonucleico (A.D.N.) *m.*

depressant *n.* sedante *m.*

diet *n.* alimentación *f.*

Dietary Reference Intakes (D.R.I.s) *n.pl.* Aportes dietéticos de referencia *m.*

diffusion *n.* difusión *f.*

digestion *n.* digestión *f.*

digestive system *n.* sistema digestivo *m.*

disease *n.* enfermedad *f.*

dislocation *n.* dislocación *f.*

disperse *v.* dispersar

E

ear *n.* oído *m.;* **inner e.** oído interno; **middle e.** oído medio

eardrum *n.* tímpano *m.*

ecosystem *n.* ecosistema *m.*

egg *n.* óvulo *m.,* huevo *m.*

elbow *n.* codo *m.*

embryo *n.* embrión *m.*

emergent layer *n.* capa emergente *f.*

endangered species *n.* especie en peligro de extinción *f.*

endocrine gland *n.* glándula endocrina *f.*

endoplasmic reticulum *n.* retículo endoplasmático *m.*

endothermic *adj.* endotérmico, -ca

environmental *adj.* medioambiental; **e. factor** *n.* factor medioambiental *m.*

enzyme *n.* enzima *f.*

epidermis *n.* epidermis *m.*

epiglottis *n.* epiglotis *f.*

epithelial tissue *n.* tejido epitelial *m.*

esophagus *n.* esófago *m.*

estrogen *n.* estrógeno *m.*

evolution *n.* evolución *f.*

excretion *n.* excreción *f.*

excretory system *n.* sistema excretorio *m.*

exosphere *n.* exosfera *f.*

exothermic *adj.* exotérmico, -ca

extinct *adj.* extinto, -ta

extinction *n.* extinción *f.*

eye *n.* ojo *m.*

eyelid *n.* párpado *m.*

F

Fallopian tube *n.* trompa de Falopio *f.*

family *n.* (taxonomy) familia *f.*

fang *n.* colmillo *m.*

fats *n.pl.* grasas *f.*

feather *n.* pluma *f.*

female *n. & adj.* hembra *f.*

fermentation *n.* fermentación *f.*

fertilization *n.* fecundación *f.*

fetus *n.* feto *m.*

fin *n.* aleta *f.;* **dorsal f.** aleta dorsal

finger *n.* dedo *m.*

fingernail *n.* uña *f.*

fish *n.* pez *m.,* peces *m.pl.*

flagellum *n.* flagelo *m.*

flatworm *n.* platelminto *m.*

flower *n.* flor *f.*

follicle *n.* folículo *m.*

food *n.* alimento *m.,* (for plants) abono *m.*

foot *n.* (human) pie *m.,* (animal)

SCIENCE

pata *f.*

frond *n.* fronda *f.*

fruit *n.* (botany) fruto *m.*, (food) fruta *f.*

fruiting body *n.* cuerpo fructífero *m.*

function *n.* función *f.*

fungi *n.pl.* hongos *m.*

fur *n.* pelaje *m.*

G

gallbladder *n.* vesícula biliar *f.*

gametophyte *n.* gametofito *m.*, gametófito *m.*

ganglion *n.* ganglio *m.*

gene *n.* gen *m.;* **g. therapy** terapia genética *f.*

genetic *adj.* genético, -ca; **g. code** *n.* código genético *m.;* **g. disorder** trastorno genético *m.;* **g. engineering** ingeniería genética *f.*

genetics *n.* genética *f.*

genitals *n.pl.* genitales *m.*

genome *n.* genoma *m.*

genotype *n.* genotipo *m.*

genus *n.* género *m.*

germination *n.* germinación *f.*

gill *n.* branquia *f.*

gland *n.* glándula *f.*

glucose *n.* glucosa *f.*

Golgi body *n.* aparato de Golgi *m.*

gradualism *n.* gradualismo *m.*, gradualidad *f.*

grain *n.* grano *m.*

grow *v.* crecer

growth *n.* crecimiento *m.*

guard cells *n.pl.* células guardianas *f.*

gymnosperms *n.pl.* gimnospermas *f.*

H

habitat *n.* hábitat *m.*

hair *n.* cabello *m.*, pelo *m.*

hand *n.* mano *f.*

head *n.* cabeza *f.*

health care *n.* cuidado de la salud *m.*

hearing *n.* audición *f.*, sentido de oido *m.*

heart *n.* corazón *m.;* **h. attack** infarto cardiaco, infarto cardíaco *m.;* **h. chambers** *pl.* cámaras del corazón *f.;* **h. muscle** músculo cardiaco, músculo cardíaco *m.*

heel *n.* (foot) talón *m.*

hemoglobin *n.* hemoglobina *f.*

herbivore *n.* herbívoro *m.*

heredity *n.* herencia *f.*

heterotroph *n.* heterótrofo *m.*

heterozygous *adj.* heterocigótico, -ca

hibernation *n.* hibernación *f.*

hip *n.* cadera *f.*

histamine *n.* histamina *f.*

hive *n.* colmena *f.*

homeostasis *n.* homeostasis *f.*

homologous structures *n.pl.* estructuras homólogas *f.*

homozygous *adj.* homocigótico, -ca

hoof *n.* (horse) casco *m.*, (cow, sheep) pezuña *f.*

hormone *n.* hormona *f.*

horn *n.* (deer) cuerno *m.*

host *n.* huésped *m.*

human *adj.* humano, -na

human *n.* humano *m.*

hybrid *n.* híbrido *m.*

hybridization *n.* hibridación *f.*
hydroponics *n.* hidroponia *f.*
hyphae *n.pl.* hifas *f.*
hypothalamus *n.* hipotálamo *m.*

I
immune *adj.* inmunológico, -ca; **i. response** *n.* respuesta inmunológica *f.*, reacción inmunológica *f.*; **i. system** sistema inmunológico *m.*
immunity *n.* inmunidad *f.*
inbreeding *n.* endogamia *f.*
incisor *n.* incisivo *m.*
index finger *n.* dedo índice *m.*
infectious disease *n.* enfermedad infecciosa, enfermedad contagiosa *f.*
inflammatory response *n.* reacción inflamatoria *f.*
inhabit *v.* habitar
inherit *v.* heredar
inheritance *n.* herencia *f.*
inherited *adj.* heredado, -da
inner ear *n.* oído interno *m.*
insect *n.* insecto *m.*
instinct *n.* instinto *m.*
insulin *n.* insulina *f.*
integumentary system *n.* sistema tegumentario *m.*
interneuron *n.* interneurona *f.*
interphase *n.* interfase *f.*
interrelationship *n.* interrelación *f.*
intestine *n.* intestino *m.;* **large i.** intestino grueso; **small i.** intestino delgado
invertebrate *n.* invertebrado *m.*
involuntary *adj.* involuntario, -ria; **i. muscle** *n.* músculo involuntario *m.*
iris *n.* (eye) iris *m.*

J
jaw *n.* mandibula *f.*, maxilar *m.*
jawbone *n.* quijada *f.*, maxilar *m.*
joint *n.* articulación *f.*

K
karyotype *n.* cariotipo *m.*
kidney *n.* riñón *m.*
kingdom *n.* (taxonomy) reino *m.*
knee *n.* rodilla *f.*

L
labor *n.* (birth) parto *m.*
lactation *n.* lactancia *f.*
larva *n.* larva *f.*
larynx *n.* laringe *f.*
leaf *n.* hoja *f.*
leg *n.* (animal) pata *f.*, (human) pierna *f.*
lens *n.* (eye) cristalino *m.*
life cycle *n.* ciclo de vida *m.*
ligament *n.* ligamento *m.*
lipid *n.* lípido *m.*
liver *n.* hígado *m.*
livestock *n.* ganado *m.*
living *adj.* vivo, -va; viviente
lung *n.* pulmón *m.*
lymph *n.* linfa *f.;* **l. node** ganglio linfático *m.*
lymphatic system *n.* sistema linfático *m.*
lymphocyte *n.* linfocito *m.*
lysosome *n.* lisosoma *m.*

SCIENCE

SCIENCE

M

macroscopic *adj.* macroscópico, -ca

male *n. & adj.* macho *m.*

mammal *n.* mamífero *m.*

mandible *n.* mandíbula *f.,* maxilar *m.*

marrow *n.* médula *f.*

medicine *n.* medicamento *m.,* fármaco *m.*

meiosis *n.* meiosis *f.*

melanin *n.* melanina *f.*

menstruation *n.* menstruación *f.*

metabolism *n.* metabolismo

metamorphosis *n.* metamorfosis *f.*

microorganism *n.* microorganismo *m.*

microscopic *adj.* microscópico, -ca

middle ear *n.* oído medio *m.*

migration *n.* migración *f.*

milk *n.* leche *f.*

mimicry *n.* mimetismo *m.*

minerals *n.pl.* minerales *m.*

mitochondria *n.* mitocondria *f.*

mitosis *n.* mitosis *f.*

mixed-breed *adj.* de raza mixta

molar *n.* muela *f.*

molecule *n.* molécula *f.*

mold *n.* moho *m.*

mortality *n.* mortalidad *f.*

moss *n.* musgo *m.*

motor neuron *n.* neurona motora *f.*

mouth *n.* boca *f.*

mucus *n.* mucosidad *f.*

multicellular *adj.* multicelular

muscle *n.* músculo *m.;* **cardiac m.** músculo cardíaco; **m. tissue** tejido muscular *m.;* **skeletal m.** músculo esquelético; **smooth m.** músculo liso; **striated m.** músculo estriado; **voluntary m.** músculo voluntario

muscular system *n.* sistema muscular *m.*

mutation *n.* mutación *f.*

mutualism *n.* mutualismo *m.*

N

nasal *adj.* nasal

natural selection *n.* selección natural *f.*

nephron *n.* nefrona *f.*

nerve *n.* nervio *m.;* **n. impulse** impulso nervioso *m.*

nervous *adj.* nervioso, -sa; **n. system** *n.* sistema nervioso *m.;* **n. tissue** tejido nervioso *m.*

nest *n.* nido *m.*

nest *v.* anidar

neuron *n.* neurona *f.;* **motor n.** neurona motora; **sensory n.** neurona sensorial

neurotransmitter *n.* neurotransmisor *m.*

niche *n.* nicho *m.*

nicotine *n.* nicotina *f.*

nonliving *adj.* inanimado, -da

nucleic acid *n.* ácido nucleico *m.*

nucleus *n.* núcleo *m.*

nutrient *n.* nutriente *m.*

nutrition *n.* nutrición *f.,* alimentación *f.*

O

offspring *n.* descendencia *f.;* crías *f.pl.*

omnivore *n.* omnívoro *m.*

optic nerve *n.* nervio óptico *m.*

order *n.* (taxonomy) orden *m.*

organ *n.* órgano *m.;* **o. malfunction** disfunción del órgano *f.;* **o. system** sistema de órganos *m.*

organelle *n.* orgánulo *m.*

organic *adj.* orgánico, -ca

organism *n.* organismo *m.*

origin *n.* origen *m.*

osmosis *n.* ósmosis *f.*

ovary *n.* ovario *m.*

overproduction *n.* sobreproducción *f.*

oviparous *adj.* ovíparo, -ra

ovoviviparous *adj.* ovovivíparo, -ra

ovulation *n.* ovulación *f.*

ovule *n.* óvulo *m.*

P

pancreas *n.* páncreas *m.*

paramecium *n.* paramecio *m.*

parasite *n.* parásito *m.*

parasitism *n.* parasitismo *m.*

parent *n.* padre *m.*

passive *adj.* pasivo, -va; **p. immunity** *n.* inmunidad pasiva *f.;* **p. transport** transporte pasivo *m.*

pasteurization *n.* pasteurización *f.*

pathogen *n.* patógeno *m.*

paw *n.* garra *f.,* pata *f.*

peat *n.* turba *f.*

pedigree *n.* pedigrí *m.*

penicillin *n.* penicilina *f.*

penis *n.* pene *m.*

Percent Daily Value (P.D.V.) *n.* Valor Porcentual Diario *m.*

peripheral *adj.* periférico, -ca; **p. nervous system** *n.* sistema nervioso periférico *m.*

peristalsis *n.* peristaltismo *m.*

permeable *adj.* permeable; **selectively p.** selectivamente permeable

petal *n.* pétalo *m.*

phagocyte *n.* fagocito *m.*

pharynx *n.* faringe *f.*

phenotype *n.* fenotipo *m.*

phlegm *n.* flema *f.*

phloem *n.* floema *m.*

photoperiodism *n.* fotoperiodisidad *f.*

photosynthesis *n.* fotosíntesis *f.*

phylum *n.* filo *m.*

phytoplankton *n.* fitoplancton *m.*

pigment *n.* pigmento *m.*

pine *n.* pino *m.;* **p. cone** piña de pino *f.*

pistil *n.* pistilo *m.*

pituitary gland *n.* glándula pituitaria *f.*

placenta *n.* placenta *f.*

plant *n.* planta *f.;* **nonvascular p.** planta no vascular; **vascular p.** planta vascular

plasma *n.* plasma *m.*

platelet *n.* plaqueta *f.*

pod *n.* vaina *f.*

poison *n.* veneno *m.*

poison *v.* envenenar

pollen *n.* polen *m.*

pollinate *v.* polinizar

pollination *n.* polinización *f.*

pollinator *n.* polinizador *m.*

SCIENCE

SCIENCE

polyp *n.* pólipo *m.*

population *n.* población *f.;* **p. density** densidad de población *f.*

pore *n.* poro *m.*

porous *adj.* poroso, -sa

predator *n.* predador, -ora *m.f.;* depredador, -ora *m.f.*

pregnancy *n.* embarazo *m.*

pregnant *adj.* embarazada

prey *n.* presa *f.*

prokaryote *n.* procariota *f.*

protein *n.* proteína *f.*

protozoan *n.* protozoo *m.*

protozoic *adj.* protozoario, -ria

pseudopod *n.* seudópodo *m.*

puberty *n.* pubertad *f.*

pulse *n.* pulso *m.*

punctuated equilibrium *n.* equilibrio puntuado *m.*

Punnett square *n.* cuadrado de Punnet *m.*

pupa *n.* crisálida *f.*

pupil *n.* pupila *f.*

purebred *adj.* de pura raza

R

race *n.* raza *f.*

raptor *n.* ave de rapiña, ave rapaz *f.*

receptor *n.* receptor *m.*

recessive allele *n.* alelo recesivo *m.*

rectum *n.* recto *m.*

red blood cell *n.* glóbulo rojo *m.*

red tide *n.* marea roja *f.*

reflex *n.* reflejo *m.*

replication *n.* replicación *f.*

reproduce *v.* reproducir

reproduction *n.* reproducción *f.*

reproductive system *n.* sistema reproductor *m.*

reptile *n.* reptil *m.*

respiration *n.* respiración *f.*

respiratory system *n.* sistema respiratorio *m.*

retina *n.* retina *f.*

rhizoid *n.* rizoide *m.*

rhizome *n.* rizoma *m.*

riboflavin *n.* riboflavina *f.*

ribonucleic acid (R.N.A.) *n.* ácido ribonucleico (A.R.N.) *m.;* **messenger R.N.A.** A.R.N. mensajero; **transfer R.N.A.** A.R.N. de transferencia

ribosome *n.* ribosoma *m.*

rib *n.* costilla *f.*

role *n.* función *f.*

root *n.*, **roots** *n.pl.* raíz *f.*, raíces *f.*

root cap *n.* caliptra *f.*

roundworm *n.* lombriz intestinal *f.*, ascáride *f.*

S

sac *n.* saco *m.*, bolsa *f.*

saliva *n.* saliva *f.*

saprophyte *n.* saprófito *m.*

scale *n.* (skin) escama *f.*

scavenger *n.* animal carroñero *m.*

secretion *n.* secreción

seed *n.* semilla *f.*

selection *n.* selección *f.*

selective breeding *n.* reproducción selectiva *f.*

semen *n.* semen *m.*

semicircular canal *n.* canal semicircular *m.*

sense *n.* sentido *m.;* **s. of hearing** sentido del oído; **s. of sight** sentido de la vista; **s. of smell** sentido del olfato; **s. of taste** sentido del gusto; **s. of touch** sentido del tacto

sensory neuron *n.* neurona sensorial *f.*

sepal *n.* sépalo *m.*

sex *n.* sexo *m.;* **s. chromosomes** *pl.* cromosomas sexuales *m.*

sex-linked gene *n.* gen ligado al sexo *m.*

sexual reproduction *n.* reproducción sexual *f.*

shelter *n.* refugio *m.*

sight *n.* sentido de vista *f.*

skeletal *adj.* esquelético, -ca; **s. muscle** *n.* músculo esquelético *m.;* **s. system** sistema esquelético, sistema óseo *m.*

skeleton *n.* esqueleto *m.*

skin *n.* piel *f.*

skull *n.* cráneo *m.,* calavera *f.*

smell *n.* olfato *m.*

somatic *adj.* somático, -ca; **s. nervous system** *n.* sistema nervioso somático *m.*

speciation *n.* especiación *f.*

species *n.* especie *f.;* **endangered s.** especie en peligro de extinción *f.;* **exotic s.** especie exótica

sperm *n.* esperma *m.,* espermatozoide *m.*

spiderweb *n.* tela de araña *f.*

spinal cord *n.* médula espinal *f.*

spore *n.* espora *f.*

stamen *n.* estambre *m.*

starch *n.* almidón *m.*

stem *n.* tallo *m.;* **s. cell** célula madre *f.*

steroid *n.* esteroide *m.*

stimulant *n.* estimulante *m.*

stimulus *n.* estímulo *m.*

stomach *n.* estómago *m.*

stomata *n.pl.* estomas *m.*

stress *n.* estrés *m.*

striated muscle *n.* músculo estriado *m.*

sunlight *n.* luz solar *f.*

survival *n.* supervivencia *f.*

survive *v.* sobrevivir

swamp *n.* pantano *m.*

symbiosis *n.* simbiosis *f.*

synapse *n.* sinapsis *f.*

synthesis *n.* síntesis *f.*

T

T cell *n.* célula T *f.*

tail *n.* cola *f.*

talon *n.* garra *f.*

target cell *n.* célula diana, célula blanco *f.*

taste *n.* sentido del gusto *m.*

tendon *n.* tendón *m.*

tentacle *n.* tentáculo *m.*

testes *n.pl.,* **testicles** *n.pl.* testículos *m.*

testosterone *n.* testosterona *f.*

theory of evolution *n.* teoría de la evolución *f.*

thorax *n.* tórax *m.*

throat *n.* garganta *f.*

thumb *n.* pulgar *m.*

thyroid gland *n.* glándula tiroides *f.*
tissue *n.* tejido *m.*
tolerance *n.* tolerancia *f.*
tongue *n.* lengua *f.*
tooth *n.* diente *m.*
touch *n.* sentido del tacto *m.*
toxic *adj.* tóxico, -ca
toxin *n.* toxina *f.*
trachea *n.* tráquea *m.*
trait *n.* rasgo *m.*, característica *f.*, cualidad *f.*
transport *n.* transporte *m.*
tree *n.* árbol *m.*; **branching t.** árbol ramificado
tropism *n.* tropismo *m.*
trunk *n.* tronco *m.*
tumor *n.* tumor *m.*
tusk *n.* colmillo *m.*

U

umbilical cord *n.* cordón umbilical *m.*
unicellular *adj.* unicelular
urea *n.* urea *f.*
ureter *n.* uréter *m.*
urethra *n.* uretra *f.*
urinary bladder *n.* vejiga urinaria *f.*
urine *n.* orina *f.*
uterus *n.* útero *m.*

V

vaccination *n.* vacunación *f.*
vaccine *n.* vacuna *f.*
vacuole *n.* vacuola *f.*
valve *n.* válvula *f.*
variation *n.* variación *f.*
vascular *adj.* vascular; **v. plant** *n.* planta vascular *f.*; **v. tissue** tejido vascular *m.*
vegetable *n.* (food) verdura *f.*, (plant) vegetal *m.*
vein *n.* vena *f.*
ventricle *n.* ventrículo *m.*
vertebrae *n.pl.* vértebras *f.*
vertebrate *adj.* vertebrado, -da
vertebrate *n.* vertebrado *m.*
villi *n.pl.* vellosidades *f.*
virus *n.* virus *m.*
vitamins *n.pl.* vitaminas *f.*
viviparous *adj.* vivíparo, -ra
vocal chords *n.pl.* cuerdas vocales *f.*
vulva *n.* vulva *f.*

W

waist *n.* cintura *f.*
warm-blooded *adj.* de sangre caliente
webbed feet *n.pl.* patas palmeadas *f.*
white blood cell *n.* glóbulo blanco *m.*
windpipe *n.* tráquea *f.*
wing *n.* ala *f.*
wisdom tooth *n.* muela del juicio *f.*, cordal *m.*
womb *n.* matriz *f.*, útero *m.*
wrist *n.* muñeca *f.*

X

xylem *n.* xilema *f.*

Y

yolk *n.* yema *f.*; **y. sac** saco vitelino *m.*

Z

zygote *n.* cigoto *m.*
zoo *n.* zoológico *m.*

ANIMALS

alligator *n.* caimán *m.,* aligador *m.*

Allosaurus *n.* Alosaurio *m.*

ant *n.* hormiga *f.*

antelope *n.* antílope *m.*

Apatosaurus *n.* Apatosaurio *m.*

ape *n.* simio *m.*

armadillo *n.* armadillo *m.*

baboon *n.* babuino *m.,* papión *m.*

badger *n.* tejón *m.*

bat *n.* murciélago *m.*

bear *n.* oso, -sa *m.f.*

beaver *n.* castor *m.*

bee *n.* abeja *f.*

beetle *n.* escarabajo *m.*

bison *n.* bisonte *m.,* búfalo *m.*

bobcat *n.* lince *m.*

bull *n.* toro *m.*

bumblebee *n.* abejorro *m.*

butterfly *n.* mariposa *f.*

camel *n.* camello *m.*

caribou *n.* caribú *m.*

cat *n.* gato, -ta *m.f.*

centipede *n.* ciempiés *m.*

chameleon *n.* camaleón *m.*

cheetah *n.* guepardo *m.*

chicken *n.* pollo *m.*

chimpanzee *n.* chimpancé *m.*

chipmunk *n.* ardilla listada *f.*

clam *n.* almeja *f.*

cockroach *n.* cucaracha *f.*

conch *n.* caracola *f.*

cougar *n.* puma *m.*

cow *n.* vaca *f.*

coyote *n.* coyote *m.*

crab *n.* cangrejo *m.*

cricket *n.* grillo *m.*

crocodile *n.* cocodrilo *m.*

crow *n.* corneja *f.,* cuervo *m.*

deer *n.* ciervo *m.,* venado *m.*

dinosaur *n.* dinosaurio *m.*

dog *n.* perro, -rra *m.f.*

dolphin *n.* delfín *m.*

donkey *n.* burro *m.*

dragonfly *n.* libélula *f.*

duck *n.* pato, -ta *m.f.*

eagle *n.* águila *m.*

eel *n.* anguila *f.*

elephant *n.* elefante *m.*

elk *n.* alce *m.*

falcon *n.* halcón *m.*

ferret *n.* hurón *m.*

flamingo *n.* flamenco *m.*

flea *n.* pulga *f.*

fly *n.,* **housefly** *n.* mosca *f.*

fox *n.* zorro *m.*

frog *n.* rana *f.*

gecko *n.* geco *m.*

gerbil *n.* jerbo *m.,* gerbo *m.*

Giganotosaurus *n.* Giganotosaurio *m.*

giraffe *n.* jirafa *f.*

goat *n.* cabra *f.*

goose *n.* ganso, -sa *m.f.*

gorilla *n.* gorila *m.*

grasshopper *n.* saltamontes *m.*

hamster *n.* hámster *m.*

hare *n.* liebre *f.*

hawk *n.* halcón *m.*

hen *n.* gallina *f.*

hippopotamus *n.* hipopótamo *m.*

horse *n.* caballo *m.*

SCIENCE

hummingbird *n.* colibrí *m.*
hyena *n.* hiena *f.*
Ichthyosaurs *n.pl.* Ictiosaurios *m.*
iguana *n.* iguana *f.*
jaguar *n.* jaguar *m.*
jellyfish *n.* medusa *f.*, aguamala *f.*
kangaroo *n.* canguro *m.*
koala *n.* koala *m.*
ladybug *n.* mariquita *f.*
leopard *n.* leopardo *m.*
lice *n.pl.* piojos *m.*
lion *n.* león *m.*
lizard *n.* lagartija *f.*, lagarto *m.*
lobster *n.* langosta *f.*
mammoth *n.* mamut *m.*
manatee *n.* manatí *m.*
mare *n.* yegua *f.*
mastodon *n.* mastodonte *m.*
monkey *n.* mono, -na *m.f.;* chango *m.*
moose *n.* alce americano *m.*
mosquito *n.* mosquito *m.*
moth *n.* polilla *f.*
mouse *n.* ratón *m.*
mule *n.* mula *f.*
octopus *n.* pulpo *m.*
opossum *n.* zarigüeya *f.*
ostrich *n.* avestruz *m.*
otter *n.* nutria *f.*
panda *n.* panda *m.*
parrot *n.* loro *m.*, papagayo *m.*
pelican *n.* pelícano *m.*
penguin *n.* pingüino *m.*
pig *n.* puerco, -ca *m.f.;* cerdo, -ca *m.f.*
Plesiosaurs *n.pl.* Plesiosaurios *m.*
Pterodactyl *n.* Pterodáctilo *n.*
Pterosaur *n.* Pterosaurio *m.*
rabbit *n.* conejo *m.*

racoon *n.* mapache *m.*
rat *n.* rata *f.*
rhinoceros *n.* rinoceronte *m.*
robin *n.* petirrojo *m.*
rooster *n.* gallo *m.*
scorpion *n.* escorpión *m.*, alacrán *m.*
sea lion *n.* león marino *m.*
seahorse *n.* caballito de mar *m.*,
  hipocampo *m.*
seal *n.* foca *f.*
shark *n.* tiburón *m.*
sheep *n.* oveja *f.*, cordero *m.*
shrimp *n.* camarón *m.*, gamba *f.*
skunk *n.* zorrillo *m.*, mofeta *f.*
snail *n.* caracol *m.*
snake *n.* culebra *f.*, serpiente *f.*
sparrow *n.* gorrión *m.*
spider *n.* araña *f.*
squid *n.* calamar *m.*
squirrel *n.* ardilla *f.*
stallion *n.* caballo semental *m.*
Stegosaurus *n.* Estegosaurio *m.*
tick *n.* garrapata *f.*
tiger *n.* tigre *m.*
toad *n.* sapo *m.*
Triceratops *n.* Triceratops *m.*
turkey *n.* pavo *m.*
turtle *n.,* **tortoise** *n.* tortuga *f.*
Tyrannosaurus rex *n.* Tiranosaurio
  rex *m.*
walrus *n.* morsa *f.*
whale *n.* ballena *f.*
wolf *n.* lobo *m.*
wolverine *n.* glotón *m.*, carcayú *m.*
woodpecker *n.* pájaro carpintero *m.*
worm *n.* gusano *m.*
zebra *n.* cebra *f.*

FRUITS, NUTS & VEGETABLES

almond *n.* almendra *f.*
apple *n.* manzana *f.*
apricot *n.* albaricoque *m.*
artichoke *n.* alcachofa *f.*
asparagus *n.* espárragos *m.pl.*
avocado *n.* aguacate *m.*
banana *n.* banana *f.*, plátano *m.*, guineo *m.*
bean *n.* frijol *m.*
beet *n.* remolacha *f.*, betabel *m.*
blackberry *n.* mora *f.*
blueberry *n.* arándano azul *m.*
broccoli *n.* brócoli *m.*
cabbage *n.* repollo *m.*, col *m.*
cantaloupe *n.* melón *m.*
capers *n.pl.* alcaparras *f.*
carrot *n.* zanahoria *f.*
cashew *n.* anacardo *m.*
cauliflower *n.* coliflor *m.*
celery *n.* apio *m.*
cherry *n.* cereza *f.*
chili pepper *n.* chile *m.*, ají *m.*
coconut *n.* coco *m.*
corn *n.* maíz *m.*
cranberry *n.* arándano *m.*
cucumber *n.* pepino *m.*
date *n.* dátil *m.*
eggplant *n.* berenjena *f.*
garlic *n.* ajo *m.*
grape *n.* uva *f.*
grapefruit *n.* pomelo *m.*, toronja *f.*
green pepper *n.* pimiento verde *m.*
lemon *n.* limón *m.*
lettuce *n.* lechuga *f.*
lime *n.* lima *f.*, limón *m.*

mango *n.* mango *m.*
mushroom *n.* hongo *m.*
nut *n.* nuez *f.*
olive *n.* aceituna *f.*
onion *n.* cebolla *f.*
orange *n.* naranja *f.*
papaya *n.* papaya *f.*
pea *n.* guisante *m.*, chícharo *m.*
peach *n.* melocotón *m.*, durazno *m.*
peanut *n.* cacahuete *m.*, cacahuate *m.*, maní *m.*
pear *n.* pera *f.*
pecan *n.* pacana *f.*
pepper *n.* (spice) pimienta *f.*
pineapple *n.* piña *f.*
pistachio *n.* pistacho *m.*
plantain *n.* plátano *m.*
plum *n.* ciruela *f.*
potato *n.* papa *f.*, patata *f.*
prune *n.* ciruela pasa *f.*
pumpkin *n.* calabaza *f.*
raspberry *n.* frambuesa *f.*
soybean *n.* soja *f.*
spinach *n.* espinaca *f.*
squash *n.* calabacín *m.*, zapallo *m.*
strawberry *n.* fresa *f.*
string bean *n.* habichuela *f.*, ejote *m.*
tangerine *n.* mandarina *f.*
tomato *n.* tomate *m.*
walnut *n.* nuez *f.*
watermelon *n.* sandía *f.*
wheat *n.* trigo *m.*
yam *n.* batata *f.*, ñame *m.*
yucca *n.* yuca *f.*
zucchini *n.* calabacín *m.*

SCIENCE

SCIENCE

IN THE GARDEN

annual *n.* planta anual *f.*

bush *n.* mata *f.*, arbusto *m.*

clippers *n.pl.* tijeras de podar *f.*

compost *n.* abono orgánico *m.*, compost *m.*

compost *v.* compostar

cover *v.* cubrir

cultivate *v.* cultivar

dig *v.* cavar, excavar

fertilize *v.* fertilizar

fertilizer *n.* abono *m.*, fertilizante *m.*

flower *n.* flor *f.*

garden *n.* jardín *m.*

garden *v.* cultivar, plantar

gardener *n.* jardinero, -ra *m.f.*

germinate *v.* germinar

gloves *n.pl.* guantes *m.*

greenhouse *n.* invernadero *m.*

grow *v.* cultivar

herb *n.* hierba *f.*

hoe *n.* azada *f.*, azadón *m.*

hoe *v.* trabajar con la azada, azadonar, sachar

horticulture *n.* horticultura *f.*

hose *n.* manguera *f.*

hose *v.* regar con manguera

humus *n.* humus *m.*, mantillo *m.*

insecticide *n.* insecticida *m.*

irrigation *n.* irrigación *f.*

lawn *n.* césped *m.*, zacate *m.*; **l. mower** segadora de césped *f.*, cortacésped *m.*

machete *n.* machete *m.*

mix *v.* mezclar

mulch *n.* mantillo *m.*

organic *adj.* orgánico, -ca

perennial *n.* planta perenne, planta vivaz *f.*

pick *n.* (tool) pico *m.*, azadón *m.*

pick *v.* (fruit) recoger

pitchfork *n.* horquilla *f.*

plant *n.* planta *f.*

plant *v.* plantar

plow *n.* arado *m.*

plow *v.* arar

pot *n.* maceta *f.*

pruning shears *n.pl.* tijeras de podar *f.*

rake *n.* rastrillo *m.*

rake *v.* rastrillar

seed *n.* semilla *f.*

seedling *n.* postura *f.*

shovel *n.* pala *f.*

shovel *v.* palear

shrub *n.* mata *f.*, arbusto *m.*

soil *n.* tierra *f.*, suelo *m.*

sow *v.* sembrar

spade *n.* pala *f.*

spray *n.* rociada *f.*, espray *m.*

spray *v.* rociar

tie *v.* atar, amarrar

till *v.* cultivar, labrar

transplant *v.* trasplantar

trowel *n.* desplantador *m.*, pala de jardinero *f.*

water *n.* agua *f.*

water *v.* regar

watering can *n.* regadera *f.*

wheelbarrow *n.* carretilla *f.*

Physical Sciences

A

absolute *adj.* absoluto, -ta; **a. brightness** *n.* brillo absoluto *m.;* **a. zero** cero absoluto *m.*

acceleration *n.* aceleración *f.*

acetone *n.* acetona *f.*

acid *adj.* ácido, -da

acid *n.* ácido *m.;* **acetic a.** ácido acético; **sulfuric a.** ácido sulfúrico

acidity *n.* acidez *f.*

aerodynamic *adj.* aerodinámico, -ca

aeronautics *n.* aeronáutica *f.*

aerosol *n.* aerosol *m.*

aerospace *n.* aeroespacio *m.*

air *n.* aire *m.;* **a. resistance** resistencia del aire *f.;* **ambient a.** aire ambiental

aircraft *n.,* **airplane** *n.* aeronave *f.,* avión *m.,* aeroplano *m.*

airwaves *n.pl.* ondas de radio *f.*

alkali metals *n.pl.* metales alcalinos *m.*

alloy *n.* aleación *f.*

alpha particle *n.* partícula alfa *f.*

ambient air *n.* aire ambiental *m.*

ammonia *n.* amoníaco *m.,* amoniaco *m.*

amorphous solid *n.* sólido amorfo *m.*

amplification *n.* amplificación *f.*

amplitude *n.* amplitud *f.*

antioxidant *adj. & n.* antioxidante *m.*

Apollo Mission *n.* misión Apolo *f.*

apparent *adj.* aparente; **a. bright-**

ness *n.* brillo aparente *m.*

applied force *n.* fuerza aplicada *f.*

Archimedes' principle *n.* principio de Arquímedes *m.*

asbestos *n.* asbesto *m.,* amianto *m.*

asphalt *n.* asfalto *m.*

asteroid *n.* asteroide *m.;* **a. belt** cinturón de asteroides *m.*

astronomical distance *n.* distancia astronómica *f.*

atmosphere *n.* atmósfera *f.*

atom *n.* átomo *m.*

atomic *adj.* atómico, -ca; **a. mass** *n.* masa atómica *f.;* **a. number** número atómico *m.*

attract *v.* atraer

axis *n.* axis *m.,* eje *m.*

azimuth *n.* azimut *m.,* acimut *m.*

B

baking powder *n.* levadura en polvo *f.*

balance *n.* equilibrio *m.*

balance *v.* equilibrar

balanced forces *n.pl.* fuerzas equilibradas *f.*

ballistics *n.* balística *f.*

battery *n.* pila *f.,* batería *f.*

Bernoulli's principle *n.* principio de Bernoulli *m.*

beta particle *n.* partícula beta *f.*

bicarbonate of soda *n.* bicarbonato de sodio *m.*

SCIENCE

Big Bang *n.* Gran Explosión *f.*, Big Bang *m.*

binary star *n.* estrella binaria *f.*

black hole *n.* agujero negro *m.*

bleach *n.* blanqueador *m.*

boil *v.* hervir

boiling *adj.* hirviente

boiling *n.* ebullición *f.;* **b. point** punto de ebullición *m.*

bond *v.* enlace *m.;* **chemical b.** enlace químico

Boyle's law *n.* ley de Boyle *f.*

brightness *n.* brillo *m.;* **absolute b.** brillo absoluto; **apparent b.** brillo aparente

brittle *adj.* frágil

buoyancy *n.* flotabilidad *f.*

buoyant *adj.* flotante; **b. force** *n.* fuerza de flotación *f.*

burn *v.* quemar

C

cable *n.* cable *m.*

candela *n.* candela *f.*

catalyst *n.* catalizador *m.*

celestial object *n.* objeto celeste *m.*

cement *n.* cemento *m.*

centrifugal force *n.* fuerza centrífuga *f.*

centripetal force *n.* fuerza centrípeta *f.*

ceramics *n.* cerámica *f.*

change of state *n.* cambio de estado *m.*

charcoal *n.* carbón *m.*

Charles's law *n.* ley de Charles *f.*

chemical *adj.* químico, -ca; **c. bond** *n.* enlace químico *m.;* **c. change** cambio químico *m.;* **c. energy** energía química *f.;* **c. formula** fórmula química *f.;* **c. property** propiedad química *f.;* **c. symbol** símbolo químico *m.*

chloride *n.* cloruro *m.*

chlorofluorocarbon *n.* clorofluoro-carbono *m.*

chloroform *n.* cloroformo *m.*

chromosphere *n.* cromósfera *f.,* cromosfera *f.*

chronometer *n.* cronómetro *m.*

circuit *n.* circuito *m.;* **closed c.** circuito cerrado; **open c.** circuito abierto; **parallel c.** circuito paralelo; **series c.** circuito en serie; **short c.** corto circuito

collision *n.* colisión *f.*

combustion *n.* combustión *f.*

comet *n.* cometa *m.*

composite material *n.* material compuesto *m.*

compound *n.* compuesto *m.*

concave *adj.* cóncavo, -va; **c. lens** *n.* lente cóncavo (-va) *m.f.;* **c. mirror** espejo cóncavo *m.*

condensation *n.* condensación *f.*

condense *v.* condensar

conduct *v.* conducir

conduction *n.* conducción *f.*

conductivity *n.* conductividad *f.*

conductor *n.* conductor *m.*

conservation of mass *n.* conservación de la masa *f.*

constellation *n.* constelación *f.*

container *n.* recipiente *m.*

convection *n.* convección *f.;* **c. current** corriente de convección *f.;* **c. zone** zona de convección *f.*

converge *v.* converger

convex *adj.* convexo, -xa; **c. lens** *n.* lente convexo (-xa) *m.f.;* **c. mirror** espejo convexo *m.*

cool *v.* enfriar

Coriolis effect *n.* efecto de Coriolis *m.*

corona *n.* corona *f.*

corrosion *n.* corrosión *f.*

cosmic *adj.* cósmico, -ca; **c. background radiation** *n.* radiación cósmica de fondo *f.*

cosmos *n.* cosmos *m.*

crescent moon *n.* luna creciente *f.*

crystal *n.* cristal *m.*

crystalline *adj.* cristalino, -na; **c. solid** *n.* sólido cristalino *m.*

current *n.* corriente *f.*

D

dark *adj.* oscuro, -ra; **d. energy** *n.* energía oscura *f.;* **d. matter** materia oscura *f.*

deceleration *n.* desaceleración *f.*

decibel *n.* decibelio *m.,* decibel *m.*

deflect *v.* desviar

density *n.* densidad *f.*

deplete *v.* agotar

desiccate *v.* secarse, desecar

desiccated *adj.* desecado, -da

detergent *n.* detergente *m.*

diatomic molecule *n.* molécula diatónica *f.*

dissolve *v.* disolver

dissonance *n.* disonancia *f.*

distance *n.* distancia *f.*

distillation *n.* destilación *f.*

distort *v.* distorsionar

divergent lens *n.* lente divergente *f.*

Doppler effect *n.* efecto de Doppler *m.*

ductile *adj.* dúctil

dwarf *adj. & n.* enano, -na *m.f.;* **red d.** enana roja; **white d.** enana blanca

E

echo *n.* eco *m.*

eclipse *n.* eclipse *m.;* **lunar e.** eclipse lunar; **solar e.** eclipse solar

eclipsing binary *n.* binaria eclipsante *f.*

electrical *adj.* eléctrico, -ca; **e. charge** *n.* carga eléctrica *f.;* **e. conductivity** conductividad eléctrica *f.;* **e. energy** energía eléctrica *f.*

electricity *n.* electricidad *f.*

electrode *n.* electrodo *m.*

electromagnet *n.* electroimán *m.*

electromagnetic *adj.* electromagnético, -ca; **e. energy** *n.* energía electromagnética *f.;* **e. radiation** radiación electromagnética *f.*

electron *n.* electrón *m.*

element *n.* elemento *m.;* **radioactive e.** elemento radiactivo

ellipse *n.* elipse *m.*

elliptical orbit *n.* órbita elíptica *f.*

emission *n.* emisión *f.*

emit *v.* emitir

endothermic change *n.* cambio endotérmico *m.*

S*CIENCE*

energy *n.* energía *f.;* **dark e.** energía oscura; **electrical e.** energía eléctrica; **e. transfer** transferencia de energía *f.;* **e. transformation** transformación energética *f.;* **kinetic e.** energía cinética; **potential e.** energía potencial; **thermal e.** energía térmica

entropy *n.* entropía *f.*

escape velocity *n.* velocidad de escape *f.*

evaporation *n.* evaporación *f.*

exothermic change *n.* cambio exotérmico *m.*

expansion *n.* expansión *f.*

expel *v.* expulsar

explosion *n.* explosión *f.*

explosive *adj.* explosivo, -va

F

fall *v.* caer

float *v.* flotar

fluid *n.* fluido *m.,* líquido *m.*

foam *n.* espuma *f.*

focus *n.* foco *m.*

force *n.* fuerza *f.;* **applied f.** fuerza aplicada; **net f.** fuerza neta; **output f.** fuerza resultante; **unbalanced f.** *pl.* fuerzas desequilibradas

form *n.* forma *f.,* estado *m.*

fossil fuel *n.* combustible fósil *m.*

Foucault pendulum *n.* péndulo de Foucault *m.*

free fall *n.* caída libre *f.*

freezing *n.* congelación *f.;* **f. point** punto de congelación *m.*

frequency *n.* frecuencia *f.*

friction *n.* fricción *f.;* **fluid f.** rozamiento líquido *m.,* fricción del líquido

fulcrum *n.* fulcro *m.,* punto de apoyo *m.*

G

galaxy *n.* galaxia *f.;* **elliptical g.** galaxia elíptica; **irregular g.** galaxia irregular; **spiral g.** galaxia espiral

gamma radiation *n.* radiación gamma *f.*

gas *n.* gas *m.;* **g. giant** gigante gaseoso *m.;* **noble g.** gas noble

globular cluster *n.* cúmulo globular *m.*

gravitation *n.* gravitación *f.*

gravitational *adj.* gravitacional; **g. attraction** *n.* atracción gravitacional *f.;* **g. potential energy** energía potencial gravitatoria *f.*

gravity *n.* gravedad *f.;* **specific g.** gravedad específica; **zero g.** gravedad cero, gravedad nula

H

half-life *n.* vida media *f.*

half moon *n.* medialuna *f.*

halogen *n.* halógeno *m.*

harmonic *adj.* armónico, -ca

harmonious *adj.* armonioso, -sa

heat *n.* calor *m.;* **h. engine** motor térmico *m.;* **h. transfer** transferencia térmica, transferencia de calor *f.;* **specific h.** calor específico

heat *v.* calentar

heating *n.* calefacción *f.*

helicopter *n.* helicóptero *m.*

heliocentric *adj.* heliocéntrico, -ca

Hertzsprung-Russell diagram *n.* diagrama Hertzsprung-Russell *m.*

heterogeneous *adj.* heterogéneo, -nea; **h. mixture** *n.* mezcla heterogénea *f.*

hibernation *n.* hibernación *f.*

hologram *n.* holograma *m.*

homogeneous *adj.* homogéneo, -nea; **h. mixture** *n.* mezcla homogénea *f.*

horsepower *n.* caballos de fuerza, caballos de potencia *m.pl.*

Hubble space telescope *n.* telescopio espacial Hubble *m.*

Hubble's law *n.* ley de Hubble *f.*

hydraulic system *n.* sistema hidráulico *m.*

hydrosphere *n.* hidrosfera *f.*

I

incandescent *adj.* incandescente

incline plane *n.* plano inclinado *m.*

indicator *n.* indicador *m.*

inert *adj.* inerte, inmóvil; **i. gas** *n.* gas inerte *m.*

inertia *n.* inercia *f.*

infinite *adj.* infinito, -ta

infinity *n.* infinito *m.,* infinidad *f.*

inflammable *adj.* inflamable

inflate *v.* inflar

infrared *adj.* infrarrojo, -ja; **i. light** *n.* luz infrarroja *f.;* **i. radiation** radiación infrarroja *f.*

input work *n.* insumos de trabajo *m.pl.*

insolation *n.* insolación *f.*

insoluble *adj.* insoluble

insulator *n.* aislante *m.*

intensity *n.* intensidad *f.*

internal combustion engine *n.* motor de combustión interna *m.*

International System of Units (S.I.) *n.* Sistema Internacional de Unidades *m.*

interstellar *adj.* interestelar; **i. space** *n.* espacio interestelar *m.*

inverse *adj.* inverso, -sa

ionosphere *n.* ionosfera *f.*

isotope *n.* isótopo *m.;* **radioactive i.** isótopo radiactivo

J

jet *n.* chorro *m.;* **j. propulsion** propulsión a chorro *f.*

K

kinetic energy *n.* energía cinética *f.*

kinetics *n.* cinética *f.*

L

launch *n.* lanzamiento *m.*

launch *v.* lanzar

law *n.* ley *f.;* **l. of conservation of energy** ley de la conservación de la energía; **l. of conservation of mass** ley de la conservación de la masa; **l. of conservation of momentum** ley de la conservación del impulso; **l. of universal gravitation** ley de la gravitación; **l. of thermodynamics** *pl.* leyes de la termodinámica; **Newton's l. of**

SCIENCE

motion *pl.* leyes del movimiento de Newton

lens *n.* lente *m.f.*

lever *n.* palanca *f.*

lift *n.* sustentación *f.*

lift *v.* levantar, alzar

light *n.* luz *f.;* **infrared l.** luz infrarroja; **l. bulb** foco *m.,* bombillo *m.;* **l. source** fuente luminosa *f.;* **l. wave** onda de luz *f.;* **l. year** año luz *m.;* **visible l.** luz visible; **ultraviolet l.** luz ultravioleta

light-emitting diode (L.E.D.) *n.* diodo emisor de luz *m.*

lighting *n.* iluminación *f.*

liquid *n.* líquido *m.*

longitudinal wave *n.* onda longitudinal *f.*

loudness *n.* volumen *m.*

lubricant *n.* lubricante *m.*

lubricating oil *n.* aceite lubricante *m.*

luminescent *adj.* luminiscente

lunar *adj.* lunar; **l. cycle** *n.* ciclo lunar *m.;* **l. eclipse** eclipse lunar *m.;* **l. maria** *pl.* mares lunares *m.*

M

machine *n.* máquina *f.;* **compound m.** máquina compuesta; **simple m.** máquina simple

magnet *n.* imán *m.*

magnetic *adj.* magnético, -ca; **m. field** *n.* campo magnético *m.;* **m. force** fuerza magnética *f.;* **m. pole** polo magnético *m.*

magnetism *n.* magnetismo *m.*

magnification *n.* aumento *m.,* magnificación *f.*

magnitude *n.* magnitud *f.*

Main Sequence *n.* Secuencia Principal *f.*

malleability *n.* maleabilidad *f.*

malleable *adj.* maleable

mass *n.* masa *f.;* **m. number** número de masa *m.*

material *n.* material *m.*

matter *n.* materia *f.*

mechanical *adj.* mecánico, -ca; **m. advantage** *n.* ventaja mecánica *f.;* **m. energy** energía mecánica *f.;* **m. force** fuerza mecánica *f.*

melting *n.* fusión *f.;* **m. point** punto de fusión *m.*

metals *n.pl.* metales *m.;* **alkalai m.** metales alcalinos; **alkaline earth m.** metales alcalinotérreos; **transition m.** metales de transición

metalloid *n.* metaloide *m.*

meteor *n.* meteoro *m.*

meteorite *n.* meteorito *m.*

meteoroid *n.* meteoroide *m.*

methane *n.* metano *m.*

microgravity *n.* microgravedad *f.*

mineral oil *n.* aceite mineral *m.*

mirror *n.* espejo *m.*

mix *v.* mezclar

mixture *n.* mezcla *f.*

model *n.* modelo *m.*

molecule *n.* molécula *f.;* **diatomic m.** molécula diatónica

momentum *n.* impulso *m.*

monomer *n.* monómero *m.*

moon *n.* luna *f.;* **crescent m.** luna creciente; **full m.** luna llena; **gib-**

bous m. luna gibosa; **m. phase** fase lunar *f.;* **new m.** luna nueva
motion *n.* movimiento *m.*
movable pulley *n.* polea móvil *f.*

N
neap tide *n.* marea muerta *f.*
nebula *n.* nebulosa *f.*
net force *n.* fuerza neta *f.*
neutrino *n.* neutrino *m.*
neutron *n.* neutrón *m.;* **n. star** estrella de neutrones *f.*
newton *n.* newton *m.*
nitrate *n.* nitrato *m.*
nitrite *n.* nitrito *m.*
noble gas *n.* gas noble *m.*
nonmetal *adj.* no metálico, -ca
nuclear *adj.* nuclear; **n. energy** *n.* energía nuclear *f.;* **n. fission** fisión nuclear *f.;* **n. fusion** fusión nuclear *f.;* **n. reaction** reacción nuclear *f.*
nucleus *n.* núcleo *m.*

O
observatory *n.* observatorio *m.*
opaque *adj.* opaco, -ca
open cluster *n.* cúmulo abierto *m.*
optical *adj.* óptico, -ca; **o. fiber** *n.* fibra óptica *f.;* **o. telescope** telescopio óptico *m.*
orbit *n.* órbita *f.;* **geostationary o.** órbita geoestacionaria
orbital velocity *n.* velocidad orbital *f.*
outer space *n.* espacio exterior *m.*
output work *n.* trabajo producido *m.*
oxidation *n.* oxidación *f.*
oxidize *v.* oxidar
ozone layer *n.* capa de ozono *f.*

P
parallax *n.* paralaje *f.*
parallel circuit *n.* circuito paralelo *m.*
particle *n.* partícula *f.;* **alpha p.** partícula alfa; **beta p.** partícula beta; **p. accelerator** acelerador de partículas *m.;* **subatomic p.** partícula subatómica
particulate matter *n.* materia particulada *f.*
pascal *n.* pascal *m.*
Pascal's principle *n.* principio de Pascal *m.*
penumbra *n.* penumbra *f.*
peptide *n.* péptido *m.*
periodic table *n.* tabla periódica *f.*
pH *n.* pH *m.*
phase *n.* fase *f.*
phosphate *n.* fosfato *m.*
phosphorescence *n.* fosforescencia *f.*
photochemical smog *n.* esmog fotoquímico *m.*
photon *n.* fotón *m.*
photosphere *n.* fotosfera *f.*
physical *adj.* físico, -ca; **p. change** *n.* cambio físico *m.;* **p. property** propiedad física *f.*
plane *n.* plano *m.*
planet *n.* planeta *m.*
planetesimal *n.* planetesimal *m.*
plasma *n.* plasma *m.*
plastic *n.* plástico *m.*
polarity *n.* polaridad *f.*

SCIENCE

polymer *n.* polímero *m.*
potential energy *n.* energía potencial *f.*
power *n.* potencia *f.,* poder *m.*
precipitate *n.* precipitado *m.*
pressure *n.* presión *f.*
prism *n.* prisma *m.*
projectile *n.* proyectil *m.*
proportional *adj.* proporcional
propulsion *n.* propulsión *f.*
proton *n.* protón *m.*
protostar *n.* protoestrella *f.*
pull *n.* jalón *m.,* tirón *m.,* fuerza de atracción *f.*
pulley *n.* polea *f.*
pulsar *n.* púlsar *m.*
push *n.* empujón *m.*

Q

quantum *adj.* cuántico, -ca; **q. mechanics** *n.pl.* mecánica cuántica *f.;* **q. theory** teoría cuántica *f.*
quarter *n.* (moon) cuarto *m.;* **first q.** cuarto creciente; **last q.** cuarto menguante
quasar *n.* quásar *m.*

R

radiation *n.* radiación *f.;* **infrared r.** radiación infrarroja; **r. zone** zona radioactiva *f.;* **ultraviolet r.** radiación ultravioleta
radioactive *adj.* radiactivo, -va; **r. decay** *n.* descomposición radiactiva *f.;* **r. isotope** isótopo radiactivo *m.*
radioactivity *n.* radiactividad *f.,* radioactividad *f.*
ray *n.* rayo *m.*
react *v.* reaccionar
reactant *n.* reactante *m.*
reaction *n.* reacción *f.*
reactivity *n.* reactividad *f.*
reagent *n.* reactivo *m.*
red dwarf *n.* enana roja *f.*
reflect *v.* reflejar
reflection *n.* reflexión *f.*
refract *v.* refractar
refraction *n.* refracción *f.*
refrigerant *n.* refrigerante *m.*
remote sensing *n.* teledetección *f.*
repel *v.* repeler
revolution *n.* revolución *f.*
revolve *v.* girar
rocket *n.* cohete *m.*
rolling friction *n.* fricción de rodadura *f.,* rozamiento a la rodadura *m.*
rotate *v.* rotar
rotation *n.* rotación *f.*
rover *n.* róver *m.,* astromóvil *m.*

S

satellite *n.* satélite *m.;* **s. image** imagen satelital *f.*
saturated *adj.* saturado, -da
saturation point *n.* punto de saturación *m.*
screw *n.* tornillo *m.*
semiconductor *n.* semiconductor *m.*
series circuit *n.* circuito en serie *m.*
short circuit *n.* corto circuito *m.*
simple machine *n.* máquina simple *f.*
sink *v.* hundirse

SCIENCE

sliding friction *n.* fricción de deslizamiento *f.*

slope *n.* pendiente *f.*, inclinación *f.*

solar *adj.* solar; **s. eclipse** *n.* eclipse solar *m.;* **s. flare** destello solar *m.;* **s. nebula** nebulosa solar *f.;* **s. prominence** prominencia solar *f.;* **s. system** sistema solar *m.;* **s. wind** viento solar *m.*

solid *n.* sólido *m.*

solubility *n.* solubilidad *f.*

solute *n.* soluto *m.*

solution *n.* solución *f.*

solvent *n.* solvente *m.*, disolvente *m.*

sonar *n.* sonar *m.*

sonic *adj.* sónico, -ca; **s. boom** *n.* estampido sónico *m.*

sound *n.* sonido *m.;* **s. barrier** barrera del sonido *f.*

space *n.* espacio *m.;* **interstellar s.** espacio interestelar; **outer s.** espacio exterior; **s. exploration** exploración espacial *f.;* **s. probe** sonda espacial *f.;* **s. shuttle** trasbordador espacial *m.;* **s. spinoff** subproducto espacial *m.;* **s. station** estación espacial *f.*

specific *adj.* específico, -ca; **s. gravity** *n.* gravedad específica *f.;* **s. heat** calor específico *m.*

spectrum *n.* espectro *m.*

speed *n.* velocidad *f.*, rapidez *f.;* **average s.** velocidad promedia, velocidad media; **instantaneous s.** rapidez instantánea

spiral galaxy *n.* galaxia espiral *f.*

spontaneous combustion *n.* auto-combustión *f.*, combustión espontánea *f.*

stable *adj.* estable

star *n.* estrella *f.;* **binary s.** estrella binaria; **neutron s.** estrella de neutrones

state *n.* estado *m.;* **s. of matter** *pl.* estados de la materia

static *adj.* estático, -ca; **s. electricity** *n.* electricidad estática *f.;* **s. friction** fricción estática *f.*

steam *n.* vapor *m.*

strength *n.* fuerza *f.*

string theory *n.* teoría de cuerdas *f.*

subatomic particle *n.* partícula subatómica *f.*

sublimation *n.* sublimación *f.*

substance *n.* sustancia *f.*

substrate *n.* sustrato *m.*

sulfuric acid *n.* ácido sulfúrico

sun *n.* sol *m.*

sunspot *n.* mancha solar *f.*

superconductor *n.* superconductor *m.*

supernova *n.* supernova *f.*

surface *n.* superficie *f.;* **s. tension** tensión superficial *f.*

synthesize *v.* sintetizar

synthetic *adj.* sintético, -ca

T

telescope *n.* telescopio *m.;* **Hubble space t.** telescopio espacial Hubble; **optical t.** telescopio óptico; **radio t.** radiotelescopio; **reflecting t.** telescopio reflectivo; **refracting t.** telescopio refractor

SCIENCE

temperature *n.* temperatura *f.;*
  room t. temperatura ambiente
terrestrial planet *n.* planeta terrestre, planeta telúrico *m.*
texture *n.* textura *f.*
thermal *adj.* térmico, -ca; **t. conductivity** *n.* conductividad térmica *f.;* **t. energy** energía térmica *f.;* **t. expansion** expansión térmica *f.*
thermodynamics *n.pl.* termodinámica *f.;* **laws of t.** *pl.* leyes de la termodinámica *f.*
thrust *n.* empuje *m.,* propulsión *f.*
tracer *n.* trazadora *f.,* marcador *m.*
translucent *adj.* traslúcido, -da
transparent *adj.* transparente
turbine *n.* turbina *f.*

U
ultraviolet *adj.* ultravioleta; **u. light** *n.* luz ultravioleta *f.;* **u. radiation** radiación ultravioleta *f.*
umbra *n.* umbra *f.*
universe *n.* universo *m.*
unsaturated *adj.* no saturado, -da

V
vacuum *n.* vacío *m.*
vapor *n.* vapor *m.*
vaporization *n.* vaporización *f.*

velocity *n.* velocidad *f.;* **escape v.** velocidad de escape; **orbital v.** velocidad orbital; **terminal v.** velocidad terminal
vibrate *v.* vibrar
vibration *n.* vibración *f.*
viscosity *n.* viscosidad *f.*
viscous *adj.* viscoso, -sa
visible light *n.* luz visible *f.*
vitreous *adj.* vítreo, -rea
voltage *n.* voltaje *m.*

W
waning *adj.* (moon) menguante
watt *n.* vatio *m.*
watt-hour *n.* vatio hora *f.*
wattage *n.* potencia en vatios *f.*
wave *n.* onda *f.*
wavelength *n.* longitud de onda *f.*
waxing *adj.* (moon) creciente
wedge *n.* cuña *f.*
white dwarf *n.* enana blanca *f.*
wire *n.* alambre *m.,* cable *m.*

X
X-ray *n.* radiografía *f.,* rayos X *m.pl.*

Z
zero gravity *n.* gravedad cero, gravedad nula *f.*

ASTRONOMICAL OJBECTS

Andromeda Galaxy *n.* Galaxia Andrómeda *f.*

Aquarius *n.* Acuario *m.*

Aries *n.* Aries *m.*

Big Dipper *n.* El Carro *m.*

Callisto *n.* Calisto *m.*

Cancer *n.* Cáncer *m.*

Canis Major *n.* Can Mayor *m.*

Canis Minor *n.* Can Menor *m.*

Capricornus *n.* Capricornio *m.*

Cassiopeia *n.* Casiopea *f.*

Ceres *n.* Ceres *m.*

Corona Borealis *n.* Corona Boreal *f.*

Crab Nebula *n.* Nebulosa del Cangrejo *f.*

Europa *n.* Europa *f.*

Ganymede *n.* Ganímedes *m.*

Gemini *n.* Géminis *m.*

Halley's Comet *n.* Cometa Halley *m.*

Hercules *n.* Hércules *m.*

Jupiter *n.* Júpiter *m.*

Io *n.* Ío *m.*

Kuiper Belt *n.* Cinturón de Kuiper *m.*

Large Magellanic Cloud *n.* Gran Nube de Magallanes *f.*

Leo *n.* Leo *m.*

Libra *n.* Libra *f.*

Mars *n.* Marte *m.*

Mayall's Object *n.* Objeto Mayall *m.*

Mercury *n.* Mercurio *m.*

Milky Way Galaxy *n.* Via Láctea *f.*

Neptune *n.* Neptuno *m.*

Oort cloud *n.* nube de Oort *f.*

Orion *n.* Orión *m.*

Pegasus *n.* Pegaso *m.*

Perseus *n.* Perseo *m.*

Pinwheel Galaxy *n.* Galaxia del Molinete *f.*

Pisces *n.* Piscis *m.*

Pleiades *n.pl.* Pléyades *f.*

Pluto *n.* Plutón *m.*

Polaris (North Star) *n.* Polaris (Estrella del Norte) *m.*

Sagittarius *n.* Sagitario *m.*

Saturn *n.* Saturno *m.*

Scorpius *n.,* **Scorpio** *n.* Escorpio *m.*

Sirius *n.* Sirio *m.*

Small Magellanic Galaxy *n.* Nube Menor de Magallanes *f.*

Southern Cross *n.* Cruz del Sur *f.*

Taurus *n.* Tauro *m.*

Titan *n.* Titán *m.*

Triangulum *n.* Triángulo *m.*

Uranus *n.* Urano *m.*

Ursa Major *n.* Osa Mayor *f.*

Ursa Minor (Little Dipper) *n.* Osa Menor *f.*

Venus *n.* Venus *m.*

Virgo *n.* Virgo *m.*

SCIENCE

SCIENCE

The Periodic Table of Elements

1 H																	2 He
3 Li	4 Be											5 B	6 C	7 N	8 O	9 F	10 Ne
11 Na	12 Mg											13 Al	14 Si	15 P	16 S	17 Cl	18 Ar
19 K	20 Ca	21 Sc	22 Ti	23 V	24 Cr	25 Mn	26 Fe	27 Co	28 Ni	29 Cu	30 Zn	31 Ga	32 Ge	33 As	34 Se	35 Br	36 Kr
37 Rb	38 Sr	39 Y	40 Zr	41 Nb	42 Mo	43 Tc	44 Ru	45 Rh	46 Pd	47 Ag	48 Cd	49 In	50 Sn	51 Sb	52 Te	53 I	54 Xe
55 Cs	56 Ba		72 Hf	73 Ta	74 W	75 Re	76 Os	77 Ir	78 Pt	79 Au	80 Hg	81 Tl	82 Pb	83 Bi	84 Po	85 At	86 Rn
87 Fr	88 Ra		104 Rf	105 Db	106 Sg	107 Bh	108 Hs	109 Mt	110 Ds	111 Rg	112 Cn	113 Uut	114 Fl	115 Uup	116 Lv	117 Uus	118 Uuo

57 La	58 Ce	59 Pr	60 Nd	61 Pm	62 Sm	63 Eu	64 Gd	65 Tb	66 Dy	67 Ho	68 Er	69 Tm	70 Yb	71 Lu
89 Ac	90 Th	91 Pa	92 U	93 Np	94 Pu	95 Am	96 Cm	97 Bk	98 Cf	99 Es	100 Fm	101 Md	102 No	103 Lr

Ac **actinium** actinio *m.*
Al **aluminium** aluminio *m.*
Am **americium** americio *m.*
Sb **antimony** antimonio *m.*
Ar **argon** argón *m.*
As **arsenic** arsénico *m.*
At **astatine** astato *m.*
Ba **barium** bario *m.*
Bk **berkelium** berkelio *m.*
Be **beryllium** berilio *m.*
Bi **bismuth** bismuto *m.*
Bh **bohrium** bohrio *m.*
B **boron** boro *m.*
Br **bromine** bromo *m.*
Cd **cadmium** cadmio *m.*
Cs **caesium** cesio *m.*
Ca **calcium** calcio *m.*
Cf **californium** californio *m.*
C **carbon** carbono *m.*
Ce **cerium** cerio *m.*
Cl **chlorine** cloro *m.*

Cr **chromium** cromo *m.*
Co **cobalt** cobalto *m.*
Cn **copernicium** copernicio *m.*
Cu **copper** cobre *m.*
Cm **curium** curio *m.*
Ds **darmstadtium** darmstadtio *m.*
Db **dubnium** dubnio *m.*
Dy **dysprosium** disprosio *m.*
Es **einsteinium** einsteinio *m.*
Er **erbium** erbio *m.*
Eu **europium** europio *m.*
Fm **fermium** fermio *m.*
Fl **flerovium** flerovio *m.*
F **fluorine** flúor *m.*
Fr **francium** francio *m.*
Gd **gadolinium** gadolinio *m.*
Ga **gallium** galio *m.*
Ge **germanium** germanio *m.*
Au **gold** oro *m.*
Hf **hafnium** hafnio *m.*
Hs **hassium** hassio *m.*

• •

He	**helium** helio *m.*		Ra	**radium** radio *m.*
Ho	**holmium** holmio *m.*		Rn	**radon** radón *m.*
H	**hydrogen** hidrógeno *m.*		Re	**rhenium** renio *m.*
In	**indium** indio *m.*		Rh	**rhodium** rodio *m.*
I	**iodine** yodo *m.*		Rg	**roentgenium** roentgenio *m.*
Ir	**iridium** iridio *m.*		Rb	**rubidium** rubidio *m.*
Fe	**iron** hierro *m.*		Ru	**ruthenium** rutenio *m.*
Kr	**krypton** kriptón *m.*		Rf	**rutherfordium** rutherfordio *m.*
La	**lanthanum** lantan *m.*		Sm	**samarium** samario *m.*
Lr	**lawrencium** lawrencio *m.*		Sc	**scandium** escandio *m.*
Pb	**lead** plomo *m.*		Sg	**seaborgium** seaborgio *m.*
Li	**lithium** litio *m.*		Se	**selenium** selenio *m.*
Lv	**livermorium** livermorio *m.*		Si	**silicon** silicio *m.*
Lu	**lutetium** lutecio *m.*		Ag	**silver** plata *f.*
Mg	**magnesium** magnesio *m.*		Na	**sodium** sodio *m.*
Mn	**manganese** manganeso *m.*		Sr	**strontium** estroncio *m.*
Mt	**meitnerium** meitnerio *m.*		S	**sulfur** azufre *m.*
Md	**mendelevium** mendelevio *m.*		Ta	**tantalum** tántalo *m.*
Hg	**mercury** mercurio *m.*		Tc	**technetium** tecnecio *m.*
Mo	**molybdenum** molibdeno *m.*		Te	**tellurium** teluro *m.*
Nd	**neodymium** neodimio *m.*		Tb	**terbium** terbio *m.*
Ne	**neon** neón *m.*		Tl	**thallium** talio *m.*
Np	**neptunium** neptunio *m.*		Th	**thorium** torio *m.*
Ni	**nickel** niquel *m.*		Tm	**thulium** tulio *m.*
Nb	**niobium** niobio *m.*		Sn	**tin** estaño *m.*
N	**nitrogen** nitrógeno *m.*		Ti	**titanium** titanio *m.*
No	**nobelium** nobelio *m.*		W	**tungsten** wolframio *m.*
Os	**osmium** osmio *m.*		Uuo	**ununoctium** ununoctio *m.*
O	**oxygen** oxígeno *m.*		Uup	**ununpentium** unumpentio *m.*
Pd	**palladium** paladio *m.*		Uus	**ununseptium** ununseptio *m.*
P	**phosphorus** fósforo *m.*		Uut	**ununtrium** ununtrio *m.*
Pt	**platinum** platino *m.*		U	**uranium** uranio *m.*
Pu	**plutonium** plutonio *m.*		V	**vanadium** vanadio *m.*
Po	**polonium** polonio *m.*		Xe	**xenon** xenón *m.*
K	**potassium** potasio *m.*		Yb	**ytterbium** yterbio *m.*
Pr	**praseodymium** praseodimio *m.*		Y	**yttrium** ytrio *m.*
Pm	**promethium** prometio *m.*		Zn	**zinc** cinc *m.*
Pa	**protactinium** protactinio *m.*		Zr	**zirconium** circonio *m.*

SCIENCE

Inquiry & Process

A
absorb *v.* absorber
analyze *v.* analizar
apparatus *n.* aparato *m.*

B
balance *n.* (scale) balanza *f.*
bar graph *n.* gráfico (-ca) de barras *m.f.*; barra gráfica *f.*
barometer *n.* barómetro *m.*
base *n.* (microscope) base *f.*
beaker *n.* vaso de precipitación, vaso de precipitado *m.*
Bunsen burner *n.* mechero de Bunsen *m.*
burete *n.* bureta *f.*

C
calculator *n.* calculadora *f.*
calibrate *v.* calibrar
categorize *v.* categorizar
category *n.* categoría *f.*
cause-and-effect relationship *n.* relación causa-efecto *f.*
Celsius, centigrade *adj.* Celsius, centígrado; **C. scale** *n.* escala Celsius *f.*
characteristics *n.pl.* características *f.*
chart *n.* cuadro *m.*, gráfico, -ca *m.f.*; **T-chart** gráfico (-ca) en forma de T; **tally c.** gráfico (-ca) de conteo
chronological *adj.* cronológico, -ca
chronometer *n.* cronómetro *m.*
clamp *n.* grapa *f.*

classification *n.* clave *f.*; **c. key** clave de clasificación
classify *v.* clasificar
collaborate *v.* colaborar
compare *v.* comparar
compass *n.* brújula *f.*
conclusion *n.* conclusión *f.*
conditions *n.pl.* condiciones *f.*
confer *v.* conferir
consistent *adj.* consistente
constant *adj. & n.* constante *f.*
construct *v.* construir
control *n.* control *m.*
control *v.* controlar
controlled *adj.* controlado, -da; **c. experiment** *n.* experimento controlado *m.*; **c. variable** variable controlada *f.*
coverslip *n.* cubreobjetos *m.*
criteria *n.pl.* criterios *m.*
crucible *n.* crisol *m.*

D
data *n.pl.* datos *m.*; **collect d.** *v.* recopilar datos; **d. sheet** hoja de registro *f.*; **d. table** tabla de datos *f.*
deduction *n.* deducción *f.*
demonstrate *v.* demostrar, probar
dependent variable *n.* variable dependiente *f.*
design *n.* diseño *m.*
device *n.* dispositivo *m.*, aparato *m.*
diagram *n.* diagrama *m.*

SCIENCE

diaphragm *n.* diafragma *m.*
discover *v.* descubrir
discovery *n.* descubrimiento *m.*
dissect *v.* disecar
dissection *n.* disección *f.*
drop *n.* gota *f.*
dropper *n.* gotero *m.*

E

equation *n.* ecuación *f.*
Erlenmeyer flask *n.* matraz de Erlenmeyer *m.*
estimate *n.* estimado *m.*
estimate *v.* estimar
evaluate *v.* evaluar
evidence *n.* evidencia *f.*, prueba *f.*
experiment *n.* experimento *m.*
experiment *v.* experimentar
experimentation *n.* experimentación *f.*
extract *v.* extraer
extrapolate *v.* extrapolar
event *n.* hecho *m.*, evento *m.*
eyepiece *n.* (microscope) ocular *m.*

F

fact *n.* hecho *m.*
Fahrenheit *adj.* Fahrenheit; **F. scale** escala Fahrenheit *f.*
findings *n.pl.* resultados *m.*
flame *n.* llama *f.*
flask *n.* matraz *m.*, frasco *m.*
focusing knob *n.* perilla de enfoque *f.*
forceps *n.* fórceps *m.*
formula *n.* fórmula *f.*
formulate *v.* formular

fume *n.* humo *m.*
funnel *n.* embudo *m.*

G

generate *v.* generar
glass *n.* vidro *m.*, cristal *m.*
gloves *n.pl.* guantes *m.*
goggles *n.pl.* gafas protectoras *f.*, anteojos de seguridad *m.*
graduated cylinder *n.* probeta graduada *f.*, cilindro graduado *m.*
graph *n.* gráfico, -ca *m.f.*
graph *v.* graficar
graphic representation *n.* representación gráfica *f.*
gyroscope *n.* giroscopio *m.*

H

hazard *n.* peligro *m.*
headlamp *n.* faro *m.*
hypothesis *n.* hipótesis *f.*
hypothesize *v.* formular hipótesis

I

ignite *v.* encender
illuminate *v.* iluminar
illumination *n.* iluminación *f.*
illustrate *v.* ilustrar
image *n.* imagen *f.*
immerse *v.* sumergir
impermeable *adj.* impermeable
implication *n.* implicación *f.*
incidence *n.* incidencia *f.*
incision *n.* incisión *f.*
incubate *v.* incubar
incubation *n.* incubación *f.;* **i. period** período de incubación *m.*

SCIENCE

SCIENCE

independent variable *n.* variable independiente *f.*

indicate *v.* indicar

indication *n.* indicación *f.*

infer *v.* inferir

inference *n.* inferencia *f.*

inspect *v.* inspeccionar

instrument *n.* instrumento *m.*

integrity *n.* (data) integridad *f.*

interaction *n.* interacción *f.*

interpret *v.* interpretar

interpretation *n.* interpretación *f.*

invent *v.* inventar, descubrir

investigate *v.* investigar

investigation *n.* investigación *f.*

irreversible *adj.* irreversible

isolate *v.* aislar

K

Kelvin scale *n.* escala Kelvin *f.*

L

laboratory *n.* laboratorio *m.;* **l. coat** bata de laboratorio *f.;* **l. equipment** equipo de laboratorio *m.*

line *n.* línea *f.;* **l. graph** gráfico (-ca) de líneas *m.f.;* **l. plot** diagrama de líneas *m.*

litmus *n.* tornasol *m.;* **l. paper** papel tornasol *m.*

log *n.* registro *m.*

logical *adj.* lógico, -ca

M

magnify *v.* ampliar

magnifying glass *n.* lupa *f.*

manometer *n.* manómetro *m.*

materials *n.pl.* materiales *m.*

measure *v.* medir

measurement *n.* medición *f.*

method *n.* método *m.*

metric *adj.* métrico, -ca; **m. ruler** *n.* regla métrica *f.;* **m. system** sistema métrico *m.*

microscope *n.* microscopio *m.;* **m. light** foco *m.;* **m. stage** platina del microscopio *f.*

model *n.* modelo *m.;* **mathematical m.** modelo matemático *m.*

modify *v.* modificar

N

needle *n.* aguja *f.*

numerical *adj.* numérico, -ca

O

object *n.* objeto *m.*

objective lens *n.* (microscope) lente objetivo *m.*

observe *v.* observar

occurrence *n.* incidencia *f.,* hecho *m.*

organize *v.* organizar

origin *n.* origen *m.*

outcome *n.* resultado *m.*

P

pattern *n.* patrón *m.*

peer review *n.* evaluación por homólogos *f.*

petri dish *n.* placa de Petri *f.*

phenomena *n.pl.* fenómenos *m.*

pictograph *n.* pictografía *f.*

pictographic *adj.* pictográfico, -ca

pipette *n.,* **pipet** *n.* pipeta *f.*

. . . .

placebo *n.* placebo *m.*
predict *v.* predecir
prediction *n.* predicción *f.*
probability *n.* probabilidad *f.*
probe *n.* sonda *f.*
procedure *n.* procedimiento *m.*
process *n.* proceso *m.*
proof *n.* prueba *f.*
property *n.* propiedad *f.*

Q

quantify *v.* cuantificar
quantitative *adj.* cuantitativo, -va
quantity *n.* cantidad *f.*

R

record *v.* grabar
relationship *n.* relación *f.*
relay *v.* reportar, pasar, transmitir
replicable *adj.* replicable
replicate *v.* replicar, reproducir
response *n.* respuesta *f.*
risk *n.* riesgo *m.*

S

scale *n.* (range) escala *f.*, (instrument) balanza *f.*
scalpel *n.* bisturí *m.*, escalpelo *m.*
scientific *adj.* científico, -ca; **s. inquiry** *n.* investigación científica *f.*; **s. law** ley científica *f.*; **s. method** método científico *m.*; **s. name** nombre científico *m.*; **s. notation** notación científica *f.*; **s. reasoning** razonamiento científico *m.*; **s. theory** teoría científica *f.*
scissors *n.pl.* tijeras *f.*

slide *n.* (microscope) portaobjetos *m.*; **s. cover** cubreobjetos *m.*
sort *v.* ordenar, clasificar, organizar
specimen *n.* ejemplar *m.*, espécimen *m.*
spectrograph *n.* espectrógrafo *m.*
substance *n.* sustancia *f.*
symbol *n.* símbolo *m.*
syringe *n.* jeringa *f.*, jeringuilla *f.*

T

tape measure *n.* cinta métrica *f.*
technological *adj.* tecnológico, -ca
technology *n.* tecnología *f.*
test tube *n.* tubo de ensayo *m.*, probeta *f.*
theoretical *adj.* teórico, -ca; **t. model** *n.* modelo teórico *m.*
theory *n.* teoría *f.*
tongs *n.pl.* tenazas *f.*, pinzas *f.*
tool *n.* herramienta *f.*, utensilio *m.*, instrumento *m.*
tray *n.* charola *f.*, bandeja *f.*
trend *n.* tendencia *f.*
trial *n.* ensayo *m.*, prueba *f.*
tweezers *n.pl.* pinzas *f.*

U

unit *n.* unidad *f.*

V

variable *n.* variable *f.*; **dependent v.** variable dependiente; **independent v.** variable independiente
Venn diagram *n.* diagrama de Venn *m.*
voltmeter *n.* voltímetro *m.*

SCIENCE

81

FIELDS OF SCIENCE & MEDICINE

acoustics *n.* acústica *f.*

anatomy *n.* anatomía *f.*

anesthesiology *n.* anestesiología *f.*

anthropology *n.* antropología *f.*

archaeology *n.* arqueología *f.*

astronomy *n.* astronomía *f.*

astrophysics *n.* astrofísica *f.*

biology *n.* biología *f.*

botany *n.* botánica *f.*

cardiology *n.* cardiología *f.*

chemistry *n.* química *f.*

computer science *n.* informática *f.,* ciencias de la computación *f.pl.*

cosmology *n.* cosmología *f.*

criminology *n.* criminología *f.*

dentistry *n.* odontología *f.*

dermatology *n.* dermatología *f.*

ecology *n.* ecología *f.*

economics *n.* economía *f.*

endocrinology *n.* endocrinología *f.*

engineering *n.* ingeniería *f.*

entomology *n.* entomología *f.*

environmental science *n.* ciencias ambientales *f.pl.*

epidemiology *n.* epidemiología *f.*

food science *n.* ciencia alimentaria *f.*

forensic science *n.* ciencia forense *f.*

forestry *n.* silvicultura *f.,* ciencias forestales *f.pl.*

gastroenterology *n.* gastroenterología *f.*

geochemistry *n.* geoquímica *f.*

geography *n.* geografía *f.*

geology *n.* geología *f.*

geriatrics *n.* geriatría *f.*

obstetrics & gynecology *n.* obstetricia y ginecología *f.*

herpetology *n.* herpetología *f.*

hydrology *n.* hidrología *f.*

ichthyology *n.* ictiología *f.*

immunology *n.* immunología *f.*

linguistics *n.* lingüística *f.*

marine biology *n.* biología marina *f.*

mathematics *n.pl.* matemáticas *f.*

mechanics *n.* mecánica *f.*

meterology *n.* meteorología *f.*

neurology *n.* neurología *f.*

oceanography *n.* oceanografía *f.*

oncology *n.* oncología *f.*

ophthalmology *n.* oftalmología *f.*

optics *n.* óptica *f.*

ornithology *n.* ornitología *f.*

orthopedics *n.* ortopedia *f.*

paleontology *n.* paleontología *f.*

pathology *n.* patología *f.*

pediatrics *n.* pediatría *f.*

periodontics *n.* periodoncia *f.*

pharmacology *n.* farmacología *f.*

physics *n.* física *f.*

physiology *n.* fisiología *f.*

political science *n.* ciencia política *f.*

psychiatry *n.* psiquiatría *f.*

psychology *n.* psicología *f.*

radiology *n.* radiología *f.*

seismology *n.* sismología *f.*

sociology *n.* sociología *f.*

statistics *n.* estadística *f.*

taxonomy *n.* taxonomía *f.*

toxicology *n.* toxicología *f.*

zoology *n.* zoología *f.*

SCIENCE

SOCIAL STUDIES

Civics & Government

∙∙

A

abortion rights *n.pl.* derechos al aborto *m.*

absentee voting *n.* voto ausente *m.*

abstinence *n.* abstinencia *f.*

abuse of power *n.* abuso de poder *m.*

acceptance speech *n.* discurso de aceptación *m.*

acculturate *v.* aculturar

acculturation *n.* aculturación *f.*

accusation *n.* acusación *f.*

accuse *v.* inculpar, acusar

activist *n.* activista *m.f.*

adjourn *v.* aplazar

adjournment *n.* aplazamiento *m.*

advice and consent *n.* consejo y consentimiento *m.*

advise and consent *v.* aconsejar y consentir

affirmative action *n.* acción afirmativa *f.*

age discrimination *n.* discriminación basada en la edad *f.*

alien *n.* extranjero, -ra *m.f.*

allegiance *n.* lealtad *f.*

ally *n.* aliado, -da *m.f.*

ambassador *n.* embajador, -ora *m.f.*

American (U.S.) *adj. & n.* americano, -na *m.f.;* estadounidense *m.f.*

American Dream *n.* sueño americano *m.*

amnesty *n.* amnistía *f.*

anti-immigrant *adj.* antiinmigrante; natitivsta; xenófobo, -ba

appoint *v.* nombrar, designar

appointee *n.* nombrado, -da *m.f.;* designado, -da *m.f.*

appointment *n.* nombramiento *m.*

apportionment *n.* prorrateo *m.,* distribución *f.*

appropriation *n.* apropiación *f.*

arbitration *n.* arbitraje *m.*

argument *n.* (reasoning) argumento *m.,* argumentación *f.;* (conflict) discusión *f.,* pelea *f.,* debate *m.*

arrest *n.* detención *f.,* arresto *m.*

arrest *v.* detener, arrestar

assimilate *v.* asimilar

assimilation *n.* asimilación *f.*

SOCIAL STUDIES

Attorney General *n.* Secretario de Justicia *m.*
authoritarian *adj.* autoritario, -ria
authority *n.* autoridad *f.*
autopsy *n.* autopsia *f.*

B
ballot *n.* votación *f.;* **b. box** urna *f.;* **b. initiative** iniciativa electoral, iniciativa de votación *f.;* **secret b.** votación secreta
behavior pattern *n.* patrón de comportamiento *m.*
belief *n.* creencia *f.*
bias *n.* parcialidad *f.*, prejuicio *m.*
bicameral *adj.* bicameral
bill *n.* proyecto de ley *m.;* **passage of a b.** aprobación de un proyecto de ley *f.*
bipartisan *adj.* bipartidista
birth rate *n.* índice de natalidad *m.*
block grant *n.* subvención global *f.*
body politic *n.* cuerpo político *m.*
Border Patrol *n.* patrulla fronteriza *f.*
branches of government *n.pl.* ramas del gobierno *f.*, poderes del estado *m.*
budget *n.* presupuesto *m.;* **balanced b.** presupuesto equilibrado
Bully Pulpit *n.* púlpito magnífico *m.*
bureaucracy *n.* burocracia *f.*
bureaucrat *n.* burócrata *m.f.*

C
cabinet *n.* gabinete *m.*
campaign *n.* campaña *f.;* **c. contribution** contribución política *f.*

candidate *n.* candidato, -ta *m.f.*
capital *n.* ciudad capital *f.;* **c. punishment** pena de muerte *f.*
capitol *n.* (building) capitolio *m.*
Capitol Hill *n.* Capitolio *m.*
caucus *n.* camarilla política *f.*
censorship *n.* censura *f.*
census *n.* censo *m.*
Central Intelligence Agency (C.I.A.) *n.* Agencia Central de Inteligencia *f.*
charge *n.* acusación *f.*, procesamiento *m.*
charge *v.* (crime) inculpar, acusar
chauvinist *adj. & n.* (sexist) machista *m.;* (nationalist) chovinista *m.f.*
checks and balances *n.pl.* controles y equilibrios, controles y contrapesos *m.*
Chief Justice *n.* Presidente (-ta) del Tribunal Supremo *m.f.*
citizen *n.* ciudadano, -na *m.f.*
citizenry *n.* ciudadanía *f.;* **informed c.** ciudadanía informada
citizenship *n.* ciudadanía *f.;* **c. by birth** ciudadanía por nacimiento
city *n.* ciudad *f.;* **c. council** consejo municipal *m.*, ayuntamiento *m.;* **c. manager** gestor (-ora) de la ciudad *m.f.;* **c. planning** planificación urbana *f.*
civic *adj.* cívico, -ca; **c. life** *n.* vida cívica *f.;* **c. mindedness** civismo *m.*, conciencia cívica *f.;* **c. participation** participación ciudadana *f.;* **c. responsibility** responsabilidad cívica *f.*
civics *n.pl.* cívica *f.*

civil *adj.* civil; **c. disobedience** *n.* desobediencia civil *f.;* **c. law** derecho civil *m.;* **c. liberties** *pl.* libertades civiles *f.;* **c. rights** *pl.* derechos civiles *m.;* **c. rights enforcement** aplicación de derechos civiles *f.;* **c. rights laws** *pl.* leyes de derechos civiles *f.;* **c. service** servicio civil *m.;* **c. society** sociedad civil *f.*

civilian control of the military *n.* control civil del ejército *m.*

civility *n.* civilidad *f.,* urbanidad *f.*

class *n.* clase *f.;* **c. action suit** juicio de acción popular *m.;* **c. conflict** lucha de clases *f.;* **c. consciousness** conciencia de clase *f.;* **middle c.** clase media; **ruling c.** clase dominante; **upper c.** clase aristócrata, clase alta; **upper middle c.** clase media alta

climate change *n.* cambio climático *m.*

cloture vote *n.* voto para terminar debate, voto de clausura *m.*

commander-in-chief *n.* comandante en jefe *m.*

common *adj.* común; **c. good** *n.* bien común *m.;* **c. law** ley común *f.;* **c. man** hombre común *m.*

communist *adj. & n.* comunista *m.f.*

community *n.* comunidad *f.*

compromise *n.* arreglo *m.,* compromiso *m.*

compromise *v.* llegar a un arreglo

conflict *n.* conflicto *m.;* **c. management** gestión de conflicto *f.,*

manejo de conflictos *m.;* **c. resolution** resolución de conflicto *f.*

Congress *n.* Congreso *m.*

Congressional *adj.* congresional; **C. committee** *n.* comité del Congreso *m.;* **C. district** distrito congresional *m.;* **C. hearing** audiencia del Congreso *f.*

Congressional Record *n.* registro del Congreso *m.*

conscientious objector *n.* objetor (-ra) de conciencia *m.f.*

conscription *n.* conscripción *f.,* reclutamiento forzado *m.*

consensus *n.* consenso *m.*

consent of the governed *n.* consentimiento del pueblo *m.*

conservatism *n.* conservadurismo *m.*

conservative *adj. & n.* conservador, -ora *m.f.*

constituency *n.* circunscripción electoral *f.*

constituent *n.* constituyente *m.f.*

constitution *n.* constitución *f.*

constitutional *adj.* constitucional; **c. amendment** *n.* enmienda constitucional *f.;* **c. law** derecho constitucional *m.*

contempt of court *n.* desacato al tribunal *m.*

contraception *n.* anticoncepción *f.*

coroner *n.* médico (-ca) forense *m.f.*

correctional facility *n.* centro penitenciario *m.,* prisión *f.,* cárcel *f.*

corrupt *adj.* corrupto, -ta; corrompido, -da

corruption *n.* corrupción *f.*

SOCIAL STUDIES

85

SOCIAL STUDIES

country *n.* país *m.;* **c. of origin** país de origen

county *n.* condado *m.*

court *n.* tribunal *m.,* juzgado *m.,* corte *f.;* **circuit c.** tribunal de circuito; **c. of appeals** corte de apelaciones; **c. order** mandato judicial *m.;* **lower c.** tribunal de primera instancia

crime *n.* crimen *m.*

criminal *adj. & n.* criminal *m.f.;* **c. law** derecho penal *m.*

cultural *adj.* cultural; **c. heritage** *n.* patrimonio cultural *m.;* **c. identity** identidad cultural *f.;* **c. pluralism** pluralismo cultural *m.;* **c. preservation** preservación cultural *f.;* **c. tradition** tradición cultural *f.*

culture *n.* cultura *f.*

curfew *n.* toque de queda *m.*

current events *n.pl.* acontecimientos actuales *m.*

custom *n.* costumbre *f.*

customs *n.* aduana *f.;* **c. search** *n.* inspección aduanal *f.*

D

death penalty *n.* pena de muerte, pena capital *f.*

debate *n.* debate *m.*

debate *v.* discutir, debatir

Declaration of Independence *n.* Declaración de la Independencia *f.*

declaratory judgment *n.* sentencia declarativa *f.*

defendant *n.* demandado, -da *m.f.;* acusado, -da *m.f.*

defense counsel *n.* abogado (-da) defensor (-ora) *m.f.*

delegate *n.* delegado, -da *m.f.*

delegate *v.* delegar

delegated powers *n.pl.* poderes delegados *m.*

delegation *n.* delegación *f.*

demagogic *adj.* demagógico, -ca

demagogue *n.* demagogo, -ga *m.f.*

democracy *n.* democracia *f.;* **direct d.** democracia directa; **representative d.** democracia representativa

democratic *adj.* democrático, -ca; **d. government** *n.* gobierno democrático *m.;* **d. values** *pl.* valores democráticos *m.*

Democratic Party *n.* Partido Demócrata *m.*

demographic change *n.* cambio demográfico *m.*

demographics *n.pl.* demografía *f.*

demonstration *n.* manifestación *f.,* concentración *f.*

department *n.* departamento *m.*

Department of Agriculture *n.* Departamento de Agricultura *m.;* **D. of Defense** Departamento de Defensa; **D. of Education** Departamento de Educación; **D. of Health and Human Services** Departamento de Salud y Servicios Humanos; **D. of Homeland Security** Departamento de Seguridad Nacional; **D. of Justice** Departamento de Justicia; **D. of Labor** Departamento de Trabajo; **D. of State** Departamento de Estado; **D. of the Interior** Departamento del Interior

deport *v.* deportar, expulsar

deregulation *n.* desregulación *f.,* desregularización *f.*

desegregation *n.* abolición de la segregación *f.*

detention without trial *n.* detención sin juicio *f.*

dictatorship *n.* dictadura *f.*

diplomacy *n.* diplomacia *f.*

diplomat *n.* diplomático, -ca *m.f.*

diplomatic *adj.* diplomático, -ca; **d. immunity** *n.* inmunidad diplomática *f.;* **d. recognition** reconocimiento diplomático *m.*

disagreement *n.* desacuerdo *m.*

discrimination *n.* discriminación *f.;* **age d.** discriminación basada en la edad; **d. based on disability** discriminación por razones de discapacidad; **ethnic d.** discriminación étnica; **gender d.** discriminación por razones de género; **language d.** discriminación basada en el idioma; **racial discrimination** discriminación racial; **religious d.** discriminación basada en la religión; **sex d.** discriminación sexual

disenfranchise *v.* privar del derechos de voto

dispute *n.* disputa *f.,* conflicto *m.,* pelea *f.*

dissent *n.* disentimiento *m.*

dissident *n.* disidente *m.f.*

district attorney *n.* fiscal *m.f.*

diversity *n.* diversidad *f.;* **ethnic d.** diversidad étnica; **linguistic d.** diversidad lingüística; **racial d.** diversidad racial

divided *adj.* dividido, -da; **d. government** *n.* gobierno dividido *m.;* **d. loyalties** *pl.* conflicto de lealtades *m.,* lealtades divididas *f.*

docket *n.* (court) expediente *m.*

document *n.* documento *m.*

document *v.* documentar

documentary *n.* documental *m.*

domestic policy *n.* política nacional *f.*

double jeopardy *n.* doble enjuiciamiento *m.,* doble riesgo *m.*

DREAM Act *n.* Ley DREAM *f.*

dress code *n.* código de vestimenta *m.,* norma de vestir *f.*

driver's license *n.* licencia de conducir, licencia de manejar *f.*

drug *n.* (medicinal) medicamento *m.,* (illegal) droga *f.;* **d. addiction** toxicomanía *f.;* **d. trafficker** narcotraficante *m.f.;* **d. trafficking** narcotráfico *m.*

due process *n.* debido proceso *m.;* **d. p. of law** debido proceso legal

Due Process Clause *n.* cláusula de debido proceso *f.*

E

ecology *n.* ecología *f.*

ecosystem *n.* ecosistema *m.*

editorial board *n.* consejo editorial *m.,* comité de redacción *m.*

education *n.* educación *f.;* **compul-**

sory e. educación obligatoria; **e. reform** reforma educativa *f.;* **private e.** educación privada; **public e.** educación pública

egalitarian *adj.* igualitario, -ria

elect *v.* elegir

elected representative *n.* representante elegido *m.*

election *n.* elección *f.;* **e. day** día de elección *m.;* **e. results** *pl.* resultados de las elecciones *m.;* **general e.** elección general; **primary e.** elección primaria; **recall e.** elección de destitución

elector *n.* elector, -ora *m.f.*

electoral district *n.* circunscripción electoral *f.,* distrito electoral *m.*

Electoral College *n.* colegio electoral *m.*

elite *adj. & n.* élite *f.,* elite *f.*

embassy *n.* embajada *f.*

emigrate *v.* emigrar

eminent domain *n.* derecho de expropiación *m.*

enact *v.* promulgar

Endangered Species Act *n.* Ley sobre Especies en Peligro de Extinción *f.*

endorsement *n.* aprobación *f.,* respaldo *m.*

English Common Law *n.* derecho consuetudinario de Inglaterra, derecho común inglés *m.*

English-only law *n.* ley de solo inglés *f.*

entitlement *n.* (right) derecho *m.;* (government program) econó-mico subsidio *m.;* **e. program** programa de ayuda social *m.*

enumerated powers *n.pl.* poderes enumerados *m.*

environment *n.* medio ambiente *m.*

Environmental Protection Agency (E.P.A.) *n.* Agencia de Protección Ambiental *f.*

envoy *n.* enviado, -da *m.f.*

Equal Employment Opportunity Commission (E.E.O.C.) *n.* Comisión para la Igualdad de Oportunidades en el Empleo *f.*

Equal Protection Clause *n.* cláusula de igual protección *f.*

equality *n.* igualdad *f.*

established religion *n.* religión establecida *f.*

Establishment Clause *n.* cláusula de establecimiento *f.*

ethical *adj.* ético, -ca; **e. dilemma** *n.* dilema ético *m.*

ethics *n.pl.* ética *f.*

ethnic *adj.* étnico, ca; **e. discrimination** *n.* discriminación étnica *f.;* **e. diversity** diversidad étnica *f.;* **e. minority** minoría étnica *f.*

ethnicity *n.* etnicidad *f.*

ethnocentric *adj.* etnocentrico, -ca

ethnocentrism *n.* etnocentrismo *m.*

European American *adj. & n.* europeo americano, -na *m.f.*

evidence *n.* evidencia *f.*

exclusionary rule *n.* regla de exclusión *f.*

executive *adj. & n.* ejecutivo, -va *m.f.;* **e. branch** rama executiva *f.,* poder ejecutivo *m.;* **e. privilege** privilegio ejecutivo *m.*

exit poll *n.* encuesta de salida *f.*

extremist *adj. & n.* extremista *m.f.*

eyewitness account *n.* relato de un testigo *m.*

F

fact checker *n.* verificador (-ora) de hechos *m.f.*

fair trial *n.* juicio justo, juicio imparcial *m.*

false arrest *n.* detención ilegal *f.,* arresto ilegal *m.*

family *n.* familia *f.;* **f. history** historia familiar *f.;* **f. life** vida familiar *f.*

fascism *n.* fascismo *m.*

fascist *adj. & n.* fascista *m.f.*

federal *adj.* federal; **f. budget** *n.* presupuesto federal *m.;* **f. court** tribunal federal *m.;* **f. deficit** déficit federal *m.;* **f. judiciary** judicatura federal *f.,* poder judicial federal *m.;* **f. spending** gasto federal *m.;* **f. supremacy clause** cláusula de supremacía federal *f.;* **f. troops** *pl.* tropas federales *f.*

Federal Bureau of Investigation (F.B.I.) *n.* Oficina Federal de Investigaciones *f.;* **F. Election Commission (F.E.C.)** Comisión de Elecciones Federales *f.*

federalism *n.* federalismo *m.*

felon *n.* felón, -ona *m.f.;* criminal *m.f.*

felony *n.* crimen *m.,* delito grave *m.*

feminism *n.* feminismo *m.*

filibuster *n.* (Senate) filibustero *m.*

fine *n.* multa *f.*

fine *v.* multar

First Amendment *n.* Primera Enmienda *f.*

First Lady *n.* Primera Dama *f.*

flag *n.* bandera *f.*

folk hero *n.* héroe popular *m.,* heroína popular *f.*

Food and Drug Administration (F.D.A.) *n.* Administración de Medicamentos y Alimentos *f.*

foreign *adj.* extranjero, -ra; **f. aid** *n.* ayuda extranjera, ayuda exterior *f.;* **f. policy** política exterior *f.;* **f. relations** *pl.* relaciones extranjeras *f.*

foreigner *n.* extranjero, -ra *m.f.*

foundation *n.* fundación *f.*

Fourteenth Amendment *n.* Decimocuarta Enmienda *f.*

Fourth of July *n.* Día de la Independencia *m.*

free press *n.* prensa libre *f.*

freedom *n.* libertad *f.;* **f. of assembly** libertad de reunión; **f. of association** libertad de asociación; **f. of choice** libertad de elección; **f. of expression** libertad de expresión; **f. of religion** libertad religiosa

fugitive *n.* prófugo, -ga *m.f.;* fugitivo, -va *m.f.*

fundamentalism *n.* fundamentalismo *m.;* **Christian f.** fundamentalismo cristiano; **Islamic f.** fundamentalismo islámico

fundamentalist *n.* fundamentalista *m.f.*

SOCIAL STUDIES

G

gender discrimination *n.* discriminación por razones de género *f.*

generation *n.* generación *f.*

genocide *n.* genocidio *m.*

gentrification *n.* aburguesamiento *m.*

geopolitics *n.* geopolítica *f.*

gerrymandering *n.* gerrymandering *m.*

global warming *n.* calentamiento global *m.*

G.O.P. (Grand Old Party) *n.* Partido Republicano *m.*

government *n.* gobierno *m.;* **central g.** gobierno central; **divided g.** gobierno dividido; **federal g.** gobierno federal; **g. policy** política gubernamental *f.;* **limited g.** gobierno limitado; **state g.** gobierno estatal; **tribal g.** gobierno tribal

governor *n.* gobernador, -ora *m.f.*

grassroots *n.* base popular *f.;* **g. campaign** campaña de base popular, campaña a nivel popular *f.*

green card *n.* tarjeta de residencia permanente *f.*

Green Party *n.* Partido Verde *m.*

gun control *n.* control de armas *m.*

H

habeas corpus *n.* hábeas corpus *m.*

hate *n.,* **hatred** *n.* odio *m.;* **h. crime** crimen motivado por el odio *m.;* **h. speech** discurso de odio *m.,* incitación al odio *f.*

health *n.* salud *f.;* **h. care** cuidado de la salud *m.;* **h. insurance** seguro de salud *m.;* **h. services** *pl.* servicios de salud *m.*

hero *n.* héroe *m.f.*

heroic *adj.* heroico, -ca

heroine *n.* heroína *f.*

heroism *n.* heroísmo *m.*

Hispanic *adj. & n.* hispano, -na *m.f.;* hispánico, -ca *m.f.*

homeless *adj.* sin hogar

homeless *n.pl.* personas sin hogar *f.*

house arrest *n.* detención domiciliaria *f.,* arresto domiciliario *m.*

House of Representatives *n.* Cámara de los Representantes *f.*

household *n.* hogar *m.*

housing *n.* vivienda *f.;* **h. development** desarrollo de viviendas *m.*

human rights *n.pl.* derechos humanos *m.*

hunger *n.* hambre *m.*

I

ideological *adj.* ideológico, -ca; **i. conflict** *n.* conflicto ideológico *m.*

ideology *n.* ideología *f.*

immigrant *n.* inmigrante *m.f.;* **undocumented i.** inmigrante indocumentado, -da *m.f.*

immigrate *v.* inmigrar

immigration *n.* inmigración *f.;* **illegal i.** inmigración ilegal; **i. laws** *pl.* leyes de inmigración *f.;* **i. policy** política migratoria *f.;* **i. quota** cuota migratoria *f.*

Immigration & Customs Enforcement (ICE) *n.* Servicio de Inmigración y Control de Aduanas *m.*

SOCIAL STUDIES

impeach *v.* destituir

impeachment *n.* proceso de destitución *m.*

inalienable rights *n.pl.* derechos inalienables *m.*

inaugural address *n.* discurso inaugural *m.*

inauguration *n.* inauguración *f.,* toma de posesión *f.,* investidura *f.*

income tax *n.* impuesto sobre la renta *m.*

incumbent *n.* titular *m.f.*

independence *n.* independencia *f.*

Independence Day *n.* Día de la Independencia *m.*

independent *adj.* independiente

indictment *n.* acusación *f.,* procesamiento *m.*

indigeneous *adj.* indígeno, -na; autóctono, -na

indigent *adj.* indigente

individual *adj. & n.* individual *m.;* individuo, -dua *m.f.;* **i. liberty** libertad individual *f.;* **i. responsibility** responsabilidad individual *f.;* **i. rights** *pl.* derechos individuales *m.*

indoctrinate *v.* adoctrinar

indoctrination *n.* adoctrinamiento *m.*

institute *n.* instituto *m.*

institute *v.* instituir

institution *n.* institución *f.*

interdependent *adj.* interdependiente

interest group *n.* grupo de interés *m.*

international *adj.* internacional; **i. law** *n.* derecho internacional *m.;* **i. organization** organización internacional *f.*

interrogate *v.* interrogar

interrogation *n.* interrogatorio *m.*

invasion of privacy *n.* invasión de la privacidad *f.*

Islamic fundamentalism *n.* fundamentalismo islámico *m.*

isolationism *n.* aislacionismo *m.*

isolationist *n.* aislacionista *m.f.*

J

jihad *n.* yihad *f.,* jihad *f.*

journalist *n.* periodista *m.f.*

judge, justice *n.* juez *m.f.,* jueza *f.;* **chief j.** juez presidente

judgment *n.* juicio *m.*

judicial *adj.* judicial; **j. branch** *n.* rama judicial *f.,* poder judicial *m.;* **j. review** revisión judicial *f.;* control jurisdiccional *m.;* **j. supremacy** supremacía judicial *f.*

judiciary *n.* poder judicial *m.*

jurisdiction *n.* jurisdicción *f.*

jury *n.* jurado *m.;* **j. duty** servicio de jurado *m.;* **trial by j.** juicio por jurado *m.*

justice *n.* justicia *f.;* **j. system** sistema de justicia *m.*

juvenile *adj.* juvenil

L

labor *n.* trabajo *m.;* **l. law** legislación laboral *f.;* **l. movement** movimiento laboral, movimiento obrero *m.;* **l. union** sindicato *m.*

lame duck *n.* funcionario invalidado *m.,* pato cojo *m.*

SOCIAL STUDIES

landmark decision *n.* decisión histórica *f.*

language discrimination *n.* discriminación basada en el idioma *f.*

Latin American *adj. & n.* latinoamericano, -na *m.f.*

law *n.* ley *f.*, derecho *m.;* **civil l.** derecho civil; **civil rights l.** ley de derechos civiles; **criminal l.** derecho penal; **due process of l.** debido proceso legal *m.;* **l. and order** ley y orden; **l. enforcement** aplicación de la ley *f.*, cumplimiento de la ley *m.;* **respect for l.** respeto del derecho, respeto por la ley *m.;* **rule of l.** estado de derecho *m.*, imperio de la ley *m.;* **sign into l.** *v.* firmar en ley

lawmaker *n.* legislador, -ora *m.f.*

lawsuit *n.* pleito *m.*, litigio *m.*, proceso *m.*, demanda *f.*

lawyer *n.* abogado, -da *m.f.*

leader *n.* líder *m.f.*

leadership *n.* liderazgo *m.*

left-wing *adj.* izquierdista, de izquierda

legal *adj.* legal; **l. claim** *n.* demanda *f.;* **l. recourse** recurso legal *m.*

legalize *v.* autorizar

legislate *v.* legislar

legislation *n.* legislación *f.*

legislative branch *n.* rama legislativa *f.*

legislator *n.* legislador, -ora *m.f.*

legislature *n.* legislatura *f.*

letter to the editor *n.* carta al editor *f.*

libel *n.* difamación *f.*

liberal *adj. & n.* liberal *m.f.;* **l. democracy** democracia liberal *f.*

libertarian *adj. & n.* libertario, -ria *m.f.*

Libertarian Party *n.* Partido Libertario *m.*

liberty *n.* libertad *f.;* **l. and justice for all** libertad y justicia para todos

Library of Congress *n.* Biblioteca del Congreso *f.*

licensing *n.* concesión de licencias *f.*

lifestyle *n.* estilo de vida *m.*

line of demarcation *n.* línea de demarcación *f.*

linguistic diversity *n.* diversidad lingüística *f.*

lobby *n.* grupo de presión *m.*

lobby *v.* presionar, cabildear, ejercer presiones

lobbying *n.* cabildeo *m.*, presión política *f.*

lobbyist *n.* cabildero, -ra *m.f.*

loyal opposition *n.* oposición leal *f.*

M

Machiavellian *adj.* maquiavélico, -ca

majority *adj.* mayoritaria

majority *n.* mayoría *f.;* **m. leader** líder de la mayoría *m.f.;* **m. rule** regla de la mayoría *f.*, gobierno de la mayoría *m.;* **simple m.** mayoría simple; **two-thirds m.** mayoría de dos tercios

male chauvinist *adj & n.* machista *m.*

mandate *n.* mandato *m.*, orden *f.;*

unfunded m. mandato sin financiamiento

mandate *v.* encomendar, encargar

marriage equality *n.* matrimonio
igualitario *m.*

matriarch *n.* matriarca *f.*

matriarchal *adj.* matriarcal

mayor *n.* alcalde, -esa *m.f.;* presidente (-ta) municipal *m.f.*

meritocracy *n.* meritocracia *f.*

middle class *n.* clase media *f.*

migrant worker *n.* trabajador (-ra)
migratorio (-ria) *m.f.*

migrate *v.* emigrar

migration *n.* migración *f.*

militarism *n.* militarismo *m.*

militarist *adj. & n.* militarista *m.f.*

minimum wage *n.* salario mínimo *m.*

minority *adj & n.* minoría *f.;* **ethnic
m.** minoría étnica; **m. leader**
líder de la minoría *m.f.;* **m. rights**
pl. derechos de las minorías *m.;*
racial m. minoría racial

misdemeanor *n.* delito menor *m.*

mobility *n.* movilidad *f.*

moderate *adj. & n.* moderado, -da
m.f.

monogamy *n.* monogamia *f.*

monument *n.* monumento *m.*

moral values *n.pl.* principios
morales *m.*

mother country *n.* patria *f.*

muckraker *n.* periodista de investigación *m.f.*

mudslinging *n.* vilipendio *m.*, calumnia *f.*

multicultural *adj.* multicultural

multiculturalism *n.* multiculturalismo *m.*

N

national *adj.* nacional; **n. anthem**
n. himno nacional *m.;* **n. debt**
deuda pública *f.;* **n. flag** bandera
nacional *f.;* **n. forest** bosque nacional *m.;* **n. holiday** día festivo
nacional *m.*, feriado nacional *m.;*
n. identity identidad nacional *f.;*
n. origin origen nacional *m.;* **n.
park** parque nacional *m.;* **n. security** seguridad nacional *f.*

**National Aeronautics and Space
Administration (NASA)** *n.* Administración Nacional de Aeronáutica y el Espacio *f.*

National Guard *n.* Guardia Nacional *f.*

National Security Council *n.* Consejo Nacional de Seguridad *m.*

nativist *adj. & n.* nativista *m.f.;* xenófobo, -ba *m.f.*

naturalization *n.* naturalización *f.*

newcomer *n.* recién llegado (-da)
m.f.

newspaper *n.* periódico *m.*

nomination *n.* nominación *f.*

nominee *n.* candidato, -ta *m.f.*

nonprofit organization *n.* organización sin fines de lucro, organización no lucrativa *f.*

nonviolent *adj.* no violenta; **n. direct action** *n.* acción directa no
violenta, acción directa pacífica *f.;*
n. resistance resistencia no vio-

93

SOCIAL STUDIES

lenta, resistencia pacífica *f.*

nuclear power *n.* energía nuclear *f.*

O

oath of office *n.* juramento al cargo *m.*

op-ed *n.* opinión editorial *f.*, artículo de opinion *m.*

open-mindedness *n.* ausencia de prejuicios *f.*, imparcialidad *f.*

opinion *n.* opinión *f.;* **o. poll** encuesta *f.*

order *n.* (mandate) orden *f.*, (sequence, operation) orden *m.;* **numerical o.** orden numérico; **public o.** orden público

order *v.* ordenar, decretar, encargar

outlaw *n.* proscrito, -ta *m.f.*

outlaw *v.* prohibir

P

pacifism *n.* pacifismo *m.*

pacifist *adj. & n.* pacifista *m.f.*

pardon *n.* perdón *m.*

parliamentary democracy *n.* democracía parlamentaria *f.*

party *n.* partido *m.*

patriarch *n.* patriarca *m.*

patriarchal *adj.* patriarcal

patriot *n.* patriota *m.f.*

patriotic *adj.* patriótico, -ca

patriotism *n.* patriotismo *m.*

penalize *v.* penalizar

penalty *n.* pena *f.*, castigo *m.;* **death p.** pena de muerte

Pentagon *n.* Pentágono *m.*

perjury *n.* perjurio *m.*

persecution *n.* persecución *f.*

petition *n.* petición *f.*

petition *v.* solicitar, elevar una petición

philanthropist *n.* filántropo, -pa *m.f.*

philanthropy *n.* filantropía *f.*

picket *n.* piquete *m.*

picket *v.* piquetear, organizar un piquete

plaintiff *n.* demandante *m.f.*, querellante *m.f.*

plea bargain *n.* negociación de cargos y condenas *f.*

pledge of allegiance *n.* juramento a la bandera *m.*

pluralism *n.* pluralismo *m.*

plurality *n.* pluralidad *f.*

pocket veto *n.* veto de bolsillo *m.*

point of order *n.* cuestión de orden *f.*

point of view *n.* punto de vista *m.*

polarization *n.* polarización *f.*

police *n.* policía *f.*

policy *n.* política *f.;* **domestic p.** política nacional; **foreign p.** política exterior; **government p.** política gubernamental; **immigration p.** política migratoria; **public p.** políticas públicas *pl.*

policymaker *n.* formulador (-ora) de políticas *m.f.*

political *adj.* político, -ca; **p. action committee** *n.* comité de acción política *m.;* **p. appointment** nombramiento político *m.;* **p. cartoon** caricatura política *f.;* **p. convention** convención política *f.;* **p. life** vida política *f.;* **p. machine** maquinaria política *f.;* **p. participation** participación política *f.;* **p. party** partido político *m.;* **p. philosophy** filosofía política *f.;* **p. platform** plataforma política *f.;* **p. spin** giro político *m.*

politics *n.* política *f.*

polling place *n.* centro electoral, centro de votación *m.*

polls *n.pl.* urnas *f.*

pollution *n.* polución *f.,* contaminación *f.;* **air p.** contaminación atmosférica

polygamy *n.* poligamia *f.*

popular *adj.* popular; **p. culture** *n.* cultura popular *f.;* **p. vote** voto popular *m.*

populism *n.* populismo *m.*

populist *adj. & n.* populista *m.f.*

poverty *n.* pobreza *f.*

power *n.* poder *m.;* **p. bloc** bloque de poder *m.;* **p. elite** élite del poder *f.;* **p. of the purse** poder del bosillo

preamble *n.* preámbulo *m.*

precinct *n.* circunscripción *f.*

prejudice *n.* prejuicio *m.*

president *n.* presidente *m.f.,* presidenta *f.*

presidential *adj.* presidencial; **p. election** *n.* elección presidencial *f.;* **p. primary** primario presidencial *m.*

President's Cabinet *n.* gabinete presidencial *m.*

presumption of innocence *n.* presunción de inocencia *f.*

prior restraint *n.* restricción previa *f.*

prison *n.* prisión *f.,* cárcel *f.*

privacy *n.* privacidad *f.,* intimidad *f.;* **invasion of p.** invasión de la privacidad *f.*

private *adj.* privado, -da; personal; **p. education** *n.* educación privada *f.;* **p. life** vida privada *f.*

privatization *n.* privatización *f.*

privilege *n.* privilegio *m.*

probable cause *n.* causa probable *f.*

probation *n.* libertad condicional *f.*

proclaim *v.* proclamar, declarar

proclamation *n.* proclamación *f.*

progressive *adj. & n.* progresista *m.;* **p. movement** movimiento progresista *m.*

propaganda *n.* propaganda *f.*

propagandize *v.* hacer propaganda

property rights *n.pl.* derechos de propiedad *m.*

proposal *n.* propuesta *f.*

prosecution *n.* enjuiciamiento *m.*

prosecutor *n.* fiscal *m.f.*

protest *n.* protesta *f.*

protest *v.* protestar

public *adj.* público, -ca; **p. agenda** *n.* agenda pública *f.;* **p. education** educación pública *f.;* **p. financing of elections** financiamiento público de las elecciones *m.;* **p. good** bien común, bien público *m.;* **p. housing** vivienda pública *f.;* **p. life** vida pública *f.;* **p. office** cargos públicos *m.pl.;* **p. official** funcionario público *m.;* **p. opinion** opinión pública *f.;* **p. policy** políticas

SOCIAL STUDIES

95

SOCIAL STUDIES

públicas *f.pl.;* **p. project** proyecto público *m.;* **p. servant** funcionario público *m.;* **p. service announcement** anuncio de servicio público *m.;* **p. transit** transporte público *m.;* **p. trial** juicio público *m.;* **p. utilities** *pl.* servicios públicos *m.*

pundit *n.* comentarista político (-ca) *m.f.*

punishment *n.* pena *f.,* castigo *m.;* **capital p.** pena de muerte; **corporal p.** castigo corporal

pure food and drug laws *n.pl.* leyes de pureza de alimentos y drogas *f.*

pursuit of happiness *n.* búsqueda de la felicidad *f.*

Q

qualifications *n.pl.* calificaciones *f.*

quality of life *n.* calidad de vida *f.*

quorum *n.* quórum *m.*

quota *n.* cuota *f.*

R

race *n.* raza *f.;* **r. relations** *pl.* relaciones raciales *f.*

racial *adj.* racial; **r. discrimination** *n.* discriminación racial *f.;* **r. diversity** diversidad racial *f.;* **r. group** grupo racial *m.*

radical *adj. & n.* radical *m.f.*

radicalism *n.* radicalismo *m.*

rally *n.* concentración *f.,* mitin *m.,* manifestación *f.*

rapid transit *n.* tránsito rápido *m.*

ratification *n.* ratificación *f.*

ratify *v.* ratificar

reactionary *adj. & n.* reaccionario, -ra *m.f.*

reapportionment *n.* nueva repartición *f.*

reasoning *n.* razonamiento *m.,* argumento *m.,* argumentación *f.*

recall election *n.* elección de destitución *f.*

redistricting *n.* reestructuración distrital *f.*

redress of grievances *n.* reparación de agravios *f.*

referendum *n.* referéndum *m.*

reform *n.* reforma *f.*

reform *v.* reformar

reformer *n.* reformador, -ora *m.f.*

refugee *n.* refugiado, -da *m.f.*

regime *n.* régimen *m.*

regulation *n.* regulación *f.,* reglamento *m.,* norma *f.,* regla *f.*

regulatory agency *n.* agencia reguladora *f.,* organismo regulador *m.*

religion *n.* religión *f.*

religious *adj.* religioso, -sa; **r. belief** *n.* creencia religiosa *f.;* **r. discrimination** discriminación basada en la religión *f.;* **r. freedom** libertad religiosa *f.;* **r. revival** renacimiento religioso *m.*

repeal *n.* revocación *f.,* abrogación *f.*

repeal *v.* derogar, abrogar

represent *v.* representar

representation *n.* representación *f.*

representative *n.* representante *m.f.;* **r. democracy** democracia representativa *f.*

republic *n.* república *f.*

Republican Party *n.* Partido Republicano *m.*

residential district *n.* área residencial *f.*

resignation *n.* renuncia *f.*, resignación *f.*

resistance *n.* resistencia *f.*

resolution *n.* resolución *f.*

respect *n.* respeto *m.*; **r. for the rights of others** respeto al derecho ajeno

responsibility *n.* responsabilidad *f.*

revoke *v.* revocar

right *n.* derecho *m.*; **civil r.** *pl.* derechos civiles; **property r.** *pl.* derechos de propiedad; **r. of appeal** derecho de apelación; **r. to a fair trial** derecho a un juicio justo; **r. to counsel** derecho a obtener un abogado; **r. to criticize the government** derecho a criticar al gobierno; **r. to face an accuser** derecho a enfrentar un acusador; **r. to vote** derecho al voto; **unalienable r.** *pl.* derechos inalienables

right-wing *adj.* derechista, de derecha

roll call vote *n.* votación nominal *f.*

rule of law *n.* imperio de la ley *m.*, estado de derecho *m.*, principio de legalidad *m.*

rules *n.pl.* normas *f.*; reglas *f.*

ruling class *n.* clase dominante *f.*

S

sales tax *n.* impuesto sobre las ventas *m.*

same-sex marriage *n.* matrimonio entre personas del mismo sexo *m.*

school *n.* escuela *f.*; **s. board** junta de educación *f.*, consejo escolar *m.*; **s. choice** libre elección de escuela *f.*; **s. prayer** oración en las escuelas *f.*; **s. vouchers** *pl.* bonos escolares *m.*

search warrant *n.* orden de registro *f.*

secret ballot *n.* votación secreta *f.*

Secretary of Defense *n.* Secretario (-ria) de Defensa *m.f.*; **S. of Education** Secretario (-ria) de Educación; **S. of State** Secretario (-ria) de Estado

secular *adj.* secular

secularism *n.* secularismo *m.*

segregation *n.* segregación *f.*; **de facto s.** segregación de facto; **de jure s.** segregación de jure

self-discipline *n.* autodisciplina *f.*

self-governance *n.*, **self-government** *n.* autogobierno *m.*, autogobernación *f.*

self-sufficiency *n.* autosuficiencia *f.*

Senate *n.* Senado *m.*

senator *n.* senador, -ora *m.f.*

senior citizen *n.* persona de la tercera edad, persona de edad avanzada *f.*; anciano, -na *m.f.*; jubilado, -da *m.f.*

sentence *n.* pena *f.*, sentencia *f.*; **commute a s.** *v.* conmutar una sentencia

separation *n.* separación *f.*; **s. of church and state** separación de

SOCIAL STUDIES

iglesia y estado; **s. of powers** separación de poderes

sex discrimination *n.* discriminación sexual *f.*

sexism *n.* sexismo *m.*

Sharia law *n.* ley de la Sharia *f.*

Silent Majority *n.* mayoría silenciosa *f.*

slander *n.* calumnia *f.*

slate *n.* lista de candidatos *f.*

slogan *n.* eslogan *m.*

slum *n.* barrio bajo *m.*, barriada *f.*

slumlord *n.* casero abusivo *m.*

social *adj.* social; **s. class** *n.* clase social *f.*; **s. gospel** evangelío social *m.*; **s. justice** justicia social *f.*; **s. reform** reforma social *f.*; **s. welfare** *n.* bienestar social *m.*

Social Security *n.* Seguro Social *m.*

socialist *adj. & n.* socialista *m.f.*

society *n.* sociedad *f.*; **civil s.** sociedad civil

socioeconomic *adj.* socioeconómico, -ca; **s. status** *n.* condición socioeconómica *f.*

sociologist *n.* sociólogo, -ga *m.f.*

sociology *n.* sociología *f.*

solidarity *n.* solidaridad *f.*

soup kitchen *n.* comedor de beneficiencia *m.*

sovereign state *n.* estado soberano *m.*

sovereignty *n.* soberanía *f.*

Speaker of the House *n.* Presidente (-ta) de la Cámara *m.f.*

standard of living *n.* nivel de vida *m.*

standardize *v.* normalizar, estandarizar

state *n.* estado *m.*; **s. constitution** constitución estatal *f.*; **s. court** corte estatal *f.*; **s. elections** *pl.* elecciones estatales *f.*; **s. government** gobierno estatal *m.*; **s. legislature** legislatura estatal *f.*; **s. senator** senador (-ora) estatal *m.f.*; **s. sovereignty** soberanía del estado *f.*

State of the Union Address *n.* discurso sobre el Estado de la Unión *m.*

statehood *n.* estadidad *f.*, condición de estado *f.*

states' rights *n.pl.* derechos de los estados *m.*

Statue of Liberty *n.* Estatua de la Libertad *f.*

status quo *n.* statu quo *m.*

statute *n.* estatuto *m.*; **s. of limitations** estatuto de prescripción legal

stump speech *n.* discurso de campaña *m.*

subpoena *n.* citación *f.*

sue *v.* demandar

Supreme Court *n.* Corte Suprema de Justicia *f.*

survey *n.* encuesta *f.*

symbol *n.* símbolo *m.*

T

tax *n.* impuesto *m.*, tributo *m.*; **corporate t.** impuesto sobre sociedades; **income t.** impuesto sobre la renta; **sales t.** impuesto

• •

sobre las ventas; **t. code** código impositivo *m.;* **t. cut** reducción de impuestos *f.;* **t. reform** reforma fiscal *f.*

taxpayer *n.* contribuyente *m.f.*

testify *v.* declarar, testificar

testimony *n.* testimonio *m.*

theory of evolution *n.* teoría de la evolución *f.*

tolerance *n.* tolerancia *f.*

trade union *n.* sindicato *m.*

treaty *n.* tratado *m.*

trial *n.* juicio *m.,* enjuiciamiento *m.,* proceso *m.;* **detention without t.** detención ilegal *f.,* arresto illegal *m.;* **fair t.** juicio justo, juicio imparcial; **public t.** juicio público; **speedy t.** juicio rápido; **t. by jury** juicio con jurado

tribal government *n.* gobierno tribal *m.*

two-party system *n.* sistema bipartidista *m.*

U

U.S. Air Force *n.* Fuerza Aéria de EE.UU. *f.*

U.S. Army *n.* Ejército de EE.UU. *m.*

U.S. Marine Corps *n.* Cuerpo de Infantería de Marina de EE.UU. *m.*

U.S. Navy *n.* Armada de EE.UU. *f.*

underclass *n.* clase marginada *f.*

undocumented worker *n.* trabajador (-ra) indocumentado (-da) *m.f.*

unification *n.* unificación *f.*

United States (U.S.) *n.* Estados

Unidos (EE.UU.) *m.pl.*

universal suffrage *n.* sufragio universal *m.*

unlawful detention *n.* detención ilegal *f.*

upper class *n.* clase aristócrata, clase alta *f.*

upward mobility *n.* movilidad ascendente *f.*

urban *adj.* urbano, -na; **u. decay** *n.* degradación de zonas urbanas *f.;* **u. growth** crecimiento urbano *m.;* **u. planning** planificación urbana *f.*

V

verdict *n.* veredicto *m.*

veto *n.* veto *m.;* **v. override** anulación del veto *f.*

veto *v.* vetar

vice-president *n.* vicepresidente *m.f.,* vicepresidenta *f.*

vigilante *adj. & n.* justiciero *m.*

volunteer *n.* voluntario, -ria *m.f.*

volunteerism *n.* voluntarismo *m.*

vote, voting *n.* voto *m.,* votación *f.;* **absentee v.** voto ausente; **v. fraud** votación fraudulenta, fraude electoral *m.;* **v. rights** *pl.* derechos de voto *m.*

vote *v.* votar; **register to v.** registrarse para votar

voter *n.* votante *m.f.;* **v. eligibility** elegibilidad del votante *f.;* **v. registration** registro de votantes *m.;* **v. suppression** supresión de votantes *f.;* **v. turnout** participa-

SOCIAL STUDIES

ción electoral *f.*, concurrencia de votantes *f.*

W

war crime *n.* crimen de guerra *m.*
War Powers Act *n.* Ley de Poderes de Guerra *f.*
welfare *n.* asistencia social *f.;* **w. reform** reforma de asistencia social *f.;* **w. state** estado de bienestar *m.*
White House *n.* Casa Blanca *f.*

women's liberation movement *n.* movimiento feminista *m.*
World Court *n.* Corte Internacional *f.*
writ *n.* orden *f.*, mandato *m.;* **w. of habeas corpus** mandato de hábeas corpus

X

xenophile *n.* xenófilo, -la *m.f.*
xenophobe *n.* xenófobo, -ba *m.f.*
xenophobia *n.* xenofobia *f.*
xenophobic *adj.* xenófobo, -ba

Economics & Finance

A

American Federation of Labor – Congress of Industrial Organizations (A.F.L.-C.I.O.) *n.* Federación Estadounidense del Trabajo y Congreso de Organizaciones Industriales *f.*
abundance *n.* abundancia *f.*
account *n.* cuenta de inversión *f.;* **bank a.** cuenta bancaria; **investment a.** cuenta de inversión; **savings a.** cuenta de ahorros
accountant *n.* contador, -ora *m.f.*
accounting *n.* contabilidad *f.*
accumulation of capital *n.* acumulación de capital *f.*
adjustable-rate mortgage *n.* hipoteca de tasa ajustable *f.*
advertising *n.* publicidad *f.*
affirmative action *n.* acción afirma-

tiva *f.*
affluence *n.* riqueza *f.*, opulencia *f.*
affluent *adj.* opulento, -ta; acomodado, -da; rico, -ca
Agency for International Development (A.I.D.) *n.* Agencia para el Desarrollo Internacional *f.*
agrarian society *n.* sociedad agraria *f.*
agreement *n.* acuerdo *m.*, convenio *m.;* **binding a.** acuerdo vinculante, convenio obligatorio
agriculture *n.* agricultura *f.*
allocate *v.* asignar
alternative energy *n.* energía alternativa *f.*
Alternative Minimum Tax *n.* Impuesto Mínimo Alternativo *m.*
amortization *n.* amortización *f.*
annual percentage rate *n.* tasa de

porcentaje anual *f.*

annuity *n.* anualidad *f.*

antitrust law *n.* ley antimonopolio *f.*

apprentice *n.* aprendiz *m.f.*

appropriate *v.* asignar

appropriation *n.* apropiación *f.*

arable land *n.* tierra cultivable *f.*

arbitrage *n.* arbitraje *m.*

artisan *n.* artesano, -na *m.f.*

assembly line *n.* línea de montaje *f.*

assets *n.pl.* activos *f.;* **a. allocation** asignación de activos *f.*

association *n.* sociedad *f.*

audit *n.* auditoría *f.*

audit *v.* auditar

auditor *n.* auditor, -ora *m.f.*

austerity *n.* austeridad *f.*

automatic teller machine (A.T.M.) *n.* cajero automático *m.*

automation *n.* automatización *f.*

automobile industry *n.* industria automovilística *f.*

aviation *n.* aviación *f.*

B

balance *n.* saldo *m.,* balanza *f.;* **b. of payments** balanza de pagos; **b. of trade** balanza comercial; **b. sheet** balanza general; **minimum b.** saldo mínimo *m.*

balance a checkbook *v.* balancear una chequera

bank *n.* banco *m.;* **b. account** cuenta bancaria *f.;* **b. balance** saldo bancario *m.;* **b. deposit** depósito bancario *m.;* **b. failure** fracaso bancario *m.;* **b. fraud** fraude bancario *m.;*

b. statement extracto bancario *m.;* **central b.** banco central; **commercial b.** banco comercial; **investment b.** banco de inversión

banking *adj.* bancario, -ria; **b. crisis** *n.* crisis bancaria *f.*

banking *n.* banca *f.;* **online b.** banca en línea, banca online

bankrupt *adj.* en quiebra, en bancarrota

bankruptcy *n.* quiebra *f.,* bancarrota *f.;* **b. law** ley de quiebras, ley de bancarrota *f.*

bargaining power *n.* poder de negociación *m.*

barter *n.* trueque *m.,* intercambio *m.*

barter *v.* trocar, intercambiar

bear market *n.* mercado bajista *m.*

behavioral economics *n.* economía conductual *f.*

benefit *n.* beneficio *m.*

black market *n.* mercado negro *m.*

blue-collar worker *n.* obrero (-ra) manual *m.f.*

board of directors *n.* junta directiva *f.*

bond *n.* bono *m.;* **b. market** mercado de bonos, mercado obligacionista *m.;* **b. yield** rendimiento de bonos *m.;* **corporate b.** bono corporativo, bono de empresa; **government b.** bono gubernamental, bono del estado; **high yield b.** bono de alto rendimiento; **junk b.** bono basura; **municipal b.** bono municipal

bookkeeping *n.* teneduría de libros

SOCIAL STUDIES

f., contabilidad *f.*

boom and bust *n.* auge y caída *m.*

borrow *v.* pedir prestado

borrower *n.* prestatario, -ria *m.f.*

boss *n.* jefe, -fa *m.f.*; patrón, -na *m.f.*

bounce a check *v.* rebotar un cheque

brand *n.* marca *f.*

broker *n.* corredor (-ra) de bolsa *m.f.*

brokerage firm *n.* firma de corretaje *f.*

budget *n.* presupuesto *m.*; **balanced b.** presupuesto equilibrado; **b. deficit** déficit presupuestario *m.*

build *v.* construir

building *n.* edificio *m.*; **b. code** código de construcción *m.*; **b. society** sociedad de crédito hipotecario *f.*

bull market *n.* mercado alcista *m.*

Bureau of Labor Statistics *n.* Oficina de Estadísticas Laborales *f.*

business *n.* negocio *m.*; **b. cycle** ciclo económico *m.*; **b. ethics** *pl.* ética empresarial *f.*; **b. loan** préstamo empresarial *m.*; **b. plan** plan de negocios *m.*; **b. school** escuela de negocios *f.*; **do b.** *v.* negociar, comerciar

buy *v.* comprar; **b. on margin** comprar acciones a préstamo

buyer *n.* comprador, -ora *m.f.*

C

capacity *n.* capacidad *f.*

capital *n.* capital *m.*; **c. equipment** bienes de equipo *m.pl.*; **c. flight** fuga de capitales *f.*; **c. gains** plus-

valías *f.pl.*; **c. gains tax** impuesto sobre las plusvalías *m.*; **c. goods** bienes de capital *m.pl.*; **c. investment** inversión de capital *f.*; **c. markets** *pl.* mercados de capitales *m.*; **finance c.** capital financiero *m.*; **human c.** capital humano; **working c.** capital de trabajo

capital-intensive *adj.* intensivo (-va) de capital

capitalism *n.* capitalismo *m.*; **crony c.** capitalismo favoritista; **state c.** capitalismo de estado

capitalist *adj. & n.* capitalista *m.f.*; **venture c.** capitalista de riesgo

career *n.* carrera *f.*

cartel *n.* cartel *m.*

cash *n.* efectivo *m.*; dinero *m.*; **c. box** caja *f.*; **c. crop** cultivo comercial *m.*; **c. flow** flujo de caja *m.*; **c. management** manejo de efectivo *m.*; **c. price** precio al contado *m.*; **c. register** caja registradora *f.*

cash *v.* cobrar; **c. a check** cobrar un cheque

casualty insurance *n.* seguro de accidentes, seguro de daños *m.*

central bank *n.* banco central *m.*

certificate of deposit *n.* certificado de depósito *m.*

certified financial planner *n.* asesor (-ora) financiero certificado *m.f.*

chain store *n.* cadena de tiendas *f.*

Chamber of Commerce *n.* Cámara de Comercio *f.*

charitable *adj.* caritativo, -va; **c. contribution** *n.* donación *f.*, con-

SOCIAL STUDIES

tribución caritativa *f.;* **c. organization** organización caritativa, organización de caridad *f.*

charity *n.* caridad *f.*

check *n.* cheque *m.;* **bounce a c.** *v.* rebotar un cheque; **cash a c.** cobrar un cheque; **endorse a c.** endosar un cheque; **write a c.** escribir un cheque

checkbook *n.* chequera *f.*

checking account *n.* cuenta de cheques *f.*

chief executive officer *n.* director (-ora) ejecutivo (-va) *m.f.*

child labor *n.* trabajo infantil *m.*

class *n.* clase *f.;* **leisure c.** clase ociosa; **middle c.** clase media; **upper c.** clase alta; **working c.** clase obrera

Code of Federal Regulations *n.* Código de Regulaciones Federales *m.*

coffee trade *n.* comercio del café *m.*

coin *n.* moneda *f.*

coin *v.* acuñar

collateral *n.* garantía financiera *f.*

collective bargaining *n.* negociación colectiva *f.*

commerce *n.* comercio *m.*

commercial *adj.* comercial; **c. bank** *n.* banco comercial *m.;* **c. law** derecho comercial *m.*

commission *n.* comisión *f.*

commodity *n.* mercancía *f.*

Commodity Futures Trading Commission *n.* Comisión del Comercio en Futuros sobre Mercancía *f.*

common stock *n.* acciones ordinarias *f.pl.*

company *n.* empresa *f.,* compañía *f.,* sociedad *f.;* **public c.** empresa pública

compensation *n.* indemnización *f.,* compensación *f.*

compete *v.* competir

competition *n.* competencia *f.,* rivalidad *f.*

competitive *adj.* competitivo, -va

competitiveness *n.* competitividad *f.*

compound interest *n.* interés compuesto *m.*

comptroller *n.* contralor, -ora *m.f.*

computer *n.* ordenador *m.;* computador, -ora *m.f.*

computer-aided design *n.* diseño asistido por ordenador *m.*

conglomerate *n.* conglomerado *m.*

consume *v.* consumir

consumer *n.* consumidor, -ora *m.f.;* **c. confidence** confianza del consumidor *f.;* **c. debt** deuda del consumidor *f.;* **c. goods** *pl.* bienes de consumo *m.;* **c. protection** protección del consumidor *f.;* **c. spending** gasto del consumo *m.;* **c. staples** *pl.* bienes de consumo básico

Consumer Price Index (C.P.I.) *n.* Índice de Precios al Consumidor *m.;* **C. Product Safety Commission (C.P.S.C.)** Comisión de Seguridad de Productos del Consumidor *f.*

consumerism *n.* consumismo *m.*

consumption *n.* consumo *m.;* **con-**

spicuous **c.** consumo conspicuo, consumo ostentoso

contract *n.* contrato *m.;* **c. law** ley de contratos *f.;* **c. negotiation** negociación de contratos *f.*

contract *v.* contratar

contracting party *n.* contratante *m.f.*

contractor *n.* contratista *m.f.;* **independent c.** contratista independiente

cooperative *n.* cooperativa *f.*

copyright *n.* derechos de autor *m.pl.;* **c. infringement** violación de los derechos de autor *f.*

corporate *adj.* corporativo, -va; **c. bond** *n.* bono corporativo, bono de empresa *m.;* **c. governance** administración empresarial *f.;* **c. raider** tiburón empresarial *m.*

corporation *n.* corporación *f.*

cost *n.* precio *m.,* costo *m.;* **c. basis** base de costo *f.;* **c. of living** costo de la vida; **c. of living adjustment (COLA)** ajuste de costo de vida *m.;* **c. of production** costo de producción; **c. overrun** sobrecosto *m.;* **opportunity c.** costo de oportunidad

cost-benefit analysis *n.* análisis de costos y beneficios *m.*

cottage industry *n.* industria artesanal *f.*

counterfeit *adj.* falsificado, -da

counterfeiting *n.* falsificación *f.*

craft *n.* arte *m.;* **c. guild** gremio de artesanía *m.;* **c. union** sindicato de artesanos *m.*

crafts *n.pl.* artesanía *f.*

credit *n.* crédito *m.;* **c. card** tarjeta de crédito *f.;* **c. counseling** asesoría de crédito *f.;* **c. rating** valoración de crédito *f.;* **c. risk** riesgo de crédito *m.;* **c. union** cooperativa de crédito *f.;* **line of c.** línea de crédito *f.*

credit *v.* acreditar

creditor *n.* acreedor, -ora *m.f.*

crop *n.* cosecha *f.,* cultivo *m.;* **c. rotation** rotación de cultivos *f.*

currency *n.* moneda *f.;* **c. exchange** cambio de divisas *m.;* **c. manipulation** manipulación monetaria *f.;* **foreign c.** divisa *f.*

customer *n.* cliente, -ta *m.f.;* **c. loyalty** fidelidad del cliente *f.;* **c. service** servicio de atención al cliente *m.*

D

dead-end job *n.* trabajo sin porvenir *m.*

deal *n.* arreglo *m.,* acuerdo *m.*

dealer *n.* distribuidor, -ora *m.f.*

debit card *n.* tarjeta de débito *f.*

debt *n.* deuda *f.;* **consumer d.** deuda del consumidor; **d. crisis** crisis de la deuda *f.;* **federal d.** deuda federal; **sovereign d.** deuda soberana

debtor *n.* deudor, -ora *m.f.*

deduction *n.* deducción *f.;* **itemized d.** deducción fiscal detallada; **standard d.** deducción estándar

default *n.* incumplimiento *m.*

default *v.* faltar al pago

deficit *n.* déficit *m.;* **budget d.** déficit presupuestario; **d. reduction** reducción del déficit *f.;* **d. spending** déficit de gasto, gasto deficitario *m.;* **federal d.** déficit federal

defined *adj.* definido, -da; **d. benefit plan** *n.* plan de prestación definida *m.;* **d. contribution plan** plan de contribución definida

deflation *n.* deflación *f.*

defraud *v.* defraudar, estafar

deindustrialization *n.* desindustrialización *f.*

demand *n.* demanda *f.;* **supply and d.** oferta y demanda *f.*

denomination *n.* denominación *f.*

Department of Commerce *n.* Departamento de Comercio *m.;* **D. of Housing and Urban Development** Departamento de Vivienda y Desarrollo Urbano; **D. of Labor** Departamento de Trabajo; **D. of the Treasury** Departamento del Tesoro

dependent *n.* dependiente *m.f.*

deposit *n.* depósito *m.;* **bank d.** depósito bancario

deposit *v.* depositar

depositor *n.* depositante *m.f.*

depreciation *n.* depreciación *f.*

depression *n.* depresión *f.*

derivative *n.* derivado *m.*

devaluation *n.* devaluación *f.*

devalue *v.* devaluar

development *n.* desarrollo *m.*

disability insurance *n.* seguro contra discapacidad *m.*

disaster relief *n.* alivio de desastre *m.*

discount *n.* descuento *m.*

disincentive *n.* desincentivo *m.*

diversification *n.* diversificación *f.*

diversified *adj.* diversificado, -da

diversify *v.* diversificar

diversity training *n.* entrenamiento sobre diversidad *m.*

dividend *n.* dividendo *m.*

division of labor *n.* división del trabajo *f.*

Dodd-Frank Act *n.* ley Dodd-Frank *f.*

double-entry bookkeeping *n.* contabilidad de partida doble *f.*

Dow Jones Industrial Average *n.* Índice Dow Jones *m.*

dumping *n.* (goods) dúmping *m.*

durable goods *n.pl.* bienes duraderos *m.*

duty *n.* derecho *m.*, impuesto *m.*, arancel *m.*

E

earn *v.* ganar

earnings *n.pl.* ingresos *m.*, ganancias *f.*

economic *adj.* económico, -ca; **e. aid** *n.* ayuda económica *f.;* **e. democracy** democracia económica *f.;* **e. growth** crecimiento económico *m.;* **e. incentive** incentivo económico *m.;* **e. indicator** indicador económico *m.;* **e. inequality** desigualdad económica *f.;* **e. restructuring** reestructura-

SOCIAL STUDIES

SOCIAL STUDIES

ción económica *f.;* **e. sanctions** *pl.* sanciones económicas *f.;* **e. security** seguridad económica *f.;* **e. slump** recesión económica *f.;* **e. stimulus** estímulo económico *m.*

economics *n.* economía *f.;* **Keynesian e.** economía keynesiana; **labor e.** economía laboral; **laissez-faire e.** economía laissez-faire; **neoclassical e.** economía neoclásica; **trickle-down e.** economía del goteo; **welfare e.** economía del bienestar social

economist *n.* economista *m.f.*

economy *n.* economía *f.;* **capitalist e.** economía capitalista; **command e.** economía dirigida; **e. of scale** economía de escala; **free market e.** economía de libre mercado; **global e.** economía global; **mixed e.** economía mixta; **planned e.** economía planificada; **political e.** economía política; **socialist e.** economía socialista; **underground e.** economía sumergida; **world e.** economía mundial

efficiency *n.* eficiencia *f.*

efficient *adj.* eficiente; **e. market hypothesis** *n.* hipótesis del mercado eficiente *f.*

eight-hour day *n.* jornada de ocho horas *f.*

embargo *n.* embargo *m.*

emerging markets *n.pl.* mercados emergentes *m.*

eminent domain *n.* dominio eminente *m.*

employee *n.* empleado, -da *m.f.*

employer *n.* empleador, -ora *m.f.;* empresario, -ria *m.f.;* patrón, -na *m.f.*

employment *n.* empleo *m.;* **full-time e.** empleo a tiempo completo; **part-time e.** empleo a tiempo parcial; **temporary e.** trabajo temporal *m.;* **termination of e.** terminación del empleo *f.*

endowment *n.* dotación *f.*

energy *n.* energía *f.;* **alternative e.** energía alternativa; **e. independence** independencia energética *f.;* **renewable e.** energía renovable

engineering *n.* ingeniería *f.*

enterprise *n.* empresa *f.*

entertainment industry *n.* industria del espectáculo *f.*

entrepreneur *n.* empresario, -ria *m.f.*

entrepreneurial *adj.* emprendedor, empresarial

entrepreneurship *n.* espíritu empresarial *m.,* iniciativa empresarial *f.*

environmental degradation *n.* degradación ambiental *f.*

equilibrium *n.* equilibrio *m.*

equities *n.pl.* (assets) acciones *f.*

equity *n.* (fairness) equidad *f.*

ergonomics *n.pl.* ergonomía *f.*

estate *n.* herencia *f.,* patrimonio *m.,* propiedad *f.;* **e. planning** planificación patrimonial *f.;* **e. tax** impuesto sobre sucesiones *m.*

Euro zone *n.* eurozona *f.,* Zona euro *f.*

exchange *n.* intercambio *m.;* **e. rate** tipo de cambio *m.*

exchange *v.* intercambiar

expansion *n.* expansión *f.*

expense *n.* gasto *m.*

exploit *v.* aprovechar, explotar

exploitation *n.* explotación *f.*

export *v.* exportar

exporting *n.* exportación *f.*

externalities *n.pl.* externalidades *f.*

extractive industries *n.pl.* industrias extractivas *f.*

F

factor of production *n.* factor de producción *m.*

factory *n.* fábrica *f.;* **f. system** sistema de fábrica *m.*

Fair Labor Standards Act *n.* Ley de Normas Razonables de Trabajo *f.*

fair trade *n.* comercio equitativo, comercio justo *m.*

farm *n.* granja *f.,* finca *f.,* estancia *f.,* rancho *m.;* **f. laborer** jornalero del campo *m.;* **f. subsidies** *pl.* subsidios agrícolas *m.*

farmer *n.* agricultor, -ora *m.f.;* granjero, -ra *m.f.*

farmland *n.* tierras de cultivo *f.pl.*

federal *adj.* federal; **f. budget** *n.* presupuesto federal *m.;* **f. debt ceiling** límite de endeudamiento federal *m.*

Federal Aviation Administration (F.A.A.) *n.* Administración Federal de Aviación *f.;* **F. Deposit Insurance Corporation (F.D.I.C.)** Corporación Federal de Seguro de Depósitos *f.;* **F. Housing Administration (F.A.A.)** Administración de Vivienda Federal; **F. Reserve Board** Junta de la Reserva Federal *f.;* **F. Trade Commission (F.T.C.)** Comisión Federal de Comercio *f.*

fee *n.* honorario *m.,* precio *m.,* cuota *f.*

finance *n.* finanza *f.;* **f. capital** capital financiero *m.;* **personal f.** finanza personal

finance *v.* financiar

financial *adj.* financiero, -ra; **f. literacy** *n.* educación financiera *f.,* conocimientos financieros *m.pl.;* **f. panic** pánico financiero *m.;* **f. reform** reforma financiera *f.;* **f. regulation** regulación financiera *f.;* **f. services** *pl.* servicios financieros *m.*

financing *n.* financiación *f.*

finished product *n.* producto acabado, producto terminado *m.*

firm *n.* firma *f.,* empresa *f.*

fiscal *adj.* fiscal; **f. austerity** *n.* austeridad fiscal *f.;* **f. policy** política fiscal *f.;* **f. year** año fiscal *m.*

fixed income *n.* ingresos fijos *m.pl.*

fixed-rate mortgage *n.* hipoteca de tasa fija *f.*

flat tax *n.* impuesto fijo *m.*

flextime *n.* horario flexible *m.*

food production *n.* producción de alimentos *f.*

foreclose *v.* ejecutar una hipoteca

foreclosure *n.* ejecución hipotecaria *f.*

foreign *adj.* extranjero, -ra; **f. exchange** *n.* cambio de divisas *m.;* **f. trade** comercio exterior, comercio extranjero *m.*

forgery *n.* falsificación *f.*

franchise *n.* franquicia *f.*

fraud *n.* fraude *m.*

free *adj.* libre; **f. enterprise** *n.* libre empresa *f.;* **f. enterprise system** sistema de libre empresa *m.;* **f. market** mercado libre *m.;* **f. trade** libre comercio *m.*

fringe benefits *n.pl.* beneficios complementarios *m.*

full employment *n.* pleno empleo *m.*

funding *n.* financiamiento *m.*

funds *n.pl.* fondos *m.;* **deposit of f.** depósito de fondos *m.;* **withdrawal of f.** retiro de fondos *m.*

fungible *adj.* fungible

G

game theory *n.* teoría de juegos *f.*

general strike *n.* huelga general *f.*

gift tax *n.* impuesto sobre donaciones *m.*

glass ceiling *n.* techo de cristal *m.*

Glass-Steagall Act *n.* ley Glass-Steagall *f.*

globalization *n.* globalización *f.*

gold standard *n.* patrón oro *m.*

goods *n.pl.* bienes *m.;* **durable g.** bienes duraderos; **g. and services** bienes y servicios; **luxury g.** bienes de lujo

government *n.* gobierno *m.;* **g.**

bond bono gubernamental, bono del estado *m.;* **g. spending** gasto público *m.;* **limited g.** gobierno limitado

greater fool theory *n.* teoría del más tonto *f.*

greenbacks *n.pl.* dólares *m.*

Gross Domestic Product (G.D.P.) *n.* producto interno bruto *m.*

growth rate *n.* tasa de crecimiento *f.*

H

harvest *n.* cosecha *f.*

health *n.* salud *f.;* **h. insurance** seguro medico, seguro de salud *m.;* **universal h. care** cuidado de salud universal *m.*

hedge *v.* cubrirse

hedge fund *n.* fondo de cobertura *m.*

high-tech *adj.* de alta tecnología

high yield bond *n.* bono de alto rendimiento *m.*

hire *v.* contratar

hiring *n.* contratación *f.*

hoarding *n.* acaparamiento *m.*

home *n.* vivienda *f.;* **h. equity loan** segunda hipoteca *f.;* **h. ownership** propiedad de la vivienda *f.*

homeowners insurance *n.* seguro de propietarios *m.*

household *n.* hogar *m.;* **h. consumption** consumo de los hogares, consumo familiar *m.;* **h. income** ingresos de los hogares, ingresos familiares *m.pl.*

housing *n.* vivienda *f.;* **h. bubble** burbuja inmobiliaria *f.*

human *adj.* humano, -na; **h. capital** *n.* capital humano *m.;* **h. resources** *pl.* recursos humanos *m.*

I

import *n.* importación *f.;* **i. duty** derecho de importación *m.*

import *v.* importar

imported *adj.* importado, -da

incentive *n.* incentivo *m.;* **negative i.** incentivo negativo; **positive i.** incentivo positivo

income *n.* ingresos *m.pl.,* salario *m.,* renta *f.;* **fixed i.** ingresos fijos; **gross i.** ingresos brutos; **i. distribution** distribución del ingresos *f.;* **i. inequality** desigualdad de ingresos *f.;* **i. tax** impuesto sobre la renta *m.*

incorporate *v.* incorporar

incorporated *adj.* incorporado, -da

incorporation *n.* incorporación *f.*

indebtedness *n.* endeudamiento *m.*

indemnification *n.* indemnización *f.*

indemnify *v.* indemnizar

index *n.* índice *m.;* **i. fund** fondo indexado *m.*

Individual Retirement Account (I.R.A.) *n.* Cuenta de Retiro Individual *f.*

industrial *adj.* industrial; **i. accident** *n.* accidente laboral *m.;* **i. center** centro industrial *m.;* **i. development** desarrollo industrial *m.;* **i. policy** política industrial *f.;* **i. production** producción industrial *f.;* **i. relations** *pl.* relaciones laborales *f.;* **i. union** sindicato industrial *m.*

industrialization *n.* industrialización *f.*

industry *n.* industria *f.;* **automobile i.** industria automovilística; **cottage i.** industria artesanal; **entertainment i.** industria del espectáculo; **heavy i.** industria pesada; **light i.** industria ligera; **petroleum i.** industria petrolera; **service i.** industria de servicios; **textile i.** industria textil

inflation *n.* inflación *f.;* **i. rate** tasa de inflación *f.*

inflation-adjusted *adj.* ajustado (-da) por inflación

information technology *n.* tecnología de la información *f.*

infrastructure *n.* infraestructura *f.*

inheritance *n.* herencia *f.*

inherited wealth *n.* riquezas heredadas *f.pl.,* fortunas heredadas *f.pl.*

initial public offering *n.* oferta pública inicial *f.*

innovation *n.* innovación *f.*

insider trading *n.* tráfico de información privilegiada *m.*

insolvency *n.* insolvencia *f.,* bancarrota *f.*

institutional investor *n.* inversor (-ra) institucional *m.f.*

insurance *n.* seguro *m.;* **casualty i.** seguro de accidentes, seguro de daños; **health i.** seguro de salud; **homeowners i.** seguro de propi-

SOCIAL STUDIES

SOCIAL STUDIES

etarios; **i. claim** reclamación de seguro *f.;* **i. claims adjuster** ajustador (-ora) de reclamaciones de seguros *m.f.;* **i. coverage** cobertura de seguro *f.;* **i. policy** póliza de seguro *f.;* **i. premium** prima de seguro *f.;* **life i.** seguro de vida *m.*

insure *v.* asegurar

intellectual property *n.* propiedad intelectual *f.*

interest *n.* interés *m.;* **compound i.** interés compuesto; **i. rate** tasa de interés *f.;* **mortgage i.** interés hipotecario; **simple i.** interés simple

intern *n.* pasante *m.f.,* alumno (-na) en prácticas *m.f.*

Internal Revenue Service (I.R.S.) *n.* Servicio de Impuestos Internos *m.*

International Monetary Fund (I.M.F.) *n.* Fondo Monetario Internacional *m.*

international trade *n.* comercio internacional *m.*

internship *n.* pasantía *f.*

Interstate Commerce Commission (I.C.C.) *n.* Comisión Interestatal de Comercio *f.*

interstate highway system *n.* red de autopistas interestatales *f.*

intrinsic value *n.* valor intrínseco *m.*

invention *n.* invención *f.*

inventory *n.* inventario *m.*

invest *v.* invertir

investing *n.* inversión *f.;* **socially responsible i.** inversión socialmente responsable

investment *n.* inversión *f.;* **direct**

foreign **i.** inversión extranjera directa; **i. adviser** asesor (-ora) de inversiones *m.f.;* **i. bank** banco de inversión *m.;* **i. income** ingresos de inversión *m.pl.;* **i. portfolio** cartera de inversión *f.;* **return on i.** rendimiento de la inversión *m.,* rentabilidad de la inversión *f.*

investor *n.* inversor, -ora *m.f.;* inversionista *m.f.;* **institutional i.** inversor institucional

Invisible Hand theory *n.* teoría de la mano invisible *f.*

itemized deduction *n.* deducción fiscal detallada *f.*

J

job *n.* trabajo *m.;* **dead-end j.** trabajo sin porvenir; **j. application** solicitud de empleo *f.;* **j. search** búsqueda de trabajo *f.;* **j. security** seguridad laboral *f.;* **j. training program** programa de capacitación laboral *m.*

jobless recovery *n.* recuperación sin empleo *f.*

junk bond *n.* bono basura *m.*

K

Keogh plan *n.* plan Keogh *m.*

Keynesian economics *n.* economía keynesiana *f.*

L

labor *n.* labor *f.,* trabajo *m.;* **child l.** trabajo infantil; **forced l.** trabajo forzado; **l. economics** economía

laboral *f.;* **l. force** fuerza laboral *f.;*
l. law derecho laboral *m.;* **l. leader**
líder sindical *m.f.;* **l. market** mercado de trabajo, mercado laboral
m.; **l. power** fuerza de trabajo *f.;* **l.**
theory of value teoría del valor-
trabajo *f.;* **l. union** sindicato obrero *m.;* **manual l.** trabajo manual
m., labor manual *f.;* **organized l.**
obreros sindicados *m.pl.*

labor-management relations *n.pl.*
relaciones laborales, relaciones
obrero-patronales *f.*

laissez-faire economics *n.* economía laissez-faire *f.*

land reform *n.* reforma agraria *f.*

landlord *n.* arrendador, -ora *m.f.*

late fee *n.* recargo por tardanza *m.*

law of diminishing returns *n.* ley de
los rendimientos decrecientes *f.*

layoff *n.* despido *m.*

legal entity *n.* entidad legal *f.*

leisure *n.* ocio *m.,* esparcimiento *m.,*
tiempo libre *m.;* **l. class** clase ociosa *f.*

lender *n.* prestamista *m.f.*

lending *n.* préstamo *m.;* **predatory**
l. préstamos abusivos, préstamos
predatorios *pl.*

leverage *n.* apalancamiento *m.*

leveraged buyout *n.* compra apalancada *f.*

liability *n.* deuda *f.,* obligación *f.,* responsabilidad *f.;* **limited l.** responsabilidad limitada

licensing *n.* concesión de licencias *f.*

line of credit *n.* línea de crédito *f.*

liquidation *n.* liquidación *f.*

liquidity *n.* liquidez *f.*

livelihood *n.* sustento *m.,* subsistencia *f.*

living wage *n.* salario de subsistencia *m.*

loan *n.* préstamo *m.;* **business l.**
préstamo empresarial; **home eq-**
uity l. préstamo con garantía hipotecaria; **mortgage l.** préstamo
hipotecario; **student l.** préstamo
estudiantil; **subprime l.** préstamo
subprime

loan *v.* prestar

lockout *n.* cierre patronal *m.*

loss *n.* pérdida *f.*

Luddites *n.pl.* luditas *m.,* ludistas *m.*

luxury goods *n.pl.* bienes de lujo *m.*

M

machine tool *n.* herramienta de
maquinaria *f.*

machinery *n.* maquinaria *f.*

macroeconomics *n.* macroeconomía *f.*

manage *v.* administrar, manejar

management *n.* gestión *f.,* administración *f.,* dirección *f.;* **scientific**
m. gestión científica

manager *n.* gerente *m.f.;* director,
-ora *m.f.;* administrador, -ora *m.f.*

manufacturer *n.* fabricante *m.*

manufacturing *n.* fabricación *f.*

marginal *adj.* marginal; **m. cost** *n.*
costo marginal *m.;* **m. tax rate**
tasa de impuesto marginal *f.;* **m.**
utility utilidad marginal *f.*

SOCIAL STUDIES

maritime rights *n.pl.* derechos marítimos *m.*

market *n.* mercado *m.;* **bear m.** mercado bajista; **black m.** mercado negro; **bond m.** mercado de bonos, mercado obligacionista; **bull m.** mercado alcista; **emerging m.** mercado emergente; **global m.** mercado mundial; **m. economics** economía de mercado *f.;* **m. failure** fracaso del mercado *m.;* **m. research** estudio de mercado *m.;* **m. sector** sector del mercado *m.;* **m. share** cuota de mercado *f.;* **m. value** valor de mercado *m.*

market-driven *adj.* impulsado (-da) por el mercado

marketing *n.* comercialización *f.,* mercadotecnia *f.*

mass media *n.pl.* medios de comunicación, medios de difusión *m.*

means of production *n.* medio de producción *m.*

mechanization *n.* mecanización *f.*

mercantilism *n.* mercantilismo *m.*

merchant *n.* comerciante *m.f.*

merger *n.* fusión *f.*

mergers and acquisitions *n.pl.* fusiones y adquisiciones *f.*

meritocracy *n.* meritocracia *f.*

microeconomics *n.* microeconomía *f.*

middle class *n.* clase media *f.*

mill *n.* molino *m.*

minimum wage *n.* salario mínimo *m.*

mining *n.* minería *f.;* **strip m.** minería a cielo abierto

mobility *n.* movilidad *f.*

mode of production *n.* modo de producción *m.*

monetarism *n.* monetarismo *m.*

monetary policy *n.* política monetaria *f.*

money *n.* dinero *m.;* **m. laundering** lavado de dinero *m.;* **m. market fund** fondo del mercado monetario *m.;* **m. supply** oferta monetaria *f.*

monopolistic *adj.* monopolístico, -ca

monopoly *n.* monopolio *m.*

moral hazard *n.* riesgo moral *m.*

mortgage *n.* hipoteca *f.;* **fixed-rate m.** hipoteca de tasa fija; **m. interest** interés hipotecario *m.;* **m. loan** préstamo hipotecario *m.;* **m. payment** pago de la hipoteca *m.*

multinational corporation *n.* corporación multinacional *f.*

municipal bond *n.* bono municipal *m.*

mutual fund *n.* fondo mutuo *m.*

N

needs *n.pl.* necesidades *f.*

negotiate *v.* negociar

negotiation *n.* negociación *f.*

neoclassical economics *n.* economía neoclásica *f.*

net *adj.* neto, -ta; **n. asset value (N.A.V.)** *n.* valor neto de los activos, valor del activo neto *m.;* **n. income** ingresos netos *m.pl.;* **n. loss** pérdida neta *f.;* **n. profit** beneficio neto *m.;* **n. worth** valor neto *m.,* patrimonio neto *m.*

New York Stock Exchange *n.* Bolsa de Valores de Nueva York *f.*

nonprofit organization *n.* organización sin fines de lucro *f.*

nonunion *adj.* no sindicalizado; **n. workforce** *n.* personal no sindicalizado *m.*

North American Free Trade Agreement (NAFTA) *n.* Tratado de Libre Comercio de América del Norte (TLCAN) *m.*

O

occupation *n.* ocupación *f.*

occupational *adj.* ocupacional; **o. disease** *n.* enfermedad ocupacional *f.;* **o. injury** accidente de trabajo *m.*

Occupational Safety and Health Administration (OSHA) *n.* Administración de Seguridad y Salud Ocupacional *f.*

Office of Management and Budget (O.M.B.) *n.* Oficina de Administración y Presupuesto *f.*

oligopoly *n.* oligopolio *m.*

online banking *n.* banca en línea, banca online *f.*

opportunity cost *n.* costo de oportunidad *m.*

option *n.* opción *f.*

organized labor *n.* obreros sindicados *m.pl.*

output *n.* salida *f.*

outsource *v.* externalizar

outsourcing *n.* externalización *f.*

overdraft protection *n.* protección contra sobregiros *f.*

overfishing *n.* sobrepesca *f.*

overproduction *n.* sobreproducción *f.*

overtime pay *n.* pago de horas extras *m.*

own *v.* poseer

owner *n.* propietario, -ria *m.f.*

ownership *n.* propiedad *f.*

P

paradox of thrift *n.* paradoja del ahorro *f.*

part-time employment *n.* empleo a tiempo parcial *m.*

partner *n.* socio, -cia *m.f.*

partnership *n.* asociación *f.,* sociedad *f.;* **limited p.** sociedad limitada

patent *n.* patente *f.*

pay equity *n.* equidad de sueldos *f.*

paycheck *n.* cheque de pago *m.*

payment *n.* pago *m.*

payroll *n.* nómina *f.;* **p. tax** impuesto de nómina *m.*

pension *n.* pensión *f.;* **p. fund** fondo de pensión *m.*

per capita *adj.* por cápita; **p. c. income** *n.* ingresos por cápita *m.pl.*

percentage *n.* porcentaje *m.;* **annual p. rate** tasa de porcentaje anual *f.*

personal finance *n.* finanza personal *f.*

personnel *n.* personal *m.*

petroleum industry *n.* industria

SOCIAL STUDIES

petrolera *f.*

picket line *n.* línea de piquete *f.*

planned *adj.* planificado, -da; **p. economy** *n.* economía planificada *f.*; **p. obsolescence** obsolescencia planificada *f.*

Ponzi scheme *n.* esquema Ponzi *m.*

poor *adj. & n.* pobre *m.f.*

possession *n.* posesión *f.*

poverty *n.* pobreza *f.*; **p. rate** tasa de pobreza *f.*

precious metals *n.pl.* metales preciosos *m.*

predatory lending *n.* préstamos abusivos, préstamos predatorios *m.pl.*

preferred stock *n.* acciones preferentes *f.pl.*

present value *n.* valor actual *m.*

price *n.* precio *m.*; **p. decrease** disminución de precios *f.*; **p. increase** aumento de los precios *m.*; **p. war** guerra de precios *f.*

price-earnings ratio *n.* relación precio-beneficio *f.*

prime rate *n.* interés preferencial *m.*

principal *n.* principal *m.*

private *adj.* privado, -da; **p. equity** *n.* capital privado *m.*; **p. market** mercado privado *m.*; **p. property** propiedad privada *f.*; **p. sector** sector privado *m.*

privatization *n.* privatización *f.*

privatize *v.* privatizar

produce *v.* producir

producer *n.* productor, -ora *m.f.*

product *n.* producto *m.*; **finished p.** producto acabado, producto terminado; **p. design** diseño de productos *m.*; **p. liability** responsabilidad por productos defectuosos *f.*; **p. line** línea de productos *f.*; **p. placement** emplazamiento de producto *m.*

production *n.* producción *f.*, fabricación *f.*; **mass p.** producción en masa; **means of p.** medio de producción *m.*; **mode of p.** modo de producción *m.*; **p. method** método de producción *m.*; **p. site** sitio de fabricación *m.*, planta de producción *f.*

productivity *n.* productividad *f.*

profession *n.* oficio *m.*

profit *n.* ganancia *f.*, beneficio *m.*; **net p.** beneficio neto; **p. maximization** maximización de beneficio *f.*; **p. motive** afán de lucro *m.*, motivo por ganancia *m.*

profitability *n.* rentabilidad *f.*

progressive income tax *n.* impuesto progresivo sobre la renta *m.*

promotion *n.* promoción *f.*

property *n.* propiedad *f.*; **intellectual p.** propiedad intelectual; **personal p.** bienes personales *m.pl.*, propiedad personal *f.*; **p. management** administración inmobiliaria *f.*; **p. ownership** propiedad de bienes *f.*; **p. rights** *pl.* derechos de propiedad *m.*; **p. tax** impuesto sobre la propiedad *m.*; **rental p.** propiedad para alquiler *f.*

prosperity *n.* prosperidad *f.*

protectionism *n.* proteccionismo *m.*

protectionist *adj.* proteccionista

protective tariff *n.* arancel proteccionista *m.*, tarifa protectora *f.*

proxy *n.* poder *m.; by p. adv.* por
poderes

public *adj.* público, -ca; **p. company**
n. empresa pública *f.;* **p. offering**
oferta pública *f.;* **p. property** propiedad pública *f.;* **p. sector** sector
público *m.;* **p. utility** utilidad pública *f.*

purchase *n.* compra *f.*

purchase *v.* comprar

purchasing power *n.* poder adquisitivo *m.*

pyramid scheme *n.* esquema piramidal *m.*

Q

qualified *adj.* calificado, -da

quota *n.* cuota *f.*

R

ranching *n.* ganadería *f.*

rank and file *n.* base del sindicato *f.*

rate of return *n.* tasa de rentabilidad, tasa de rendimiento *f.*

rational choice theory *n.* teoría de
la elección racional *f.*

raw materials *n.pl.* materias primas *f.*

real estate *n.* propiedad inmobiliaria *f.;* bienes raíces, bienes inmuebles *m.pl.;* **r. e. agency** inmobiliaria *f.;* **r. e. agent** agente inmobiliario (-ria) *m.;* **r. e. investment**

trust (REIT) fideicomiso de inversión inmobiliaria *m.*

recession *n.* recesión *f.*

recovery *n.* recuperación *f.*

refinance *v.* refinanciar

refund, repayment *n.* reembolso *m.*

regressive tax *n.* impuesto regresivo *m.*

regulate *v.* regular

regulation *n.* regulación *f.*, reglamento *m.*

regulator *n.* regulador, -ora *m.f.*

rent *n.* pago de alquiler *m.;* **r. control** control de alquileres *m.*

rent *v.* alquilar

rental property *n.* propiedad para
alquiler *f.*

replacement worker *n.* rompehuelgas *m.*

resource *n.* recurso *m.;* **limited r.** *pl.*
recursos limitados; **renewable r.**
pl. recursos renovables; **r. conservation** conservación de los recursos *f.;* **r. depletion** agotamiento
de recursos *m.*

retail *adj.* al por menor; **r. price** *n.*
precio al por menor *m.;* **r. sales**
ventas al por menor *f.pl.*

retailing *n.* menudeo *m.*, venta al
por menor *f.*

retired *adj.* jubilado, -da

retirement *n.* jubilación *f.*, retiro
m.; **r. plan** plan de jubilación *m.*

return on investment *n.* rentabilidad de la inversión *f.*

revenue *n.* ingresos *m.pl.*

reward *n.* recompensa *f.*

SOCIAL STUDIES

SOCIAL STUDIES

reward *v.* recompensar

right-to-work laws *n.pl.* leyes del derecho al trabajo *f.*

risk *n.* riesgo *m.;* **r. management** gestión de riesgos *f.;* **r. pool** fondo común para riesgos *m.;* **r. reduction** reducción del riesgo *f.*

robotics *n.* robótica *f.*

S

salary *n.* sueldo *m.*

sales *n.pl.* ventas *f.;* **s. force** personal de ventas *m.,* equipo de ventas *m.;* **s. tax** impuesto sobre las ventas *m.*

salesperson *n.* vendedor, -ora *m.f.*

save *v.* ahorrar

savings *n.pl.* ahorros *m.;* **s. account** cuenta de ahorros *f.;* **s. and loan association** asociación de ahorro y préstamo *f.;* **s. rate** tasa de ahorros *f.*

scam *n.* estafa *f.*

scarce *adj.* escaso, -sa; **s. resource** *n.* recurso escaso *m.*

scarcity *n.* escasez *f.*

scientific management *n.* gestión científica *f.*

Securities and Exchange Commission (S.E.C.) *n.* Comisión de Bolsa y Valores *f.*

securities *n.pl.* títulos *m.,* valores *m.*

self-employed *adj.* autónomo, -ma

self-employment *n.* trabajo autónomo, trabajo por cuenta propia *m.*

sell *v.* vender; **s. short** vender al descubierto

seller *n.* vendedor, -ora *m.f.;* **s. financing** financiación por el vendedor *f.*

service *n.* servicio *m.;* **s. charge** cargo por servicio *m.;* **s. economy** economía de servicios *f.;* **s. industry** industria de servicios *f.*

shareholder *n.* accionista *m.f.*

shares *n.pl.* acciones *f.*

shift work *n.* trabajo por turnos *m.*

shipping *n.* envío *m.*

shop *n.* tienda *f.,* bodega *f.*

shopkeeper *n.* comerciante *m.f.*

shopper *n.* comprador, -ora *m.f.*

shopping mall *n.* centro comercial *m.*

shortage *n.* escasez *f.*

sick leave *n.* baja por enfermedad *f.*

simple interest *n.* interés simple *m.*

skill *n.* habilidad *f.,* destreza *f.*

skilled *adj.* experto, -ta; calificado, -da

Small Business Administration (S.B.A.) *n.* Administración de Pequeños Negocios *f.*

Social Security *n.* Seguro Social *m.;* **S. S. benefits** *pl.* beneficios de Seguro Social *m.,* prestaciones de Seguro Social *f.*

socialist *adj. & n.* socialista *m.f.;* **s. economy** economía socialista *f.*

socially responsible investing *n.* inversión socialmente responsables *f.*

sole proprietorship *n.* propiedad exclusiva *f.*

speculation *n.* especulación *f.*

speculator *n.* especulador, -ora *m.f.*

spending *n.* gasto *m.*

staffing *n.* personal *m.*

standard of living *n.* nivel de vida *m.*

stock *n.* acciones *f.pl.;* **common s.** acciones ordinarias; **preferred s.** acciones preferentes; **s. option** opción de acciones *f.;* **s. split** división de acciones *f.*

stock market *n.* mercado de valores, mercado de acciones, mercado bursátil *m.;* **s. m. bubble** burbuja bursátil, burbuja del mercado de valores *f.;* **s. m. crash** derrumbe bursátil *m.,* caída del mercado de valores *f.;* **s. m. rally** repunte del mercado de valores *f.*

stockholder *n.* accionista *m.f.*

strike *n.* huelga *f.;* **general s.** huelga general

strikebreaker *n.* rompehuelgas *m.*

store *n.* tienda *f.,* bodega *f.*

student loan *n.* préstamo estudiantil *m.*

subcontractor *n.* subcontratista *m.f.*

subprime *adj.* subprime; **s. loan** *n.* préstamo subprime *m.*

subsidy *n.* subsidio *m.*

subsistence farming *n.* agricultura de subsistencia *f.*

supervisor *n.* supervisor, -ora *m.f.*

supply *n.pl.* suministro *m.,* oferta *f.;* **law of s. and demand** ley de la oferta y la demanda *f.;* **s. chain** cadena de suministro *f.*

supply-side economics *n.* economía de oferta *f.*

surcharge *n.* recargo *m.*

surplus *n.* excedente *m.,* superávit *m.;* **s. food** excedente alimenticio; **s. value** plusvalía *f.*

sustainable *adj.* sostenible; **s. development** *n.* desarrollo sostenible *m.*

swindle *v.* estafar

T

tariff *n.* arancel *m.,* tarifa *f.*

tax *n.* impuesto *m.,* tributo *m.;* **flat t.** impuesto fijo; **gift t.** impuesto sobre donaciones; **income t.** impuesto sobre la renta; **payroll t.** impuesto sobre nómina; **progressive t.** impuesto progresivo; **regressive t.** impuesto regresivo; **sales t.** impuesto sobre las ventas; **t. code** código impositivo *m.;* **t. cut** reducción de impuestos *f.;* **t. deduction** deducción de impuestos *f.;* **t. evasion** evasión fiscal *f.;* **t. exemption** exención de impuestos *f.;* **t. haven** paraíso fiscal *m.;* **t. loophole** laguna tributaria *f.;* **t. preparation** preparación de la declaración de impuestos *f.;* **t. reform** reforma fiscal *f.;* **t. shelter** refugio tributario *m.;* **value-added t.** impuesto sobre el valor añadido *m.*

tax *v.* cobrar impuestos

tax-deferred *adj.* de impuestos diferidos

taxation *n.* tributación *f.*

technological change *n.* cambio tecnológico *m.*

technology *n.* tecnología *f.;* **infor-**

SOCIAL STUDIES

117

SOCIAL STUDIES

mation t. tecnología de la información

telecommuting *n.* teletrabajo *m.*, trabajo a distancia *m.*

tenant *n.* inquilino, -na *m.f.*; arrendatario, -ria *m.f.*

textile industry *n.* industria textil *f.*

time-motion study *n.* estudio de tiempo y movimientos *m.*

tools *n.pl.* instrumentos *m.*

tort law *n.* derecho de responsabilidad civil *m.*

trade *n.* comercio *m.*; **fair t.** comercio justo; **foreign t.** comercio exterior; **free t.** libre comercio; **t. agreement** acuerdo comercial *m.*; **t. balance** balanza comercial *f.*; **t. barrier** barrera al comercio *f.*; **t. name** nombre comercial *m.*; **t. route** ruta comercial *f.*; **t. union** sindicato *m.*; **t. war** guerra comercial *f.*

trade *v.* comerciar, negociar

trademark *n.* marca *f.*

training *n.* formación *f.*, práctica *f.*, entrenamiento *m.*

transport *n.* transporte *m.*

treasury *n.* tesorería *f.*; **public t.** tesoro público *m.*

Treasury *n.* Tesoro *m.*; **T. bill** letra del Tesoro *f.*; **T. bond** bono ordinario del Tesoro *m.*

trickle-down economics *n.* economía del goteo *f.*

trust *n.* fideicomiso *m.*

Truth in Lending Act *n.* Ley de Veracidad en los Préstamos *f.*

U

U.S. International Trade Commission *n.* Comisión de Comercio Internacional de Estados Unidos *f.*

underclass *n.* subclase *f.*

underdevelopment *n.* subdesarrollo *m.*

underground economy *n.* economía sumergida *f.*

underwriting *n.* verificación *f.*

unemployment *n.* desempleo *m.*; **cyclical u.** desempleo cíclico; **u. insurance** seguro de desempleo *m.*; **u. rate** tasa de desempleo *f.*

unfair trade practices *n.pl.* prácticas comerciales desleales *f.*

unfunded liability *n.* responsabilidad sin fondos *f.*

union *n.* sindicato *m.*; **craft u.** sindicato de artesanos; **industrial u.** sindicato industrial; **u. busting** campaña antisindicalista *f.*; **u. organizing** organización sindical *f.*; **u. shop** taller sindical *m.*

unionization *n.* sindicalización *f.*

unionize *v.* sindicar

unionized *adj.* sindicalizado, -da

unskilled *adj.* no calificado, -da

usury *n.* usura *f.*

utilities *n.pl.* servicios *m.*, utilidades *f.*

V

valuation *n.* valoración *f.*, estimación *f.*

value *n.* valor *m.*; **intrinsic v.** valor intrínseco; **market v.** valor de mercado; **present v.** valor actual; **v. added tax** impuesto sobre el valor añadido *m.*

venture capitalist *n.* capitalista de riesgo *m.f.*

vocation *n.* vocación *f.*

vocational training *n.* formación profesional *f.*

volatility *n.* volatilidad *f.*

W

wage *n.* salario *m.;* **living w.** salario de subsistencia; **minimum w.** salario mínimo; **w. and price controls** *pl.* controles de precios y salarios *m.;* **w. rate** tasa salarial *f.;* **w. slavery** esclavitud asalariada *f.*

Wall Street *n.* Wall Street *f.*

wants *n.* deseos *m.*

warehouse *n.* almacén *m.,* bodega *f.*

wealth *n.* riqueza *f.*

wealthy *adj.* rico, -ca; acaudalado, -da

weights and measures *n.pl.* pesos y medidas *m.*

welfare *n.* bienestar *m.;* **w. economics** economía del bienestar social *f.;* **w. state** estado del bienestar *m.*

wholesale *adj.* al por mayor; **w. price** *n.* precio al por mayor *m.*

wholesaler *n.* mayorista *m.f.,* comerciante al por mayor *m.f.*

windfall *n.* ganancia imprevista *f.*

withdrawal of funds *n.* retiro de fondos *m.*

work *n.* trabajo *m.;* **shift w.** trabajo por turnos; **w. ethic** ética laboral *f.;* **w. rules** *pl.* reglas del trabajo *f.;* **w. week** semana de trabajo *f.*

work *v.* trabajar

worker *n.* trabajador, -ora *m.f.;* obrero, -ra *m.f.;* **blue collar w.** obrero (-ra) manual; **pink collar w.** trabajadora de cuello rosa *f.;* **replacement w.** rompehuelgas *m.;* **white-collar w.** oficinista *m.f.*

workers compensation *n.* compensación al trabajador *f.*

workforce *n.* fuerza laboral *f.;* **non-union w.** personal no sindicalizado *m.*

working class *n.* clase obrera *f.;* **w. conditions** *pl.* condiciones de trabajo *f.*

workplace *n.* lugar de trabajo *m.;* **w. democracy** democracia laboral *f.*

workshop *n.* taller *m.*

World Bank *n.* Banco Mundial *m.;* **W. Trade Organization (W.T.O.)** Organización Mundial del Comercio *f.*

wrongful discharge *n.* despido injustificado *m.*

Y

yield *n.* rendimiento *m.*

Z

zero sum game *n.* juego de suma cero *m.*

zoning *n.* distribución en zonas *f.,* zonificación *f.*

SOCIAL STUDIES

Geography

A

ablation zone *n.* zona de ablación *f.*

aboriginal peoples *n.pl.* pueblos aborígenes *m.*

Aborigine *n.* aborigen *m.f.*

abrasion *n.* abrasión *f.,* corrosión *f.*

abyssal plain *n.* llanura abisal *f.*

accumulation *n.* acumulación *f.*

acid rain *n.* lluvia ácida *f.*

adaptation *n.* adaptación *f.*

Adriatic Sea *n.* mar Adriático *m.*

Aegean Sea *n.* mar Egeo *m.*

Afghan *adj. & n.* afgano, -na *m.f.*

Afghanistan *n.* Afganistán *m.*

Africa *n.* África *f.*

African *adj. & n.* africano, -na *m.f.*

Afrikaner *adj. & n.* afrikáner, afrikánder, bóer

aftershock *n.* réplica de terremoto *f.*

air pollution *n.* contaminación del aire *f.*

Alaska Pipeline *n.* Oleoducto Trans-Alaska *m.*

Albania *n.* Albania *f.*

Albanian *adj. & n.* albanés, -esa *m.f.*

Aleutian Islands *n.pl.* islas Aleutianas *f.*

Algeria *n.* Argelia *f.*

Algerian *adj. & n.* argelino, -na *m.f.*

alluvial *adj.* aluvial; **a. fan** *n.* abanico aluvial *m.;* **a. plain** llanura aluvial *f.*

alpine *adj.* alpino, -na

Alps *n.pl.* Alpes *m.*

altitude *n.* altitud *f.*

Amazon Basin *n.* cuenca del Amazonas *f.;* **A. River** río Amazonas *m.*

Amazonia *n.* Amazonía *f.*

American *adj. & n.* americano, -na; norteamericano, -na; estadounidense *m.f.*

Amerindian *adj.* amerindio, -dia *m.f*

Anatolia *n.* Anatolia *f.*

Andean *adj. & n.* andino, -na *m.f.*

Andes Mountains *n.pl.* cordillera de los Andes *f.*

Andorra *n.* Andorra *f.*

Andorran *adj. & n.* andorrano, -na *m.f.*

Angola *n.* Angola *f.*

Angolan *adj. & n.* angoleño, -ña; angolano, -na *m.f.*

Antarctic *adj.* antártico, -ca; **A. Circle** *n.* Círculo Polar Antártico *m.;* **A. Peninsula** península Antártica *f.*

Antarctic *n.* Antártico, -ca *m.f.,* Antártida *f.*

Antilles *n.pl.* Antillas *f.*

Apennine Mountains *n.pl.* montes Apeninos *m.,* montañas de los Apeninos *f.*

Appalachia *n.* Apalachia *f.,* Apalaches *m.pl.*

Appalachian Mountains *n.pl.* montañas Apalaches *f.,* cordillera de los Apalaches *f.*

• •

aquaculture *n.* acuicultura *f.*

aqueduct *n.* acueducto *m.*

aquifer *n.* acuífero *m.*

aquiferous *adj.* acuífero, -ra

Arabian Sea *n.* mar de Arabia *m.;* **A. Peninsula** península arábiga *f.*

arable land *n.* tierra cultivable *f.*

archipelago *n.* archipiélago *m.*

Arctic *adj.* ártico, -ca; **A. Circle** *n.* Círculo Polar Ártico *m.;* **A. Ocean** océano Ártico *m.;* **A. region** región ártica *f.*

Arctic *n.* Ártico *m.*

Argentina *n.* Argentina *f.*

Argentine *adj. & n.,* **Argentinean** *adj. & n.* argentino, -na *m.f.*

arid climate *n.* clima árido *m.*

Armenia *n.* Armenia *f.*

Armenian *adj. & n.* armenio, -nia *m.f.*

arroyo *n.* arroyo *m.*

Asia *n.* Asia *f.*

Asian *adj. & n.* asiático, -ca *m.f.*

astrolabe *n.* astrolabio *m.*

Athens *n.* Atenas *f.*

Atlantic Ocean *n.* océano Atlántico *m.*

atlas *n.* atlas *m.*

atmosphere *n.* atmósfera *f.,* ambiente *m.*

atmospheric pressure *n.* presión atmosférica *f.*

atoll *n.* atolón *m.*

Australasia *n.* Australasia *f.*

Australia *n.* Australia *f.*

Australian *adj. & n.* australiano, -na *m.f.*

Austria *n.* Austria *f.*

Austrian *adj. & n.* austriaco, -ca; austríaco, -ca *m.f.*

autumnal equinox *n.* equinoccio de otoño *m.*

avalanche *n.* avalancha *f.*

Azerbaijan *n.* Azerbaiyán *m.*

azimuthal projection *n.* proyección azimutal *f.*

Azores *n.pl.* islas Azores *f.*

B

badlands *n.pl.* tierras baldías *f.,* páramos *m.*

Bahamas *n.pl.* Bahamas *f.*

Bahamian *n.* bahamés, -esa; bahameño, -ña *m.f.*

Balkans *n.pl.* Balcanes *m.*

Baltic Sea *n.* mar Báltico *m.*

Bangladesh *n.* Bangladesh *m.*

Bangladeshi *adj. & n.* bangladesí *m.f.*

bank *n.* (river) orilla *f.,* ribera *f.*

Bantu *n.* Bantú *m.*

Barbados *n.* Barbados *m.*

barrier island *n.* isla barrera *f.,* isla de barrera *f.*

basalt *n.* basalto *m.*

basin *n.* cuenca *f.*

Basque *adj. & n.* vasco, -ca *m.f.;* **B. Country** *n.* País Vasco *m.*

Bavaria *n.* Baviera *f.*

bay *n.* bahía *f.*

Bay Area *n.* Área de la bahía de San Francisco *f.;* **B. of Bengal** bahía de Bengala *f.;* **B. of Biscay** golfo de Vizcaya *m.*

beach *n.* playa *f.*

Beijing *n.* Pekín *m.,* Beijing *m.*

SOCIAL STUDIES

Belarus *n.* Bielorrusia *f.*

Belgian *adj. & n.* belga *m.f.*

Belgium *n.* Bélgica *f.*

Belize *n.* Belice *m.*

Belizean *adj. & n.* beliceño, -ña *m.f.*

Benin *n.* Benín *m.;* **Bight of B.** golfo de Benín *m.*

Bering Strait *n.* estrecho de Bering *m.*

Bermuda *n.* Bermudas *f.pl.*

Bermudan *adj. & n.* bermudeño, -na; bermudiano, -na *m.f.*

Bhutan *n.* Bután *m.*

biodiversity *n.* biodiversidad *f.*

biome *n.* bioma *m.*

biosphere *n.* biosfera *f.*

Black Hills *n.pl.* Colinas Negras *f.*

Black Sea *n.* mar Negro *m.*

Boers *n.pl.* bóers, afrikaners *m.f.*

bog *n.* pantano *m.,* ciénaga *f.*

Bolivia *n.* Bolivia *f.*

Bolivian *n.* boliviano, -na *m.f.*

border *n.* frontera *f.*

Bosnia and Herzegovina *n.* Bosnia-Herzegovina *f.*

Bosnian *adj. & n.* bosnio, -na *m.f.*

Bosphorus Strait *n.* estrecho del Bósforo *m.*

Botswana *n.* Botsuana *f.*

Botswanan *adj. & n.* botsuano, -na *m.f.*

boulder *n.* roca *f.,* peña *f.,* peñasco *m.,* canto rodado *m.*

boundary *n.* límite *m.,* frontera *f.*

Brazil *n.* Brasil *m.*

Brazilian *adj. & n.* brasileño, -ña *m.f.*

bridge *n.* puente *m.*

Britain *n.* Gran Bretaña *f.*

British *adj. & n.* británico, -ca *m.f.;* **B. Isles** *n.pl.* islas Británicas *f.*

brook *n.* arroyo *m.*

Brunei Darussalam *n.* Brunei Darussalam *m.*

Bulgaria *n.* Bulgaria *f.*

Bulgarian *adj. & n.* búlgaro, -ra *m.f.*

Burgundy *n.* Borgoña *f.*

Burma *n.* Birmania *f.,* Myanmar *f.*

Burmese *adj. & n.* birmano, -na *m.f.*

Burundi *n.* Burundi *m.*

C

Cambodia *n.* Camboya *f.*

Cambodian *adj. & n.* camboyano, -na *m.f.*

Cameroon *n.* Camerún *m.*

Canada *n.* Canadá *m.*

Canadian *adj. & n.* canadiense *m.f.*

canal *n.* canal *m.*

Canary Islands *n.pl.* islas Canarias *f.*

canyon *n.* cañón *m.*

cape *n.* cabo *m.*

Cape Cod *n.* cabo Cod *m.;* **C. Hatteras** cabo Hatteras; **C. Horn** cabo de Hornos; **C. of Good Hope** cabo de Buena Esperanza; **C. Verde** cabo Verde

cardinal points *n.pl.* puntos cardinales *m.*

Caribbean *adj. & n.* Caribe *m.;* **C. Basin** cuenca del Caribe *f.;* **C. Sea** mar Caribe *m.*

Carpathian Mountains *n.pl.* montes Cárpatos *m.*

cartographer *n.* cartógrafo *m.*

cartography *n.* cartografía *f.*

Caspian Sea *n.* mar Caspio *m.*
Catalonia *n.* Cataluña *f.*
Catalonian *adj. & n.* catalán, -ana *m.f.*
Caucasus Mountains *n.pl.* cordillera del Cáucaso *f.,* montañas del Cáucaso *f.*
cave *n.* cueva *f.*
cavern *n.* caverna *f.*
Central African Republic *n.* República Centroafricana *f.*
Central America *n.* Centroamérica *f.*
Central American *adj. & n.* centroamericano, -na *m.f.*
Ceylon *n.* Ceilán *m.,* Sri Lanka *m.*
Chad *n.* Chad *m.*
chasm *n.* sima *f.,* abismo *m.,* grieta *f.*
Chesapeake Bay *n.* bahía de Chesapeake *f.*
Chicano *n.* chicano, -na *m.f.*
Chile *n.* Chile *m.*
Chilean *adj. & n.* chileno, -na *m.f.*
China *n.* China *f.*
Chinese *adj. & n.* chino, -na *m.f.*
choropleth map *n.* mapa de coropletas *m.*
city *n.* ciudad *f.;* **c. center** centro de la ciudad, centro urbano *m.;* **port c.** ciudad portuaria *f.*
clear-cut forest *n.* bosque talado *m.*
clearing *n.* apertura *f.,* claro *m.*
cliff *n.* acantilado *m.,* risco *m.,* precipicio *m.*
climate *n.* clima *m.,* ambiente *m.;* **c. change** cambio climático *m.;* **c. region** región climática *f.*
coal *n.* carbón *m.*
coast *n.* costa *f.,* litoral *m.*

coastal plain *n.* llanura costera *f.*
coastline *n.* línea costera *f.*
Colombia *n.* Colombia *f.*
Colombian *adj. & n.* colombiano, -na *m.f.*
Colorado River *n.* río Colorado *m.*
Columbia River *n.* río Columbia *m.*
Comoros *n.pl.* Comoras *f.*
compass *n.* brújula *f.;* **c. points** *n.pl.* puntos cardinales *m.*
Congo River *n.* río Congo *m.;* **Democratic Republic of C.** República Democrática del Congo *f.;* **Republic of C.** República del Congo
Congolese *adj. & n.* congoleño, -ña *m.f.*
conservation *n.* conservación *f.*
conservationist *adj. & n.* conservacionista *m.f.*
continent *n.* continente *m.*
continental *adj.* continental; **c. divide** *n.* división continental *f.;* **c. drift** deriva continental *f.;* **c. shelf** plataforma continental *f.*
contour map *n.* mapa de contorno *m.*
coral reef *n.* arrecife coralino, arrecife de coral *m.*
Coral Sea *n.* mar del Coral *m.*
core *n.* (Earth) núcleo *m.*
Corsica *n.* Córcega *f.*
Costa Rica *n.* Costa Rica *f.*
Costa Rican *adj. & n.* costarricense *m.f.*
cove *n.* ensenada *f.*
crater *n.* cráter *m.*
Crete *n.* Creta *f.*
crevice *n.,* **crevasse** *n.* grieta *f.*

SOCIAL STUDIES

123

SOCIAL STUDIES

Crimea *n.* Crimea *f.*

Croat *adj. & n.*, **Croatian** *adj. & n.* croata *m.f.*

Croatia *n.* Croacia *f.*

crop *n.* cosecha *f.*, cultivo *m.;* **c. yield** rendimiento de los cultivos, rendimiento de la cosecha *m.*

crust *n.* (Earth) corteza *f.*

Cuba *n.* Cuba *f.*

Cuban *adj. & n.* cubano, -na *m.f.*

Cumberland Plateau *n.* meseta de Cumberland *f.*

Curaçao *n.* Curazao *m.*, Curasao *m.*

Cypriot *adj. & n.* chipriota *m.f.*

Cyprus *n.* Chipre *f.*

Czech *adj. & n.* checo, -ca *m.f.*

Czech Republic *n.* República Checa *f.*

D

dam *n.* presa *f.*, represa *f.*

dam *v.* represar, embalsar

Danish *adj. & n.* danés, -esa *m.f.*

Danube River *n.* río Danubio *m.*

Dardanelles *n.pl.* Dardanelos *m.*

Death Valley *n.* valle de la Muerte *m.*

debris *n.* escombros *m.pl.*, residuos *m.pl.*

decomposition *n.* descomposición *f.*

Deep South *n.* extremo sur de Estados Unidos *m.*

dell *n.* vallecito *m.*

delta *n.* delta *m.*

demographic *adj.* demográfico, -ca; **d. change** *n.* cambio demográfico *m.;* **d. information** información demográfica *f.*

demographics *n.pl.* estadísticas demográficas *f.*

dendrochronology *n.* dendrocronología *f.*

Denmark *n.* Dinamarca *f.*

denuded *adj.* denudado, -da

depression *n.* depresión *f.*

desert *n.* desierto *m.*

dike *n.* dique *m.*, presa *f.*

diurnal *adj.* diurno, -na

Djibouti *n.* Yibuti *m.*

dock *n.* muelle *m.*

Dominica *n.* Dominica *f.*

Dominican *adj. & n.* dominicano, -na *m.f.*

Dominican Republic *n.* República Dominicana *f.*

downstream *adj. & adv.* aguas abajo, río abajo

drainage basin *n.* cuenca hidrográfica, cuenca de drenaje *f.*

dredge *v.* dragar

dredging *n.* dragado *m.*

drought *n.* sequía *f.*

dune *n.* duna *f.*

dust storm *n.* tormenta de polvo *f.*

Dutch *adj. & n.* holandés, -esa *m.f.*

Dutch West Indies *n.pl.* Antillas Neerlandesas, Antillas Holandesas *f.*

E

earthquake *n.* terremoto *m.*, temblor de tierra *m.*, sismo *m.;* **e. zone** zona sísmica *f.*

east *adj.* oriental, este

east *n.* este *m.*

East Asia *n.* Asia del Este *f.*

East Indies *n.pl.* Indias Orientales *f.*

East Timor *n.* Timor Oriental *m.*

East Timorese *adj. & n.* timorense *m.f.*

Easter Island *n.* Isla de Pascua *f.*

Eastern Europe *n.* Europa Oriental, Europa del Este *f.*

Eastern Hemisphere *n.* hemisferio oriental, hemisferio este *m.*

ebb tide *n.* reflujo de marea *m.*

ecosystem *n.* ecosistema *m.*

ecozone *n.* ecozona *f.*

Ecuador *n.* Ecuador *m.*

Ecuadoran *adj. & n.* ecuatoriano, -na *m.f.*

Egypt *n.* Egipto *m.*

Egyptian *adj. & n.* egipcio, -cia *m.f.*

El Salvador *n.* El Salvador *m.*

elevation *n.* elevación *f.*

England *n.* Inglaterra *f.*

English *adj. & n.* inglés, -esa *m.f.;* **E. Channel** canal de la Mancha *m.*

environment *n.* medio ambiente *m.*

environmental *adj.* ambiental; **e. protection** protección ambiental *f.*

equator *n.* ecuador *m.*

Equatorial Guinea *n.* Guinea Ecuatorial *f.*

equinox *n.* equinoccio *m.;* **autumnal e.** equinoccio de otoño; **vernal e., spring e.** equinoccio de primavera

Erie Canal *n.* canal de Erie *m.*

Eritrea *n.* Eritrea *f.*

Eritrean *adj. & n.* eritreo, -rea *m.f.*

erode *v.* erosionar

erosion *n.* erosión *f.*

erupt *v.* estallar, erupcionar

eruption *n.* erupción *f.*

Estonia *n.* Estonia *f.*

Estonian *adj. & n.* estonio, -nia *m.f.*

estuary *n.* estuario *m.,* desembocadura *f.*

Ethiopia *n.* Etiopía *f.*

Ethiopian *adj. & n.* etíope *m.f.*

Eurasia *n.* Eurasia *f.*

Europe *n.* Europa *f.;* **Eastern E.** Europa Oriental, Europa del Este; **Northern E.** norte de Europa *m.;* **Southern E.** sur de Europa *m.;* **Western E.** Europa Occidental, Europa del Oeste *f.*

European *adj. & n.* europeo, -pea *m.f.*

Everglades *n.pl.* Everglades *m.*

F

Falkland Islands *n.pl.* islas Malvinas *f.*

farmland *n.* tierras de cultivo *f.pl.*

fault *n.* falla geológica *f.;* **f. line** línea de falla, línea divisoria *f.*

fauna *n.* fauna *f.*

fertile *adj.* fértil

fertility *n.* fertilidad *f.;* **f. rate** tasa de fecundidad *f.*

fertilization *n.* fertilización *f.*

Fiji *n.* Fiyi *f.,* islas Fiji *f.pl.*

Filipino *adj. & n.* filipino, -na *m.f.*

Finland *n.* Finlandia *f.*

Finnish *adj. & n.* finlandés, -sa *m.f.*

fissure *n.* grieta *f.*

fjord *n.* fiordo *m.*

Flemish *adj. & n.* flamenco, -ca *m.f.*

SOCIAL STUDIES

SOCIAL STUDIES

flood *n.* inundación *f.;* **f. control measures** control de inundaciones *m.*

floodplain *n.* llanura de inundación *f.*

flora *n.* flora *f.*

Florida Keys *n.pl.* cayos de la Florida *m.*

fog *n.* niebla *f.*

foggy *adj.* neblinoso, -sa; brumoso, -sa; lleno (-na) de niebla

foothills *n.pl.* estribaciones *f.*

forest *n.* bosque *m.,* selva *f.;* **clear-cut f.** bosque talado; **f. canopy** dosel del bosque *m.;* **rain f.** selva tropical

forestry *n.* silvicultura *f.,* ciencias forestales *f.pl.*

French *adj. & n.* francés, -sa *m.f.*

front *n.* frente *m.*

G

Gabon *n.* Gabón *m.*

Galapagos Islands *n.pl.* islas Galápagos *f.*

Galilee *n.* Galilea *f.*

Gambia *n.* Gambia *f.*

Ganges River *n.* río Ganges *m.*

Gaza Strip *n.* Franja de Gaza *f.*

geographer *n.* geógrafo *m.*

geographic *adj.* geográfico, -ca; **g. dispersion** *n.* dispersión geográfica *f.;* **g. feature** accidente geográfico *m.;* **g. information systems** *pl.* sistemas de información geográfica *m.;* **g. region** región geográfica *f.*

geology *n.* geología *f.*

Georgia *n.* Georgia *f.*

Georgian *adj. & n.* georgiano, -na *m.f.*

geothermal energy *n.* energía geotérmica *f.*

German *adj. & n.* alemán, -na *m.f.*

Germany *n.* Alemania *f.*

Ghana *n.* Ghana *f.*

Ghanaian *adj. & n.* ghanés, -sa *m.f.*

glacial lake *n.* lago glaciar *m.*

glacier *n.* glaciar *m.*

global warming *n.* calentamiento global *m.*

gorge *n.* desfiladero *m.,* cañón *m.*

grain *n.* grano *m.*

Grand Canyon *n.* Gran Cañón *m.*

granite *n.* granito *m.*

grasslands *n.pl.* pastizales *m.,* praderas *f.*

grazing *n.* pastoreo *m.*

Great American Desert *n.* Gran Desierto Americano *m.*

Great Barrier Reef *n.* Gran Barrera de Coral *f.*

Great Basin *n.* Gran Cuenca *f.*

Great Britain *n.* Gran Bretaña *f.*

Great Lakes *n.pl.* Grandes Lagos *m.*

Great Salt Lake *n.* Gran Lago Salado *m.*

Greater Antilles *n.pl.* Antillas Mayores *f.*

Greece *n.* Grecia *f.*

Greek *adj. & n.* griego, -ga *m.f.*

greenhouse effect *n.* efecto invernadero *m.*

Greenland *n.* Groenlandia *f.*

Greenlander *adj. & n.* groenlandés, -esa *m.f.*

Grenada *n.* Granada *f.*

Grenadian *adj. & n.* granadino, -na *m.f.*

groundwater *n.* aguas subterráneas *f.pl.*

Guadeloupe *n.* Guadalupe *f.*

Guam *n.* Guam *f.*

Guatemala *n.* Guatemala *f.*

Guatemalan *adj. & n.* guatemalteco, -ca *m.f.*

Guinea *n.* Guinea *f.*

Guinean *adj. & n.* guineano, -na *m.f.*

gulch *n.* barranco *m.*, quebrada *f.*

Gulf Coast *n.* costa del golfo de México *f.;* **G. of Alaska** golfo de Alaska *m.;* **G. of California** golfo de California; **G. of Guinea** golfo de Guinea; **G. of Mexico** golfo de México; **G. of St. Lawrence** golfo de San Lorenzo; **G. Stream** corriente del golfo *f.*

gully *n.* hondonada *f.*, barranco *m.*

Guyana *n.* Guyana *f.*

Guyanese *adj. & n.* guyanés, -esa *m.f.*

H

habitat *n.* hábitat *m.*

Haiti *n.* Haití *m.*

Haitian *adj. & n.* haitiano, -na *m.f.*

harbor *n.* puerto *m.*

harvest *n.* cosecha *f.*

hatchery *n.* criadero *m.*, vivero *m.*, incubadora *f.*

Hawaiian Islands *n.pl.* islas Hawaianas *f.*

hay *n.* zacate *m.*

headwater *n.* cabecera de río *f.*

heat island *n.* isla de calor, isla térmica *f.*

Hebrides *n.pl.* Hébridas *f.*

hemisphere *n.* hemisferio *m.*

high plains *n.pl.* mesetas *f.*, llanuras altas *f.*

highlands *n.pl.* tierras altas *f.*

hill *n.* colina *f.*, cerro *m.*, loma *f.*

hillside *n.* ladera *f.*

hilly *adj.* montañoso, -sa

Himalayas *n.pl.* Himalaya *f.*

Hindu Kush *n.* Hindú Kush *m.*

hinterland *n.* interior del país *m.*

Hispaniola *n.* Española *f.*

Holland *n.* Holanda *f.*

hollow *n.* hoyo *m.*, hueco *m.*, hondonada *f.*

Honduran *adj. & n.* hondureño, -ña *m.f.*

Honduras *n.* Honduras *f.*

Hudson River *n.* río Hudson *m.*

Humboldt Current *n.* corriente de Humboldt *f.*

humid *adj.* húmedo, -da

humidity *n.* humedad *f.*

Hungarian *adj. & n.* húngaro, -ra *m.f.*

Hungary *n.* Hungría *f.*

hydroelectric power *n.* energía hidroeléctrica *f.*

hydrosphere *n.* hidrosfera *f.*, hidrósfera *f.*

I

Iberian Peninsula *n.* península ibérica *f.*

ice *n.* hielo *m.;* **i. sheet** capa de hielo *f.*

SOCIAL STUDIES

127

ice age *n.* edad de hielo *f.,* era glacial *f.*

iceberg *n.* iceberg *m.*

Iceland *n.* Islandia *f.*

Icelander *adj. & n.* islandés, -sa *m.f.*

icy *adj.* helado, -da

India *n.* India *f.*

Indian *adj. & n.* indio, -dia *m.f.;* hindú *m.f.;* **I. Ocean** océano Índico *m.;* **I. subcontinent** subcontinente indio *m.*

indigenous *adj.* indígena; autóctono, -na *m.f.*

Indochina *n.* Indochina *f.*

Indonesia *n.* Indonesia *f.*

Indonesian *adj. & n.* indonesio, -sia *m.f.*

Indus Valley *n.* valle del Indo *m.*

infant mortality rate *n.* tasa de mortalidad infantil *f.*

inhabit *v.* habitar

inhabitant *n.* habitante *m.f.*

inhabited *adj.* habitado, -da

inlet *n.* ensenada *f.,* brazo de mar *m.*

International Date Line *n.* Línea de Fecha Internacional *f.*

intertidal zone *n.* zona intermareal *f.*

invasive species *n.pl.* especies invasoras *f.*

Iran *n.* Irán *m.*

Iranian *adj. & n.* iraní *m.f.*

Iraq *n.* Iraq *m.*

Iraqi *adj. & n.* iraquí *m.f.*

Ireland *n.* Irlanda *f.*

Irish *adj. & n.* irlandés, -esa *m.f.;* **I Sea** *n.* mar de Irlanda *m.*

irrigate *v.* regar

irrigation *n.* riego *m.*

islet *n.* isleta *f.*

Israel *n.* Israel *m.*

Israeli *adj. & n.* israelí *m.f.*

isthmus *n.* istmo *m.*

Isthmus of Panama *n.* istmo de Panamá *m.*

Italian *adj. & n.* italiano, -na *m.f.;* **I. Peninsula** *n.* península italiana *f.*

Italy *n.* Italia *f.*

J

Jamaica *n.* Jamaica *f.*

Jamaican *adj. & n.* jamaicano, -na; jamaiquino, -na *m.f.*

Japan *n.* Japón *m.*

Japanese *adj. & n.* japonés, -esa *m.f.*

Jerusalem *n.* Jerusalén *m.*

jet stream *n.* corriente en chorro *f.*

jetty *n.* embarcadero *m.*

Jordan *n.* Jordania *f.*

Jordan River *n.* río Jordán *m.*

Jordanian *adj. & n.* jordano, -na *m.f.*

jungle *n.* selva *f.,* jungla *f.*

K

Kalahari Desert *n.* desierto del Kalahari *m.*

Kazakh *adj. & n.* kazajo, -ja *m.f.*

Kazakhstan *n.* Kazajistán *m.*

Kenai Peninsula *n.* península de Kenai *f.*

Kenya *n.* Kenia *f.*

Kenyan *adj. & n.* keniano, -na *m.f.*

key *n.* (island) cayo *m.;* (map) clave *f.,* leyenda *f.*

SOCIAL STUDIES

Khyber Pass *n.* paso Khyber, paso de Khyber *m.*

Korea *n.* Corea *f.;* **North K.** Corea del Norte; **S. Korea** Corea del Sur

Korean *adj. & n.* coreano, -na *m.f.*

Kurd *adj. & n.* kurdo, -da *m.f.*

Kurdish *adj.* kurdo, -da

Kurdistan *n.* Kurdistán *m.*

Kuwait *n.* Kuwait *m.*

Kuwaiti *adj. & n.* kuwaití *m.f.*

Kyrgyzstan *n.* Kirguistán *m.*

L

Labrador *n.* Labrador *m.;* **L. Current** corriente del Labrador *f.*

lagoon *n.* laguna *f.*

lake *n.* lago *m.*

Lake Baikal *n.* lago Baikal *m.;* **L. Champlain** lago Champlain; **L. Erie** lago Erie; **L. Huron** lago Hurón; **L. Michigan** lago Michigan; **L. Ontario** lago Ontario; **L. Superior** lago Superior; **L. Tanganyika** lago Tanganica; **L. Victoria** lago Victoria

land *n.* tierra *f.;* **l. bridge** puente terrestre *m.,* istmo *m.;* **l. mass** masa de tierra *f.;* **l. use** uso de la tierra *m.*

landfill *n.* vertedero *m.*

landlocked *adj.* sin litoral marítimo

landmark *n.* punto de referencia *m.,* hito *m.*

landscape *n.* paisaje *m.*

landslide *n.* deslizamiento *m.,* desplazamiento de tierra *m.*

Laos *n.* Laos *m.*

Laotian *adj. & n.* laosiano, -na *m.f.*

Lapland *n.* Laponia *f.*

Latin America *n.* América Latina *f.*

Latin American *adj. & n.* latinoamericano, -na *m.f.*

latitude *n.* latitud *f.*

Latvia *n.* Letonia *f.*

Latvian *adj. & n.* letón, -na *m.f.*

Lebanese *adj. & n.* libanés, -esa *m.f.*

Lebanon *n.* Líbano *m.*

leeward *adj.* de sotavento

leeward *n.* sotavento *m.*

Lesotho *n.* Lesoto *m.*

Lesser Antilles *n.pl.* Antillas Menores *f.*

levee *n.* dique *m.*

Liberia *n.* Liberia *f.*

Liberian *adj. & n.* liberiano, -na *m.f.*

Libya *n.* Libia *f.*

Libyan *adj. & n.* libio, -bia *m.f.*

Liechtenstein *n.* Liechtenstein *m.*

limestone *n.* caliza *f.*

lithosphere *n.* litósfera *f.*

Lithuania *n.* Lituania *f.*

Lithuanian *adj. & n.* lituano, -na *m.f.*

littoral zone *n.* zona litoral *f.*

lodestone *n.* imán *m.*

London *n.* Londres *m.*

Long Island Sound *n.* estrecho de Long Island *m.*

longitude *n.* longitud *f.*

Luxembourg *n.* Luxemburgo *m.*

Luxembourger *adj. & n.* luxemburgués, -sa *m.f.*

M

Macedonia *n.* Macedonia *f.*

Macedonian *adj. & n.* macedonio,

SOCIAL STUDIES

-nia *m.f.*

Madagascar *n.* Madagascar *m.*

Malagasy *adj. & n.,* **Madagascan** *adj. & n.* malgache *m.f.*

Malawi *n.* Malaui *m.*

Malaysia *n.* Malasia *f.*

Malaysian *adj. & n.* malasio, -sia *m.f.*

Maldives *n.pl.* Maldivas *f.*

Mali *n.* Malí *m.*

Malta *n.* Malta *f.*

Maltese *adj. & n.* maltés, -sa *m.f.*

Manchuria *n.* Manchuria *f.*

mangrove swamp *n.* manglar *m.*

manioc *n.* mandioca *f.*

mantle *n.* manto *m.*

map *n.* mapa *m.;* **choropleth m.** mapa de coropletas; **contour m.** mapa de contorno; **m. projection** proyección cartográfica *f.;* **physical m.** mapa físico; **political m.** mapa político; **relief m.** mapa de relieve

marina *n.* puerto deportivo *m.*

marine *adj.* marino, -na; **m. climate** *n.* clima marino *m.;* **m. vegetation** vegetación marina *f.*

Marshall Islands *n.pl.* islas Marshall *f.*

Marshallese *adj. & n.* marshalés, -esa *m.f.*

Massachusetts Bay *n.* bahía de Massachusetts *f.*

Mauritania *n.* Mauritania *f.*

Mauritanian *adj. & n.* mauritano, -na *m.f.*

Mecca *n.* la Meca *f.*

Mediterranean region *n.* región mediterránea *f.;* **M. Sea** mar Mediterráneo *m.*

megalopolis *n.* megalópolis *m.*

Mekong Delta *n.* delta del Mekong *m.;* **M. River** río Mekong *m.*

Mercator projection *n.* proyección Mercator *f.*

meridian *n.* meridiano *m.;* **prime m.** primero meridiano, meridiano de Greenwich; **principal m.** *pl.* meridianos principales

Mesoamerica *n.* Mesoamérica *f.*

Mexican *adj. & n.* mexicano, -na *m.f.*

Mexico *n.* México *m.*

microclimate *n.* microclima *m.*

Micronesia *n.* Micronesia *f.*

Micronesian *adj. & n.* micronesio, -sia *m.f.*

Middle East *n.* Medio Oriente *m.*

Midwest *n.* Medio Oeste *m.*

migration *n.* migración *f.*

migratory *adj.* migratorio, -ria

mine *n.* mina *f.*

miner *n.* minero *m.*

mineral *adj. & n.* mineral *m.;* **m. deposit** depósito mineral *m.*

mining *n.* minería *f.*

Mississippi River *n.* río Misisipi *m.*

Missouri River *n.* río Misuri *m.*

mist *n.* nublina *f.*

Mogollon Rim *n.* borde Mogollón *m.*

Moldova *n.* Moldavia *f.*

Monaco *n.* Mónaco *m.*

Mongolia *n.* Mongolia *f.*

Mongolian *adj. & n.* mongol, -ola *m.f.*

monsoon *n.* monzón *m.*

Montenegro *n.* Montenegro *m.*

moraine *n.* morrena, morrena glaciar *f.*

Moroccan *adj. & n.* marroquí *m.f.*

Morocco *n.* Marruecos *m.*

Moscow *n.* Moscú *m.*

mound *n.* montículo *m.*

Mount Everest *n.* monte Everest *m.;* **M. Kilimanjaro** monte Kilimanjaro; **M. McKinley** monte McKinley

mountain *n.* montaña *f.;* **m. range** cordillera *f.*

mouth of a river *n.* desembocadura de un río *f.*

Mozambican *adj. & n.* mozambiqueño, -ña *m.f.*

Mozambique *n.* Mozambique *m.*

mud *n.* lodo *m.*

muddy *adj.* lodoso, -sa

Myanmar *n.* Myanmar *f.,* Birmania *f.*

Myanmarese *adj. & n.* birmano, -na *m.f.*

N

Namibia *n.* Namibia *f.*

Namibian *adj. & n.* namibio, -bia *m.f.*

nation *n.* nación *f.*

natural resource *n.* recurso natural *m.*

nature *n.* naturaleza *f.*

navigable river *n.* río navegable *m.*

navigate *v.* navegar

Nepal *n.* Nepal *m.*

Nepalese *adj. & n.* nepalés, -sa; nepalí *m.f.*

Netherlander *adj. & n.* holandés, -sa *m.f.*

Netherlands *n.* Países Bajos *m.pl.,* Holanda *f.*

New Delhi *n.* Nueva Dehli *f.*

New England *n.* Nueva Inglaterra *f.*

New York *n.* Nueva York *f.*

New Zealand *n.* Nueva Zelandia *f.*

New Zealander *adj. & n.* neozelandés, -sa *m.f.*

Newfoundland *n.* Terranova *f.*

Nicaragua *n.* Nicaragua *f.*

Nicaraguan *adj. & n.* nicaragüense *m.f.*

Niger *n.* Níger *m.*

Nigeria *n.* Nigeria *f.*

Nigerian *adj. & n.* (from Nigeria) nigeriano, -na *m.f.*

Nigerien *adj. & n.* (from Niger) nigerino, -na *m.f.*

Nile Delta *n.* delta del Nilo *m.;* **N. River** río Nilo *m.*

nitrogen cycle *n.* ciclo del nitrógeno *m.*

nomad *n.* nómada *m.f.*

nomadic *adj.* nómada

Nordic *adj.* nórdico, -ca

Normandy *n.* Normandía *f.*

north *adj. & n.* norte *m.*

North Africa *n.* norte de África *m.*

North Atlantic *n.* Atlántico Norte *m.*

North Korea *n.* Corea del Norte *f.*

North Pole *n.* Polo Norte *m.*

North Sea *n.* mar del Norte *m.*

northeast *adj. & n.* noreste *m.*

Northern Europe *n.* norte de Europa *m.,* Europa del Norte *f.*

Northern Hemisphere *n.* hemisfe-

SOCIAL STUDIES

131

SOCIAL STUDIES

rio norte *m.*

Northern Ireland *n.* Irlanda del Norte *f.*

northwest *adj. & n.* noroeste *m.*

Norway *n.* Noruega *f.*

Norwegian *adj. & n.* noruego, -ga *m.f.*

Nova Scotia *n.* Nueva Escocia *f.*

O

obsidian *n.* obsidiana *f.*

occidental *adj.* occidental

ocean *n.* océano; **o. circulation** circulación oceánica *f.;* **o. currents** corrientes oceánicas *f.pl.;* **o. pollution** contaminación marina *f.*

Oceania *n.* Oceanía *f.*

oceanic *adj.* oceánico, -ca; **o. ridge** *n.* dorsal oceánica *f.;* **o. trench** fosa oceánica *f.,* zanja oceánica *f.*

Ogallala Aquifer *n.* acuífero de Ogallala *m.*

Ohio River *n.* río Ohio *m.*

oil *n.* petróleo *m.;* **o. field** yacimiento petrolífero *m.;* **o. shale** pizarra bituminosa *f.,* esquisto bituminoso *m.;* **o. spill** derrame de petróleo *m.*

old-growth forest *n.* selva virgen *f.*

Oman *n.* Omán *m.*

open range *n.* pradera abierta *f.*

oriental *adj.* oriental

Orinoco River *n.* río Orinoco *m.*

outback *n.* despoblado *m.,* interior *m.*

overfishing *n.* sobrepesca *f.,* pesca excesiva *f.*

overgrazing *n.* sobrepastoreo *m.,*

pastoreo excesivo *m.*

overpopulation *n.* superpoblación *f.*

ozone layer *n.* capa de ozono *f.*

P

Pacific Northwest *n.* Noroeste Pacífico *m.;* **P. Ocean** océano Pacífico *m.;* **P. Rim** cuenca del Pacífico *f.*

Pakistan *n.* Pakistán, Paquistán *m.*

Pakistani *adj. & n.* paquistaní *m.f.*

Palestine *n.* Palestina *f.*

Palestinian *adj. & n.* palestino, -na *m.f.;* **P. territories** *pl.* territorios palestinos *m.*

pampas *n.pl.* pampas *f.*

Panama *n.* Panamá *m.;* **P. Canal** canal de Panamá *m.*

Panamanian *adj. & n.* panameño, -ña *m.f.*

Pan-American Highway *n.* carretera Panamericana *f.*

Pangaea *n.* Pangea *f.*

Papua New Guinea *n.* Papúa Nueva Guinea *f.*

Papua New Guinean *adj. & n.* papú *m.f.*

Paraguay *n.* Paraguay *m.*

Paraguayan *adj. & n.* paraguayo, -ya *m.f.*

parallel *n.* (latitude) paralelo *m.*

Paris *n.* París *m.*

pasture *n.* pasto *m.,* zacate *m.*

Patagonia *n.* Patagonia *f.*

peak *n.* picacho *m.*

peat *n.* turba *f.;* **p. bog** turbera *f.*

peninsula *n.* península *f.*

permafrost *n.* permagel *m.*

Persian Gulf *n.* golfo Pérsico *m.*

Peru *n.* Perú *m.*

Peruvian *adj. & n.* peruano, -na *m.f.*

Philippine archipelago *n.* archipiélago filipino, archipiélago de las Filipinas *m.*

Philippines *n.pl.* Filipinas *f.*

piedmont *n.* piedemonte *m.,* pie de monte *m.*

pier *n.* muelle *m.,* embarcadero *m.*

place *n.* lugar *m.;* **p. name** nombre de un lugar *m.*

plain *n.* llanura *f.*

plankton *n.* plancton *m.*

plant species *n.* especie de plantas, especie vegetal *f.*

plateau *n.* meseta *f.,* altiplano *m.*

Poland *n.* Polonia *f.*

polar ice cap *n.* casquete polar *m.*

Pole, Polish *adj. & n.* polaco, -ca *m.f.*

pollute *v.* contaminar

pollution *n.* contaminación *f.,* polución *f.*

Polynesia *n.* Polinesia *f.*

Polynesian *adj. & n.* polinesio, -sia *m.f.*

population density *n.* densidad de población *f.*

porous *adj.* poroso, -sa

port *n.* puerto *m.;* **p. city** ciudad portuaria *f.*

Portugal *n.* Portugal *m.*

Portuguese *adj. & n.* portugués, -esa *m.f.*

prairie *n.* pradera *f.*

precipice *n.* precipicio *m.*

precipitation *n.* precipitación *f.*

prevailing wind *n.* viento predominante *m.*

prime meridian *n.* primero meridiano, meridiano de Greenwich *m.*

principal meridians *n.pl.* meridianos principales *m.*

province *n.* provincia *f.*

Puerto Rican *adj.* puertorriqueño, -ña *m.f.*

Puerto Rico *n.* Puerto Rico *m.*

Puget Sound *n.* estrecho de Puget *m.*

Pyrenees *n.pl.* Pirineos *m.*

Q

Qatar *n.* Qatar *m.*

quarry *n.* cantera *f.*

Quebec *n.* Quebec *m.*

Quebecois *adj. & n.* quebequés, -esa *m.f.;* quebequense *m.f.*

R

rain *n.* lluvia *f.;* **r. forest** selva tropical *f.;* **r. shadow** sombra pluviométrica, sombra pluvial *f.*

rain *v.* llover

rainfall *n.* precipitación *f.*

rainy *adj.* lluvioso, -sa

ravine *n.* cañada *f.*

Red Sea *n.* mar Rojo *m.*

reef *n.* arrecife *m.*

reforestation *n.* reforestación *f.,* repoblación forestal *f.*

region *n.* región *f.*

relief map *n.* mapa de relieve *m.*

replacement rate *n.* tasa de reemplazo *f.,* índice de sustitución *m.*

SOCIAL STUDIES

133

reservoir *n.* depósito *m.*, embalse *m.*, represa *f.*

resource *n.* recurso *m.;* **natural r.** recurso natural; **nonrenewable r.** recurso no renovable; **renewable r.** recurso renovable; **r. management** administración de recursos *f.*

rice paddy *n.* arrozal *m.*

Richter scale *n.* escala de Richter *f.*

ridge *n.* cresta *f.*, cordillera *f.*, cerro *m.*, caballete *m.*

rim *n.* borde *m.*

Ring of Fire *n.* Cinturón de Fuego del Pacífico *m.*

Rio Grande Valley *n.* valle del Río Grande *m.*

riptide *n.* aguas revueltas *f.pl.*, contracorriente *f.*

river *n.* río *m.;* **mouth of a r.** desembocadura de un río *f.;* **navigable r.** río navegable; **r. delta** delta del río *m.;* **r. valley** valle del río *f.;* **source of a r.** fuente de un río *f.*, nacimiento de un río *m.*

Rocky Mountains *n.pl.* montañas Rocosas *f.*

Roma *adj. & n.*, **Romany** *adj. & n.* romaní *m.f.;* gitano, -na *m.f.*

Romania *n.* Rumania *f.*

Romanian *adj. & n.* rumano, -na *m.f.*

Rome *n.* Roma *f.*

runoff *n.* escorrentía *f.*

Russia *n.* Rusia *f.*

Russian *adj. & n.* ruso, -sa *m.f.*

Rust Belt *n.* cinturón industrial, cinturón de óxido *m.*

Rwanda *n.* Ruanda *f.*

Rwandan *adj. & n.* ruandés, -esa *m.f.*

S

Sahara Desert *n.* desierto del Sahara *m.*

St. Lawrence River *n.* río de San Lorenzo *m.*

salt *n.* sal *f.;* **s. marsh** salina *f.;* **s. water** agua salada *f.*

Salvadoran *adj. & n.* salvadoreño, -ña *m.f.*

Sami *adj. & n.* sami *m.f.*

Samoa *n.* Samoa *f.*

Samoan *adj. & n.* samoano, -na *m.f.*

sand *n.* arena *f.;* **s. dune** duna de arena *f.*

sandy *adj.* arenoso, -sa

Sardinia *n.* Cerdeña *f.*

Saudi Arabia *n.* Arabia Saudita *f.*

Saudi *adj. & n.*, **Saudi Arabian** *adj. & n.* saudí, saudita *m.f.*

savannah *n.* sabana *f.*, pampa *f.*

Scandinavia *n.* Escandinavia *f.*

Scot *n.* escocés, -esa *m.f.*

Scotland *n.* Escocia *f.*

Scottish *adj.* escocés, -esa; **S. Highlands** *pl.* Tierras Altas de Escocia *f.*

sea *n.* mar *m.;* **s. bed** fondo del mar *m.;* **s. level** nivel del mar *m.;* **s. swell** oleaje del mar *m.*, marejada *f.*

sediment *n.* sedimento *m.*

sedimentary *adj.* sedimentario, -ria

Seine River *n.* río Sena *m.*

semiarid area *n.* área semiárida *f.*

Senegal *n.* Senegal *m.*

Senegalese *adj. & n.* senegalés, -esa

m.f.

Serbia *n.* Serbia *f.*

Serbian *adj. & n.* serbio, -bia *m.f.*

Siberia *n.* Siberia *f.*

Sicily *n.* Sicilia *f.*

Sierra Leone *n.* Sierra Leona *f.*

Sierra Nevada Mountains *n.pl.* montañas de Sierra Nevada *f.*

Sinai Peninsula *n.* península del Sinaí *f.*

Singapore *n.* Singapur *m.*

Singaporean *adj. & n.* singapurense *m.f.*

sinkhole *n.* sumidero *m.*

sirocco *n.* siroco *m.*

slope *n.* cuesta *f.*, pendiente *f.*; (downward) declive *m.*, bajada *f.*, falda *f.*

Slovak *adj. & n.*, **Slovakian** *adj. & n.* eslovaco, -ca *m.f.*

Slovakia *n.*, **Slovak Republic** *n.* Eslovaquia *f.*

Slovenia *n.* Eslovenia *f.*

Slovene *adj. & n.*, **Slovenian** *adj. & n.* esloveno, -na *m.f.*

snow *n.* nieve *f.*

snow *v.* nevar

snowy *adj.* nevado, -da

soil *n.* suelo *m.*; **s. conservation** conservación de suelos *f.*; **s. erosion** erosión del suelo *f.*

solar power *n.* energía solar *f.*

Solomon Islands *n.pl.* islas Salomón *f.*

Somali *adj. & n.*, **Somalian** *adj. & n.* somalí *m.f.*

Somalia *n.* Somalia *f.*

Sonoran Desert *n.* desierto de Sonora *m.*

source of a river *n.* fuente de un río *f.*, nacimiento de un río *m.*

south *adj. & n.* sur *m.*

South Africa *n.* Sudáfrica *f.*

South African *adj. & n.* sudafricano, -na *m.f.*

South America *n.* América del Sur *f.*, Sudamérica *f.*

South American *adj. & n.* sudamericano, -na *m.f.*

South Asia *n.* Asia Meridional *f.*

South China Sea *n.* mar de China Meridional *m.*

South Korea *n.* Corea del Sur

South Pacific *n.* Pacífico Sur *m.*

South Pole *n.* Polo Sur *m.*

southeast *adj. & n.* sureste, sudeste *m.*

Southeast Asia *n.* sudeste de Asia *m.*

Southern Europe *n.* sur de Europa *m.*, Europa del Sur *f.*

Southern Hemisphere *n.* hemisferio sur *m.*

Southern Ocean *n.* océano Austral *m.*

southwest *adj. & n.* suroeste, sudoeste *m.*

Spain *n.* España *f.*

Spanish *adj.* español, -ola

Spaniard *n.* español, -ola *m.f.*

spring *n.* fuente *f.*, manantial *m.*; **thermal s.** fuente termal

Sri Lanka *n.* Sri Lanka *m.*, Ceilán *m.*

Sri Lankan *adj. & n.* esrilanqués, -esa *m.f.*; ceilandés, -esa *m.f.*

SOCIAL STUDIES

135

SOCIAL STUDIES

staple crop *n.* cultivo básico *m.*

steppe *n.* estepa *f.*

storm *n.* tormenta *f.*

stormy *adj.* tormentoso, -sa

strait *n.* estrecho *m.*

Strait of Gibraltar *n.* estrecho de Gibraltar *m.;* **S. of Hormuz** estrecho de Ormuz; **S. of Magellan** estrecho de Magallanes

stream *n.* arroyo *m.,* riachuelo *m.*

subcontinent *n.* subcontinente *m.*

subduction *n.* subducción *f.;* **s. zone** zona de subducción *f.*

Sub-Saharan Africa *n.* África subsahariana *f.*

subsidence *n.* hundimiento *m.*

subsistence agriculture *n.* agricultura de subsistencia *f.*

suburb *n.* suburbio *m.*

succulents *n.pl.* suculentas *f.*

Sudan *n.* Sudán *m.*

Sudanese *adj. & n.* sudanés, -esa *m.f.*

Suez Canal *n.* canal de Suez *m.*

summer solstice *n.* solsticio de verano *m.*

summit *n.* picacho *m.*

Sun Belt *n.* Franja del Sur *f.,* Cinturón del Sol *m.*

surf *n.* olas rompientes *f.pl.*

Suriname *n.* Surinam *m.*

surroundings *n.pl.* entorno *m.*

sustainability *n.* sostenibilidad *f.*

swamp *n.* pantano *m.,* ciénaga *f.*

Swaziland *n.* Suazilandia *f.*

Swede *n.* sueco, -ca *m.f.*

Swedish *adj.* sueco, -ca

Sweden *n.* Suecia *f.*

Swiss *adj. & n.* suizo, -za *m.f.*

Switzerland *n.* Suiza *f.*

Syria *n.* Siria *f.*

Syrian *adj. & n.* sirio, -ria *m.f.*

T

Tahiti *n.* Tahití *m.*

Taiwan *n.* Taiwán *m.*

Taiwanese *adj. & n.* taiwanés, -esa *m.f.*

Tajikistan *n.* Tayikistán *m.*

Tanzania *n.* Tanzania *f.*

Tanzanian *adj. & n.* tanzano, -na *m.f.*

tar *n.* brea *f.;* **t. pit** pozo de brea *m.*

Tasmania *n.* Tasmania *f.*

tectonic plate *n.* placa tectónica *f.*

terrace *n.* terraza *f.;* **t. farming** cultivo en terrazas *m.*

territory *n.* territorio *m.*

Thai *adj. & n.* tailandés, -esa *m.f.*

Thailand *n.* Tailandia *f.*

thermal springs *n.pl.* fuentes termales *f.*

Tibet *n.* Tíbet *m.*

Tibetan *adj. & n.* tibetano, -na *m.f.;* **T. Plateau** meseta Tibetana *f.*

tidal wave *n.* maremoto *m.,* tsunami *m.*

tide *n.* marea *f.*

timber extraction *n.* extracción de madera *f.*

time zone *n.* huso horario *m.,* zona horaria *f.*

Timor *n.* Timor *m.*

Togo *n.* Togo *m.*

Tokyo *n.* Tokio *m.*

Tonga *n.* Tonga *f.*

topography *n.* topografía *f.*

tornado *n.* tornado *m.*

toxic waste *n.* residuos tóxicos *m.pl.*

trade winds *n.pl.* vientos alisios *m.*

trail *n.* camino *m.*, sendero *m.*

tree *n.* árbol *m.;* **t. canopy** copa del árbol *f.*, dosel arbóreo *m.;* **t. line** límite del bosque *m.*

tributary *n.* afluente *m.*

Trinidad and Tobago *n.* Trinidad y Tobago *f.*

Trinidadian *adj. & n.* trinitense *m.f.*

Tropic of Cancer *n.* trópico de Cáncer *m.;* **T. of Capricorn** trópico de Capricornio

tropical rain forest *n.* pluviselva *f.*, selva tropical *f.*

tropics *n.* trópicos *m.*

tundra *n.* tundra *f.*

Tunisia *n.* Túnez *m.*

Tunisian *adj. & n.* tunecino, -na *m.f.*

tunnel *n.* túnel *m.*

Turk *n.* turco, -ca *m.f.*

Turkish *adj.* turco, -ca

Turkey *n.* Turquía *f.*

Turkmen *adj. & n.* turkmeno, -na; turcomano, -na *m.f.*

Turkmenistan *n.* Turkmenistán *m.*

typhoon *n.* tifón *m.*

U

Uganda *n.* Uganda *f.*

Ugandan *adj. & n.* ugandés, -sa *m.f.*

Ukraine *n.* Ucrania *f.*

Ukrainian *adj. & n.* ucraniano, -na *m.f.*

uninhabited *adj.* deshabitado, -da

United Arab Emirates *n.pl.* Emiratos Árabes Unidos *m.*

United Kingdom *n.* Reino Unido *m.*

United States *n.* Estados Unidos *m.pl.*

unpopulated *adj.* despoblado, -da

Ural Mountains *n.pl.* montes Urales *m.*

urban *adj.* urbano, -na; **u. center** *n.* centro urbano *m.;* **u. growth** crecimiento urbano *m.;* **u. heat island** isla de calor urbano *f.;* **u. sprawl** expansión urbana *f.*

Uruguay *n.* Uruguay *m.*

Uruguayan *adj. & n.* uruguayo, -ya *m.f.*

Uzbek *adj. & n.* uzbeko, -ka *m.f.*

Uzbekistan *n.* Uzbekistán *m.*

V

Vatican City *n.* Ciudad del Vaticano *f.*

vegetation *n.* vegetación *f.*

Venezuela *n.* Venezuela *f.*

Venezuelan *adj. & n.* venezolano, -na *m.f.*

vernal equinox *n.* equinoccio de primavera *m.*

Victoria Falls *n.pl.* cataratas Victoria *f.*

Vietnam *n.* Vietnam *m.*

Vietnamese *adj. & n.* vietnamita *m.f.*

village *n.* aldea *f.*, caserío *m.*, villa *f.*

Virgin Islands *n.pl.* islas Vírgenes *f.*

volcanic *adj.* volcánico, -ca

volcanism *n.* vulcanismo *m.*

volcano *n.* volcán *m.*

Volga River *n.* río Volga *m.*

SOCIAL STUDIES

SOCIAL STUDIES

W

Wales *n.* Gales *m.*

wash *n.* cañada *f.*

water *n.* agua *f.;* **w. cycle** ciclo del agua *m.;* **w. pollution** contaminación del agua *f.;* **w. supply** abastecimiento de agua *m.*

waterfall *n.* cascada *f.*

watershed *n.* línea divisoria de las aguas *f.*

waterway *n.* vía navegable *f.*

wave *n.* (ocean) ola *f.*

Welsh *adj. & n.* galés, -esa *m.f.*

west *adj. & n.* oeste *m.*

West Bank *n.* Cisjordania *f.*

West Indies *n.pl.* Indias Occidentales *f.,* Antillas *f.*

Western Europe *n.* Europa Occidental, Europa del Oeste *f.*

Western Hemisphere *n.* hemisferio occidental *m.*

wetlands *n.pl.* humedales *m.*

wilderness area *n.* área silvestre *f.,* zona salvaje *f.,* reserva natural *f.*

wildlife *n.* vida salvaje, vida silvestre *f.*

wind *n.* viento *m.*

windswept *adj.* azotado (-da) por el viento

windward *adj.* a barlovento

windward *n.* barlovento *m.*

Windward Islands *n.pl.* islas de Barlovento *f.*

windy *adj.* ventoso, -sa

winter solstice *n.* solsticio de invierno *m.*

woodland, woods *n.* bosque *m.*

work animals *n.pl.* animales de trabajo *m.*

Y

Yangtze River *n.* río Yangtzé *m.*

Yemen *n.* Yemen *m.*

Yemeni *adj. & n.* yemení *m.f.*

Yucatan Peninsula *n.* península de Yucatán *f.*

Yugoslav *n.* yugoslavo, -va *m.f.*

Yugoslavian *adj.* yugoslavo, -va

Yugoslavia *n.* Yugoslavia *f.*

Yukon *n.* Yukón *m.*

Z

Zaire *n.* Zaire *m.*

Zairian *adj. & n.* zaireño, -ña *m.f.*

Zambia *n.* Zambia *f.*

Zambian *adj. & n.* zambiano, -na *m.f.*

Zimbabwe *n.* Zimbabue *m.*

Zimbabwean *adj. & n.* zimbabués, -esa; zimbabuense *m.f.*

Zuiderzee *n.* Zuiderzee *f.*

History

• •

A

abdicate *v.* abdicar

abolition *n.* abolición *f.*

abolitionist *adj. & n.* abolicionista *m.f.;* **a. movement** movimiento abolicionista *m.*

Acropolis *n.* Acrópolis *f.*

African American *adj. & n.* afro-americano, -na *m.f.*

African National Congress *n.* Congreso Nacional Africano *m.*

Afrocaribbean *adj. & n.* afrocari-beño, -ña *m.f.*

Age of Discovery *n.* era de los descubrimientos *f.;* **A. of Enlightenment** siglo de las luces *m.;* **A. of Reason** era de la razón *f.*

aggression *n.* agresión *f.;* **act of a.** acto de agresión *m.*

aggressor *n.* agresor, -ora *m.f.*

agnostic *adj. & n.* agnóstico, -ca *m.f.*

agrarian reform *n.* reforma agraria *f.*

agreement *n.* acuerdo *m.*

agriculture *n.* agricultura *f.*

air force *n.* fuerza aérea *f.*

aircraft carrier *n.* portaaviones *m.*

airplane *n.* avión *m.*

alchemy *n.* alquimia *f.*

Alexander the Great *n.* Alejandro Magno *m.*

Alexandria *n.* Alejandría *f.*

Alien and Sedition Acts *n.pl.* Leyes de Extranjería y Sedición *f.*

alliance *n.* alianza *f.*

Alliance for Progress *n.* Alianza para el Progreso *f.*

Allied Powers *n.pl.* Potencias Aliadas *f.*

ambassador *n.* embajador, -ora *m.f.*

ambush *n.* emboscada *f.*

ambush *v.* emboscar

America *n.* América *f.*

American *adj. & n.* americano, -na *m.f.;* norteamericano, -na *m.f.;* **A. Civil War** guerra civil estadounidense *f.;* **A. Indians** *pl.* indios americanos *m.;* **A. Revolution** Revolución americana *f.*

American Civil Liberties Union (A.C.L.U.) *n.* Unión Americana de Libertades Civiles *f.*

Americanization *n.* americanización *f.*

anarchism *n.* anarquismo *m.*

anarchist *adj. & n.* anarquista *m.f.*

anarcho-syndicalist *adj. & n.* anarco-sindicalista *m.f.*

anarchy *n.* anarquía *f.*

ancestor *n.* antepasado *m.;* **a. worship** culto de los antepasados *m.*

ancient *adj.* antiguo, -gua;

ancient Egypt *n.* antiguo Egipto *m.;* **a. Greece** antigua Grecia *f.;* **a. Rome** antigua Roma *f.*

Anglo-Saxon *adj. & n.* anglosajón, -na *m.f.*

SOCIAL STUDIES

annexation *n.* anexión *f.*

Anno Domini (A.D.) *adv.* después de Cristo (d.C.)

antebellum *adj.* prebélico, -ca

anthropologist *n.* antropólogo, -ga *m.f.*

anthropology *n.* antropología *f.*

anticlericalism *n.* anticlericalismo *m.*

antiquity *n.* antigüedad *f.*

anti-Semitism *n.* antisemitismo *m.*

antislavery *adj.* en contra de la esclavitud, abolicionista

antiwar movement *n.* movimiento contra la guerra *m.*

apartheid *n.* apartheid *m.*

aqueduct *n.* acueducto *m.*

Arab *adj. & n.* árabe *m.f.*

Arab-Israeli conflict *n.* conflicto árabe-israelí *m.*

Arabic *adj.* arábigo, -ga

archduke *n.* archiduque *m.*

archeological *adj.* arqueológico, -ca; **a. dig** *n.* excavación arqueológica *f.;* **a. evidence** evidencia arqueológica *f.;* **a. site** yacimiento arqueológico *m.*

archeologist *n.* arqueólogo, -ga *m.f.*

archeology *n.* arqueología *f.*

archery *n.* tiro con arco *m.*

architect *n.* arquitecto, -ta *m.f.*

architecture *n.* arquitectura *f.*

aristocrat *n.* aristócrata *m.f.*

Aristotle *n.* Aristóteles *m.*

armed forces *n.pl.* fuerzas armadas *f.*

armor *n.* armadura *f.*

arms control *n.* control de armas, control de armamentos *m.*

army *n.* ejército *m.*

Articles of Confederation *n.pl.* Artículos de la Conferación *m.*

artifact *n.* artefacto *m.*

artillery *n.* artillería *f.*

Asian American *adj. & n.* asiático (-ca) americano (-na) *m.f.*

Asian Pacific Islander *n.* isleño (-ña) de Asia y el Pacífico *m.f.*

assassinate *v.* asesinar

assassination *n.* asesinato *m.*

Assyria *n.* Asiria *f.*

Assyrian Empire *n.* Imperio asirio *m.*

astrolabe *n.* astrolabio *m.*

atheism *n.* ateísmo *m.*

atheist *n.* ateo, -tea *m.f.*

Athens *n.* Atenas *f.*

atomic bomb *n.* bomba atómica *f.*

atrocities *n.pl.* atrocidades *f.*

attack on Pearl Harbor *n.* ataque a Pearl Harbor *m.*

Augustus Caesar *n.* Augusto César *m.*

Austro-Hungarian Empire *n.* Imperio austro-húngaro *m.*

authoritarian *adj. & n.* autoritario, -ra *m.f.*

authoritarianism *n.* autoritarismo *m.*

autocracy *n.* autocracia *f.*

automobile *n.* automóvil *m.*

aviation *n.* aviación *f.*

Axis Powers *n.pl.* potencias del Eje *f.,* fuerzas del Eje *f.*

ayatollah *n.* ayatolá *m.*

Aztec *adj. & n.* azteca *m.f.;* **A. Empire** *n.* Imperio azteca *m.*

B

Babylon *n.* Babilonia *f.*

Babylonian Empire *n.* Imperio babilónico *m.*

Bacon's Rebellion *n.* rebelión de Bacon *f.*

balance of power *n.* equilibrio de poder *m.*

Balfour Declaration *n.* Declaración de Balfour *f.*

Balkanization *n.* balcanización *f.*

barbarian *adj. & n.* bárbaro, -ra *m.f.*

barbed wire *n.* alambre de espino *m.*

baron *n.* barón *m.*

baroness *n.* baronesa *f.*

battalion *n.* batallón *m.*

battering ram *n.* ariete *m.*

battle *n.* batalla *f.*

Battle of Britain *n.* batalla de Inglaterra *f.;* **B. of Gallipoli** batalla de Galípoli; **B. of Gettysburg** batalla de Gettysburg; **B. of Iwo Jima** batalla de Iwo Jima; **B. of Midway** batalla de Midway; **B. of the Bulge** batalla de las Ardenas; **B. of the Little Bighorn** batalla de Little Bighorn; **B. of the Plains of Abraham** batalle de las llanuras de Abrahán

Bay of Pigs *n.* bahía de Cochinos *f.*

Beat Generation *n.* generación beat *f.*

Before Christ (B.C.) *adv.* antes de Cristo (a.C.); **B. the Common Era (B.C.E)** antes de la Era Común (a.E.C)

behead *v.* decapitar

Bering land bridge *n.* puente terrestre de Bering *m.*

Berlin Wall *n.* Muro de Berlín *m.*

betray *v.* traicionar

big stick policy *n.* política del garrote *f.*

bigotry *n.* intolerancia *f.*

bilingual education *n.* educación bilingüe *f.*

bilingualism *n.* bilingüismo *m.*

Bill of Rights *n.* Carta de Derechos *f.*

biological weapon *n.* arma biológica *f.*

Black Death *n.* peste negra *f.*

Black Legend *n.* leyenda negra *f.*

Black Panthers *n.pl.* Panteras Negras *f.*

blacklist *n.* lista negra *f.*

Bleeding Kansas *n.* guerra fronteriza de Kansas *f.,* Kansas Sangrante *f.*

blimp *n.* zepelín *m.,* dirigible *m.*

blitzkrieg *n.* guerra relámpago *f.*

blockade *n.* bloqueo *m.*

Boer War *n.* guerra Bóer *f.*

Bolsheviks *n.pl.* bolcheviques *m.f.*

bomb *n.* bomba *f.;* **atomic b.** bomba atómica; **hydrogen b.** bomba de hidrógeno

bomb *v.* bombar

bombardment *n.* bombardeo *m.*

Bonus Army *n.* ejército del bono *m.*

border state *n.* estado fronterizo *m.*

Boston Massacre *n.* masacre de Boston *m.;* **B. Tea Party** motín del té de Boston *f.*

SOCIAL STUDIES

boundary dispute *n.* disputa fronteriza *f.*

bourgeois *adj. & n.* burgués, -esa *m.f.*

bourgeoisie *n.* burguesía *f.;* **petite b.** pequeña burguesía

bow and arrow *n.* arco y flecha *m.*

Boxer Rebellion *n.* rebelión de los bóxers *f.*

British *adj.* británico, -ca; **B. Empire** *n.* Imperio británico *m.;* **B. Raj** raj británico *m.*

bronze *n.* bronce *m.*

Bronze Age *n.* Edad de Bronce *f.*

Brown v. Board of Education *n.* Brown contra la Junta de Educación *m.*

bubonic plague *n.* peste bubónica *f.*

Buddha *n.* Buda *m.*

Buddhism *n.* budismo *m.*

Buffalo Soldiers *n.pl.* soldados búfalo *m.*

burial chamber *n.* cámara funeraria *f.*

Byzantine Empire *n.* Imperio bizantino *m.*

Byzantium *n.* Bizancio *m.*

C

calendar *n.* calendario *m.;* **Gregorian c.** calendario Gregoriano; **Julian c.** calendario Juliano

California Gold Rush *n.* fiebre del oro en California *f.*

caliph *n.* califa *m.*

caliphate *n.* califato *m.*

Camp David Accords *n.pl.* Acuerdos de Camp David *m.*

cannon *n.* cañón *m.;* **c. ball** bala de cañón *f.;* **c. fire** cañonazos *m.pl.;* **c. fodder** carne de cañón *f.*

capitalism *n.* capitalismo *m.*

capitalist *adj. & n.* capitalista *m.f.*

capture *v.* capturar

caravan *n.* caravana *f.*

caravel *n.* carabela *f.*

Carthage *n.* Cartago *m.*

Carthaginian, *adj. & n.* cartaginés, -esa *m.f.*

caste system *n.* sistema de castas *m.*

castle *n.* castillo *m.*

casualty *n.* víctima *f.;* **c. rate** tasa de víctimas *f.*

catacombs *n.pl.* catacumbas *f.*

catapult *n.* catapulta *f.*

cathedral *n.* catedral *f.;* **Gothic c.** catedral gótica *f.*

Catherine the Great *n.* Catalina la Grande *f.*

Catholic *adj. & n.* católico, -ca; **C. Church** *n.* Iglesia católica *f.;* **C. Reformation** Reforma católica *f.*

cause *n.* causa *f.;* **c. of war** causa de la guerra

cause *v.* causar

cavalry *n.* caballería *f.*

cave paintings *n.pl.* pinturas rupestres *f.*

ceasefire *n.* alto de fuego *m.*

Celtic *adj.* céltico, -ca

Celts *adj. & n.pl.* celtas *m.f.*

centurion *n.* centurión *m.*

century *n.* siglo *m.*

chariot *n.* carro de batalla *m.,*

cuadriga *f.*

Charlemagne *n.* Carlomagno *m.*

charter *n.* carta *f.*

chattel slavery *n.* propiedad de esclavos *f.*

chauvinism *n.* (national) chovinismo *m.*

chemical warfare *n.* guerra química *f.*

Cherokee Nation *n.* Nación Cherokee *f.*

child labor *n.* trabajo infantil *m.*

Chinatown *n.* barrio chino *m.*

Chinese Revolution *n.* Revolución china *f.*

Christian *adj. & n.* cristiano, -na *m.f.*

Christianity *n.* cristianismo *m.*

Christopher Columbus *n.* Cristóbal Colón *m.*

chronology *n.* cronología *f.*

Church of England *n.* Iglesia de Inglaterra *f.*

circumnavigate *v.* circunnavegar

civil disobedience *n.* desobediencia civil *f.*

civil rights *n.pl.* derechos civiles *m.;* **c. r. movement** movimiento de derechos civiles *m.*

Civil Rights Act *n.* Ley de Derechos Civiles *f.*

civil war *n.* guerra civil *f.*

Civil War *n.* guerra civil estadounidense *f.*

Civilian Conservation Corps (C.C.C.) *n.* Cuerpo Civil de Conservación *m.*

civilization *n.* civilización *f.;* **classi-** cal c. civilización clásica

civilized *adj.* civilizado, -da

class *n.* clase *f.;* **c. consciousness** conciencia de clase *f.;* **c. system** sistema de clases *m.;* **c. warfare** lucha de clases *f.;* **middle c.** clase media; **working c.** clase obrera, clase trabajadora

Clean Air Act *n.* Ley del Aire Puro *f.*

clergy *n.* clero *m.*

coalition government *n.* gobierno de coalición *m.*

Code Napoleon *n.* Código de Napoleón *m.*

Cold War *n.* guerra fría *f.*

Coliseum *n.* Coliseo *m.*

collective farm *n.* granja colectiva *f.*

collectivism *n.* colectivismo *m.*

colonial *adj.* colonial; **c. power** *n.* potencia colonial *f.,* poder colonial *m.*

Colonial Period *n.* período colonial *m.*

colonialism *n.* colonialismo *m.*

colonist *n.* colonizador, -ora *m.f.;* colono, -na *m.f.*

colonization *n.* colonización *f.*

colonize *v.* colonizar

colony *n.* colonia *f.*

combat *n.* combate *m.*

combatant *n.* combatiente *m.f.*

Committee of Correspondence *n.* Comité de Correspondencia *m.*

Common Market *n.* mercado común *m.*

commonwealth *n.* mancomunidad *f.*

communication *n.* comunicación *f.*

SOCIAL STUDIES

communism *n.* comunismo *m.*

communist *adj. & n.* comunista *m.f.*

Communist Manifesto *n.* Manifiesto Comunista *m.;* **American C. Party** Partido Comunista de Estados Unidos *m.;* **C. Party of the Soviet Union** Partido Comunista de la Unión Soviética

compass *n.* brújula *f.*

compromise *n.* compromiso *m.*

concentration camp *n.* campo de concentración *m.*

concessions *n.pl.* concesiones *f.*

Confederacy *n.* Confederación *f.*

Confederate Army *n.* ejército de la Confederación *m.;* **C. States of America** Estados Confederados de América *m.*

confederation *n.* confederación *f.*

conflict *n.* conflicto *m.;* **regional c.** conflicto regional

Confucianism *n.* confucianismo *m.*

Congress *n.* Congreso *m;* **C. of Vienna** Congreso de Viena

conquer *v.* conquistar

conquest *n.* conquista *f.*

Conservative Party *n.* Partido Conservador *m.*

constitutional *adj.* constitucional; **c. amendment** *n.* enmienda constitucional *f.;* **c. democracy** democracia constitucional *f.;* **c. monarchy** monarquía constitucional *f.;* **c. rights** *pl.* derechos constitucionales *m.*

Constitutional Convention *n.* convención constitucional *f.*

containment *n.* contención *f.*

contemporary *adj. & n.* contemporáneo, -nea *m.f.*

Continental Army *n.* ejército continental *m.;* **C. Congress** Congreso Continental *m.*

convent *n.* convento *m.*

convert *n.* converso, -sa *m.f.*

convert *v.* convertir

coronation *n.* coronación *f.*

cotton *n.* algodón *m.;* **c. gin** desmotadora de algodón *f.;* **c. mill** molino de algodón *m.;* **King C.** Rey Algodón *m.*

count *n.* conde *m.*

counterinsurgency *n.* contrainsurgencia *f.*

counterintelligence *n.* contraespionaje *m.*

counterrevolution *n.* contrarrevolución *f.*

counterterrorism *n.* antiterrorismo *m.*

countess *n.* condesa *f.*

coup d'état *n.* golpe de estado *m.*

covert action *n.* acción encubierta *f.*

Coxey's Army *n.* ejército de Coxey *m.*

creation myth *n.* mito de la creación *m.*

Crimean War *n.* guerra de Crimea *f.*

crimes against humanity *n.pl.* crímenes contra la humanidad *m.*

crisis *n.* crisis *f.*

Cro-Magnon *n.* CroMagnon *m.,* Cromañón *m.*

crossbow *n.* ballesta *f.*

crown *n.* corona *f.;* **c. prince** príncipe heredero *m.;* **c. princess** princesa heredera *f.*

crown *v.* coronar

crucifixion *n.* crucifixión *f.*

crusader *n.* cruzado *m.*

Crusades *n.pl.* Cruzadas *f.*

Cuban exiles *n.pl.* cubanos exilios *m.;* **C. Missile Crisis** Crisis de los misiles en Cuba *f.;* **C. Revolution** Revolución cubana *f.*

cuneiform *adj. & n.* cuneiforme *m.*

czar *n.* zar *m.*

Czar Nicholas II *n.* zar Nicolás II *m.*

Czarist Russia *n.* Rusia zarista *f.*

D

D-Day *n.* Día D *m.*

Dark Ages *n.pl.* Edad de las Tinieblas *f.*

dark horse *n.* caballo negro *m.*

death rate *n.* tasa de mortalidad *f.*

decade *n.* década *f.*

decentralization *n.* descentralización *f.*

Declaration of Independence *n.* Declaración de Independencia *f.;* **D. of the Rights of Man and of the Citizen** Declaración de los Derechos del Hombre y del Ciudadano

decolonization *n.* descolonización *f.*

defeat *n.* derrota *f.*

defeat *v.* derrotar, vencer

Deism *n.* deísmo *m.*

Demilitarized Zone (D.M.Z.) *n.* zona desmilitarizada *f.*

demobilization *n.* desmovilización *f.*

democracy *n.* democracia *f.*

Democratic-Republican Party *n.* Partido Demócrata-Republicano *m.*

democratization *n.* democratización *f.*

depose *v.* deponer

depth charge *n.* carga de profundidad *f.*

desegregation *n.* abolición de la segregación *f.*

deserter *n.* desertor, -ora *m.f.*

desertion *n.* deserción *f.*

despot *n.* déspota *m.f.*

détente *n.* distensión *f.*

deterrence *n.* disuasión *f.*

developed country *n.* nación desarrollada *f.*

developing country *n.* nación en vías de desarrollo *f.*

diaspora *n.* diáspora *f.*

diplomacy *n.* diplomacia *f.;* **gunboat d.** diplomacia de las cañoneras; **shuttle d.** diplomacia itinerante, diplomacia de lanzadera

disappeared *adj. & n.* desaparecido, -da *m.f.*

disarmament *n.* desarme *m.*

discovery *n.* descubrimiento *m.*

disease *n.* enfermedad *f.;* **infectious d.** enfermedad infecciosa

displaced persons *n.pl.* personas desplazadas *f.*

dissidents *n.pl.* disidentes *m.f.*

divine right of kings *n.* derecho divino de los reyes *m.*

doge *n.* dux *m.*

domesticated animals *n.pl.* animales domésticos *m.*

SOCIAL STUDIES

145

SOCIAL STUDIES

Domino Theory *n.* teoría del dominó *f.*

draft riot *n.* disturbio de reclutamiento *m.*

Dred Scott decision *n.* decisión del caso Dred Scott *f.*

duchess *n.* duquesa *f.*

dugout ship *n.* piragua *f.*

duke *n.* duque *m.*

Dust Bowl *n.* cuenca de polvo *f.*

dynasty *n.* dinastía *f.*

E

earl *n.* conde *m.*

Edwardian *adj. & n.* eduardiano, -na *m.f.*

electricity *n.* electricidad *f.*

Elizabethan *adj. & n.* isabelino, -na *m.f.*

Ellis Island *n.* Isla de Ellis *f.*

emancipation *n.* emancipación *f.*

Emancipation Proclamation *n.* proclamación de la emancipación *f.*

embargo *n.* embargo *m.;* **oil e.** embargo de petróleo

embassy *n.* embajada *f.*

emigration *n.* emigración *f.*

emperor *n.* emperador *m.*

empire *n.* imperio *m.*

empress *n.* emperatriz *f.*

enclosure *n.* recinto *m.,* cercado *m.*

encomienda system *n.* sistema de encomienda *m.*

English Parliament *n.* parlamento inglés *m.*

Enlightenment *n.* Siglo de las Luces *m.,* período de la Ilustración *m.*

enslave *v.* esclavizar

epidemic *adj.* epidémico, -ca

epidemic *n.* epidemia *f.,* epidémico *m.*

equilibrium *n.* equilibrio *m.*

era *n.* época *f.,* era *f.,* edad *f.*

Era of Good Feelings *n.* época de los buenos sentimientos *f.;* **Neolithic E.** Neolítico *m.;* **Progressive E.** era progresista *f.*

escape *v.* escapar

Espionage Act *n.* Ley de Espionaje *f.*

Estates General *n.* Estados Generales *m.pl.*

ethnic *adj.* étnico, -ca; **e. cleansing** *n.* limpieza étnica *f.;* **e. conflict** conflicto étnico *m.*

eugenics *n.* eugenesia *f.*

European Economic Community *n.* Comunidad Económica Europea *f.;* **E. Union** Unión Europea *f.*

evacuation *n.* evacuación *f.*

event *n.* evento *m.*

Evil Empire *n.* imperio del mal *m.*

evolution *n.* evolución *f.;* **theory of e.** teoría de la evolución *f.*

excavate *v.* excavar

excavation *n.* excavación *f.*

execution *n.* ejecución *f.;* **e. by firing squad** fusilamiento *m.*

exile *n.* exilio *m.*

exile *v.* exiliar

exodus *n.* éxodo *m.*

expansion *n.* expansión *f.*

expansionism *n.* expansionismo *m.*

expedition *n.* expedición *f.*

• •

exploration *n.* exploración *f.*

explorer *n.* explorador, -ora *m.f.*

F

faction *n.* facción *f.*

Fair Deal *n.* Trato Justo *m.*

fallout shelter *n.* refugio de lluvia radiactivas *m.*

famine *n.* hambre *m.,* hambruna *f.*

fascism *n.* fascismo *m.*

fascist *adj. & n.* fascista *m.f.*

Federalist Papers *n.pl.* Documentos Federalistas *m.;* **F. Party** Partido Federalista *m.*

Fertile Crescent *n.* Creciente Fértil *m.*

feudal *adj.* feudal; **f. lord** *n.* señor feudal *m.*

feudalism *n.* feudalismo *m.*

Filipino Insurrection *n.* insurrección filipina *f.*

Final Solution *n.* Solución Final *f.*

firing squad *n.* pelotón de ejecución *m.*

First Americans *n.pl.* primeros (-ras) americanos (-nas) *m.f.*

first inhabitants *n.pl.* primeros (-ras) habitantes *m.f.*

Five Civilized Tribes *n.pl.* cinco tribus civilizadas *f.*

Five Year Plan *n.* plan quinquenal *m.*

flank attack *n.* ataque de flanco *m.*

forced relocation *n.* traslado forzoso *m.,* reubicación forzosa *f.*

former *adj.* antiguo, -gua; **f. master** *n.* antiguo (-gua) amo (ma) *m.f.;* **f. slave** antiguo (-gua) esclavo (-va) *m.f.*

fort *n.,* **fortress** *n.* fuerte *m.,* fortaleza *f.,* presidio *m.*

Fort Sumter *n.* Fuerte Sumter *m.*

fortification *n.* fortificación *f.*

Founders *n.pl.* (U.S.) Fundadores *m.*

Four Freedoms *n.pl.* Cuatro Libertades *f.*

Framers of the U.S. Constitution *n.pl.* autores de la Constitución *m.*

Franco-Prussian War *n.* guerra franco-prusiana *f.*

Free Silver *n.* movimiento Free Silver *f.*

free state *n.* estado libre de esclavitud *m.*

freedmen *n.pl.* libertos *m.*

Freedmen's Bureau *n.* Oficina de Libertos *f.*

freedom *n.* libertad *f.;* **f. riders** *n.pl.* pasajeros de la libertad *m.;* **political f.** libertad política

French and Indian War *n.* guerra franco-india *f.;* **F. Revolution** Revolución francesa *f.*

friendly fire *n.* fuego amigo *m.*

frontier *n.* frontera *f.*

frontiersman *n.* hombre de la frontera *m.*

Fugitive Slave Act *n.* Ley de los Esclavos Fugitivos *f.*

fundamental rights *n.pl.* derechos fundamentales *m.*

G

G.I. Bill *n.* Ley G.I. *f.*

Gadsden Purchase *n.* Compra de Gadsden *f.,* Venta de La Mesilla *f.*

SOCIAL STUDIES

147

SOCIAL STUDIES

Gaelic *adj.* gaélico, -ca

garrison *n.* presidio *m.*

gas mask *n.* careta antigás *f.*

Gauls *n.pl.* galos *m.*

gay liberation movement *n.* movimiento de la liberación gay *m.;* **g. rights** *pl.* derechos de los homosexuales *m.*

Geneva Conventions *n.pl.* Convenios de Ginebra *m.*

Genghis Khan *n.* Gengis Kan *m.*

genocide *n.* genocidio *m.*

gentry *n.* aristocracia *f.,* clase alta *f.*

germ warfare *n.* guerra bacteriológica *f.*

Gettysburg Address *n.* Discurso de Gettysburg *m.*

Gilded Age *n.* época dorada *f.*

gladiator *n.* gladiador *m.*

glasnost *n.* glasnost *m.*

Glorious Revolution *n.* Revolución Gloriosa *f.*

god *n.* dios *m.;* **gods** *pl.* dioses

goddess *n.* diosa *f.*

Gothic *adj.* gótico, -ca; **G. cathedral** *n.* catedral gótica *f.*

Goths *n.pl.* godos *m.*

govern *v.* gobernar

government *n.* gobierno *m.;* **coalition g.** gobierno de coalición *m.;* **provisional g.** gobierno provisional *m.;* **puppet g.** gobierno títere, gobierno marioneta *m.*

grandfather clause *n.* cláusula de derechos adquiridos *f.*

Great Awakening *n.* Gran despertar *m.*

Great Depression *n.* Gran Depresión *f.*

Great Leap Forward *n.* Gran Salto Adelante *m.*

Great Plague *n.* Gran Plaga *f.*

Great Proletarian Cultural Revolution *n.* Gran Revolución Cultural Proletaria *f.*

Great Pyramid of Giza *n.* Gran Pirámide de Gizeh *f.*

Great Society *n.* Gran Sociedad *f.*

Great Wall of China *n.* Gran Muralla de China *f.*

Greek city-state *n.* ciudad-estado griego *f.;* **G. democracy** democracia griega *f.;* **G. philosopher** filósofo griego *m.*

Greek Orthodox Christianity *n.* cristianismo ortodoxo griego *m.*

Green Mountain Boys *n.pl.* muchachos de las Montañas Verdes *m.*

Green Revolution *n.* Revolución Verde *f.*

Gregorian calendar *n.* calendario Gregoriano *m.*

guerrilla warfare *n.* guerra de guerrillas *f.*

guillotine *n.* guillotina *f.*

Gulf of Tonkin Resolution *n.* Resolución del golfo de Tonkin *f.*

gun *n.* pistola *f.,* arma de fuego *f.;* **machine g.** ametralladora *f.*

gunboat diplomacy *n.* diplomacia de las cañoneras *f.*

gunpowder *n.* pólvora *f.*

Gutenberg Bible *n.* Biblia de Gutenberg *f.*

H

Han Dynasty *n.* Dinastía Han *f.*

Hanging Gardens of Babylon *n.pl.* jardines colgantes de Babilonia *m.*

Hapsburg Empire *n.* Imperio de los Habsburgo *m.*

Harlem Renaissance *n.* Renacimiento de Harlem *m.*

Haymarket Riot *n.* motín de Haymarket *m.*

hegemonic power *n.* potencia hegemónica *f.*

hegemony *n.* hegemonía *f.*

Hellenist culture *n.* cultura helenística *f.*

Helsinki Accords *n.pl.* Acuerdos de Helsinki *m.*

heresy *n.* herejía *f.*

heretic *n.* hereje *m.f.*

hierarchy *n.* jerarquía *f.*

hieroglyphics *n.pl.* jeroglíficos *m.*

Hindu *adj. & n.* hindú *m.f.*

Hispanic *adj. & n.* hispano, -na *m.f.;* hispánico, -ca *m.f.*

historian *n.* historiador, -ora *m.f.*

historic *adj.,* **historical** *adj.* histórico, -ca; **h. document** *n.* documento histórico *m.;* **h. event** acontecimiento histórico *m.;* **h. figure** figura histórica *f.,* personaje histórico *m.;* **h. period** período histórico *m.;* **h. preservation** preservación histórica *f.*

history *n.* historia *f.*

Hittites *n.pl.* hititas *m.*

Holocaust *n.* holocausto *m.*

Holy Land *n.* Tierra Santa *f.*

Holy Roman Empire *n.* Sacro Imperio Romano *m.*

home country *n.* país de origen *m.*

Homestead Act *n.* Ley de Heredad *f.*

homesteader *n.* granjero *m.,* hacendado *m.*

Hoovervilles *n.pl.* barrios de chabolas *m.*

hostilities *n.pl.* hostilidades *f.*

House of Commons *n.* Cámara de los Comunes *f.;* **H. of Lords** Cámara de los Lores; **H. of Representatives** Cámara de los Representantes; **H. Un-American Activities Committee** Comité de Actividades Antiamericanas *m.*

human rights *n.pl.* derechos humanos *m.*

humanism *n.* humanismo *m.*

Hundred Flowers Movement *n.* Movimiento de las Cien Flores *m.*

Hundred Years War *n.* guerra de los Cien Años *f.*

Hungarian Revolution *n.* Revolución húngara *f.*

Huns *n.pl.* hunos *m.f.*

hunter-gatherer *n.* cazador-recolector *m.f.*

hydrogen bomb *n.* bomba de hidrógeno *f.*

I

immigration *n.* inmigración *f.;* **i. restrictions** *pl.* restricciones de inmigración *f.*

imperial *adj.* imperial; **i. power** *n.*

SOCIAL STUDIES

poder imperial *m.;* **i. presidency** presidencia imperial *f.*

imperialism *n.* imperialismo *m.*

impressment *n.* leva *f.,* reclutamiento forzoso *m.*

Inca *adj. & n.* inca *m.f.;* **I. Empire** Imperio inca *m.*

incursion *n.* incursión *f.*

indentured servitude *n.* servidumbre por deuda *f.*

independence *n.* independencia *f.*

independent *adj.* independiente

Indian *adj. & n.* indio, -dia *m.f.;* indígena *m.f.;* **I. reservation** reserva indígena *f.;* **I. uprising** levantamiento indio *m.*

Indian Removal Act *n.* Ley de Remoción de los Indios *f.;* **I. Territory** territorio indio *m.;* **I. Wars** *pl.* guerras indias *f.*

indigenous *adj.* autóctono, -na; indígena; **i. culture** *n.* cultura indígena *f.;* **i. peoples** *pl.* pueblos indígenas *m.*

Indo-European languages *n.* lenguas indoeuropeas *f.*

Industrial Revolution *n.* revolución industrial *f.*

Industrial Workers of the World (I.W.W.) *n.pl.* Trabajadores Industriales del Mundo *m.*

infantry *n.* infantería *f.*

infectious disease *n.* enfermedad infecciosa *f.*

Information Age *n.* éra de la información *f.*

Inquisition *n.* Inquisición *f.*

insurrection *n.,* **insurgency** *n.* insurrección *f.*

intelligentsia *n.* intelectualidad *f.*

internment *n.* internamiento *m.;* **i. camp** campo de internamiento, campo de reclusión *m.;* **i. of Japanese Americans** internamiento de japoneses-americanos *m.*

intervention *n.* intervención *f.*

interventionist *n.* intervencionista *m.f.*

invasion *n.* invasión *f.*

invention *n.* invención *f.*

Iran-Contra Affair *n.* asunto Irán-Contra *m.*

Iranian hostage crisis *n.* Crisis de los rehenes en Irán *f.*

Iraq War *n.* guerra de Iraq *f.*

Irish Potato Famine *n.* Gran Hambruna irlandesa *f.*

Iron Curtain *n.* cortina de hierro *f.*

Iroquois Confederacy *n.* confederación Iroquois, confederación iraquesa *f.*

irrigation *n.* riego *m.*

Islam *n.* Islam *m.*

isolationism *n.* aislacionismo *m.*

isolationist *adj. & n.* aislacionista *m.*

ivory trade *n.* comercio de marfil *m.*

J

Jacksonian Democracy *n.* democracia jacksoniana *f.*

Jacobins *n.pl.* Jacobinos *m.*

Jazz Age *n.* era del jazz *f.*

Jeffersonian Democracy *n.* democracia jeffersoniana *f.*

Jesus Christ *n.* Jesucristo *m.*

Jim Crow laws *n.pl.* leyes de Jim Crow *f.*

jingoism *n.* patrioterismo *m.*

Joan of Arc *n.* Juana de Arco *f.*

Judaism *n.* Judaísmo *m.*

Judeo-Christian ethic *n.* ética judeocristiana *f.*

Julian calendar *n.* calendario Juliano *m.*

Julius Caesar *n.* Julio César *m.*

K

Kansas-Nebraska Act *n.* Ley de Kansas-Nebraska *f.*

karma *n.* karma *m.*

Kennedy assassination *n.* asesinato de Kennedy *m.*

Kennewick Man *n.* hombre de Kennewick *m.*

king *n.* rey *m.*

King Cotton *n.* Rey Algodón *m.*

King Philip's War *n.* guerra del rey Felipe *f.*

kingdom *n.* reino *m.*

knight *n.* caballero *m.*

Knights of Labor *n.pl.* Caballeros del Trabajo *m.*

Know-Nothing Party *n.* Partido Know Nothing *m.*

Koran *n.* Corán *m.*

Korean War *n.* guerra de Corea *f.*

Ku Klux Klan *n.* Ku Klux Klan *m.*

L

labor movement *n.* movimiento obrero *m.*

Labor Party *n.* Partido Laborista *m.*

land reform *n.* reforma agraria *f.*

laissez-faire *adj. & n.* laissez-faire *m.*

language region *n.* región lingüística *f.*

Lawrence Textile Strike *n.* huelga textil de Lawrence *f.*

League of Nations *n.* Sociedad de Naciones *f.*

Lend-Lease *n.* Ley de Préstamo y Arriendo *f.*

Lewis and Clark expedition *n.* expedición de Lewis y Clark *f.*

liberate *v.* libertar

liberation theology *n.* teología de la liberación *f.*

liberty *n.* libertad *f.*

Liberty Bell *n.* campana de la libertad *f.*

Lincoln-Douglas Debate *n.* debate Lincoln-Douglas *m.*

literacy rate *n.* tasa de alfabetización, tasa de alfabetismo *f.;* índice de alfabetización *f.*

Long March *n.* Larga Marcha *f.*

Lost Colony *n.* Colonia Perdida *f.*

Lost Generation *n.* Generación Perdida *f.*

Louisiana Purchase *n.* Compra de Louisiana *f.*

loyalist *adj. & n.* partidario (-ria) del régimen *m.f.*, lealista *m.*

lynch *v.* linchar

lynching *n.* linchamiento *m.*

M

machine gun *n.* ametralladora *f.*

SOCIAL STUDIES

151

SOCIAL STUDIES

Maginot Line *n.* Línea Maginot *f.*

Magna Carta *n.* Carta Magna *f.*

mammoth hunt *n.* caza de mamuts *f.*

Manhattan Project *n.* proyecto Manhattan *m.*

Manifest Destiny *n.* destino manifiesto *m.*

Maoism *n.* maoísmo *m.*

Maoist *adj. & n.* maoísta *m.f.*

Marbury v. Madison *n.* Marbury contra Madison *m.*

Mariel boatlift *n.* éxodo del Mariel *m.*

Marshall Plan *n.* plan Marshall *m.*

martyr *n.* mártir *m.f.*

Marxism *n.* marxismo *m.;* **Marxism-Leninism** marxismo-leninismo *m.*

massacre *n.* masacre *f.,* matanza *f.*

Mayan *adj. & n.* maya *m.f.;* **M. Empire** Imperio maya *m.*

Mayflower Compact *n.* Pacto del Mayflower *m.*

McCarthyism *n.* macartismo *m.*

medieval *adj.* medieval; **m. society** *n.* sociedad medieval *f.*

Melting Pot *n.* crisol de razas *m.*

mercenary *adj. & n.* mercenario *m.f.*

Mesopotamia *n.* Mesopotamia *f.*

Mexican American *adj. & n.* mexicano (-na) americano (-na) *m.f.*

Mexican-American War *n.* guerra mexicano-estadounidense *f.*

Middle Ages *n.pl.* Edad Media *f.*

Middle Passage *n.* travesía del Atlántico, travesía intermedia *f.*

migration *n.* migración *f.;* **involuntary m.** migración involuntaria

militant *adj. & n.* militante *m.f.*

military *adj.* militar; **m. campaign** *n.* campaña militar *f.;* **m. draft** reclutamiento *m.;* **m. force** fuerza militar *f.;* **m. intervention** intervención militar *f.;* **m. strategy** estrategia militar *f.*

Military Industrial Complex *n.* complejo militar industrial *m.*

millennium *n.* milenio *m.*

minefield *n.* campo de minas *m.*

Ming Dynasty *n.* Dinastía Ming *f.*

Miranda Rule *n.* regla Miranda *f.*

missile *n.* misil *m.*

missing in action *adj. & n.* desaparecido (-da) en acción *m.f.*

mission *n.* misión *f.*

missionary *n.* misionero, -ra *m.f.*

Missouri Compromise *n.* Compromiso de Misuri *m.*

moat *n.* foso *m.*

modernization *n.* modernización *f.*

Mohammed *n.* Mahoma *m.*

monarch *n.* monarca *m.f.*

monarchist *adj. & n.* monárquico, -ca *m.f.*

monarchy *n.* monarquía *f.*

monastery *n.* monasterio *m.*

Mongol Empire *n.* Imperio mongol *m.*

monk *n.* monje *m.*

monotheism *n.* monoteísmo *m.*

Monroe Doctrine *n.* Doctrina Monroe *f.*

Moon landing *n.* alunizaje *m.*

Moors *n.pl.* moros *m.*

Mormon *adj. & n.* mormón -na *m.f.;* **M. Church** Iglesia Mormona *f.*

mortality rate *n.* tasa de mortalidad *f.*

Moses *n.* Moisés *m.*

mosque *n.* mezquita *f.*

Mound Builders *n.pl.* constructores de montículos *m.*

Mount Olympus *n.* monte Olimpo *m.*

mummification *n.* momificación *f.*

mummy *n.* momia *f.*

Muslim *adj. & n.* musulmán, -na *m.f.*

mustard gas *n.* gas mostaza *m.*

mutual aid society *n.* sociedad de ayuda mutua *f.*

My Lai Massacre *n.* masacre de My Lai *f.*

myth *n.* mito *m.*

N

Napoleon *n.* Napoleón *m.*

Napoleonic Wars *n.pl.* guerras napoleónicas *f.*

nation *n.* nación *f.;* **n. building** construcción nacional, construcción de la nación *f.*

national anthem *n.* himno nacional *m.*

National Association for the Advancement of Colored People (N.A.A.C.P.) *n.* Asociación Nacional para el Progreso de las Personas de Color *f.*

National Liberation Front (N.L.F.) *n.* Frente de Liberación Nacional *m.*

national liberation movement *n.* movimiento de liberación nacional *m.*

National Recovery Act *n.* Ley de Recuperación Nacional *f.*

nationalism *n.* nacionalismo *m.*

nationality *n.* nacionalidad *f.*

native *adj. & n.* nativo, -va; indígena; oriundo, -da *m.f.*

Native American *adj. & n.* nativo (-va) americano (-na) *m.f.;* **N. A. languages** *n.pl.* lenguas indígenas *f.*

nativism *n.* nativismo *m.*

nativist *adj. & n.* nativista *m.f.*

natural law *n.* ley natural *f.*

Navajo Nation *n.* Nación Navajo *f.*

naval *adj.* naval; **n. blockade** *n.* bloqueo naval *m.;* **n. warfare** guerra naval *f.*

navigation *n.* navegación *f.*

navy *n.* marina *f.*, armada *f.*

Nazi *adj. & n.* nazi *m.f.*

Nazi Germany *n.* Alemania nazi *f.*

Nazism *n.* nazismo *m.*

Neanderthal *n.* Neandertal *m.f.*

Nebuchadnezzar *n.* Nabucodonosor *m.*

negotiations *n.pl.* negociaciones *f.*

Neolithic *adj.* neolítico, -ca; **N. Era** *n.* Neolítico *m.*

Nero *n.* Nero *m.*

nerve gas *n.* gas nervioso *m.*

neutral *adj.* neutral

neutrality *n.* neutralidad *f.*, neutralismo *m.*

New Amsterdam *n.* Nueva Ámsterdam *f.*

SOCIAL STUDIES

New Deal *n.* Nuevo Trato *m.*

New Economic Policy *n.* Nueva Política Económica *f.*

New Left *n.* Nueva Izquierda *f.*

nirvana *n.* nirvana *m.*

nobility *n.* nobleza *f.*

noble *adj. & n.* noble *m.*

Noble Savage *n.* salvaje noble *m.*, buen salvaje *m.*

nobleman *n.* noble *m.*, hidalgo *m.* caballero *m.*

nomad *n.* nómada *m.f.*

nomadic *adj.* nómada *m.f.*

nonaligned *adj.* no alineados, neutral

Norman Conquest *n.* conquista normanda *f.*

Normandy Landing *n.* desembarco de Normandía *m.*

North Atlantic Treaty Organization (NATO) *n.* Organización del Tratado del Atlántico del Norte *f.*

Northwest Ordinance *n.* Ordenanza del Noroeste *f.;* **N. Passage** paso del Noroeste *m.*

Nubian Empire *n.* Imperio de Nubia *m.*

nuclear *adj.* nuclear; **n. war** *n.* guerra nuclear *f.;* **n. weapon** arma nuclear *f.*

Nuclear Test Ban Treaty *n.* Tratado de Prohibición Completa de Pruebas Nucleares *m.*

nullification doctrine *n.* doctrina de anulación *f.*

nun *n.* monja *f.*

Nuremburg Trials *n.pl.* juicios de Nuremberg *m.*

O

occupied territory *n.* territorio ocupado *m.*

oil embargo *n.* embargo de petróleo *m.*

oligarch *n.* oligarca *m.*

oligarchy *n.* oligarquía *f.*

Open Door Policy *n.* política de puertas abiertas *f.*

Operation Desert Storm *n.* operación Tormenta del Desierto *f.*

Opium War *n.* guerra del Opio *f.*

oral tradition *n.* tradición oral *f.*

Oregon Trail *n.* ruta de Oregón *f.*

Organization of Petroleum Exporting Countries (OPEC) *n.* Organización de Países Exportadores de Petróleo *f.*

organized crime *n.* crimen organizado *m.*

origin *n.* origen *m.*

Ottoman Empire *n.* Imperio otomano *m.*

overpopulation *n.* superpoblación *f.*

overthrow *v.* derrocar

P

pact *n.* pacto *m.*

Paleolithic *adj.* paleolítico, -ca; **P. Era** *n.* Paleolítico *m.*

Palestine Liberation Organization (P.L.O.) *n.* Organización de Liberación Palestina *f.*

Palmer Raids *n.pl.* incursiones Palmer *f.*

Pan-Arabism *n.* panarabismo *m.*

pandemic *n.* pandemia *f.*

papacy *n.* papado *m.*

papyrus *n.* papiro *m.*

paratrooper *n.* paracaidista *m.f.*

Paris Commune *n.* Comuna de París *f.*

Paris Peace Accords *pl.* Acuerdos de Paz de París *m.*

parliament *n.* parlamento *m.*

partisan *adj.* parcial

partisan *n.* partisano, -na *m.f.*

Parthenon *n.* Partenón *m.*

Partition of Poland *n.* reparto de Polonia *m.*

past *adj.* pasado, -da

past *n.* pasado *m.;* **recent p.** pasado reciente

patriarch *n.* patriarca *m.*

patriarchal *adj.* patriarcal

Pax Romana *n.* Pax Romana *f.*

peace *n.* paz *m.;* **p. march** marcha por la paz *f.;* **p. treaty** tratado de paz *m.*

Peace Corps *n.* Cuerpo de Paz *m.*

peaceful coexistence *n.* coexistencia pacífica *f.*

peacekeeper *n.* mantenedor (-ora) de la paz *m.f.;* pacificador, -ora *m.f.*

peasant *n.* campesino, -na *m.f.*

peasantry *n.* campesinado *m.*

peculiar institution *n.* institución peculiar *f.*

Peloponnesian War *n.* guerra del Peloponeso *f.*

penal colony *n.* colonia penal *f.*

Pentagon Papers *n.pl.* papeles del Pentágono *m.*

persecution *n.* persecución *f.*

Persian Gulf War *n.* guerra del golfo Pérsico *f.*

Peter the Great *n.* Pedro el Grande *m.*

petite bourgeoisie *n.* pequeña burguesía *f.*

petroleum *n.* petróleo *m.*

pharaoh *n.* faraón *m.*

Phoenicia *n.* Fenicia *f.*

pictograph *n.* pictografía *f.,* pictograma *m.*

pilgrim *n.* peregrino, -na *m.f.*

pillage, plunder *n.* pillaje *m.*

pioneer *n.* pionero, -ra *m.f.*

pirates *n.pl.* piratas *m.f.*

pistol *n.* pistola *f.*

plague *n.* plaga *f.*

plantation *n.* hacienda *f.,* colonia *f.*

Plato's Republic *n.* República de Platón *f.*

Plessy v. Ferguson *n.* Plessy contra Ferguson *m.*

plunder *v.,* **pillage** *v.* saquear, pillar

Plymouth Colony *n.* Colonia de Plymouth *f.*

pogrom *n.* pogromo *m.,* matanza *f.*

political *adj.* político, -ca; **p. freedom** *n.* libertad política *f.;* **p. ideology** ideología política *f.;* **p. machine** maquinaria política *f.;* **p. opportunist** oportunista político (-ca) *m.f.*

poll tax *n.* impuesto de capitación *m.*

polytheism *n.* politeísmo *m.*

Pompeii *n.* Pompeya *f.*

SOCIAL STUDIES

155

SOCIAL STUDIES

pope *n.* papa *m.*

popular uprising *n.* levantamiento popular *m.*

population *n.* población *f.;* **p. explosion** explosión demográfica *f.;* **p. growth** crecimiento de la población *m.*

Populist Movement *n.* Movimiento Populista *m.,* populismo *m.*

pottery *n.* cerámica *f.*

pragmatism *n.* pragmatismo *m.*

preacher *n.* predicador, -ora *m.f.*

Pre-Columbian *adj.* precolombino, -na

prehistoric *adj.* prehistórico, -ca

prehistory *n.* prehistoria *f.*

present day *n.* día de hoy *m.*

priest *n.* sacerdote *m.*

primary source *n.* fuente primaria *f.*

prime minister *n.* primer ministro *m.*

primitive *adj.* primitivo, -va

prince *n.* príncipe *m.;* **crown p.** príncipe heredero

princess *n.* princesa *f.;* **crown p.** princesa heredera

printing press *n.* imprenta *f.*

prison *n.* presidio *m.*

privateer *n.* corsario *m.*

Progressive Era *n.* era progresista *f.*

Prohibition *n.* prohibición *f.*

proletariat *n.* proletariado *m.*

prosperity *n.* prosperidad *f.*

protest *n.* protesta *f.*

Protestant Christianity *n.* cristianismo protestante *m.*

provisional government *n.* gobierno provisional *m.*

proviso *n.* condición *f.,* cláusula *f.*

Pueblo Revolt *n.* revuelta de los indios Pueblo *f.*

Puerto Rican *adj. & n.* puertorriqueño, -ña *m.f.*

Pullman Strike *n.* huelga de Pullman *f.*

Punic Wars *n.pl.* guerras púnicas *f.*

puppet government *n.* gobierno títere, gobierno marioneta *m.*

Puritan *adj. & n.* puritano, -na *m.f.*

Puritanism *n.* puritanismo *m.*

Q

Quaker *adj. & n.* cuáquero, -ra *m.f.*

queen *n.* reina *f.*

R

raid *n.* incursión *f.*

raid *v.* invadir

raiders *n.pl.* invasores *m.f.*

rape *n.* violación *f.*

rape *v.* violar

raze *v.* arrasar

realm *n.* reino *m.*

rebel *n.* rebelde *m.f.*

rebel *v.* rebelarse

reconnaissance *n.* reconocimiento *m.*

Reconquest of Spain *n.* reconquista de España *f.*

Reconstruction *n.* reconstrucción *f.*

recruits *n.pl.* reclutas *m.f.*

Red Army *n.* ejército rojo *m.*

Red Guard *n.* guardia rojo *m.*

Red Scare *n.* miedo a los rojos *m.*

redistribution of wealth *n.* redistribución de la riqueza *f.*

Reformation *n.* Reforma *f.*

refugees *n.pl.* refugiados *m.*

regime *n.* régimen *m.*

regiment *n.* regimiento *m.*

regional conflict *n.* conflicto regional *m.*

reign *n.* reinado *m.*

reign *v.* reinar

Reign of Terror *n.* reinado del terror *m.*

reincarnation *n.* reencarnación *f.*

reinforcements *n.pl.* refuerzos *m.*

Renaissance *n.* Renacimiento *m.*

reparation *n.* reparación *f.*

repel *v.* repeler, rechazar

republic *n.* república *f.*

republican *adj. & n.* repúblicano, -na *m.f.*

resettlement *n.* reasentamiento *m.*

resistance *n.* resistencia *f.*

restoration *n.* restauración *f.*

retreat *n.* retirada *f.*

retreat *v.* retirar

reunification *n.* reunificación *f.*

revisionism *n.* revisionismo *m.;* **historical r.** revisionismo histórico

revolt *n.* revuelta *f.,* sublevación *f.*

revolt *v.* rebelarse, sublevarse

revolution *n.* revolución *f.*

revolutionary *adj. & n.* revolucionario, -ria *m.f.*

Revolutionary War *n.* guerra revolucionaria *f.*

rifle *n.* rifle *m.*

Roaring Twenties *n.pl.* bulliciosos años veinte *m.*

robber barons *n.pl.* magnates ladrones *m.,* barones ladrones *m.*

Roe v. Wade *n.* Roe contra Wade *m.*

Roman Catholicism *n.* Catolicismo romano *m.*

Roman Empire *n.* Imperio romano *m.;* **R. Forum** Foro Romano *m.;* **R. Republic** República romana *f.*

Romance language *n.* lengua romance *f.*

Rosetta Stone *n.* Piedra de Rosetta *f.*

Royal Air Force (R.A.F.) *n.* Fuerza Aérea Real *f.*

royal court *n.* corte real *f.*

royalist *adj. & n.* realista *m.f.;* monárquico, -ca *m.f.*

royalty *n.* realeza *f.*

ruin *n.* ruina *f.*

rule *v.* reinar, gobernar

ruler *n.* gobernante *m.f.*

ruling *adj.* gobernante

Russian Revolution *n.* Revolución rusa *f.*

Rust Belt *n.* Cinturón de Óxido *m.*

S

sail *n.* vela *f.*

sail *v.* navegar

Salem witch trials *n.pl.* juicios por brujería de Salem *m.*

sanctions *n.pl.* sanciones *f.*

satellite *n.* satélite *m.*

scandal *n.* escándalo *m.*

Scopes trial *n.* juicio Scopes *m.*

scorched-earth policy *n.* política de tierra quemada *f.*

sculpture *n.* escultura *f.*

SOCIAL STUDIES

SOCIAL STUDIES

secession *n.* secesión *f.*

secondary source *n.* fuente secundaria *f.*

sectionalism *n.* seccionalismo *m.*

Semitic languages *n.pl.* lenguas semíticas *f.*

Senate *n.* Senado *m.*

separate but equal *adj.* separados (-das) pero iguales

separatist *adj. & n.* separatista *m.f.*

serf *n.* siervo *m.*

serfdom *n.* servidumbre *f.*

settlement *n.* colonia *f.*, poblado *m.*; **s. house** casa de asentamiento *f.*

settler *n.* colono, -na *m.f.*

Seven Years War *n.* guerra de Siete Años *f.*

Shah of Iran *n.* Sha de Irán *m.*

shantytown *n.* barrio de chabola *m.*

sharecropper *n.* aparcero, -ra *m.f.*

Shay's Rebellion *n.* rebelión de Shay *f.*

Sherman Antitrust Act *n.* Ley Sherman antimonopolio *f.*

Shi'ite *adj. & n.* chiita *m.f.*

ship *n.* barco *m.*, buque *m.*; **dugout s.** piragua *f.*

shoot *v.* disparar

shot *n.*, **shooting** *n.* tiro *m.*, disparo *m.*

shuttle diplomacy *n.* diplomacia itinerante, diplomacia de lanzadera *f.*

siege *n.* asedio *m.*, sitio *m.*; **state of s.** estado de sitio *m.*

Siege of Stalingrad *n.* asedio de Stalingrado *m.*; **S. of Vicksburg** asedio de Vicksburg

Silk Road *n.* camino de seda *m.*

sink *v.* hundir

Sino-Soviet split *n.* ruptura sino-soviética *f.*

Sioux Nation *n.* Nación Sioux *f.*

sit-down strike *n.* huelga de brazos caídos *f.*

sit-in *n.* sentada *f.*

skirmish *n.* escaramuza *f.*

slave *n.* esclavo, -va *m.f.*; **s. codes** *pl.* códigos de esclavos, códigos de esclavitud *m.*; **s. holder** esclavista *m.f.*; **s. labor** trabajo esclavizante *m.*; **s. rebellion** rebelión de esclavos *f.*; **s. state** estado esclavo *m.*; **s. trade** trata de esclavos *f.*

Slave Power *n.* poder esclavista *m.*

slavery *n.* esclavitud *f.*

slum *n.* barrio bajo, barrio marginal *m.*

smallpox epidemic *n.* epidemia de viruela *f.*

smuggling *n.* contrabando *m.*

Social Contract *n.* contrato social *m.*

Social Darwinism *n.* darwinismo social *m.*

social democracy *n.* democracia social *f.*

socialism *n.* socialismo *m.*

socialist *adj. & n.* socialista *m.f.*

Socrates *n.* Sócrates *m.*

soldier *n.* soldado *m.*, militar *m.f.*

Sons of Liberty *n.pl.* Hijos de la Libertad *m.*

source *n.* fuente *f.*; **p. source** fuente

primaria; **s. source** fuente secundaria

sovereign *adj. & n.* soberano, -na *m.f.*

Soviet bloc *n.* bloque soviético *m.;*
S. Empire Imperio soviético *m.;*
S. Union Unión Soviética *f.*

space exploration *n.* exploración
del espacio *f.*

Spanish-American War *n.* guerra
española-americana *f.*

Spanish Armada *n.* Armada Española *f.;* **S. Civil War** guerra civil española *f.;* **S. Republic** República
española *f.*

Sparta *n.* Esparta *f.*

spear *n.* lanza *f.*

specialization *n.* especialización *f.*

sphere of influence *n.* esfera de influencia *f.,* ámbito de influencia *m.*

spice trade *n.* comercio de especias *m.*

squire *n.* (landowner) terrateniente
m., hacendado *m.;* (knight's attendant) escudero *m.*

Stalinism *n.* estalinismo *m.*

Star-Spangled Banner *n.* La bandera tachonada de estrellas *f.*

statehood *n.* estadidad *f.*

states' rights *n.pl.* derechos de los
estados *m.*

steam engine *n.* máquina de
vapor *f.*

steamboat *n.* barco de vapor *m.*

steamship *n.* buque de vapor *m.*

Stone Age *n.* Edad de Piedra *f.*

subdue *v.* someter

subjugate *v.* subyugar

submarine *n.* submarino *m.*

succession *n.* sucesión *f.;* **order of
s.** orden de sucesión *m.*

suffrage *n.* sufragio *m.;* **s. movement** movimiento sufragista *m.;*
women's s. sufragio femenino *m.*

suffragette *n.* sufragista *m.f.*

sugar cane *n.* caña de azúcar *f.*

suicide bomber *n.* atacante suicida
m.f.

Sunni *adj. & n.* sunita, suní *m.f.*

superpower *n.* superpotencia *f.*

supporter *n.* partidario, -ria *m.f.*

surrender *n.* rendición *f.*

surrender *v.* rendir, entregar

sweatshop *n.* taller de explotación *m.*

sword *n.* espada *f.*

synagogue *n.* sinagoga *f.*

syndicalism *n.* sindicalismo *m.*

T

tactic *n.* táctica *f.*

Taj Mahal *n.* Taj Mahal *m.*

Tamerlane *n.* Tamerlán *m.*

tank *n.* tanque *m.*

taxation without representation *n.*
impuestos sin representación *m.pl.*

technology *n.* tecnología *f.*

telegraph *n.* telégrafo *m.*

temperance *n.* templanza *f.;* **t.
movement** movimiento por la
templanza *m.*

temple *n.* templo *m.*

Ten Commandments *n.pl.* diez
mandamientos *m.*

territorial expansion *n.* expansión
territorial *f.*

SOCIAL STUDIES

territory *n.* territorio *m.;* **occupied t.** territorio ocupado

terrorism *n.* terrorismo *m.*

terrorist *adj. & n.* terrorista *m.f.*

Teutonic *adj.* teutónico, -ca

theocracy *n.* teocracia *f.*

Third Reich *n.* Tercer Reich *m.*

Third World *n.* tercer mundo *m.*

throne *n.* trono *m.*

Tigris-Euphrates River Valley *n.* valle del río Tigris y Éufrates *m.*

timeline *n.* cronología *f.,* línea de tiempo *f.*

tomb *n.* tumba *f.,* sepulcro *m.*

totalitarian *adj.* totalitario, -ria; **t. regime** *n.* régimen totalitario *m.*

totalitarianism *n.* totalitarismo *m.*

trade route *n.* ruta comercial *f.*

Trail of Tears *n.* Sendero de Lágrimas *m.*

traitor *n.* traidor, -ora *m.f.*

transcendentalism *n.* transcendentalismo *m.*

transcendentalist *adj. & n.* transcendentalista *m.f.*

transcontinental railroad *n.* ferrocarril transcontinental *m.*

treason *n.* traición *f.*

treaty *n.* tratado *m.*

Treaty of Guadalupe Hidalgo *n.* Tratado de Guadalupe Hidalgo *m.;* **T. of Paris** Tratado de París; **T. of Versailles** Tratado de Versalles

trench warfare *n.* guerra de trincheras *f.*

triangular trade *n.* comercio triangular *m.*

tribalism *n.* tribalismo *m.*

tribe *n.* tribu *f.*

tribute *n.* homenaje *m.*

Triple Entente *n.* Triple Entente *f.*

Trojan Horse *n.* caballo de Troya *m.;* **T. War** guerra de Troya *f.*

troops *n.pl.* tropas *f.*

truce *n.* tregua *f.*

trustbuster *n.* oficial antimonopolista *m.*

tyranny *n.* tiranía *f.*

tyrant *n.* tirano, -na *m.f.;* caudillo *m.*

U

U.S. Congress *n.* Congreso de EE.UU. *m.;* **U.S. Constitution** Constitución de EE.UU. *f.;* **U.S. v. Texas** EE.UU. contra Texas *m.*

unalienable rights *n.pl.* derechos inalienable *m.*

unconditional surrender *n.* rendición incondicional *f.*

Underground Railroad *n.* ferrocarril subterráneo *m.*

unification *n.* unificación *f.;* **u. of Germany** unificación de Alemania *f.*

Union Army *n.* ejército de la Unión *m.*

Union of Soviet Socialist Republics (U.S.S.R.) *n.* Unión de Repúblicas Socialistas Soviéticas *f.*

United Nations *n.* Naciones Unidas *f.pl.;* **U.N. Charter** Carta de las Naciones Unidas *f.;* **U.N. Children's Fund (UNICEF)** Fondo de las Naciones Unidas para la Infancia *m.*

Universal Declaration of Human Rights *n.* Declaración Universal de los Derechos Humanos *f.*

uprising *n.* sublevación *f.*

Urban League *n.* Liga Urbana *f.*

urbanization *n.* urbanización *f.*

utilitarianism *n.* utilitarismo *m.*

utopia *n.* utopía *f.*

utopian *adj.* utópico, -ca; **u. community** *n.* comunidad utópica *f.;* **u. socialism** socialismo utópico *m.*

V

vanguard party *n.* partido de vanguardia *m.*

viceroy *n.* virrey *m.*

Victorian *adj. & n.* victoriano, -na *m.f.*

victory *n.* victoria *f.*

Vietcong *n.* Vietcong *m.f.*

Vietnam War *n.* guerra de Vietnam *f.*

vigilante *n.* vigilante *m.f.*

vigilantism *n.* vigilantismo *m.*

Vikings *n.pl.* Vikingos *m.*

Virginia House of Burgesses *n.* Cámara de la Burguesía de Virginia *f.*

viscount *n.* vizconde *m.*

Volstead Act *n.* Ley de Volstead *f.*

Voting Rights Act *n.* Ley de Derecho al Voto *f.*

voyage *n.* viaje *m.*

Voyage of the Beagle *n.* viaje del Beagle *m.; * **v. of Columbus** *pl.* viajes de Colón

W

war *n.,* **warfare** *n.* guerra *f.;* **chemical w.** guerra química; **civil w.** guerra civil; **guerrilla w.** guerra de guerrillas; **naval w.** guerra naval; **trench w.** guerra de trincheras; **w. crime** crimen de guerra *m.;* **w. of attrition** guerra de desgaste

War of 1812 *n.* guerra de 1812 *f.;* **W. on Poverty** guerra contra la pobreza; **W. Powers Act** Ley de Poderes de Guerra *f.;* **W. of the Roses** *pl.* guerras de las Rosas

warlord *n.* caudillo *m.*

Warsaw Pact *n.* Pacto de Varsovia *m.*

warship *n.* buque de guerra *m.*

Washington's Farewell Address *n.* Discurso de despedida de Washington *m.*

water rights *n.pl.* derechos de agua *m.*

Watergate scandal *n.* escándalo de Watergate *m.*

Wealth of Nations, The *n.* La riqueza de las naciones *f.*

weapon *n.* arma *f.;* **biological w.** arma biológica; **nuclear w.** arma nuclear

weaponry *n.* armamento *m.*

weaving *n.* tejeduría *f.,* tejedura *f.*

Weimar Republic *n.* República de Weimar *f.*

Western culture *n.* cultura occidental *f.*

Westward Expansion *n.* expansión hacia el oeste *f.*

wheel *n.* rueda *f.*

SOCIAL STUDIES

SOCIAL STUDIES

Whig Party *n.* Partido Whig *m.*

Whiskey Rebellion *n.* rebelión del whisky *f.*

White Citizens Councils *n.pl.* Consejos de Ciudadanos Blancos *m.*

William the Conqueror *n.* Guillermo el Conquistador *m.*

Wilmot Proviso *n.* Cláusula Wilmot *f.*

women's liberation movement *n.* movimiento de liberación de las mujeres *m.*

women's suffrage *n.* sufragio femenino *m.*

working class *n.* clase obrera, clase trabajadora *f.*

Works Progress Administration (W.P.A.) *n.* Administración de Trabajos en Progreso *f.*

world power *n.* potencia mundial *f.*

World War I *n.* primera guerra mundial *f.;* **W.W. II** segunda guerra mundial

writing system *n.* sistema de escritura *m.*

written *adj.* escrito, -ta; **w. language** *n.* lenguaje escrito *m.;* **w. record** constancia escrita *f.*

Y

Yalta Conference *n.* Conferencia de Yalta *f.*

yellow journalism *n.* periodismo amarillo *m.,* prensa sensacionalista *f.*

Yellow Peril *n.* peligro amarillo *m.*

Z

Zapotec civilization *n.* civilización zapoteca *f.*

zeppelin *n.* zepelín *m.,* dirigible *m.*

Zionism *n.* sionismo *m.*

Zionist *adj. & n.* sionista *m.f.*

Zulu Empire *n.* Imperio zulú *m.*

FINE ARTS

Performing Arts

A

accent *n.* acento *m.*

accompaniment *n.* acompaña-miento *m.*

accompanist *n.* acompañante *m.f.*

accompany *v.* acompañar, corear

accordion *n.* acordeón *m.*

acoustic instrument *n.* instrumento acústico *m.*

act *n.* acto *m.*

act *v.* actuar

action *n.* acción *f.;* **falling a.** acción decreciente; **rising a.** acción en aumento

actor *n.* actor *m.,* actriz *f.;* **supporting a.** actor (-triz) de reparto

adaptation *n.* adaptación *f.*

ad-lib *adv.* a modo de improvisación, improvisadamente

ad-lib *n.* improvisación *f.*

ad-lib *v.* improvisar

aesthetics *n.* estética *f.*

alignment *n.* alineamiento *m.*

alto *n.* contralto *m.*

amphitheater *n.* anfiteatro *m.*

animation *n.* animación *f.*

antagonist *n.* antagonista *m.f.*

applaud *v.* aplaudir

applause *n.* aplauso *m.*

archetype *n.* arquetipo *m.*

arena stage *n.* teatro arena, teatro circular *m.*

arrangement *n.* (music) arreglo *m.*

art form *n.* modalidad artística *f.,* disciplina artística *f.*

artist *n.* artista *m.f.*

aside *n.* (theater) aparte *m.*

atmosphere *n.* atmósfera *f.*

audience *n.* público *m.*

audition *n.* audición *f.*

auditorium *n.* auditorio *m.,* sala *f.*

autoharp *n.* autoarpa *f.*

avant-garde *n.* vanguardismo *m.f.*

B

backstage *adv.* entre bastidores, tras bambalinas

bagpipe *n.* gaita *f.*

FINE ARTS

balance *n.* equilibrio *m.*

balance *v.* equilibrar, balancear

ballad *n.* balada *f.*

ballet *n.* ballet *m.;* **b. barre** barra de ballet *f.*

band *n.* banda *f.,* orquesta de vientos *m.,* conjunto musical *m.,* grupo *m.*

bandora *n.* bandolina *f.*

banjo *n.* banjo *m.,* banyo *m.*

bar *n.* (music) compás *m.;* **b. line** barra *f.;* **double b. line** doble barra

baritone *n.* barítono *m.*

bass *n.* (instrument or vocal) bajo *m.;* **b. clef** clave de fa *f.;* **b. drum** tambor grave *m.,* bombo *m.,* tambora *f.;* **b. guitar** bajo eléctrico

bassoon *n.* fagot *m.,* fagote *m.*

beat *n.* pulso *m.,* tiempo *m.,* ritmo *m.*

bell *n.* campanilla *f.*

bit part *n.* papel secundario *m.*

black humor *n.* humor negro *m.*

black-out *n.* (theater) oscuro *m.*

blocking *n.* (theater) montaje *m.*

blues *n.* blues *m.*

bongo drums *n.pl.* bongós *m.*

bow *n.* (theater) agradecimiento *m.,* (ballet) reverencia *f.,* (for instrument) arco *m.*

bow *v.* agradecer, hacer una reverencia

brass instrument *n.* instrumento de viento-metal *m.*

break a leg! (theater idiom) ¡mucha mierda!

breath control *n.* control de la respiración *m.*

Broadway musical *n.* musical de Broadway *m.*

bugle *n.* clarín *m.*

C

call and response *n.* llamada y respuesta *f.*

canon *n.* (music) canon *m.*

cast *n.,* **casting** *n.* reparto *m.*

cast *v.* asignar un papel, dar un papel

castanets *n.pl.* castañuelas *f.*

catharsis *n.* catarsis *f.*

cellist *n.* violonchelista *m.f.*

cello *n.* violonchelo *m.*

center stage *adv.* al centro del escenario

character *n.* personaje *m.*

characterization *n.* caracterización *f.*

choir *n.* coro *m.*

chord *n.* acorde *m.;* **c. progression** progresión de acordes *f.*

choral *adj.* coral

choreograph *v.* montar una coreografía

choreographer *n.* coreógrafo, -fa *m.f.*

choreography *n.* coreografía *f.*

chorus *n.* (refrain) estribillo *m.,* coro *m.*

clap *v.* aplaudir

clarinet *n.* clarinete *m.*

clarinetist *n.* clarinetista *m.f.*

classical *adj.* clásico, -ca

climax *n.* clímax *m.*

coda *n.* coda *f.*

collapse *v.* (dance) colapsar

comedian *n.* comediante, -ta *m.f.*

comedy *n.* comedia *f.;* **c. routine** rutina de comedia *f.;* **c. sketch** sketch cómico *m.*

comic *adj. & n.* cómico, -ca *m.f.*

compose *v.* componer

composer *n.* compositor, -ra *m.f.*

composition n. composición *f.*

concept *n.* concepto *m.*

concert *n.* concierto *m.*

concerto *n.* concierto *m.*

conduct *v.* dirigir

conductor *n.* director (-ora) de orquesta *m.f.*

conflict *n.* conflicto *m.*

conga drum *n.* conga *f.*

consonance *n.* consonancia *f.*

contemporary music *n.* música contemporánea *f.*

contralto *n.* contralto *m.*

cornet *n.* corneta *f.*

costume *n.* vestuario *m.*

countermelody *n.* contramelodía *f.*

country music *n.* música country *f.*

cowbell *n.* cencerro *m.*

cue *n.* (theater) pie *m.*

cue *v.* dar el pie

curtain call *n.* llamado a escena *m.*

cymbal *n.* platillo *m.*, címbalo *m.*

D

dance *n.* danza *f*, baile *m.;* **ballroom d.** baile de salón; **d. combination** combinación *f.;* **d. step** paso de danza *m.;* **folk d.** baile folclórico; **modern d.** danza moderna

dance *v.* danzar, bailar

dancer *n.* bailarín, -na *m.f.*

design *n.* diseño *m.*

dialogue *n.* diálogo *m.*

diction *n.* dicción *f.*, locución *f.*

direction *n.* dirección *f.*

director *n.* director, -ora *m.f.*

discordant *adj.* discordante; **d. note** *n.* nota discordante *f.*

dissonance *n.* disonancia *f.*

downstage *adv.* hacia el frente del escenario

drama *n.* drama *m.;* **children's d.** teatro infantil, teatro de niños *m.*

dramatic *adj.* dramático, -ca; **d. art** *n.* arte dramático *m.*

dramatist *n.* dramaturgo, -ga *m.f.*

dramatization *n.* dramatización *f.*

dramatize *v.* enscenificar, dramatizar

dress rehearsal *n.* ensayo general *m.*

drum *n.* tambor *m.;* **d. set, d. kit** batería *f.*

drummer *n.* baterista *m.f.*

drumstick *n.* baqueta *f.*

dubbed *adj.* doblado, -da

duet *n.* dúo *m.*

dulcimer *n.* dulcémele *m.*, salterio *m.*

duple meter *n.* compás doble *m.*

duration *n.* duración *f.*

dynamics *n.* dinámica *f.*

E

echo *n.* eco *m.*

effects *n.pl.* efectos *m.*

eighth note *n.* corchea *f.*

electronic *adj.* electrónico, -ca; **e. instrument** *n.* instrumento electrónico *m.;* **e. sound** sonido electrónico *m.*

FINE ARTS

165

FINE ARTS

elevation *n.* altura *f.*

embellishment *n.* adorno *m.,* embellecimiento *m.*

emotion *n.* emoción *f.*

emotional *adj.* emocional; **e. response** *n.* respuesta emocional *f.*

empathy *n.* empatía *f.*

emphasis *n.* énfasis *m.*

English horn *n.* corno inglés *m.*

ensemble *n.* (music) conjunto *m.*

entertainer *n.* animador, -ora *m.f.;* artista *m.f.*

entrance *n.* (stage) entrada *f.*

enunciation *n.* enunciación *f.,* articulación *f.*

exit *n.* salida *f.*

exposition *n.* exposición *f.*

expression *n.* expresión *f.*

F

farce *n.* farsa *f.*

film *n.* película *f.,* cine *m.;* **horror f.** película de terror

flat *adj.* (music) bemol

flat *n.* (theater) bastidor *m.*

flexibility *n.* flexibilidad *f.*

float *v.* flotar

flute *n.* flauta *f.*

folk *adj.* folclórico, -ca; **f. dance** *n.* baile folclórico *m.,* danza folclórica *f.;* **f. song** canción folclórica *f.*

folktale *n.* cuento folclórico, cuento tradicional *m.*

follow *v.* (dance) seguir

force *n.* fuerza *f.*

foreshadow *v.* presagiar

form *n.* forma *f.*

four-four time *n.* compás de cuatro por cuatro *m.*

fourth wall *n.* cuarta pared *f.*

French horn *n.* corno francés *m.*

fret *n.* (guitar) traste *m.*

G

genre *n.* género *m.*

gesture *n.* gesto *m.*

glide *v.* deslizarse

gospel *n.* (music) gospel *m.*

guitar *n.* guitarra *f.;* **accoustic g.** guitarra acústica; **bass g.** bajo eléctrico *m.;* **classical g.** guitarra clásica; **electric g.** guitarra eléctrica

guitarist *n.* guitarrista *m.f.*

H

half note *n.* blanca *f.*

hand drum *n.* percusión de mano *f.*

harmonica *n.* armónica *f.*

harmony *n.* armonía *f.*

harp *n.* arpa *f.*

harpist *n.* arpista *m.f.*

harpsichord *n.* clavecín *m.*

heritage *n.* herencia *f.*

high-pitched *adj.* agudo, -da

horn *n.* trompa *f.,* cuerno *m.*

house *n.* (theater) auditorio *m.,* sala *f.*

hymn *n.* himno *m.*

I

improvise *v.* improvisar, repentizar

improvisation *n.* improvisación *f.*

in step *adv.* acompasadamente

inflection *n.* inflexión *f.*

instrument *n.* instrumento *m.;*
   acoustic i. instrumento acústico;
   brass i. instrumento de viento-
   metal; **electronic i.** instrumento
   electrónico; **i. family** familia de
   instrumentos *f.;* **keyboard i.** instrumento de teclas; **percussion i.**
   instrumento de percusión; **string
   i.** instrumento de cuerdas; **wind i.**
   instrumento de viento

instrumental score *n.* partitura
   instrumental *f.,* composición instrumental *f.,* pieza instrumental *f.*

instrumentation *n.* instrumentación *f.*

intermission *n.* intermedio *m.*

interpretation *n.* interpretación *f.*

interval *n.* (music) intervalo *m.*

intonation *n.* entonación *f.*

isolation *n.* (dance) aislamiento *m.*

J

jazz *n.* jazz *m.*

K

kazoo *n.* mirlitón *m.*

kettledrum *n.* timbal *m.*

key *n.* tono *m.,* tonalidad *f.;* **major k.**
   tono mayor; **minor k.** tono menor

keyboard *n.* teclado *m.;* **k. instrument** instrumento de teclas *m.*

keyboardist *n.* tecladista *m.f.*

kinesthetic awareness *n.* inteligencia kinestésica, inteligencia cine-
   stésica *f.*

L

landing *n.* (dance) caída *f.*

Latin dance *n.* danza latinoamericana *f.,* baile latino *m.*

lead *v.* (dance) guiar, conducir

leap *v.* saltar

ledger lines *n.pl.* líneas adicionales *f.*

level *n.* nivel *m.*

lighting *n.* iluminación *f.*

locomotion *n.* locomoción *f.*

locomotor *adj.* (dance) locomotor,
   -ora, -triz

lullaby *n.* canción de cuna *f.*

lyrical *adj.* lírico, -ca

lyrics *n.pl.* letra *f.,* letras *f.*

M

make up *v.* maquillar

makeup *n.* maquillaje *m.*

malapropism *n.* malapropismo *m.,*
   yerro *m.*

mallet *n.* (music) baqueta *f.*

mandolin *n.* mandolina *f.*

maracas *n.pl.* maracas *f.*

march *n.* (music) marcha *f.*

marimba *n.* marimba *f.*

marionette *n.* marioneta *f.*

mask *n.* máscara *f.*

mass media *n.pl.* medios de difusión, medios de comunicación *m.*

measure *n.* (music) compás *m.,* medida *f.*

melodrama *n.* melodrama *m.*

melody *n.* melodía *f.*

meter *n.* (music) compás *m.*

metronome *n.* metrónomo *m.*

mezzo-soprano *n.* (singer) mezzo-

FINE ARTS

167

FINE ARTS

soprano *f.,* (voice) mezzosoprano *m.*

middle C *n.* media C *f.*

mime *n.* mímica *f.,* mimo *m.*

mimic *v.* imitar

mirroring *adj.* reflejando, -da

modern dance *n.* danza moderna *f.*

monologue *n.* monólogo *m.*

monotone *n.* monótono *m.,* monotonía *f.*

mood *n.* atmósfera *f.,* ambiente *m.*

motif *n.* motivo *m.,* tema *f.*

motivation *n.* motivación *f.*

movement *n.* movimiento *m.*

movie theater *n.* sala de cine *f.*

music *n.* música *f.;* **m. in four parts** música en cuatro partes

musical *adj. & n.* músical *m.;* **m. arrangement** *n.* arreglo musical *m.;* **m. comedy** comedia musical *f.;* **m. instrument** instrumento musical *m.;* **m. notes** notas musicales *f.pl.;* **m. phrase** frase musical *f.;* **m. piece** pieza musical *f.;* **m. scale** escala musical *f.;* **m. score** partitura *f.;* **m. staff** pentagrama *m.;* **m. theater** teatro musical *m.*

musician *n.* músico, -ca *m.f.*

mute *n.* (music) sordina *f.*

myth *n.* mito *m.*

mythology *n.* mitología *f.*

N

narrative *n.* narrativa *f.*

nonlocomotor *adj.* (dance) no locomotor (-ora, -triz)

notation *n.* anotación *f.*

note *n.* nota *f.;* **dotted n.** nota punteada; **eighth n.** corchea *f.;* **half n.** blanca *f.;* **quarter n.** negra *f.;* **sixteenth n.** semicorchea *f.;* **whole n.** redonda *f.*

O

oboe *n.* oboe *m.*

octave *n.* octava *f.*

offstage *adv.* fuera de escena, tras bambalinas, entre bastidores

onstage *adv.* sobre el escenario

opening night *n.* noche de apertura, noche de estreno *f.,* estreno *m.*

opera *n.* ópera *f.*

operatic *adj.* operístico, -ca

oral tradition *n.* tradición oral *f.*

orchestra *n.* orquesta *f.;* **chamber o.** orquesta de cámara; **philharmonic o.** orquesta filarmónica; **string o.** orquesta de cuerdas

organ *n.* órgano *m.;* **barrel o.** organillo *m.*

out of tune *adj.* desafinado, -da

P

pan pipes *n.pl.* zampoña *f.*

pantomime *n.* pantomima *f.*

participation theater *n.* teatro participativo *m.*

partner *n.* pareja *f.*

patriotic song *n.* canción patriótica *f.*

pentatonic *adj.* pentatónico, -ca; **p. scale** *n.* escala pentatónica *f.*

percussion *n.* percusión *f.;* **p. instrument** *n.* instrumento de percusión *m.*

percussive *adj.* percusivo, -va

perform *v.* (music) ejecutar, (theater, dance) interpretar

performance *n.* actuación *f.*, función *f.*

performer *n.* artista *m.f.*, (music) intérprete *m.*

performing arts *n.pl.* artes de la interpretación, artes interpretativas *f.*

phrase *n.* (music) frase *f.*

pianist *n.* pianista *m.f.*

piano *n.* piano *m.*

piece *n.* (music, theater) pieza *f.*

pitch *n.* tono *m.*

play *n.* obra *f.*, pieza *f.;* **morality p.** teatro moralista *f.;* **one-act p.** obra en un acto *f.*

play by ear *v.* tocar de oído

playwright *n.* autor, -ra *m.f.;* dramaturgo, -ga *m.f.*

plot *n.* argumento *m.*

polyphonic *adj.* polifónico, -ca

pop *n.* (music) música pop *m.*

posture *n.* postura *f.*

practice *n.* práctica *f.*, ensayo *m.*

practice *v.* practicar, ensayar

pratfall *n.* caída cómica *f.*

premiere *n.* estreno *m.*

presentation *n.* presentación *f.*

preview *n.* preestreno *m.*

producer *n.* productor *m.f.*

production *n.* producción *f.*

progression *n.* progresión *f.;* **chord p.** progresión de acordes

prologue *n.* prólogo *m.*

prop *n.* (theater) utilería *f.*

proscenium stage *n.* proscenio *m.*

protagonist *n.* protagonista *m.f.*

puppet *n.* títere *m.*, marioneta *f.;* **hand p.** títere de mano

puppeteer *n.* titiritero, -ra *m.f.*

puppetry *n.* arte de titiritero *m.*

Q

quarter note *n.* negra *f.*

quartet *n.* cuarteto *m.*

quintet *n.* quinteto *m.*

R

range *n.* registro *m.*

rattle *n.* cascabel *m.*

Readers Theater *n.* Teatro Leído *m.*

recorder *n.* (music) flauta dulce *f.;* (technology) grabadora *f.;* **digital r.** grabadora digital

recording *n.* grabación *f.;* **tape r.** grabación en cinta

refrain *n.* estribillo *m.*

reggae *n.* música reggae *f.*

register *n.* registro *m.*

rehearsal *n.* ensayo *m.*

rehearse *v.* ensayar

repeat sign *n.* (music) repetición *f.*

repertoire *n.* repertorio *m.*

rest *n.* (music) silencio *m.;* **half-note r.** silencio de blanca; **whole-note r.** silencio de redonda

rhythm *n.* ritmo *m.*

rock music *n.* rock *m.*

role *n.* papel *m.*

role-play *n.* representación *f.*

role-play *v.* representar, dramatizar

FINE ARTS

FINE ARTS

romantic *adj.* romántico, -ca
rondo *n.* rondó *m.*
round *n.* (music) canon *m.*
run-through *n.* (theater) corrida *f.*
run through *v.* correr a través de

S

satirical *adj.* satírico, -ca
satire *n.* sátira *f.*
saxophone *n.* saxofón *m.*, saxófono *m.*
scale *n.* escala *f.*
scat *n.* (music) improvisación vocal *f.*
scenario *n.* escenario *m.*, guión *m.*, argumento *m.*
scene *n.* escena *f.*
scenery *n.* (theater) escenografía *f.*
score *n.* (music) partitura *f.*
script *n.* guión *m.*, libreto *m.*
sea chantey *n.* canción marinera *f.*
sequence *n.* secuencia *f.*
set *n.* (theater) escenografía *f.;* **s. design** diseño de escenografía, diseño escenográfico *m.*
set *v.* (to music) incorporar a la música, poner al ritmo de la música
setting *n.* localidad *f.*, espacio teatral *m.*
sharp *adj.* (music) sostenido
sight-read *v.* repentizar
sitar *n.* cítara *f.*
sixteenth note *n.* semicorchea *f.*
skip *v.* saltar, brincar
slapstick *n.* bufonadas *f.pl.*, payasadas *f.pl.*

slide *v.* deslizarse
slur *n.* (musical notation) ligadura *f.*
smooth *adj.* suave
snare drum *n.* tarola *f.*
social dance *n.* danza social *f.*
soliloquy *n.* soliloquio *m.*
solo *n.* solo *m.*
soloist *n.* solista *m.f.*
sonata *n.* sonata *f.*
song *n.* canción *f.*
soprano *n.* soprano *m.*
soul music *n.* soul *m.*
sound effects *n.pl.* efectos de sonido *m.*
soundtrack *n.* banda sonora *f.*
space *n.* espacio *m.*
spatial *adj.* espacial
spin *v.* girar
spinning *n.* giro *m.*
spiritual *adj.* espiritual
square dance *n.* square dance *f.*
staff *n.* (music) pentagrama *m.*
stage *n.* escenario *m.;* **center s.** centro del escenario *m.;* **s. fright** miedo escénico *m.;* **s. hand** tramoyista *m.;* **s. left** lado izquierdo del escenario *m;* **s. manager** jefe de piso *m.;* **s. right** lado derecho del escenario
stage *v.* escenificar, representar, poner en escena
stand-up routine *n.* rutina cómica *f.*
stem *n.* (musical notation) plica *f.*
step *n.* (dance) paso *m.*, (music) intervalo *m.*
story *n.* cuento *m.*, historia *f.*
storyline *n.* trama *f.*, argumento *m.*

storyteller *n.* cuentacuentos *m.f.,* narrador (-ora) de cuentos *m.f.*

stretch *v.* estirarse

strings *n.pl.* cuerdas *f.;* **s. instrument** instrumento de cuerdas *ms.*

structure *n.* estructura *f.*

strum *v.* (strings) rasguear

style *n.* estilo *m.*

subplot *n.* subargumento *m.*

subtitles *n.pl.* (cinema) subtítulos *m.*

suite *n.* (music) suite *f.*

superhero *n.* superhéroe *m.,* superheroína *f.*

suspense *n.* suspenso *m.*

sustain *v.* sostener

sway *v.* tambalear, columpiar

swing *n.* (music) swing *m.*

symbol *n.* símbolo *m.*

symphony *n.* sinfonía *f.*

syncopated *adj.* sincopado, -da

syncopation *n.* síncope *m.*

synthesizer *n.* sintetizador *m.*

T

tambourine *n.* pandereta *f.*

tap dance *n.* tap *m.*

technique *n.* técnica *f.*

tempo *n.* tiempo *m.*

tenor *n.* tenor *m.*

tension *n.* tensión *f.*

theater *n.* teatro *m.;* **children's t.** teatro infantil, teatro de niños; **musical t.** teatro musical; **Readers T.** Teatro Leído

theater-in-the-round *n.* teatro circular *m.*

theme *n.* tema *f.*

thespian *n.* actor *m.,* actriz *f.*

three-quarter time *n.* compás de tres cuartos *m.*

ticket *n.* boleto *m.;* **t. office** boletería *f.,* taquilla *f.*

tie *n.* (musical notation) ligadura *f.*

timbre *n.* timbre *m.*

timing *n.* (dance) sincronización *f.*

timpani *n.* tímpano *m.*

tonality *n.* tonalidad *f.*

tone *n.* tono *m.*

traditional art forms *n.pl.* formas tradicionales de arte *f.*

tragedy *n.* tragedia *f.*

transition *n.* transición *f.*

treble clef *n.* clave de sol *f.*

triangle *n.* triángulo *m.*

trickster *n.* pillo *m.,* pícaro *m.*

trio *n.* trío *m.*

triple meter *n.* compás triple *m.*

triplet *n.* (music) tresillo *m.*

trombone *n.* trombón *m.*

trumpet *n.* trompeta *f.*

tuba *n.* tuba *f.*

tune *n.* melodía *f.*

tune *v.* afinar

two-four time *n.* compás de dos cuartos *m.*

typecasting *n.* encasillamiento actoral *m.*

U

ukulele *n.* ukelele *m.*

understudy *n.* suplente *m.f.*

unison *n.* unísono *m.*

universal concept *n.* concepto universal *m.*

FINE ARTS

FINE ARTS

upstage *adv.* hacia el fondo del escenario

upstage *v.* eclipsar, deslucir

V

variation *n.* (music) variación *f.*

vaudeville *n.* (theater) vodevil *m.*, teatro de carpa *m.*, (music) canción satírica de cabaret *f.*

verse *n.* verso *m.*

villain *n.* villano *m.*

viola *n.* viola *f.*

violin *n.* violín *m.*

violinist *n.* violinista *m.f.*

vocal *adj.* vocal; **v. pitch** *n.* tono vocal *m.;* **v. score** partitura vocal *f.*

voice *n.* voz *f.*

volume *n.* volumen *m.*

W

waltz *n.* vals *m.*

warm up *n.* calentamiento *m.*

weight shift *n.* cambio del peso *m.*

whistle *n.* silbato *m.*, pito *m.*

whistle *v.* silbar, pitar, chiflar

whole note *n.* redonda *f.*

wind instrument *n.* instrumento de viento *m.*

wings *n.pl.* (theater) alas *f.*

woodwind *n.* instrumento de viento-madera *m.*

work of art *n.* obra de arte *f.*

work song *n.* canción de trabajo *f.*

writer *n.* escritor, -ora *m.f.*

X

xylophone *n.* xilófono *m.*

Visual Arts

A

abstract *adj.* abstracto, -ta

aerial perspective *n.* perspectiva aérea *f.*

animation *n.* animación *f.*

architecture *n.* arquitectura *f.*

art *n.* arte *m.f.;* **a. material** material de arte *m.*

artifact *n.* artefacto *m.*, objeto de arte *m.*

artist *n.* artista *m.f.*

arts and crafts *n.* artesanía *f.*

artwork *n.* obra de arte *f.*

asymmetrical *adj.* asimétrico, -ca

asymmetry *n.* asimetría *f.*

B

background *n.* fondo *m.*

balance *n.* equilibrio *m.*

balance *v.* equilibrar

balanced *adj.* equilibrado, -da

bead *n.* cuenta *f.*, chaquira *f.*, abalorio *m.*

blend *n.* mezcla *f.*, combinación *f.*

blend *v.* mezclar, combinar

brush *n.* pincel *m.*

C

caligrapher *n.* calígrafo, -fa *m.f.*

caligraphy *n.* caligrafía *f.*

camera *n.* cámara *f.*

canvas *n.* lienzo *m.*

cardboard *n.* cartón *m.*

caricature *n.* caricatura *f.*

cartoon *n.* dibujos animados *m.pl.*

cartoonist *n.* dibujante *m.*

cast *v.* fundir

casting *n.* (process) fundición *f.*, (object) pieza fundida *f.*

ceramic *n.* cerámica *f.*

chalk *n.* tiza *f.*, gis *m.*

chalk *v.* escribir con tiza, marcar con gis

chalky *adj.* yesoso, -sa

charcoal *n.* (for drawing) carboncillo *m.*

cityscape *n.* paisaje urbano *m.*

clay *n.* arcilla *f.*, barro *m.*

coil *n.* rollo *m.*

coil *v.* enrollar

collage *n.* collage *m.*

color *n.* color *m.;* **c. scheme** esquema del color *f.;* **c. variation** variación del color *f.;* **c. wheel** rueda de colores *f.*

color *v.* colorear

colors *n.pl.* colores *m.;* **complementary c.** colores complementarios; **cool c.** colores frescos; **intermediate c.** colores intermedios; **neutral c.** colores neutrales; **pastel c.** colores pasteles; **primary c.** colores primarios; **secondary c.** colores secundarios; **soft c.** colores suaves; **tertiary c.** colores terciarios; **warm c.** colores cálidos

comic strip *n.,* **comics** *n.pl.* historietas *f.*, tebeos *m.*, tiras cómicas *f.*

compose *v.* componer

composition *n.* composición *f.*

construction *n.* construcción *f.;* **c. paper** papel de construcción *m.*, cartoncillo para manualidades *m.*

contour *n.* contorno *m.;* **c. drawing** dibujo de contorno *m.;* **c. line** línea de contorno *f.*

contrast *n.* contraste *m.*

copper *n.* (metal) cobre *m.*

craft *n.* arte manual *m.*

crayon *n.* crayón *m.*

crystal *n.* cristal *m.*

D

decal *n.* calcamonía *f.*

depth *n.* profundidad *f.*

design *n.* diseño *m.*

dimension *n.* dimensión *f.*

diminishing size *n.* reducción dimensional *f.*

diorama *n.* diorama *m.*

directionality *n.* direccionalidad *f.*

display *n.* exhibición *f.*, exposición *f.*

display *v.* exhibir, exponer

draw *v.* dibujar

drawing *n.* dibujo *m.;* **d. paper** papel de dibujo *m.*

dry-brush *n.* técnica de brocha seca *f.*

dye *n.* tinta *f.*

dye *v.* entintar, teñir

dyed *adj.* entintado, -da; tinto, -ta

dyeing *n.* tinta *f.*, tinte *m.*

FINE ARTS

FINE ARTS

E

easel *n.* caballete *m.*

enamel *n.* esmalte *m.*

enamel *v.* esmaltar

engrave *v.* grabar

engraving *n.* grabado *m.*

eraser *n.* borrador *m.*

etch *v.* grabar al agua fuerte

etching *n.* (art) aguafuerte *m.*, (process) grabado *m.*

F

fiber *n.* fibra *f.*

fire *v.* (ceramics) cocer

flexible *adj.* flexible

fold *n.* doblez *m.*, pliegue *m.*

fold *v.* doblar, plegar

folded *adj.* doblado, -da; plegado, -da

folk art *n.* arte folclórico *m.*

foreground *n.* primer plano *m.*

form *n.* forma *f.*

format *n.* formato *m.*

fresco *n.* fresco *m.*

fringe *n.* franja *f.*

G

geometric *adj.* geométrico, -ca; **g. design** *n.* diseño geométrico *m.;* **g. shape** forma geométrica *f.*

glass *n.* vidrio *m.,* cristal *m.*

glaze *n.* (ceramics) vidriado *m.*

glaze *v.* vidriar

glazed *adj.* vidriado, -da

glue *n.* goma de pegar *f.*

glue *v.* pegar

graphic *adj.* gráfico, -ca; **g. arts** *n.pl.* artes gráficas *f.;* **g. design** diseño gráfico *m.*

H

highlight *n.* toque de luz *m.*

highlight *v.* resaltar, iluminar

horizon *n.* horizonte *m.*

horizontal *adj.* horizontal

hue *n.* matiz *m.,* tonalidad *f.*

I

illusion *n.* ilusión *f.*

ink *n.* tinta *f.*

intensity *n.* intensidad *f.*

K

kiln *n.* (ceramics) horno *m.*

L

landscape *n.* paisaje *m.*

loom *n.* telar *m.*

M

Manila paper *n.* papel de Manila *m.*

mask *n.* máscara *f.*

masking tape *n.* cinta adhesiva protectora *f.*

medium *adj.* medio, -dia

metal *n.* metal *m.*

miniature *adj.* en miniatura

miniature *n.* miniatura *f.*

mix *v.* mezclar

monochromatic *adj.* monocromático, -ca

mosaic *n.* mosaico *m.*

mural *n.* mural *m.,* pintura mural *m.*

muralist *n.* muralista *m.f.*

museum *n.* museo *m.*

N

negative space *n.* espacio negativo *m.*

nonrepresentational *adj.* no representativo (-va)

O

oil paint *n.* óleo *m.*, pintura al óleo *f.*

optical *adj.* óptico, -ca; o. illusion *n.* ilusión óptica *f.*

ordered pattern *n.* patrón ordenado *m.*

overlap *v.* superponer, traslapar

P

paint *n.* pintura *f.*

paint *v.* pintar

paint box *n.* caja de pinturas *f.*

paintbrush *n.* pincel *m.*, brocha *f.*

painter *n.* pintor, -ra *m.f.*

painting *n.* pintura *f.*, cuadro *m.*

palette *n.* paleta *f.*

papier mâché *n.* papel maché *m.*

parallel *adj.* paralelo, -la

pastels *n.pl.* pasteles *m.*, tonos pasteles *m.*, pinturas al pastel *f.*

pattern *n.* patrón *m.*

perspective *n.* perspectiva *f.*

photograph *n.*, photography *n.* foto *f.*, fotografía *f.*

photograph *v.* fotografiar

photographer *n.* fotógrafo, -fa *m.f.*

photographic *adj.* fotográfico, -ca

picture *n.* imagen *f.*, dibujo *m.*

placement *n.* ubicación *f.*

plaster *n.* yeso *m.*

plasterer *n.* yesero, -ra *m.f.*

plastic *n.* plástico *m.*

portfolio *n.* portafolio *m.*

portrait *n.* retrato *m.*

portraitist *n.* retratista *m.f.*

positive space *n.* espacio positivo *m.*

poster *n.* afiche *m.*, cartel *m.*

pottery *n.* alfarería *f.*

print *n.* impresión fotográfica *f.*, copia *f.*

print *v.* imprimir

printing *n.* impresión *f.*

proportion *n.* proporción *f.*

public art *n.* arte público *m.*

Q

quilt *n.* colcha *f.*

quilt *v.* acolchar, hacer una colcha

R

random pattern *n.* patrón aleatorio *m.*

realism *n.* realismo *m.*

realistic *adj.* realista

relief sculpture *n.* escultura a relieve *f.*

representation *n.* representación *f.*

representational *adj.* representativo, -va

rubbing *n.* calco *m.*

S

scissors *n.pl.* tijeras *f.*

sculpt *v.* esculpir

sculptor *n.* escultor, -ra *m.f.*

sculpture *n.* escultura *f.*

FINE ARTS

175

FINE ARTS

seascape *n.* paisaje marino *m.*

self-portrait *n.* autoretrato *m.*

shade of color *n.* tonalidad de color *f.,* matiz de color *m.*

shading *n.* sombreado *m.*

shadow *n.* sombra *f.;* **s. edge** contorno de sombra *m.,* borde de sombra *m.*

shape *n.* forma *f.*

silk-screen *n.* serigrafía *f.*

size *n.* tamaño *m.*

sketch *n.* bosquejo *m.,* esbozo *m.;* **thumbnail s.** esbozo en miniatura *m.*

sketchbook *n.* cuaderno de bosquejos *m.,* bloc de bosquejos *m.*

slab *n.* losa *f.*

smock *n.* bata *f.,* guardapolvo *m.,* blusón *m.*

special effects *n.pl.* efectos especiales *m.*

spectrum *n.* gama *f.*

still life *n.* naturaleza muerta *f.*

stone *n.* piedra *f.*

stucco *n.* estuco *m.*

style *n.* estilo *m.*

stylized *adj.* estilizado, -da

symbol *n.* símbolo *m.*

symbolize *v.* simbolizar

symmetrical *adj.* simétrico, -ca

symmetry *n.* simetría *f.*

T

tempera paint *n.* pintura al temple *f.*

terra cotta *n.* terracota *f.*

texture *n.* textura *f.*

tie-dye *n.* teñido anudado *m.*

tin *n.* (metal) hojalata *f.*

tint *n.* tinte *m.,* matiz de color *m.*

tint *v.* teñir, matizar

tripod *n.* trípode *m.*

typography *n.* tipografía *f.*

V

vertical *adj.* vertical

viewer *n.* visor fotográfico *m.*

W

wash *n.* (painting) mano *f.,* capa *f.*

watercolor *n.* acuarela *f.*

wax *n.* parafina *f.,* cera *f.;* **w. paper** papel encerado *m.*

weave *v.* tejer

weaver *n.* tejedor, -ora *m.f.*

wire *n.* cable *m.,* alambre *m.*

wood *n.* madera *f.*

COLORS

aquamarine *n.* aguamarina *f.*

black *adj.* negro, -gra

black *n.* negro *m.*

blue *adj. & n.* azul *m.;* **light b.** azul claro; **navy b.** azul marino

brown *adj. & n.* marrón *m.;* **dark b.** marrón oscuro; **light b.** marrón claro

burgundy *n.* color vino tinto, color borgoña *m.*

copper *adj.* cobrizo, -za

copper *n.* color cobrizo *m.*

• •

cyan *adj. & n.* cián *m.*

emerald *adj. & n.* verde esmeralda *m.*

flesh color *n.* color carne *m.*

golden *adj.* dorado, -da

gray *adj. & n.* gris *m.*

green *adj. & n.* verde *m.*

indigo *adj. & n.* añil *m.*

lavender *adj. & n.* lavanda *f.*

magenta *adj. & n.* magenta *f.*

mahogany *n.* caoba *f.*

maroon *adj. & n.* granate *m.*

orange *adj.* anaranjado, -da

orange *n.* anaranjado *m.*

pink *adj.* rosado, -da; rosa

pink *n.* rosa *m.*

plum *adj. & n.* ciruela *f.*

purple *adj.* morado, -da; púrpura

purple *n.* morado *m.,* púrpura *m.*

red *adj.* rojo, -ja; colorado, -da

red *n.* rojo *m.,* colorado *m.*

rose *adj. & n.* rosa *m.*

salmon *adj. & n.* salmón *m.*

scarlet *adj. & n.* escarlata *m.*

sepia *adj. & n.* sepia *m.*

silver *adj.* plateado

silver *n.* plata *f.*

teal *adj. & n.* verde azulado *m.*

tan *adj. & n.* marrón claro *m.*

turquoise *adj. & n.* turquesa *m.*

violet *adj. & n.* violeta *m.*

white *adj.* blanco, -ca

white *n.* blanco *m.*

yellow *adj.* amarillo, -lla

yellow *n.* amarillo *m.*

SHAPES

circle *n.* círculo *m.*

circular *adj.* circular

cone *n.* cono *m.*

conical *adj.* cónico, -ca

cube *n.* cubo *m.*

cubic *adj.* cúbico, -ca

curved *adj.* curvo, -va; arqueado, -da

cylinder *n.* cilindro *m.*

cylindrical *adj.* cilíndrico, -ca

diagonal *adj. & n.* diagonal *f.*

dot *n.* punto *m.;* **small d.** puntillo *m.*

dotted *adj.* punteado, -da

hexagon *n.* hexágono *m.*

hexagonal *adj.* hexagonal

intersecting *adj.* intersecado, -da; cruzado, -da

line *n.* línea *f.;* **contour l.** línea de contorno; **converging l.** *pl.* líneas convergentes; **intersecting l.** *pl.* líneas intersecadas; **straight l.** línea recta

linear *adj.* lineal

octagon *n.* octágono *m.,* octógono *m.*

octagonal *adj.* octagonal

one-dimensional *adj.* unidimensional

pentagon *n.* pentágono *m.*

pentagonal *adj.* pentagonal

pyramid *n.* pirámide *f.*

piramidal *adj.* piramidal

rectangle *n.* rectángulo *m.*

rectangular adj. rectangular

sphere *n.* esfera *f.*

spherical *adj.* esférico, -ca
spiral *n.* espiral *f.*
square *adj.* cuadrado, -da
square *n.* cuadrado *m.,* cuadro *m.*
straight *adj.* recto, -ta
three-dimensional *adj.* tridimensional

two-dimensional *adj.* bidimensional
triangle *n.* triángulo *m.*
triangular *adj.* triangular
wavy *adj.* ondeado, -da
zigzag *n.* zigzag *m.*
zigzag *v.* zigzaguear

FINE ARTS

TECHNOLOGY

A

access *n.* acceso

access *v.* acceder

add *v.* agregar; **a. printer** agregar impresora; **a. program** agregar programa

address *n.* (email) dirección de correo *f.*, (Web) dirección de Web, dirección de página Web

address book *n.* libreta de direcciones *f.*

align *v.* alinear

antivirus *adj. & n.* antivirus *m.*

application *n.* aplicación *f.*; **a. package** paquete de programas *m.*

ASCII *n.* ASCII *m.*

at sign (@) *n.* arroba *f.*

attach *v.* (to email) adjuntar

attached file *n.* archivo adjunto *m.*

attachment *n.* mensaje adjunto, mensaje anexo *m.*

authentication *n.* autenticación *f.*

B

back button *n.* botón para regresar *m.*

back up *v.* hacer una copia de seguridad

background *n.* fondo *m.*

backslash (\) *n.* barra invertida, barra inversa *f.*, contrabarra *f.*

backup *n.* apoyo *m.*, copia de seguridad *f.*, respaldo *m.;* **b. disk** disco de respaldo, disco de seguridad *m.;* **remote b.** copia de seguridad remota *f.*

bandwidth *n.* ancho de banda *m.*, amplitud de banda *f.*

bar *n.* barra *f.*

battery *n.* batería *f.*, pila *f.*

blog *n.* blog *m.*

bold, boldface *n.* (type) negrita *f.*

bookmark *n.* favorito *m.*, marcador *m.*, marcapáginas *m.*

boot disk *n.* disco de inicio *m.*

bounce back *v.* (email) rebotar

box *n.* (on Web forms) casilla *f.*

broadband *n.* banda ancha *f.*

browser *n.* navegador *m.*, explorador de Web *m.*

bug *n.* fallo *m.*, error lógico *m.*, defecto *m.*

built-in *adj.* incorporado, -da

burner *n.* quemador *m.*

TECHNOLOGY

button *n.* botón *m.*

byte *n.* byte *m.*

C

cable *n.* cable *m.*

camcorder *n.* videocámara *f.*

card *n.* tarjeta *f.*

cartridge *n.* cartucho *m.*

CD-ROM *n.* CD-ROM *m.*

cell phone *n.* teléfono celular, teléfono móvil *m.*

chat *n.* charla *f.*, chateo *m.;* **c. room** sala de charla, sala de discusión *f.*

chat *v.* chatear, charlar

check email *v.* revisar el correo electrónico; **c. the box** *v.* marcar la casilla, seleccionar la casilla

click *n.* clic *m.*

click *v.* hacer clic, presionar, pulsar

clipboard *n.* portapapeles *m.*

cloud computing *n.* computación en la nube *f.*

compatible *adj.* compatible

compression *n.* compresión *f.*

computer *n.* computadora *f.*, computador *m.*, ordenador *m.;* **c. chip** chip de computadora *m.*, microprocesador *m.;* **laptop c.** ordenador portátil, computadora portátil

computer-based learning *n.* aprendizaje por computadora *m.*

connect *v.* conectar

connection *n.* conexión *f.*

control panel *n.* tablero de mando *m.*, panel de control *m.*

convert *v.* convertir

cookies *n.pl.* cookies *f.*

copy *v.* copiar

corrupted *adj.* dañado, -da

C.P.U. *n.* U.C.P. *m.*

crash *n.* congelamiento *m.*, bloqueo *m.*

crash *v.* congelar, bloquear

cursor *n.* cursor *m.*

cut and paste *v.* cortar y pegar

cyberspace *n.* ciberespacio *m.*

D

data *n.pl.* datos *m.*

database *n.* base de datos *f.*

dead *adj.* (link) fuera de servicio

default *n.* opción por defecto, opción predeterminada *f.*

delete *v.* borrar

deleted items *n.pl.* elementos eliminados *m.*

desktop *n.* (computer) escritorio *m.*, pantalla *f.*

diagnostic program *n.* programa de diagnóstico *m.*

digital *adj.* digital; **d. signature** *n.* firma digital *f.*

directory *n.* directorio *m.*

disk *n.* disco *m.*, disquete *m.;* **d. drive** unidad de disco *f.*, lector de disco *m.*, disquetera *f.;* **floppy d.** disquete flexible *m.;* **system d.** disco de sistema *m.*

document *n.* documento *m.*

domain *n.* dominio *m.*

dot com *n.* punto com *m.*

download *n.* descarga *f.*

download *v.* bajar, descargar

drag *v.* arrastrar; **d. and drop** arrastrar y pegar

driver *n.* (software) controlador de dispositivo *m.*

drop-down list *n.* menú desplegable, menú contextual *m.*

D.V.D. *n.* D.V.D. *m.*

E

email *n.* correo electrónico *m.*, email *m.*; **e. address** dirección de correo electrónico *f.*; **e. recipient** destinatario *m.*; **encrypted e.** correo codificado, correo cifrado; **junk e.** correo basura, spam *m.*

email *v.* enviar un correo electrónico; **check e.** revisar el correo electrónico

encrypt *v.* codificar, cifrar

encrypted *adj.* codificado, -da; cifrado, -da

encryption *n.* codificación *f.*, encriptación *f.*

erase *v.* borrar

error *n.* error *m.*

export *v.* exportar

extension *n.* extensión *f.*

external *adj.* externo, -na; **e. memory** *n.* memoria externa *f.*

F

F.A.Q. (Frequently Asked Questions) *n.pl.* preguntas frecuentes *f.*

fax, facsimile *n.* fax *m.*, facsímil *m.*; **f. machine** *n.* equipo de fax *m.*, aparato de facsímil *m.*

fax *v.* enviar un fax

file *n.* fichero *m.*, archivo, archivo de datos *m.*; **attached f.** archivo adjunto; **compressed f.** archivo compromido; **f. conversion** conversión de archivos *f.*; **f. deletion** borrado de archivos *m.*, eliminación de archivos *f.*; **f. server** servidor de archivos *m.*; **f. transfer** transferencia de ficheros, tranferencia de archivos *f.*

filename *n.* nombre del archivo *m.*

firewall *n.* cortafuegos *m.*, antiintrusos *m.*, muro de fuegos *m.*

flash drive *n.* dispositivo portátil de memoria, dispositivo de memoria flash *m.*, memoria extraible, memoria removible *f.*

folder *n.* carpeta *f.*; **f. name** nombre de la carpeta *m.*

font *n.* tipo de letra *m.*, fuente *f.*

form *n.* formulario *m.*

format *n.* formato *m.*

format *v.* formatear, dar formato a

forward button *n.* botón para avanzar *m.*

frames *n.pl.* (Web pages) marcos *m.*

G

gigahertz *n.* gigahertz *m.*

go back *v.* regresar

graphics *n.pl.* gráficos *m.*

H

hacker *n.* hacker *m.f.*, pirata informático (-ca) *m.f.*

hacking *n.* piratería informática *f.*

hard disk *n.*, **hard drive** *n.* disco duro *m.*

TECHNOLOGY

TECHNOLOGY

hardware *n.* dispositivo físico *m.*

hertz *n.* hertz *m.*

hidden *adj.* oculto, -ta

high *adj.* alta; **h. resolution** *n.* alta resolución *f.*, alta definición *f.*; **h. speed** alta velocidad *f.*

home page *n.* página raíz, página inicial, página principal *f.*

hyperlink *n.* hipervínculo *m.*, hiperenlace *m.*

I

icon *n.* ícono, icono *m.*

image *n.* imagen *f.*

import *v.* importar

inbox *n.* bandeja de entrada *f.*

ink *n.* tinta *f.*

insert *v.* insertar

install *v.* instalar

instant messaging (I.M.) *n.* mensajería instantánea *f.*

interface *n.* interfaz *f.*

internal *adj.* interno, -na

Internet *n.* Internet *m.*, Red *f.*; **I. access** acceso a Internet *m.*; **I. cafe** cibercafé *m.*; **I. service provider** I.S.P. *m.*, proveedor de servicios Internet *m.*

italic *adj. & f.* cursiva

italics *n.pl.* itálicas *f.*, cursivas *f.*, bastardillas *f.*

K

key *n.* tecla *f.*

keyboard *n.* teclado *m.*

keyword *n.* palabra clave *f.*

kilobyte *n.* kilobyte *m.*

L

LAN (local area network) *n.* LAN *f.*, red de área local *f.*

laptop computer *n.* ordenador portátil *m.*, computadora portátil *f.*

L.C.D. *n.* L.C.D. *f.*

link *n.* enlace *m.*, vínculo *m.*

listserv *n.* servidor de listas *m.*, listserv *m.*

lurker *n.* participante silencioso (-sa) *m.f.*, lurker *m.f.*

lurking *n.* acecho *m.*, lurking *m.*

M

mailbox *n.* buzón de correo *m.*

malware *n.* aplicación maligna *f.*, programa maligno *m.*

maximize *v.* maximizar

megabyte *n.* megabyte *m.*

megahertz *n.* megahertz *m.*

memory *n.* memoria *f.*; **external m.** memoria externa; **m. stick** memoria extraíble *f.*, dispositivo portátil de memoria *m.*; **virtual m.** memoria virtual

menu *n.* menú *m.*; **m. bar** barra de menú *f.*; **pop-up m.** menú desplegable, menú contextual

message *n.* mensaje *m.*; **instant m.** mensaje instantáneo; **m. heading** encabezado de mensaje *m.*; **outgoing m.** mensaje saliente; **text m.** mensaje de texto

minimize *v.* minimizar

modem *n.* módem *m.*

monitor *n.* monitor *m.*; **color m.** monitor de color

monochrome *adj.* monocromático, -ca; monocromo, -ma

motherboard *n.* tarjeta madre *f.*

mouse *n.* ratón *m.;* **m. button** botón del ratón *m.;* **m. pad** almohadilla *f.,* alfombrilla *f.*

multimedia *adj. & n.* multimedia *f.*

multitasking *n.* multitarea *f.*

N

navigate *v.* navegar

netiquette *n.* etiqueta de la Red, etiqueta de Internet *f.*

network *n.* red *f.*

networking *n.* conexión de redes *f.*

newsgroup *n.* grupo de noticias *m.*

O

offline *adj.* desconectado, -da

online *adj.* en línea; conectado, -da

operating system *n.* sistema operativo *m.*

outbox *n.* bandeja de salida *f.*

P

padlock *n.* (on Web sites) ícono de cerradura *m.*

page *n.* página *f.;* **home p.** página inicial, página raíz, página principal; **main p.** página principal; **p. layout** diseño de página *m.;* **Web p.** página Web

paper *n.* papel *m.;* **p. feed** alimentación de papel *f.;* **p. jam** atasco en el suministro de papel *m.*

password *n.* contraseña *f.,* clave *f.*

paste *v.* pegar

peripheral device *n.* dispositivo periférico *m.*

photocopier *n.* fotocopiadora *f.*

photocopy *n.* fotocopia *f.*

photocopy *v.* fotocopiar

piracy *n.* piratería *f.*

plug and play *n. & v.* enchufar y usar *m.*

pop-up window *n.* ventana emergente *f.;* **p. menu** menú desplegable, menú contextual *m.*

port *n.* puerto *m.;* **serial p.** puerto de serie; **U.S.B. p.** puerto U.S.B.

portal *n.* portal *m.*

power *n.* energía *f.,* corriente *f.;* **p. failure** fallo de alimentación, fallo de corriente *m.;* **p. supply** fuente de alimentación *f.,* suministro de alimentación *m.*

power off *adj.* apagado, -da; **p. on** encendido, -da

preferences *n.pl.* preferencias *f.*

press *v.* pulsar; **p. a key** *v.* pulsar una tecla

print *v.* imprimir

printer *n.* impresora *f.;* **p. driver** controlador de impresora *m.;* **inkjet p.** impresora de chorro de tinta; **laser p.** impresora láser

privacy *n.* privacidad *f.*

processor *n.* procesador *m.*

program *n.* programa *m.*

program *v.* programar

public domain *n.* dominio público *m.*

Q

quit *v.* salir

TECHNOLOGY

R

RAM *n.* RAM *f.*

reboot *v.* reiniciar

record *v.* grabar

recorder *n.* grabadora *f.*

recording *n.* grabación *f.;* **digital r.** grabación digital

recover *v.* recuperar

recycling bin *n.* papelera de reciclaje *f.*

redo *v.* rehacer

remote *adj.* remoto, -ta; **r. backup** *n.* copia de seguridad remota *f.*

remove *v.* eliminar; **r. item** eliminar elemento; **r. program** eliminar programa

rename *v.* cambiar el nombre

repair *v.* reparar

replace *v.* reemplazar

replacement *n.* reemplazo *m.*

reply *v.* responder; **r. to all** responder a todos

restore *v.* restaurar

retrieve *v.* recuperar; **r. database** recuperar la base de datos

run *v.* correr, ejecutar

S

save *v.* (document) salvar, guardar

scan *v.* escanear

scanner *n.* escáner *m.*

screen *n.* pantalla *f.*

screensaver *n.* protector de pantalla *m.*

scroll bar *n.* barra de desplazamiento *f.*

search *n.* búsqueda *f.;* **s. engine** buscador *m.,* motor de búsqueda *m.,* servidor de búsqueda *m.*

search *v.* buscar

secure *adj.* seguro, -ra; **s. Web site** *n.* sitio Web seguro, sitio Web protegido *m.*

select *v.* seleccionar, escoger

sent box *n.* (email) bandeja de correos enviados *f.*

server *n.* servidor *m.;* **secure s.** servidor seguro, servidor protegido

shared access *n.* acceso compartido *m.*

shareware *n.* aplicación gratuita *f.,* programa gratuito *m.*

slash (/) *n.* barra, barra oblicua *f.*

smart board *n.* pizarra digital interactiva *f.,* pantalla digital interactiva *f.*

snail mail *n.* correo caracol *m.*

social network *n.* red social *f.*

software *n.* programa *m.,* aplicación *f.*

spam *n.* spam *m.*

spreadsheet *n.* hoja de cálculo *f.*

spyware *n.* aplicación espía *f.,* software espía *m.*

static electricity charge *n.* carga eléctrica estática *f.*

storage *n.* almacenamiento *m.;* **s. archive** archivo de almacenamiento *m.*

store *v.* almacenar

streaming *adj.* de transferencia continua

subfolder *n.* subcarpeta *f.*

subject *n.* (email) asunto *m.*

• •

submenu *n.* submenú *m.*

subscribe *v.* suscribirse

surf *v.* navegar

surfer *n.* cibernauta *m.f.*

system *n.* sistema *m.;* **s. disk** disco de sistema *m.*

T

tab *n.* pestaña *f.*

tablet *n.* tableta *f.,* tablet *m.*

tabbing *n.* tabulación *f.*

tabulate *v.* tabular

template *n.* plantilla *f.*

text *v.* mandar un mensaje de texto, enviar un mensaje de texto

text message *n.* texto *m.,* mensaje de texto *m.;* **compose a t. m.** *v.* redactar un texto

thumbnail *n.* miniatura de una imagen *f.,* previa en miniatura *f.*

toolbar *n.* barra de herramientas *f.*

Trojan horse *n.* caballo de Troya *m.,* troyano *m.*

typeface *n.* tipografía *f.,* tipo de letra, tipo de fuente *m.*

type format *n.* (bold or italic) formato de letra, formato de fuente *m.*

U

undelete *v.* restaurar

uninstall *v.* desintalar

update *n.* actualización *f.*

update *v.* actualizar

updated *adj.* actualizado, -da

upgrade *v.* actualizar

upload *v.* subir, cargar

U.R.L. *n.* dirección Web *f.,* U.R.L. *f.*

user *n.* usuario *m.;* **u. account** cuenta de usuario *f.;* **u. name** nombre de usuario *m.*

V

video *n.* video *m.;* **v. call** video llamada *f.;* **v. conferencing** videoconferencia *f.;* **v. game** videojuego *m.*

videotape *n.* cinta de video *f.*

virtual *adj.* virtual; **v. community** *n.* comunidad virtual *f.;* **v. memory** memoria virtual *f.*

virus *n.* virus *m.*

voice mail *n.* correo de voz *m.*

VRAM *n.* video RAM *m.*

W

Web *n.* Web; **W. address** dirección de página Web, dirección de Web *f.;* **W. page** página Web *f.;* **W. site** sitio Web *m.;* **World Wide W.** Red informática mundial *f.*

webcam *n.* cámara web *f.*

Wi-Fi *n.* Wi-Fi *m.*

window *n.* ventana *f.*

wireless *adj.* inalámbrico, -ca; **w. network** *n.* red inalámbrica *f.;* **w. signal** señal inalámbrica *f.*

word processing *n.* procesamiento de texto *m.*

word processor *n.* procesador de texto *m.*

word wrap *n.* ajuste de línea *m.*

worm *n.* gusano *m.*

Z

zip *v.* comprimir

SCHOOL LIFE

Holidays & Celebrations

BIRTHDAY *n.* cumpleaños *m.*

balloons *n.pl.* globos *m.*

birthday cake *n.* pastel de cumpleaños *m.*, tarta de cumpleaños *f.;* **b. party** fiesta de cumpleaños *f.;* **b. present** regalo de cumpleaños *m.*

fifteenth birthday celebration *n.* fiesta de quince *f.*, quinceañera *f.*

games *n.pl.* juegos *m.*

guests *n.pl.* invitados *m.*

Happy Birthday! *n.* ¡feliz cumpleaños! *m.*

hosts *n.pl.* anfitriones *m.*

invitations *n.pl.* invitaciones *f.*

make a wish *v.* pedir un deseo

surprise party *n.* fiesta sorpresa *f.*

Sweet Sixteen *n.* dulces dieciséis *m.pl.*

thank you notes *n.pl.* notas de agradecimiento *f.*

CHANUKAH *n.* Janucá *f.*

candle *n.* vela *f.*

dreidel *n.* dreidel *m.*, sevivón *m.*

gelt *n.* guelt *m.*

Maccabees *n.pl.* Macabeos *m.*

menorah *n.* menorá *f.*, menora *f.*

latkes *n.pl.* tortitas de papas *f.*

religious freedom *n.* libertad religiosa *f.*

shamash *n.* vela auxiliar más alta *f.*

CHRISTMAS *n.* Navidad *f.*

angels *n.pl.* ángeles *m.*

Baby Jesus *n.* el Niño Jesús *m.*

chestnuts *n.pl.* castaños *m.*

Christmas Day *n.* Día de Navidad *m.;* **C. carol** villancico *m.;* **C. caroling** parranda *f.;* **C. Eve** Nochebuena *f.;* **C. music** aguinaldo *m.;* **C. present** regalo de Navidad, regalo navideño *m.;* **C. spirit** espíritu navideño *m.;* **C. stocking** calceta de Navidad *f.*, calcetín de Navidad *m.;* **C. tree** árbol de Navidad *m.*

eggnog *n.* rompope *m.*, ponche de huevo *m.*

elves *n.pl.* elfos *m.*

holly *n.* acebo *m.*

humbug *n.* bobadas *f.pl.,* tonterías *f.pl.*

Jack Frost *n.* Jack Frío *m.,* Padre Invierno *m.*

jingle bells *n.pl.* cascabeles *m.*

Joseph *n.* José *m.*

Latino celebration of the Nativity *n.* Las Posadas *f.pl.*

manger *n.* pesebre *m.*

Midnight Mass *n.* misa del gallo *f.*

mistletoe *n.* muérdago *m.*

nativity *n.* natividad *f.,* pastorela *f.*

Noel *n.* Navidad *f.*

ornaments *n.pl.* (tree) adornos *m.*

poinsettia *n.* flor de nochebuena *f.*

reindeer *n.pl.* renos *m.*

Santa Claus *n.* Papá Noel *m.*

shepherds *n.pl.* pastores *m.*

sleigh *n.* trineo *m.*

snowman *n.* muñeco de nieve *m.*

St. Nick *n.* San Nicolás *m.*

Star of Bethlehem *n.* estrella de Belén *f.*

Three Kings Day *n.* Día de Reyes, Día de Reyes Magos *m.*

three wise men *n.pl.* tres reyes magos *m.*

Twelfth Night *n.* Noche de Reyes *f.*

Virgin Mary *n.* la Virgen María *f.*

wreath *n.* corona *f.,* ramo *m.*

Yule log *n.* tronco de Navidad *m.,* leño de Navidad *m.*

DAY OF THE DEAD *n.* Día de los muertos *m.*

altar *n.* altar *m.*

ancestor *n.* antepasado, -da *m.f.;* ancestro *m.*

candles *n.pl.* velas *f.*

cemetery *n.* pantión *m.,* cementerio *m.*

grave *n.* tumba *f.*

marigold *n.* cempasúchil *m.,* caléndula *f.,* flor de muertos *f.*

offerings *n.pl.* ofrendas *f.*

prayer *n.* oración *f.*

skeleton *n.* esqueleto *m.*

skull *n.* cráneo *m.,* calavera *f.;* **sugar s.** calavera de azucar

tombstone *n.* lápida *f.*

HALLOWEEN *n.* Noche de Brujas *f.*

bat *n.* murciélago *m.*

black cat *n.* gato negro *m.*

caldron *n.* caldero *m.*

cobweb *n.* telaraña *f.*

costume *n.* disfraz *m.*

devil *n.* diablo *m.*

flying broomstick *n.* escoba voladora *f.*

ghost *n.* fantasma *m.*

ghoul *n.* demonio necrófago *m.,* espíritu maligno *m.*

goblin *n.* duende *m.*

goosebumps *n.pl.* piel de gallina *f.*

haunted house *n.* casa embrujada *f.*

jack-o'-lantern *n.* calabaza iluminada *f.*

mask *n.* máscara *f.*

monster *n.* monstruo *m.*

mummy *n.* momia *f.*

SCHOOL LIFE

SCHOOL LIFE

pumpkin *n.* calabaza *f.*

scary movies *n.pl.* películas de terror *f.*

spell *n.* hechizo *m.*, encanto *m.*; **cast a s.** *v.* hechizar

spooky *adj.* espeluznante, escalofriante

trick or treat *n.* truco o trato *m.*

vampire *n.* vampiro *m.*

werewolf *n.* hombre lobo *m.*, licántropo *m.*

witch *n.* bruja *f.*

wizard *n.* brujo *m.*, hechicero *m.*, mago *m.*

zombie *n.* zombi *m.f.*

NEW YEAR *n.* Año Nuevo *m.*

champagne *n.* champaña *m.*

cheers *n.pl.* aclamaciones *f.*

confetti *n.* confeti *m.*

countdown *n.* cuenta regresiva *f.*

fireworks *n.pl.* fuegos artificiales *m.*, cuetes *m.*

Happy New Year! *n.* ¡feliz año nuevo! *m.*

New Year's Day *n.* Día de año nuevo *m.*

New Year's Eve *n.* Víspera de año nuevo *f.*

resolution *n.* buenos propósitos *m.pl.*

streamer *n.* serpentina *f.*

stroke of midnight *n.* filo de la medianoche *m.*

toast *n.* brindis *m.*

ST. PATRICK'S DAY *n.* Día de San Patricio *m.*

bagpipes *n.pl.* gaitas *f.*

four-leaf clover *n.* trébol de cuatro hojas *m.*

Ireland *n.* Irlanda *f.*

Irish *adj. & n.* irlandés, -esa *m.f.*

leprechaun *n.* duende *m.*

lucky charm *n.* amuleto de buena suerte *m.*

pot o' gold *n.* olla de oro *f.*

shamrock *n.* trébol *m.*

three wishes *n.pl.* tres deseos *m.*

wear green *v.* ponerse ropa de color verde

THANKSGIVING *n.* Día de Acción de Gracias

corn on the cob *n.* mazorca de maíz *f.*, elote *m.*

cranberry *n.* arándano *m.*

gobble *n.* (turkey) gluglú *m.*

gobble *v.* gluglutear

gravy *n.* salsa *f.*

harvest festival *n.* festividad de la cosecha *f.*

leftovers *n.pl.* sobras *f.*

Native American *n.* nativo (-va) americano (-na) *m.f.*

pilgrim *n.* peregrino *m.*

pumpkin pie *n.* pastel de calabaza *m.*, tarta de calabaza *f.*

say grace *v.* dar las gracias

stuffing *n.* relleno *m.*

thankful for *adj.* agradecido (-da) por

turkey *n.* pavo *m.*

yam *n.* ñame *m.*, batata *f.*, boniato *m.*

OTHER HOLIDAYS *n.pl.*
Otras Fiestas *f.*

Cesar Chavez Holiday *n.* Día de César Chávez *m.*

Chinese New Year *n.* Año Nuevo Chino *m.*

Columbus Day *n.* Día de Colón, Día de la Raza *m.*

Easter *n.* Pascua *f.*

Fifth of May *n.* Cinco de Mayo *m.*

Father's Day *n.* Día del Padre *m.*

Fourth of July *n.* Día de Independencia *m.*

Indigenous Peoples' Day *n.* Día Internacional de los Pueblos Indígenas *m.*

Juneteenth *n.* Diecinueve de Junio *m.*

Kwanzaa *n.* Kwanzaa *f.*

Labor Day *n.* Día del Trabajo *m.*

Lares Rebellion *n.* El Grito de Lares *m.*

Lincoln's Birthday *n.* Natalicio de Lincoln *m.*

Martin Luther King's Birthday *n.* Natalicio de Martin Luther King *m.*

May Day *n.* Primero de Mayo *m.*

Memorial Day *n.* Día de los Caídos *m.*

Mexican Independence Day *n.* Día de la Independencia de México *m.*

Mother's Day *n.* Día de la Madre *m.*

Presidents' Day *n.* Día de los Presidentes *m.*

Pulaski's Birthday *n.* Natalicio de Pulaski *m.*

Ramadan *n.* Ramadán *m.*

Valentine's Day *n.* Día de San Valentín, Día de los Enamorados *m.*

Veterans Day *n.* Día de los Veteranos *m.*

Washington's Birthday *n.* Natalicio de Washington *m.*

Yom Kipur *n.* Iom Kipur *m.*, Día de Expiación *m.*

School Routines & Activities

A

absence *n.* ausencia *f.*

activity centers *n.pl.* centros de actividades *m.*

after-school tutoring *n.* tutoría después de clases *f.*

assembly *n.* asamblea *f.*; **a. schedule** horario de asamblea *m.*;

awards a. asamblea de premios

attendance *n.* asistencia *f.*

auditorium *n.* auditorio *m.*

B

backpack *n.* mochila *f.*

bathroom rules *n.pl.* normas para el uso de los baños *f.*

SCHOOL LIFE

189

SCHOOL LIFE

bell *n.* campana *f.*, campanilla *f.*; **b. schedule** horario escolar *m.*

Bilingual Parent Committee *n.* Comité de Padres Bilingües *m.*

birth certificate *n.* certificado de nacimiento *m.*

blackboard, chalkboard *n.* pizarra *f.*, pizarrón *m.*

board work *n.* trabajo en el pizarrón *m.*

book fair *n.* feria del libro *f.*

C

chess club *n.* club de ajedrez *m.*

cleanup time *n.* tiempo de limpieza *m.*

curriculum *n.* plan de estudios *m.*, programa de estudios *m.*

D

debate team *n.* equipo de debate *m.*

disaster drill *n.* simulacro de desastre *m.*

drama club *n.* club de drama, club de teatro *m.*

E

enrollment form *n.* formulario de matrícula *m.*

exam *n.* exámen *m.*

F

Family Night *n.* Noche de Familias *f.*

field day *n.* día de campo *m.*

final exam *n.* exámen final *m.*

fire drill *n.* simulacro de incendio *m.*

first semester *n.* primer semestre *m.*

G

gather in groups *v.* reunirse en grupos, formar grupos

geography bee *n.* torneo de geografía *m.*

grade *n.* (level) grado *m.*

grades *n.pl.* (marks) calificaciones *f.*, notas *f.*

graduation *n.* graduación *f.*; **g. ceremony** ceremonia de graduación *f.*

guardian *n.* tutor, -ra *m.f.*; guardián, -ana *m.f.*

guidance counselor *n.* consejero, -ra *m.f.*

H

hall pass *n.* pase de pasillo *m.*

homecoming *n.* regreso al hogar *m.*

homeroom *n.* salón principal *m.*

homework *n.* tarea *f.*

honor roll *n.* lista de honor *f.*

I

inclement weather *n.* mal tiempo *m.*

L

line up *v.* ponerse en fila

Local School Council *n.* Consejo Local de la Escuela *m.*

lunch ticket *n.* boleto de almuerzo *m.*

lunchroom *n.* cafetería *f.*

M

marching band *n.* banda de marcha *f.*

midterm exam *n.* exámen parcial, examen de medio periodo *m.*

N

naptime *n.* hora de la siesta *f.*

newsletter *n.* boletín informativo *m.*

notetaking *n.* toma de apuntes, toma de notas *f.*

O

open house *n.* casa abierta *f.*

P

Parent Teacher Association (P.T.A.) *n.* Asociación de Padres y Maestros *f.*

peer tutoring *n.* tutoría entre iguales *f.*

permission *n.* permiso *m.;* **p. slip** hoja de permiso *f.*

picture day *n.* día de fotografía *m.*

pledge of allegiance *n.* juramento de la bandera, juramento de lealdad *m.*

principal's office *n.* oficina del (de la) director (-ora) *f.*

R

raise your hand *v.* levantar la mano, alzar la mano

read aloud *v.* leer en voz alta

read-aloud *n.* lectura en voz alta *f.*

reading corner *n.* rincón de lectura *m.*

recess *n.* recreo *m.*

registration *n.* inscripción *f.,* matrícula *f.*

report card *n.* tarjeta de informe *f.,* boleta de calificaciones *f.*

S

school assembly *n.* asamblea escolar *f.;* **s. board meeting** junta del consejo escolar *f.;* **s. dance** baile escolar *m.;* **s. rules** *pl.* normas escolares *f.*

School Site Council *n.* Consejo de la Escuela *m.*

science club *n.* club de ciencias *m.;* **s. fair** feria de ciencias *f.*

second semester *n.* segundo semestre *m.*

senior prom *n.* baile de graduación *m.*

shortened-day schedule *n.* horario de día corto *m.*

show and tell *v.* mostrar y contar

silent reading *n.* lectura silenciosa, lectura en silencio *f.*

snack *n.* merienda *f.,* bocadillo *m.*

spelling bee *n.* torneo de ortografía *m.*

spirit week *n.* semana de espíritu escolar *f.*

spring break *n.* vacaciones de primavera *f.pl.*

state achievement tests *n.pl.* evaluaciones estatales *f.*

story time *n.* tiempo de cuentos *m.,* hora del cuento *f.*

student advisory group *n.* grupo asesor estudiantil *m.;* **s. aide** alumno (-na) ayudante *m.f.;* **s. body** estudiantado *m.;* **s. council** consejo estudiantil *m.;* **s. government election** elección del gobierno estudiantil *f.;* **s. newspa-**

SCHOOL LIFE

per periódico estudiantil *m.*

summer *n.* verano *m.;* **s. school** escuela de verano *f.;* **s. vacation** vacaciones de verano *f.*

T

take notes *v.* tomar apuntes, tomar notas

talent show *n.* concurso de talentos *m.*

teacher in-service day *n.* día para la formación del profesorado *m.*

technology club *n.* club de tecnología *m.*

W

wash your hands *v.* lavarse las manos

white board *n.* tablero blanco *m.,* pizarra blanca *f.,* pizarrón blanco *m.*

winter vacation *n.* vacaciones de invierno *f.*

work in pairs *v.* trabajar en parejas

Y

yearbook *n.* anuario *m.;* **y. sale** venta del anuario *f.*

Field Trips & Transportation

A

admission tickets *n.pl.* boletos de admisión *m.,* entradas *f.*

amusement park *n.* parque de atracciones *m.*

aquarium *n.* acuario *m.*

arrival time *n.* hora de llegada *f.*

art museum *n.* museo de arte *m.*

assigned seats *n.pl.* asientos asignados *m.*

attend a performance *v.* asistir a una función

B

bag lunch *n.* bolsa de almuerzo *f.*

botanical garden *n.* jardín botánico *m.*

buddy *n.* compañero, -ra *m.f.*

bus *n.* autobus *m.,* guagua *f.;* **b. fare** tarifa del autobús *f.;* **b. stop** parada del autobús *f.;* **conduct on the b.** conducta en el autobús *f.;* **free b. pass** pase gratis de autobús *m.;* **public b.** autobús público; **school b.** autobús escolar; **school b. routes** *pl.* rutas del autobús escolar *f.*

C

chaperon *n.* chaperón, -na *m.f.;* acompañante *m.f.*

children's theater *n.* teatro para niños, teatro infantil *m.*

crosswalk *n.* paso de peatones *m.*

D

dance concert *n.* espectáculo de danza, espectáculo danzario *m.*

departure time *n.* hora de salida *f.*

drop-off point *n.* lugar de entrega *m.*, punto de desembarque *m.*

F

fair *n.* feria *f.*

farm *n.* granja *f.*, finca *f.*

L

lost and found *n.* objetos perdidos y encontrados *m.pl.*

M

money for incidentals *n.* fondo para gastos imprevistos *m.*

motion sickness *n.* mareo *m.*

museum *n.* museo *m.;* **anthropology m.** museo antropológico; **art m.** museo de arte; **m. exhibits** *pl.* piezas de museo *f.;* **m. of natural history** museo de historia natural; **science m.** museo de ciencias

music concert *n.* concierto de música *m.*

O

observatory *n.* observatorio *m.*

overnight *adv.* de la noche a la mañana; **o. stay** *n.* pernoctación *f.*

P

park *n.* parque *m.*

partner *n.* pareja *f.*

permission slip *n.* autorización *f.*, permiso firmado *m.*

pick-up location *n.* lugar de recogida *m.*

planetarium *n.* planetario *m.*

public library *n.* biblioteca pública *f.*

S

school bus *n.* autobús escolar *m.;* **s. b. routes** *pl.* rutas del autobús escolar *f.*

science museum *n.* museo de ciencias *m.*

seat belt *n.* cinturón de seguridad *m.*

senior citizen's center *n.* centro de tercera edad, centro para jubilados *m.*

student identification card *n.* credencial de estudiante *f.*, carnet de estudiante *f.*

T

transportation *n.* transporte *m.*

V

van *n.* camioneta *f.*

Z

zoo *n.* zoológico *m.*

SCHOOL LIFE

School Library

••

A

alphabetical order *n.* orden alfabético *m.*

art prints *n.pl.* impresiones artísticas *f.*

audio book *n.* audiolibro *m.*

author *n.* autor *m.*

B

bar code *n.* código de barra *m.*

bibliography *n.* bibliografía *f.*

book *n.* libro *m.;* **b. cart** cesta de libros *f.,* carrito de libros *m.;* **b. jacket** sobrecubierta del libro *f.,* forro del libro *m.;* **b. mark** señalador *m.,* marcador *m.;* **b. spine** lomo del libro *m.*

bookcase *n.* librero *m.*

bookends *n.pl.* soportalibros *m.,* sujetalibros *m.,* apoyalibros *m.*

bookshelves *n.pl.* estanterías *f.*

browse *v.* hojear

C

call number *n.* número de catálogo *m.*

card catalog *n.* fichero *m.,* catálogo de fichas *m.*

catalog search *n.* búsqueda en el catálogo *f.*

check out books *v.* sacar libros

copyright date *n.* fecha de propiedad literaria *f.*

cubicle *n.* cubículo *m.*

D

Dewey decimal system *n.* sistema decimal de Dewey *m.*

digital materials *n.pl.* materiales digitales *m.*

due date *n.* fecha de vencimiento, fecha de caducidad *f.*

E

e-book *n.* libro electrónico *m.*

encyclopedia *n.* enciclopedia *f.*

F

fiction *adj. & n.* ficción *f.*

H

hardback *n.* libro de tapa dura *m.,* encuadernación dura *f.*

headphones *n.pl.* audífonos *m.*

I

illustration *n.* ilustración *f.*

illustrator *n.* ilustrador *m.*

index *n.* índice *m.*

J

journal *n.* diario *m.,* revista *f.*

K

keyword *n.* palabra clave *f.;* **k. search** búsqueda por palabra clave *f.*

SCHOOL LIFE

L

laminator *n.* laminador *m.*
librarian *n.* bibliotecaria *f.*
library *n.* biblioteca *f.;* **l. card** tarjeta de la biblioteca *f.,* carnet de biblioteca *m.;* **l. hours** *pl.* horario de la biblioteca *m.*

M

magazine *n.* revista *f.*
maps *n.pl.* mapas *m.*

N

newspaper *n.* periódico *m.*
nonfiction *adj. & n.* no ficción *f.*

O

online catalog *n.* catálogo en línea *m.*
overdue *adj.* atrasado, -da

P

pamphlets *n.pl.* folletos *m.*
paperback *n.* libro de tapa flexible, libro en rústica *m.*
periodical *n.* publicación periódica *f.*

photocopier *n.* fotocopiadora *f.*

R

reference materials *n.pl.* materiales de referencia, materiales de consulta *m.*
research *n.* investigación *f.*

S

science fiction *n.* ciencia ficción *f.*
search the catalog *v.* buscar en el catálogo
shelf *n.* estante *m.*
spine *n.* (book) lomo *m.*
study room *n.* sala de estudio *f.,* cuarto de estudio *m.*
subject *n.* sujeto *m.*

T

title *n.* título *m.;* **t. page** página de título *f.,* hoja de presentación *f.*

Y

young adult novels *n.pl.* novelas para jóvenes, novelas juveniles *f.*

SCHOOL LIFE

Playground & Sports

A

aerobics *n.* aeróbico *m.*
anaerobic exercise *n.* ejercicio anaeróbico *m.*
athletics *n.* atletismo *m.*

B

ball *n.* pelota *f.*
bench *n.* banco *m.*
baseball *n.* béisbol *m.*
basketball *n.* baloncesto *m.;* **b. court** pista de baloncesto *f.*

SCHOOL LIFE

bat *n.* bate *m.*
block *v.* bloquear
bounce *v.* botar, rebotar
boxing *n.* boxeo *m.*

C

calisthenics *n.pl.* calistenia *f.*
cardiovascular exercise *n.* ejercicio cardiovascular *m.*
catch *v.* atrapar
champions *n.pl.* campeones *m.*
championship *n.* campeonato *m.*
cheat *v.* engañar, hacer trampa
cheating *n.* trampa *f.*, engaño *m.*
chin-ups *n.pl.* dominadas *f.*
climb *v.* trepar, subir, escalar
coach *n.* entrenador, -ora *m.f.*
coach *v.* entrenar
competition *n.* competencia *f.*, rivalidad *f.*
contact sport *n.* deporte de contacto *m.*
court *n.* cancha *f.*, pista *f.*

D

dive *n.* clavado *m.*, salto de cabeza *m.*
dive *v.* tirarse de cabeza, bucear
dodge *v.* esquivar
dodgeball *n.* balón prisionero *m.*
dribble *v.* regatear, driblar
duck *v.* agacharse

E

exercise *n.* ejercicio *m.*

F

football *n.* fútbol americano *m.*

foul *n.* falta *f.*
four-square *n.* juego de cuatro cuadros *m.*
freeze tag *n.* juego de los encantados *m.*

G

game *n.* juego *m.*
goal *n.* gol *m.*
gymnasium *n.* gimnasio *m.*
gymnastics *n.* gimnástica *f.*, gimnasia *f.*

H

handspring *n.* voltereta sobre manos *f.*, salto de paloma *m.*
handstand *n.* parada de manos *f.*
hide-and-seek *n.* escondite *m.*
hit *v.* pegar, golpear
hopscotch *n.* tejo *m.*, rayuela *f.*

J

jump *n.* salto *m.;* **j. rope** cuerda de saltar *f.*, comba *f.*
jump *v.* saltar

K

kick *v.* patear
kickball *n.* kickbol *m.*

L

leapfrog *n.* pídola *f.*
locker *n.* casillero *m.*, taquilla *f.;* **l. room** vestuario *m.*, vestidores *m.pl.*

M

match *n.* partido *m.*

monkey bars *n. pl.* barras de mono *f.*

N

net *n.* red *f.*

O

out *adj.* eliminado, -da

out *adv.* fuera; **o. of bounds** fuera de los límites

out *n.* eliminación *f.*

P

pass *v.* pasar

pick sides *v.* tomar partido

play *v.* jugar

players *n.pl.* jugadores, -ras *m.f.*

playground *n.* patio de recreo *m.*

push-ups *n.pl.* flexiones *f.*

R

race *n.* carrera *f.;* **relay r.** carrera de relevos

rebound *n.* rebote *m.*

referee *n.* árbitro *m.*

rules *n.pl.* reglas *f.*

run *n.* (baseball) carrera *f.*

run *v.* correr

runner-up *n.* subcampeón, -na *m.f.;* segundo lugar *m.f.*

S

sandbox *n.* arenero *m.,* caja de arena *f.*

score *n.* cuenta *f.,* puntaje *m.,* resultado *m.*

score *v.* apuntar, marcar, anotar

scoreboard *n.* marcador *m.*

scorekeeper *n.* tanteador *m.*

seesaw *n.* subibaja *m.,* balancín *m.*

shoot *v.* tirar, chutar

sit-ups *n.pl.* abdominales *m.*

slide *n.* resbaladero *m.,* tobogán *m.*

slide *v.* resbalar, deslizarse

soccer *n.* fútbol *m.*

softball *n.* softbol *m.*

somersault *n.* voltereta *f.,* salto mortal *m.*

Special Olympics *n.pl.* Olimpiadas Especiales *f.*

spin *v.* girar

sportsmanship *n.* espíritu deportivo *m.,* deportividad *f.*

sprint *v.* esprintar, correr a toda velocidad

stretch *v.* estirar

stretching *n.* elongación *f.*

substitution *n.* substitución *f.*

swim *v.* nadar

swimming *n.* natación *f.*

swing *n.* columpio *m.*

swing *v.* columpiarse; **s. at the ball** dar a la pelota

T

tag *n.* (game) pega *f.;* **freeze t.** juego de los encantados *m.*

take turns *v.* turnarse, alternarse

team *n.* equipo *m.*

teammates *n.pl.* compañeros, -ras *m.f.*

teeter-totter *n.* subibaja *m.,* balancín *m.*

tennis *n.* tenis *m.;* **t. court** pista de tenis *f.*

SCHOOL LIFE

197

SCHOOL LIFE

tetherball *n.* tetherball *m.*, espiro *m.*
throw *v.* lanzar, tirar
tie *n.* (game) empate *m.*
tie *v.* empatar
time out *n.* tiempo muerto *m.;* **call a t. o.** *v.* solicitar un tiempo muerto; **take a t. o.** tomar un descanso, tomar un tiempo muerto
track and field events *n.pl.* pruebas de atletismo *f.*

turn *v.* voltear
twist *v.* torcerse, retorcerse

V
volleyball *n.* voleibol *m.*

W
weight lifting *n.* levantamiento de pesas *m.*
wrestling *n.* lucha *f.*

Student Health

A
abdomen *m.* abdomen
abdominal pain *n.* dolor abdominal *m.*
abscess *n.* absceso *m.*
acute pain *n.* dolor agudo *m.*
addiction *n.* adicción *f.*
AIDS *n.* SIDA *m.*
allergy *n.* alergia *f.*
anemia *n.* anemia *f.*
anorexia *n.* anorexia *f.*
anxiety *n.* ansiedad *f.*
appendicitis *n.* apendicitis *f.*
asthma *n.* asma *f.*
athlete's foot *n.* pie de atleta *m.*

B
backache *n.* dolor de espalda *m.*
bad breath *n.* mal aliento *m.*, halitosis *f.*
bee sting *n.* picadura de abeja *f.*, picada de abeja *f.*

birth control pills *n.pl.* píldoras anticonceptivas *f.*
birth defect *n.* defecto de nacimiento *m.*, anomalía congénita *f.*
birthmark *n.* lunar *m.*
bite *n.* (dog) mordisco *m.;* (insect) picadura *f.;* (snake) mordedura *f.*
bleeding *adj.* sangrante
bleeding *n.* hemorragia *f.*, sangramiento *m.*
blister *n.* ampolla *f.*
blood clot *n.* coágulo *m.*
blood pressure *n.* presión arterial *f.*, tensión arterial *f.;* **high b. p.** presión alta, hipertensión arterial *f.*
boil *n.* furúnculo *m.*, grano enterrado *m.*
bowel movement *n.* evacuación intestinal *f.*
bowlegged *adj.* estevado, -da
braces *n.pl.* frenillos *m.*, frenos dentales *m.*, aparatos ortodóncicos *m.*

breathing difficulties *n.pl.* problemas respiratorios *m.*

breathless *adj.* falta de aliento

broken bone *n.* hueso roto, hueso fracturado *m.;* **b. leg** pierna quebrada, pierna rota *f.;* fractura de pierna *f.*

bronchitis *n.* bronquitis *m.*

bruise *n.* contusión *f.,* moretón *m.,* hematoma *m.*

bulimia *n.* bulimia *f.*

bump *n.* golpe *m.*

bump against *v.* chocar contra

burn *n.* quemadura *f.*

C

cancer *n.* cáncer *m.*

cavity *n.* cavidad *f.*

check-up *n.* chequeo de salud *m.,* reconocimiento médico *m.*

chicken pox *n.* varicela *f.*

chills *n.pl.* escalofríos *m.*

chronic *adj.* crónico, -ca; **c. condition** *n.* condición crónica *f.;* **c. illness** enfermedad crónica *f.*

club foot *n.* pie zambo, pie equinovaro *m.*

cold *n.* resfriado *m.,* catarro *m.;* **catch c.** *v.* coger un catarro, pescar un resfriado

color blindness *n.* daltonismo *m.*

communicable disease *n.* enfermedad contagiosa, enfermedad transmisible *f.*

complications *n.pl.* complicaciones *f.*

concussion *n.* concusión *f.,* conmoción cerebral *f.*

condoms *n.pl.* condones *m.*

confidentiality *n.* confidencialidad *f.*

conjunctivitis *n.* conjuntivitis *f.*

constipation *n.* estreñimiento *m.*

contact lenses *n.pl.* lentes de contacto *m.*

contagious *adj.* contagioso, -sa

convulsion *n.* convulsión *f.*

cough *n.* tos *f.*

cramps *n.pl.* calambres *m.*

cross-eyed *adj.* bizco, -ca

cut *n.* cortadura *f.*

cyst *n.* quiste *m.*

D

dental floss *n.* hilo dental *m.*

depressed *adj.* deprimido, -da

depression *n.* depresión *f.*

diabetes *n.* diabetes *m.*

diarrhea *n.* diarrea *f.*

diet *n.* dieta *f.*

digestion *n.* digestión *f.*

disability *n.* discapacidad *f.;* **physical d.** discapacidad física; **temporary d.** discapacidad temporal

disabled *adj.* discapacitado, -da

discomfort *n.* incomodidad *f.*

disease *n.* enfermedad *f.;* **spread of d.** propagación de la enfermedad *f.*

dizziness *n.* mareo *m.,* vértigo *m.*

dizzy *adj.* mareado, -da

doctor *n.* médico, -ca *m.f.*

dose *n.* dosis *m.*

Down's Syndrome *n.* síndrome de Down *m.*

drowsy *adj.* soñoliento, -ta

drugs *n.pl.* (illegal) drogas *f.;* **be**

SCHOOL LIFE

under the influence of d. *v.* estar bajo la influencia de drogas

dyslexia *n.* dislexia *f.*

E

ear *n.* oído *m.;* (external) oreja *f.,* pabellón auditivo *m.;* **inner e.** oído interno

earache *n.* dolor de oído *m.*

eardrum *n.* tímpano *m.,* membrana timpánica *f.*

enlarged glands *n.pl.* glándulas inflamadas *f.*

epidemic *n.* epidemia *f.*

epilepsy *n.* epilepsia *f.*

exhaustion *n.* agotamiento *m.*

eyelid *n.* párpado *m.*

eyestrain *n.* vista fatigada *f.,* fatiga ocular *f.*

F

faint *v.* desmayarse

fatigue *n.* cansancio *m.*

fever *n.* fiebre *f.,* calentura *f.*

flatulence *n.* flatulencia *f.,* gases *m.pl.*

flesh wound *n.* herida superficial *f.*

flu *n.* gripe *f.,* gripa *f.,* influenza *f.*

food poisoning *n.* intoxicación alimentaria *f.*

foreign body *n.* cuerpo extraño *m.*

foster home *n.* casa de acogida *f.*

fracture *n.* fractura *f.,* quebradura *f.*

frostbite *n.* congelación *f.*

G

gash *n.* cuchillada *f.,* herida profunda *f.*

glasses *n.pl.* gafas *f.,* anteojos *m.,* lentes *m.*

gums *n.pl.* encías *f.*

H

hay fever *n.* fiebre del heno *f.*

head lice *n.pl.* piojos *m.*

headache *n.* dolor de cabeza *m.*

health history *n.* historia clínica *f.*

healthy *adj.* sano, -na; saludable

hearing aid *n.* aparato auditivo *m.*

heart murmur *n.* soplo cardíaco *m.*

heartburn *n.* acidez *f.,* ardor de estómago *m.*

hemorrhage *n.* hemorragia *f.*

hepatitis *n.* hepatitis *f.*

hernia *n.* hernia *f.*

herpes *n.* herpes *m.*

H.I.V. *n.* V.I.H. *m.*

hives *n.pl.* ronchas *f.,* urticaria *f.*

hoarseness *n.* ronquera *f.*

hookworm *n.* anquilostoma *m.*

hurt *v.* hacer daño, lastimar, doler

hypertension *n.* presión alta *f.,* hipertensión arterial *f.*

hypoglycemia *n.* hipoglucemia *f.,* bajón de azúcar *m.*

I

immunization *n.* inmunización *f.*

incubation period *n.* periodo de incubación *m.*

indigestion *n.* indigestión *f.*

infection *n.* infección *f.*

inflammation *n.* inflamación *f.*

injury *n.* daño *m.,* lesión *f.,* herida *f.*

intestinal worms *n.pl.* lombrices

intestinales *f.*

irritation *n.* irritación *f.*

itch *n.* comezón *f.*, picazón *f.*

K

knot on the head *n.* chichón *m.*

L

lack of appetite *n.* inapetencia *f.*

laryngitis *n.* laringitis *f.*

lesion *n.* lesión *f.*

limp *n.* cojera *f.*

limp *v.* cojear

M

malnourished *adj.* malnutrido, -da; desnutrido, -da

measles *n.* sarampión *m.;* **German m.** rubéola *f.*

medical *adj.* médico, -ca; **m. exam** *n.* reconocimiento médico *m.;* **m. information card** tarjeta de información médica *f.;* **m. records** *pl.* expedientes médicos *m.;* **m. treatment** tratamiento médico *m.*

medication *n.* medicación *f.*

medicine *n.* medicina *f.*

mentrual period *n.* periodo menstrual *m.*, la regla *f.*

menstruation *n.* menstruación *f.*

migraine *n.* migraña *f.*

mole *n.* verruga *f.*, lunar *m.*

mouthwash *n.* enjuague bucal *m.*

mumps *n.pl.* paperas *f.*

N

nausea *n.* náusea *f.*, náuseas *f.pl.*

nearsighted *adj.* miope

nearsightedness *n.* miopía *f.*

neurological *adj.* neurológico, -ca

numbness *n.* insensibilidad *f.*, entumecimiento *m.*

O

obese *adj.* obeso, -sa

overdose *n.* sobredosis *f.*

overweight *adj. & n.* sobrepeso *m.*

P

pain *n.* dolor *m.;* **acute p.** dolor agudo

pale *adj.* pálido, -da

physical disability *n.* discapacidad física *f.;* **p. examination** examen médico *m.;* **p. restrictions** *pl.* restricciones físicas *f.*

pimple *n.* grano *m.*

pinkeye *n.* conjuntivitis *f.*

pneumonia *n.* neumonía *f.*, pulmonía *f.*

poison ivy *n.* hiedra venenosa *f.*

pregnant *adj.* embarazada

pulse *n.* pulso *m.;* **take your p.** *v.* tomarse el pulso

pus *n.* pus *m.*

R

rash *n.* erupción de la piel *f.*, sarpullido *m.*

referral to a specialist *n.* remisión a un especialista *f.*

relapse *n.* recaída *f.*

ringworm *n.* tiña *f.*

rubella *n.* rubéola *f.*

runny nose *n.* secreción nasal *f.*, moqueo *m.*, nariz mocosa *f.*

SCHOOL LIFE

201

rupture *n.* ruptura *f.*, hernia *f.*

S

safety procedures *n.pl.* procedimientos de seguridad *m.*

sanitary napkin *n.* compresa *f.*, toalla femenina *f.*

scab *n.* costra *f.*

scar *n.* cicatriz *f.*

school nurse *n.* enfermera de la escuela *f.*

scoliosis *n.* escoliosis *f.*

scratch *n.* rasguño *m.*, arañazo *m.*

scratch *v.* rascar

seizures *n.pl.* convulsiones *f.*

severe case *n.* caso grave *m.*

sexual abuse *n.* abuso sexual *m.*

shock *n.* choque *m.*

short of breath *adj.* falta de aliento

skin sore *n.* úlcera en la piel *f.*, llaga en la piel *f.*

sliver *n.* astilla *f.*

smallpox *n.* viruela *f.*

snakebite *n.* mordedura de serpiente *f.*

sneeze *n.* estornudo *m.*

sore *adj.* dolorido, -da; irritado, -da; **s. throat** *n.* dolor de garganta *m.*

sore *n.* úlcera *f.*, llaga *f.*

spasm *n.* espasmo *m.*

splinter *n.* astilla *f.*

sprain *n.* esguince *m.*, torcedura *f.*

stomach ache *n.* dolor de estómago *m.*

strep throat *n.* faringitis estreptocócica *f.*

stress *n.* estrés *m.*

stutter, stammer *v.* tartamudear

stutterer *n.* tartamudo, -da *m.f.*

sty *n.* orzuelo *m.*

suicide *n.* suicidio *m.*

sunburn *n.* quemadura del sol *f.*

sunstroke *n.* insolación *f.*

sweaty *adj.* sudoroso, -sa

swelling *n.* hinchazón *f.*

swollen *adj.* hinchado, -da

symptoms *n.pl.* síntomas *f.*

T

take orally *v.* tomar por vía oral, tomar oralmente; **t. your pulse** tomarse el pulso; **t. your temperature** tomarse la temperatura

temperature *n.* temperatura *f.*; **high t.** calentura *f.*, fiebre *f.*

tetanus *n.* tétano *m.*

throb *v.* latir, palpitar

tingling sensation *n.* hormigueo *m.*, cosquilleo *m.*

tonsillitis *n.* amigdalitis *f.*

tooth-brushing *n.* cepillado dental *m.*

toothache *n.* dolor de los muelas *m.*

trauma *n.* trauma *m.*

tumor *n.* tumor *m.*

typhoid fever *n.* fiebre tifoidea *f.*

U

unconscious *adj.* desmayado, -da; inconsciente

unhealthy, unsanitary *adj.* insalubre; antihigiénico, -ca

urinate *v.* orinar

urine *n.* orina *f.*

V

vaccinate *v.* vacunar

vaccination *n.* vacunación *f.*

vaccine *n.* vacuna *f.;* **v. exemption form** formulario de exención de vacunas *m.*

venereal disease *n.* enfermedad venérea *f.*

virus *n.* virus *m.*

vomit *v.* vomitar *v.*

W

wart *n.* verruga *f.*

wasp sting *n.* picadura de avispa *f.*

wellness *n.* bienestar físico *m.*

welts *n.pl.* verdugones *m.*

whooping cough *n.* tos ferina *f.*

wound *n.* herida *f.*

Special Needs

A

accommodations *n.pl.* alojamientos *m.,* acomodaciones *f.*

advocate *n.* defensor, -ra *m.f.*

age *n.* edad *f.;* **a. equivalent** *adj.* equivalente a la edad; **chronological a.** edad cronológica; **mental a.** edad mental

American Sign Language (A.S.L.) *n.* Lenguaje Americano de Señas *m.*

Americans with Disabilities Act (A.D.A.) *n.* Acta para los Norteamericanos con Discapacidades *f.*

annual review *n.* revisión anual *f.*

appropriate *adj.* apropiado, -da

aptitude *n.* aptitud *f.*

Asperger's syndrome *n.* síndrome de Asperger *m.*

assessment *n.* evaluación *f.*

assistive technology *n.* tecnología de apoyo *f.*

attention deficit disorder (A.D.D.) *n.* trastorno por déficit de atención *m.;* **a. d. hyperactivity disorder (A.D.H.D.)** trastorno por déficit de atención e hiperactividad

attention span *n.* capacidad de atención *f.,* período de atención *m.*

auditory discrimination *n.* discriminación auditiva *f.*

autism spectrum disorder *n.* trastorno del espectro del autismo *m.*

B

behavior disorder *n.* trastorno de la conducta *m.*

blind *adj.* ciego, -ga

blindness *n.* ceguera *f.*

bullying *n.* acoso *m.,* intimidación *f.*

C

capacity *n.* capacidad *f.*

case manager *n.* coordinador (-ora) del caso *m.f.*

SCHOOL LIFE

cerebral palsy *n.* parálisis cerebral *f.*

chronological age *n.* edad cronológica *f.*

cognitive *adj.* cognitivo, -va

cognitively delayed *adj.* cognitivamente atrasado (-da)

consent *n.* consentimiento *m.*

counseling *n.* asesoramiento *m.;* **c. services** servicios de consejería *m.pl.*

creativity *n.* creatividad *f.*

D

deaf *adj.* sordo, -da

deaf-blindness *n.* sordoceguera *f.*

deafness *n.* sordera *f.*

deformity *n.* deformidad *f.*

developmental delay *n.* retraso del desarrollo *m.;* **d. disability** discapacidad del desarrollo *f.*

dexterity *n.* destreza *f.*

disability *n.* discapacidad *f.,* inhabilidad *f.,* incapacidad *f.;* **intellectual d.** discapacidad intelectual; **learning d.** discapacidad en el aprendizaje; **multiple d.** *pl.* discapacidades múltiples

due process hearing *n.* audiencia del proceso legal debido *f.*

E

early intervention *n.* intervención temprana *f.*

educable mentally handicapped (E.M.H.) *adj.* discapacitado (-da) intelectual educable

eligibility *n.* elegibilidad *f.*

emotional disturbance *n.* trastorno emocional *m.*

English as a second language *n.* inglés como segunda idioma *m.*

evaluation *n.* evaluación *f.;* **independent e.** evaluación independiente

expressive language *n.* lenguaje expresivo *m.*

F

fetal alcohol syndrome *n.* síndrome de alcoholismo fetal *m.*

fine motor skills *n.pl.* habilidades motrices finas *f.,* motricidad fina *f.*

G

gifted and talented *adj.* dotado (-da) y talentoso (-sa)

grade-level expectations *n.pl.* expectativas de nivel de grado *f.*

gross motor skills *n.pl.* habilidades motrices gruesas *f.,* motricidad gruesa *f.*

guardianship *n.* tutela *f.,* custodia *f.*

H

handicapped *adj.* impedido, -da; discapacitado, -da

hearing impairment *n.* impedimento auditivo *m.*

highly creative *adj.* muy creativo, -va

hyperactivity *n.* hiperactividad *f.*

I

impartial hearing *n.* audiencia imparcial *f.*

● ●

inappropriate *adj.* inadecuado, -da; impropio, -pia

inattention *n.* falta de atención *f.*, desatención *f.*

inclusion *n.* inclusión *f.*

Individualized Education Program (I.E.P.) *n.* Programa de Educación Individualizada *m.;* **I.E.P. team** equipo del I.E.P. *m.*

Individuals with Disabilities Education Act (I.D.E.A.) *n.* Acta para la Educación de Individuos con Discapacidades *f.*

intellectual disability *n.* discapacidad intelectual *f.*

interpreter services *n.pl.* servicios de intérprete *m.*

intervention *n.* intervención *f.*

L

language impairment *n.* trastorno del lenguaje *m.*

learning disability (L.D.) *n.* discapacidad en el aprendizaje *f.*

least restrictive environment *n.* ambiente menos restrictivo *m.*

lip reading *n.* lectura de los labios *f.*

M

mental age *n.* edad mental *f.*

modifications *n.pl.* modificaciones *f.*

monitoring *n.* monitoreo *m.*

mood swings *n.pl.* cambios de humor *m.*

motor sensory function *n.* funcionamiento motor y sensorial *m.*

multisensory *adj.* multisensorial

N

neurosis *n.* neurosis *f.*

O

occupational therapy *n.* terapia ocupacional *f.*

orientation and mobility services *n.pl.* servicios de orientación y movilidad *m.*

orthopedic impairment *n.* impedimento ortopédico *m.*

outburst *n.* explosión de cólera *f.*, arrebato *m.*, arranque *m.*

P

paraprofessional *n.* paraprofesional *m.f.*

physical therapy (P.T.) *n.* terapia física *f.*

placement *n.* colocación *f.*

positive behavioral supports *n.pl.* apoyos positivos de la conducta *m.*

procedural safeguards *n.pl.* garantías procesales *f.*

progress monitoring *n.* seguimiento *m.*, monitoreo del progreso *m.*

psychological *adj.* sicológico, -ca; psicológico, -ca

psychologist *n.* sicólogo, -ga *m.f.;* psicólogo, -ga *m.f.*

pullout programs *n.* programas de separación de clase *m.pl.*

R

reassessment *n.* reevaluación *f.*

receptive language *n.* lenguaje receptivo *m.*

SCHOOL LIFE

SCHOOL LIFE

referral *n.* remisión *f.*
remedial program *n.* programa de recuperación *m.*
resource services *n.pl.* servicios de recursos *m.*
Response to Intervention (R.T.I.) *n.* Respuesta a la Intervención *f.*
revocation of consent *n.* revocación del consentimiento *f.*

S

school counselor *n.* consejero (-ra) escolar *m.f.*
screening test *n.* examen de selección *m.*
self-contained classroom *n.* salón autocontenido *m.*
self-control *n.* autocontrol *m.*
self-discipline *n.* autodisciplina *f.*
social promotion *n.* promoción social *f.*
special education *n.* educación es-

pecial *f.*
speech impairment *n.* trastorno del habla *m.;* **s. therapy** logopedia *f.,* terapia del habla *f.*
strength *n.* fortaleza *f.,* fuerza *f.*

T

traumatic brain injury *n.* lesión cerebral traumática *f.*
tutoring *n.* tutoría *f.,* clases particulares *f.pl.*

U

universal design *n.* diseño universal *m.*

V

visual impairment *n.* impedimento visual *m.,* trastorno visual *m.*

W

weakness *n.* debilidad *f.*

Conduct & Discipline

A

absences *n.pl.* ausencias *f.;* **excessive a.** ausencias excesivas; **unexcused a.** ausencias sin excusa
accomplice *n.* cómplice *m.f.*
after-school detention *n.* detención después de clases *f.*
appeal *n.* apelación *f.*
appeal *v.* apelar

arrest *n.* arresto *m.,* detención *f.*
arrest *v.* arrestar
assault *n.* asalto *m.*
assault *v.* asaltar

B

bully *n.* intimidador, -ra *m.f.;* matón, -na *m.f.;* peleonero, -ra *m.f.*
bully *v.* intimidar, acosar

• •

burden of proof *n.* carga de la prueba *f.*

C

charge *n.* cargo *m.*

charge *v.* acusar

cheat *v.* hacer trampa, copiar

cheater *n.* mentiroso, -sa *m.f.;* tramposo, -sa *m.f.;* copión, -na *m.f.*

confession *n.* confesión *f.*

confiscate *v.* confiscar

contradict *v.* contradecir

custody *n.* custodia *f.*

D

drug paraphernalia *n.* parafernalia de drogas *f.*

E

evidence *n.* prueba *f.,* evidencia *f.*

expulsion *n.* expulsión *f.*

F

fistfight *n.* pelea a puñetazos *f.*

forgery *n.* falsificación *f.*

G

gang signs *n.pl.* señales de pandillas *f.,* signos de pandillas *m.*

graffiti *n.pl.* grafiti *m.*

H

harassment *n.* acoso *m.*

hearing *n.* audiencia *f.*

horseplay *n.* juego rudo *m.,* payasadas *f.pl.*

I

infraction *n.* infracción *f.,* violación *f.*

insubordination *n.* insubordinación *f.*

insulting *adj.* insultante; ofensivo, -va

M

misconduct *n.* mala conducta *f.*

N

narcotic *n.* narcótico *m.*

O

obscenity *n.* obscenidad *f.,* indecencia *f.,* grosería *f.*

P

parental permission *n.* permiso de los padres *m.*

penalty *n.* pena *f.,* sanción *f.*

pocketknife *n.* navaja *f.,* cortaplumas *m.*

probation *n.* libertad condicional *f.*

progressive discipline *n.* disciplina progresiva *f.*

punish *v.* castigar

punishment *n.* castigo *m.*

R

rowdy *adj.* revoltoso, -sa

S

safety *n.* seguridad *f.*

search *n.* registro *m.*

security *n.* seguridad *f.*

smoke *v.* fumar

SCHOOL LIFE

SCHOOL LIFE

smoking *n.* fumar *m.*

spit *v.* escupir

steal *v.* robar

suspect *n.* sospechoso, -sa *m.f.*

suspension *n.* suspensión *f.*

suspicion *n.* sospecha *f.*, desconfianza *f.*

T

talk back *v.* replicar, contestar con insolencia

tardiness *n.* tardanza *f.*

tattoo *n.* tatuaje *m.*

taunt *v.* burlar

testimony *n.* atestación *f.*, declaración *f.*

theft *n.* robo *m.*

threaten *v.* amenazar

transfer *v.* transferir

trespass *v.* invadir, entrar ilegalmente, traspasar

troublemaker *n.* perturbador *m.*

truancy *n.* absentismo escolar *m.*

V

vandalize *v.* destrozar

victim *n.* víctima *m.f.*

violation *n.* violación *f.*

violent behavior *n.* comportamiento violento *m.*

vulgarity *n.* vulgaridad *f.*, grosería *f.*

W

waiver of rights *n.* renuncia de derechos *f.*

warning *n.* advertencia *f.*

weapon *n.* arma *f.*

withdraw from school *v.* separarse de la escuela, retirarse de la escuela

witness *n.* testigo *m.*

wrongdoing *n.* delito *m.*, infracción *f.*

Z

zero tolerance policy *n.* política de tolerencia cero *f.*

ESPAÑOL-INGLÉS

ARTES DEL LENGUAJE

Gramática y Composición

A

abreviar *v.* to abridge, condense
abreviatura *f.* abbreviation
acento *m.* (símbolo) accent, (sílaba) stress; **a. agudo** acute accent; **a. diacrítico** diacritical marks; **a. ortográfico** accent mark
acrónimo *m.* acronym
adjetivo *m.* adjective; **a. comparativo** comparative adjective; **a. compuesto** compound adjective; **a. indefinido** indefinite adjective; **a. predicativo** predicate adjective; **a. superlativo** superlative adjective
adverbio *m.* adverb
afijo *m.* affix
afirmativo, -va *adj.* affirmative
alfabeto *m.* alphabet
ampersand *m.* ampersand
anexar *v.* to append
anotación *f.* entry
antecedente *m.* antecedent
antónimo *m.* antonym
apellido *m.* surname, last name

apodo *m.* nickname
apositivo *m.* appositive
apóstrofo *m.* apostrophe
apuntes *m.pl.* notes
arcaico, -ca *adj.* archaic
argumento *m.* argumentation, topic
artículo *m.* article; **a. definido** definite article; **a. indefinido** indefinite article
asterisco *m.* asterisk
ataque personal *m.* personal attack
atribución *f.* attribution

B

bastardilla *f.* italics *pl.;* **en b.** *adj.* italicized; **poner in b.** *v.* to italicize
bibliografía *f.* bibliography
biblioteca *f.* library
bibliotecario *m.* library catalog
bitácora *f.* log
boceto *m.* outline
boletín informativo *m.* newsletter
borrador *m.* draft; **hacer un b. de** *v.* to draft

borrar *v.* to delete

C

cambio de tiempo *m.* tense shift

cancioncilla *f.* jingle, ditty

carácter *m.* (letra) character

carta *f.* (escritura) letter; **c. de negocio** business letter

caso *m.* case; **c. nominativo, primer c.** subjective case; **c. objetivo** objective case

catálogo bibliográfico *m.* library catalog

categoría gramatical *f.* part of speech

circunlocución *f.* circumlocution

cita *f.* quotation, citation; **c. directa** direct quote; **c. dividida** divided quotation

claridad *f.* clarity

cláusula *f.* clause; **c. condicional** conditional clause; **c. dependiente** dependent clause; **c. independiente** independent clause; **c. relativa, c. de relativo** relative clause; **c. subordinada** subordinate clause

cliché *m.* cliché

cognado *m.* cognate; **c. falso** false cognate

coherencia *f.* coherence

colaboración *f.* collaboration

colaborar *v.* to collaborate

coloquial *adj.* colloquial

coloquialismo *m.* colloquialism

columna *f.* column

coma *f.* comma

comandar *v.* to command

comando *m.* command

combinación *f.* combination; **c. de oraciones** sentence combining; **c. de vocales** vowel combination

comillas *f.pl.* quotation marks

comparación *f.* comparison

compartido, -da *adj.* shared; **escritura c.** *f.* shared writing; **lectura c.** *f.* shared reading

compendiar *v.* to condense

compilar *v.* to compile

complemento *m.* object, complement; **c. de la preposición** object of the preposition; **c. directo** direct object; **c. indirecto** indirect object

componer *v.* to compose

composición *f.* composition

comprensión *f.* comprehension

comunicación *f.* communication

concepto *m.* concept

conciso, -sa *adj.* concise

concordancia entre sujeto y verbo *f.* subject-verb agreement

concreto, -ta *adj.* concrete

condensar *v.* to condense

conecciones personales *f.pl.* personal connections

conjunción *f.* conjunction; **c. coordinante** coordinating conjunction; **c. correlativa** correlative conjunction; **c. subordinada** subordinating conjunction

connotación *f.* connotation

consecutivo, -va *adj.* consecutive

consonante *f.* consonant; **c. final**

ending consonant; **c. inicial** beginning consonant; **unión de c.** *f.* consonant blend

consonántico, -ca *adj.* consonant; **grupo c.** *m.* consonant blend

construcción inadecuada *f.* awkward construction

contenido *m.* content

contracción *f.* contraction

contradicción *f.* contradiction

contraste *m.* contrast

corchetes *m.pl.* brackets

correcto, -ta *adj.* correct

corregir *v.* to correct, edit, proofread, revise

correlación como causalidad *f.* correlation as causation

crítica constructiva *f.* constructive criticism

cronológico, -ca *adj.* chronological

cuadro *m.* (texto) table

cuerpo *m.* body

cursiva *f.* italics *pl.,* cursive; **poner en c.** *v.* to italicize

cursivo, -va *adj.* italicized, cursive

curriculum vitae *m.* résumé

D

debate *m.* debate

declaración *f.* declarative sentence

decodificar *v.* to decode; **estrategias para d.** *f.pl.* decoding strategies

definición *f.* definition

deletrear *v.* to spell; **d. mal** to misspell

deletreo *m.* spelling

denotación *f.* denotation

derrotero *m.* outline

despedida *f.* (carta) closing

detalles *m.pl.* details; **d. de apoyo, d. secundarios** supporting details; **d. relacionados que lo apoyen** relevant supporting details

diario *m.* log; **d. de lectura** reading log

diccionario *m.* dictionary; **d. de apellidos** surname dictionary; **d. de citas** quotation dictionary; **d. de ideas afines** thesaurus; **d. de rimas** rhyming dictionary; **d. geográfico** geographic dictionary; **d. ilustrado** picture dictionary; **entrada del d.** *f.* dictionary entry

dificultad *f.* problem

diminutivo, -va *adj.* diminutive

diptongo *m.* diphthong

discurso *m.* speech

discusión *f.* discussion

documentación *f.* documentation

dos puntos *m.pl.* colon

E

editar *v.* to edit

elipsis *f.* ellipsis

elíptico, -ca *adj.* elliptical

encabezado *m.* headline

encabezamiento *m.* heading

enciclopedia *f.* encyclopedia

entrada *f.* entry

entrevista *f.* interview

enumeración *f.* enumeration

enunciación *f.* enunciation

enunciar *v.* to enunciate

epíteto *m.* epithet

ARTES DEL LENGUAJE

error *m.* error; **e. de ortografía**
misspelling; **e. tipográfico** misprint, typographical error
esbozo *m.* outline
escribir *v.* to write; **e. incorrectamente** to misspell
escrito, -ta *adj.* written
escritura *f.* writing; **e. a mano**
handwriting; **e. colaborativa** collaborative writing; **e. compartida**
shared writing; **e. creativa** creative writing; **e. expositiva** expository writing; **plan de e.** *m.*
prewriting
eslogan *m.* slogan
espacio *m.* space
estrategias *f.pl.* strategies; **e. para
decodificar** decoding strategies
estructura *f.* structure; **e. de la
oración** sentence structure; **e.
paralela** parallel structure
etimología *f.* etymology
evidencia *f.* evidence
exageración *f.* overstatement, exag-
geration
exposición *f.* exposition
expositivo, -va *adj.* expository; **escritura e.** *f.* expository writing;
texto e. *m.* expository text

F
figura del discurso *f.* figure of
speech
firma *f.* signature
fonema *m.* phoneme
forma gramatical *f.* grammatical
form

formato *m.* format
fragmento de oración *m.* sentence
fragment
frase *f.* phrase; **f. adjetiva** adjective
phrase; **f. preposicional** prepositional phrase; **f. verbal** verb
phrase
fuente *f.* source; **f. primaria, f.
principal** primary source; **f. secundaria** secondary source
futuro, -ra *adj.* future
futuro *m.* future tense; **f. perfecto**
future perfect tense

G
generalidad *f.* generality
generalización *f.* generalization
generalizar *v.* to generalize
género *m.* gender
gerundio *m.* gerund
glosario *m.* glossary
grafema *m.* grapheme
gráfico, -ca *m.f.* chart, graph
gramática *f.* grammar
gramatical *adj.* grammatical; **categoría g.** *f.* part of speech; **regla g.**
f. grammatical rule
guión *m.* hyphen, dash

H
hecho *m.* fact
hoja de vida *f.* résumé
hojear *v.* to skim
homófono *m.* homophone
homógrafo *m.* homograph
homónimo *m.* homonym

ARTES DEL LENGUAJE

● ●

I

idea principal *f.* main idea

idioma *m.* language; **adquisición del i.** *f.;* language acquisition; **i. de llegada** target language

idiomático, -ca *adj.* idiomatic; **expresión i.** *f.* idiom

impresora *f.* printer

imprimir *v.* to print

indicativo, -va *adj.* indicative; **modo i.** *m.* indicative mood

infinitivo *m.* infinitive; **i. dividido** split infinitive

inflexión *f.* inflection

informe *m.* report

inglés estándar *m.* standard English

instrucciones *f.pl.* directions

interjección *f.* interjection

itálicas *f.pl.* italics

J

jerga *f.* jargon, slang

L

legible *adj.* legible

letra *f.* letter, print; **l. bastardilla** italics *pl.;* **l. cursiva** cursive writing; **l. de imprenta** typeface; **l. mayúscula** capital letter; **l. minúscula** lower case letter

léxico *m.* lexicon

libelo *m.* libel

libro *m.* book; **l. de sinónimos** thesaurus; **l. de texto** textbook

lingüística *f.* linguistics

literal *adj.* literal; **traducción l.** *f.* literal translation

lógica *f.* logic

lógico, -ca *adj.* logical

LL

lluvia de ideas *f.* brain-storming; **hacer ll. de i.** *v.* to brainstorm

M

manual de estilo *m.* style manual

margen *m.* margin

materiales de referencia *f.pl.* reference materials

matiz *m.* nuance, shade of meaning

mayúscula *f.* capital letter; **escribir con m.** *v.* to capitalize; **uso de mayúsculas** *m.* capitalization

mayúsculo, -la *adj.* uppercase, capitalized

medios de difusión, medios de comunicación *m.pl.* mass media

mezcla *f.* blend

mezclar *v.* to blend

minúscula *f.* lower case letter

minúsculo, -la *adj.* lower case

modismo *m.* idiom

modo *m.* mood; **m. imperativo** imperative mood; **m. indicativo** indicative mood; **m. subjuntivo** subjunctive mood

morfología *f.* morphology

N

narración personal *f.* personal narrative

negación doble *f.* double negative

negativo, -va *adj.* negative

ARTES DEL LENGUAJE

ARTES DEL LENGUAJE

negrita *f.* boldface

neologismo *m.* neologism

no verbal *adj.* nonverbal

nombre *m.* noun, name, first name, given name; **n. de soltera** maiden name; **n. propio** proper noun; **segundo n.** middle name

nombrete *m.* nickname

nota *f.* note, memo; **n. al final** endnote; **n. al pie de página** footnote; **n. explicativa** explanatory note

número *m.* number

O

objetivo, -va *adj.* objective; **caso o.** *m.* objective case

objeto *m.* object; **o. directo** direct object; **o. indirecto** indirect object; **o. preposicional, o. de la preposición** object of the preposition

obras citadas *f.pl.* works cited

obseno, -na *adj.* obscene

obsoleto, -ta *adj.* obsolete

opinión *f.* opinion

oración *f.* sentence, clause; **estructura de o.** sentence structure *f.*; **fragmento de o.** *m.* sentence fragment; **o. compleja** complex sentence; **o. completa** complete sentence; **o. compuesta** compound sentence; **o. compuesta compleja** compound-complex sentence; **o. condicional** conditional clause; **o. declarativa** declarative sentence; **o. dependiente** dependent clause; **o. exclamativa** exclamatory sentence; **o. imperativa** imperative

sentence; **o. inconexa, o. seguida** run-on sentence; **o. independiente** independent clause; **o. interrogativa** interrogative sentence; **o. principal** topic sentence; **o. relativa** relative clause; **o. simple** simple sentence; **o. subordinada** subordinate clause

oral *adj.* oral

orden *f.* (mandato) command

orden *m.* (secuencia) order; **o. cronológico** chronological order

ordenar *v.* to command

organización *f.* organization; **patrones de o.** *m.pl.* organizational patterns

organizador gráfico *m.* graphic organizer

ortografía *f.* spelling

P

página *f.* page

palabra *f.* word; **p. a simple vista** sight word; **p. afín** cognate; **p. compuesta** compound word; **p. extranjera** foreign word

parafrasear *v.* to paraphrase

paráfrasis *f.* paraphrase

paralelismo *m.* parallelism

paréntesis *m.* parenthesis

participio *m.* participle; **pasado p.** past participle; **presente p.** present participle

párrafo *m.* paragraph

pasado, -da *adj.* past

pasado *m.* past tense; **p. perfecto** past perfect tense

patronímico *m.* patronymic

persona *f.* person; **primera p.** first person; **segunda p.** second person; **tercera p.** third person

personal *adj.* personal

petición de principio *m.* begging the question

plagio *m.* plagiarism

plan de escritura *m.* prewriting

plural *adj. & m.* plural

portafolio *m.* portfolio

posesivo, -va *adj.* possessive

predicado *m.* predicate; **p. nominal** predicate nominative

predicativo, -va *adj.* predicate; **adjetivo p.** *m.* predicate adjective

prefijo *m.* prefix

pregunta *f.* question

preguntar *v.* to question

preposición *f.* preposition; **complemento de la p., objeto de la p.** *m.* object of the preposition

presentación oral *f.* oral presentation

presente *adj. & m.* present tense; **p. perfecto** present perfect tense

primera persona *f.* first person

problema *m.* problem

procesamiento de texto *m.* word processing

pronombre *m.* pronoun; **p. demonstrativo** demonstrative pronoun; **p. indefinido** indefinite pronoun; **p. interrogativo** interrogative pronoun; **p. reflexivo** reflexive pronoun; **p. relativo** relative pronoun

pronunciación *f.* pronunciation

prueba *f.* evidence

puesta en común *f.* brainstorming

punto *m.* period

punto y coma *m.* semicolon

puntos suspensivos *m.pl.* ellipsis

puntuación *f.* punctuation

R

raíz de la palabra *f.* root word

raya *f.* dash

razonamiento *m.* reasoning; **r. circular** circular reasoning; **r. deductivo** deductive reasoning; **r. inductivo** inductive reasoning

recopilar *v.* to compile

recurso mnemotécnico *m.* mnemonic device

redacción *f.* writing, drafting, composition

redactar *v.* to compose, draft; **r. de nuevo** to redraft

redundancia *f.* redundancy

redundante *adj.* redundant

reescribir *v.* to rewrite, redraft

reescrito, -ta *adj.* rewritten

referencia cruzada *f.* cross-reference

reflexión *f.* reflection

registro *m.* log; **r. de lectura** reading log

regla gramatical *f.* grammatical rule

relación grafofonética *f.* letter-sound relationship

relevante *adj.* relevant

repetir *v.* to repeat

reportaje *m.* news story, reportage

reporte *m.* report

ARTES DEL LENGUAJE

ARTES DEL LENGUAJE

resumen *m.* abstract, summary
resumir *v.* to summarize, condense
retroalimentación *f.* feedback
revisado, -da *adj.* revised
revisar *v.* to revise
revisión *f.* revision
rima *f.* rhyme; **diccionario de rimas** *m.* rhyming dictionary
romana *f.* Roman type
rúbrica *f.* rubric

S

saludo *m.* salutation, (carta) greeting
sangrado, -da *adj.* indented
sangrar *v.* to indent
sangría *f.* indentation
secuencia de pensamiento *f.* train of thought
segunda persona *f.* second person
semántica *f.* semantics
seminario socrático *m.* Socratic seminar
separación silábica *f.* hyphenation
significado *m.* denotation
signo *m.* mark, sign; **s. de exclamación, s. de admiración** exclamation mark; **s. de interrogación** question mark; **s. et** ampersand
sílaba *m.* syllable
silabeo *m.* syllabication
símbolo & *m.* ampersand
singular *adj. & m.* singular
sinónimo *m.* synonym
sinopsis *f.* synopsis, abstract
sintaxis *f.* syntax
sobregeneralización *f.* overgeneralization

subjetivo, -va *adj.* subjective; **caso s.** *m.* subjective case
subtítulo *m.* subhead
sufijo *m.* suffix
sujeto *m.* subject; **concordancia entre s. y verbo** *f.* subject-verb agreement
sustantivo *m.* noun
sustitución *f.* substitution; **s. de consonante** consonant substitution

T

tabla *f.* table, chart
tarjeta de catálogo *f.* card catalog
tema *m.* theme, subject, topic
tensión *f.* tension
tercera persona *f.* third person
tesauro *m.* thesaurus
tiempo *m.* tense; **cambio de t.** tense shift
tilde *f.* tilde, accent mark
titular *m.* headline
título *m.* heading, title
trabajo de investigación *m.* research paper
traducción *f.* translation; **t. literal** literal translation; **t. simultánea** simultaneous translation
traducir *v.* to translate
transición *f.* transition

U

uso *m.* usage

V

validez *f.* validity

● ●

válido, -da *adj.* valid

variante *f.* variant

verbal *adj.* verbal; **no v.** nonverbal

verbo *m.* verb; **v. atributivo** linking verb; **v. auxiliar** auxiliary verb; **v. compuesto** compound verb; **v. copulativo** linking verb; **v. de acción** action verb; **v. intransitivo** intransitive verb; **v. irregular** irregular verb; **v. regular** regular verb; **v. transitivo** transitive verb

virguilla *f.* apostrophe

vocabulario *m.* vocabulary

vocal *f.* vowel; **sonido de v.** *m.* vowel sound; **v. corta** short vowel; **v. larga** long vowel

voz *f.* voice; **v. activa** active voice; **v. pasiva** passive voice

vulgar *adj.* vulgar

vulgaridad *f.,* **vulgarismo** *m.* vulgarity

Y

yuxtaposición *f.* juxtaposition

Literatura

● ●

A

abreviado, -da *adj.* abridged

abstracto, -ta *adj.* abstract

acción *f.* action; **a. ascendente** rising action; **a. descendente** falling action

adaptación *f.* adaptation

adaptado, -da *adj.* adapted

adivinanza *f.* riddle

agradecimientos *m.pl.* acknowledgments

alegoría *f.* allegory

aliteración *f.* alliteration

almanaque *m.* almanac

alusión *f.* allusion

ambiente *m.* ambience

ambigüedad *f.* ambiguity

análisis *m.* analysis; **a. crítico** critical analysis; **a. estructural** structural analysis

analogía *f.* analogy

anécdota *f.* anecdote

anónimo, -ma *adj.* anonymous

antagonista *m.f.* antagonist

antecedentes *m.pl.* background

anticlímax *f.* anticlimax

antihéroe *m.* antihero

antología *f.* anthology

apelación *f.* appeal; **a. a la autoridad** appeal to authority; **a. emocional** emotional appeal

apéndice *f.* appendix

apócrifo, -fa *adj.* apocryphal

argumento *m.* plot, story line, topic; **a. decisivo, a. final** clincher; **a. secundario** subplot; **desarrollo del a.** *m.* plot development

arquetipo *m.* archetype

artefacto *m.* artifact

articulación *f.* articulation

artículo *m.* article

artífice de la palabra *m.f.* word-smith

asonancia *f.* assonance

asunto *m.* motif, theme, topic

audiencia *f.*, **auditorio** *m.* audience

autobiografía *f.* autobiography

autógrafo *m.* autograph

autor, -ora *m.f.* author

B

balada *f.* ballad

bardo *m.* bard, poet

bibliografía *f.* bibliography; **b. comentada** annotated bibliography

biografía *f.* biography

bosquejo corto *m.* vignette

C

cadencia *f.* cadence

calendario *m.* almanac

calidad *f.* quality; **c. estética** aesthetic quality

caligrafía *f.* script, calligraphy

canción infantil, canción de cuna *f.* nursery rhyme

canon *m.* (literatura) canon

capítulo *m.* chapter

carácter *m.* character, quality; **desarrollo de c.** *m.* character development; **rasgo de c.** *m.* character trait

característica del texto *f.* text feature

caracterización *f.* characterization

causa y efecto *f.* cause and effect

causalidad *f.* causation

censura *f.* censorship

censurar *v.* to censor

ciencia ficción *f.* science fiction

claridad de la prosa *f.* prose clarity

clásico, -ca *adj.* classical; **texto c.** classical text

clásicos *m.pl.* classics

clave *f.* clue; **c. de contexto** contextual clue

clímax *m.* climax

coautor, -ora *m.f.* coauthor

colección *f.* collection; **c. de cuentos, c. de historias** collection of stories

comedia *f.* comedy

comienzo *m.* onset

comparar y contrastar *v.* to compare and contrast

conclusión *f.* conclusion, denouement

condensado, -da *adj.* condensed; **versión c.** *f.* condensed version

conferencia *f.* lecture

conflicto *m.* conflict; **c. externo** external conflict; **c. interno** internal conflict; **c. interpersonal** interpersonal conflict

consonancia *f.* consonance

contexto *m.* context

contraportada *f.* (libro) back cover

convención *f.* convention

copla *f.* couplet

coro *m.* chorus, refrain

credibilidad *f.* credibility

creíble *adj.* credible

criterios *m.pl.* criteria

crítica *f.* criticism, critique; **c. liter-**

aria literary criticism

crónicas *f.pl.* chronicles

cronología *f.* chronology

cubierta *f.* (libro) front cover; **c. dura** hardcover

cuento *m.* story, tale; **c. corto** short story; **c. de fantasmas** ghost story; **c. de hadas** fairy tale; **c. fantastico** tall tale; **c. largo** feature story; **c. picaresco, c. de travesuras** trickster tale; **c. sobrenatural** supernatural tale; **c. tradicional** folktale

culpabilidad por asociación *f.* guilt by association

cultura *f.* culture

D

decepción *f.* anticlimax

dedicatoria *f.* (libro) dedication

derechos de autor *m.* copyright

desarrollo *m.* development; **d. de carácter** character development; **d. del argumento** plot development

descripción *f.* description; **d. física** physical description

desenlace *m.* denouement

detalles sensorios *m.pl.* sensory details

dialecto *m.* dialect

diálogo *m.* dialogue; **d. dramático** dramatic dialogue

diario *m.* diary, journal, newspaper

diarista *m.f.* diarist

dicción *f.* diction

discurso *m.* discourse, oration; **d.**

directo direct address

disertación *f.* discourse

docudrama *m.* drama-documentary

drama *m.* drama

dramático, -ca *adj.* dramatic

E

edición *f.* edition

editar *v.* to publish

editor *m.* editor, publisher

editorial *f.* publisher, publishing house

editorial *m.* (artículo) editorial

elaboración *f.* elaboration

elegía *f.* elegy

elementos literarios *m.pl.* literary elements

énfasis *m.* emphasis

engañoso, -sa *adj.* fallacious

ensayo *m.* essay

entonación *f.* intonation

épico, -ca *adj.* epic; **poema é.** *m.* epic poem

epígrafe *m.* epigraph

episódico, -ca *adj.* episodic

episodio *m.* episode

epopeya *f.* epic poem

error de cita *m.* misquotation

escandir *v.* to scan

escena *f.* scene, stage; **e. retrospectiva** flashback

escenario *m.* setting

escritor, -ora *m.f.* writer; **e. de misterio** mystery writer; **e. fantasma** ghost writer

escritura *f.* writing

esencia *f.* gist, essence

ARTES DEL LENGUAJE

ARTES DEL LENGUAJE

estanza *f.* stanza
estereotípico, -ca *adj.* stereotypical
estereotipo *m.* stereotype
estético, -ca *adj.* aesthetic; **calidad e.** *f.* aesthetic quality; **propósito e.** *m.* aesthetic purpose
estilizado, -da *adj.* stylized
estilo *m.* style
estribillo *m.* refrain
estructura *f.* structure; **e. del cuento** story structure; **e. del texto** text structure; **e. jerárquica** hierarchic structure
eufemismo *m.* euphemism
evocador, -ora *adj.;* **evocativo, -va** *adj.* evocative
evocar *v.* to evoke
explícito, -ta *adj.* explicit
expresivo, -va *adj.* expressive; **escritura e.** *f.* expressive writing
extracto *m.* excerpt

F
fábula *f.* fable
falacia *f.* fallacy; **f. del hombre de paja** straw man
falaz *adj.* fallacious
fantasía *f.* fantasy
farsa *f.* farce
ficción *f.* fiction; **ciencia f.** science fiction; **f. histórica** historical fiction; **narración de f.** *f.* fictional narrative
figura retórica *f.* figure of speech
figurativo, -va *adj.* figurative; **lenguaje f.** *m.* figurative language
fin *m.* end, conclusion

final *m.* end, ending; **f. abierto** open ending
fluidez *f.* fluency
flujo de conciencia *m.* stream of consciousness
folleto *m.* brochure

G
género *m.* genre
gótico, -ca *adj.* Gothic

H
haiku *m.* haiku
héroe *m.* hero
heroína *f.* heroine
hipérbole *f.* hyperbole
hipótesis *f.* hypothesis
histórico, -ca *adj.* historical; **narración h.** *f.* historical narrative
humor *m.* humor

I
idioma *f.* language
ilustración *f.* illustration
ilustrar *v.* to illustrate
imagen *f.* image; **i. sensorial** sensory image
imágenes *f.pl.,* **imaginería** *f.* imagery
imitación *f.* pastiche
implícito, -ta *adj.* implicit, inferential
impreso, -sa *adj.* published
incongruencia *f.* incongruity
índice *m.* table of contents, index
inédito, -ta *adj.* unpublished
inferencia *f.* inference

• •

inferencial *adj.* inferential, implicit

influencia *f.* bias; **i. del (de la) autor (-ora)** author's bias

información secundaria *f.* supporting detail

interpretación *f.* interpretation

introducción *f.* introduction, prologue

ironía *f.* irony

J

juego de palabras *m.* pun, wordplay

L

lapso de tiempo *m.* time lapse

lector, -ora *m.f.* reader

lectura *f.* reading; **l. compartida** shared reading; **l. en coro** choral reading; **l. en voz alta** read-aloud; **l. guiada** guided reading

leer *v.* to read; **l. de nuevo** to reread; **l. en voz alta** to read aloud

lengua *f.* language; **l. de origen** source language; **l. vernácula** vernacular

lenguaje *m.* language; **l. descriptivo** descriptive language; **l. figurativo** figurative language; **l. formal** formal language; **l. informal** informal language; **patrón del l.** *m.* language pattern

léxico *m.* lexicon

leyenda *f.* legend

libraco *m.* potboiler

librería *f.* bookstore

libro *m.* book; **l. de capítulos** chapter book; **l. en rústica, l. en edi-**ción de bolsillo paperback; **l. ilustrado** picture book; **l. sin texto** wordless book

limerick *f.* limerick

lírico, -ca *adj.* lyrical; **poema l.** *m.* lyric poem

literario, -ria *adj.* literary; **crítica l.** *f.* literary criticism; **elementos l.** *m.pl.* literary elements; **recurso l.** *m.* literary device

literatura *f.* literature; **l. factual, l. no ficcional** nonfiction; **l. neoclásica** neoclassic literature

lomo *m.* (libro) spine

M

manido, -da *adj.* trite

manuscrito *m.* manuscript

matiz *m.* nuance

melodrama *m.* melodrama

melodramático, -ca *adj.* melodramatic

memoria *f.* memoir

metacognición *f.* metacognition

metáfora *f.* metaphor

metonimia *f.* metonymy

metro *m.* meter

misterio *m.* mystery

mito *m.* myth

mitología *f.* mythology

modernismo *m.* modernism

momento crucial *m.* turning point

monólogo *m.* monologue; **m. interior** interior monologue, stream of consciousness

moraleja *f.* (cuento) moral

motivo *m.* motive

ARTES DEL LENGUAJE

N

narración *f.* narrative, narration; **n. de ficción** fictional narrative; **n. historica** historical narrative

narrador, -ora *m.f.* narrator; **n. limitado (-da)** limited narrator; **n. omnisciente** omniscient narrator

narrativo, -va *adj.* narrative

naturalismo *m.* naturalism

nombre artístico *m.* nom de plume, pseudonym

novela *f.* novel, fiction; **n. corta** novella; **n. de suspenso** thriller; **n. picaresca** picaresque novel; **n. policiaca** crime novel, detective story; **n. romántica, n. rosa** love story; **n. utópica** utopian novel

noveleta *f.* novella

novelista *m.f.* novelist

O

objeto de arte artifact *m.*

obra *f.* work; **o. literarias** *pl.* literary works

oda *f.* ode

omnisciente *adj.* omniscient; **o. limitado** limited omniscient

onomatopeya *f.* onomatopoeia

oración *f.* oration

oratoria *f.* oratory

oxímoron *m.* oxymoron

P

página de presentación *f.* title page

palabra *f.* word; **juego de palabras** *m.* pun, word play; **p. clave** key word

palíndromo *m.* palindrome

panfleto *m.* pamphlet

papel del carácter *m.* character foil

parábola *f.* parable

paradoja *f.* paradox

parodia *f.* parody

pasaje *m.* passage

pastiche *m.* pastiche

pastoral *adj.* pastoral

pathos *m.* pathos

patrón *m.* patrón; **p. del lenguaje** language pattern

pendiente resbaladiza *f.* slippery slope

pentámetro yámbico *m.* iambic pentameter

periódico *m.* newspaper

periodista *m.f.* journalist, reporter

personaje *m.* character; **desarrollo del p.** *m.* character development; **p. estático** static character; **p. plano** flat character; **p. principal** main character; **p. redondo** round character; **p. secundario** minor character

personificación *m.* personification

perspectiva *f.* perspective

persuasivo, -va *adj.* persuasive

pista *f.* clue

poema *m.* poem; **p. épico** epic poem; **p. lírico** lyric poem

poesía *f.* poetry; **p. estructurada** structured poetry

poeta *m.f.* poet

portada *f.* (libro) cover, title page

predecir *v.* to foreshadow

predicción *f.* prediction

prefacio *m.* preface

pregunta *f.* question; **p. retórica** rhetorical question

premisa *f.* premise

presagiar *v.* to foreshadow

prólogo *m.* foreword, prologue

propaganda *f.* propaganda

propósito *m.* purpose, **p. del (de la) autor (-ora)** author's purpose; **p. estético** aesthetic purpose

prosodia *f.* prosody

protagonista *m.f.* protagonist

proverbio *m.* proverb

publicación *f.* publication; **p. periódica** periodical

publicador *m.* publisher

publicar *v.* to publish

público *m.* audience

punto de vista *m.* point of view, perspective; **p. d. v. omnisciente** omniscient point of view; **p. d. v. limitado** limited point of view

R

rasgo de carácter *m.* character trait

realismo *m.* realism; **r. mágico** magical realism

recontar *v.* to retell

recurso *m.* device; **r. literario** literary device; **r. persuasivo** persuasive device; **r. retórico** rhetorical device

relato *m.* story; **r. absurdo** tall tale

releer *v.* to reread

reparto de personajes *m.* cast of characters

repetición *m.* repetition

repetido, -da *adj.* repeated

reportero, -ra *m.f.* reporter

reseña de cine *f.* film review

resolución *f.* resolution

retórica *f.* rhetoric

revista *f.* diary, journal, magazine

ritmo *m.* rhythm

romanticismo *m.* Romanticism

romántico, -ca *adj.* Romantic; **período literario r.** *m.* Romantic period literature

S

sacar conclusiones *v.* to draw conclusions

saga *f.* saga, legend

sarcasmo *m.* sarcasm

sátira *f.* satire

secuencia *f.* sequence

segmento *m.* excerpt

semántica *f.* semantics

serial *m.* serial

sermón *m.* sermon

sesgado, -da *adj.* biased, slanted

seudónimo *m.* pseudonym, nom de plume

significado *m.* meaning; **s. múltiples** *pl.* multiple meanings

simbolismo *m.* symbolism

símbolo *m.* symbol

simil *m.* simile

síntesis *m.* synthesis

sistema de creencias *m.* belief system

ARTES DEL LENGUAJE

ARTES DEL LENGUAJE

soliloquio *m.* soliloquy

solución *f.* solution; **s. del conflicto** conflict resolution

soneto *m.* sonnet

subestimación *f.* understatement

sugerencia *f.* suggestion

surrealismo *m.* surrealism

surrealista *adj. & m.f.* surrealist

suspenso *m.* suspense, cliffhanger

T

tabla de contenidos *f.* table of contents

tema *m.* theme, motif; **t. explícito** explicit theme; **t. implícito** implicit theme; **t. principal** primary theme; **t. recurrente** recurring theme; **t. universal** universal theme

tesis *f.* thesis

teutónico, -ca *adj.* Teutonic

texto *m.* text, textbook; **característica del t.** *f.* text feature; **t. clásico** classical text; **t. contemporáneo** contemporary text; **t. expositivo** expository text; **t. informativo** informational text; **t. narrativo** narrative text; **t. persuasivo** persuasive text; **t. popular** popular text

título *m.* title

tonalidad *f.* nuance

tono *m.* tone

trabalenguas *m.* tongue-twister

tradado *m.* treatise

tradición oral *f.* oral tradition

tragedia *f.* tragedy

tragicomedia *f.* tragicomedy

trasfondo *m.* background

trillado, -da *adj.* trite, hackneyed

U

utopía *f.* utopia

utópico, -ca *adj.* utopian; **novela u.** utopian novel *f.*

V

vanguardia *f.* avant-garde

verboso, -sa *adj.* verbose

vernáculo, -la *adj.* vernacular; **lengua v.** *f.* vernacular

verosimilitud *f.* verisimilitude

versión *f.* version; **v. condensada** condensed version

verso *m.* verse; **v. libre** blank verse, free verse

victoriano, -na *adj.* Victorian; **novela v.** *f.* Victorian novel

villano *m.* villain

vocabulario *m.* lexicon

volumen *m.* volume

volver a contar *v.* to retell

Idiomas

alemán *m.* German
amárico, amhárico *m.* Amharic
apache *m.* Apache
árabe *m.* Arabic
armenio *m.* Armenian
aymará *m.* Aymara
bengalí *m.* Bengali
camboyano *m.* Cambodian
cantonés *m.* Cantonese
castellano *m.* Castilian
catalán *m.* Catalan
coreano *m.* Korean
crow *m.* Crow
checo *m.* Czech
cheroqui *m.* Cherokee
cheyenne *m.* Cheyenne
choctaw *m.* Choctaw
danés *m.* Danish
eritreo *m.* Eritrean
español *m.* Spanish
finés, finlandés *m.* Finnish
francés *m.* French; criollo f. *m.*
 French Creole
gaélico *m.* Gaelic
gallego *m.* Galician
griego *m.* Greek
gujarati *m.* Gujarati
hawaiano *m.* Hawaiian
haytian criollo *m.* Haitian Creole
hebreo *m.* Hebrew
hindú *m.* Hindi
hmong *m.* Hmong
holandés *m.* Dutch

hopi *m.* Hopi
húngaro *m.* Hungarian
indonesio *m.* Indonesian
inglés *m.* English; i. antiguo Old
 English
iñupiaq *m.* Inupiak
italiano *m.* Italian
japonés *m.* Japanese
keres *m.* Keres
kurdo *m.* Kurdish
ladino *m.* Ladino
lakota *m.* Lakota
lao *m.* Laotian
latín *m.* Latin
malayo *m.* Malay
mandarín *m.* Mandarin
maorí *m.* Maori
maya *m.* Maya
mixteco *m.* Mixtec
náhuatl *m.* Nahuatl
navajo *m.* Navajo
neerlandés *m.* Dutch
noruego *m.* Norwegian
ojibwa *m.* Ojibwa
papago *m.* Papago
persa *m.* Farsi (Persian)
pima *m.* Pima
polaco *m.* Polish
portugués *m.* Portuguese
punjabí *m.* Punjabi
quechua *m.* Quechua
rumano *m.* Romanian
ruso *m.* Russian

ARTES DEL LENGUAJE

samoano *m.* Samoan

serbocroata *m.* Serbo-Croatian

somalí *m.* Somali

sudanés *m.* Sudanese

sueco *m.* Swedish

tagalo *m.* Tagalog

tailandés *m.* Thai

tamil *m.* Tamil

tewa *m.* Tewa

turco *m.* Turkish

ucraniano *m.* Ukrainian

urdu *m.* Urdu

vasco *m.* Basque

vietnamita *m.* Vietnamese

xhosa *m.* Xhosa

yídish *m.* Yiddish

yupik *m.* Yup'ik

zapoteco *m.* Zapotec

zulú *m.* Zulu

zuni *m.* Zuñi

ARTES DEL LENGUAJE

MATEMÁTICAS

Aritmética y Álgebra

A

abajo de *adv. & prep.* under, below
abscisa *f.* abscissa
acercarse *v.* to approximate
acertar *v.* to guess correctly
adentro de *adv. & prep.* inside
adición *f.* addition
afuera de *adv. & prep.* outside
aislar *v.* to isolate
al menos *adj.* at least
álgebra *f.* algebra
algebraico, -ca *adj.* algebraic
algoritmo *m.* algorithm
alto, -ta *adj.* high; **el más a., la más a.** highest; **más a.** higher
antes de *adv. & prep.* before
aplicaciones *f.pl.* applications
aplicar *v.* to apply
aproximadamente *adv.* approximately
aproximado, -da *adj.* approximate
aproximarse *v.* to approximate
aritmética *f.* arithmetic
aritmético, -ca *adj.* arithmetic; **se-cuencia a.** *f.* arithmetic sequence; **serie a.** *f.* arithmetic series
arreglo *m.* array
atinar *v.* to guess correctly

B

bajo, -ja *adj.* low; **el más b., la más b.** lowest; **más b.** lower
bajo *adv.* under
balance *m.,* **balanza** *f.* balance
base *f.* base; **b. de una potencia** base of a power; **b. diez** base ten
bastante *adv.* enough
binomio *m.* binomial
borde *m.* border
buscar *v.* to look for

C

cada *adj.* each
calculadora *f.* calculator
calcular *v.* to calculate
calendario *m.* calendar
cambio *m.* (dinero) change
casi *adv.* almost
categoría *f.* category

MATEMÁTICAS

centésimo, -ma *adj;* hundredth; **c. parte** *f.* hundredth part

centésimo *m.* percent, hundredth

cercano, -na *adj.* near; **el más c., la más c.** nearest; **más c.** nearer

certero, -ra *adj.* certain

certeza *f.* certainty

ciclo *m.* cycle

cierto, -ta *adj.* certain

clasificar *v.* to classify, sort

clave *f.* key

cociente *m.* quotient

coeficiente *m.* coefficient

columna *f.* column

coma decimal *f.* decimal point

combinación *f.* combination

combinar *v.* to combine

como máximo *adj.* at most

comparar *v.* to compare

compilar *v.* to gather

completo, -ta *adj.* full

común *adj.* common

conclusión *f.* conclusion

conexión *f.* connection

conjetura *f.* guess, conjecture

conjunto *m.* set

consecutivamente *adv.* consecutively

consecutivo, -va *adj.* consecutive

constante *adj. & f.* constant

construcción *f.* construction

contar *v.* to count

coordenada *f.* coordinate; **c. cartesiana** Cartesian coordinate; **c. x** x-coordinate; **c. y** y-coordinate

correcto, -ta *adj.* right, correct

correlación *f.* correlation

coseno *m.* cosine (cos); **proporción del c.** *f.* cosine ratio

cotangente *f.* cotangent (cot)

crecer *v.* to grow

creciente *adj.* growing

crecimiento *m.* growth; **c. exponencial** exponential growth

cronograma *m.* schedule, timetable

cuadrado *m.* square; **c. inverso** inverse square; **c. perfecto** perfect square

cuadrante *m.* quadrant

cuadrar *v.* to square

cuadrático, -ca *adj.* quadratic

cuadrícula de coordenadas *f.* coordinate grid

¿Cuál es el volumen de ...? What is the volume of ...?

¿Cuántos? *adv.* How many?; **¿C. más?** How many more?

cuarto, -ta *adj. & m.f.* quarter

cubo *m.* cube; **c. perfecto** perfect cube

cubicar *v.* to cube

cuenta salteada *f.* skip-count

CH

cheque *m.* (dinero) check

D

debajo de *adv. & prep.* under, below

decenas *f.pl.* tens

decimal *adj. & m.* decimal; **coma d.** *f.,* **punto d.** *m.* decimal point; **d. finito** terminating decimal; **d. mixto** mixed decimal; **d. periódico** repeating decimal

● ●

décima parte *f.* (proporción) tenth

décimo *m.* (serie) tenth

demostrar *v.* to show

denominador *m.* denominator; **d. común** common denominator

dentro de *adv. & prep.* inside

derecho, -cha *adj.* straight

descomposición en factores primos *f.* prime factorization

descuento *m.* discount

desigual *adj.* unlike, unequal

desigualdad *f.* inequality

después de *adv. & prep.* after

determinar *v.* to determine

diagrama de Venn *m.* Venn Diagram

dibujo a escala *m.* scale drawing

diferencia *f.* difference, gap

diferente *adj.* different

dígito *m.* digit; **d. significativos** *pl.* significant digits

disimil *adj.* unlike

distancia *f.* gap, space; **d. horizontal** run; **d. vertical** rise

dividendo *m.* dividend

dividir *v.* to divide

divisible *adj.* divisible

división *f.* division

divisor *m.* divisor

doblar *v.* to double

doble *adj. & m.* double

docena *f.* dozen

dominio *m.* domain

E

ecuación *f.* equation; **e. algebraica** algebraic equation; **e. cuadrática** quadratic equation; **e. lineal** linear equation

eje *m.* axis; **e. horizontal**. horizontal axis; **e. vertical** vertical axis; **e. x** x-axis; **e. y** y-axis

ejercicios *m.pl.* excercises

elemento *m.* element

eliminar *v.* to eliminate

encima *adv. & prep.,* **por encima de** *adv. & prep.* above, over

encontrar *v.* to find

entero *m.* integer, whole number; **e. negativo** negative integer; **e. positivo** positive integer

entrada *f.* input

entre *prep.* between

enunciado condicional *m.* conditional statement

equivalente *adj. & m.* equivalent

escoger *v.* to choose

espacio *m.* space, gap

esquina *f.* corner

estándar *adj.* standard; **forma e.** *f.* standard form; **notación e.** *f.* standard notation

estimación *f.* estimation; **e. frontal, e. por la izquierda** front-end estimation; **e. y verificación** guess and check

estimar *v.* to estimate

evaluar *v.* to evaluate

exactamente *adv.* exactly

exacto, -ta *adj.* accurate

examinar *v.* to examine

explicación *f.* explanation

explicar *v.* to explain

exponencial *adj.* exponential

MATEMÁTICAS

MATEMÁTICAS

exponente *m.* exponent; **e. negativo** negative exponent; **e. positivo** positive exponent

expresar *v.* to express

expresión *f.* expression; **e. algebraica** algebraic expression; **e. mínima de una fracción** simplest form of a fraction

F

factor *m.* factor; **árbol de factores** *m.* factor tree; **f. común** common factor; **f. común mayor** greatest common factor; **f. de crecimiento** growth factor; **f. de escala** scale factor; **f. exponencial** exponential factor

factorial *adj.* factorial

factorización *f.* factorization; **f. en primos** prime factorization

falso, -sa *adj.* false

faltante *adj.* missing

fila *f.* row

finito, -ta *adj.* finite

fondo *m.* bottom

forma *f.* form; **f. de cuña** wedge; **f. desarrollada** expanded form; **f. estándar** standard form; **f. más simple** simplest form; **f. pendiente-intercepto** slope intercept; **f. reducida** reduced form

fórmula *f.* formula; **f. cuadrática** quadratic formula

fracción *f.* fraction; **f. impropia** improper fraction; **f. con denominadores distintos** *pl.* unlike fractions; **f. mixtas** *pl.* mixed fractions

función *f.* function; **f. cuadrática** quadratic function; **f. lineal** linear function

G

general *adj.* general

generalización *f.* generalization

generalizar *v.* to generalize

generar *v.* to generate

gradual *adj.* gradual

gráfica *f.,* **gráfico** *m.* graph

graficar *v.* to chart

grande *adj.* large; **el más g., la más g.** largest; **más g.** larger

grupo *m.* cluster, group

H

hallar *v.* to find

hecho *m.* fact; **familia de hechos** *f.* fact family; **h. aditivo** addition fact; **h. de división** division fact; **h. de multiplicación** multiplication fact; **h. de resta, h. de sustracción** subtraction fact; **h. numérico** number fact

horario *m.* schedule, timetable

I

identidad *f.* identity; **i. aditiva** additive identity; **i. multiplicativa** multiplicative identity

igual *adj.* equal

igualar *v.* to equal

igualdad *f.* equality

impar *adj.* odd

imposible *adj.* impossible

improbable *adj.* unlikely

impuesto sobre las ventas *m.* sales tax

infinito, -ta *adj.* infinite

integral *adj.* integral

intercambio *m.* trade

intercepto en x *m.* x-intercept; **i. en y** y-intercept

interés *m.* interest; **i. compuesto** compound interest; **i. simple** simple interest

intervalo *m.* gap

inverso, -sa *adj.* inverse; **operación i.** *f.* inverse operation

inverso *m.* inverse; **i. aditivo** additive inverse; **i. multiplicativo** multiplicative inverse

J

juntar *v.* to join

L

lapso *m.* span

lejano, -na *adj.* far; **el más l., la más l.** farthest; **más l.** farther

línea *f.* line; **l. de tiempo** timeline; **l. numérica** number line

lineal *adj.* linear; **no l.** nonlinear

lista *f.* list

listar *v.* to list

liviano, -na *adj.* light

localizar *v.* to locate

logaritmo *m.* logarithm

M

más *adj. & adv.* more, most; **m. que** more than

más *prep.* plus

matemáticas *f.* mathematics

matriz *f.* array, matrix

máximo, -ma *adj.* most; **m. común divisor** *m.* greatest common factor

máximo *m.* maximum; **como m.** at most

mayor *adj.* most; **m. parte** *f.* most; **m. número de** most; **m. que** *adv.* greater than

mayoría *f.* most

media *f.* average

medio, -dia *adj.* half, middle

menor *adj.* less; **el m., m. número de** fewest; **m. que** *adv.* less than

menos *adj. & adv.* less; **m. que** fewer than, less than; **por lo m.** at least

menos *prep.* minus

meta *f.* goal

método *m.* method; **m. de eliminación** elimination method; **m. de sustitución** subsition method

mezclar *v.* to mix

milésimo, -ma *adj.* thousandth

milésimo *m.* thousandth

mínimo, -ma *adj.* least, minimum; **lo m.** *adv. & m.* least; **m. cantidad de** *adj.* fewest; **m. común denominador** *m.* least common denominator

mínimo *m.* minimum

mismo, -ma *adj.* same; **el m. que** *adv.* same as

mitad *adj. & f.* half

mixto, -ta *adj.* mixed

modelo a escala *m.* scale model

moneda *f.* coin, currency

MATEMÁTICAS

monomio *m.* monomial
multiplicación *f.* multiplication
multiplicador *m.* multiplier
multiplicar *v.* to multiply; **m. en cruz** to cross multiply
multiplicativo, -va *adj.* multiplicative
múltiplo *m.* multiple; **mínimo común m.** least common multiple; **m. común** common multiple

N

nada *pron.* nothing
negativo, -va *adj.* negative; **entero n.** *m.* negative integer; **exponente n.** *m.* negative exponent; **número n.** *m.* negative number
ninguno *pron.* none
no más que *adv.,* **no mayor que** *adv.* no more than
no menos que *adv.,* **no menor que** *adv.* no less than
notación *f.* notation; **n. científica** scientific notation; **n. de sumatoria** summation notation; **n. estándar** standard notation
numerador *m.* numerator
numeral *adj.* numeral
numérico, -ca *adj.* numerical
número *m.* number, numeral, whole number; **n. árabe** Arabic numeral; **n. áureo** golden ratio; **n. cardinal** cardinal number; **n. compuesto** composite number; **n. de referencia** benchmark number; **n. decimal** decimal number; **n. entero** whole number; **n. imaginario** imaginary number; **n. impar** odd number; **n. irracional** irrational number; **n. mixto** mixed number; **n. negativo** negative number; **n. ordinal** ordinal number; **n. par** even number; **n. primo** prime number; **n. racional** rational number; **n. real** real number; **n. romano** Roman numeral; **n. naturales** *pl.* natural numbers

O

objetivo *m.* goal
opuesto, -ta *adj.* opposite
orden *f.* command, order
orden *m.* sequence, order, array; **o. de operaciones** order of operations
ordenado, -da *adj.* ordered
ordenar *v.* to order, sort
organizar *v.* to arrange
orígen *m.* origin

P

par *adj.* even
par *m.* pair; **p. coordenado** coordinated pair; **p. nulo** zero pair; **p. ordenado** ordered pair
parábola *f.* parabola
parte *f.* part, piece; **p. inferior** bottom; **p. superior** top
paso *m.* step
patrón *m.* pattern
pendiente *f.* slope
pequeño, -ña *adj.* small; **el más p., la más p.** smallest; **más p.** smaller

● ●

percentil *m.* percentile

perfecto, -ta *adj.* perfect

pesado, -da *adj.* heavy; **el más p., la más p.** heaviest; **más p.** heavier

pie *m.* bottom

plan *m.* plan

planificar *v.* to plan

plano coordenado *m.* coordinated plane

pocos, -cas *adj. & m.f.pl.* few

polinomio *m.* polynomial

por *prep.* (multiplicación) times

por ciento *adv.* percent

porcentaje *m.* percentage

porción *f.* piece

positivo, -va *adj.* positive

potencia *f.* (exponente) power; **p. de diez** power of ten; **segunda p.** square

practicar *v.* to practice

precio *m.* price; **p. de oferta** sale price; **p. unitario** unit price

precisión *f.* precision

preciso, -sa *adj.* precise, accurate

predecir *v.* to predict

predicción *f.* prediction

primer *m.* first

primero, -ra *adj.* first

primo, -ma *adj.* prime

principio *m.* principle; **p. fundamental de conteo** fundamental counting principle

problema *m.* problem; **p. narrativo** story problem

producto *m.* product; **p. cruzado** cross product; **p. parcial** partial product

progresión *f.* progression; **p. aritmética** arithmetic sequence, arithmetic progression; **p. geométrica** geometric sequence, geometric progression

promedio *m.* mean, average

propiedad *f.* property; **p. asociativa** associative property; **p. conmutativa** communicative property; **p. de orden** order property; **p. distributiva** distributive property

proporción *f.* proportion, ratio; **p. del coseno** cosine ratio; **p. del seno** sine ratio

puntaje *m.* score

punto *m.* point; **p. decimal** decimal point; **p. periódico** repeating decimal

R

radical *adj. & m.* radical

raíz *f.* root; **r. cuadrada** square root; **r. cúbica** cube root

razonable *adj.* reasonable; **no r.** unreasonable

razonamiento *m.* reasoning

reagrupar *v.* to regroup

recíproca *f.* reciprocal

recopilar *v.* to gather

recursivo, -va *adj.* recursive

redondear *v.* to round

reemplazar *v.* to replace

regla *f.* rule; **r. recursiva** recursive rule

relación *f.* relation

representar *v.* to represent

MATEMÁTICAS

MATEMÁTICAS

residuo *m.*, **resto** *m.*, **restante** *m.* remainder
resolver *v.* to solve
respuesta *f.* answer
resta *f.* subtraction
restar *v.* to subtract
resultados *m.pl.* results

S

saldo *m.* balance
salida *f.* output
salteada *f.* skip-count
secuencia *f.* sequence, progression; **s. aritmética** arithmetic sequence; **s. de Fibonacci** Fibonacci sequence; **s. de números** number sequence; **s. geométrica** geometric sequence
semejante *adj.* alike
seno *m.* sine (sin)
separado, -da *adj.* separate
separar *v.* to isolate
serie *f.* series; **s. aritmética** arithmetic series; **s. geométrica** geometric series
signo *m.* sign; **s. de adición, s. de suma** plus sign, addition sign; **s. de división** division sign; **s. de menos, s. de resta, s. de sustracción** minus sign, subtraction sign; **s. de multiplicación** multiplication sign; **s. radical** radical sign
símbolo *m.* symbol
simplificar *v.* to simplify
simulación *f.* simulation
sistema *m.* system; **s. de desigualdades lineales** system of linear

inequalities; **s. de ecuaciones** system of equations; **s. métrico** metric system
sobre *prep.* over
solución *f.* solution, answer
suficiente *adj.* enough
suma *f.* sum, addition
sumando *m.* addend
sumar *v.* to add
sumas y restas *f.pl.* addition and subtraction
sumatoria *f.* summation; **notación s.** summation notation
suponer *v.* to guess
suposición *f.* guess
sustituir *v.* to subsitute
sustracción *f.* subtraction
sustraer *v.* to subtract

T

tabla *f.* table; **t. de funciones** function table
tangente *f.* tangent (tan)
tantos como *adv.* as many as
tasa *f.* rate; **t. de cambio** rate of change; **t. unitaria** unit rate
tendencia *f.* trend
término *m.* term; **t. no semejantes** *pl.* unlike terms
termómetro *m.* thermometer
tiempo transcurrido *m.* elasped time
todo, -da *adj.* all
tope *m.* top, maximum, limit
total *m.* total
trigonometría *f.* trigonometry
trinomio, -ma *adj.* trinomial

trinomio *m.* trinomial
triple *adj.* triple
triplicar *v.* to triple

U
último, -ma *adj.* last
único, -ca *adj.* single
unidad *f.* unit
unidades *f.pl.* ones

unir *v.* to join

V
vacío, -cía *adj.* empty
valor *m.* value; **v. absoluto** absolute value; **v. posicional** place value
variable *adj. & f.* variable
verdadero, -ra *adj.* true
verificar *v.* to check, verifys

Geometría

A
adyacente *adj.* adjacent
agudo, -da *adj.* acute
alterno, -na *adj.* alternate
altitud *f.* altitude
alto, -ta *adj.* tall; **el más, la más a.** tallest; **más a.** taller
altura *f.* height; **a. de un triángulo** height of a triangle
ancho, -cha *adj.* wide
ancho *m.* width
anchura *f.* width
ángulo *m.* angle; **á. adyacente** adjacent angle; **á. agudo** acute angle; **á. central** central angle; **á. de rotación** angle of rotation; **á. exterior** exterior angle; **á. interno** interior angle; **á. llano** straight angle; **á. obtuso** obtuse angle; **á. recto** right angle; **á. suplementario** supplementary angle; **á. vertical** vertical angle
ángulos alternos *m.pl.* alternate angles; **á. complementarios** complementary angles; **á. correspondientes** corresponding angles; **á. externos alternos** alternate exterior angles; **á. internos alternos** alternate interior angles; **á. opuestos** opposite angles
apotema lateral *f.* slant height; **a. l. de una pirámide** regular slant height of a regular pyramid
arco *m.* arc; **a. mayor** major arc; **a. menor** minor arc
área *f.* area; **á. de superficie** surface area
arista *f.* (prisma) edge
axioma *m.* axiom

B
base *f.* base
bidimensional *adj.* two-dimensional
bisecar *v.* to bisect
bisectriz *adj. & f.* bisector; **b. del**

ángulo angle bisector; **b. perpendicular** perpendicular bisector
boceto *m.* sketch
borde *m.* edge

C

capacidad *f.* capacity
cara *f.* face
cateto *m.* (triángulo recto) leg
centro *m.* center
cilindro *m.* cylinder
cinta métrica *f.* tape measure
circular *adj.* circular
círculo *m.* circle
circunferencia *f.* circumference
clasificar *v.* to classify
comparar *v.* to compare
compás *m.* compass
completo, -ta *adj.* full
comprobar *v.* to prove
cóncavo, -va *adj.* concave
congruente *adj.* congruent
cono *m.* cone
construir *v.* to construct
convexo, -xa *adj.* convex
corto, -ta *adj.* short; **el más c., la más c.** shortest; **más c.** shorter
correspondiente *adj.* corresponding; **partes c.** *f.pl.* corresponding parts
cuadrado, -da *adj.* square
cuadrado *m.* square
cuadrante *m.* quadrant
cuadrícula *f.* grid
cuadrilátero, -ra *adj.* quadrilateral
cuadrilátero *m.* quadrilateral
cúbico, -ca *adj.* cubic

cubo *m.* cube
cuerda *f.* chord
cuerpo geométrico *m.* solid
curva *f.* curve
curvo, -va *adj.* curved

D

decágono *m.* decagon
demostrar *v.* to prove
densidad *f.* density
describir *v.* to describe
deslizamiento *m.* slide
diagonal *adj.* diagonal
diámetro *m.* diameter
dibujar v. to draw
dibujo *m.* drawing, sketch
dilatación *f.* dilation
dimensión *f.* dimension
diseñar *v.* to design, draw
diseño *m.* design
distancia *f.* distance

E

elipse *m.* ellipse
elíptico, -ca *adj.* elliptical
esfera *f.* sphere
estimar *v.* to estimate
extremos *m.pl.* endpoints

F

figura *f.* figure; **f. abierta** open figure; **f. cerrada** closed figure; **f. plana** plane figure; **f. semejante** simlar figure; **f. sólida** solid figure
forma *f.* shape
frente *m.* front; **al f.** *adj. & adv.* in front

MATEMÁTICAS

G

geometría *f.* geometry; **g. euclidea**
  Euclidean geometry
geométrico, -ca *adj.* geometric
girar *v.* to turn
giro *m.* turn
grado *m.* degree; **g. de un ángulo**
  degree of an angle
gráfica circular *f.* circle graph

H

hemisferio *m.* hemisphere
heptágono *m.* heptagon
hexágono *m.* hexagon
hipérbola *f.* hyperbola
hipotenusa *f.* hypotenuse
horizontal *adj.* horizontal

I

identificar *v.* to identify
imagen en espejo *f.* mirror image
intersectar *v.* to intersect
invertir *v.* to flip
isósceles *adj.* isosceles

L

lado *m.* side; **l. derecho** right side;
  l. izquierdo left side; **l. corre-**
  spondientes *pl.* corresponding
  sides
largo, -ga *adj.* long; **el más l., la más**
  l. longest; **más l.** longer; **¿Qué tan**
  l. es ... ? How long is ... ?
línea *f.* line; **l. de simetría** line of
  symmetry; **l. secante** secant line;
  segmento de l. *m.* line segment
líneas paralelas, líneas rectas *f.pl.*

parallel lines; **l. perpendiculares**
  perpendicular lines
longitud *f.* length

LL

lleno, -na *adj.* full

M

masa *f.* mass
medida *f.* measurement
medir *v.* to measure
métrico, -ca *adj.* metric; **sistema**
  m. *m.* metric system
modelar *v.* to model
modelo *m.* model; **m. a escala**
  scale model

O

obtuso, -sa *adj.* obtuse; **ángulo o.**
  m. obtuse angle
octágno *m.* octagon

P

paralelo, -la *adj.* parallel
paralelogramo *m.* parallelogram
partes correspondientes *f.pl.* corresponding parts
partición *f.* grid
pendiente *f.* slope
pentágono *m.* pentagon
perímetro *m.* perimeter
perpendicular *adj.* perpendicular
peso *m.* weight; **p. bruto** gross
  weight
pi *m.* pi
pirámide *f.* pyramid
poliedro *m.* polyhedron

MATEMÁTICAS

239

MATEMÁTICAS

polígono *m.* polygon; **p. irregular** irregular polygon; **p. regular** regular polygon; **p. semejante** similar polygon

postulado *m.* postulate

prisma *m.* prism; **p. rectangular** rectangular prism; **p. triangular** triangular prism

profundidad *f.* depth

prueba *f.* proof

punto *m.* point; **p. de rotación** point of rotation; **p. medio** midpoint

R

radio *m.* radius

rayo *m.* ray

rectangular *adj.* rectangular

rectángulo *m.* rectangle

recto, -ta *adj.* right; **trapecio r., trapezoide r.** *m.* right trapezoid; **triángulo r.** *m.* right triangle

red *f.* net

reflejo *m.* reflection

reflexión con desplazamiento y traslación *f.* glide reflection

regla *f.* ruler

reloj *m.* clock; **en sentido contrario a las agujas del r.** *adj. & adv.* counterclockwise; **en sentido de las agujas del r.** clockwise

rombo *m.* rhombus

rompecabezas chino *m.* tangram

rotación *f.* rotation

S

sector *m.* sector

segmento *m.* segment; **s. de línea** line segment

semejante *adj.* similar

semicírculo *m.* semicircle

simetría *f.* symmetry; **s. lineal** linear symmetry; **s. rotacional** rotational symmetry

similar *adj.* similar

sistema *m.* system; **s. anglosajón de unidades** customary system; **s. métrico** metric system

sólido, -da *adj.* solid

sólido *m.* solid; **s. geométricos** *pl.* geometric solids

sombreado, -da *adj.* shaded; **sin sombra** unshaded

superficie *f.* surface; **area de s.** *f.* surface area

T

tablero de dardos *m.* dart board

tamaño *m.* size

tangente *f.* tangent

teorema *m.* theorem; **t. de Pitágoras** Pythagorean Theorem

teselación *f.,* **teselado** *m.* tessellation

teselar *v.* to tessellate

tetraedro *m.* tetrahedron

transformación *f.* transformation

transportador *m.* protractor

transversal *adj.& f.* transversal

trapecio *m.,* **trapezoide** *m.* trapezoid; **t. isósceles** isosceles trapezoid; **t. recto, t. rectángulo** right trapezoid

traslación *f.* slide

trazar *v.* to trace

triángulo *m.* triangle; **altura de un t.** *f.* height of a triangle; **t. agudo** acute triangle; **t. de Pascal** Pascal's triangle; **t. equilátero** equilateral triangle; **t. escaleno** scalene triangle; **t. isósceles** isosceles triangle; **t. obtuso** obtuse triangle; **t. recto, t. rectángulo** right triangle

tridimensional *adj.* three-dimensional

trío pitagórico *m.* Pythagorean triple

tubo *m.* tube

U

unidad *f.* unit; **u. cuadrada** square unit; **u. cúbica** cubic unit

unidimensional *adj.* one-dimensional

V

vertical *adj.* vertical

vértice *m.* vertex

voltear *v.* to turn

volumen *m.* volume

Probabilidad y Análisis de Datos

A

alcance *m.* range

aleatorio, -ria *adj.* random

aleatoriamente *adv.* randomly

análisis *m.* analysis

analizar *v.* to analyze

arrojar datos *v.* to produce data

C

causalidad *f.* causality

consecuencia *f.* outcome

correlación *f.* correlation; **c. negativa** negative correlation; **c. positiva** positive correlation

cuartil *m.* quartile; **c. inferior** lower quartile; **c. superior** upper quartile

D

datos *m.pl.* data

dependiente *adj.* dependent

desviación típica, desviación estandar *f.* standard deviation

diagrama *m.* plot, diagram; **d. de caja y bigotes** box and whiskers plot; **d. de dispersión, d. de puntos** scatter plot; **d. de líneas** line plot; **d. de tallo y hojas** stem and leaf plot

distribución asimétrica *f.* skewed distribution

E

encuesta *f.* survey

MATEMÁTICAS

241

error *m.* error; **máximo e. posible** greatest possible error

estadística *f.* statistics

etiqueta *f.* label

etiquetar *v.* to label

eventos *m.pl.* events; **e. dependientes** dependent events; **e. independientes** independent events

experimental *adj.* experimental

experimento *m.* experiment

extremo *m.* extreme; **e. inferior** lower extreme; **e. superior** upper extreme

F

flecha *f.* arrow

G

graficar *v.* to graph

gráfico, -ca *m.f.* graph; **g. circular** pie chart; **g. de barras** bar graph; **g. de líneas** line graph

grupo de control *m.* control group

H

histograma *m.* histogram

I

independiente *adj.* independent

intervalo *m.* interval

L

línea *f.* line; **l. de ajuste** line of best fit

líneas alabeadas *f.pl.* skew lines

M

marca de conteo *f.* tally mark

margen de error *m.* margin of error

máximo *m.* maximum

media *f.* mean

mediana *f.* median

mediano, -na *adj.* median

medida *f.* measure; **m. de tendencia central** measure of central tendency

medio, -dia *adj.* mean

mínimo *m.* minimum

modo *m.* mode

muestra *f.* sample; **m. aleatoria** random sample; **m. de conveniencia** convenience sample; **m. sesgada** biased sample

N

nombrar *v.* to label

O

oportunidad *f.* chance

P

permutación *f.* permutation

pictografía *f.* pictograph

población *f.* population

posibilidad *f.* possibility

posible *adj.* possible

pregunta *f.* question; **p. capciosa, p. sesgada** biased question

probabilidad *f.* probability; **p. experimental** experimental probability; **p. teórica** theoretical probability

probable *adj.* likely, probable; **igualmente p.** equally likely

promedio *m.* average, mean

R

rango *m.* range

resultado *m.* outcome

riesgo *m.* chance

rotular *v.* to label

rótulo *m.* label

S

sesgado, -da *adj.* biased; **muestra s.** *f.* biased sample; **pregunta s.** *f.* biased question

suceso *m.* event; **s. compuesto** compound event; **s. mutuamente excluyentes** *pl.* mutually exclusive events

T

tabla de frecuencias *f.* frequency table

V

valor *m.* value; **v. atípico** outlier

variable *f.* variable; **v. dependiente** dependent variable; **v. independiente** independent variable

Números y Medidas

NÚMEROS

	Cardinal	Ordinal
0	zero	
1	one	first
2	two	second
3	three	third
4	four	fourth
5	five	fifth
6	six	sixth
7	seven	seventh
8	eight	eighth
9	nine	ninth
10	ten	tenth

MATEMÁTICAS

11	eleven	eleventh
12	twelve	twelfth
13	thirteen	thirteenth
14	fourteen	fourteenth
15	fifteen	fifteenth
16	sixteen	sixteenth
17	seventeen	seventeenth
18	eighteen	eighteenth
19	nineteen	nineteenth
20	twenty	twentieth
21	twenty-one	twenty-first
30	thirty	thirtieth
31	thirty-one	thirty-first
40	forty	fortieth
50	fifty	fiftieth
60	sixty	sixtieth
70	seventy	seventieth
80	eighty	eightieth
90	ninety	ninetieth
100	one hundred	hundredth
101	one hundred one	one hundred first
200	two hundred	two hundredth
300	three hundred	three hundredth
400	four hundred	four hundredth
500	five hundred	five hundredth
600	six hundred	six hundredth
700	seven hundred	seven hundredth
800	eight hundred	eight hundredth
900	nine hundred	nine hundredth
1,000	one thousand	thousandth
1,001	one thousand one	one thousand first
1,000,000	one million	millionth
1,000,000,000	one billion	billionth
1,000,000,000,000	one trillion	trillionth

MATEMÁTICAS

LONGITUDES

pulgada *f.* inch

pie *m.* foot

yarda *f.* yard

milla *f.* mile

milímetro *m.* millimeter

centímetro *m.* centimeter

metro *m.* meter

kilómetro *m.* kilometer

ÁREAS

pulgada cuadrada *f.* square inch

pie cuadrado *m.* square foot

yarda cuadrada *f.* square yard

milla cuadrada *f.* square mile

acre *m.* acre

centímetro cuadrado *m.* square centimeter

metro cuadrado *m.* square meter

kilómetro cuadrado *m.* square kilometer

VOLUMENES

cucharadita *f.* teaspoon

cucharada *f.* tablespoon

taza *f.* cup

pinta *f.* pint

cuarto de galón *m.* quart

galón *m.* gallon

mililitro *m.* milliliter

decilitro *m.* deciliter

litro *m.* liter

kilolitro *m.* kiloliter

PESOS

onza *f.* ounce

libra *f.* pound

tonelada *f.* ton

miligramo *m.* milligram

gramo *m.* gram

kilogramo *m.* kilogram

TIEMPO

segundo *m.* second

minuto *m.* minute

hora *f.* hour

minutero *m.* minute hand

media hora *f.* half-hour

día *m.* day

semana *f.* week

mes *m.* month

MATEMÁTICAS

● ●

horario, manecilla de las horas *f.* hour hand
segundero *m.* second hand
cuarto de hora *m.* quarter-hour

año *m.* year
década *f.* decade
siglo *m.* century
milenio *m.* millennium

DINERO

centavo *m.*, **penique** *m.* penny
níquel *m.* nickel
diez centavos *m.pl.* dime

veinticinco centavos *m.pl.* quarter
medio dólar *m.* half dollar
dólar *m.* dollar

ENERGÍA

amperio *m.* ampere
miliamperio *m.* milliampere
hertz *m.* hertz
megahertz *m.* megahertz
julio *m.* joule

voltio *m.* volt
vatio *m.* watt
kilovatio *m.* kilowatt
megavatio *m.* megawatt
gigavatio *m.* gigawatt

MATEMÁTICAS

CIENCIA

Ciencias de la Tierra

A

abanico alubial *m.* alluvial fan

abrasión *f.* abrasion

acantilado *m.* cliff

acuático, -ca *adj.* aquatic

acuífero *m.* aquifer

afluente *m.* tributary

agrimensura *f.* survey, surveying

agua *f.* water; **a. atmosférica** atmospheric water; **a. dulce** freshwater; **a. mineral** mineral water; **a. salada** saltwater; **a. salobre** brackish water; **a. superficial** surface water; **a. termal** hot spring; **a. subterráneas, a. freáticas** *pl.* groundwater; **cuerpo de a.** *m.* body of water; **fuente de a.** *f.* water source; **vapor de a.** *m.* water vapor

aguanieve *f.* sleet

aire *m.* air, wind; **contaminación del a.** *f.* air pollution; **dirección del a.** *f.* wind direction; **masa del a.** *f.* air mass; **movimiento del a.** *m.* air movement

alpino, -na *adj.;* **alpestre** *adj.* alpine

anemómetro *m.* anenometer

Anillo de Fuego *m.* Ring of Fire

anticiclón *m.* anticyclone

arado *m.* plowing; **a. de conservación** conservation plowing; **a. de contorno** contour plowing

arcilla *f.* clay

arena *f.* sand

arenisca *f.* sandstone

árido, -da *adj.* arid

ártico, -ca *adj.* arctic; **tundra á.** arctic tundra

arrecife de coral *m.* coral reef

arroyo *m.* stream

arroyuelo *m.* rill

atmósfera *f.* atmosphere

aurora *f.* aurora; **a. boreal** aurora borealis

avalancha *f.* avalanche

B

banco de arena *m.* shoal

barlovento *m.* windward; **de b.** *adj.*

247

windward

barómetro *m.* barometer; **b. aneroide** aneroid barometer

barranco *m.* gully

barrera *f.* barrier

barro *m.* clay

basura *f.* litter

batolito *m.* batholith

bifurcarse *v.* to diverge

bloque *m.* (piedra) block, brick; **b. colgante** hanging wall; **b. yacente** footwall

boca *f.* vent, opening

borde *m.* boundary; **b. de transformación** transform boundary; **b. divergente** divergent boundary

bosque *m.* forest; **b. boreal** boreal forest, taiga; **b. caducifolio, b. deciduo** deciduous forest; **b. nuboso** cloud forest; **b. pluvial templado** temperate rainforest

brillo *m.* luster

brisa *f.* breeze; **b. marina** sea breeze; **b. terrestre** land breeze

brumoso, -sa *adj.* foggy, misty

C

cabo *m.* cape, headland

caja glacial *f.* glacial till

calcita *f.* calcite

caldera volcánica *f.* caldera

calefacción *f.* heating

calentamiento *m.* warming; **c. global** global warming

caliza *f.* limestone

cámara magmática *f.* magma chamber

canto rodado *m.* boulder

cañón *m.* canyon, gorge

capa *f.* layer; **c. de hielo** ice sheet; **c. de ozono** ozone layer; **c. superior del suelo** topsoil; **c. profundas de la tierra, c. interiores de la tierra** *pl.* layers of the Earth

carbón mineral *m.* coal

carga *f.* load

cascada *f.* waterfall

casquete de hielo *m.* ice cap

catástrofe natural *f.* natural disaster

cellisca *f.* sleet

cementación *f.* cementation

ceniza *f.* ash; **cono de c.** *m.* cinder cone

ciclo *m.* cycle; **c. de la roca** *m.* rock cycle

cielo *m.* sky

ciénaga *f.* marsh

Cinturón de Fuego *m.* Ring of Fire

cirro *m.* cirrus

cizallamiento *m.* shearing

clima *m.* climate

colina *f.* hill

combustible *m.* fuel

compactación *f.* compaction

composición *f.* composition; **c. del suelo** soil composition

compresión *f.* compression

condiciones meteorológicas *f.pl.* weather conditions

congelación *f.* freezing; **punto de c.** *m.* freezing point

conglomerado *m.* conglomerate

conífera *f.* conifer

CIENCIA

conservación *f.* conservation; **c. del suelo** *f.* soil conservation

conservar *v.* to conserve

contaminación *f.* pollution; **c. atmosférica** air pollution

contaminante *m.* pollutant

contorno *m.* contour; **intervalo de c.** *m.* contour interval

convección *f.* convection

cordillera *f.* mountain range; **c. oceánica central** mid-ocean ridge

corteza terrestre *f.* earth's crust

corriente *f.* current; **c. de convección** convection current; **c. de resaca** rip current; **c. en chorro** jet stream; **c. piroclástica** pyroclastic flow

cráter *m.* crater

crecer *v.* (río) to rise

cristal *m.* crystal

cristalización *f.* crystallization

cronológico, -ca *adj.* chronological

cuarzo *m.* quartz

cuello volcánico *m.* volcanic neck

cuenca *f.* basin; **c. de polvo** dust bowl; **c. hidrográfica** drainage basin, watershed

cueva *f.* cave

cúmulo *m.* cumulus

cuña de hielo *f.* ice wedging

curva *f.* curve; **c. de nivel** contour line; **c. de nivel índice** index contour

CH

charca *f.* pond

chimenea volcánica *f.* volcanic pipe

D

datación relativa *f.* relative dating

deflación *f.* deflation

deforestación *f.* deforestation

delta *m.* delta

densidad *f.* density

deriva *f.* drift; **d. continental** continental drift; **d. litoral** longshore drift

derretimiento *m.,* **descongelación** *f.* thawing, melting

descomponedor *m.* decomposer

descomposición *f.* decomposition; **d. radiactiva** radioactive decay

desfiladero *m.* gorge

desgaste *m.* weathering; **d. mecánico** mechanical weathering; **d. químico** chemical weathering

deshielo *m.* deglaciation

desierto *m.* desert

deslave *m.,* **desprendimiento de tierras** *m.* landslide

deslizamiento *m.* shearing

diamante *m.* diamond

dique *m.* levee, dyke

dirección del viento *f.* wind direction

divergir *v.* to diverge

dorsal centro-oceánica *m.* mid-ocean ridge

duna *f.* dune; **d. de arena** sand dune

dureza *f.* hardness

E

ecología *f.* ecology

ecológico, -ca *adj.* ecological

ecuador *m.* equator

edad *f.* age; **e. absoluta** absolute age; **e. de hielo** ice age; **e. relativa** relative age

efecto invernadero *m.* greenhouse effect

El Niño *m.* El Niño

elemento *m.* element

elevación *f.* elevation

energía *f.* energy; **e. cinética** kinetic energy; **e. solar** solar energy, solar power

enfriamiento del viento *m.* wind chill

epicentro *m.* epicenter

época *f.* epoch

Época del Eoceno Eocene Epoch *f.;* **É. del Holoceno** Holocene Epoch; **É. del Paleoceno** Paleocene Epoch; **É. del Pleistoceno** Pleistocene Epoch

equinoccio *m.* equinox; **e. de otoño** autumnal equinox; **e. de primavera** vernal equinox

era *f.* era

Era Cenozoica *f.* Cenozoic Era; **E. Críptica** Cryptic Era; **E. Mesozoica** Mesozoic Era; **E. Paleozoica** Paleozoic Era

erosión *f.* erosion, weathering

erupción *f.* eruption; **hacer e., entrar en e.** *v.* to erupt

escala *f.* scale; **e. de dureza de Mohs** Mohs hardness scale; **e. de magnitud de momento** moment magnitude scale; **e. de Mercalli** Mercalli scale; **e. de Richter**

Richter scale; **e. geocronológica** geologic time scale

escarcha *f.* frost

escurrimiento *m.* runoff

esfuerzo *m.* stress

esmeralda *f.* emerald

esmog *m.* smog

esquisto *m.* shale

estación *f.* season

estalactita *f.* stalactite

estalagmita *f.* stalagmite

estapa *f.* steppe

estratósfera, estratosfera *f.* stratosphere

evolución *f.* evolution

expansión *f.* expansion; **e. del piso marino** sea-floor spreading

explosión *f.* explosion

exposición *f.* exposure

extinción en masa, extinción masiva *f.* mass extinction

extinto, -ta *adj.* extinct

extracción glaciar *f.* plucking

extrusión *f.* extrusion

F

falla *f.* fault; **f. inversa** reverse fault; **f. normal** normal fault; **f. transcurrente, f. de rumbo** strike-slip fault

feldespato *m.* feldspar

fierro *m.* iron

fisura *f.* fissure

flujo piroclástico *m.* pyroclastic flow

fluorita *f.* fluorite

foco *m.* focus

foliado, -da *adj.* foliated

formación *f.* formation

fosa oceánica profunda *f.* deep-ocean trench

fósil *adj. & m.* fossil; **combustibles f.** *pl.* fossil fuels; **f. petrificado** petrified fossil; **registro f.** *m.* fossil record; **vestigio f.** trace fossil

fractura *f.* fracture

frente *m.* front; **f. caliente** warm front; **f. frío** cold front

fricción *f.* friction

frontera convergente *f.* convergent boundary

fuego *m.* fire

fuente de agua *f.* water source

fuerza *f.* stress, force

fundición *f.* smelting

G

gas *m.* gas; **g. invernadero** greenhouse gas; **g. natural** natural gas; **g. atmosféricos** *pl.* atmospheric gases

géiser *m.* geyser

gema *f.* gem, gemstone

geocéntrico, -ca *adj.* geocentric

geoda *f.* geode

geográfico, -ca *adj.* geographical; **accidente g.** *m.* geographical feature

geológico, -ca *adj.* geological

geotérmico, -ca *adj.* geothermal; **actividad g.** *f.* geothermal activity

gigantes gaseosos *m.pl.* gas giants

glaciar *m.* glacier

globo terráqueo *m.* (mapa) globe

gota de rocío *f.* dewdrop

gradiente *m.* gradient

grado *m.* degree

grafito *m.* graphite

granito *m.* granite

granizar *v.* to hail

granizo *m.* hail

grava *f.*, **gravilla** *f.* gravel

grueso, -sa *adj.* coarse

guijarro *m.* pebble

H

halo *m.* halo

helado, -da *adj.* freezing

hemisferio *m.* hemisphere

hidrómetro *m.* hydrometer

hidrósfera, hidrosfera *f.* hydrosphere

hielo *m.* ice

hierro *m.* iron

higrómetro *m.* hygrometer

horizonte de suelo *m.* soil horizon

hueco, -ca *adj.* hollow

humedad *f.* moisture, humidity; **h. relativa** relative humidity

humedales *m.pl.* wetlands

humo *m.* smoke

huracán *m.* hurricane

huso horario *m.* time zone

I

iceberg *m.* iceberg

impacto *m.* impact

inactivo, -va *adj.* dormant

incendio *m.* fire; **i. forestal** forest fire

inclemencia climática *f.* severe weather

CIENCIA

CIENCIA

inorgánico, -ca *adj.* inorganic
intrusión *f.* intrusion
inundación *f.* flood
invasión *f.* invasion
invierno *m.* winter
isla *f.* island; **arco de islas** *m.* island arc
isobara *f.* isobar
isoterma *f.* isotherm

L

ladrillo *m.* brick
lago *m.* lake; **l. glacial** glacial lake; **l. oxbow, l. de meandro** oxbow lake
laguna *f.* lagoon
latitud *f.* latitude
lava *f.* lava; **colada de l.** *f.,* **corriente de l.** *f.* lava flow; **l. cordada** pahoehoe
ley de la superposición *f.* law of superposition
licuefacción *f.* liquefaction
litósfera *f.,* **litosfera** *f.* lithosphere
lodo *m.* mud
loess *m.* loess
longitud *f.* longitude
luminoso, -sa *adj.* luminous
lustre *m.* luster

LL

llanura *f.* plain; **ll. aluvial** flood plain
llovizna *f.* drizzle, mist
lluvia *f.* rain; **ll. ácida** acid rain; **ll. fuerte** heavy rain

M

magma *m.* magma
magnitud *f.* magnitude
manantial termal *m.* hot spring
manto *m.* mantle
mapa *m.* map *m.;* **m. meteorológico** weather map; **m. topográfico** topographic map
mar *m.* sea, ocean; **nivel del m.** sea level *m.*
marea *f.* tide; **m. alta** high tide; **m. baja** low tide; **m. viva** spring tide
maremoto *m.* tsunami, tidal wave
marfil *m.* ivory
marga *f.* loam
marino, -na *adj.* marine
marisma *f.* salt marsh
marmita de gigante *f.* kettle
mármol *m.* marble
masa *f.* mass; **m. de aire** air mass; **m. terrestre** land mass
masivo, -va *adj.* massive
meandro *m.* meander
medio ambiente *m.* environment
mena *f.* ore
meridiano *m.* meridian; **m. cero, m. de Greenwich** prime meridian
meseta *f.* plateau
mesosfera *f.* mesosphere
metálico, -ca *adj.* metallic
meteorólogo, -ga *m.f.* meteorologist
mica *f.* mica
mineral *m.* mineral; **m. metalífero** ore mineral
modelo meteorológico *m.* station model

molde *m.* mold

montaña *f.* mountain

montañoso, -sa *adj.* mountainous, hilly

monzón *m.* monsoon

morrena glaciar *f.* moraine

movimiento *m.* motion, movement; **m. aparente** apparent movement; **m. de aire** air movement; **m. glacial** glacial movement

N

neblinoso, -sa *adj.* foggy

nevar *v.* to snow

niebla *f.* fog; **lleno de n.** *adj.* foggy; **n. tóxica** smog

nieve *f.* snow

nimbo *m.* nimbus

nubarrón *m.* storm cloud

nube *f.* cloud; **n. estrato** stratus cloud

nublado, -da *adj.* cloudy; **parcialmente n.** partly cloudy

núcleo *m.* core; **n. interno** inner core

O

obsidiana *f.* obsidian

océano *m.* ocean

ola *f.* (de agua) wave

onda *f.* (física) wave; **o. P** P-wave; **o. S** S-wave; **o. sísmica** seismic wave; **o. superficial** surface wave

órbita geoestacionaria *f.* geostationary orbit

origen *m.* origin

orilla *f.* shore

otoño *m.* autum, fall

ozono *m.* ozone; **agotamiento del o.** *m.,* **disminución del o.** *f.;* ozone depletion; **capa de o.** *f.* ozone layer

P

paisaje *m.* landscape

Pangea *f.* Pangaea

pantanal *m.* marshland

pantano *m.* marsh

pastizal *m.* grassland; **p. templado** temperate grassland

patrón meteorológico *m.* weather pattern

pendiente *f.* slope

península *f.* península

peñasco *m.* cliff, boulder

período, periodo *m.* period

Período Cámbrico, Período Cambriano *m.* Cambrian Period; **P. Cretácico, P. Cretáceo** Cretaceous Period; **P. Cuaternario** Quaternary Period; **P. Jurásico** Jurassic Period; **P. Pérmico** Permian Period; **P. Triásico** Triassic Period

permeable *adj.* permeable

petróleo *m.* oil, petroleum

piedra *f.* rock, stone; **p. caliza** limestone; **p. preciosa** gem, gemstone

pirita *f.* pyrite (fool's gold)

pizarra *f.* slate

placa *f.* plate; **p. tectónicas** *pl.* plate tectonics

playa *f.* beach

pleamar *f.* high tide

CIENCIA

CIENCIA

plegamiento anticlinal *m.* anticline
pliegue *m.* fold
pluviómetro *m.* rain gauge
polo *m.* pole; **P. Norte** North Pole;
　P. Sur South Pole
poza de marea *f.* tide pool
pradera *f.* grassland
precipitación *f.* precipitation
prehistórico, -ca *adj.* prehistoric
presa *f.* dam
presión *f.* pressure; **alta p.** high
　pressure; **baja p.** low pressure; **p.
　atmosférica** air pressure; **p. baro-
　métrica** barometric pressure
primavera *f.* spring
proceso *m.* process; **p. físico** physi-
　cal process; **p. natural** natural
　process
profundidad *f.* depth
promontorio *m.* headland
pronóstico *m.* forecast; **p. del tiem-
　po** weather forecast
proyección cartográfica *f.* map pro-
　jection
punto *m.* point; **p. caliente** hot spot;
　p. de condensación dew point; **p.
　de congelación** freezing point
putrefacción *f.* decomposition

R

racha *f.* streak
radiación *f.* radiation
radiactividad *f.,* **radioactividad** *f.*
　radioactivity
radiactivo, -va *adj.* radioactive;
　datación r. *f.* radioactive dating
rayo *m.* lightning

reciclar *v.* to recycle
recurso *m.* resource; **r. limitado**
　limited resource; **r. renovable** re-
　newable resource; **r. naturales** *pl.*
　natural resources
refinería *f.* refinery
registro fósil *m.* fossil record
relámpago *m.* lightning
relieve *m.* relief
remolino *m.* whirlpool
represa *f.* dam
resaca *f.* undertow
restos *m.pl.* remains; **r. animales**
　animal remains; **r. de plantas**
　plant remains
reutilizar *v.* to reuse
riachuelo *m.* stream, rill
río *m.* river
roca *f.* rock, boulder; **lecho de r.**
　m. bedrock; **r. clástica** clastic
　rock; **r. extrusiva** extrusive rock;
　r. ígnea igneous rock; **r. intrusi-
　va** intrusive rock; **r. metamór-
　fica** metamorphic rock; **r. orgáni-
　ca** organic rock; **r. química, r. de
　precipitación química** chemical
　rock; **r. sedimentaria** sedimen-
　tary rock
rocío *m.* dew
rotura *f.* fracture

S

sabana *f.* savanna
sal *f.* salt
salinidad *f.* salinity
salir *v.* (sol) to rise
sedimentación *f.* deposition

sedimento *m.* silt, sediment

seísmo *m.,* **sismo** *m.* earthquake

selva *f.* rainforest; **s. tropical** tropical rainforest

sequía *f.* drought

serpentear *v.* (río) to meander

sinclinal *adj.* syncline

sismógrafo *m.* seismograph

sismograma *m.* seismogram

sistema de posicionamiento global *m.* global positioning system (G.P.S.)

sobrepoblación *f.* overpopulation

soleado, -da *adj.* sunny

solsticio *m.* solstice; **s. de invierno** winter solstice; **s. de verano** summer solstice

sotavento *m.* leeward; **de s.** *adj.* leeward

subducción *f.* subduction

subir *v.* (marea) to rise

subsuelo *m.* subsoil

suelo *m.* ground, soil; **capa superior del s.** *f.* topsoil; **conservación del s.** *f.* soil conservation; **s. ácido** acid soil *m.;* **textura del s.** *f.* soil texture

suministro *m.* supply

T

taiga *f.* boreal forest

talco *m.* talc

talud continental *m.* continental slope

tectónica de placas *f.* plate tectonics

temblor *m.* tremor; **t. de tierra** earthquake

temperatura *f.* temperature

temporada *f.* season

tensión *f.* tension

tepe *m.* sod

termómetro *m.* thermometer

terremoto *m.* earthquake; **réplica de t.** *f.* aftershock

terreno *m.* land, terrain, soil

textura *f.* texture

tiempo *m.* weather; **t. geológico** geological time; **t. severo** severe weather

tierra *f.* land, soil, earth; **estructura de la t.** *f.* soil composition; **lengua de t.** *f.* spit of land; **t. pantanosas** *pl.* wetlands

tifón *m.* typhoon

topacio *m.* topaz

topografía *f.* topography

tormenta *f.* storm; **t. de nieve** blizzard, snowstorm; **t. de polvo** dust storm; **t. de viento** wind storm; **t. eléctrica** thunderstorm

tornado *m.* tornado

trópicos *m.pl.* tropics

tropósfera *f.,* **troposfera** *f.* troposphere

truenos *m.pl.* thunder

tsunami *m.* tsunami, tidal wave

tubería *f.* volcanic pipe

tundra *f.* tundra

turbulencia *f.* turbulence

U

umbral submarino *m.* sill

CIENCIA

255

CIENCIA

V

vaho *m.* moisture

valle *m.* valley; **v. del rift** rift valley; **glaciar del v.** valley glacier

vapor de agua *m.* water vapor

veleta *f.* wind vane

vena *f.* vein

ventisca *f.* blizzard

ventoso, -sa *adj.* windy

verano *m.* summer

vertedero de basura *m.* landfill

vestigio fósil *m.* trace fossil

veta *f.* streak

viento *m.* wind; **enfriamiento del v.** *m.* wind chill; **velocidad del v.** *f.* wind speed; **v. fuerte** high wind; **v. alisios** *pl.* trade winds

viscosidad *f.* viscosity

volcán *m.* volcano; **v. compuesto** composite volcano; **v. en escudo** shield volcano

volcánico, -ca *adj.* volcanic; **caldera v.** *f.* caldera; **cuello v.** *m.* volcanic neck; **chimenea v.** *f.* volcanic pipe

Y

yacimiento *m.* deposit

yeso *m.* gypsum

Z

zona *f.* zone; **z. de divergencia, z. divergente** divergent zone; **z. horaria** time zone; **z. intermareal** intertidal zone; **z. litoral** littoral zone; **z. pelágica** pelagic zone; **z. de clima templado** *pl.* temperate zones; **z. polares** polar zones

Ciencias de la Vida

A

abdomen *m.* abdomen

absorción *f.* absorption

ácido *m.* acid; **á. desoxirribonucleico (A.D.N.)** deoxyribonucleic acid (D.N.A.); **á. nucleico** *m.* nucleic acid; **á. ribonucleico (A.R.N.)** ribonucleic acid (R.N.A.); **A.R.N. de transferencia** transfer R.N.A.; **A.R.N. mensajero** messenger R.N.A.

acuático, -ca *adj.* aquatic

adaptación *f.* adaptation

adulto, -ta *adj. & m.f.* adult

ala *f.* wing

alelo *m.* allele; **a. dominante** dominant allele; **a. recesivo** recessive allele; **a. múltiples** *pl.* multiple alleles

aleta *f.* fin; **a. dorsal** dorsal fin

algas *f.pl.* algae; **floración de a.** *f.* algal bloom

alimentación *f.* diet, nutrition

alimento *m.* food

almidón *m.* starch

ameba *f.* amoeba

••

aminoácidos *m.pl.* amino acids

anfibio *m.* amphibian

anidar *v.* to nest

animal carroñero *m.* scavenger

anticoncepción *f.* contraception

aparato de Golgi *m.* Golgi body

Aportes dietéticos de referencia (A.D.R.s) *m.pl.* Dietary Reference Intakes (D.R.I.s)

arácnido *m.* arachnid

árbol ramificado *m.* branching tree

arteria *f.* artery; **a. coronaria** coronary artery

articulación *f.* joint

ascáride *f.* roundworm

audición *f.* hearing

autótrofo *m.* autotroph

auxina *f.* auxin

ave *f.* bird; **a. de corral** fowl; **a. de rapiña** raptor, bird of prey

B

bacteria *f.* bacteria

bacteriófago *m.* bacteriophage

barriga *f.* belly

bíceps *m.pl.* biceps

biodegradable *adj.* biodegradable

biodiversidad *f.* biodiversity

biomagnificación *f.* biomagnification

biosfera *f.* biosphere

boca *f.* mouth

bolsa *f.* sac

bosque *m.* forest

branquia *f.* gill

brazo *m.* arm

C

cabello *m.* hair

cabeza *f.* head

cadera *f.* hip

calavera *f.* skull

caliptra *f.* root cap

camuflaje *m.* camouflage

canal semicircular *m.pl.* semicircular canal

cáncer *m.* cancer

caninos *m.pl.* (dientes) canines

capa emergente *f.* emergent layer

capilar *m.* capillary

capullo *m.* cocoon

característica *f.* characteristic, trait

carbohidrato *m.* carbohydrate

carcinógeno *m.* carcinogen

cariotipo *m.* karyotype

carnívoro *m.* carnivore

carpelo *m.* carpel

cartílago *m.* cartilage

casco *m.* (caballo) hoof

célula *f.* cell; **c. diana, c. blanco** target cell; **c. madre** stem cell; **c. T** T cell; **c. guardianas** *pl.* guard cells

celular *adj.* cellular; **ciclo c.** *m.* cell cycle; **crecimiento c.** *m.* cell growth; **división c.** *f.* cell division; **membrana c.** *f.* cell membrane; **pared c.** *f.* cell wall; **teoría c.** *f.* cell theory

celulosa *f.* cellulose

cerebelo *m.* cerebellum

cerebro *m.* brain, cerebrum

ciclo *m.* cycle; **c. de vida** life cycle

cigoto *m.* zygote

CIENCIA

CIENCIA

cilios *m.pl.* cilia

cintura *f.* waist

circular *v.* to circulate

citocinesis *f.* cytokinesis

citoplasma *m.* cytoplasm

clase *f.* (taxonomía) class

clasificación *f.* classification

clavícula *f.* clavicle

clon *m.* clone

clorofila *f.* chlorophyll

cloroplasto *m.* chloroplast

cóclea *f.* cochlea

código *m.* code

codo *m.* elbow

codominancia *f.* codominance

cola *f.* tail

colesterol *m.* cholesterol

colmena *f.* hive

colmillo *m.* fang, tusk

colon *m.* colon

columna vertebral *f.* backbone

comensalismo *m.* commensalism

competencia *f.*, **competición** *f.* competition

comportamiento *m.* behavior

conjugación *f.* conjugation

controlar *v.* to control

contusión *f.* concussion

corazón *m.* heart; **cámaras del c.** *f.pl.* heart chambers

cordal *m.* wisdom tooth

cordón umbilical *m.* umbilical cord

cornamenta *f.* antlers *pl.*

córnea *f.* cornea

corola *f.* corolla

corteza *f.* bark

costilla *f.* rib

cráneo *m.* skull

crecer *v.* to grow

crecimiento *m.* growth; **c. celular** cell growth

crías *f.pl.* offspring

crisálida *f.* pupa, chrysalis

cristalino *m.* (ojo) lens

cromosoma *m.* chromosome; **c. sexuales** *pl.* sex chromosomes

cuadrado de Punnet *m.* Punnett square

cualidad *f.* trait

cuerdas vocales *f.pl.* vocal chords

cuerno *m.* (venado) horn, antler

cuerpo fructífero *m.* fruiting body

cuidado de la salud *m.* health care

D

dedo *m.* finger; **d. índice** index finger

dendrita *f.* dendrite

depredador, -ora *m.f.* predator

descendencia *f.* offspring

descomponer *v.* to break down, decompose, rot

descomposición *f.* decay, decomposition

diente *m.* tooth; **d. de leche** *pl.* baby teeth

difusión *f.* diffusion

digestión *f.* digestion

dióxido de carbono *m.* carbon dioxide

disfunción del órgano *f.* organ malfunction

dislocación *f.* dislocation

disminuir *v.* to decrease

dispersar *v.* to disperse
división celular *f.* cell division

E

ecosistema *m.* ecosystem
embarazada *adj.* pregnant
embarazada *f.* pregnant woman
embarazo *m.* pregnancy
embrión *m.* embryo
endogamia *f.* inbreeding
endotérmico, -ca *adj.* endothermic
enfermedad *f.* disease; **e. infecciosa, e. contagiosa** infectious disease
envenenar *v.* to poison
enzima *f.* enzyme
epidermis *m.* epidermis
epiglotis *f.* epiglottis
equilibrio puntuado *m.* punctuated equilibrium
escama *f.* (piel) scale
esófago *m.* esophagus
especiación *f.* speciation
especie *f.* species; **e. en peligro de extinción** *f.* endangered species; **e. exótica** exotic species
esperma *m.,* **espermatozoide** *m.* sperm
espina dorsal *f.* backbone
espora *f.* spore
esqueleto *m.* skeleton
estambre *m.* stamen
estanque *m.* pond
esteroide *m.* steroid
estimulante *m.* stimulant
estímulo *m.* stimulus
estómago *m.* stomach

estomas *m.pl.* stomata
estrés *m.* stress
estrógeno *m.* estrogen
estructura *f.* structure; **e. homólogas** *pl.* homologous structures
evolución *f.* evolution
excreción *f.* excretion
exosfera *f.* exosphere
exotérmico, -ca *adj.* exothermic
extinción *f.* extinction
extinto, -ta *adj.* extinct

F

fagocito *m.* phagocyte
familia *f.* (taxonomía) family
faringe *f.* pharynx
fármaco *m.* (medicina) drug
fecundación *f.* fertilization
fenotipo *m.* phenotype
fermentación *f.* fermentation
feto *m.* fetus
filo *m.* phylum
fisión binaria *f.* binary fission
fitoplancton *m.* phytoplankton
flagelo *m.* flagellum
flema *f.* phlegm
floema *m.* phloem
flor *f.* flower
folículo *m.* follicle
fotoperiodisidad *f.* photoperiodism
fotosíntesis *f.* photosynthesis
fronda *f.* frond
fruta *f.* (para comer) fruta
fruto *m.* (botánica) fruit
función *f.* function, role

CIENCIA

CIENCIA

G

gametofito, gametófito *m.* gametophyte

ganado *m.* livestock

ganglio *m.* ganglion; **g. linfático** lymph node

garganta *f.* throat

garra *f.* claw, talon, paw

gen *m.* gene; **g. ligado al sexo** sex-linked gene

género *m.* genus

genética *f.* genetics

genitales *m.pl.* genitals

genoma *m.* genome

genotipo *m.* genotype

germinación *f.* germination

gimnospermas *f.pl.* gymnosperms

glándula *f.* gland; **g. endocrina** endocrine gland; **g. pituitaria** pituitary gland; **g. tiroides** thyroid gland

glóbulo *m.* blood cell; **g. blanco** white blood cell; **g. rojo** red blood cell

glucosa *f.* glucose

gradualismo *m.,* **gradualidad** *f.* gradualism

grano *m.* grain

grasas *f.pl.* fats

H

habitar *v.* to inhabit

hábitat *m.* habitat

hembra *adj. & f.* female

hemoglobina *f.* hemoglobin

herbívoro *m.* herbivore

heredado, -da *adj.* inherited

heredar *v.* to inherit

herencia *f.* heredity, inheritance

heterocigótico, -ca *adj.* heterozygous

heterótrofo *m.* heterotroph

hibernación *f.* hibernation

hibridación *f.* hybridization

híbrido, -da *adj.* hybrid

híbrido *m.* hybrid

hidroponia *f.* hydroponics

hifas *f.pl.* hyphae

hígado *m.* liver

hipotálamo *m.* hypothalamus

histamina *f.* histamine

hoja *f.* leaf

homeostasis *f.* homeostasis

homocigótico, -ca *adj.* homozygous

homólogo, -ga *adj.* homologous; **estructuras h.** *pl.* homologous structures

hongos *m.pl.* fungi

hormona *f.* hormone

hueso *m.* bone; **h. compacto** compact bone; **h. esponjoso** spongy bone

huésped *m.* host

huevo *m.* egg

humano, -na *adj.* human

humano *m.* human

I

impulso nervioso *m.* nerve impulse

inanimado, -da *adj.* nonliving, inanimate

incisivo *m.* incisor

infarto cardiaco, infarto cardíaco

m. heart attack

ingeniería genética *f.* genetic engineering

inmunidad *f.* immunity; **i. pasiva** passive immunity

insecto *m.* insect, bug

instinto *m.* instinct

insulina *f.* insulin

interfase *f.* interphase

interneurona *f.* interneuron

interrelación *f.* interrelationship

intestino *m.* intestine; **i. delgado** small intestine; **i. grueso** large intestine

invertebrado, -da *adj.* invertebrate

invertebrado *m.* invertebrate

involuntario, -ria *adj.* involuntary

iris *m.* (ojo) iris

L

lactancia *f.* lactation

laringe *f.* larynx

larva *f.* larva

leche *f.* milk

lengua *f.* tongue

ligamento *m.* ligament

linfa *f.* lymph

linfocito *m.* lymphocyte

lípido *m.* lipid

lisosoma *m.* lysosome

lombriz intestinal *f.* roundworm

luz solar *f.* sunlight

M

macroscópico, -ca *adj.* macroscopic

macho *m. & adj.* male

mamífero *m.* mammal

mandibula *f.* jaw, mandible

mano *f.* hand

manto *m.* canopy

marea roja *f.* red tide

matriz *f.* womb

maxilar *m.* jaw, jawbone

medicamento *m.* medicine, drug

medioambiental *adj.* environmental; **factor m.** *m.* environmental factor

médula *f.* marrow, medulla; **m. espinal** spinal cord

meiosis *f.* meiosis

mejilla *f.* cheek

melanina *f.* melanin

membrana celular *f.* cell membrane

menstruación *f.* menstruation

metabolismo *m.* metabolism

metamorfosis *f.* metamorphosis

microorganismo *m.* microorganism

microscópico, -ca *adj.* microscopic

migración *f.* migration

mimetismo *m.* mimicry

minerales *m.pl.* minerals

mitocondria *f.* mitochondria

mitosis *f.* mitosis

moho *m.* mold

molécula *f.* molecule

monóxido de carbono *m.* carbon monoxide

mortalidad *f.* mortality

mucosidad *f.* mucus

muela *f.* molar; **m. del juicio** wisdom tooth

muerte *f.* death

CIENCIA

CIENCIA

muerto, -ta *adj. & m.f.* dead
multicelular *adj.* multicellular
muñeca *f.* wrist
músculo *m.* muscle; **m. cardiaco,
m. cardíaco** heart muscle; **m. esquelético** skeletal muscle; **m. estriado** striated muscle; **m. involuntario** involuntary muscle; **m.
liso** smooth muscle; **m. voluntario** voluntary muscle
musgo *m.* moss
mutación *f.* mutation
mutualismo *m.* mutualism

N
nacimiento *m.* birth
nalgas *f.pl.* buttocks
nasal *adj.* nasal
nefrona *f.* nephron
nervio *m.* nerve; **n. óptico** optic
nerve
neurona *f.* neuron; **n. motora**
motor neuron; **n. sensorial** sensory neuron
neurotransmisor *m.* neurotransmitter
nicotina *f.* nicotine
nicho *m.* niche
nido *m.* nest
nomenclatura binomial *f.* binomial
nomenclature
núcleo *m.* nucleus
nutriente *m.* nutrient

O
oído *m.* ear; **o. interno** inner ear; **o.
medio** middle ear

ojo *m.* eye
olfato *m.* (sentido) smell
omnívoro *m.* omnivore
orden *m.* (taxonomía) order
organelo *m.* organelle
orgánico, -ca *adj.* organic
organismo *m.* organism; **o. descomponedor** decomposer
órgano *m.* organ; **disfunción del o.**
f. organ malfunction
orgánulo *m.* organelle
origen *m.* origin
orina *f.* urine
ósmosis *f.* osmosis
ovario *m.* ovary
ovíparo, -ra *adj.* oviparous
ovovivíparo, -ra *adj.* ovoviviparous
ovulación *f.* ovulation
óvulo *m.* ovule, egg

P
padre *m.* parent
pájaro *m.* bird
páncreas *m.* pancreas
pantano *m.* swamp
panza *f.* belly
paramecio *m.* paramecium
parasitismo *m.* parasitism
parásito *m.* parasite
pared celular *f.* cell wall
párpado *m.* eyelid
parto *m.* (nacimiento) labor
pasteurización *f.* pasteurization
pata *f.* (animal) leg, paw, foot, hoof;
p. palmeadas *pl.* webbed feet
patógeno *m.* pathogen
pecho *m.* chest

pedigrí *m.* pedigree
pelaje *m.* fur
pelo *m.* hair
pene *m.* penis
penicilina *f.* penicillin
peristaltismo *m.* peristalsis
permeable *adj.* permeable; **selecti-**
  vamente p. selectively permeable
pétalo *m.* petal
pez *m.*, **peces** *m.pl.* fish
pezuña *f.* (vaca, oveja) hoof
pico *m.* beak, bill; **p. encorvado**
  curved bill; **p. ganchudo** hooked
  bill; **p. recto** straight bill
pie *m.* foot
piel *f.* skin
pierna *f.* (humano) leg
pigmento *m.* pigment
pistilo *m.* pistil
placenta *f.* placenta
plantas *f.* plant; **p. no vascular**
  nonvascular plant; **p. vascular**
  vascular plant
plaqueta *f.* platelet
plasma *m.* plasma
platelminto *m.* flatworm
pluma *f.* feather
población *f.* population; **densidad**
  de p. *f.* population density
polen *m.* pollen
polinización *f.* pollination
polinizador *m.* pollinator
polinizar *v.* to pollinate
pólipo *m.* polyp
poro *m.* pore
poroso, -sa *adj.* porous
portador, -ora *m.f.* carrier

predador, -ora *m.f.* predator
presa *f.* prey
procariota *f.* prokaryote
proteína *f.* protein
protozoario, -ria *adj.* protozoan
protozoo *m.* protozoan
pubertad *f.* puberty
pulgar *m.* thumb
pulmón *m.* lung
pulso *m.* pulse
pupila *f.* pupil

Q
quijada *f.* jawbone

R
raíz *f.*, **raíces** *f.pl.* root, roots
rama *f.* branch
rasgo *m.* trait
raza *f.* breed, race; **de pura r.** *adj.*
  purebred; **de r. mixta** mixed-
  breed
reacción *f.*, **respuesta** *f.* reaction,
  response; **r. inflamatoria** inflammatory response; **r. inmunológ-**
  ica immune response
receptor *m.* receptor
recto *m.* rectum
reflejo *m.* reflex
refugio *m.* shelter
reino *m.* (taxonomía) kingdom
replicación *f.* replication
reproducción *f.* reproduction, breeding; **r. asexual** asexual reproduction; **r. selectiva** selective breeding; **r. sexual** sexual reproduction
reproducir *v.* to reproduce

CIENCIA

CIENCIA

reptil *m.* reptile
respiración *f.* respiration
retículo endoplasmático *m.* endoplasmic reticulum
retina *f.* retina
riboflavina *f.* riboflavin
ribosoma *m.* ribosome
riñón *m.* kidney
rizoide *m.* rhizoid
rizoma *m.* rhizome
rodilla *f.* knee

S

saco *m.* sac; **s. vitelino** yolk sac
saliva *f.* saliva
sangre *f.* blood; **de s. caliente** *adj.* warm blooded; **de s. fría** cold blooded
saprofito *m.*, **saprófito** *m.* saprophyte
secreción *f.* secretion
sedante *m.* depressant
selección *f.* selection; **s. natural** natural selection
semen *m.* semen
semilla *f.* seed
sentido *m.* sense; **s. de la vista** sense of sight; **s. del gusto** sense of taste; **s. del oído** sense of hearing; **s. del olfato** sense of smell; **s. del tacto** sense of touch;
sépalo *m.* sepal
seudópodo *m.* pseudopod
simbiosis *f.* symbiosis
sinapsis *f.* synapse
síntesis *f.* synthesis
sistema *m.* system; **s. cardiovascular** cardiovascular system; **s. circulatorio** circulatory system; **s. de órganos** organ system; **s. digestivo** digestive system; **s. esquelético** skeletal system; **s. excretorio** excretory system; **s. inmunológico** immune system; **s. linfático** lymphatic system; **s. muscular** muscular system; **s. nervioso central** central nervous system; **s. nervioso periférico** peripheral nervous system; **s. nervioso somático** somatic nervous system; **s. reproductor** reproductive system; **s. respiratorio** respiratory system; **s. tegumentario** integumentary system
sobreproducción *f.* overproduction
sobrevivir *v.* to survive
somático, -ca *adj.* somatic
supervivencia *f.* survival

T

talón *m.* (pie) heel
tallo *m.* stem
tejido *m.* tissue; **t. conectivo** connective tissue; **t. epitelial** epithelial tissue; **t. muscular** muscle tissue; **t. nervioso** nervous tissue; **t. vascular** vascular tissue
tela de araña *f.* spiderweb
tendón *m.* tendon
tentáculo *m.* tentacle
teoría *f.* theory; **t. celular** cell theory; **t. de la evolución** f. theory of evolution
terapia genética *f.* gene therapy

• •

testículos *m.pl.* testes, testicles

testosterona *f.* testosterone

tímpano *m.* eardrum

tobillo *m.* ankle

tolerancia *f.* tolerance

tórax *m.* thorax

tóxico, -ca *adj.* toxic

toxina *f.* toxin

transporte *m.* transport; **t. activo** active transport; **t. pasivo** passive transport

tráquea *f.* windpipe, trachea

trastorno genético *m.* genetic disorder

trompa de Falopio *f.* Fallopian tube

tronco *m.* trunk

tropismo *m.* tropism

tumor *m.* tumor

turba *f.* peat

U

unicelular *adj.* unicellular

uña *f.* fingernail

urea *f.* urea

uréter *m.* ureter

uretra *f.* urethra

útero *m.* uterus, womb

V

vacuna *f.* vaccine

vacunación *f.* vaccination

vacuola *f.* vacuole

vaina *f.* pod

Valor Porcentual Diario *m.* Percent Daily Value (P.D.V.)

válvula *f.* valve

variación *f.* variation

vegetal *adj. & m.* (planta) vegetable

vejiga *f.* bladder; **v. urinaria** urinary bladder

vellosidades *f.pl.* villi

vena *f.* vein

veneno *m.* poison, venom

ventrículo *m.* ventricle

verdura *f.* (alimento) vegetable

vertebrado, -da *adj.* vertebrate

vértebras *f.pl.* vertebrae

vertebrado *m.* vertebrate

vesícula biliar *f.* gallbladder

virus *m.* virus; **v. activo** active virus

vista *f.* sight

vitaminas *f.pl.* vitamins

vivíparo, -ra *adj.* viviparous

vivo, -va *adj.;* **viviente** *adj.* living, alive

vulva *f.* vulva

X

xilema *f.* xylem

Y

yema *f.* yolk

Z

zoológico *m.* zoo

CIENCIA

ANIMALES

abeja *f.* bee

abejorro *m.* bumblebee

alce *m.* elk; **a. americano** moose

aligador *m.* alligator

águila *m.* eagle

almeja *f.* clam

Alosaurio *m.* Allosaurus

anguila *f.* eel

antílope *m.* antelope

Apatosaurio *m.* Apatosaurus

araña *f.* spider

ardilla *f.* squirrel; **a. listada** chipmunk

armadillo *m.* armadillo

avestruz *m.* ostrich

babuino *m.* baboon

ballena *f.* whale

bisonte *m.*, **búfalo** *m.* bison

burro *m.* donkey

caballito de mar *m.* seahorse

caballo *m.* horse; **c. semental** stallion

cabra *f.* goat

caimán *m.* alligator

calamar *m.* squid

camaleón *m.* chameleon

camarón *m.* shrimp

camello *m.* camel

cangrejo *m.* crab

canguro *m.* kangaroo

caracol *m.* snail

caracola *f.* conch

caribú *m.* caribou

castor *m.* beaver

cebra *f.* zebra

cerdo, -da *m.f.* pig, sow

ciempiés *m.* centipede

ciervo *m.* deer

cocodrilo *m.* crocodile

colibrí *m.* hummingbird

conejo *m.* rabbit

cordero *m.* sheep

corneja *f.*, **cuervo** *m.* crow

coyote *m.* coyote

cucaracha *f.* cockroach

culebra *f.* snake

chango *m.* monkey

chimpancé *m.* chimpanzee

delfín *m.* dolphin

dinosaurio *m.* dinosaur

elefante *m.* elephant

escarabajo *m.* beetle

escorpión *m.* scorpion

Estegosaurio *m.* Stegosaurus

flamenco *m.* flamingo

foca *f.* seal

gallina *f.* hen

gallo *m.* rooster

gamba *f.* shrimp

ganso, -sa *m.f.* goose

garrapata *f.* tick

gato, -ta *m.f.* cat

geco *m.* gecko

gorila *m.* gorilla

grillo *m.* cricket

guepardo *m.* cheetah

gusano *m.* worm

halcón *m.* falcon, hawk

hámster *m.* hamster

hiena *f.* hyena

hipocampo *m.* seahorse

hipopótamo *m.* hippopotamus

hormiga *f.* ant
hurón *m.* ferret
Ictiosaurios *m.pl.* Ichthyosaurs
iguana *f.* iguana
jaguar *m.* jaguar
jerbo *m.* gerbil
jirafa *f.* giraffe
koala *m.* koala
lagartija *f.*, **lagarto** *m.* lizard
langosta *f.* lobster
león *m.* lion; **l. marino** sea lion
leopardo *m.* leopard
libélula *f.* dragonfly
liebre *f.* hare
lince *m.* bobcat, lynx
lobo *m.* wolf
loro *m.* parrot
mamut *m.* mammoth
manatí *m.* manatee
mapache *m.* racoon
mariposa *f.* butterfly
mariquita *f.* ladybug
mastodonte *m.* mastodon
medusa *f.* jellyfish
mofeta *f.* skunk
mono, -na *m.f.* monkey
morsa *f.* walrus
mosca *f.* fly, housefly
mosquito *m.* mosquito
mula *f.* mule
murciélago *m.* bat
nutria *f.* otter
oso, -sa *m.f.* bear
oveja *f.* sheep
pájaro carpintero *m.* woodpecker
panda *m.* panda
papagayo *m.* parrot

papión *m.* baboon
pato, -ta *m.f.* duck
pavo *m.* turkey
pingüino *m.* penguin
perro, -rra *m.f.* dog
petirrojo *m.* robin
piojos *m.pl.* lice
Plesiosaurios *m.pl.* Plesiosaurs
polilla *f.* moth
pollo *m.* chicken
Pterodáctilo *m.* Pterodactyl
Pterosaurio *m.* Pterosaur
puerco, -ca *m.f.* pig
pulga *f.* flea
pulpo *m.* octopus
puma *m.* cougar
rana *f.* frog
rata *f.* rat
ratón *m.* mouse
rinoceronte *m.* rhinoceros
saltamontes *m.* grasshopper
sapo *m.* toad
serpiente *f.* snake
simio *m.* ape
tiburón *m.* shark
tigre *m.* tiger
Tiranosaurio rex *m.* Tyrannosaurus
   rex
toro *m.* bull
tortuga *f.* turtle, tortoise
Triceratops *m.* Triceratops
vaca *f.* cow
venado *m.* deer
yegua *f.* mare
zarigüeya *f.* opossum
zorrillo *m.* skunk
zorro *m.* fox

CIENCIA

FRUTAS, NUECES Y VERDURAS

CIENCIA

aceituna *f.* olive
aguacate *m.* avocado
ají *m.* chili pepper
ajo *m.* garlic
albaricoque *m.* apricot
alcaparras *f.pl.* capers
almendra *f.* almond
anacardo *m.* cashew
apio *m.* celery
arándano *m.* cranberry; **a. azul** blueberry
banana *f.* banana
batata *m.* yam, sweet potato
berenjena *f.* eggplant
betabel *m.* beet
brócoli *m.* broccoli
cacahuate *m.*, **cacahuete** *m.* peanut
calabacín *m.* zucchini, squash
calabaza *f.* pumpkin
cebolla *f.* onion
cereza *f.* cherry
ciruela *f.* plum; **c. pasa** prune
coco *m.* coconut
col *m.* cabbage
coliflor *m.* cauliflower
chícharo *m.* pea
chile *m.* chili pepper
dátil *m.* date
durazno *m.* peach
ejote *m.* string bean
espárragos *m.pl.* asparagus
espinaca *f.* spinach
frambuesa *f.* raspberry
fresa *f.* strawberry
frijol *m.* bean
guisante *m.* pea

habichuela *f.* string bean
hongo *m.* mushroom
lechuga *f.* lettuce
lima *f.* lime
limón *m.* lemon, lime
maíz *m.* corn
mandarina *f.* tangerine
maní *m.* peanut
manzana *f.* apple
melocotón *m.* peach
melón *m.* cantaloupe
mora *f.* blackberry
naranja *f.* orange
nuez *f.* nut, walnut
ñame *m.* yam
pacana *f.* pecan
papa *f.*, **patata** *f.* potato
papaya *f.* papaya
pepino *m.* cucumber
pera *f.* pear
pimienta *f.* (especia) pepper
pimiento verde *m.* green pepper
piña *f.* pineapple
pistacho *m.* pistachio
plátano *m.* plantain, banana
pomelo *m.* grapefruit
remolacha *f.* beet
repollo *m.* cabbage
sandía *f.* watermelon
soja *f.* soybean
tomate *m.* tomato
toronja *f.* grapefruit
uva *f.* grape
yuca *f.* yucca
zanahoria *f.* carrot
zapallo *m.* winter squash

EN EL JARDÍN

abono *m.* fertilizer; **a. orgánico**
  compost

agua *f.* water

arado *m.* plow

arar *v.* to plow

arbusto *m.* bush, shrub

atar, amarrar *v.* to tie up

azada *f.* hoe; **trabajar con la a.** *v.* to
  hoe

azadón *m.* pickaxe, large hoe

azadonar *v.* to hoe

carretilla *f.* wheelbarrow

cavar *v.,* **excavar** *v.* to dig

césped *m.* lawn

compost *m.* compost

compostar *v.* to compost

cortacésped *m.* lawn mower

cubrir *v.* to cover

cultivar *v.* to cultivate, garden, till

desplantador *m.* trowel

espray *m.* spray

fertilizante *m.* fertilizer

fertilizar *v.* to fertilize

flor *f.* flower

germinar *v.* to germinate

guantes *m.pl.* gloves

hierba *f.* herb

horquilla *f.* pitchfork

horticultura *f.* horticulture

humus *m.* humus

insecticida *m.* insecticide

invernadero *m.* greenhouse

irrigación *f.* irrigation

jardín *m.* garden

jardinero, -ra *m.f.* gardener

labrar *v.* to till

maceta *f.* pot

machete *m.* machete

manguera *f.* hose; **regar con m.** *v.*
  to hose

mantillo *m.* humus, compost

mata *f.* bush, shrub

mezclar *v.* to mix

orgánico, -ca *adj.* organic

pala *f.* spade, shovel; **p. de jardinero** trowel

palear *v.* to shovel

pico *m.* pickaxe

planta *f.* plant; **p. anual** annual; **p.
  perenne, p. vivaz** perennial

plantar *v.* to plant, garden

postura *f.* seedling

rastrillar *v.* to rake

rastrillo *m.* rake

recoger *v.* to pick

regadera *f.* watering can

regar *v.* to water

rociada *f.* spray

rociar *v.* to spray

sachar *v.* to hoe, weed

segadora de césped *f.* lawn mower

sembrar *v.* to sow

semilla *f.* seed

suelo *m.,* **tierra** *f.* soil

tijeras de podar *f.pl.* clippers, pruning shears

trasplantar *v.* to transplant

zacate *m.* lawn

CIENCIA

Ciencias Físicas

CIENCIA

A

aceite *m.* oil; **a. lubricante** lubricating oil; **a. mineral** mineral oil

aceleración *f.* acceleration

acelerador de partículas *m.* particle accelerator

acetona *f.* acetone

acidez *f.* acidity

ácido, -da *adj.* acid

ácido *m.* acid; **a. acético** acetic acid; **a. sulfúrico** sulfuric acid

aerodinámico, -ca *adj.* aerodynamic

aeroespacio *m.* aerospace

aeronáutica *f.* aeronautics

aeronáutico, -ca *adj.* aeronautic

aeronave *f.* aircraft

aeroplano *m.,* **avión** *m.* airplane

aerosol *m.* aerosol

agujero negro *m.* black hole

aire *m.* air; **a. ambiental** ambient air; **resistencia del a.** *f.* air resistance

aislante *m.* insulator

alambre *m.* wire

aleación *f.* alloy

alzar *v.* to lift

amianto *m.,* **asbesto** *m.* asbestos

amoníaco *m.,* **amoniaco** *m.* ammonia

amplificación *f.* amplification

amplitud *f.* amplitude

antioxidante *adj. & m.* antioxidant

año luz *m.* light year

armónico, -ca *adj.* harmonic

armonioso, -sa *adj.* harmonious

asfalto *m.* asphalt

asteroide *m.* asteroid

astromóvil *m.* rover

atmósfera *f.* atmosphere

átomo *m.* atom

atracción gravitacional *f.* gravitational attraction

atraer *v.* to attract

aumento *m.* magnification

autocombustión *f.* spontaneous combustion

axis *m.* axis

azimut *m.,* **acimut** *m.* azimuth

B

balística *f.* ballistics

barómetro *m.* barometer

batería *f.* battery

bicarbonato de sodio *m.* baking soda

binaria eclipsante *f.* eclipsing binary

blanqueador *m.* bleach

bombillo *m.* light bulb

brillo *m.* brightness; **b. absoluto** absolute brightness; **b. aparente** apparent brightness

C

caballos de fuerza, caballos de

potencia *m.pl.* horsepower
cable *m.* (eléctrico) cable, wire
caer *v.* to fall
caída libre *f.* free fall
calefacción *f.* heating
calentar *v.* to heat
calor *m.* heat; **c. específico** specific heat
cambio *m.* change; **c. de estado** change of state; **c. endotérmico** endothermic change; **c. exotérmico** exothermic change; **c. físico** physical change; **c. químico** chemical change
candela *f.* candela
carbón *m.* charcoal
carga eléctrica *f.* electrical charge
catalizador *m.* catalyst
cemento *m.* cement
cerámica *f.* ceramic
cero absoluto *m.* absolute zero
cinética *f.* kinetics
cinturón de asteroides *m.* asteroid belt
circuito *m.* circuit; **c. abierto** open circuit; **c. cerrado** closed circuit; **c. en serie** series circuit; **c. paralelo** parallel circuit; **corto c.** short circuit
clorofluorocarbono *m.* chlorofluorocarbon
cloroformo *m.* chloroform
cloruro *m.* chloride
cohete *m.* rocket
colisión *f.* collision
combustible *m.* fuel; **c. fósil** fossil fuel

combustión *f.* combustion; **c. espontánea** spontaneous combustion
cometa *m.* comet
compuesto *m.* compound
cóncavo, -va *adj.* concave
condensación *f.* condensation
condensar *v.* to condense
conducción *f.* conduction
conducir *v.* to conduct
conductividad *f.* conductivity; **c. eléctrica** electrical conductivity; **c. térmica** thermal conductivity
conductor *m.* conductor
congelación *f.* freezing; **punto de c.** *m.* freezing point
conservación *f.* conservation
constelación *f.* constellation
convección *f.* convection
converger *v.* to converge
convexo, -xa *adj.* convex
corona *f.* corona
corriente *f.* current; **c. de convección** convection current
corrosión *f.* corrosion
cósmico, -ca *adj.* cosmic; **radiación c. de fondo** *f.* cosmic background radiation
cosmos *m.* cosmos
creciente *adj.* (lunar) waxing; **cuarto c.** *m.* first quarter
creciente *n.* crescent *m.*
cristal *m.* crystal
cristalino, -na *adj.* crystalline
cromósfera *f.*, **cromosfera** *f.* chromosphere
cronómetro *m.* chronometer

CIENCIA

271

cúmulo *m.* cluster; **c. abierto** open cluster; **c. globular** globular cluster

cuña *f.* wedge

CH

chorro *m.* jet; **propulsión a c.** *f.* jet propulsion

D

decibelio *m.*, **decibel** *m.* decibel

densidad *f.* density

desaceleración *f.* deceleration

descomposición radiactiva *f.* radioactive decay

desecado, -da *adj.* desiccated

desecar *v.* to desiccate

destello solar *m.* solar flare

destilación *f.* distillation

desviar *v.* to deflect

detergente *m.* detergent

diagrama Hertzsprung-Russell *m.* Hertzsprung-Russell diagram

diodo emisor de luz *m.* light-emitting diode (L.E.D.)

disolvente *m.* solvent

disolver *v.* to dissolve

disonancia *f.* dissonance

distancia *f.* distance; **d. astronómica** astronomical distance

distorsionar *v.* to distort

dúctil *adj.* ductile

E

ebullición *f.* boiling; **punto de e.** *m.* boiling point

eclipse *m.* eclipse; **e. lunar** lunar eclipse; **e. solar** solar eclipse

eco *m.* echo

efecto *m.* effect; **e. de Coriolis** Coriolis effect; **e. de Doppler** Doppler effect

eje *m.* axis

electricidad *f.* electricity; **e. estática** static electricity

electrodo *m.* electrode

electroimán *m.* electromagnet

electrón *m.* electron

elemento *m.* element

elipse *m.* ellipse

emisión *f.* emission

emitir *v.* to emit

empuje *m.* thrust

enano, -na *adj. & m.f.* dwarf; **e. blanca** white dwarf; **e. roja** red dwarf

energía *f.* energy; **e. cinética** kinetic energy; **e. eléctrica** electrical energy; **e. electromagnética** electromagnetic energy; **e. mecánica** mechanical energy; **e. nuclear** nuclear energy; **e. oscura** dark energy; **e. potencial** potential energy; **e. química** chemical energy; **e. térmica** thermal energy

enfriar *v.* to cool

enlace *m.* bond; **e. químico** chemical bond

entropía *f.* entropy

equilibrar *v.* to balance

equilibrio *m.* balance, equilibrium

esmog fotoquímico *m.* photochemical smog

espacio *m.* space; **e. exterior** outer

space; **e. interestelar** interstellar space

espectro *m.* spectrum

espejo *m.* mirror; **e. cóncavo** concave mirror; **e. convexo** convex mirror

espuma *f.* foam

estable *adj.* stable

estación espacial *f.* space station

estado *m.* state, form; **e. de la materia** *pl.* states of matter

estrella *f.* star; **e. binaria** binary star; **e. de neutrones** neutron star

evaporación *f.* evaporation

expansión *f.* expansion; **e. térmica** thermal expansion

exploración espacial *f.* space exploration

explosión *f.* explosion

explosivo, -va *adj.* explosive

expulsar *v.* to expel

F

fase *f.* phase; **f. lunar** moon phase

fibra óptica *f.* optical fiber

físico, -ca *adj.* physical; **cambio f.** *m.* physical change

fisión *f.* fission; **f. nuclear** nuclear fission

flotabilidad *f.* buoyancy

flotante *adj.* buoyant

flotar *v.* to float

fluido *m.* fluid

foco *m.* focus, light bulb

forma *f.* form, shape

fórmula química *f.* chemical formula

fosfato *m.* phosphate

fosforescencia *f.* phosphorescence

fotón *m.* photon

fotosfera *f.* photosphere

frágil *adj.* brittle, fragile

frecuencia *f.* frequency

fricción *f.* friction; **f. de deslizamiento** sliding friction; **f. de rodadura** rolling friction; **f. del líquido** fluid friction; **f. estática** static friction

fuerza *f.* force, strength; **f. aplicada** applied force, input force; **f. centrífugo** centrifugal force; **f. centrípeta** centripetal force; **f. de atracción** pull; **f. de flotación** buoyant force; **f. luminosa** light source; **f. magnética** magnetic force; **f. mecánica** mechanical force; **f. neta** net force; **f. resultante** output force; **f. desequilibradas** *pl.* unbalanced forces; **f. equilibradas** *pl.* balanced forces

fulcro *m.* fulcrum

fusión *f.* melting, fusion; **f. nuclear** nuclear fusion

G

galaxia *f.* galaxy; **g. elíptica** elliptical galaxy; **g. espiral** spiral galaxy; **g. irregular** irregular galaxy

gas *m.* gas; **g. inerte** inert gas; **g. noble** noble gas

girar *v.* to revolve

Gran Explosión *f.* Big Bang

gravedad *f.* gravity; **g. cero, g. nula**

CIENCIA

zero gravity; **g. específica** specific gravity

gravitación *f.* gravitation

H

halógeno *m.* halogen
helicóptero *m.* helicopter
heliocéntrico, -ca *adj.* heliocentric
hervir *v.* to boil
heterogéneo, -nea *adj.* heterogeneous
hibernación *f.* hibernation
hidrosfera *f.* hydrosphere
hirviente *adj.* boiling
holograma *m.* hologram
homogéneo, -nea *adj.* homogeneous
hundirse *v.* to sink

I

iluminación *f.* lighting
imagen satelital *f.* satellite image
imán *m.* magnet
impulso *m.* momentum
incandescente *adj.* incandescent
inclinación *f.* slope
indicador *m.* indicator
inercia *f.* inertia
inerte *adj.,* **inmóvil** *adj.* inert
infinito, -ta *adj.* infinite
infinito *m.,* **infinidad** *f.* infinity
inflamable *adj.* inflammable
inflar *v.* to inflate
infrarrojo, -ja *adj.* infrared
insolación *f.* insolation
insoluble *adj.* insoluble
intensidad *f.* intensity

interestelar *adj.* interstellar
inverso, -sa *adj.* inverse
ionosfera *f.* ionosphere
isótopo *m.* isotope; **i. radiactivo** radioactive isotope

J

jalón *m.* pull

L

lanzamiento *m.* launch
lanzar *v.* to launch
lente *m.f.* lens; **l. cóncavo (-va)** concave lens; **l. convexo (-xa)** convex lens; **l. divergente** divergent lens
levadura en polvo *f.* baking powder
levantar *v.* to lift
ley *f.* law; **l. de Boyle** Boyle's law; **l. de Charles** Charles's law; **l. de Hubble** Hubble's law; **l. de la conservación de la energía** law of conservation of energy; **l. de la conservación de la masa** law of conservation of mass; **l. de la conservación del impulso** law of conservation of momentum; **l. de la gravitación** universal law of universal gravitation; **l. de la termodinámica** *pl.* laws of thermodynamics; **l. del movimiento de Newton** *pl.* Newton's laws of motion
líquido *m.* liquid, fluid
lubricante *adj. & m.* lubricant
luminiscente *adj.* luminescent
luna *f.* moon; **l. creciente** crescent

CIENCIA

moon; **l. gibosa** gibbous moon; **l. llena** full moon; **l. nueva** new moon

lunar *adj.* lunar; **ciclo l.** *m.* lunar cycle; **eclipse l.** *m.* lunar eclipse

luz *f.* light; **l. infrarroja** infrared light; **l. ultravioleta** ultraviolet light; **l. visible** visible light

M

magnético, -ca *adj.* magnetic; **campo m.** *m.* magnetic field

magnetismo *m.* magnetism

magnificación *f.* magnification

magnitud *f.* magnitude

maleabilidad *f.* malleability

maleable *adj.* malleable

mancha solar *f.* sunspot

máquina *f.* machine; **m. compuesta** compound machine; **m. simple** simple machine

marcador *m.* tracer

marea muerta *f.* neap tide

mares lunares *m.pl.* lunar maria

masa *f.* mass; **m. atómica** atomic mass; **número de m.** *m.* mass number

materia *f.* matter; **m. oscura** dark matter; **m. particulada** particulate matter

material *m.* material; **m. compuesto** composite material

mecánica cuántica *f.* quantum mechanics *pl.*

medialuna *f.* half moon

menguante *adj.* (lunar) waning; **cuarto m.** *m.* last quarter

metales *m.pl.* metals; **m. alcalinos** alkali metals; **m. alcalinotérreos** alkaline earth metals; **m. de transición** transition metals

metálico, -ca *adj.* metalic, metal; **no metálico, -ca** nonmetal

metaloide *m.* metalloid

metano *m.* methane

meteorito *m.* meteorite

meteoro *m.* meteor

meteoroide *m.* meteoroid

mezcla *f.* mixture; **m. heterogénea** heterogeneous mixture; **m. homogénea** homogeneous mixture

mezclar *v.* to mix

microgravedad *f.* microgravity

modelo *m.* model

molécula *f.* molecule; **m. diatónica** diatomic molecule

monómero *m.* monomer

motor *m.* engine; **m. de combustión interna** internal combustion engine; **m. térmico** heat engine

movimiento *m.* motion

N

nebulosa *f.* nebula; **n. solar** solar nebula

neutrino *m.* neutrino

neutrón *m.* neutron

newton *m.* newton

nitrato *m.* nitrate

nitrito *m.* nitrite

núcleo *m.* nucleus

número *m.* number; **n. atómico** atomic number; **n. de masa** mass number

CIENCIA

CIENCIA

O

objeto celeste *m.* celestial object

observatorio *m.* observatory

onda *f.* wave; **longitud de o.** *f.* wavelength; **o. de luz** light wave; **o. longitudinal** longitudinal wave; **o. de radio** *pl.* airwaves

opaco, -ca *adj.* opaque

órbita *f.* orbit

oxidación *f.* oxidation

oxidar *v.* to oxidize

ozono *m.* ozone; **capa de o.** ozone layer *f.*

P

palanca *f.* lever

paralaje *f.* parallax

partícula *f.* particle; **p. alfa** alpha particle; **p. beta** beta particle; **p. subatómica** subatomic particle

pascal *m.* pascal

pendiente *f.* slope

péndulo de Foucault *m.* Foucault pendulum

penumbra *f.* penumbra

péptido *m.* peptide

peso *m.* weight; **p. atómico** atomic weight

pH *m.* pH

pila *f.* battery

planeta *m.* planet; **p. terrestre, p. telúrico** terrestrial planet

planetesimal *m.* planetesimal

plano *m.* plane; **p. inclinado** incline plane

plasma *m.* plasma

plástico *m.* plastic

poder *m.* power

polaridad *f.* polarity

polea *f.* pulley; **p. móvil** movable pulley

polímero *m.* polymer

polo magnético *m.* magnetic pole

potencia *f.* power; **p. en vatios** wattage

precipitado *m.* precipitate

presión *f.* pressure

principio *m.* principle; **p. de Arquímedes** Archimedes' principle; **p. de Bernoulli** Bernoulli's principle; **p. de Pascal** Pascal's principle

prisma *m.* prism

prominencia *f.* prominence

propiedad *f.* property; **p. física** physical property; **p. química** chemical property

proporcional *adj.* proportional

propulsión *f.* propulsion, lift; **p. a chorro** jet propulsion

protoestrella *f.* protostar

protón *m.* proton

proyectil *m.* projectile

púlsar *m.* pulsar

punto *m.* point; **p. de apoyo** fulcrum; **p. de congelación** freezing point; **p. de ebullición** boiling point; **p. de fusión** melting point; **p. de saturación** saturation point

Q

quásar *m.* quasar

quemar *v.* to burn

químico, -ca *adj.* chemical; **cambio q.** *m.* chemical change; **fórmula**

q. *f.* chemical formula; **símbolo q.** *m.* chemical symbol

R

radiación *f.* radiation; **r. cósmica de fondo** cosmic background radiation; **r. electromagnética** electromagnetic radiation; **r. gamma** gamma radiation; **r. infrarroja** infrared radiation; **r. ultravioleta** ultraviolet radiation

radiactividad *f.,* **radioactividad** *f.* radioactivity

radiactivo, -va *adj.* radioactive; **descomposición r.** *f.* radioactive decay; **isótopo r.** *m.* radioactive isotope

radiografía *f.* radiography, X-ray

radiotelescopio *m.* radio telescope

rapidez *f.* speed; **r. instantánea** instantaneous speed

rayo *m.* ray; **r. X** *pl.* X-rays

reacción *f.* reaction; **r. nuclear** nuclear reaction

reaccionar *v.* to react

reactante *m.* reactant

reactividad *f.* reactivity

reactivo *m.* reagent

recipiente *m.* container

reflejar *v.* to reflect

reflexión *f.* reflection

refracción *f.* refraction

refractar *v.* to refract

refrigerante *m.* refrigerant

repeler *v.* to repel

revolución *f.* revolution

rotación *f.* rotation

rotar *v.* to rotate

róver *m.* rover

rozamiento *m.* friction; **r. a la rodadura** rolling friction; **r. líquido** fluid friction

S

satélite *m.* satellite

saturado, -da *adj.* saturated; **no saturado, -da** unsaturated

secarse *v.* to desiccate

secuencia principal *f.* main sequence

semiconductor *m.* semiconductor

sintético, -ca *adj.* synthetic

sintetizar *v.* to synthesize

Sistema Internacional de Unidades (S.I.) *m.* International System of Units

solar *adj.* solar; **destello s.** *m.* solar flare; **eclipse s.** *m.* solar eclipse; **mancha s.** *f.* sunspot; **nebulosa s.** *f.* solar nebula; **sistema s.** *m.* solar system

sólido *m.* solid; **s. amorfo** amorphous solid; **s. cristalino** crystalline solid

solubilidad *f.* solubility

solución *f.* solution

soluto *m.* solute

solvente *m.* solvent

sonar *m.* sonar

sonda espacial *f.* space probe

sónico, -ca *adj.* sonic; **estampido s.** *m.* sonic boom

sonido *f.* sound; **barrera del s.** sound barrier

CIENCIA

CIENCIA

sublimación *f.* sublimation
subproducto espacial *m.* space spinoff
superconductor *m.* superconductor
superficie *f.* surface
supernova *f.* supernova
sustancia *f.* substance
sustentación *f.* (aeronáutica) lift
sustrato *m.* substrate

T

tabla periódica *f.* periodic table
teledetección *f.* remote sensing
telescopio *m.* telescope; **t. espacial Hubble** Hubble space telescope; **t. óptico** optical telescope; **t. reflectivo** reflecting telescope; **t. refractor** refracting telescope
temperatura *f.* temperature; **t. ambiente** room temperature
tensión superficial *f.* surface tension
teoría *f.* theory; **t. cuántica** quantum theory; **t. de cuerdas** string theory
térmico, -ca *adj.* thermal
termodinámica *f.* thermodynamics
terrestre *adj.* terrestrial
textura *f.* texture
tirón *m.* pull
tornillo *m.* screw
trabajo *m.* work; **insumos de t.** *m.pl.* input work; **t. producido** output work
transferencia *f.* transfer; **t. de energía** energy transfer; **t. térmica, t. de calor** heat transfer
transformación energética *f.* energy transformation
transparente *adj.* transparent
trasbordador espacial *m.* space shuttle
traslúcido, -da *adj.* translucent
trazadora *f.* tracer
turbina *f.* turbine

U

ultravioleta *adj.* ultraviolet
umbra *f.* umbra
universo *m.* universe

V

vacío *m.* vacuum
vapor *m.* steam, vapor
vaporización *f.* vaporization
vatio *m.* watt; **v. hora** *f.* watt-hour
velocidad *f.* velocity; **v. de escape** escape velocity; **v. media** average speed; **v. orbital** orbital velocity; **v. terminal** terminal velocity
ventaja mecánica *f.* mechanical advantage
vibración *f.* vibration
vibrar *v.* to vibrate
vida media *f.* half-life
viento solar *m.* solar wind
viscosidad *f.* viscosity
viscoso, -sa *adj.* viscous
vítreo, -rea *adj.* vitreous
voltaje *m.* voltage
volumen *m.* loudness

Z

zona de convección *f.* convection zone

• •

OBJETOS ASTRONÓMICOS

Acuario *m.* Aquarius

Aries *m.* Aries

Calisto *m.* Callisto

Can Mayor *m.* Canis Major

Can Menor *m.* Canis Minor

Cáncer *m.* Cancer

Capricornio *m.* Capricornus

Carro, El *m.* Big Dipper

Casiopea *f.* Cassiopeia

Ceres *m.* Ceres

Cinturón de Kuiper *m.* Kuiper Belt

Cometa Halley *m.* Halley's Comet

Corona Boreal *f.* Corona Borealis

Cruz del Sur *f.* Southern Cross

Escorpio *m.* Scorpius, Scorpio

Europa *f.* Europa

Galaxia Andrómeda *f.* Andromeda Galaxy; **G. del Molinete** Pinwheel Galaxy

Ganímedes *m.* Ganymede

Géminis *m.* Gemini

Gran Nube de Magallanes *f.* Large Magellanic Cloud

Hércules *m.* Hercules

Ío *m.* Io

Júpiter *m.* Jupiter

Leo *m.* Leo

Libra *f.* Libra

Marte *m.* Mars

Mercurio *m.* Mercury

Nebulosa del Cangrejo *f.* Crab Nebula

Neptuno *m.* Neptune

nube de Oort *f.* Oort cloud; **N. Menor de Magallanes** Small Magellanic Galaxy

Objeto Mayall *m.* Mayall's Object

Orión *m.* Orion

Osa Mayor *f.* Ursa Major

Osa Menor *f.* Ursa Minor (Little Dipper)

Pegaso *m.* Pegasus

Perseo *m.* Perseus

Piscis *m.* Pisces

Pléyades *f.pl.* Pleiades

Plutón *m.* Pluto

Polaris (Estrella del Norte) *m.* Polaris (North Star)

Sagitario *m.* Sagittarius

Saturno *m.* Saturn

Sirio *m.* Sirius

Tauro *m.* Taurus

Titán *m.* Titan

Triángulo *m.* Triangulum

Urano *m.* Uranus

Venus *m.* Venus

Via Láctea *f.* Milky Way Galaxy

Virgo *m.* Virgo

CIENCIA

CIENCIA

La Tabla Periódica de los Elementos

1																	2
H																	He
3 Li	4 Be											5 B	6 C	7 N	8 O	9 F	10 Ne
11 Na	12 Mg											13 Al	14 Si	15 P	16 S	17 Cl	18 Ar
19 K	20 Ca	21 Sc	22 Ti	23 V	24 Cr	25 Mn	26 Fe	27 Co	28 Ni	29 Cu	30 Zn	31 Ga	32 Ge	33 As	34 Se	35 Br	36 Kr
37 Rb	38 Sr	39 Y	40 Zr	41 Nb	42 Mo	43 Tc	44 Ru	45 Rh	46 Pd	47 Ag	48 Cd	49 In	50 Sn	51 Sb	52 Te	53 I	54 Xe
55 Cs	56 Ba		72 Hf	73 Ta	74 W	75 Re	76 Os	77 Ir	78 Pt	79 Au	80 Hg	81 Tl	82 Pb	83 Bi	84 Po	85 At	86 Rn
87 Fr	88 Ra		104 Rf	105 Db	106 Sg	107 Bh	108 Hs	109 Mt	110 Ds	111 Rg	112 Cn	113 Uut	114 Fl	115 Uup	116 Lv	117 Uus	118 Uuo

57 La	58 Ce	59 Pr	60 Nd	61 Pm	62 Sm	63 Eu	64 Gd	65 Tb	66 Dy	67 Ho	68 Er	69 Tm	70 Yb	71 Lu
89 Ac	90 Th	91 Pa	92 U	93 Np	94 Pu	95 Am	96 Cm	97 Bk	98 Cf	99 Es	100 Fm	101 Md	102 No	103 Lr

Ac **actinio** *m.* actinium
Al **aluminio** *m.* aluminium
Am **americio** *m.* americium
Sb **antimonio** *m.* antimony
Ar **argón** *m.* argon
As **arsénico** *m.* arsenic
At **astato** *m.* astatine
S **azufre** *m.* sulfur
Ba **bario** *m.* barium
Bk **berilio** *m.* beryllium
Be **berkelio** *m.* berkelium
Bi **bismuto** *m.* bismuth
Bh **bohrio** *m.* bohrium
B **boro** *m.* boron
Br **bromo** *m.* bromine
Cd **cadmio** *m.* cadmium
Ca **calcio** *m.* calcium
Cf **californio** *m.* californium
C **carbono** *m.* carbon
Ce **cerio** *m.* cerium
Cs **cesio** *m.* caesium

Zn **cinc** *m.* zinc
Zr **circonio** *m.* zirconium
Cl **cloro** *m.* chlorine
Co **cobalto** *m.* cobalt
Cu **cobre** *m.* copper
Cn **copernicio** *m.* copernicium
Cr **cromo** *m.* chromium
Cm **curio** *m.* curium
Ds **darmstadtio** *m.* darmstadtium
Dy **disprosio** *m.* dysprosium
Db **dubnio** *m.* dubnium
Es **einsteinio** *m.* einsteinium
Er **erbio** *m.* erbium
Sc **escandio** *m.* scandium
Sn **estaño** *m.* tin
Sr **estroncio** *m.* strontium
Eu **europio** *m.* europium
Fm **fermio** *m.* fermium
Fl **flerovio** *m.* flerovium
F **flúor** *m.* fluorine
P **fósforo** *m.* phosphorus

• •

Fr	**francio** *m.* francium	**Pu**	**plutonio** *m.* plutonium
Gd	**gadolinio** *m.* gadolinium	**Po**	**polonio** *m.* polonium
Ga	**galio** *m.* gallium	**K**	**potasio** *m.* potassium
Ge	**germanio** *m.* germanium	**Pr**	**praseodimio** *m.* praseodymium
Hf	**hafnio** *m.* hafnium	**Pm**	**prometio** *m.* promethium
H	**hassio** *m.* hassium	**Pa**	**protactinio** *m.* protactinium
He	**helio** *m.* helium	**Ra**	**radio** *m.* radium
H	**hidrógeno** *m.* hydrogen	**Rn**	**radón** *m.* radon
Fe	**hierro** *m.* iron	**Re**	**renio** *m.* rhenium
Ho	**holmio** *m.* holmium	**Rh**	**rodio** *m.* rhodium
In	**indio** *m.* indium	**Rg**	**roentgenio** *m.* roentgenium
Ir	**iridio** *m.* iridium	**Rb**	**rubidio** *m.* rubidium
Kr	**kriptón** *m.* krypton	**Ru**	**rutenio** *m.* ruthenium
La	**lantan** *m.* lanthanum	**Rf**	**rutherfordio** *m.* rutherfordium
Lr	**lawrencio** *m.* lawrencium	**Sm**	**samario** *m.* samarium
Li	**litio** *m.* lithium	**Sg**	**seaborgio** *m.* seaborgium
Lv	**livermorio** *m.* livermorium	**Se**	**selenio** *m.* selenium
Lu	**lutecio** *m.* lutetium	**Si**	**silicio** *m.* silicon
Mg	**magnesio** *m.* magnesium	**Na**	**sodio** *m.* sodium
Mn	**manganeso** *m.* manganese	**Tl**	**talio** *m.* thallium
Mt	**meitnerio** *m.* meitnerium	**Ta**	**tántalo** *m.* tantalum
Md	**mendelevio** *m.* mendelevium	**Tc**	**tecnecio** *m.* technetium
Hg	**mercurio** *m.* mercury	**Te**	**teluro** *m.* tellurium
Mo	**molibdeno** *m.* molybdenum	**Tb**	**terbio** *m.* terbium
Nd	**neodimio** *m.* neodymium	**Ti**	**titanio** *m.* titanium
Ne	**neón** *m.* neon	**Th**	**torio** *m.* thorium
Np	**neptunio** *m.* neptunium	**Tm**	**tulio** *m.* thulium
Nb	**niobio** *m.* niobium	**Uup**	**unumpentio** *m.* ununpentium
Ni	**niquel** *m.* nickel	**Uuo**	**ununoctio** *m.* ununoctium
N	**nitrógeno** *m.* nitrogen	**Uus**	**ununseptio** *m.* ununseptium
No	**nobelio** *m.* nobelium	**Uut**	**ununtrio** *m.* ununtrium
Au	**oro** *m.* gold	**U**	**uranio** *m.* uranium
Os	**osmio** *m.* osmium	**V**	**vanadio** *m.* vanadium
O	**oxígeno** *m.* oxygen	**W**	**wolframio** *m.* tungsten
Pd	**paladio** *m.* palladium	**Xe**	**xenón** *m.* xenon
Ag	**plata** *f.* silver	**I**	**yodo** *m.* iodine
Pt	**platino** *m.* platinum	**Yb**	**yterbio** *m.* ytterbium
Pb	**plomo** *m.* lead	**Y**	**ytrio** *m.* yttrium

CIENCIA

Investigación y Proceso

∙∙

A

absorber *v.* to absorb
aguja *f.* needle
aislar *v.* to isolate
ampliar *v.,* **aumentar** *v.* to magnify
analizar *v.* to analyze
anteojos de seguridad *m.pl.* goggles
aparato *m.* apparatus, device
argumento científico *m.* scientific argument

B

bandeja *f.* tray
barra gráfica *f.* bar graph
base *f.* (microscopio) base
balanza *f.* balance, scale
bata de laboratorio *f.* lab coat
bisturí *m.* scalpel
brújula *f.* compass
bureta *f.* burete

C

calculadora *f.* calculator
calibrar *v.* to calibrate
cantidad *f.* quantity
características *f.pl.* characteristics
categoría *f.* category
categorizar *v.* to categorize
Celsius, centígrado *adj.* Celsius
científico, -ca *adj.* scientific
cilindro graduado *m.* graduated cylinder
cinta métrica *f.* tape measure

clasificación *f.* classification; **clave de c.** *f.* classification key
clasificar *v.* to classify, sort, organize
colaborar *v.* to collaborate
comparar *v.* to compare
conclusión *f.* conclusion
condiciones *f.pl.* conditions
conferir *v.* to confer
consistente *adj.* consistent
constante *adj. & f.* constant
construir *v.* to construct
control *m.* control
controlar *v.* to control
crisol *m.* crucible
cristal *m.* glass
criterios *m.pl.* criteria
cronológico, -ca *adj.* chronological
cronómetro *m.* chronometer
cuadro *m.* chart
cuantificar *v.* to quantify
cuantitativo, -va *adj.* quantitative
cubreobjetos *m.* (microscopio) slide cover, coverslip

CH

charola *f.* tray

D

datos *m.pl.* data; **recopilar d.** *v.* to collect data; **tabla de d.** *f.* data table
deducción *f.* deduction
demostrar *v.* to demonstrate
descubrimiento *m.* discovery

descubrir *v.* to discover, invent

diafragma *m.* diaphragm

diagrama *m.* diagram; **d. de líneas** line plot; **d. de Venn** Venn diagram

disecar *v.* to dissect

disección *f.* dissection

diseño *m.* design

dispositivo *m.* device

E

ecuación *f.* equation

ejemplar *m.,* **espécimen** *m.* specimen

embudo *m.* funnel

encender *v.* to ignite

ensayo *m.* trial

equipo de laboratorio *m.* laboratory equipment

escala *f.* scale; **e. Celsius** Celsius scale; **e. Fahrenheit** Fahrenheit scale

escalpelo *m.* scalpel

espectrógrafo *m.* spectrograph

estimado *m.* estimate

estimar *v.* to estimate

evaluación por homólogos *f.* peer review

evaluar *v.* to evaluate

evidencia *f.* evidence

experimentación *f.* experimentation

experimentar *v.* to experiment

experimento *m.* experiment; **e. controlado** controlled experiment

extraer *v.* to extract

extrapolar *v.* to extrapolate

F

Fahrenheit *adj.* Fahrenheit

faro *m.* headlamp

fenómeno *m.* phenomena

foco *m.* (microscopio) light

fórceps *m.* forceps

fórmula *f.* formula

formular *v.* to formulate

frasco *m.* flask

G

gafas protectoras *f.pl.* goggles

generar *v.* to generate

giroscopio *m.* gyroscope

gota *f.* drop

gotero *m.* dropper

grabar *v.* to record

gráfico, -ca *m.f.* graph, chart; **g. de barras** bar graph; **g. de conteo** tally chart; **g. de líneas** line graph; **g. en forma de T** T-chart

graficar *v.* to graph

grapa *f.* clamp

guantes *m.pl.* gloves

H

hecho *m.* event, fact, occurrence

herramienta *f.* tool

hipótesis *f.* hypothesis; **formular h.** *v.* to hypothesize

humo *m.* fume

I

iluminación *f.* illumination

iluminar *v.* to illuminate

ilustrar *v.* to illustrate

imagen *f.* image

CIENCIA

CIENCIA

impermeable *adj.* impermeable
implicación *f.* implication
incidencia *f.* incidence, occurrence
incisión *f.* incision
incubación *f.* incubation; **período de i.** incubation period *m.*
incubar *v.* to incubate
indicación *f.* indication
indicar *v.* to indicate
inferencia *f.* inference
inferir *v.* to infer
inspeccionar *v.* to inspect
instrumento *m.* instrument, tool
integridad *f.* (datos) integrity
interacción *f.* interaction
interpretación *f.* interpretation
interpretar *v.* to interpret
inventar *v.* to invent
investigación *f.* investigation; **i. científica** scientific inquiry
investigar *v.* to investigate
irreversible *adj.* irreversible

J

jeringa *f.,* **jeringuilla** *f.* syringe

L

laboratorio *m.* laboratory
lente objetivo *m.* (microscopio) objective lens
ley científica *f.* scientific law
lógico, -ca *adj.* logical
lupa *f.* magnifying glass

LL

llama *f.* flame

M

manómetro *m.* manometer
materiales *m.pl.* materials
matraz *m.* flask; **m. de Erlenmeyer** Erlenmeyer flask
mechero de Bunsen *m.* Bunsen burner
medición *f.* measurement
medir *v.* to measure
método *m.* method; **m. científico** scientific method
microscopio *m.* microscope
modelo *m.* model; **m. matemático** mathematical model; **m. teórico** theoretical model
modificar *v.* to modify

N

nombre científico *m.* scientific name
notación científica *f.* scientific notation
numérico, -ca *adj.* numerical

O

objeto *m.* object
observar *v.* to observe
ocasión *f.* occurrence
ocular *m.* (microscopio) eyepiece
ordenar *v.,* **organizar** *v.* to sort, organize
origen *m.* origin

P

papel tornasol *m.* litmus paper
patrón *m.* pattern
peligro *m.* hazard

• •

perilla de enfoque *f.* focusing knob

pictografía *f.,* **pictograma** *m.* pictograph

pictográfico, -ca *adj.* pictographic

pinzas *f.pl.* tweezers, tongs

pipeta *f.* pipette, pipet

placa de Petri *f.* petri dish

placebo *m.* placebo

platina *f.* (microscopio) stage

portaobjetos *m.* (microscopio) slide

predecir *v.* to predict

predicción *f.* prediction

probabilidad *f.* probability

probar *v.* to demonstrate

probeta *f.* test tube; **p. graduada** graduated cylinder

procedimiento *m.* procedure

proceso *m.* process

propiedad *f.* property

prueba *f.* test, proof, trial

R

razonamiento científico *m.* scientific reasoning

registro *m.* log

regla métrica *f.* metric ruler

relación *f.* relationship; **r. causa-efecto** cause-and-effect relationship

replicable *adj.* replicable

replicar *v.,* **reproducir** *v.* to replicate

reportar *v.* to relay

representación gráfica *f.* graphic representation

respuesta *f.* response

resultados *m.pl.* findings

riesgo *m.* risk

S

secundario, -ria *adj.* secondary

símbolo *m.* symbol

sistema métrico *m.* metric system

sonda *f.* probe

sumergir *v.* to immerse

sustancia *f.* substance

T

tabla de datos *f.* data table

tecnología *f.* technology

tecnológico, -ca *adj.* technological

tenazas *f.pl.* tongs

tendencia *f.* trend

teoría *f.* theory

tijeras *f.pl.* scissors

tornasol *m.* litmus; **papel t.** litmus paper *m.*

tubo de ensayo *m.* test tube

U

unidad *f.* unit

V

variable *f.* variable; **v. controlada** controlled variable; **v. dependiente** dependent variable; **v. independiente** independent variable

vaso de precipitación, vaso de precipitado *m.* beaker

vidrio *m.* glass

voltímetro *m.* voltmeter

CIENCIA

CAMPOS DE LA CIENCIA Y MEDICINA

CIENCIA

acústica *f.* acoustics
anatomía *f.* anatomy
anestesiología *f.* anesthesiology
antropología *f.* anthropology
arqueología *f.* archaeology
astrofísica *f.* astrophysics
astronomía *f.* astronomy
biología *f.* biology; **b. marina** marine biology
botánica *f.* botany
cardiología *f.* cardiology
ciencia alimentaria *f.* food science; **c. forense** forensic science; **c. política** political science
ciencias ambientales *f.pl.* environmental science; **c. de la computación** computer science; **c. forestales** forestry
cosmología *f.* cosmology
dermatología *f.* dermatology
ecología *f.* ecology
endocrinología *f.* endocrinology
entomología *f.* entomology
epidemiología *f.* epidemiology
estadística *f.* statistics
farmacología *f.* pharmacology
física *f.* physics
fisiología *f.* physiology
gastroenterología *f.* gastroenterology
geografía *f.* geography
geología *f.* geology
geoquímica *f.* geochemistry
geriatría *f.* geriatrics

herpetología *f.* herpetology
hidrología *f.* hydrology
ictiología *f.* ichthyology
immunología *f.* immunology
informática *f.* computer science
ingeniería *f.* engineering
lingüística *f.* linguistics
matemáticas *f.pl.* mathematics
mecánica *f.* mechanics
meteorología *f.* meterology
neurología *f.* neurology
obstetricia y ginecología *f.* obstetrics and gynecology
oceanografía *f.* oceanography
odontología *f.* dentistry
oftalmología *f.* ophthalmology
oncología *f.* oncology
óptica *f.* optics
ornitología *f.* ornithology
ortopedia *f.* orthopedics
paleontología *f.* paleontology
patología *f.* pathology
pediatría *f.* pediatrics
periodoncia *f.* periodontics
psicología *f.* psychology
psiquiatría *f.* psychiatry
química *f.* chemistry
radiología *f.* radiology
silvicultura *f.* forestry
sismología *f.* seismology
sociología *f.* sociology
taxonomía *f.* taxonomy
toxicología *f.* toxicology
zoología *f.* zoology

ESTUDIOS SOCIALES
Cívica y Gobierno

A

abogado, -da *m.f.* lawyer; **a. defensor (-ora)** defense counsel

abrogación *f.* repeal, abrogation

abrogar *v.* to repeal

abstinencia *f.* abstinence

aburguesamiento *m.* gentrification

abuso de poder *m.* abuse of power

acción *f.* action; **a. afirmativa** affirmative action; **a. directa pacífica, a. directa no violenta** nonviolent direct action

aconsejar y consentir *v.* to advise and consent

acontecimientos actuales *m.pl.* current events

activista *m.f.* activist

aculturación *f.* acculturation

aculturar *v.* to acculturate

acusación *f.* indictment

acusado, -da *m.f.* defendant

acusar *v.* to accuse, charge

Administración de Medicamentos y Alimentos *f.* Food and Drug Administration (F.DA.); **A. Nacional de Aeronáutica y el Espacio** National Aeronautics and Space Administration (NASA)

adoctrinamiento *m.* indoctrination

adoctrinar *v.* to indoctrinate

aduana *f.* customs

agencia *f.* agency **a. reguladora** regulatory agency

Agencia Central de Inteligencia *f.* Central Intelligence Agency (C.I.A.); **A. de Protección Ambiental** Environmental Protection Agency (E.P.A.)

agenda pública *f.* public agenda

aislacionismo *m.* isolationism

aislacionista *m.f.* isolationist

alcalde, -esa *m.f.* mayor

aliado, -da *m.f.* ally

americano, -na *adj. & m.f.* American

amnistía *f.* amnesty

anciano, -na *m.f.* senior citizen

anticoncepción *f.* contraception

antiinmigrante *adj.* anti-immigrant,

nativist

anuncio de servicio público *m.* public service announcement

aplazamiento *m.* adjournment

aplazar *v.* to adjourn

aplicación *f.* enforcement; **a. de derechos civiles** civil rights enforcement; **a. de la ley** law enforcement

aprobación *f.* passage, endorsement; **a. de un proyecto de ley** passage of a bill

apropiación *f.* appropriation

arbitraje *m.* arbitration

argumento *m.,* **argumentación** *f.* (razonamiento) argument

Armada de EE.UU. *f.* U.S. Navy

arreglo *m.* compromise; **llegar a un a.** *v.* to compromise

arrestar *v.* to arrest

arresto *m.* arrest, detention; **a. domiciliario** house arrest; **a. ilegal** false arrest

asimilación *f.* assimilation

asimilar *v.* to assimilate

asistencia social *f.* welfare

ausencia de prejuicios *f.* open-mindedness

autóctono, -na *adj.* indigenous

autodisciplina *f.* self-discipline

autogobierno *m.,* **auto-gobernación** *f.* self-governance

autopsia *f.* autopsy

autoridad *f.* authority

autoritario, -ria *adj.* authoritarian; **régimen a.** *m.* authoritarian regime

autorizar *v.* to legalize, authorize

autosuficiencia *f.* self-sufficiency

ayuda extranjera, ayuda exterior *f.* foreign aid

ayuntamiento *m.* city council

B

bandera *f.* flag; **b. nacional** national flag

barriada *f.,* **barrio bajo** *m.* slum

base popular *f.* grassroots

Biblioteca del Congreso *f.* Library of Congress

bicameral *adj.* bicameral

bien común, bien público *m.* common good, public good

bienestar social *m.* social welfare

bipartidista *adj.* bipartisan

bloque de poder *m.* power bloc

bosque nacional *m.* national forest

burocracia *f.* bureaucracy

burócrata *m.f.* bureaucrat

búsqueda de la felicidad *f.* pursuit of happiness

C

cabildeo *m.* lobbying

cabildero, -ra *m.f.* lobbyist

calentamiento global *m.* global warming

calidad de vida *f.* quality of life

calificaciones *f.pl.* qualifications

calumnia *f.* slander, mudslinging

Cámara de Representantes *f.* House of Representatives

camarilla política *f.* caucus

cambio *m.* change; **c. climático** cli-

ESTUDIOS SOCIALES

mate change; **c. demográfico** demographic change

campaña *f.* campaign; **c. de a nivel popular** grassroots campaign; **c. política** political campaign

candidato, -ta *m.f.* candidate, nominee

capitalista *adj. & m.* capitalist

capitolio *m.* (edificio) capitol

Capitolio *m.* Capitol Hill

cárcel *f.* prison, correctional facility

cargos públicos *m.pl.* public office

caricatura política *f.* political cartoon

carta al editor *f.* letter to the editor

Casa Blanca *f.* White House

casero abusivo *m.* slumlord

castigo *m.* punishment, penalty; **c. corporal** corporal punishment

causa probable *f.* probable cause

censo *m.* census

censura *f.* censorship

centro electoral, centro de votación *m.* polling place

circunscripción electoral *f.* precinct, electoral district, constituency

citación *f.* subpoena

ciudad *f.* city; **c. capital** capital city

ciudadanía *f.* citizenry, citizenship; **c. informada** informed citizenry; **c. por nacimiento** citizenship by birth

ciudadano, -na *m.f.* citizen

cívica *f.* civics *pl.*

cívico, -ca *adj.* civic

civilidad *f.* civility

civismo *m.* civic mindedness

clase *f.* class; **c. aristócrata, c. alta** upper class; **c. dominante** ruling class; **c. marginada** underclass; **c. media** middle class; **c. media alta** upper middle class; **c. social** social class; **conciencia de c.** *f.* class consciousness; **lucha de clases** *f.* class conflict

cláusula *f.* clause; **c. de debido proceso** Due Process Clause; **c. de establecimiento** Establishment Clause; **c. de igual protección** Equal Protection Clause; **c. de supremacía federal** federal supremacy clause

código de vestimenta *m.* dress code

colegio electoral *m.* Electoral College

comandante en jefe *m.* commander-in-chief

comedor de beneficiencia *m.* soup kitchen

comentarista político (-ca) *m.f.* pundit

Comisión de Elecciones Federales *f.* Federal Election Commission (F.E.C.); **C. para la Igualdad de Oportunidades en el Empleo** Equal Employment Opportunity Commission (E.E.O.C.)

comité *m.* committee; **c. de acción política** political action committee; **c. de redacción** editorial board; **c. del Congreso** Congressional committee

compromiso *m.* compromise

comunidad *f.* community

ESTUDIOS SOCIALES

comunista *adj. & m.f.* communist

concentración *f.* rally, demonstration

concesión de licencias *f.* licensing

conciencia cívica *f.* civic mindedness

concurrencia *f.* attendance; **c. de votantes** voter turnout

condado *m.* county

condición socioeconómica *f.* socioeconomic status

conflicto ideológico *m.* ideological conflict

Congreso *m.* Congress; **audiencia del C.** *f.* Congressional hearing

conmutar *v.* to commute

conscripción *f.* conscription

consejo *m.* council, advice; **c. editorial** editorial board; **c. escolar** school board; **c. municipal** city council

consejo y consentimiento *m.* advice and consent

Consejo Nacional de Seguridad *m.* National Security Council

consentimiento del pueblo *m.* consent of the governed

conservador, -ora *adj. & m.f.* conservative

conservadurismo *m.* conservatism

constitución *f.* constitution

constituyente *m.f.* constituent

contaminación *f.* pollution; **c. atmosférica** air pollution

contribución política *f.* campaign contribution

contribuyente *m.f.* taxpayer

control *m.* control; **c. civil del ejército** civilian control of the military; **c. de armas** gun control

controles y equilibrios *m.pl.,* **frenos y contrapesos** *m.pl.* checks and balances

convención política *f.* political convention

convicto, -ta *m.f.* criminal

corte *f.* court; **c. de apelaciones** court of appeals; **c. estatal** state court; **c. federal** federal court

Corte Internacional *f.* World Court; **C. Suprema de Justicia** Supreme Court

corrupción *f.* corruption

corrupto, -ta *adj.;* **corrompido, -da** *adj.* corrupt

costumbre *f.* custom

crecimiento urbano *m.* urban growth

creencia *f.* belief; **c. religiosa** religious belief

crimen *m.* crime; **c. de guerra** war crime; **c. motividado por el odio** hate crime

criminal *adj. & m.f.* criminal

cuerpo político *m.* body politic

Cuerpo de Infantería de Marina de EE.UU. *m.* U.S. Marine Corps

cuestión de orden *f.* point of order

cuidado de la salud *m.* health care

cultura popular *f.* popular culture

cumplimiento de la ley *m.* law enforcement

cuota *f.* quota; **c. migratoria** immigration quota

CH

chovinista *adj. & m.f.* chauvinist, national chauvinist

D

debate *m.* debate

debatir *v.* to debate

debido proceso *m.* due process; **d. p. legal** due process of law

Decimocuarta Enmienda *f.* Fourteenth Amendment

decisión histórica *f.* landmark decision

Declaración de la Independencia *f.* Declaration of Independence

declarar *v.* to proclaim, testify

decretar *v.* to order, decree

degradación de zonas urbanas *f.* urban decay

delegación *f.* delegation

delegado, -da *m.f.* delegate

delegar *v.* to delegate

delito *m.* crime, offense; **d. grave** felony; **d. menor** misdemeanor

demagógico, -ca *adj.* demagogic

demagogo, -ga *m.f.* demagogue

demanda *f.* legal claim, lawsuit; **presentar una d.** *v.* to file suit

demandado, -da *m.f.* defendant

demandante *m.f.* plaintiff

demandar *v.* to sue

democracia *f.* democracy; **d. directa** direct democracy; **d. liberal** liberal democracy; **d. parlamentaria** parliamentary democracy; **d. representativa** representative democracy

democrático, -ca *adj.* democratic; **valores d.** *m.pl.* democratic values

demografía *f.* demographics *pl.*

Departamento de Agricultura *m.* Department of Agriculture; **D. de Defensa** Department of Defense; **D. de Educación** Department of Education; **D. de Estado** Department of State; **D. de Justicia** Department of Justice; **D. de Salud y Servicios Humanos** Department of Health and Human Services; **D. de Seguridad Nacional** Department of Homeland Security; **D. de Trabajo** Department of Labor; **D. del Interior** Department of the Interior

deportar *v.* to deport

derechista, de derecha *adj.* right-wing

derecho *m.* law, right, entitlement; **d. a criticar al gobierno** right to criticize the government; **d. a enfrentar un acusador** right to face an accuser; **d. a obtener un abogado** right to counsel; **d. a un juicio justo** right to a fair trial; **d. al voto** right to vote; **d. civil** civil law; **d. común inglés, d. consuetudinario de Inglaterra** English Common Law; **d. constitucional** constitutional law; **d. de apelación** right of appeal; **d. de expropiación** eminent domain; **d. internacional** international law; **d. penal** criminal law; **estado de d.** *m.* rule of law

ESTUDIOS SOCIALES

derechos *m.pl.* rights; **d. al aborto** abortion rights; **d. civiles** civil rights; **d. de autor** copyright; **d. de las minorías** minority rights; **d. de los estados** states' rights; **d. de propiedad** property rights; **d. de voto** voting rights; **d. human-os** human rights; **d. inalienables** inalienable rights, unalienable rights; **d. individuales** individual rights

derogar *v.* to repeal

desacato al tribunal *m.* contempt of court

desacuerdo *m.* disagreement

desarrollo de viviendas *m.* housing development

deshechos nucleares *m.pl.* nuclear waste

designado, -da *m.f.* appointee

designar *v.* to appoint

desobediencia civil *f.* civil disobedience

desregulación *f.,* **desregulariza-ción** *f.* deregulation

destituir *v.* to impeach

detención *f.* arrest; **d. domiciliaria** house arrest; **d. ilegal** unlawful detention, false arrest; **d. sin juicio** detention without trial

detener *v.* to arrest

deuda pública *f.* national debt

Día de Elecciones *m.* Election Day; **D. de la Independencia** Fourth of July, Independence Day

día festivo nacional *m.* national holiday

dictadura *f.* dictatorship

difamación *f.* slander, libel

dilema ético *m.* ethical dilemma

diplomacia *f.* diplomacy

diplomático, -ca *adj. & m.f.* diplomat

discriminación *f.* discrimination; **d. basada en el idioma** language discrimination; **d. basada en la edad** age discrimination; **d. basada en la religión** religious discrimination; **d. étnica** ethnic discrimination; **d. por razones de discapacidad** discrimination based on disability; **d. por razones de género** gender discrimination; **d. racial** racial discrimination; **d. sexual** sex discrimination

discurso *m.* speech; **d. de acepta-ción** acceptance speech; **d. de campaña** stump speech; **d. de odio** hate speech; **d. inaugural** inaugural address; **d. sobre el Estado de la Unión** State of the Union Address

discusión *f.* argument, discussion

discutir *v.* to debate, discuss

disentimiento *m.* dissent

disidente *m.f.* dissident

distribución *f.* apportionment

distrito congresional *m.* Congressional district

diversidad *f.* diversity; **d. étnica** ethnic diversity; **d. lingüística** linguistic diversity; **d. racial** racial diversity

dividido, -da *adj.* divided; **leal-tades d.** *pl.* divided loyalties

doble enjuiciamiento *m.,* **doble riesgo** *m.* double jeopardy

documental *m.* documentary

documentar *v.* to document

documento *m.* document

drogas *f.pl.* illegal drugs

E

ecología *f.* ecology

ecosistema *m.* ecosystem

educación *f.* education; **e. obligatoria** compulsory education; **e. privada** private education; **e. pública** public education

ejecutivo, -va *adj. & m.f.* executive

Ejército de EE.UU. *m.* U.S. Army

elección *f.* election; **e. de destitución** recall election; **e. general** general election; **e. presidencial** presidential election; **e. primaria** primary election; **resultados de la e.** *m.pl.* election results

elector, -ora *m.f.* elector

elegir *v.* to elect

élite *adj. & f.,* **elite** *adj. & f.* elite; **é. del poder** power elite

embajada *f.* embassy

embajador, -ora *m.f.* ambassador

emigrar *v.* to migrate, emigrate

encargar *v.,* **encomendar** *v.* to mandate, order

encuesta *f.* survey, opinion poll; **e. de salida** exit poll

energía nuclear *f.* nuclear power

enjuiciamiento *m.* indictment, prosecution

enmienda constitucional *f.* constitutional amendment

enviado, -da *m.f.* envoy

escuela *f.* school; **libre elección de e.** *f.* school choice

eslogan *m.* slogan

estadidad *f.* statehood

estado *m.* state; **e. de bienestar** welfare state; **e. de derecho** rule of law; **e. soberano** sovereign state

Estados Unidos (EE.UU.) *m.pl.* United States (U.S.)

estadounidense *adj. & m.f.* American (U.S.)

estatal *adj.* state; **corte e.** *f.* state court; **gobierno e.** *m.* state government; **legislatura e.** *f.* state legislature; **senador (-ora) e.** *m.f.* state senator

Estatua de la Libertad *f.* Statue of Liberty

estatuto *m.* statute; **e. de prescripción legal** statute of limitations

estilo de vida *m.* lifestyle

ética *f.pl.* ethics

ético, -ca *adj.* ethical; **dilema é.** *m.* ethical dilemma

etnicidad *f.* ethnicity

etnocentrico, -ca *adj.* ethnocentric

etnocentrismo *m.* ethnocentrism

europeo americano, -na *adj. & m.f.* European American

evangelío social *m.* social gospel

evidencia *f.* evidence

expediente *m.* (tribunal) docket

expulsar *v.* to deport

extranjero, -ra *adj. & m.f.* foreign,

ESTUDIOS SOCIALES

foreigner, alien

extremista *adj. & m.f.* extremist

F

familia *f.* family

fascista *adj. & m.f.* fascist

federalismo *m.* federalism

feminismo *m.* feminism

feriado nacional *m.* national holiday

filantropía *f.* philanthropy

filántropo, -pa *m.f.* philanthropist

filibustero *m.* (Senado) filibuster

filosofía política *f.* political philosophy

financiamiento público de las elecciones *m.* public financing of elections

fiscal *m.f.* prosecutor

fraude electoral *m.* vote fraud

Fuerza Aéria de EE.UU. *f.* U.S. Air Force

funcionario *m.* public official, civil servant; **f. invalidado** lame duck

fundación *f.* foundation

fundamentalismo *m.* fundamentalism; **f. cristiano** Christian fundamentalism; **f. islámico** Islamic fundamentalism

fundamentalista *m.f.* fundamentalist

G

gabinete *m.* cabinet; **g. presidencial** President's Cabinet

gasto federal *m.* federal spending

generación *f.* generation

genocidio *m.* genocide

geopolítica *f.* geopolitics

gerrymandering *m.* gerrymandering

gestión de conflicto *f.* conflict management

gestor (-ora) de la ciudad *m.f.* city manager

giro político *m.* political spin

gobernación por el pueblo *f.* rule by the people

gobernador, -ora *m.f.* governor

gobierno *m.* government; **g. central** central government; **g. democrático** democratic government; **g. dividido** divided government; **g. estatal** state government; **g. federal** federal government; **g. limitado** limited government; **g. tribal** tribal government; **rama del g.** *f.* branch of government

grupo *m.* group; **g. de interés** interest group; **g. de presión** lobby; **g. racial** racial group

Guardia Nacional *f.* National Guard

H

hábeas corpus *m.* habeas corpus; **mandato de h. c.** *m.* writ of habeas corpus;

hambre *m.* hunger

héroe *m.*, **heroína** *f.* hero, heroine; **h. popular** *m.f.* folk hero

heroico, -ca *adj.* heroic

heroísmo *m.* heroism

himno nacional *m.* national anthem

hispánico, -ca *adj.* Hispanic

hispano, -na *adj. & m.f.* Hispanic

historia familiar *f.* family history

hogar *m.* household; **sin h.** *adj.* homeless

hombre común *m.* common man

I

identidad *f.* identity; **i. cultural** cultural identity; **i. nacional** national identity

ideología *f.* ideology

ideológico, -ca *adj.* ideological

igualdad *f.* equality

igualitario, -ria *adj.* egalitarian

imparcialidad *f.* open-mindedness

impuesto *m.* tax; **i. sobre la renta** income tax; **i. sobre las ventas** sales tax; **i. sobre sociedades** corporate tax

inauguración *f.* inauguration

incitación al odio *f.* hate speech

inculpar *v.* to accuse, charge

independencia *f.* independence

independiente *adj.* independent

índice de natalidad *m.* birth rate

indígeno, -na *adj.* indigenous

indigente *adj.* indigent

individuo, -dua *m.f.* individual

iniciativa electoral, iniciativa de votación *f.* ballot initiative

inmigración *f.* immigration; **i. ilegal** illegal immigration

inmigrante *m.f.* immigrant; **i. indocumentado (-da)** undocumented immigrant

inmigrar *v.* to immigrate

inmunidad diplomática *f.* diplomatic immunity

inspección aduanal *f.* customs search

institución *f.* institution

instituir *v.* to institute

instituto *m.* institute

interdependiente *adj.* interdependent

interrogar *v.* to interrogate

interrogatorio *m.* interrogation

intimidad *f.* privacy, private life

investidura *f.* inauguration

izquierdista, de izquierda *adj.* left-wing

J

judicatura *f.* judiciary

judicial *adj.* judicial; **poder j.** *m.* judicial branch, judiciary; **revisión j.** *f.* judicial review; **supremacía j.** *f.* judicial supremacy

juez *m.f.*, **jueza** *f.* judge, justice

juicio *m.* trial, lawsuit; **j. de acción popular** class action suit; **j. imparcial** fair trial; **j. justo, j. público** public trial; **j. rápido** speedy trial

junta directiva escolar *f.* school board

jurado *m.* jury; **juicio por j.** *m.* trial by jury; **servicio de j.** *m.* jury duty

juramento *m.* oath, pledge; **bajo j.** *adj. & adv.* under oath; **j. a la bandera** pledge of allegiance; **j. al cargo** oath of office

jurisdicción *f.* jurisdiction

justicia *f.* justice; **j. social** social justice; **sistema de j.** *m.* justice sys-

ESTUDIOS SOCIALES

Estudios Sociales

tem

juvenil *adj.* juvenile, youthful

juzgado *m.* court, tribunal

L

latinoamericano, -na *adj. & m.f.* Latin American

lealtad *f.* allegiance, loyalty; **l. divididas** *pl.* divided loyalties

legislación *f.* legislation; **l. laboral** labor law

legislador, -ora *m.f.* legislator, lawmaker

legislar *v.* to legislate

legislatura *f.* legislature; **l. estatal** state legislature

ley *f.* law; **firmar en l.** *v.* to sign into law; **imperio de la l.** *m.* rule of law; **l. común** common law; **l. de la Sharia** Sharia law; **l. de solo inglés** English-only law; **l. y orden** law and order; **proyecto de l.** *m.* bill

Ley de Poderes de Guerra *f.* War Powers Act; **L. DREAM** DREAM Act; **L. sobre Especies en Peligro de Extinción** Endangered Species Act

leyes de derechos civiles *f.pl.* civil rights laws; **l. de inmigración** immigration laws; **l. de pureza de alimentos y drogas** pure food and drug laws

liberal *adj. & m.f.* liberal

libertad *f.* freedom, liberty; **l. condicional** probation; **l. de asociación** freedom of association; **l. de**

elección freedom of choice; **l. de expresión** freedom of expression; **l. de reunión** freedom of assembly; **l. individual** individual liberty; **l. religiosa** freedom of religion; **l. y justicia para todos** liberty and justice for all

libertades civiles *f.pl.* civil liberties

libertario, -ra *adj. & m.f.* libertarian

licencia de conducir, licencia de manejar *f.* driver's license

líder *m.f.* leader; **l. de la mayoría** Majority Leader; **l. de la minoría** Minority Leader; **l. mundial** world leader

liderazgo *m.* leadership

línea de demarcación *f.* line of demarcation

lista de candidatos *f.* election slate

litigio *m.* lawsuit, dispute

lucha de clases *f.* class conflict

M

machista *adj. & m.* male chauvinist

mandato *m.* mandate, order, writ; **m. de hábeas corpus** writ of habeas corpus; **m. judicial** court order; **m. sin financiamiento** unfunded mandate

manejo de conflicto *m.* conflict management

manifestación *f.* demonstration, rally

maquiavélico, -ca *adj.* Machiavellian

maquinaria política *f.* political machine

matriarca *f.* matriarch

matriarcal *adj.* matriarchal

matrimonio *m.* marriage; **m. entre personas del mismo sexo** same-sex marriage; **m. igualitario** marriage equality

mayoría *f.* majority; **líder de la m.** Majority Leader *m.f.;* **m. de dos tercios** two-thirds majority; **m. silenciosa** Silent Majority; **m. simple** simple majority; **regla de la m.** *f.* majority rule

médico (-ca) forense *m.f.* coroner

medio ambiente *m.* environment

meritocracia *f.* meritocracy

migración *f.* migration

militarismo *m.* militarism

militarista *adj. & m.f.* militarist

minoría *f.* minority; **derechos de las minorías** *m.pl.* minority rights; **líder de la m.** Minority Leader *m.f.;* **m. étnica** ethnic minority

mitin *m.* rally, meeting

moderado, -ra *adj. & m.f.* moderate

monogamia *f.* monogamy

monumento *m.* monument

movilidad *f.* mobility; **m. ascendente** upward mobility

movimiento *m.* movement; **m. feminista** women's liberation movement; **m. laboral** labor movement; **m. progresista** progressive movement

multa *f.* fine

multar *v.* to fine

multicultural *adj.* multicultural

multiculturalismo *m.* multiculturalism

N

narcotraficante *m.f.* drug trafficker

narcotráfico *m.* drug trafficking

nativista *adj. & m.f.* nativist

naturalización *f.* naturalization

negociación de cargos y condenas *f.* plea bargain

nombrado, -da *m.f.* appointee

nombramiento *m.* appointment; **n. político** political appointment

nombrar *v.* to appoint

nominación *f.* nomination

norma *f.* rule, regulation; **n. de vestir** dress code

normalizar *v.* to standardize, normalize

O

objetor (-ra) de conciencia *m.f.* conscientious objector

Oficina Federal de Investigaciones *f.* Federal Bureau of Investigation (F.B.I.)

opinión *f.* opinion; **o. editorial** op-ed; **o. pública** public opinion

oposición leal *f.* loyal opposition

oración en la escuela *f.* school prayer

orden *f.* order, mandate, writ; **o. de registro** search warrant

orden *m.* (secuencia, funcionamiento) order; **o. numérico** numerical order; **o. público** public order

ordenar *v.* to order

ESTUDIOS SOCIALES

ESTUDIOS SOCIALES

organismo regulador *m.* regulatory agency

organización *f.* organization; **o. internacional** international organization; **o. no lucrativa, o. sin fines de lucro** nonprofit organization

origen nacional *m.* national origin

P

pacifismo *m.* pacifism
pacifista *adj. & m.f.* pacifist
país de origen *m.* country of origin
parcialidad *f.* bias
parque nacional *m.* national park
participación *f.* participation; **p. ciudadana** civic participation; **p. electoral** voter turnout; **p. política** political participation
partido *m.* political party
Partido Demócrata *m.* Democratic Party; **P. Libertario** Libertarian Party; **P. Republicano** Republican Party, G.O.P.; **P. Verde** Green Party
patria *f.* mother country
patriarca *m.* patriarch
patriarcal *adj.* patriarchal
patrimonio cultural *m.* cultural heritage
patriota *m.f.* patriot
patriótico, -ca *adj.* patriotic
patriotismo *m.* patriotism
patrón de comportamiento *m.* behavior pattern
patrulla fronteriza *f.* Border Patrol
pelea *f.* argument, conflict
pena *f.* penalty, sentence; **p. de**

muerte capital punishment
penalizar *v.* to penalize
Pentágono *m.* Pentagon
perdón *m.* pardon
periódico *m.* newspaper
periodista *m.f.* journalist; **p. de investigación** investigative reporter, muckraker
perjurio *m.* perjury
persecución *f.* persecution
persona *f.* person; **p. de la tercera edad, p. de edad avanzada** senior citizen; **p. sin hogar** homeless person
petición *f.* petition; **elevar una p.** *v.* to petition
piquete *m.* picket
piquetear *v.* to picket
planificación urbana *f.* city planning
pleito *m.* lawsuit
pluralidad *f.* plurality
pluralismo cultural *m.* cultural pluralism
pobreza *f.* poverty
poder *m.* power; **p. del bolsillo, p. del dinero** power of the purse; **p. ejecutivo** executive power, executive branch; **p. judicial** judiciary, judicial system, judicial branch; **p. legislativo** legislative authority, legislative branch
poderes delegados *m.pl.* delegated powers; **p. del estado** branches of government; **p. enumerados** enumerated powers
polarización *f.* polarization

policía *f.* police

poligamia *f.* polygamy

política *f.* policy, politics; **contribución p.** *f.* campaign contribution; **p. exterior** foreign policy; **p. gubernamental** government policy; **p. migratoria** immigration policy; **p. nacional** domestic policy; **p. pública** public policy

político, -ca *adj.* political; **caricatura p.** *f.* political cartoon; **comentarista p.** *m.f.* pundit, commentator; **cuerpo p.** *m.* body politic; **filosofía p.** *f.* political philosophy; **giro p.** *m.* political spin; **maquinaria p.** *f.* political machine; **nombramiento p.** *m.* political appointment; **plataforma p.** *f.* political platform; **presión p.** *f.* lobbying

polución *f.* pollution

populismo *m.* populism

populista *adj. & m.f.* populist

preámbulo *m.* preamble

prejuicio *m.* prejudice, bias

prensa libre *f.* free press

preservación cultural *f.* cultural preservation

presidente, -ta *m.f.* president, chairman, chairwoman

Presidente (-ta) de la Cámara *m.f.* Speaker of the House; **P. del Tribunal** Chief Justice

presionar *v.* to lobby

presunción de inocencia *f.* presumption of innocence

presupuesto *m.* budget; **p. equilibrado** balanced budget

primario presidencial *m.* presidential primary

Primera Dama *f.* First Lady

Primera Enmienda *f.* First Amendment

principio *m.* principle; **p. de legalidad** rule of law; **p. morales** *pl.* moral values

prisión *f.* correctional facility

privacidad *f.* privacy; **invasión de la p.** *f.* invasion of privacy

privado, -da *adj.* private

privatización *f.* privatization

privilegio ejecutivo *m.* executive privilege

proceso *m.* process, trial, lawsuit; **debido p. legal** due process of law; **p. de destitución** impeachment

proclamación *f.* proclamation

proclamar *v.* to proclaim

prófugo, -ga *m.f.* fugitive

programas de ayuda social *m.* entitlement programs

progresista *adj. & m.* progressive; **movimiento p.** progressive movement *m.*

prohibir *v.* to outlaw

promulgar *v.* to enact

propaganda *f.* propaganda; **hacer p.** *v.* to propagandize

propuesta *f.* proposal

prorrateo *m.* apportionment

proscrito, -ta *m.f.* outlaw

protección ambiental *f.* environmental protection

protesta *f.* protest

ESTUDIOS SOCIALES

protestar *v.* to protest

proyecto *m.* project, plan; **p. de ley** bill; **p. público** public project

púlpito magnifico *m.* Bully Pulpit

punto de vista *m.* point of view

Q

quórum *m.* quorum

R

radical *adj. & m.f.* radical

radicalismo *m.* radicalism

rama *f.* branch; **r. del gobierno** branch of government; **r. ejecutiva** executive branch; **r. judicial** judicial branch; **r. legislativa** legislative branch

ratificación *f.* ratification

ratificar *v.* to ratify

raza *f.* race

razonamiento *m.* reasoning

reaccionario, -ra *adj. & m.f.* reactionary

recién llegado (-da) *m.f.* newcomer

reclutamiento forzado *m.* conscription

reconocimiento diplomático *m.* diplomatic recognition

recurso legal *m.* legal recourse

reestructuración distrital *f.* redistricting

referéndum *m.* referendum

reforma *f.* reform; **r. de asistencia social** welfare reform; **r. educativa** education reform; **r. social** social reform

reformador, -ora *m.f.* reformer

reformar *v.* to reform

refugiado, -da *m.f.* refugee

régimen *m.* regime

registrarse para votar *v.* to register to vote

registro de votantes *m.* voter registration

Registro del Congreso *m.* Congressional Record

regla *f.* rule, regulation; **r. de exclusión** exclusionary rule; **r. de la mayoría** majority rule

reglamento *m.,* **regulación** *f.* regulation

relaciones extranjeras *f.pl.* foreign relations; **r. raciales, r. interraciales** race relations

religión *f.* religion; **r. establecida** established religion

renacimiento religioso *m.* religious revival

renuncia *f.* resignation

reparación de agravios *f.* redress of grievances

repartición *f.* distribution; **nueva r.** reapportionment

representación *f.* representation

representante *m.f.* representative; **r. elegido** elected representative

representar *v.* to represent

república *f.* republic

resignación *f.* resignation

resistencia *f.* resistance; **r. no violenta** nonviolent resistance

resolución *f.* resolution; **r. de conflicto** conflict resolution

respaldo *m.* endorsement

respeto *m.* respect; **r. al derecho ajeno** respect for the rights of others; **r. de la ley** respect for law

responsabilidad *f.* responsibility; **r. cívica** civic responsibility; **r. individual** individual responsibility

restricción previa *f.* prior restraint

revisión judicial *f.* judicial review

revocación *f.* repeal

revocar *v.* to revoke, repeal

S

Secretario (-ria) de Defensa *m.f.* Secretary of Defense; **S. de Educación** Secretary of Education; **S. de Estado** Secretary of State; **S. de Justicia** Attorney General

secular *adj.* secular

secularismo *m.* secularism

segregación *f.* segregation; **abolición de la s.** *f.* desegregation; **s. de facto** de facto segregation; **s. de jure** de jure segregation

seguridad nacional *f.* national security

seguro *m.* insurance; **s. de salud** health insurance

Seguro Social *m.* Social Security

Senado *m.* Senate; **filibustero en el S.** *m.* Senate filibuster

senador, -ora *m.f.* senator; **s. estatal** state senator

sentencia *f.* sentence, judgment; **s. declarativa** declaratory judgment

separación *f.* separation; **s. de iglesia y estado** separation of church and state; **s. de poderes** separation of powers

servicio *m.* service; **s. civil** civil service; **s. militar obligatorio** conscription; **s. públicos** *pl.* public utilities, public services

Servicio de Inmigración y Control de Aduanas *m.* Immigration and Customs Enforcement

sexismo *m.* sexism

símbolo *m.* symbol

sin hogar *adj.* homeless

sindicato *m.* trade union

sistema *m.* system; **s. bipartidista** two-party system; **s. de justicia** justice system

soberanía *f.* sovereignty; **s. del estado** state sovereignty

socialista *adj. & m.f.* socialist

sociedad civil *f.* civil society

socioeconómico, -ca *adj.* socioeconomic; **condición s.** *f.* socioeconomic status

sociología *f.* sociology

sociólogo, -ga *m.f.* sociologist

solicitar *v.* to petition

solidaridad *f.* solidarity

statu quo *m.* status quo

subsidio *m.* entitlement program

subvención global *f.* block grant

sueño americano *m.* American Dream

sufragio universal *m.* universal suffrage

supremacía judicial *f.* judicial supremacy

supresión de votantes *f.* voter suppression

ESTUDIOS SOCIALES

T

tarjeta verde, tarjeta de residencia permanente *f.* green card

tema de actualidad *m.* hot topic, issue of current interest

teoría de la evolución *f.* theory of evolution

testificar *v.* to testify, give evidence

testigo *m.* witness; **relato de un t.** *m.* eyewitness testimony

testimonio *m.* testimony

titular *m.f.* incumbent

tolerancia *f.* tolerance

toma de posesión *f.* inauguration

toque de queda *m.* curfew

trabajador, -ora *m.f.* worker; **t. indocumentado (-da)** undocumented worker; **t. migratorio (-ria)** migrant worker

tradición cultural *f.* cultural tradition

tránsito rápido *m.* rapid transit

toxicomanía *f.* drug addiction

tribunal *m.* court; **t. de circuito** circuit court; **t. de primera instancia** lower court; **t. estatal** state court; **t. federal** federal court

tropas federales *f.pl.* federal troops

U

unificación *f.* unification

urbanidad *f.* civility

urnas *f.pl.* polls, ballot boxes

V

veredicto *m.* verdict

verificador (-ora) de hechos *m.f.* fact checker

vetar *v.* to veto

veto *m.* veto; **anulación del v.** *f.* veto override; **v. de bolsillo** pocket veto

vicepresidente *m.f.,* **vicepresidenta** *f.* vice-president

vida *f.* life; **v. cívica** civic life; **v. familiar** family life; **v. privada** private life; **v. pública** public life

vilipendio *m.* mudslinging

vivienda *f.* housing; **v. pública** public housing

voluntario, -ria *m.f.* volunteer

voluntarismo *m.* volunteerism

votación *f.* ballot; **v. fraudulenta** vote fraud; **v. nominal** roll call vote; **v. secreta** secret ballot

votante *m.f.* voter; **elegibilidad del v.** *f.* voter eligibility

votantes *m.f.pl.* voters; **concurrencia de v.** *f.* voter turnout; **supresión de v.** *f.* voter suppression

votar *v.* to vote

voto *m.* vote; **privar de derechos de v.** *v.* to disenfranchise; **v. de clausura** cloture vote; **v. en ausencia, v. ausente** absentee voting; **v. popular** popular vote

X

xenófilo, -la *m.f.* xenophile

xenofobia *f.* xenophobia

xenófobo, -ba *adj. & m.f.* xenophobic, nativist; xenophobe, nativist

Y

yihad *m.f.* jihad

Economía y Finanza

● ●

A

abundancia *f.* abundance

acaparamiento *m.* hoarding

acaudalado, -da *adj.* wealthy

accidente de trabajo *m.* occupational injury

acción afirmativa *f.* affirmative action

acciones *f.pl.* equities, shares, stocks; **a. ordinarias** common stock; **a. preferentes** preferred stock

accionista *m.f.* shareholder, stockholder

acomodado, -da *adj.* affluent

acreditar *v.* to credit

acreedor, -ora *m.f.* creditor

activos *f.pl.* assets; **asignación de a.** asset allocation

acuerdo *m.* agreement, deal; **a. comercial** trade agreement; **a. vinculante** binding agreement

acumulación de capital *f.* accumulation of capital

acuñar *v.* (moneda) to coin

administración *f.* management, administration; **a. empresarial** corporate governance; **a. inmobiliaria** property management

Administración de Pequeños Negocios *f.* Small Business Administration (S.B.A.); **A. de Seguridad y Salud Ocupacional** Occupational Safety and Health Administration (OSHA); **A. de Vivienda Federal** Federal Housing Administration (F.H.A.); **A. Federal de Aviación** Federal Aviation Administration (F.A.A.)

administrador, -ora *m.f.* manager

administrar *v.* to manage

afán de lucro *m.* profit motive

Agencia para el Desarrollo Internacional *f.* Agency for International Development (A.I.D.)

agente *m.f.* agent; **a. inmobiliario (-ria)** real estate agent

agotamiento de recursos *m.* resource depletion

agricultor, -ora *m.f.* farmer

agricultura *f.* agriculture; **a. de subsistencia** subsistence farming

ahorrar *v.* to save

ahorros *m.pl.* savings; **tasa de a.** *f.* savings rate

ajustado (-da) por inflación *adj.* inflation-adjusted

ajustador (-ora) de reclamaciones de seguros *m.f.* insurance claims adjuster

ajuste de costo de vida *m.* cost of living adjustment (COLA)

al por mayor *adj.* wholesale

al por menor *adj.* retail

alivio de desastre *m.* disaster relief

almacén *m.* warehouse

alquilar *v.* to rent

ESTUDIOS SOCIALES

alquiler *m.* rent; **control de alquileres** *m.* rent control

alumno (-na) en prácticas *m.f.* intern

amortización *f.* amortization

análisis de costos y beneficios *m.* cost-benefit analysis

antisindicalista *adj.* antiunion; **campaña a.** *f.* union busting

anualidad *f.* annuity

año fiscal *m.* fiscal year

apalancamiento *m.* leverage

aprendiz *m.f.* apprentice

apropiación *f.* appropriation

arancel *m.* tariff; **a. de importación** import duty; **a. proteccionista** protective tariff

arbitraje *m.* arbitrage

artesanía *f.* crafts

artesano, -na *m.f.* artisan

arreglo *m.* deal

arrendador, -ora *m.f.* landlord

arrendatario, -ria *m.f.* tenant

asegurar *v.* to insure

asesor, -ora *m.f.* adviser; **a. de inversiones** investment adviser; **a. financiero certificado** certified financial planner

asesoría de crédito *f.* credit counseling

asignación de activos *f.* asset allocation

asignar *v.* to allocate, appropriate

asociación *f.* partnership, association; **a. de ahorro y préstamo** savings and loan association

auditar *v.* to audit

auditor, -ora *m.f.* auditor

auditoría *f.* audit

auge y caída *m.* boom and bust

aumento de los precios *m.* price increase

austeridad *f.* austerity; **a. fiscal** fiscal austerity

automatización *f.* automation

autónomo, -ma *adj.* self-employed

aviación *f.* aviation

ayuda económica *f.* economic aid

B

baja por enfermedad *f.* sick leave

balancear una chequera *v.* to balance a checkbook

balanza *f.* balance; **b. comercial** balance of trade; **b. de pagos** balance of payments; **b. general** balance sheet

banca *f.* banking; **b. en línea, b. online** online banking

bancario, -ria *adj.* banking; **crisis b.** *f.* banking crisis; **cuenta b.** *f.* bank account; **extracto b.** *m.* bank statement; **fracaso b.** *m.* bank failure; **fraude b.** *m.* bank fraud

bancarrota *f.* bankruptcy, insolvency; **en b.** *adj.* bankrupt

banco *m.* bank; **b. central** central bank; **b. comercial** commercial bank; **b. de inversión** investment bank

Banco Mundial *m.* World Bank

barreras comerciales *f.* trade barriers

base de costo *f.* cost basis

base del sindicato *f.* rank and file

beneficios *m.pl.* benefits, profits; **b. complementarios** fringe benefits; **b. de Seguro Social** Social Security benefits; **maximización de b.** *f.* profit maximization

bienes *m.pl.* goods; **b. de capital** capital goods; **b. de consumo** consumer goods; **b. de consumo básico** consumer staples; **b. de equipo** capital equipment; **b. de lujo** luxury goods; **b. duraderos** durable goods; **b. inmuebles, b. raíces** real estate; **b. personales** personal property

bienes y servicios *m.pl.* goods and services

bienestar *m.* welfare; **estado del b.** *m.* welfare state

bodega *f.* warehouse, small shop, corner grocery

bolsa *f.* stock market

Bolsa de Valores de Nueva York *f.* New York Stock Exchange

bono *m.* bond; **b. basura** junk bond; **b. corporativo, b. de empresa** corporate bond; **b. de alto rendimiento** high yield bond; **b. gubernamental, b. del estado** government bond; **b. municipal** municipal bond; **b. ordinario del Tesoro** Treasury bond

burbuja *f.* bubble; **b. bursátil, b. del mercado de valores** stock market bubble; **b. inmobiliaria** housing bubble

C

cadena de tiendas *f.* chain store

caída del mercado de valores *f.* stock market crash

caja *f.* cash box; **c. registradora** cash register *f.;* **flujo de c.** *m.* cash flow

cajero automático *m.* automatic teller machine (A.T.M.)

calificado, -da *adj.* qualified, skilled; **no c.** unskilled

Cámara de Comercio *f.* Chamber of Commerce

cambio *m.* change, exchange; **c. de divisas** currency exchange, foreign exchange; **c. tecnológico** technological change; **tipo de c.** *m.* exchange rate

capacidad *f.* capacity

capacitación laboral *f.* job training

capital *m.* capital; **acumulación de c.** *f.* accumulation of capital; **c. de trabajo** working capital; **c. financiero** finance capital; **c. humano** human capital; **c. privado** private equity; **intensivo (-va) de c.** *adj.* capital-intensive; **inversión de c.** *f.* capital investment

capitalismo *m.* capitalism; **c. de estado** state capitalism; **c. favoritista** crony capitalism

capitalista *adj. & m.f.* capitalist; **c. de riesgo** venture capitalist

cargo *m.* charge; **c. por servicio** service charge

caridad *f.* charity

cartel *m.* cartel

cartera de inversión *f.* investment portfolio

carrera *f.* career

centro *m.* center; **c. comercial** shopping mall; **c. industrial** industrial center

certificado de depósito *m.* certificate of deposit

ciclo económico *m.* business cycle

cierre patronal *m.* lockout

clase *f.* class; **c. alta** upper class; **c. media** middle class; **c. obrera** working class

cliente, -ta *m.f.* customer; **fidelidad del c.** *f.* customer loyalty

cobertura de seguro *f.* insurance coverage

cobrar *v.* to cash, charge, collect; **c. impuestos** to tax; **c. un cheque** to cash a check

código *m.* code; **c. de construcción** building code; **c. impositivo** tax code

Código de Regulaciones Federales *m.* Code of Federal Regulations

comercialización *f.* marketing

comerciante *m.f.* merchant, shopkeeper; **c. al por mayor** wholesaler

comerciar *v.* to trade, do business

comercio *m.* trade, commerce, trading; **c. del café** coffee trade; **c. equitativo, comercio justo** fair trade; **c. exterior** foreign trade; **c. interestatal** interstate commerce; **c. internacional** international trade; **libre c.** free trade; **prácti-**

cas desleales de c. *f.pl.* unfair trade practices

comisión *f.* commission

Comisión de Bolsa y Valores *f.* Securities and Exchange Commission (S.E.C.); **C. de Comercio Internacional de Estados Unidos** U.S. International Trade Commission (U.S.I.T.C.); **C. de Seguridad de Productos del Consumidor** Consumer Product Safety Commission (C.P.S.C.); **C. del Comercio en Futuros sobre Mercancía** Commodity Futures Trading Commission (C.F.T.C.); **C. Federal de Comercio** Federal Trade Commission (F.T.C.); **C. Interestatal de Comercio** Interstate Commerce Commission (I.C.C.)

compañía *f.* company

compensación *f.* compensation; **c. al trabajador** workers compensation

competencia *f.* competition

competir *v.* to compete

competitividad *f.* competitiveness

competitivo, -va *adj.* competitive

compra *f.* purchase; **c. apalancada** leveraged buyout

comprador, -ora *m.f.* buyer, shopper

comprar *v.* to buy, purchase; **c. acciones a préstamo** to buy stock on margin

computador, -ora *m.f.* computer

concesión de licencias *f.* licensing

conglomerado *m.* conglomerate

conocimientos financieros *m.pl.* financial literacy

conservación de los recursos *f.* resource conservation

construir *v.* to build

consumidor, -ora *m.f.* consumer; **confianza del c.** *f.* consumer confidence

consumir *v.* to consume, use

consumismo *m.* consumerism

consumo *m.* consumption; **c. conspicuo, c. ostentoso** conspicuous consumption; **c. de los hogares, c. familiar** household consumption

contabilidad *f.* accounting, bookkeeping; **c. de partida doble** double-entry bookkeeping

contador, -ora *m.f.* accountant

contralor, -ora *m.f.* comptroller

contratación *f.* hiring

contratante *m.f.* contracting party

contratar *v.* to hire, recruit, contract

contratista independiente *m.f.* independent contractor

contrato *m.* contract

contribución caritativa *f.* charitable contribution

controles de precios y salarios *m.pl.* wage and price controls

convenio *m.* agreement, deal; **c. obligatorio** binding agreement

cooperativa *f.* cooperative; **c. de crédito** credit union

corporación *f.* corporation; **c. multinacional** multinational corporation

Corporación Federal de Seguro de

Depósitos *f.* Federal Deposit Insurance Corporation (F.D.I.C.)

corredor (-ra) de bolsa *m.f.* broker

cosecha *f.* crop, harvest

costo *m.* cost; **c. de la vida** cost of living; **c. de oportunidad** opportunity cost; **c. de producción** cost of production; **c. marginal** marginal cost

crecimiento *m.* growth; **c. económico** economic growth; **tasa de c.** *f.* growth rate

credibilidad *f.* credibility

crédito *m.* credit; **asesoría de c.** *f.* credit counseling

cubrirse *v.* to hedge

cuenta *f.* account; **c. bancaria** bank account; **c. de ahorros** savings account; **c. de cheques** checking account; **c. de inversión** investment account

Cuenta de Retiro Individual *f.* Individual Retirement Account (IRA)

cuidado de salud universal *m.* universal health care

cultivable *adj.* arable; **tierra c.** *f.* arable land

cultivo *m.* crop, farming; **c. comercial** cash crop; **rotación de cultivos** *f.* crop rotation; **tierras de c.** *f.pl.* farmland

cuota *f.* share, quota, fee; **c. de mercado** market share

CH

cheque *m.* check; **c. de pago** paycheck; **cobrar un c.** *v.* to cash a

ESTUDIOS SOCIALES

check; **endosar un c.** to endorse a check; **escribir un c.** to write a check; **rebotar un c.** to bounce a check

chequera *f.* checkbook

D

deducción *f.* deduction; **d. de impuestos** tax deduction; **d. estándar** standard deduction; **d. fiscal detallada** itemized deduction

déficit *m.* deficit; **d. de gasto** deficit spending; **d. federal** federal deficit; **reducción del d.** *f.* deficit reduction

deflación *f.* deflation

defraudar *v.* to defraud

degradación ambiental *f.* environmental degradation

demanda *f.* demand; **oferta y d.** supply and demand *f.*

democracia *f.* democracy; **d. económica** economic democracy; **d. laboral** workplace democracy

denominación *f.* denomination

Departamento de Comercio *m.* Department of Commerce; **D. de Trabajo** Department of Labor; **D. de Vivienda y Desarrollo Urbano** Department of Housing and Urban Development; **D. del Tesoro** Department of the Treasury

dependiente *m.f.* dependent

depositante *m.f.* depositor

depositar *v.* to deposit

depósito *m.* deposit; **d. bancario** bank deposit

depreciación *f.* depreciation

depresión *f.* depression

derecho law, right, duty *m.;* **d. comercial** commercial law; **d. de importación** import duty; **d. de responsabilidad civil** tort law; **d. laboral** labor law

derechos *m.pl.* rights; **d. de autor** copyright; **d. de propiedad** property rights; **d. marítimos** maritime rights; **violación de los d. de autor** *f.* copyright infringement

derivado *m.* derivative

derrumbe bursátil *m.* stock market crash

desarrollo *m.* development; **d. industrial** industrial development; **d. sostenible** sustainable development

descuento *m.* discount

desempleo *m.* unemployment; **d. cíclico** cyclical unemployment; **tasa de d.** *f.* unemployment rate

deseos *m.* wants

desigualdad económica *f.* economic inequality

desincentivo *m.* disincentive

desindustrialización *f.* deindustrialization

despido *m.* dismissal, layoff; **d. injustificado** wrongful discharge

destreza *f.* skill, know-how

deuda *f.* debt, liability; **crisis de la d.** *f.* debt crisis; **d. del consumidor** consumer debt; **d. soberana** sovereign debt

deudor, -ora *m.f.* debtor

• •

devaluación *f.* devaluation

devaluar *v.* to devalue

dinero *m.* money; **lavado de d.** money laundering

dirección *f.* management

director, -ora *m.f.* manager; **d. ejecutivo (-va)** chief executive officer

diseño *m.* design; **d. asistido por ordenador** computer-aided design; **d. de productos** product design

distribución *f.* distribution; **d. del ingreso** income distribution; **d. en zonas** zoning

distribuidor, -ora *m.f.* dealer

diversificación *f.* diversification

diversificado, -da *adj.* diversified

diversificar *v.* to diversify

dividendo *m.* dividend

divisa *f.* foreign currency

división *f.* division; **d. de acciones** stock split; **d. del trabajo** division of labor

dólares *m.* dollars, greenbacks

dominio eminente *m.* eminent domain

donación *f.* charitable contribution, endowment, grant

dúmping *m.* (bienes) dumping

E

economía *f.* economy, economics; **e. conductual** behavioral economics; **e. de escala** economy of scale; **e. de mercado** market economy; **e. de oferta** supply-side economics; **e. de servicios** service economy;

e. del bienestar social welfare economics; **e. del goteo** trickledown economics; **e. del mercado** market economy; **e. dirigida** command economy; **e. global** global economy; **e. keynesiana** Keynesian economics; **e. laboral** labor economics; **e. laissez-faire** laissez-faire economics; **e. mixta** mixed economy; **e. mundial** world economy; **e. neoclásica** neoclassical economics; **e. planificada** planned economy; **e. socialista** socialist economy; **e. sumergida** underground economy

económico, -ca *adj.* economic; **crecimiento e.** *m.* economic growth; **estímulo e.** *m.* economic stimulus; **indicador e.** *m.* economic indicator; **reestructuración e.** *f.* economic restructuring; **sanciones e.** *f.pl.* economic sanctions; **seguridad e.** *f.* economic security

economista *m.f.* economist

edificio *m.* building

educación financiera *f.* financial literacy

efectivo *m.* cash

eficiencia *f.* efficiency

eficiente *adj.* efficient

ejecución hipotecaria *f.* foreclosure

ejecutar una hipoteca *v.* to foreclose

embargo *m.* embargo

emplazamiento de producto *m.* product placement

ESTUDIOS SOCIALES

empleado, -da *m.f.* employee

empleador, -ora *m.f.;* **empresario, -ria** *m.f.* employer

empleo *m.* employment; **e. a tiempo completo** full-time employment; **e. a tiempo parcial** part-time employment; **pleno e.** full employment; **solicitud de e.** *f.* job application; **terminación del e.** *f.* termination of employment

emprendedor, -ora *adj.;* **empresarial** *adj.* entrepreneurial; **espíritu e.** *m.* entrepreneurship

empresa *f.* enterprise, company; **e. pública** public company; **gran e.** large firm; **libre e.** free enterprise

empresario, -ria *m.f.* entrepreneur

endeudamiento *m.* debt, indebtedness; **límite de e. federal** *m.* federal debt ceiling

energía *f.* energy; **e. alternativa** alternative energy; **e. renovable** renewable energy

enfermedad ocupacional *f.* occupational disease

entidad legal *f.* legal entity

entrenamiento *m.* training; **e. sobre diversidad** diversity training

envío *m.* shipping

equidad *f.* equity, fairness; **e. de sueldos** pay equity

equilibrio *m.* equilibrium

equipo de ventas *m.* sales force

ergonomía *f.* ergonomics

escapatoria de impuestos, escapatoria tributaria *f.* tax loophole

escasez *f.* scarcity, shortage

escaso, -sa *adj.* scarce

esclavitud asalariada *f.* wage slavery

escuela de negocios *f.* business school

esparcimiento *m.* leisure

especulación *f.* speculation

especulador, -ora *m.f.* speculator

esquema *m.* scheme; **e. piramidal** pyramid scheme; **e. Ponzi** Ponzi scheme

estafa *f.* scam

estafar *v.* to swindle, defraud

estancia *f.* farm

estimación *f.* valuation

estímulo económico *m.* economic stimulus

estudio *m.* study; **e. de mercado** market research; **e. de tiempo y movimientos** time-motion study

ética *f.* ethics; **é. empresarial** business ethics; **é. laboral** work ethic

eurozona *f.* Euro zone

evasión fiscal, evasión tributaria *f.* tax evasion

excedente *m.* surplus

exención del impuesto *f.* tax exemption

expansión *f.* expansion

experto, -ta *adj.* skilled

explotación *f.* exploitation

explotar *v.* to exploit

exportación *f.* exporting

exportar *v.* to export

externalidades *f.* externalities

externalización *f.* outsourcing

externalizar *v.* to outsource

• •

extracto bancario *m.* bank statement

extranjero, -ra *adj.* foreign; **inversión e. directa** *f.* direct foreign investment

F

fábrica *f.* factory

fabricación *f.* manufacturing, production; **sitio de f.** *m.* manufacturing site

fabricante *m.* manufacturer

falsificación *f.* forgery

falsificado, -da *adj.* counterfeit

faltar al pago *v.* to default

Federación Estadounidense del Trabajo y Congreso de Organizaciones Industriales *f.* A.F.L.-C.I.O.

fideicomiso *m.* trust; **f. de inversión inmobiliaria** real estate investment trust (REIT)

fidelidad del cliente *f.* customer loyalty

financiación *f.* financing; **f. por el vendedor** seller financing

financiamiento *m.* funding

financiar *v.* to finance

finanza personal *f.* personal finance

finca *f.* farm

firma *f.* firm, business; **f. de corretaje** brokerage firm

fiscal *adj.* fiscal; **año f.** *m.* fiscal year; **austeridad f.** *f.* fiscal austerity; **paraíso f.** *m.* tax haven; **política f.** *f.* fiscal policy; **reforma f.** *f.* tax reform; **refugio f.** *m.* tax shelter

flujo de caja *m.* cash flow

fondo *m.* fund; **f. común para riesgos** risk pool; **f. de cobertura** hedge fund; **f. de pensión** pension fund; **f. del mercado monetario** money market fund; **f. indexado** index fund; **f. mutuo** mutual fund

Fondo Monetario Internacional *m.* International Monetary Fund (I.M.F.)

formación *f.* training; **f. profesional** vocational training

fracaso *m.* failure; **f. bancario** bank failure; **f. del mercado** market failure

franquicia *f.* franchise

fraude *m.* fraud

fuerza de trabajo *f.* labor power; **f. laboral** workforce

fuga de capitales *f.* capital flight

fungible *adj.* fungible

fusión *f.* merger

fusiones y adquisiciones *f.pl.* mergers and acquisitions

G

ganadería *f.* ranching

ganancia *f.* profit, earnings; **g. imprevista** windfall; **motivo por g.** *m.* profit motive

ganar *v.* to earn

garantía financiera *f.* collateral

gasto *m.* expense, spending; **g. de consumo** consumer spending; **g. deficitario** deficit spending; **g.**

Estudios Sociales

público government spending
gerente *m.f.* manager
gestión *f.* management; **g. cientí-fica** scientific management; **g. de riesgos** risk management
globalización *f.* globalization
granja *f.* farm
granjero, -ra *m.f.* farmer
gremio de artesanía *m.* craft guild
guerra comercial *f.* trade war

H

habilidades *f.* skills
herencia *f.* inheritance, estate
hipoteca *f.* mortgage; **h. de tasa ajustable** adjustable-rate mortgage; **h. de tasa fija** fixed-rate mortgage; **h. subprime** subrime mortage; **pago de la h.** *m.* mortgage payment; **segunda h.** second mortgage, home equity loan
hipótesis del mercado eficiente *f.* efficient market hypothesis
hogar *m.* household
honorario *m.* fee
horario flexible *m.* flextime
huelga *f.* strike; **h. general** general strike

I

importación *f.* import; **derecho de i.** *m.* import duty
importado, -da *adj.* imported
importar *v.* to import
impuesto *m.* tax, duty; **de i. diferi-do** *adj.* tax-deferred; **exención del i.** *f.* tax exemption; **i. fijo** flat tax; **i. progresivo sobre la renta** progressive income tax; **i. regresi-vo** regressive tax; **i. sobre dona-ciones** gift tax; **i. sobre el valor añadido** value added tax; **i. sobre la nómina** payroll tax; **i. sobre la propiedad** property tax; **i. sobre la renta** income tax; **i. sobre las plusvalías** capital gains tax; **i. so-bre las ventas** sales tax; **i. sobre sucesiones** estate tax; **prepara-ción de impuestos** *f.* tax prepara-tion; **reducción de impuestos** *f.* tax cut; **tasa de i. marginal** *f.* marginal tax rate
Impuesto Mínimo Alternativo *m.* Alternative Minimum Tax
incentivo *m.* incentive; **i. econó-mico** economic incentive; **i. nega-tivo** negative incentive; **i. positi-vo** positive incentive
incorporación *f.* incorporation
incorporado, -da *adj.* incorporated
incorporar *v.* to incorporate
incumplimiento *m.* default
indemnización *f.* compensation, in-demnification
indemnizar *v.* to indemnify
independencia energética *f.* en-ergy independence
indicador económico *m.* economic indicator
índice *m.* index
Índice de Precios al Consumidor *m.* Consumer Price Index (C.P.I.); **Í. Dow Jones** Dow Jones Indus-trial Average

● ●

industria *f.* industry; **i. artesanal** cottage industry; **i. automovilística** automobile industry; **i. de servicios** service industry; **i. del espectáculo** entertainment industry; **i. ligera** light industry; **i. pesada** heavy industry; **i. petrolera** petroleum industry; **i. textil** textile industry; **i. extractivas** *pl.* extractive industries

industrialización *f.* industrialization

inflación *f.* inflation; **ajustado por i.** *adj.* inflation-adjusted; **tasa de i.** *f.* inflation rate

infraestructura *f.* infrastructure

ingeniería *f.* engineering

ingresos *m.pl.* earnings, revenue, income; **i. brutos** gross income; **i. de inversión** investment income; **i. de los hogares, i. familiares;** household income; **i. fijos** fixed income; **i. netos** net income; **i. por cápita** per capita income

iniciativa empresarial *f.* entrepreneurship

inmobiliaria *f.* real estate agency

innovación *f.* innovation

inquilino, -na *m.f.* tenant

insolvencia *f.* insolvency

instrumentos *m.* tools

intensivo (-va) de capital *adj.* capital-intensive

intercambiar *v.* to barter, exchange

intercambio *m.* barter, exchange

interés *m.* interest; **i. compuesto** compound interest; **i. hipotecario** mortgage interest; **i. preferencial** prime rate; **i. simple** simple interest; **tasa de i.** *f.* interest rate

invención *f.* invention

inventario *m.* inventory

inversión *f.* investment, investing; **cartera de i.** investment portfolio; **i. de capital** capital investment; **i. extranjera directa** direct foreign investment; **i. socialmente responsable** socially responsible investing

inversor, -ora *m.f.;* **inversionista** *m.f.* investor; **i. institucional** institutional investor

invertir *v.* to invest

J

jefe, -fa *m.f.* boss

jornada de ocho horas *f.* eight-hour day

jornalero del campo *m.* farm laborer

jubilación *f.* retirement

jubilado, -da *adj.* retired

juego de suma cero *m.* zero sum game

Junta de la Reserva Federal *f.* Federal Reserve Board

junta directiva *f.* board of directors

L

labor *f.* labor; **l. manual** manual labor

laguna tributaria *f.* tax loophole

lavado de dinero *m.* money laundering

ESTUDIOS SOCIALES

ESTUDIOS SOCIALES

letra del Tesoro *f.* Treasury bill

ley *f.* law **l. antimonopolio** antitrust law; **l. de contratos** contract law; **l. de los rendimientos decrecientes** law of diminishing returns; **l. de quiebras, l. de bancarrota** bankruptcy law; **l. del derecho al trabajo** *pl.* right-to-work laws

Ley de Normas Razonables de Trabajo *f.* Fair Labor Standards Act; **L. de Veracidad en los Préstamos** Truth in Lending Act; **L. Dodd-Frank** Dodd-Frank Act; **L. Glass-Steagall** Glass-Steagall Act

líder sindical *m.f.* labor leader

línea *f.* line; **l. de crédito** line of credit; **l. de montaje** assembly line; **l. de piquete** picket line; **l. de productos** product line

liquidación *f.* liquidation

liquidez *f.* liquidity

luditas *m.pl.*, **ludistas** *m.pl.* Luddites

lugar de trabajo *m.* workplace

M

macroeconomía *f.* macroeconomics

manejar *v.* to manage

manejo *m.* management; **m. de efectivo** cash management; **m. de la propiedad** property management

manipulación monetaria *f.* currency manipulation

maquinaria *f.* machinery; **herramienta de m.** *f.* machine tool

marca *f.* brand, trademark

materias primas *f.* raw materials

maximización de beneficio *f.* profit maximization

mayorista *m.f.* wholesaler

mecanización *f.* mechanization

medios de comunicación, medios de difusión *m.pl.* mass media

mercado *m.* market; **fracaso del m.** *m.* market failure; **impulsado (-da) por el m.** *adj.* market-driven; **m. alcista** bull market; **m. bajista** bear market; **m. bursátil, m. de valores** stock market; **m. de bonos, m. obligacionista** bond market; **m. de trabajo, m. laboral** labor market; **m. libre** free market; **m. mundial** global market; **m. negro** black market; **m. privado** private market; **m. de capitales** *pl.* capital markets; **m. emergentes** *pl.* emerging markets; **repunte del m. de valores** *f.* stock market rally

mercadotecnia *f.* marketing

mercancía *f.* commodity

mercantilismo *m.* mercantilism

meritocracia *f.* meritocracy

metales preciosos *m.* precious metals

microeconomía *f.* microeconomics

minería *f.* mining; **m. a cielo abierto** strip mining

molino *m.* mill

moneda *f.* coin, currency

monetarismo *m.* monetarism

monopolio *m.* monopoly

monopolístico, -ca *adj.* monopolistic

motivo por ganancia *m.* profit motive

movilidad *f.* mobility; **m. ascendente** upward mobility

N

necesidades *f.* needs

negociación *f.* negotiation; **n. colectiva** collective bargaining; **n. de contratos** contract negotiation

negociar *v.* to trade, negotiate, do business

negocio *m.* business

nivel de vida *m.* standard of living

nombre comercial *m.* trade name

nómina *f.* payroll

O

obligación *f.* liability, bond, security

obrero, -ra *m.f.* worker; **o. manual** blue-collar worker; **o. sindicados** *pl.* organized labor

obsolescencia planificada *f.* planned obsolescence

obstáculos comerciales *m.* trade barriers

ocio *m.* leisure

ocupación *f.* occupation

oferta *f.* offering, supply; **o. monetaria** money supply; **o. pública inicial** initial public offering; **o. y demanda** supply and demand

Oficina de Administración y Presupuesto *f.* Office of Management and Budget (O.M.B.); **O. de Estadísticas Laborales** Bureau of Labor Statistics (B.L.S.)

oficinista *m.f.* office worker, white-collar worker

oficio *m.* profession, trade

oligopolio *m.* oligopoly

opción *f.* option; **o. de acciones** stock option

opulencia *f.* affluence

opulento, -ta *adj.* affluent

ordenador *m.* computer

organización *f.* organization; **o. caritativa, o. de caridad** charitable organization; **o. sindical** union organizing

Organización Mundial del Comercio *f.* World Trade Organization (W.T.O.)

P

pago *m.* payment; **p. de alquiler** rent; **p. de horas extras** overtime pay; **p. de la hipoteca** mortgage payment

pánico financiero *m.* financial panic

paradoja del ahorro *f.* paradox of thrift

paraíso fiscal *m.* tax haven

pasantía *f.* internship

patente *f.* patent

patrimonio *m.* estate; **p. neto** net worth

patrón, -na *m.f.* employer, boss

patrón oro *m.* gold standard

pedir prestado *v.* to borrow

pensión *f.* pension

pérdida *f.* loss

personal *m.* staffing, personnel; **p.**

ESTUDIOS SOCIALES

de ventas sales force; **p. no sindicalizado** nonunion workforce

pesos y medidas *m.pl.* weights and measures

plan *m.* plan; **p. de contribución definida** defined contribution plan; **p. de jubilación** retirement plan; **p. de negocios** business plan; **p. de prestación definida** defined benefit plan; **p. Keogh** Keogh plan

planificación *f.* planning; **p. patrimonial** estate planning

pleno empleo *m.* full employment

plusvalía *f.* surplus value, added value

plusvalías *f.pl.* capital gains

pobre *adj. & m.f.* poor

pobreza *f.* poverty; **tasa de p.** *f.* poverty rate

poder *m.* power, proxy; **p. adquisitivo** purchasing power; **p. de negociación** bargaining power

política *f.* policy; **p. fiscal** fiscal policy; **p. industrial** industrial policy; **p. monetaria** monetary policy

póliza de seguro *f.* insurance policy

por cápita *adj.* per capita

por poderes *adv.* by proxy

porcentaje *m.* percentage; **tasa de p. anual** *f.* annual percentage rate

poseer *v.* to own

posesión *f.* possession

prácticas comerciales desleales *f.* unfair trade practices

precio *m.* price, cost, fee; **disminución de precios** *f.* price decrease;

guerra de precios *f.* price war; **p. al contado** cash price; **p. al por mayor** wholesale price; **p. al por menor** retail price

preparación de impuestos *f.* tax preparation

prestamista *m.f.* lender

préstamo *m.* loan, lending; **p. empresarial** business loan; **p. estudiantil** student loan; **p. hipotecario** mortgage loan; **p. predatorio** predatory lending; **p. subprime** subprime loan

prestar *v.* to loan

prestatario, -ria *m.f.* borrower

presupuesto *m.* budget; **p. equilibrado** balanced budget; **p. federal** federal budget

prima de seguro *f.* insurance premium

principal *m.* principal

privatización *f.* privatization

privatizar *v.* to privatize

producción *f.* production; **factor de p.** *m.* factor of production; **medio de p.** *m.* means of production; **método de p.** *m.* production method; **modo de p.** *m.* mode of production; **planta de p.** *f.* manufacturing plant, production site; **p. de alimentos** food production; **p. en masa** mass production; **p. industrial** industrial production

producir *v.* to produce

productividad *f.* productivity

producto *m.* product; **p. acabado, p. terminado** finished product; **p.**

interno bruto Gross Domestic Product (G.D.P.)

productor, -ora *m.f.* producer

promoción *f.* promotion

propiedad *f.* ownership; **p. de bienes** property ownership; **p. de la vivienda** home ownership; **p. exclusiva** sole proprietorship; **p. intelectual** intellectual property; **p. para alquiler** rental property; **p. privada** private property; **p. pública** public property

propietario, -ria *m.f.* owner

prosperidad *f.* prosperity

protección *f.* protection; **p. contra sobregiros** overdraft protection; **p. del consumidor** consumer protection

proteccionismo *m.* protectionism

proteccionista *adj.* protectionist

publicidad *f.* advertising

Q

quiebra *f.* bankruptcy; **en q.** *adj.* bankrupt

R

rebotar un cheque *v.* to bounce a check

recargo *m.* surcharge; **r. por tardanza** late fee

recesión económica *f.* recession, economic slump

reclamación de seguro *f.* insurance claim

recompensa *f.* reward

recompensar *v.* to reward

recuperación *f.* recovery; **r. sin empleo** jobless recovery

recursos *m.pl.* resources; **conservación de los r.** *f.* resource conservation; **r. escasos** scarce resources; **r. humanos** human resources; **r. limitados** limited resources; **r. renovables** renewable resources

red *f.* system, network; **r. de autopistas interestatales** interstate highway system; **r. de protección social** social safety net

reducción *f.* reduction; **r. de impuestos** tax cut; **r. del déficit** deficit reduction; **r. del riesgo** risk reduction

reembolso *m.* refund, repayment

reestructuración económica *f.* economic restructuring

refinanciar *v.* to refinance

reforma *f.* reform; **r. agraria** land reform; **r. financiera** financial reform; **r. fiscal, r. tributaria** tax reform

refugio fiscal, refugio tributario *m.* tax shelter

reglas del trabajo *f.pl.* work rules

regulación *f.*, **reglamento** *m.* regulation; **r. financiero (-ra)** financial regulation

regulador, -ora *m.f.* regulator

regular *v.* to regulate

relación precio-beneficio *f.* price-earnings ratio

relaciones laborales, relaciones obrero-patronales *f.* labor-man-

ESTUDIOS SOCIALES

ESTUDIOS SOCIALES

agement relations

rendimiento *m.* yield, return; **r. de bonos** bond yield; **r. de la inversión** return on investment; **tasa de r.** *f.* rate of return

rentabilidad *f.* profitability, yield; **r. de la inversión** return on investment

repunte del mercado de valores *f.* stock market rally

responsabilidad *f.* liability; **r. limitada** limited liability; **r. por productos defectuosos** product liability; **r. sin fondos** unfunded liability

retiro *m.* retirement; **r. de fondos** withdrawal of funds

rico, -ca *adj.* rich, wealthy

riesgo *m.* risk; **r. de crédito** credit risk; **r. moral** moral hazard

riqueza *f.* affluence, wealth; **r. heredada** inherited wealth

rivalidad *f.* competition

robótica *f.* robotics

rompehuelgas *m.* strikebreaker, replacement worker

ruta comercial *f.* trade route

S

salario *m.* wage, income; **s. de subsistencia** living wage; **s. mínimo** minimum wage

saldo *m.* balance; **s. bancario** bank balance; **s. mínimo** minimum balance

salida *f.* output

sanciones económicas *f.* economic

sanctions

sector *m.* sector; **s. del mercado** market sector; **s. privado** private sector; **s. público** public sector

seguridad *f.* security; **s. económica** economic security; **s. laboral** job security

seguro *m.* insurance; **cobertura de s.** *f.* insurance coverage; **póliza de s.** *f.* insurance policy; **prima de s.** *f.* insurance premium; **reclamación de s.** *f.* insurance claim; **s. de accidentes, s. de daños** casualty insurance; **s. de desempleo** unemployment insurance; **s. contra discapacidad** disability insurance; **s. de propietarios** homeowners insurance; **s. de salud, s. medico** health insurance; **s. de vida** life insurance

Seguro Social *m.* Social Security; **beneficios de S. S.** *m.pl.,* **prestaciones de S. S.** *f.pl.* Social Security benefits

semana de trabajo *f.* work week

servicio de atención al cliente *m.* customer service

Servicio de Impuestos Internos *m.* Internal Revenue Service (I.R.S.)

servicios *m.pl.* services, utilities; **industria de s.** *f.* service industry; **s. financieros** financial services

sindicalización *f.* unionization

sindicalizado, -da *adj.* unionized; **no s.** nonunion

sindicar *v.* to unionize

sindicato *m.* trade union; **s. de**

artesanos craft union; **s. industrial** industrial union

sistema *m.* system; **s. de fábrica** factory system; **s. de libre empresa** free enterprise system

sobrecosto *m.* cost overrun

sobrepesca *f.* overfishing

sobreproducción *f.* overproduction

sociedad *f.* company, association, partnership; **s. agraria** agrarian society; **s. de crédito hipotecario** building society; **s. limitada** limited partnership

socio, -cia *m.f.* partner

sostenible *adj.* sustainable

subclase *f.* underclass

subcontratista *m.f.* subcontractor

subdesarrollo *m.* underdevelopment

subprime *adj.* subprime; **hipoteca s.** *f.* subrime mortage; **préstamo s.** *m.* subprime loan

subsidios *m.pl.* subsidies; **s. agrícolas** farm subsidies

subsistencia *f.*, **sustento** *m.* livelihood

sueldo *m.* salary

suministro *m.* supply; **cadena de s.** *f.* supply chain

superávit *m.* surplus

supervisor, -ora *m.f.* supervisor

T

taller sindical *m.* union shop

tarifa *f.* tariff; **t. protectora** protective tariff

tarjeta *f.* card; **t. de crédito** credit card; **t. de débito** debit card

tasa *f.* rate; **t. de ahorros** savings rate; **t. de crecimiento** growth rate; **t. de desempleo** unemployment rate; **t. de impuesto marginal** marginal tax rate; **t. de inflación** inflation rate; **t. de interés** interest rate; **t. de pobreza** poverty rate; **t. de porcentaje anual** annual percentage rate; **t. de rentabilidad, t. de rendimiento** rate of return; **t. salarial** wage rate

techo de cristal *m.* glass ceiling

tecnología *f.* technology; **de alta t.** *adj.* high-tech; **t. de la información** information technology

teletrabajo *m.* telecommuting

teneduría de libros *f.* bookkeeping

teoría *f.* theory; **t. de juegos** game theory; **t. de la elección racional** rational choice theory; **t. de la mano invisible** Invisible Hand theory; **t. del más tonto** greater fool theory; **t. del valor-trabajo** labor theory of value

terminación del empleo *f.* termination of employment

tesoro *m.*, **tesorería** *f.* treasury; **t. público** public treasury

Tesoro (EE.UU.) *m.* Treasury; **bono ordinario del T.** *m.* Treasury bond; **letra del T.** *f.* Treasury bill

tiburón empresarial *m.* corporate raider

tienda *f.* store; **t. de ventas al por**

ESTUDIOS SOCIALES

ESTUDIOS SOCIALES

menor retail outlet
tipo de cambio *m.* exchange rate
títulos *m.pl.* securities
trabajador, -ora *m.f.* worker; **t. de cuello rosa** pink collar worker; **t. manual** blue-collar worker
trabajar *v.* to work
trabajo *m.* work, job, labor; **búsqueda de t.** *f.* job search; **condiciones de t.** *f.pl.* working conditions; **división del t.** *f.* division of labor; **lugar de t.** *m.* workplace; **reglas del t.** *f.pl.* work rules; **semana de t.** *f.* work week; **t. a distancia** telecommuting; **t. forzado** forced labor; **t. infantil** child labor; **t. manual** manual labor; **t. por cuenta propia, t. autónomo** self-employment; **t. por turnos** shift work; **t. sin porvenir** dead-end job; **t. temporal** temporary employment
tráfico de información privilegiada *m.* insider trading
transporte *m.* transport
Tratado de Libre Comercio de América del Norte (TLCAN) *m.* North American Free Trade Agreement (NAFTA)
tributación *f.* taxation
trocar *v.* to barter
trueque *m.* barter

U
usura *f.* usury
utilidad *f.* utility; **u. marginal** marginal utility; **u. pública** public utility

V
valor *m.* value; **v. actual** present value; **v. añadido** value added; **v. de mercado** market value; **v. intrínseco** intrinsic value; **v. neto** net worth; **v. del activo neto** net asset value (N.A.V.)
valoración *f.* valuation; **v. de crédito** credit rating
valores *m.pl.* securities
vendedor, -ora *m.f.* seller, salesperson
vender *v.* to sell; **v. al descubierto** to sell short
venta *f.* sale; **v. al por menor** retailing
verificación *f.* underwriting
vivienda *f.* housing
vocación *f.* vocation
volatilidad *f.* volatility

W
Wall Street *f.* Wall Street

Z
Zona euro *f.* Euro zone
zonificación *f.* zoning

Geografía

• •

A

abismo *m.* chasm

aborigen *adj. & m.f.* Aborigine; **pueblos a.** *m.pl.* aboriginal peoples

abrasión *f.* abrasion

acantilado *m.* cliff

accidente geográfico *m.* geographic feature

acueducto *m.* aqueduct

acuicultura *f.* aquaculture

acuífero, -ra *adj.* aquiferous

acuífero *m.* aquifer; **a. de Ogallala** Ogallala Aquifer

acumulación *f.* accumulation

adaptación *f.* adaptation

Afganistán *m.* Afghanistan

Afgano, -na *adj. & m.f.* Afghan

afluente *m.* tributary

África *f.* Africa; **Á. subsahariana** Sub-Saharan Africa; **norte de Á.** *m.* North Africa

africano, -na *adj. & m.f.* African

afrikáner *adj. & m.f.,* **afrikánder** *adj. & m.f.* Afrikaner, Boer

agricultura *f.* agriculture; **a. de subsistencia** subsistence agriculture

agua *f.* water; **abastecimiento de a.** *m.* water supply; **a. revueltas** *pl.* riptide; **a. salada** salt water; **a. subterráneas** *pl.* groundwater

aguas abajo *adj. & adv.* downstream

albanés, -esa *adj. & m.f.* Albanian

Albania *f.* Albania

aldea *f.* village

alemán, -na *adj. & m.f.* German

Alemania *f.* Germany

Alpes *m.pl.* Alps

alpino, -na *adj.* alpine

altiplano *m.* plateau

altitud *f.* altitude

Amazonía *f.* Amazonia

ambiental *adj.* environmental; **protección a.** *f.* environmental protection

ambiente *m.* environment, atmosphere

América del Sur *f.* South America; **A. Latina** *f.* Latin America

americano, -na *adj. & m.f.* American

amerindio, -dia *adj. & m.f.* Amerindian

Anatolia *f.* Anatolia

andino, -na *adj. & m.f.* Andean

Andorra *f.* Andorra

andorrano, -na *adj. & m.f.* Andorran

Angola *f.* Angola

angoleño, -ña *adj. & m.f.;* **angolano, -na** *adj. & m.f.* Angolan

animales de trabajo *m.pl.* work animals

antártico, -ca *adj.* Antarctic; **Círculo Polar A.** *m.* Antarctic Circle; **península A.** *f.* Antarctic Peninsula

Antártico, -ca *m.f.,* **Antártida** *f.* Antarctic

Antillas *f.pl.* Antilles, West Indies;

ESTUDIOS SOCIALES

A. Mayores Greater Antilles; **A. Menores** Lesser Antilles; **A. Neerlandesas, A. Holandesas** Dutch West Indies
Apalaches *m.pl.* Appalachia; **montañas A.** *f.pl.* Appalachian Mountains
apertura *f.* clearing
Arabia Saudita *f.* Saudi Arabia
árbol *m.* tree; **copa del a.** *f.* tree canopy
archipiélago *m.* archipelago; **a. filipino, a. de las Filipinas** Philippine archipelago
área *f.* area; **á. semiárida** semiarid area; **á. silvestre** wilderness area
Área de la bahía de San Francisco *f.* Bay Area
arena *f.* sand; **duna de a.** *f.* sand dune
arenoso, -sa *adj.* sandy
Argelia *f.* Algeria
argelino, -na *adj. & m.f.* Algerian
Argentina *f.* Argentina
argentino, -na *adj. & m.f.* Argentine, Argentinean
Armenia *f.* Armenia
armenio, -nia *adj. & m.f.* Armenian
ártico, -ca *adj.* Arctic; **Círculo Polar Á.** *m.* Arctic Circle; **océano Á.** *m.* Arctic Ocean; **región á.** Arctic region *f.*
Ártico *m.* Arctic
arrecife *m.* reef; **a. coralino, a. de coral** coral reef
arroyo *m.* arroyo, brook, stream
arrozal *m.* rice paddy

Asia *f.* Asia; **A. del Este** East Asia; **A. Meridional** South Asia; **sudeste de A.** *m.* Southeast Asia
asiático, -ca *adj. & m.f.* Asian, Asiatic
astrolabio *m.* astrolabe
Atenas *f.* Athens
Atlántico Norte *m.* North Atlantic; **océano Á.** *m.* Atlantic Ocean
atlas *m.* atlas
atmósfera *f.* atmosphere
atolón *m.* atoll
aurora boreal *f.* aurora borealis
Australasia *f.* Australasia
Australia *f.* Australia
australiano -na *adj. & m.f.* Australian
Austria *f.* Austria
austriaco, -ca *adj. & m.f.;* **austríaco, -ca** *adj. & m.f.* Austrian
autóctono, -na *adj. & m.f.* indigenous, native
avalancha *f.* avalanche
Azerbaiyán *m.* Azerbaijan
azotado (-da) por el viento *adj.* windswept

B

Bahamas *f.pl.* Bahamas
bahamés, -esa *adj. & m.f.,* **bahameño, -ña** *adj. & m.f.* Bahamian
bahía *f.* bay
bahía de Bengala *f.* Bay of Bengal; **b. de Chesapeake** Chesapeake Bay; **b. de Massachusetts** Massachusetts Bay
bajada *f.* (abajo) slope

Balcanes *m.pl.* Balkans

Bangladesh *m.* Bangladesh

bangladesí *adj. & m.f.* Bangladeshi

Bantú *m.* Bantu

Barbados *m.* Barbados

barlovento *m.* windward; **a b.** *adj.* windward

barranco *m.* gulch, gully

basalto *m.* basalt

Baviera *f.* Bavaria

Beijing *m.* Beijing

belga *adj. & m.f.* Belgian

Bélgica *f.* Belgium

Belice *m.* Belize

beliceño, -ña *adj. & m.f.* Belizean

Benín *m.* Benin

Bermudas *f.pl.* Bermuda

bermudiano, -na *adj. & m.f.;* **bermudeño, -ña** *adj. & m.f.* Bermudan

Bielorrusia *f.* Belarus

biodiversidad *f.* biodiversity

bioma *m.* biome

biosfera *f.* biosphere

Birmania *f.* Burma, Myanmar

birmano, -na *adj. & m.f.* Burmese, Myanmarese

bóer *adj. & m.f.* Boer, Afrikaner

Bolivia *f.* Bolivia

boliviano, -na *adj. & m.f.* Bolivian

borde Mogollón *m.* Mogollon Rim

Borgoña *f.* Burgundy

Bosnia-Herzegovina *f.* Bosnia and Herzegovina

bosnio, -na *adj. & m.f.* Bosnian

bosque *m.* forest, woodland; **b. talado** clear-cut forest; **dosel del b.** *m.* forest canopy; **límite del b.** *m.* tree line

Botsuana *f.* Botswana

botsuano, -na *adj. & m.f.* Botswanan

Brasil *m.* Brazil

brasileño, -ña *adj. & m.f.* Brazilian

brea *f.* tar; **pozo de b.** *m.* tar pit

británico, -ca *adj.* British

brújula *f.* compass

brumoso, -sa *adj.* foggy

Brunei Darussalam *m.* Brunei Darussalam

Bulgaria *f.* Bulgaria

búlgaro, -ra *adj. & m.f.* Bulgarian

Burundi *m.* Burundi

Bután *m.* Bhutan

C

caballete *m.* ridge

cabecera de río *f.* headwater

cabo *m.* cape

cabo Cod *m.* Cape Cod; **c. de Buena Esperanza** Cape of Good Hope; **c. de Hornos** Cape Horn; **c. Hatteras** Cape Hatteras; **c. Verde** Cape Verde

calentamiento global *m.* global warming

caliza *f.* limestone

cambio *m.* change; **c. climático** climate change; **c. demográfico** demographic change

Camboya *f.* Cambodia

camboyano, -na *adj. & m.f.* Cambodian

Camerún *m.* Cameroon

camino *m.* road, path, trail

Canadá *m.* Canada

Estudios Sociales

canadiense *adj. & m.f.* Canadian

canal *m.* canal, channel

canal de Erie *m.* Erie Canal; **c. de la Mancha** English Channel; **c. de Panamá** Panama Canal; **c. de Suez** Suez Canal

cantera *f.* quarry

canto rodado *m.* boulder

cañada *f.* ravine, wash

cañón *m.* canyon, gorge

capa *f.* layer; **c. de hielo** ice sheet; **c. de ozono** ozone layer

carbón *m.* coal

Caribe *adj. & m.* Caribbean; **cuenca del C.** *f.* Caribbean Basin; **mar C.** *m.* Caribbean Sea

cartografía *f.* cartography

cartógrafo *m.* cartographer

carretera *f.* road; **c. Panamericana** Pan-American Highway

cascada *f.* waterfall

caserío *m.* village

casquete polar *m.* polar ice cap

catalán *adj. & m.f.* Catalonian

Cataluña *f.* Catalonia

cataratas Victoria *f.pl.* Victoria Falls

caverna *f.* cavern

cayo *m.* (isla) key

cayos de la Florida *m.pl.* Florida Keys

Ceilán *m.* Ceylon, Sri Lanka

ceilandés, -esa *adj. & m.f.* Ceylonese, Sri Lankan

Centroamérica *f.* Central America

centroamericano, -na *adj. & m.f.* Central American

Cerdeña *f.* Sardinia

cerro *m.* hill, ridge

ciclo *m.* cycle; **c. del agua** water cycle; **c. nitrógeno** nitrogen cycle

ciénaga *f.* marsh, bog, swamp

ciencias forestales *f.pl.* forestry

Cinturón de Fuego del Pacífico *m.* Ring of Fire; **C. del Sol** Sun Belt; **C. de Óxido** Rust Belt

circulación oceánica *f.* ocean circulation

Círculo Polar Antártico *m.* Antarctic Circle; **C. P. Ártico** *m.* Arctic Circle

Cisjordania *f.* West Bank

ciudad *f.* city; **c. portuaria** port city

Ciudad del Vaticano *f.* Vatican City

claro *m.* clearing

clave *f.* (mapa) key

clima *m.* climate; **c. árido** arid climate; **c. marino** marine climate

colina *f.* hill

Colinas Negras *f.pl.* Black Hills

Colombia *f.* Colombia

colombiano, -na *adj. & m.f.* Colombian

Comoras *f.pl.* Comoros

congoleño, -ña *adj. & m.f.* Congolese

conservación *f.* conservation; **c. de suelos** soil conservation

conservacionista *adj. & m.f.* conservationist

construir *v.* to build, construct

contaminación *f.* pollution; **c. del agua** water pollution; **c. del aire** air pollution; **c. del mar, c. marina** ocean pollution

contaminar *v.* to pollute

continente *m.* continent
contracorriente *f.* riptide
Córcega *f.* Corsica
cordillera *f.* mountain range, ridge
cordillera de los Andes *f.* Andes Mountains *pl.;* **c. del Cáucaso** Caucasus Mountains *pl.*
Corea *f.* Korea; **C. del Norte** North Korea; **C. del Sur** South Korea
coreano, -na *adj. & m.f.* Korean
corteza *f.* (terrestre) crust
corriente *f.* current; **c. en chorro** jet stream; **c. oceánica** ocean current
corriente de Humboldt *f.* Humboldt Current; **c. del golfo** Gulf Stream; **c. del Labrador** Labrador Current
corrosión *f.* abrasion
cosecha *f.* harvest, crop
costa *f.* coast; **c. del golfo de México** Gulf Coast
Costa Rica *f.* Costa Rica
costarricense *adj. & m.f.* Costa Rican
cráter *m.* crater
crecimiento *m.* growth; **c. de población** population growth; **c. urbano descontrolado** urban sprawl
cresta *f.* ridge
Creta *f.* Crete
criadero *m.* hatchery
Crimea *f.* Crimea
Croacia *f.* Croatia
croata *adj. & m.f.* Croat, Croatian
Cuba *f.* Cuba
cubano, -na *adj. & m.f.* Cuban
cuenca *f.* basin; **c. hidrográfica, c.**

de drenaje drainage basin
cuenca del Amazonas *f.* Amazon Basin; **c. del Pacífico** Pacific Rim
cuesta *f.* slope
cueva *f.* cave
cultivo *m.* crop; **c. básico** staple crop; **c. en terrazas** terrace farming; **rendimiento de los cultivos** *m.* crop yield
Curazao *m.,* **Curasao** *m.* Curaçao

CH

Chad *m.* Chad
checo, -ca *adj. & m.f.* Czech
chicano, -na *adj. & m.f.* Chicano
Chile *m.* Chile
chileno, -na *adj. & m.f.* Chilean
China *f.* China
chino, -na *adj. & m.f.* Chinese
Chipre *f.* Cyprus
chipriota *adj. & m.f.* Cypriot

D

danés, -esa *adj. & m.f.* Danish
Dardanelos *m.pl.* Dardanelles
declive *m.* (abajo) slope
delta *m.* delta; **d. del río** river delta
delta del Mekong *m.* Mekong Delta; **d. del Misisipi** Mississipi Delta; **d. del Nilo** Nile Delta
demográfico, -ca *adj.* demographic; **cambio d.** *m.* demographic change; **estadísticas d.** *f.pl.* demographics
dendrocronología *f.* dendrochronology
denudado, -da *adj.* denuded

ESTUDIOS SOCIALES

325

ESTUDIOS SOCIALES

depósito *m.* reservoir; **d. mineral** mineral deposit

depresión *f.* depression

deriva continental *f.* continental drift

derrame de petróleo *m.* oil spill

descomposición *f.* decomposition

desembocadura *f.* estuary; **d. de un río** mouth of a river

desfiladero *m.* gorge

deshabitado, -da *adj.* uninhabited

desierto *m.* desert

desierto de Sonora Sonoran Desert *m.;* **d. del Kalahari** Kalahari Desert; **d. del Sahara** Sahara Desert

deslizamiento, deslizamiento de tierra *m.* landslide

despoblado, -da *adj.* unpopulated

despoblado *m.* outback, deserted place

Dinamarca *f.* Denmark

dique *m.* levee, dike

diurno, -na *adj.* diurnal

división continental *f.* continental divide

Dominica *f.* Dominica

dominicano, -na *adj. & m.f.* Dominican

dorsal oceánica *f.* oceanic ridge

dosel arbóreo *m.* forest canopy

dragado *m.* dredging

dragar *v.* to dredge

duna *f.* dune; **d. de arena** sand dune

E

eclipse *m.* eclipse

ecosistema *m.* ecosystem

ecozona *f.* ecozone

ecuador *m.* equator

Ecuador *m.* Ecuador

ecuatoriano, -na *adj. & m.f.* Ecuadoran

edad de hielo *f.,* **era glacial** *f.* ice age

efecto invernadero *m.* greenhouse effect

egipcio, -cia *adj. & m.f.* Egyptian

Egipto *m.* Egypt

El Salvador *m.* El Salvador

elevación *f.* elevation

embalsar *v.* to dam

embarcadero *m.* jetty, pier

Emiratos Árabes Unidos *m.pl.* United Arab Emirates

energía *f.* energy, power; **e. geotérmica** geothermal energy; **e. hidroeléctrica** hydroelectric power; **e. solar** solar power

ensenada *f.* inlet, cove

entorno *m.* environment; **e. físico** physical environment; **e. natural** natural environment

equinoccio *m.* equinox; **e. de otoño** autumnal equinox; **e. de primavera** vernal equinox, spring equinox

Eritrea *f.* Eritrea

eritreo, -rea *adj. & m.f.* Eritrean

erosión *f.* erosion; **e. de la tierra, e. del suelo** soil erosion

erosionar *v.* to erode

erupción *f.* eruption

erupcionar *v.* to erupt

escala de Richter *f.* Richter scale

Escandinavia *f.* Scandinavia

escocés, -esa *adj. & m.f.* Scottish

Escocia *f.* Scotland; **Tierras Altas de E.** *f.pl.* Scottish Highlands

escombros *m.pl.* debris

escorrentía *f.* runoff

eslovaco, -ca *adj. & m.f.* Slovak, Slovakian

Eslovaquia *f.* Slovak Republic

Eslovenia *f.* Slovenia

esloveno, -na *adj. & m.f.* Slovenian

España *f.* Spain

español, -ola *adj. & m.f.* Spanish, Spaniard

Española *f.* Hispaniola

especie *f.* species; **e. de planta, e. vegetal** plant species; **e. invasora** invasive species

esquisto bituminoso *m.* oil shale

esrilanqués, -esa *adj. & m.f.* Sri Lankan

Estados Unidos *m.pl.* United States

estadounidense *adj. & m.f.* American

estallar *v.* to erupt

este *adj. & m.* east, eastern

estepa *f.* steppe

Estonia *f.* Estonia

estonio, -nia *adj. & m.f.* Estonian

estrecho *m.* strait

estrecho de Bering *m.* Bering Strait; **e. de Gibraltar** Strait of Gibraltar; **e. de Long Island** Long Island Sound; **e. de Magallanes** Strait of Magellan; **e. de Ormuz** Strait of Hormuz; **e. de Puget** Puget Sound; **e. del Bósforo** Bosphorus Strait

estribaciones *f.pl.* foothills

estuario *m.* estuary

etíope *adj. & m.f.* Ethiopian

Etiopía *f.* Ethiopia

Eurasia *f.* Eurasia

Europa *f.* Europe; **E. Occidental, E. del Oeste** Western Europe; **E. Oriental, E. del Este** Eastern Europe; **norte de E.** *m.* Northern Europe; **sur de E.** *m.* Southern Europe

europeo, -ea *adj. & m.f.* European

Everglades *m.pl.* Everglades

F

falda *f.* (abajo) slope

falla, falla geológica *f.* fault

fauna *f.* fauna

fértil *adj.* fertile

fertilidad *f.* fertility

fertilización *f.* fertilization

Filipinas *f.pl.* Philippines

filipino, -na *adj. & m.f.* Filipino

finlandés, -sa *adj. & m.f.* Finnish

Finlandia *f.* Finland

fiordo *m.* fjord

Fiyi *f.* Fiji

flamenco, -ca *adj. & m.f.* Flemish

flora *f.* flora

fosa oceánica *f.* oceanic trench

francés, -sa *adj. & m.f.* French

Franja de Gaza *f.* Gaza Strip; **F. del Sur** (EE.UU.) Sun Belt

frente *m.* front

frontera *f.* boundary, border

fuente *f.* source, spring; **f. de un río** source of a river; **f. termal** hot spring, thermal spring

ESTUDIOS SOCIALES

ESTUDIOS SOCIALES

G

Gabón *m.* Gabon
Gales *m.* Wales
galés, -esa *adj. & m.f.* Welsh
Galilea *f.* Galilee
Gambia *f.* Gambia
geográfico, -ca *adj.* geographic; **accidente g.** *f.* geographic feature; **dispersión g.** *f.* geographic dispersion; **región g.** *f.* geographic region; **sistemas de información g.** *m.pl.* geographic information systems
geógrafo *m.* geographer
geología *f.* geology
Georgia *f.* Georgia
georgiano, -na *adj. & m.f.* Georgian
Ghana *f.* Ghana
ghanés, -sa *adj. & m.f.* Ghanaian
gitano, -na *adj. & m.f.* gypsy, Roma, Romany
glaciar *m.* glacier
golfo de Alaska *m.* Gulf of Alaska; **g. de Benín** Bight of Benin; **g. de California** Gulf of California; **g. de Guinea** Gulf of Guinea; **g. de México** Gulf of Mexico; **g. de San Lorenzo** Gulf of St. Lawrence; **g. de Vizcaya** Bay of Biscay; **g. Pérsico** Persian Gulf
Gran Barrera de Coral *f.* Great Barrier Reef
Gran Bretaña *f.* Great Britain
Gran Cañón *m.* Grand Canyon
Gran Cuenca *f.* Great Basin
Gran Desierto Americano *m.* Great American Desert
Gran Lago Salado *m.* Great Salt Lake
Granada *f.* Grenada
granadino, -dina *adj. & m.f.* Grenadian
Grandes Lagos *m.pl.* Great Lakes
granito *m.* granite
grano *m.* grain, seed
Grecia *f.* Greece
griego, -ga *adj. & m.f.* Greek
grieta *f.* crevice, crevasse, fissure, chasm
groenlandés, -esa *adj. & m.f.* Greenlander
Groenlandia *f.* Greenland
Guadalupe *f.* Guadeloupe
Guam *f.* Guam
Guatemala *f.* Guatemala
guatemalteco, -ca *adj. & m.f.* Guatemalan
Guinea *f.* Guinea
Guinea Ecuatorial *f.* Equatorial Guinea
guineano, -na *adj. & m.f.* Guinean
Guyana *f.* Guyana
guyanés, -esa *adj. & m.f.* Guyanese

H

habitado, -da *adj.* inhabited
habitante *m.f.* inhabitant
habitar *v.* to inhabit
hábitat *m.* habitat
Haití *m.* Haiti
haitiano, -na *adj. & m.f.* Haitian
Hébridas *f.pl.* Hebrides
helado, -da *adj.* icy, frozen
hemisferio *m.* hemisphere; **h. norte**

Northern Hemisphere; **h. occidental** Western Hemisphere; **h. oriental, h. este** Eastern Hemisphere; **h. sur** Southern Hemisphere

hidrosfera, hidrósfera *f.* hydrosphere

hielo *m.* ice

Himalaya *m.* Himalayas *pl.*

hindú *m.f.* Indian, Hindu

Hindú Kush *m.* Hindu Kush

hito *m.* landmark

Holanda *f.* Holland

holandés, -sa *adj. & m.f.* Dutch, Netherlander

hondonada *f.* gully, hollow

Honduras *f.* Honduras

hondureño, -eña *adj. & m.f.* Honduran

hoyo *m.,* **hueco** *m.* hole, hollow

humedales *m.pl.* wetland

humedad *f.* humidity

húmedo, -da *adj.* humid

hundimiento *m.* subsidence

Húngaro, -ra *adj. & m.f.* Hungarian

Hungría *f.* Hungary

huso horario *m.* time zone

I

iceberg *m.* iceberg

imán *m.* lodestone

incubadora *f.* hatchery

India *f.* India

Indias *f.pl.* Indies; **I. Occidentales** West Indies; **I. Orientales** East Indies

índice de sustitución *m.* replacement rate

indígena *adj.* indigenous

indio, -da *adj. & m.f.* Indian

Indochina *f.* Indochina

Indonesia *f.* Indonesia

Indonesio, -sia *adj. & m.f.* Indonesian

Inglaterra *f.* England

inglés, -esa *adj. & m.f.* English

instinto *m.* instinct

interior, interior del país *m.* outback, hinterland

inundación *f.* flood; **control de i.** *m.pl.* flood control measures

Irán *m.* Iran

iraní *adj. & m.f.* Iranian

Iraq *m.* Iraq

iraquí *adj. & m.f.* Iraqi

Irlanda *f.* Ireland; **I. del Norte** *f.* Northern Ireland

irlandés, -esa *adj. & m.f.* Irish

isla *f.* island; **i. barrera, i. de barrera** barrier island; **i. de calor, i. térmica** heat island

Isla de Pascua *f.* Easter Island

islandés, -esa *adj. & m.f.* Icelandic, Icelander

Islandia *f.* Iceland

islas Aleutianas *f.pl.* Aleutian Islands; **i. Azores** Azores; **i. Británicas** British Isles; **i. Canarias** Canary Islands; **i. de Barlovento** Windward Islands; **i. Galápagos** Galapagos Islands; **i. Hawaianas** Hawaiian Islands; **i. Malvinas** Falkland Islands; **i. Marshall** Marshall Islands; **i. Salomón** Solomon Islands; **i. Vírgenes** Virgin Islands

ESTUDIOS SOCIALES

isleta *f.* islet
Israel *m.* Israel
israelí *adj. & m.f.* Israeli
istmo *m.* isthmus, land bridge
istmo de Panamá *m.* Isthmus of
  Panama
Italia *f.* Italy
italiano, -na *adj. & m.f.* Italian

J

Jamaica *f.* Jamaica
jamaicano, -na *adj. & m.f.; **jamaiquino, -na** *adj. & m.f.* Jamaican
Japón *m.* Japan
japonés, -esa *adj. & m.f.* Japanese
Jerusalén *m.* Jerusalem
Jordania *f.* Jordan
jordano, -na *adj. & m.f.* Jordanian
jungla *f.* jungle

K

kazajo, -ja *adj. & m.f.* Kazakh
Kazajistán *m.* Kazakhstan
Kenia *f.* Kenya
keniano, -na *adj. & m.f.* Kenyan
Kirguistán *m.* Kyrgyzstan
Kurdistán *m.* Kurdistan
kurdo, -da *adj. & m.f.* Kurd, Kurdish
Kuwait *m.* Kuwait
kuwaití *adj. & m.f.* Kuwaiti

L

Labrador *m.* Labrador
ladera *f.* hillside
lago Baikal *m.* Lake Baikal; **l.
  Champlain** Lake Champlain; **l.
  Erie** Lake Erie; **l. Hurón** Lake

Huron; **l. Michigan** Lake Michigan; **l. Ontario** Lake Ontario; **l.
Superior Lake Superior; **l. Tan-
ganica Lake Tanganyika; **l. Victo-
ria Lake Victoria
laguna *f.* lagoon
Laos *m.* Laos
laosiano, -na *m.f.* Laotian
Laponia *f.* Lapland
latinoamericano, -na *adj. & m.f.*
  Latin American
latitud *f.* latitude
Lesoto *m.* Lesotho
letón, -na *adj. & m.f.* Latvian
Letonia *f.* Latvia
leyenda *f.* (mapa) key
libanés, -esa *adj. & m.f.* Lebanese
Líbano *m.* Lebanon
Liberia *f.* Liberia
liberiano, -na *adj. & m.f.* Liberian
Libia *f.* Libya
libio, -bia *adj. & m.f.* Libyan
Liechtenstein *m.* Liechtenstein
límite *m.* boundary; **l. del bosque**
  tree line
línea *f.* line; **l. de falla, l. divisoria**
  fault line; **l. divisoria de las
  aguas** watershed
Línea de Fecha Internacional *f.* International Date Line
litoral *m.* coast, coast line; **sin l.
  marítimo** *adj.* landlocked
litosfera *f.,* **litósfera** *f.* lithosphere
Lituania *f.* Lithuania
lituano, -na *adj. & m.f.* Lithuanian
lodo *m.* mud
lodoso, -sa *adj.* muddy

loma *f.* hill
Londres *m.* London
longitud *f.* longitude
lugar *m.* place; **nombre de un l.** *m.* place name
Luxemburgo *m.* Luxembourg
luxemburgués, -sa *adj. & m.f.* Luxembourger

LL

llanura *f.* plain; **ll. abisal** abyssal plain; **ll. aluvial** alluvial plain; **ll. costera** coastal plain; **ll. de inundación** floodplain
llanuras altas *f.pl.* high plains
llover *v.* to rain
lluvia *f.* rain; **ll. ácida** acid rain
lluvioso, -sa *adj.* rainy

M

Macedonia *f.* Macedonia
macedonio, -nia *adj. & m.f.* Macedonian
Madagascar *m.* Madagascar
madera *f.* timber, lumber; **extracción de m.** *f.* timber extraction
Malasia *f.* Malaysia
malasio, -sia *adj. & m.f.* Malaysian
Malaui *m.* Malawi
Maldivas *f.pl.* Maldives
malgache *m.f.* Malagasy, Madacascan
Malí *m.* Mali
Malta *f.* Malta
maltés, -sa *adj. & m.f.* Maltese
manantial *m.* (agua) spring
Manchuria *f.* Manchuria

mandioca *f.* manioc
manglar *m.* mangrove swamp
manto *m.* mantle
mapa *m.* map; **m. de coropletas** choropleth map; **m. de relieve** relief map; **m. físico** physical map; **m. político** political map
mar *m.* sea; **brazo de m.** *m.* inlet; **fondo del m.** *m.* sea bed; **nivel del m.** *m.* sea level; **oleaje del m.** *m.* sea swell
mar Adriático Adriatic Sea *m.;* **m. Báltico** Baltic Sea; **m. Caspio** Caspian Sea; **m. de Arabia** Arabian Sea; **m. de China Meridional** South China Sea; **m. del Coral** Coral Sea; **m. del Norte** North Sea; **m. Egeo** Aegean Sea; **m. Mediterráneo** Mediterranean Sea; **m. Negro** Black Sea; **m. Rojo** Red Sea
marea *f.* tide; **reflujo de m.** *m.* ebb tide
marejada *f.* sea swell
maremoto *m.* tidal wave
marshalés, -esa *adj. & m.f.* Marshallese
marroquí *adj. & m.f.* Moroccan
Marruecos *m.* Morocco
masa de tierra *f.* land mass
Mauritania *f.* Mauritania
mauritano, -na *adj. & m.f.* Mauritanian
Meca, la *f.* Mecca
medio ambiente *m.* environment
Medio Oeste *m.* Midwest; **M. Oriente** Middle East

ESTUDIOS SOCIALES

megalópolis *m.* megalopolis

meridiano *m.* meridian; **m. de Greenwich, primero m.** prime meridian; **m. principales** *pl.* principal meridians

meseta *f.* plateau

meseta de Cumberland *f.* Cumberland Plateau; **m. Tibetana** Tibetan Plateau

Mesoamérica *f.* Mesoamerica

mexicano, -na *adj. & m.f.* Mexican

México *m.* Mexico

microclima *m.* microclimate

Micronesia *f.* Micronesia

micronesio, -sia *adj. & m.f.* Micronesian *adj.*

migración *f.* migration

migratorio, -ria *adj.* migratory

mina *f.* mine

minería *f.* mining

minero *m.* miner

Moldavia *f.* Moldova

Mónaco *m.* Monaco

mongol, -ola *adj. & m.f.* Mongolian

Mongolia *f.* Mongolia

montañas Apalaches *f.pl.* Appalachian Mountains; **m. de Sierra Nevada** Sierra Nevada Mountains; **m. del Cáucaso** Caucasus Mountains; **m. del Himalaya** Himalayan Mountains; **m. Rocosas** Rocky Mountains

monte Everest *m.* Mount Everest; **m. Kilimanjaro** Mount Kilimanjaro; **m. McKinley** Mount McKinley

Montenegro *m.* Montenegro

montes Apeninos *m.pl.* Apennine Mountains; **m. Cárpatos** Carpathian Mountains; **m. Urales** Ural Mountains

montículo *m.* mound

monzón *m.* monsoon

morrena, morrena glaciar *f.* moraine

Moscú *m.* Moscow

Mozambique *m.* Mozambique

mozambiqueño, -ña *adj. & m.f.* Mozambican

muelle *m.* dock, pier

Myanmar *f.* Myanmar, Burma

N

nación *f.* nation

Namibia *f.* Namibia

namibio, -bia *adj. & m.f.* Namibian

naturaleza *f.* nature

navegable *adj.* navigable; **vía n.** *f.* waterway

navegar *v.* to navigate

neblinoso, -sa *adj.* foggy

neozelandés, -sa *adj. & m.f.* New Zealander

Nepal *m.* Nepal

nepalés, -sa *adj. & m.f.;* **nepalí** *adj. & m.f.* Nepalese

nevado, -da *adj.* snowy

nevar *v.* to snow

Nicaragua *f.* Nicaragua

nicaragüense *adj. & m.f.* Nicaraguan

niebla *f.* fog; **lleno (-na) de n.** *adj.* foggy

nieve *f.* snow

Níger *m.* Niger

Nigeria *f.* Nigeria

nigeriano, -na *adj. & m.f.* (de Nigeria) Nigerian

nigerino, -na *adj. & m.f.* (de Níger) Nigerien

nivel del mar *m.* sea level

nómada *adj. & m.f.* nomadic, nomad

nórdico, -ca *adj.* Nordic

noreste *adj. & m.* northeast

Normandía *f.* Normandy

noroeste *adj. & m.* northwest

Noroeste Pacífico *m.* Pacific Northwest

norte *adj. & m.* north; **Polo N.** *m.* North Pole

norteamericano, -na *adj. & m.f.* American (U.S.)

Noruega *f.* Norway

noruego, -ga *adj. & m.f.* Norwegian

nublina *f.* mist

núcleo *m.* (de la Tierra) core

Nueva Dehli *f.* New Delhi

Nueva Escocia *f.* Nova Scotia

Nueva Inglaterra *f.* New England

Nueva York *f.* New York

Nueva Zelandia *f.* New Zealand

O

obsidiana *f.* obsidian

occidental *adj.* occidental, western

Oceanía *f.* Oceania

océano Ártico *m.* Arctic Ocean; **o. Atlántico** Atlantic Ocean; **o. Austral** Southern Ocean; **o. Índico** Indian Ocean; **o. Pacífico** Pacific Ocean

oeste *adj. & m.* west, western

ola *f.* (oceánico) wave; **o. rompientes** *pl.* surf

oleaje del mar *m.* sea swell

Oleoducto Trans-Alaska *m.* Alaska Pipeline

Omán *m.* Oman

oriental *adj.* oriental, eastern

orilla *f.* (de río) bank

P

Pacífico Sur *m.* South Pacific

País Vasco *m.* Basque Country

paisaje *m.* landscape

Países Bajos *m.pl.* Netherlands

Pakistán *m.,* **Paquistán** *m.* Pakistan

Palestina *f.* Palestine

palestino, -na *adj. & m.f.* Palestinian

pampas *f.pl.* pampas

Panamá *m.* Panama

panameño, -ña *adj. & m.f.* Panamanian

Pangea *f.* Pangaea

pantano *m.* marsh, bog, swamp

papú *adj. & m.f.* Papua New Guinean

Papúa Nueva Guinea *f.* Papua New Guinea

paquistaní *adj. & m.f.* Pakistani

Paraguay *m.* Paraguay

paraguayo, -ya *adj. & m.f.* Paraguayan

paralelo *m.* (latitud) parallel

páramos *m.pl.* badlands

París *m.* Paris

paso Khyber, paso de Khyber *m.* Khyber Pass

ESTUDIOS SOCIALES

333

ESTUDIOS SOCIALES

pastizales *m.pl.* grasslands
pasto *m.* pasture, grass
pastoreo *m.* grazing; **p. excesivo** overgrazing
Patagonia *f.* Patagonia
Pekín *m.* Beijing
pendiente *f.* slope
península *f.* peninsula
península Antártica *f.* Antarctic Peninsula; **p. arábiga** Arabian Peninsula; **p. de Kenai** Kenai Peninsula; **p. de Yucatán** Yucatan Peninsula; **p. del Sinaí** Sinai Peninsula; **p. ibérica** Iberian Peninsula; **p. italiana** Italian Peninsula
peña *f.,* **peñasco** *m.* boulder
permagel *m.* permafrost
Perú *m.* Peru
peruano, -na *adj. & m.f.* Peruvian
pesca *f.* fishing, fishery; **p. excesiva** overfishing
petróleo *m.* oil; **derrame de p.** *m.* oil spill; **yacimiento de p.** *m.* oil field
picacho *m.* peak, summit
piedemonte *m.,* **pie de monte** *m.* piedmont
Pirineos *m.pl.* Pyrenees
pizarra bituminosa *f.* oil shale
placa tectónica *f.* tectonic plate
plancton *m.* plankton
plataforma continental *f.* continental shelf
playa *f.* beach
pluviselva *f.* tropical rain forest
población *f.* population; **densidad de p.** *f.* population density

polaco, -ca *adj. & m.f.* Pole, Polish
Polinesia *f.* Polynesia
polinesio, -sia *adj. & m.f.* Polynesian
Polo Norte *m.* North Pole; **P. Sur** South Pole
Polonia *f.* Poland
polución *f.* pollution
poroso, -sa *adj.* porous
Portugal *m.* Portugal
portugués, -esa *adj. & m.f.* Portuguese
pozo *m.* pit; **p. de brea** tar pit
pradera *f.* prairie, grassland; **p. abierta** open range
precipicio *m.* cliff, precipice
precipitación *f.* precipitation, rainfall
presa *f.* dam, dike
primero meridiano *m.* prime meridian
protección ambiental *f.* environmental protection
provincia *f.* province
proyección *f.* projection; **p. azimutal** azimuthal projection; **p. cartográfica** map projection; **p. Mercator** Mercator projection
puente *m.* bridge; **p. terrestre** land bridge
puerto *m.* harbor, port; **p. deportivo** marina
Puerto Rico *m.* Puerto Rico
puertorriqueño, -ña *adj. & m.f.* Puerto Rican
punto de referencia *m.* landmark; **p. cardinales** *pl.* cardinal points, compass points

Q

Qatar *m.* Qatar
Quebec *m.* Quebec
quebequés, -esa *adj. & m.f.;* **quebequense** *adj. & m.f.* Quebecois
quebrada *f.* gulch

R

recursos *m.pl.* resources; **administración de r.** *f.* resource management; **r. natural** natural resources; **r. no renovable** nonrenewable resources; **r. renovable** renewable resources
reflujo de marea *m.* ebb tide
reforestación *f.* reforestation
regar *v.* to irrigate
región *f.* region; **r. ártica** Arctic region; **r. climática** climate region; **r. geográfica** geographic region; **r. mediterránea** Mediterranean region; **r. montañosa** mountainous region
Reino Unido *m.* United Kingdom
repoblación *f.* repopulation; **r. forestal** reforestation
represa *f.* dam
represar *v.* to dam
República Centroafricana *f.* Central African Republic; **R. Checa** Czech Republic; **R. del Congo** Republic of Congo; **R. Democrática del Congo** Democratic Republic of Congo; **R. Dominicana** Dominican Republic
reserva natural *f.* wilderness area

residuos *m.pl.* debris; **r. tóxicos** toxic waste
riachuelo *m.* stream
ribera *f.* (de río) bank, shore
riego *m.* irrigation
río *m.* river; **cabecera de r.** *f.* headwater; **fuente de un r.** *f.,* **nacimiento de un r.** *m.* source of a river; **r. navegable** navigable river
río abajo *adj. & adv.* downstream
río Amazonas *m.* Amazon River; **r. Colorado** Colorado River; **r. Columbia** Columbia River; **r. Congo** Congo River; **r. Danubio** Danube River; **r. de San Lorenzo** St. Lawrence River; **r. Ganges** Ganges River; **r. Hudson** Hudson River; **r. Jordán** Jordan River; **r. Mekong** Mekong River; **r. Misisipi** Mississippi River; **r. Misuri** Missouri River; **r. Nilo** Nile River; **r. Ohio** Ohio River; **r. Orinoco** Orinoco River; **r. Sena** Seine River; **r. Volga** Volga River; **r. Yangtzé** Yangtze River
risco *m.* cliff
roca *f.* boulder
Roma *f.* Rome
romaní *adj. & m.f.* Roma, Romany
Ruanda *f.* Rwanda
ruandés, -esa *adj. & m.f.* Rwandan
Rumania *f.* Romania
rumano, -na *adj. & m.f.* Romanian
Rusia *f.* Russia
ruso, -sa *adj. & m.f.* Russian

S

sabana *f.* savannah

salina *f.* salt marsh

salvadoreño, -ña *adj. & m.f.* Salvadoran

sami *adj. & m.f.* Sami

Samoa *f.* Samoa

samoano, -na *adj. & m.f.* Samoan

saudí *adj. & m.f.*, **saudita** *adj. & m.f.* Saudi, Saudi Arabian

sedimentario, -ria *adj.* sedimentary

sedimento *m.* sediment

selva *f.* jungle, forest; **s. tropical** rain forest; **s. virgen** old-growth forest

sendero *m.* trail, path

Senegal *m.* Senegal

senegalés, -esa *adj. & m.f.* Senegalese

sequía *f.* drought

Serbia *f.* Serbia

serbio, -bia *adj. & m.f.* Serbian

Siberia *f.* Siberia

Sicilia *f.* Sicily

Sierra Leona *f.* Sierra Leone

silvicultura *f.* forestry

sima *f.* chasm

Singapur *m.* Singapore

singapurense *m.f.* Singaporean

Siria *f.* Syria

sirio, -ria *adj. & m.f.* Syrian

siroco *m.* sirocco

sismo *m.* earthquake

Slovakia *f.* Slovak Republic

sobrepastoreo *m.* overgrazing

sobrepesca *f.* overfishing

solsticio *m.* solstice; **s. de invierno** winter solstice; **s. de verano** summer solstice

somalí *adj. & m.f.* Somali, Somalian

Somalia *f.* Somalia

sombra pluviométrica, sombra pluvial *f.* rain shadow

sostenibilidad *f.* sustainability

sotavento *m.* leeward; **de s.** *adj.* leeward

Sri Lanka *m.* Sri Lanka, Ceylon

Suazilandia *f.* Swaziland

subcontinente *m.* subcontinent; **s. indio** Indian subcontinent

subducción *f.* subduction; **zona de s.** *f.* subduction zone

suburbio *m.* suburb

suculentas *f.pl.* succulents

Sudáfrica *f.* South Africa

sudafricano, -na *adj. & m.f.* South African

Sudamérica *f.* South America

sudamericano, -na *adj. & m.f.* South American

Sudán *m.* Sudan

sudanés, -esa *adj. & m.f.* Sudanese

Suecia *f.* Sweden

sueco, -ca *adj. & m.f.* Swede, Swedish

Suiza *f.* Switzerland

suizo, -za *adj. & m.f.* Swiss

sumidero *m.* sinkhole

superpoblación *f.* overpopulation

sur *adj. & m.* south, southern; **extremo s. de Estados Unidos** Deep South; **Polo S.** *m.* South Pole

sureste, sudeste *adj. & m.* southeast

Surinam *m.* Suriname

suroeste, sudoeste *adj. & m.* south-west

T

Tahití *m.* Tahiti
tailandés, -esa *adj. & m.f.* Thai
Tailandia *f.* Thailand
Taiwán *m.* Taiwan
taiwanés, -esa *adj. & m.f.* Taiwanese
Tanzania *f.* Tanzania
tanzano, -na *adj. & m.f.* Tanzanian
tasa *f.* rate; **t. de fecundidad** fertility rate; **t. de mortalidad infantil** infant mortality rate; **t. de reemplazo** replacement rate
Tasmania *f.* Tasmania
Tayikistán *m.,* **Tadzhikistan** *m.* Tajikistan
temblor de tierra *m.* earthquake
Terranova *f.* Newfoundland
terraza *f.* terrace
terremoto *m.* earthquake; **réplica de t.** *f.* aftershock
territorio *m.* territory
Tíbet *m.* Tibet
tibetano, -na *adj. & m.f.* Tibetan
tierra *f.* land; **deslizamiento de t.** *m.* landslide; **erosión de la t.** *f.* soil erosion; **masa de t.** *f.* land mass; **t. cultivable** arable land, farmland; **t. altas** *pl.* highlands; **t. baldías** *pl.* badlands; **uso de la t.** *m.* land use
tifón *m.* typhoon
Timor *m.* Timor
Timor Oriental *m.* East Timor
Togo *m.* Togo

Tokio *m.* Tokyo
Tonga *f.* Tonga
topografía *f.* topography
tormenta *f.* storm; **t. de polvo** dust storm
tormentoso, -sa *adj.* stormy
tornado *m.* tornado
Trinidad y Tobago *f.* Trinidad and Tobago
trinitense *adj. & m.f.* Trinidadian
trópico de Cáncer *m.* Tropic of Cancer; **t. de Capricornio** Tropic of Capricorn
trópicos *m.pl.* tropics
tsunami *m.* tsunami
tundra *f.* tundra
tunecino, -na *adj. & m.f.* Tunisian
túnel *m.* tunnel
Túnez *m.* Tunisia
turba *f.* peat
turbera *f.* peat bog
turco, -ca *adj. & m.f.* Turk, Turkish
Turkmenistán *m.* Turkmenistan
turkmeno, -na *adj. & m.f.;* **turcomano, -na** *adj. & m.f.* Turkmen
Turquía *f.* Turkey

U

Ucrania *f.* Ukraine
ucraniano, -na *adj. & m.f.* Ukrainian
Uganda *f.* Uganda
ugandés, -sa *adj. & m.f.* Ugandan
urbano, -na *adj.* urban; **centro u.** *m.* city center, urban center; **expansión u.** *f.* urban sprawl
Uruguay *m.* Uruguay
uruguayo, -ya *adj. & m.f.* Uruguayan

ESTUDIOS SOCIALES

Uzbekistán *m.* Uzbekistan
uzbeko, -ka *adj. & m.f.* Uzbek

V

valle *m.* valley; **v. del río** river valley
valle del Indo *m.* Indus Valley; **v. de la Muerte** Death Valley; **v. del Río Grande** Rio Grande Valley
vallecito *m.* dell
vasco, -ca *adj. & m.f.* Basque
vegetación *f.* vegetation; **v. marina** marine vegetation
venezolano, -na *adj. & m.f.* Venezuelan
Venezuela *f.* Venezuela
ventoso, -sa *adj.* windy
vertedero *m.* landfill
vida salvaje, vida silvestre *f.* wildlife
viento *m.* wind; **azotado (-da) por el v.** *adj.* windswept; **v. alisios** *pl.* trade winds; **v. predominante** prevailing wind
Vietnam *m.* Vietnam
vietnamita *adj. & m.f.* Vietnamese
vivero *m.* hatchery
volcán *m.* volcano
volcánico, -ca *adj.* volcanic
vulcanismo *m.* volcanism

Y

yacimiento *m.* deposit, field; **y. de petróleo, y. petrolífero** oil field
Yemen *m.* Yemen
yemení *adj. & m.f.* Yemeni
Yibuti *m.f.* Djibouti
Yugoslavia *f.* Yugoslavia
yugoslavo, -va *adj. & m.f.* Yugoslav, Yugoslavian
Yukón *m.* Yukon

Z

zacate *m.* hay, forage
Zaire *m.* Zaire
zaireño, -ña *adj. & m.f.* Zairian
Zambia *f.* Zambia
zambiano, -na *adj. & m.f.* Zambian
zanja oceánica *f.* oceanic trench
Zimbabue *m.* Zimbabwe
zimbabuense *adj. & m.f.;* **zimbabués, -esa** *adj. & m.f.* Zimbabwean
zona *f.* zone; **z. de ablación** ablation zone; **z. de subducción** subduction zone; **z. horaria** time zone; **z. salvaje** wilderness area; **z. sísmica** earthquake zone
Zuiderzee *f.* Zuiderzee

Historia

A

abdicar *v.* to abdicate
abolición *f.* abolition; **a. de la segregación** desegregation
abolicionista *m.f.* abolitionist
acción encubierta *f.* covert action
Acrópolis *f.* Acropolis
acueducto *m.* aqueduct
acuerdo *m.* agreement
Acuerdos de Camp David *m.pl.* Camp David Accords; **A. de Helsinki** Helsinki Accords; **A. de Paz de París** Paris Peace Accords
Administración de Trabajos en Progreso *f.* Works Progress Administration (W.P.A.)
afroamericano, -na *adj. & m.f.* African American
afrocaribeño, -ña *adj. & m.f.* Afro-caribbean
agnóstico, -ca *adj. & m.f.* agnostic
agresión *f.* aggression; **acto de a.** *m.* act of aggression
agresor, -ora *m.f.* aggressor
agricultura *f.* agriculture
aislacionismo *m.* isolationism
aislacionista *adj. & m.* isolationist
alambre de espino *m.* barbed wire
Alejandría *f.* Alexandria
Alejandro Magno *m.* Alexander the Great
Alemania nazi *f.* Nazi Germany
alfabetización *f.,* **alfabetismo** *m.* literacy; **tasa de a.** *f.* literacy rate
algodón *m.* cotton; **desmotadora de a.** *f.* cotton gin; **molino de a.** *m.* cotton mill; **Rey A.** *m.* King Cotton
alianza *f.* alliance
Alianza para el Progreso *f.* Alliance for Progress
alquimia *f.* alchemy
alunizaje *m.* Moon landing
ámbito de influencia *m.* sphere of influence
América *f.* America
americanización *f.* Americanization
americano, -na *adj. & m.f.* American
ametralladora *f.* machine gun
anarco-sindicalista *adj. & m.f.* anarcho-syndicalist
anarquía *f.* anarchy
anarquismo *m.* anarchism
anarquista *adj. & m.f.* anarchist
anexión *f.* annexation
anglosajón, -na *adj. & m.f.* Anglo-Saxon
animales domésticos *m.pl.* domesticated animals
antepasados *m.pl.* ancestors; **culto de los a.** *m.* ancestor worship
antes de Cristo (a.C.) *adv.* Before Christ (B.C.); **a. de la Era Común (a.E.C)** Before the Common Era (B.C.E.)

ESTUDIOS SOCIALES

anticlericalismo *m.* anticlericalism

antigüedad *f.* antiquity

antiguo, -gua *adj.* ancient, former;
 a. amo, -ma *m.f.* former master;
 a. esclavo, -va *m.f.* former slave

antiguo Egipto *m.* ancient Egypt;
 antigua Grecia *f.* ancient Greece;
 a. Roma *f.* ancient Rome

antimonopolista *adj.* antimonopoly, antitrust; **oficial a.** *m.* trustbuster

antisemitismo *m.* anti-Semitism

antiterrorismo *m.* counterterrorism

antropología *f.* anthropology

antropólogo, -ga *m.f.* anthropologist

aparcero, -ra *m.f.* sharecropper

apartheid *m.* apartheid

árabe *adj. & m.f.* Arab

arábigo, -ga *adj.* Arabic

arco y flecha *m.* bow and arrow;
 tiro con a. *m.* archery

archiduque *m.* archduke

ariete *m.* battering ram

aristocracia *f.* gentry

aristócrata *m.f.* aristocrat

Aristóteles *m.* Aristotle

arma *f.,* **armamento** *m.* weapon, armament; **a. biológica** biological weapon; **a. de fuego** gun, firearm; **a. nuclear** nuclear weapon; **control de armamentos** *m.* arms control

armada *f.* navy

Armada Española *f.* Spanish Armada

armadura *f.* armor

arqueología *f.* archeology

arqueológico, -ca *adj.* archeological; **evidencia a.** *f.* archeological evidence; **excavación a.** *f.* archeological dig

arqueólogo, -ga *m.f.* archeologist

arquitecto, -ta *m.f.* architect

arquitectura *f.* architecture

artefacto *m.* artifact

Artículos de la Conferación *m.pl.* Articles of Confederation

artillería *f.* artillery

arrasar *v.* to raze, devastate, destroy

asedio *m.* siege

asedio de Stalingrado *m.* Siege of Stalingrad; **a. de Vicksburg** Siege of Vicksburg

asesinar *v.* to assassinate

asesinato *m.* assassination; **a. de Kennedy** Kennedy assassination

asesino, -na *m.f.* assassin

asiático (-ca) americano (-na) *adj. & m.f.* Asian American

Asiria *f.* Assyria

Asociación Nacional para el Progreso de las Personas de Color *f.* National Association for the Advancement of Colored People (N.A.A.C.P.)

astrolabio *m.* astrolabe

asunto Irán-Contra *m.* Iran-Contra Affair

atacante suicida *m.f.* suicide bomber

ataque *m.* attack; **a. a Pearl Harbor** attack on Pearl Harbor **a. de**

340

flanco flank attack
ateísmo *m.* atheism
Atenas *f.* Athens
ateo, -tea *m.f.* atheist
atrocidades *f.pl.* atrocities
Augusto César *m.* Augustus Caesar
autocracia *f.* autocracy
autóctono, -na *adj.* indigenous
automóvil *m.* automobile
autores de la Constitución *m.* Framers of the U.S. Constitution
autoritario, -ra *adj. & m.f.* authoritarian
autoritarismo *m.* authoritarianism
aviación *f.* aviation
avión *m.* airplane
ayatolá *m.* ayatollah
azteca *m.f.* Aztec

B

Babilonia *f.* Babylon
bahía de Cochinos *f.* Bay of Pigs
balcanización *f.* Balkanization
ballesta *f.* crossbow
bandera tachonada de estrellas, La *f.* The Star-Spangled Banner
bárbaro, -ra *adj. & m.f.* barbarian
barco *m.* boat, ship; **b. de vapor** *m.* steamboat
barón *m.* baron; **b. ladrones** *m.pl.* robber barons
baronesa *f.* baroness
barrio bajo, barrio marginal *m.* slum; **b. chino** Chinatown; **b. de chabolas** *m.pl.* Hoovervilles, shantytowns
batalla *f.* battle

batalla de Galípoli *f.* Battle of Gallipoli; **b. de Gettysburg** Battle of Gettysburg; **b. de Inglaterra** Battle of Britain; **b. de Iwo Jima** Battle of Iwo Jima; **b. de las Ardenas** Battle of the Bulge; **b. de las llanuras de Abrahán** Battle of the Plains of Abraham; **b. de Little Bighorn** Battle of the Little Bighorn; **b. de Midway** Battle of Midway
batallón *m.* battalion
Biblia de Gutenberg *f.* Gutenberg Bible
bilingüismo *m.* bilingualism
Bizancio *m.* Byzantium
bloque soviético *m.* Soviet bloc
bloqueo *m.* blockade; **b. naval** naval blockade
bolcheviques *m.f.pl.* Bolsheviks
bomba bomb *f.;* **b. atómica** atomic bomb; **b. de hidrógeno** hydrogen bomb
bombar *v.* to bomb
bombardeo *m.* bombardment
bronce *m.* bronze
Brown contra la Junta de Educación *m.* Brown v. Board of Education
brújula *f.* compass
Buda *m.* Buddha
budismo *m.* Buddhism
buen salvaje *m.* Noble Savage
bulliciosos años veinte *m.pl.* Roaring Twenties
buque *m.* ship, vessel; **b. de guerra** warship; **b. de vapor** steamship

• •

burgués, -esa *adj. & m.f.* bourgeois

burguesía *f.* bourgeoisie; **pequeña b.** petite bourgeoisie

C

caballería *f.* cavalry

caballero *m.* knight, nobleman

Caballeros del Trabajo *m.pl.* Knights of Labor

caballo *m.* horse; **c. negro** dark horse

caballo de Troya *m.* Trojan Horse

calendario *m.* calendar; **c. Gregoriano** Gregorian calendar; **c. Juliano** Julian calendar

califa *m.* caliph

califato *m.* caliphate

cámara *f.* chamber, house; **c. funeraria** burial chamber

Cámara de la Burguesía de Virginia *f.* Virginia House of Burgesses; **C. de los Comunes** House of Commons; **C. de los Lores** House of Lords; **C. de los Representantes** House of Reprsentatives

camino de seda *m.* Silk Road

campamento *m.* camp, encampment

campana de la libertad *f.* Liberty Bell

campaña militar *f.* military campaign

campesinado *m.* peasantry

campesino, -na *m.f.* peasant

campo *m.* camp, field countryside; **c. de concentración** concentration camp; **c. de internamiento,**

c. de reclusión internment camp; **c. de minas** minefield

caña de azúcar *f.* sugar cane

cañón *m.* cannon; **bala de c.** *f.* cannon ball; **carne de c.** *f.* cannon fodder

cañonazos *m.pl.* cannon fire

capitalismo *m.* capitalism

capitalista *adj. & m.f.* capitalist

capturar *v.* to capture

carabela *f.* caravel

caravana *f.* caravan

careta antigás *f.* gas mask

carga de profundidad *f.* depth charge

Carlomagno *m.* Charlemagne

carta *f.* charter

Carta de Derechos *f.* Bill of Rights; **C. de las Naciones Unidas** United Nations Charter; **C. Magna** Magna Carta

cartaginés, -esa *adj. & m.f.* Carthaginian

Cartago *m.* Carthage

carro de batalla *m.* chariot

casa de asentamiento *f.* settlement house

castillo *m.* castle

catacumbas *f.pl.* catacombs

Catalina la Grande *f.* Catherine the Great

catedral *f.* cathedral; **c. gótica** Gothic cathedral

Catolicismo romano *m.* Roman Catholicism

católico, -ca *adj. & m.f.* Roman Catholic

caudillo *m.* warlord, tyrant

causa *f.* cause; **c. de la guerra** cause of war

causar *v.* to cause

caza de mamuts *f.* mammoth hunt

cazador-recolector *m.f.* hunter-gatherer

celtas *adj. & m.f.pl.* Celts

céltico, -ca *adj.* Celtic

centurión *m.* centurion

cerámica *f.* pottery

cercado *m.* enclosure

cinco tribus civilizadas *f.pl.* Five Civilized Tribes

Cinturón de Óxido *m.* Rust Belt

circunnavegar *v.* to circumnavigate

ciudad-estado griego *f.* Greek city-state

civilización *f.* civilization; **c. clásica** classical civilization; **c. zapoteca** Zapotec civilization

civilizado, -da *adj.* civilized

clase *f.* class; **c. alta** gentry; **c. obrera** working class; **conciencia de c.** *f.* class consciousness

cláusula *f.* clause, proviso; **c. de derechos adquiridos** grandfather clause

Cláusula Wilmot *f.* Wilmot Proviso

clero *m.* clergy

Código de Napoleón *m.* Code Napoleon

códigos de esclavos, códigos de esclavitud *m.pl.* slave codes

coexistencia pacífica *f.* peaceful coexistence

colectivismo *m.* collectivism

Coliseo *m.* Coliseum

colonia *f.* colony, settlement, plantation; **c. penal** penal colony

Colonia Perdida *f.* Lost Colony; **C. de Plymouth** Plymouth Colony

colonial *adj.* colonial

colonialismo *m.* colonialism

colonización *f.* colonization

colonizar *v.* to colonize

colono, -na *m.f.;* **colonizador, -ora** *m.f.* colonist, settler

combate *m.* combat

combatiente *m.f.* combatant

comercio *m.* trade; **c. de especias** spice trade; **c. de marfil** ivory trade; **c. triangular** triangular trade

Comité de Actividades Antiamericanas *m.* House Un-American Activities Committee; **C. de Correspondencia** Committee of Correspondence

complejo militar industrial *m.* Military Industrial Complex

Compra de Gadsden *f.* Gadsden Purchase; **C. de Louisiana** Louisiana Purchase

compromiso *m.* compromise

Compromiso de Misuri *m.* Missouri Compromise

Comuna de París *f.* Paris Commune

comunicación *f.* communication

comunidad *f.* community; **c. utópica** utopian community

Comunidad Económica Europea *f.* European Economic Community

comunismo *m.* communism

ESTUDIOS SOCIALES

ESTUDIOS SOCIALES

comunista *adj. & m.f.* communist

concesiones *f.pl.* concessions

conciencia de clase *f.* class consciousness

conde *m.* count, earl

condesa *f.* countess

condición *f.* proviso

confederación *f.* confederation; **c. Iroquois, c. iraquesa** Iroquois Confederacy

Confederación *f.* Confederacy

Conferencia de Yalta *f.* Yalta Conference

conflicto *m.* conflict; **c. árabe-israelí** Arab-Israeli conflict; **c. étnico** ethnic conflict; **c. regional** regional conflict

confucianismo *m.* Confucianism

congreso *m.* congress

Congreso Continental *m.* Continental Congress; **C. de Viena** Congress of Vienna

Congreso de EE.UU. *m.* U.S. Congress

Congreso Nacional Africano *m.* African National Congress

conquista *f.* conquest

conquista normanda *f.* Norman Conquest

conquistar *v.* to conquer

Consejos de Ciudadanos Blancos *m.pl.* White Citizens Councils

constancia escrita *f.* written record

Constitución de EE.UU. *f.* U.S. Constitution

constitucional *adj.* constitutional;

convención c. *f.* Constitutional Convention; **enmienda c.** *f.* constitutional amendment

construcción nacional, construcción de la nación *f.* nation building

constructores de montículos *m.pl.* Mound Builders

contemporáneo, -nea *adj. & m.f.* contemporary

contención *f.* containment

contrabando *m.* smuggling

contraespionaje *m.* counterintelligence

contrainsurgencia *f.* counterinsurgency

contrarrevolución *f.* counterrevolution

contrato social *m.* Social Contract

control de armas, control de armamentos *m.* arms control

Convenios de Ginebra *m.pl.* Geneva Conventions

convento *m.* convent

converso, -sa *m.f.* convert

convertir *v.* to convert

Corán *m.* Koran

coronación *f.* coronation

coronar *v.* to crown

corsario *m.* privateer

corte real *f.* royal court

cortina de hierro *f.* Iron Curtain

Creciente Fértil *m.* Fertile Crescent

crimen *m.* crime; **c. de guerra** war crime; **c. organizado** organized crime; **c. contra la humanidad** *pl.* crimes against humanity

Crisis de los misiles en Cuba *f.* Cuban Missile Crisis; **C. de los rehenes en Irán** Iranian hostage crisis

crisol de razas *m.* Melting Pot

cristianismo *m.* Christianity; **c. ortodoxo griego** Greek Orthodox Christianity; **c. protestante** Protestant Christianity

cristiano, -na *adj. & m.f.* Christian

Cristóbal Colón *m.* Christopher Columbus

CroMagnon *m.,* **Cromañón** *m.* Cro-Magnon

cronología *f.* chronology, timeline

crucifixión *f.* crucifixion

Cruzadas *f.pl.* Crusades

cruzado *m.* crusader

cuadriga *f.* chariot

cuáquero, -ra *adj. & m.f.* Quaker

Cuatro Libertades *f.* Four Freedoms

cubanos exilios *m.pl.* Cuban exiles

cuenca de polvo *f.* Dust Bowl

Cuerpo Civil de Conservación *m.* Civilian Conservation Corps; **C. de Paz** Peace Corps

cultura *f.* culture; **c. helenística** Hellenist culture; **c. indígena** indigenous culture; **c. occidental** Western culture

cuneiforme *adj. & m.* cuneiform

CH

chiita *adj. & m.f.* Shi'ite

chovinismo *m.* (nacionalista) chauvinism

D

darwinismo social *m.* Social Darwinism

debate Lincoln-Douglas *m.* Lincoln-Douglas Debate

década *f.* decade

decapitar *v.* to behead, decapitate

decisión del caso Dred Scott *f.* Dred Scott decision

Declaración de Balfour *f.* Balfour Declaration; **D. de Independencia** Declaration of Independence; **D. de los Derechos del Hombre y del Ciudadano** Declaration of the Rights of Man and of the Citizen; **D. Universal de los Derechos Humanos** Universal Declaration of Human Rights

deísmo *m.* Deism

democracia *f.* democracy; **d. constitucional** constitutional democracy; **d. social** social democracy

democracia griega *f.* Greek democracy; **d. jacksoniana** Jacksonian Democracy; **d. jeffersoniana** Jeffersonian Democracy

democratización *f.* democratization

deponer *v.* to depose

derecho divino de los reyes *m.* divine right of kings

derechos *m.pl.* rights; **d. de agua** water rights; **d. civiles** civil rights; **d. constitucionales** constitutional rights; **d. de los estados** states' rights; **d. de los homosexuales** gay rights; **d. fundamentales**

ESTUDIOS SOCIALES

fundamental rights; **d. humanos** human rights; **d. inalienables** unalienable rights

derrocar *v.* to overthrow

derrota *f.* defeat

derrotar *v.* to defeat

desaparecido, -da *adj. & m.f.* missing, disappeared; **d. en acción** missing in action

desarme *m.* disarmament

descentralización *f.* decentralization

descolonización *f.* decolonization

descubrimiento *m.* discovery

desembarco de Normandía *m.* Normandy Landing

deserción *f.* desertion

desertor, -ora *m.f.* deserter

desmotadora de algodón *f.* cotton gin

desmovilización *f.* demobilization

desobediencia civil *f.* civil disobedience

déspota *m.f.* despot

después de Cristo (d.C.) *adv.* Anno Domini (A.D.)

destino manifiesto *m.* Manifest Destiny

Día D *m.* D-Day

día de hoy *m.* present day

diáspora *f.* diaspora

diez mandamientos *m.pl.* Ten Commandments

dinastía *f.* dynasty

Dinastía Han *f.* Han Dynasty; **D. Ming** Ming Dynasty

dios *m.* god; **dioses** *m.pl.* gods

diosa *f.* goddess

diplomacia *f.* diplomacy; **d. de las cañoneras** gunboat diplomacy; **d. de lanzadera** shuttle diplomacy

dirigible *m.* blimp, zeppelin, airship

discurso *m.* speech, address

Discurso de despedida de Washington Washington's Farewell Address; **D. de Gettysburg** Gettysburg Address

disidentes *m.f.pl.* dissidents

disparar *v.* to shoot

disparo *m.* shot

disputa fronteriza *f.* boundary dispute

distensión *f.* détente

disuasión *f.* deterrence

doctrina *f.* doctrine; **d. de anulación** nullification doctrine

Doctrina Monroe *f.* Monroe Doctrine

Documentos Federalistas *m.pl.* Federalist Papers

duque *m.* duke

duquesa *f.* duchess

dux *m.* doge

E

edad *f.* age, era, epoch

Edad de Bronce *f.* Bronze Age; **E. de Piedra** Stone Age; **E. de las Tinieblas** Dark Ages *pl.*; **E. Media** Middle Ages *pl.*

eduardiano, -na *adj. & m.f.* Edwardian

educación bilingüe *f.* bilingual education

EE.UU. contra Texas *m.pl.* U.S. v. Texas

ejecución *f.* execution

ejército *m.* army

ejército del bono *m.* Bonus Army; **e. continental** Continental Army; **e. de Coxey** Coxey's Army; **e. de la Confederación** Confederate Army; **e. de la Unión** Union Army; **e. rojo** Red Army

electricidad *f.* electricity

emancipación *f.* emancipation

embajada *f.* embassy

embajador, -ora *m.f.* ambassador

embargo *m.* embargo; **e. de petróleo** oil embargo

emboscada *f.* ambush

emboscar *v.* to ambush

emigración *f.* emigration

emperador *m.* emperor

emperatriz *f.* empress

enfermedad *f.* disease; **e. infecciosa** infectious disease

enmienda constitucional *f.* constitutional amendment

entregar *v.* to surrender

epidemia *f.* epidemic; **e. de viruela** smallpox epidemic

epidémico, -ca *adj.* epidemic

época *f.* era, epoch; **é. glacial** ice age

época de los buenos sentimientos *f.* Era of Good Feelings; **é. dorada** Gilded Age

equilibrio *m.* equilibrium; **e. de poder** balance of power

era *f.* age, era, epoch

era de la información *f.* Informa-

tion Age; **e. de la razón** Age of Reason; **e. de los descubrimientos** Age of Discovery; **e. del jazz** Jazz Age; **e. progresista** Progressive Era

escándalo *m.* scandal; **e. de Watergate** Watergate scandal

escapar *v.* to escape

escaramuza *f.* skirmish

esclavista *m.f.* slave holder

esclavitud *f.* slavery; **en contra de la e.** *adj.* antislavery

esclavizar *v.* to enslave

esclavo, -va *adj. & m.f.* slave, enslaved; **propiedad de esclavos** *f.* chattel slavery

escudero *m.* squire, knight's attendant

escultura *f.* sculpture

esfera de influencia *f.* sphere of influence

espada *f.* sword

Esparta *f.* Sparta

especialización *f.* specialization

estadidad *f.* statehood

estado *m.* state; **e. esclavo** slave state; **e. fronterizo** border state; **e. libre de esclavitud** free state

Estados Confederados de América *m.pl.* Confederate States of America

Estados Generales *m.pl.* Estates General

estalinismo *m.* Stalinism

estrategia *f.* strategy; **e. militar** military strategy

ética judeocristiana *f.* Judeo-Christian ethic

étnico, -ca *adj.* ethnic; **conflicto é.** *m.* ethnic conflict; **limpieza é.** *f.* ethnic cleansing

eugenesia *f.* eugenics

evacuación *f.* evacuation

evento *m.* event

evolución *f.* evolution; **teoría de la e.** *f.* theory of evolution

excavación *f.* excavation; **e. arqueológica** archeological dig

excavar *v.* to excavate

exiliar *v.* to exile

exilio *m.* exile

éxodo *m.* exodus

expansión *f.* expansion; **e. hacia el oeste** Westward Expansion; **e. territorial** territorial expansion

expansionismo *m.* expansionism

expedición *f.* expedition; **e. de Lewis y Clark** Lewis and Clark expedition

exploración *f.* exploration; **e. del espacio** space exploration

explorador, -ora *m.f.* explorer

explosión demográfica *f.* population explosion

F

facción *f.* faction

faraón *m.* pharaoh

fascismo *m.* fascism

fascista *adj. & m.f.* fascist

Fenicia *f.* Phoenicia

ferrocarril *m.* railroad; **f. subterráneo** Underground Railroad; **f. transcontinental** transcontinen-

tal railroad

feudal *adj.* feudal; **señor f.** *m.* feudal lord

feudalismo *m.* feudalism

fiebre del oro en California *f.* California Gold Rush

filósofo griego *m.* Greek philosopher

Fondo de las Naciones Unidas para la Infancia *m.* United Nations Children's Fund (UNICEF)

Foro Romano *m.* Roman Forum

fortaleza *f.* fort, fortress

fortificación *f.* fortification

foso *m.* moat

Frente de Liberación Nacional *m.* National Liberation Front (N.L.F.)

frontera *f.* frontier, border

fuego *m.* fire, firing; **alto de f.** *m.* ceasefire; **f. amigo** *m.* friendly fire

fuente *f.* source; **f. primaria** primary source; **f. secundaria** secondary source

fuerte *m.* fort, fortress

Fuerte Sumter *m.* Fort Sumter

fuerza aérea *f.* air force; **F. A. Real** Royal Air Force (R.A.F.)

fuerzas armadas *f.pl.* armed forces

fuerzas del Eje *f.pl.* Axis powers

Fundadores *m.pl.* (de EE.UU.) Founders

fusilamiento *m.* execution by firing squad

G

gaélico, -ca *adj.* Gaelic

galos *m.pl.* Gauls

gas *m.* gas; **g. mostaza** mustard gas; **g. nervioso** nerve gas

generación *f.* generation

generación beat *f.* Beat Generation; **g. perdida** Lost Generation

Gengis Kan *m.* Genghis Khan

genocidio *m.* genocide

gladiador *m.* gladiator

glasnost *m.* glasnost

gobernante *adj.* ruling, governing

gobernante *m.f.* ruler, leader

gobernar *v.* to rule, govern

gobierno *m.* government; **g. de coalición** coalition government; **g. marioneta, g. títere** puppet government; **g. provisional** provisional government

godos *m.pl.* Goths

golpe de estado *m.* coup d'état

gótico, -ca *adj.* Gothic

Gran Depresión *f.* Great Depression

Gran Despertar *m.* Great Awakening

Gran Hambruna irlandesa *f.* Irish Potato Famine

Gran Muralla de China *f.* Great Wall of China

Gran Pirámide de Gizeh *f.* Great Pyramid of Giza

Gran Plaga *f.* Great Plague

Gran Revolución Cultural Proletaria *f.* Great Proletarian Cultural Revolution

Gran Salto Adelante *m.* Great Leap Forward

Gran Sociedad *f.* Great Society

granja colectiva *f.* collective farm

granjero *m.* homesteader

guardia rojo *m.* Red Guard

guerra *f.* war; **g. bacteriológica** germ warfare; **g. civil** civil war; **g. de desgaste** war of attrition; **g. de guerrillas** guerrilla warfare; **g. naval** naval warfare; **g. nuclear** nuclear war; **g. química** chemical warfare; **g. relámpago** blitzkrieg; **movimiento contra la g.** *m.* anti-war movement

guerra de 1812 *f.* War of 1812; **g. Bóer** Boer War; **g. contra la pobreza** War on Poverty; **g. civil española** Spanish Civil War; **g. civil estadounidense** American Civil War; **g. de Corea** Korean War; **g. de Crimea** Crimean War; **g. de Iraq** Iraq War; **g. de los Cien Años** Hundred Years War; **g. de los Siete Años** Seven Years War; **g. de Troya** Trojan War; **g. de Vietnam** Vietnam War; **g. del golfo Pérsico** Persian Gulf War; **g. del Opio** Opium War; **g. del Peloponeso** Peloponnesian War; **g. del rey Felipe** King Philip's War; **g. española-americana** Spanish-American War; **g. franco-india** French and Indian War; **g. franco-prusiana** Franco-Prussian War; **g. fría** Cold War; **g. fronteriza de Kansas** Bleeding Kansas; **g. mexicano-estadounidense** Mexican-American War; **primera g. mundial** World War I; **g. revolucionaria** Revolutionary War; **segunda g. mundial** World War II

ESTUDIOS SOCIALES

ESTUDIOS SOCIALES

guerras de las Rosas *f.pl.* Wars of the Roses; **g. indias** Indian Wars; **g. napoleónicas** Napoleonic Wars; **g. púnicas** Punic Wars

Guillermo el Conquistador *m.* William the Conqueror

guillotina *f.* guillotine

H

hacendado *m.* homesteader, land-owner

hacienda *f.* plantation

hambre *m.*, **hambruna** *f.* hunger, famine

hegemonía *f.* hegemony

hereje *m.f.* heretic

herejía *f.* heresy

hidalgo, -ga *m.f.* nobleman, noble-woman

Hijos de la Libertad *m.pl.* Sons of Liberty

himno nacional *m.* national anthem

hindú *adj. & m.f.* Hindu

hispano, -na *adj. & m.f.;* **hispánico, -ca** *adj. & m.f.* Hispanic

historia *f.* history

historiador, -ora *m.f.* historian

histórico, -ca *adj.* historic, historical; **documento h.** *m.* historical document; **figura h.** *f.,* **personaje h.** *m.* historic figure

hititas *m.pl.* Hittites

holocausto *m.* Holocaust

hombre de Kennewick *m.* Kennewick Man; **h. de la frontera** frontiersman

homenaje *m.* tribute

hostilidades *f.pl.* hostilities

huelga *f.* strike; **h. de brazos caídos** sit-down strike

huelga de Pullman *f.* Pullman Strike; **h. textil de Lawrence** Lawrence Textile Strike

humanismo *m.* humanism

hundir *v.* to sink

hunos *m.f.pl.* Huns

I

ideología política *f.* political ideology

Iglesia católica *f.* Catholic Church; **I. de Inglaterra** Church of England; **I. Mormona** Mormon Church

imperialismo *m.* imperialism

imperio *m.* empire

Imperio asirio *m.* Assyrian Empire; **I. austro-húngaro** Austro-Hungarian Empire; **I. azteca** Aztec Empire; **I. babilónico** Babylonian Empire; **I. bizantino** Byzantine Empire; **I. británico** British Empire; **I. de los Habsburgo** Hapsburg Empire; **I. de Nubia** Nubian Empire; **i. del mal** Evil Empire; **I. inca** Inca empire; **I. maya** Mayan Empire; **I. mongol** Mongol Empire; **I. otomano** Ottoman Empire; **I. romano** Roman Empire; **I. soviético** Soviet Empire; **I. zulú** Zulu Empire; **Sacro I. Romano** Holy Roman Empire

imprenta *f.* printing press

impuesto *m.* tax; **i. de capitación,**

i. per cápita poll tax; **i. sin representación** *pl.* taxation without representation

inca *m.f.* Inca

incursión *f.* incursion, raid

incursiones Palmer *f.pl.* Palmer Raids

independencia *f.* independence

independiente *adj.* independent

índice de alfabetización *m.* literacy rate

indígena *adj. & m.f.* Indian, native; **pueblos i.** *m.pl.* indigenous peoples; **reserva i.** *f.* Indian reservation

indio, -dia *adj. & m.f.* Indian; **i. americanos** *pl.* American Indians; **levantamiento i.** *m.* Indian uprising

infantería *f.* infantry

inmigración *f.* immigration; **restricciones de i.** *f.pl.* immigration restrictions

Inquisición *f.* Inquisition

institución peculiar *f.* peculiar institution

insurrección *f.* insurrection, insurgency; **i. filipina** Filipino Insurrection

intelectualidad *f.* intelligentsia

internamiento de japoneses-americanos *m.* internment of Japanese Americans

intervención *f.* intervention; **i. militar** military intervention

intervencionista *m.f.* interventionist

intolerancia *f.* bigotry

invadir *v.* to raid

invasión *f.* invasion

invasores *m.f.pl.* raiders

invención *f.* invention

isabelino, -na *adj. & m.f.* Elizabethan

Isla de Ellis *f.* Ellis Island

Islam *m.* Islam

isleño (-ña) de Asia y el Pacífico *m.f.* Asian Pacific Islander

J

Jacobinos *m.pl.* Jacobins

jardines colgantes de Babilonia *m.pl.* Hanging Gardens of Babylon

jerarquía *f.* hierarchy

jeroglíficos *m.pl.* hieroglyphics

Jesucristo *m.* Jesus Christ

Juana de Arco *f.* Joan of Arc

Judaísmo *m.* Judaism

juicio *m.* trial

juicio Scopes *m.* Scopes trial; **j. de Nuremberg** *pl.* Nuremburg Trials; **j. por brujería de Salem** *pl.* Salem witch trials

Julio César *m.* Julius Caesar

K

Kansas Sangrante *f.* Bleeding Kansas

karma *m.* karma

Ku Klux Klan *m.* Ku Klux Klan

L

laissez-faire *adj. & m.* laissez-faire

lanza *f.* spear

ESTUDIOS SOCIALES

351

Estudios Sociales

Larga Marcha *f.* Long March

lealista *m.f.* loyalist

lenguaje escrito *m.* written language

lenguas *f.pl.* languages; **l. indígenas** indigenous languages; **l. indoeuropeas** Indo-European languages; **l. romances** Romance languages; **l. semíticas** Semitic languages

leva *f.* impressment

levantamiento *m.* uprising; **l. indio** Indian uprising; **l. popular** popular uprising

ley *f.* law; **l. natural** natural law

Ley del Aire Puro *f.* Clean Air Act; **L. de Derecho al Voto** Voting Rights Act; **L. de Derechos Civiles** Civil Rights Act; **L. de Espionaje** Espionage Act; **L. de Heredad** Homestead Act; **L. de Kansas-Nebraska** Kansas-Nebraska Act; **L. de los Esclavos Fugitivos** Fugitive Slave Act; **L. de Poderes de Guerra** War Powers Act; **L. de Préstamo y Arriendo** Lend-Lease Act; **L. de Recuperación Nacional** National Recovery Act; **L. de Remoción de los Indios** Indian Removal Act; **L. de Volstead** Volstead Act; **L. G.I.** G.I. Bill; **L. Sherman antimonopolio** Sherman Antitrust Act; **L. de Extranjería y Sedición** *pl.* Alien and Sedition Acts; **L. de Jim Crow** *pl.* Jim Crow laws

leyenda negra *f.* Black Legend

libertad *f.* freedom, liberty; **l. política** political freedom

libertar *v.* to liberate

libertos *m.pl.* freedmen

Liga Urbana *f.* Urban League

limpieza étnica *f.* ethnic cleansing

linchamiento *m.* lynching

linchar *v.* to lynch

línea de tiempo *f.* timeline, chronology

Línea Maginot *f.* Maginot Line

lista negra *f.* blacklist

lucha de clases *f.* class warfare

M

macartismo *m.* McCarthyism

magnates ladrones *m.pl.* robber barons

Mahoma *m.* Mohammed

mancomunidad *f.* commonwealth

Manifiesto Comunista *m.* Communist Manifesto

maoísmo *m.* Maoism

maoísta *adj. & m.f.* Maoist

máquina de vapor *f.* steam engine

maquinaria política *f.* political machine

Marbury contra Madison *m.* Marbury v. Madison

marina *f.* navy

mártir *m.f.* martyr

marxismo *m.* Marxism

marxismo-leninismo *m.* Marxism-Leninism

masacre *f.* massacre

masacre de Boston *f.* Boston Massacre; **m. de My Lai** My Lai Massacre

matanza *f.* massacre, pogrom

maya *adj. & m.f.* Mayan
medieval *adj.* medieval
mercado común *m.* Common Market
Mesopotamia *f.* Mesopotamia
mexicano (-na) americano (-na) *adj. & m.f.* Mexican American
mezquita *f.* mosque
miedo a los rojos *m.* Red Scare
migración *f.* migration; **m. involuntaria** involuntary migration
milenio *m.* millennium
militante *adj. & m.f.* militant
militar *adj.* military; **intervención m.** *f.* military intervention
militar *m.f.* soldier
misil *m.* missile
misión *f.* mission
misionero, -ra *m.f.* missionary
mito *m.* myth; **m. de la creación** creation myth
modernización *f.* modernization
Moisés *m.* Moses
molino de algodón *m.* cotton mill
momia *f.* mummy
momificación *f.* mummification
monarca *m.f.* monarch
monarquía *f.* monarchy; **m. constitucional** constitutional monarchy
monárquico, -ca *adj. & m.f.* monarchist, royalist
monasterio *m.* monastery
monja *f.* nun
monje *m.* monk
monoteísmo *m.* monotheism
monte Olimpo *m.* Mount Olympus
mormón, -na *m.f.* Mormon

moros *m.pl.* Moors
motín *m.* riot
motín de Haymarket *m.* Haymarket Riot; **m. del té de Boston** Boston Tea Party
movimiento *m.* movement; **m. abolicionista** abolitionist movement; **m. de derechos civiles** civil rights movement; **m. de la liberación gay** gay liberation movement; **m. de liberación de las mujeres** women's liberation movement; **m. de liberación nacional** national liberation movement; **m. obrero** labor movement; **m. por la templanza** temperance movement; **m. sufragista** suffrage movement
Movimiento de las Cien Flores *m.* Hundred Flowers Movement; **M. Free Silver** Free Silver; **M. Populista** Populist Movement
muchachos de las Montañas Verdes *m.pl.* Green Mountain Boys
Muro de Berlín *m.* Berlin Wall
musulmán, -na *m.f.* Muslim

N

Nabucodonosor *m.* Nebuchadnezzar
nación *f.* nation, country; **n. desarrollada** developed country; **n. en vías de desarrollo** developing country
Nación Cherokee *f.* Cherokee Nation; **N. Navajo** Navajo Nation; **N. Sioux** Sioux Nation
nacionalidad *f.* nationality

ESTUDIOS SOCIALES

ESTUDIOS SOCIALES

nacionalismo *m.* nationalism

nacionalista *adj. & m.f.* nationalist

Naciones Unidas *f.pl.* United Nations

Napoleón *m.* Napoleon

nativismo *m.* nativism

nativista *adj. & m.f.* nativist

nativo, -va *adj. & m.f.* native

nativo (-va) americano (-na) *adj. & m.f.* Native American

navegación *f.* navigation

navegar *v.* to sail

nazi *adj. & m.f.* Nazi; **Alemania n.** *f.* Nazi Germany

nazismo *m.* Nazism

Neandertal *m.f.* Neanderthal

negociaciones *f.pl.* negotiations

Neolítico *m.* Neolithic Era

Nero *m.* Nero

neutral *adj.,* **no alineados** *adj.* neutral, nonaligned

neutralidad *f.,* **neutralismo** *m.* neutrality

nirvana *m.* nirvana

noble *adj. & m.* noble

nobleza *f.* nobility

nómada *adj. & m.f.* nomad, nomadic

Nueva Ámsterdam *f.* New Amsterdam

Nueva Izquierda *f.* New Left

Nueva Política Económica *f.* New Economic Policy

Nuevo Trato *m.* New Deal

O

Oficina de Libertos *f.* Freedmen's Bureau

oligarca *m.* oligarch

oligarquía *f.* oligarchy

operación Tormenta del Desierto *f.* Operation Desert Storm

oportunista político (-ca) *m.f.* political opportunist

Ordenanza del Noroeste *f.* Northwest Ordinance

Organización de Liberación Palestina *f.* Palestine Liberation Organization (P.L.O.); **O. de Países Exportadores de Petróleo** Organization of Petroleum Exporting Countries (OPEC); **O. del Tratado del Atlántico del Norte** North Atlantic Treaty Organization (NATO)

origen *m.* origin

oriundo, -da *adj. & m.f.* native

P

pacificador, -ora *m.f.* peacekeeper

pacto *m.* pact, agreement

Pacto de Varsovia *m.* Warsaw Pact; **P. del Mayflower** Mayflower Compact

país *m.* country; **p. de origen** country of origin, home country

Paleolítico *m.* Paleolithic Era

panarabismo *m.* Pan-Arabism

pandemia *f.* pandemic

Panteras Negras *f.pl.* Black Panthers

papa *m.* pope

papado *m.* papacy

papeles del Pentágono *m.pl.* Pentagon Papers

papiro *m.* papyrus

paracaidista *m.f.* paratrooper

parlamento *m.* parliament; **p. inglés** English Parliament

Partenón *m.* Parthenon

partidario, -ria *m.f.* supporter, follower; **p. del régimen** loyalist

partido *m.* party; **p. de vanguardia** vanguard party

Partido Comunista de Estados Unidos *m.* American Communist Party; **P. Comunista de la Unión Soviética** Communist Party of the Soviet Union; **P. Conservador** Conservative Party; **P. Demócrata-Republicano** Democratic-Republican Party; **P. Federalista** Federalist Party; **P. Know Nothing** Know-Nothing Party; **P. Laborista** Labor Party; **P. Whig** Whig Party

partisano, -na *m.f.* partisan

pasado, -da *adj.* past

pasado *m.* past; **p. reciente** recent past

pasajeros de la libertad *m.pl.* freedom riders

paso del Noroeste *m.* Northwest Passage

patriarca *m.* patriarch

patriarcal *adj.* patriarchal

patrioterismo *m.* jingoism

Pax Romana *f.* Pax Romana

paz *m.* peace; **conversaciones de p.** *m.pl.* peace talks; **mantenedor (-ora) de la p.** *m.f.* peacekeeper; **marcha por la p.** *f.* peace march; **trato de p.** *m.* peace treaty

Pedro el Grande *m.* Peter the Great

peligro amarillo *m.* Yellow Peril

pelotón de ejecución *m.* firing squad

pequeña burguesía *f.* petite bourgeoisie

peregrino, -na *m.f.* pilgrim

periodismo amarillo *m.* yellow journalism

período *m.* period; **p. histórico** historical period

período colonial *m.* Colonial Period; **p. de la Ilustración** Englightenment

persecución *f.* persecution

personas desplazadas *f.pl.* displaced persons

peste *f.* plague, pestilence; **p. bubónica** bubonic plague; **p. negra** Black Death

petróleo *m.* petroleum

pictografía *f.,* **pictograma** *m.* pictograph

Piedra de Rosetta *f.* Rosetta Stone

pillaje *m.* pillage, plunder

pillar *v.* to pillage, plunder

pinturas rupestres *f.pl.* cave paintings

pionero, -ra *m.f.* pioneer

piragua *f.* dugout ship

piratas *m.f.pl.* pirates

pistola *f.* pistol, gun

plaga *f.* plague

plan Marshall *m.* Marshall Plan

plan quinquenal *m.* Five Year Plan

Plessy contra Ferguson *m.* Plessy v. Ferguson

población *f.* population; **crecimien-**

ESTUDIOS SOCIALES

to de p. *m.* population growth

poblado *m.* settlement

poder *m.* power; **p. esclavista** Slave Power; **p. imperial** imperial power

pogromo *m.* pogrom

politeísmo *m.* polytheism

política *f.* policy, politics; **p. de puertas abiertas** Open Door Policy; **p. de tierra quemada** scorched-earth policy; **p. del garrote** big stick policy

pólvora *f.* gunpowder

Pompeya *f.* Pompeii

populismo *m.* Populist Movement

portaaviones *m.* aircraft carrier

potencia *f.* power; **p. colonial** colonial power; **p. hegemónica** hegemonic power; **p. mundial** world power

Potencias Aliadas *f.pl.* Allied Powers; **P. del Eje** Axis Powers

pragmatismo *m.* pragmatism

prebélico, -ca *adj.* antebellum

precolombino, -na *adj.* Pre-Columbian

predicador, -ora *m.f.* preacher

prehistoria *f.* prehistory

prehistórico, -ca *adj.* prehistoric

prensa *f.* press; **p. sensacionalista** yellow journalism

preservación histórica *f.* historic preservation

presidencia imperial *f.* imperial presidency

presidio *m.* prison, garrison, fort

primer ministro *m.* prime minister

primera guerra mundial *f.* World War I, First World War

primeros (-ras) americanos (-nas) *m.f.pl.* First Americans; **p. habitantes** *m.f.pl.* first inhabitants

primitivo, -va *adj.* primitive

princesa *f.* princess; **p. heredera** crown princess

príncipe *m.* prince; **p. heredero** crown prince

proclamación de la emancipación *f.* Emancipation Proclamation

prohibición *f.* Prohibition

proletariado *m.* proletariat

propiedad de esclavos *f.* chattel slavery

prosperidad *f.* prosperity

protesta *f.* protest

proyecto Manhattan *m.* Manhattan Project

puente terrestre de Bering *m.* Bering land bridge

puertorriqueño, -ña *adj. & m.f.* Puerto Rican

puritanismo *m.* Puritanism

puritano, -na *adj. & m.f.* Puritan

R

raj británico *m.* British Raj

realeza *f.* royalty

realista *adj. & m.f.* royalist, monarchist

reasentamiento *m.* resettlement

rebelarse *v.* to rebel, revolt

rebelde *m.f.* rebel

rebelión *f.* rebellion; **r. de esclavos** slave rebellion

rebelión de Bacon *f.* Bacon's Rebellion; **r. de los bóxers** Boxer Rebellion; **r. de Shay** Shay's Rebellion; **r. del whisky** Whiskey Rebellion

recinto *m.* enclosure

reclutamiento *m.* military draft; **disturbio de r.** *m.* draft riot; **r. forzoso** impressment

reclutas *m.f.pl.* recruits

reconocimiento *m.* reconnaissance

reconquista de España *f.* Reconquest of Spain

reconstrucción *f.* Reconstruction

rechazar *v.* to repel

redistribución de la riqueza *f.* redistribution of wealth

reencarnación *f.* reincarnation

Reforma *f.* Reformation; **R. católica** Catholic Reformation

reforma agraria *f.* agrarian reform, land reform

refuerzos *m.pl.* reinforcements

refugiados *m.pl.* refugees

refugio de lluvia radiactiva *m.* fallout shelter

régimen *m.* regime; **r. totalitario** totalitarian regime

regimiento *m.* regiment

región lingüística *f.* language region

regional *adj.* regional; **conflicto r.** *m.* regional conflict

regla Miranda *f.* Miranda Rule

reina *f.* queen

reinado *m.* reign; **r. del terror** Reign of Terror

reinar *v.* to reign, rule

reino *m.* kingdom, realm

Renacimiento *m.* Renaissance; **R. de Harlem** Harlem Renaissance

rendición *f.* surrender; **r. incondicional** unconditional surrender

rendir *v.* to surrender

reparación *f.* reparation

reparto de Polonia *m.* Partition of Poland

repeler *v.* to repel

república *f.* republic

República de Platón *f.* Plato's Republic; **R. de Weimar** Weimar Republic; **R. española** Spanish Republic; **R. romana** Roman Republic

republicano, -na adj. & *m.f.* republican

reserva indígena *f.* Indian reservation

resistencia *f.* resistance

Resolución del golfo de Tonkin *f.* Gulf of Tonkin Resolution

restauración *f.* restoration

retirada *f.* retreat

retirar *v.* to retreat

reubicación forzosa *f.* forced relocation

reunificación *f.* reunification

revisionismo *m.* revisionism; **r. histórico** historical revisionism

revolución *f.* revolution

Revolución americana *f.* American Revolution; **R. china** Chinese Revolution; **R. cubana** Cuban Revolution; **R. francesa** French Revolution; **R. Gloriosa** Glorious Revolution; **R. húngara** Hungarian Revolution; **r. industrial** In-

ESTUDIOS SOCIALES

dustrial Revolution; **R. rusa** Russian Revolution; **R. Verde** Green Revolution

revolucionario, -ria *adj. & m.f.* revolutionary

revuelta *f.* revolt; **r. de los indios Pueblo** Pueblo Revolt

rey *m.* king

Rey Algodón *m.* King Cotton

riego *m.* irrigation

rifle *m.* rifle

riqueza de las naciones, La *f.* The Wealth of Nations

Roe contra Wade *m.* Roe v. Wade

Roman Catholic *adj. & n.* católico, -ca *m.f.*

rueda *f.* wheel

ruina *f.* ruin

ruptura sino-soviética *f.* Sino-Soviet split

Rusia zarista *f.* Czarist Russia

ruta *f.* route; **r. comercial** trade route; **r. de Oregón** Oregon Trail

S

sacerdote *m.* priest

Sacro Imperio Romano *m.* Holy Roman Empire

salvaje noble *m.* Noble Savage

sanciones *f.pl.* sanctions

saquear *v.* to pillage, plunder

satélite *m.* satellite

seccionalismo *m.* Sectionalism

secesión *f.* secession

segunda guerra mundial *f.* World War II, Second World War

Senado *m.* Senate

Sendero de Lágrimas *m.* Trail of Tears

sentadas *f.pl.* sit-down strikes

señor feudal *m.* feudal lord

separados (-das) pero iguales *adj.* separate but equal

separatista *adj. & m.f.* separatist

sepulcro *m.* tomb

servidumbre *f.* serfdom; **s. por deuda** indentured servitude

Sha de Irán *m.* Shah of Iran

siervo *m.* serf

siglo *m.* century

Siglo de las Luces *m.* Enlightenment

sinagoga *f.* synagogue

sindicalismo *m.* syndicalism

sionismo *m.* Zionism

sionista *adj. & m.f.* Zionist

sistema *m.* system; **s. de castas** caste system; **s. de clases** class system; **s. de encomienda** encomienda system

sitio *m.* siege; **estado de s.** state of siege *m.*

soberano, -na *adj. & m.f.* sovereign

socialismo *m.* socialism

socialista *adj. & m.f.* socialist

sociedad *f.* society; **s. de ayuda mutua** mutual aid society; **s. medieval** medieval society

Sociedad de Naciones *f.* League of Nations

Sócrates *m.* Socrates

soldado *m.* soldier; **s. mercenario** mercenary soldier

soldados búfalo *m.pl.* Buffalo Soldiers

Solución Final *f.* Final Solution
someter *v.* to subdue
sublevación *f.* revolt
sublevarse *v.* to revolt
submarino *m.* submarine
subyugar *v.* to subjugate
sucesión *f.* succession; **orden de s.** *m.* order of succession
sufragio *m.* suffrage; **s. femenino** women's suffrage
sufragista *m.f.* suffragette
suní *adj. & m.f.,* **sunita** *adj. & m.f.* Sunni
superpoblación *f.* overpopulation
superpotencia *f.* superpower
superstición *f.* superstition

T
táctica *f.* tactic
Taj Mahal *m.* Taj Mahal
taller de explotación *m.* sweatshop
Tamerlán *m.* Tamerlane
tanque *m.* tank
tasa *f.* rate; **t. de alfabetización, t. de alfabetismo** literacy rate; **t. de mortalidad** death rate, mortality rate; **t. de víctimas** casualty rate
tecnología *f.* technology
tejeduría *f.,* **tejedura** *f.* weaving
telégrafo *m.* telegraph
templanza *f.* temperance; **movimiento por la t.** *m.* temperance movement
templo *m.* temple
teocracia *f.* theocracy
teología de la liberación *f.* liberation theology
teoría del dominó *f.* Domino Theory; **t. de la evolución** theory of evolution
tercer mundo *m.* Third World
Tercer Reich *m.* Third Reich
teutónico, -ca *adj.* Teutonic
terrateniente *m.* landowner
territorio *m.* territory; **t. indio** Indian Territory; **t. ocupado** occupied territory
terrorismo *m.* terrorism
terrorista *adj. & m.f.* terrorist
Tierra Santa *f.* Holy Land
tiranía *f.* tyranny
tirano, -na *m.f.* tyrant
tiro *m.* shot, shooting; **t. con arco** archery
totalitario, -ria *m.f.* totalitarian
totalitarismo *m.* totalitarianism
Trabajadores Industriales del Mundo *m.pl.* Industrial Workers of the World (I.W.W.)
trabajo *m.* work, labor; **t. esclavizante** slave labor; **t. infantil** child labor
tradición oral *f.* oral tradition
traición *f.* treason
traicionar *v.* to betray
traidor, -ora *m.f.* traitor
transcendentalismo *m.* transcendentalism
transcendentalista *adj. & m.f.* transcendentalist
traslado forzoso *m.* forced relocation
trata de esclavos *f.* slave trade

ESTUDIOS SOCIALES

359

ESTUDIOS SOCIALES

tratado *m.* treaty; **t. de paz** peace treaty

Tratado de Guadalupe Hidalgo *m.* Treaty of Guadalupe Hidalgo; **T. de París** Treaty of Paris; **T. de Prohibición Completa de Pruebas Nucleares** Nuclear Test Ban Treaty; **T. de Versalles** Treaty of Versailles

Trato Justo *m.* Fair Deal

travesía del Atlántico, travesía intermedia *f.* Middle Passage

tribalismo *m.* tribalism

tribu *f.* tribe

trono *m.* throne

tropas *f.pl.* troops

tumba *f.* tomb

U

unificación *f.* unification; **u. de Alemania** unification of Germany

Unión Americana de Libertades Civiles *f.* American Civil Liberties Union (A.C.L.U.)

Unión de Repúblicas Socialistas Soviéticas *f.* Union of Soviety Socialist Republics (U.S.S.R.); **U. Soviética** *f.* Soviet Union

Unión Europea *f.* European Union

urbanización *f.* urbanization

utilitarismo *m.* utilitarianism

utopía *f.* utopia

utópico, -ca *adj.* utopian; **socialismo u.** *m.* utopian socialism

V

valle del río Tigris y Éufrates *m.* Tigris-Euphrates River Valley

vela *f.* sail

vencer *v.* to defeat

Venta de La Mesilla *f.* Gadsden Purchase

viaje *m.* voyage; **v. del Beagle** Voyage of the Beagle; **v. de Colón** *pl.* voyages of Columbus

víctimas *f.pl.* casualties; **tasa de v.** *f.* casualty rate

victoria *f.* victory

victoriano, -na *adj. & m.f.* Victorian

Vietcong *m.f.* Vietcong

vigilante *m.f.* vigilante

vigilantismo *m.* vigilantism

Vikingos *m.pl.* Vikings

violación *f.* rape

violar *v.* to rape

viruela *f.* smallpox

virrey *m.* viceroy

vizconde *m.* viscount

Y

yacimiento arqueológico *m.* archeological site

Z

zar *m.* czar

zar Nicolás II *m.* Czar Nicholas II

zepelín *m.* zeppelin, blimp, airship

zona desmilitarizada *f.* Demilitarized Zone (D.M.Z.)

BELLAS ARTES

Artes de la Interpretación

A

acción *f.* action; **a. decreciente** falling action; **a. en aumento** rising action

acento *m.* accent

acompañamiento *m.* accompaniment

acompañante *m.f.* accompanist

acompañar *v.* to accompany

acompasadamente *adv.* in step

acorde *m.* chord; **progresión del a.** *f.* chord progression

acordeón *m.* accordion

acto *m.* (teatro) act

actor *m.*, **actriz** *f.*, actor, thespian; **a. de reparto** supporting actor

actuación *f.* performance

actuar *v.* to act

adaptación *f.* adaptation

adorno *m.* embellishment

afinar *v.* to tune

agradecer *v.* to bow

agradecimiento *m.* (teatro) bow

agudo, -da *adj.* high-pitched

alas *f.pl.* (teatro) wings

alejarse *v.* to upstage

alineamiento *m.* alignment

altura *f.* elevation

ambiente *m.* mood

anfiteatro *m.* amphitheater

animación *f.* animation

animador, -ora *m.f.* entertainer

anotación *f.* notation

antagonista *m.f.* antagonist

aparte *m.* (teatro) aside

aplaudir *v.* to clap, applaud

aplauso *m.* applause

arco *m.* (de instrumento) bow

argumento *m.* storyline, plot, scenario

armonía *f.* harmony

armónica *f.* harmonica

arpa *f.* harp

arpista *m.f.* harpist

arquetipo *m.* archetype

arte *m.* art; **a. de titiritero** puppetry

articulación *f.* enunciation

artista *m.f.* performer, entertainer, artist

arreglo *m.* (música) arrangement

asignar un papel *v.* to cast

atmósfera *f.* atmosphere, mood

audición *f.* audition

auditorio *m.* (teatro) house, auditorium

autoarpa *f.* autoharp

autor, -ra *m.f.* playwright

B

bailar *v.* to dance

bailarín, -na *m.f.* dancer

baile *m.* dance; **b. de salón** ballroom dance; **b. latino** Latin dance

bajo *m.* (instrumento, voz) bass; **b. eléctrico** bass guitar

balada *f.* ballad

balancear *v.* to balance

ballet *m.* ballet

banda *f.* band; **b. sonora** soundtrack

bandolina *f.* bandora

banjo *m.,* **banyo** *m.* banjo

baqueta *f.* (música) mallet, drumstick

barítono *m.* baritone

barra *f.* bar line; **b. de ballet** ballet barre; **doble b.** double bar line

bastidor *m.* (teatro) flat, wing

batería *f.* drum set, drum kit

baterista *m.f.* drummer

bemol *adj.* (música) flat

blanca *f.* half note

blues *m.* blues

boletería *f.* ticket office, box office

boleto *m.* ticket

bombo *m.* bass drum

bongós *m.pl.* bongo drums

brincar *v.* to skip

bufonadas *f.pl.* slapstick

C

caída *f.* (danza) landing; **c. cómica** pratfall

calentamiento *m.* warm up

cambio del peso *m.* weight shift

campanilla *f.* bell

canción *f.* song; **c. de cuna** lullaby; **c. de trabajo** work song; **c. folclórica** folk song; **c. marinera** sea chantey; **c. patriótica** patriotic song; **c. satírica de cabaret** vaudeville

canon *m.* (música) canon

caracterización *f.* characterization

cascabel *m.* rattle

castañuelas *f.pl.* castanets

catarsis *f.* catharsis

cencerro *m.* cowbell

címbalo *m.* cymbal

cine *m.* cinema, film; **sala de c.** *f.* movie theater

cítara *f.* sitar

clarín *m.* bugle

clarinete *m.* clarinet

clarinetista *m.f.* clarinetist

clásico, -ca *adj.* classical

clave *f.* clef; **c. de fa** bass clef; **c. de sol** treble clef

clavecín *m.* harpsichord

clímax *m.* climax

coda *f.* coda

BELLAS ARTES

colapsar *v.* (danza) to collapse

combinación *f.* dance combination

comedia *f.* comedy; **rutina de c.** *f.* comedy routine

comediante, -ta *m.f.* comedian

cómico, -ca *adj. & m.f.* comic

compás *m.* (música) beat, meter, bar, measure; **c. de cuatro por cuatro** four-four time; **c. de dos cuartos** two-four time; **c. de tres cuartos** three-quarter time; **c. duple** duple meter; **c. triple** triple meter; **llevar el c.** *v.* to beat

componer *v.* to compose

composición *f.* composition; **c. instrumental** instrumental score

compositor, -ra *m.f.* composer

concepto *m.* concept; **c. universal** universal concept

conciencia kinestésica *f.* kinesthetic awareness

concierto *m.* concert, concerto

conducir *v.* (danza) to lead

conflicto *m.* conflict

congas *f.pl.* conga drums

conjunto musical *m.* band, ensemble

consola *f.* keyboard

consonancia *f.* consonance

contralto *m.* alto, contralto

contramelodía *f.* countermelody

coral *adj.* choral

corchea *f.* eighth note

corear *v.* to accompany

coreografía *f.* choreography; **montar una c.** *v.* to choreograph

coreógrafo *m.f.* choreographer

corneta *f.* cornet

corno francés *m.* French horn; **c. inglés** English horn

coro *m.* choir, chorus

corrida *f.* (teatro) run-through

cuarta pared *f.* fourth wall

cuarteto *m.* quartet

cuentacuentos *m.f.,* **cuentista** *m.f.* storyteller

cuento *m.* story; **c. folclórico, c. tradicional** folktale

cuerdas *f.pl.* (música) strings; **instrumento de c.** *m.* string instrument

cuerno *m.* horn

CH

chiflar *v.* to whistle

D

danza *f.* dance; **d. folclórica** folk dance; **d. moderna** modern dance; **d. latinoamericana** Latin dance; **d. social** social dance

danzar *v.* to dance

decorado *m.* set design

desafinado, -da *adj.* out of tune

deslizarse *v.* to slide, glide

deslucir *v.* to upstage

detrás de bastidores *adv.* backstage

diálogo *m.* dialogue

dicción *f.* diction

dinámica *f.* dynamics *pl.*

dirección *f.* direction

director, -ora *m.f.* director; **d. de orquesta** conductor

BELLAS ARTES

BELLAS ARTES

dirigir *v.* (música) to conduct
disciplina artística *f.* art form
discordante *adj.* out of tune
diseño *m.* design; **d. de escenografía** set design
disonancia *f.* dissonance
doblado, -da *adj.* (cine) dubbed
drama *m.* drama
dramático, -ca *adj.* dramatic
dramatización *f.* dramatization
dramatizar *v.* to dramatize
dramaturgo, -ga *m.f.* playwright
dulcémele *m.* dulcimer
dúo *m.* duet
duración *f.* duration

E

eclipsar *v.* to upstage
eco *m.* echo
efectos de sonido *m.pl.* sound effects
ejecutar *v.* (música) to perform
electrónico, -ca *adj.* electronic
embellesimiento *m.* embellishment
emoción *f.* emotion
emocional *adj.* emotional
empatía *f.* empathy
encasillamiento actoral *m.* typecasting
énfasis *m.* emphasis
ensayar *v.* to rehearse, practice
ensayo *m.* rehearsal, practice; **e. general** dress rehearsal
entonación *f.* intonation
entrada *f.* (escena) entrance
entre bastidores *adv.* backstage, offstage

enunciación *f.* enunciation
equilibrar *v.* to balance
equilibrio *m.* balance
escala *f.* scale
escena *f.* stage, scenery, scene; **llamado a e.** *m.* curtain call; **poner en e.** *v.* to stage
escenario *m.* stage, scenario; **al centro del e.** *adv.* center stage; **fuera de e.** offstage; **hacia el fondo del e.** upstage; **hacia el frente del e.** downstage; **lado derecho del e.** *m.* stage right; **lado izquierdo del e.** stage left; **sobre el e.** *adv.* onstage
escenificar *v.* to stage
escenografía *f.* (teatro, cine) set, scenery
escritor, -ora *m.f.* writer
espacial *adj.* spatial
espacio *m.* space
espiritual *adj.* spiritual
estética *f.* aesthetics
estilo *m.* style
estirarse *v.* to stretch
estreno *m.* premiere, opening night
estribillo *m.* refrain, chorus
estructura *f.* structure
exposición *f.* exposition
expresión *f.* expression

F

fagot, fagote *m.* bassoon
farsa *f.* farce
filarmonía *f.* love of music
flauta *f.* flute; **f. dulce** recorder
flexibilidad *f.* flexibility

flotar *v.* to float
folclórico, -ca *adj.* folk
forma *f.* form; **f. tradicionales de arte** *pl.* traditional art forms
fracasar *v.* (danza) to collapse
frase musical *f.* musical phrase
fuerza *f.* force
función *f.* performance

G

gaita *f.* bagpipe
género *m.* genre
gesto *m.* gesture
girar *v.* to swing
giro *m.* spinning
gospel *m.* (música) gospel
grabación *f.* recording; **g. en cinta** tape recording
grabadora *f.* recorder; **g. digital** digital recorder
grupo *m.* band
guiar *v.* (danza) to lead
guión *m.* scenario
guitarra *f.* guitar; **g. acústica** acoustic guitar; **g. clásica** classical guitar; **g. eléctrica** electric guitar
guitarrista *m.f.* guitarist

H

herencia *f.* heritage
himno *m.* hymn
historia *f.* story
humor negro *m.* black humor

I

iluminación *f.* lighting
imitar *v.* to mimic

improvisadamente *adv.* ad-lib
improvisar *v.* to ad-lib
improvisación *f.* improvisation, ad-lib; **i. vocal** scat
inflexión *f.* inflection
instrumentación *f.* instrumentation
instrumento *m.* instrument; **familia de instrumentos** *f.* instrument family; **i. acústico** acoustic instrument; **i. de cuerdas** string instrument; **i. de percusión** percussion instrument; **i. de teclas** keyboard instrument; **i. de viento** wind instrument; **i. de viento-madera** woodwind; **i. de viento-metal** brass instrument; **i. electrónico** electronic instrument
intermedio *m.* intermission
interpretación *f.* interpretation
interpretar *v.* (danza, teatro) to perform
intérprete *m.f.* (música) performer, singer
intervalo *m.* (música) step, interval

J

jazz *m.* jazz
jefe de piso *m.* stage manager

K

kinestésico, -ca *adj.* kinesthetic; **inteligencia k.** *f.* kinesthetic awareness

L

lectura dramatizada *f.* dramatic reading

BELLAS ARTES

365

letra *f.,* **letras** *f.pl.* lyrics
libreto *m.* libretto, script
ligadura *f.* (música) slur, tie
línea *f.* line; **l. adicional** ledger line;
  l. del cuento storyline
lírico, -ca *adj.* lyrical
locomoción *f.* locomotion
locomotor, -ora, -triz *adj.* (danza)
  locomotor; **no l.** nonlocomotor
locución *f.* diction

LL

llamada y respuesta *f.* call and response
llamado a escena *m.* curtain call

M

malapropismo *m.* malapropism
mandolina *f.* mandolin
maquillaje *m.* makeup
maquillar *v.* to apply makeup
maracas *f.pl.* maracas
marcha *f.* march
marimba *f.* marimba
marioneta *f.* marionette, puppet
máscara *f.* mask
media C *f.* middle C
medida *f.* (música) measure
**medios de difusión, medios de
  comunicación** *m.pl.* mass media
melodía *f.* tune, melody
melodrama *m.* melodrama
metrónomo *m.* metronome
mezzosoprano *f.* (cantante) mezzosoprano
mezzosoprano *m.* (voz) mezzosoprano

miedo escénico *m.* stagefright
mímica *f.,* **mimo** *m.* mime
mirlitón *m.* kazoo
mito *m.* myth
mitología *f.* mythology
modalidad artística *f.* art form
modo *m.* mood
monólogo *m.* monologue
monótono *m.,* **monotonía** *f.* monotone
montaje *m.* (teatro) blocking
motivación *f.* motivation
motivo *m.* (música, teatro) motif,
  theme
movimiento *m.* movement
¡mucha mierda! (modismo de
  teatro) break a leg!
música *f.* music; **m. contemporánea** contemporary music; **m.
  country** country music; **m. en cuatro partes** music in four parts;
  m. folclórica, m. folk folk music;
  m. pop pop; **m. reggae** reggae;
  m. rock rock music; **poner al
  ritmo de la m.** *v.* to set to music
musical *adj. & m.* musical; **m. de
  Broadway** Broadway musical
músico, -ca *m.f.* musician

N

narrador, -ra *m.f.* narrator, storyteller
narrativa *f.* narrative
negra *f.* quarter note
nivel *m.* level
noche de estreno *f.* opening night

nota *f.* note; **n. discordante** discordant note; **n. punteada** dotted note

O

oboe *m.* oboe

obra *f.* work of art, play; **o. en un acto** one-act play

octava *f.* octave

ópera *f.* opera

organillo *m.* barrel organ

organista *m.f.* organist

órgano *m.* organ

orquesta *f.* orchestra; **o. de cámara** chamber orchestra; **o. de cuerdas** string orchestra; **o. de vientos** band; **o. filarmónica** philharmonic orchestra

oscuro *m.* (teatro) black-out

P

pandereta *f.* tambourine

pantomima *f.* pantomime

papel *m.* (teatro) role; **asignar un p., dar un p.** *v.* to cast; **p. secundario** bit part

pareja *f.* partner

partitura *f.* (música) score; **p. instrumental** instrumental score; **p. vocal** vocal score

paso *m.* (danza) step

payasadas *f.pl.* slapstick

película *f.* film; **p. de terror** horror film

pentagrama *m.* (música) staff

pentatónico, -ca *adj..* pentatonic; **escala p.** *f.* pentatonic scale

percusión *f.* percussion; **p. de mano** hand drum

percusivo, -va *adj.* percussive

personaje *m.* character

pianista *m.f.* pianist

piano *m.* piano

pícaro *m.* trickster

pie *m.*(teatro) cue; **dar la p.** *v.* to cue

pieza *f.* (música, teatro) piece, play; **p. moralista** morality play

pillo *m.* trickster

pito *m.* whistle

platillo *m.* cymbal

plica *f.* (anotación música) stem

polifónico, -ca *adj.* polyphonic

postura *f.* posture

práctica *f.* practice

practicar *v.* to practice

preestreno *m.* preview

presagiar *v.* to foreshadow

presentación *f.* presentation

producción *f.* production

productor *m.f.* producer

progresión *f.* progression; **p. de acordes** chord progression

prólogo *m.* prologue

proscenio *m.* downstage, proscenium stage

protagonista *m.f.* protagonist

proyección *f.* projection; **sala de p.** *f.* movie theater

público *m.* audience

pulso *m.* (música) beat

Q

quinteto *m.* quintet

BELLAS ARTES

BELLAS ARTES

R

rasguear *v.* (cuerdas) to strum
redonda *f.* whole note
reflejando, -da *adj.* mirroring
registro *m.* register, range
reparto *m.* (teatro) cast, casting
repentizar *v.* (música) to sight-read, improvise
repertorio *m.* repertoire
repetición *f.* (música) repeat sign
representación *f.* role-play
representar *v.* to stage, role-play
respiración *f.* breathing; **control de la r.** *m.* breath control
respuesta emocional *f.* emotional response
retórica *f.* rhetoric
reverencia *f.* (ballet) bow; **hacer una r.** *v.* to bow
ritmo *m.* rhythm
rock *m.* rock music, rock 'n roll
romántico, -ca *adj.* romantic
rondó *m.* rondo
rutina cómica *f.* stand-up routine, comedy routine

S

sala *f.* (teatro) auditorium, house
salida *f.* (teatro) exit
saltar *v.* to skip, leap
salterio *m.* dulcimer
sátira *f.* satire
satírico, -ca *adj.* satirical
saxofón, saxófono *m.* saxophone
secuencia *f.* sequence
seguir *v.* (danza) to follow
semicorchea *f.* sixteenth note

silbar *v.* to whistle
silbato *m.* whistle
silencio *m.* (música) rest; **s. de blanca** half-note rest; **s. de redonda** whole-note rest
símbolo *m.* symbol
sincopado, -da *adj.* syncopated
síncope *m.* syncopation
sincronización *m.* (danza) timing
sinfonía *f.* symphony
sintetizador *m.* synthesizer
sitar *m.* sitar
sketch cómico *m.* comedy sketch
soliloquio *m.* soliloquy
solista *m.f.* soloist
solo *m.* solo
sonata *f.* sonata
sonido *m.* sound; **efectos de s.** *m.pl.* sound effects; **s. electrónico** electronic sound
soprano *m.* soprano
sostener *v.* to sustain
sostenido *adj.* (música) sharp
soul *m.* soul music
square dance *f.* square dance
suave *adj.* smooth
subargumento *m.* subplot
subtítulos *m.pl.* (cine) subtitles
suite *f.* (música) suite
superhéroe *m.*, **superheroína** *f.* superhero
suplente *m.f.* understudy
suspenso *m.* suspense
swing *m.* (música) swing

T

tambalear *v.* to sway

tambor *m.* drum; **t. grave** bass drum

tambora *f.* bass drum

tap *m.* tap dance

taquilla *f.* ticket office

tarola *f.* snare drum

teatro *m.* theater; **t. arena** arena stage; **t. circular** arena stage; **t. de carpa** vaudeville; **t. de escenario central, t. en la rotonda** theater-in-the-round; **t. de niños, t. infantil** children's theater; **t. de variedad** vaudeville; **T. Leído** Readers Theater; **t. moralista** morality play; **t. musical** musical theater; **t. participativo** participation theater

tecladista *m.f.* keyboardist

teclado *m.* keyboard

técnica *f.* technique

tema *f.* theme, motif

tenor *m.* tenor

tensión *f.* tension

tiempo *m.* (música) beat, tempo

timbal *m.* kettledrum

timbales *m.pl.* timpani

timbre *m.* timbre

tímpano *m.* timpani

títere *m.* puppet; **t. de mano** hand puppet

titiritero, -ra *m.f.* puppeteer

tocar de oído *v.* to play by ear

tonalidad *f.* tonality, key

tono *m.* (música) key, pitch, tone; **t. mayor** major key; **t. menor** minor key; **t. vocal** vocal pitch

tradición oral *f.* oral tradition

tragedia *f.* tragedy

trama *f.* storyline, plot

tramoyista *m.* stage hand

transición *f.* transition

tras bambalinas *adv.* backstage, offstage

traste *m.* (guitarra) fret

tresillo *m.* (música) triplet

triángulo *m.* triangle

trío *m.* trio

trombón *m.* trombone

trompa *f.* horn

trompeta *f.* trumpet

tuba *f.* tuba

U

unísono *m.* unison

ukelele *m.* ukulele

utilería *f.* (teatro) prop

V

vals *m.* waltz

vanguardismo *m.f.* avant-garde

vanguardista *m.f.* avant-garde artist

variación *f.* variation

verso *m.* verse

vestuario *m.* costume

villano *m.* villain

viola *f.* viola

violín *m.* violin

violinista *m.f.* violinist

violonchelista *m.f.* cellist

violonchelo *m.* cello

vocal *f.* vocal

vodevil *m.* vaudeville

volumen *m.* volume

voz *f.* voice

BELLAS ARTES

X

xilófono *m.* xylophone

Z

zampoña *f.* pan pipe

Artes Plásticas

BELLAS ARTES

A

abalorio *m.* bead
abstracto, -ta *adj.* abstract
acolchar *v.* to quilt
acuarela *f.* watercolor
afiche *m.* poster
aguafuerte *m.* etching
alambre *m.* wire
alfarería *f.* pottery
animación *f.* animation
arcilla *f.* clay
arquitectura *f.* architecture
arte *m.f.* art; **a. folclórico** folk art;
    a. manual craft; **a. público** public
    art; **a. gráficas** *pl.* graphic arts;
    material de a. *m.* art material;
    obra de a. *f.* artwork; **ojeto de a.**
    m. artifact
artefacto *m.* artifact
artesanía *f.* arts and crafts
artista *m.f* artist
asimetría *f.* asymmetry
asimétrico, -ca *adj.* asymmetrical
autoretrato *m.* self-portrait

B

barro *m.* clay
bata *f.* smock
bloc de dibujos *m.* sketchbook

blusón, -sa *m.f.* smock
bosquejo *m.* sketch
borrador *m.* eraser
brocha *f.* brush

C

caballete *m.* easel
cable *m.* wire
caja de pinturas *f.* paint box
calcamonía *f.* decal, sticker
calco *m.* rubbing
caligrafía *f.* caligraphy
calígrafo, -fa *m.f.* caligrapher
cámara *f.* camera
capa *f.* (de pintura) wash
carboncillo *m.* charcoal
caricatura *f.* caricature, cartoon
cartel *m.* poster
cartón *m.* cardboard
cartoncillo para manualidades *m.*
    construction paper
cera *f.* wax
cerámica *f.* ceramic
cinta adhesiva protectora *f.* mask-
    ing tape
cobre *m.* (metal) copper
cocer *v.* (cerámica) to fire
colcha *f.* quilt; **hacer una c.** *v.* to
    quilt
colocación *f.* placement

● ●

color *m.* color; **esquema del c.** *f.* color scheme; **variación del c.** *f.* color variation

colorear *v.* to color

colores cálidos *m.pl.* warm colors; **c. complementarios** complementary colors; **c. frescos** cool colors; **c. intermedios** intermediate colors; **c. neutrales** neutral colors; **c. pasteles** pastel colors; **c. primarios** primary colors; **c. secundarios** secondary colors; **c. suaves** soft colors; **c. terciarios** teriary colors

collage *m.* collage

combinación *f.* blend

combinar *v.* to blend

componer *v.* to compose

composición *f.* composition

concepto visual *m.* visual concept

construcción *f.* construction

contorno *m.* contour

contraste *m.* contrast

copia *f.* (fotografía) print

crayón *m.* crayon

cristal *m.* crystal, glass

cuaderno de bosquejos *m.* sketchbook

cuadro *m.* picture, canvas, square

cuenta de vitrio *f.* glass bead

CH

chaquira *f.* bead

D

dibujante *m.* cartoonist

dibujar *v.* to draw

dibujo *m.* drawing, picture; **d. de contorno** contour drawing; **d. animados** *pl.* cartoons

dimensión *f.* dimension

diorama *m.* diorama

direccionalidad *f.* directionality

diseño *m.* design; **d. gráfico** graphic design

doblado, -da *adj.* folded

doblar *v.* to fold

doblez *m.* fold

E

efectos especiales *m.pl.* special effects

enrollar *v.* to coil

entintado, -da *adj.* dyed

entintar *v.* to dye

equilibrado, -da *adj.* balanced

equilibrar *v.* to balance

equilibrio *m.* balance

esculpir *v.* to sculpt

escultor, -ra *m.f.* sculptor

escultura *f.* sculpture; **e. a relieve** relief sculpture

esmaltar *v.* to enamel, glaze

esmalte *m.* enamel

espacio *m.* space; **e. negativo** negative space; **e. positivo** positive space

espiral *f.* spiral

estilo *m.* style

estilizado, -da *adj.* stylized

estuco *m.* stucco

exhibición *f.* display

exhibir *v.*, **exponer** *v.* to display

exposición *f.* display

BELLAS ARTES

BELLAS ARTES

F

fibra *f.* fiber

fondo *m.* background

forma *f.* form, shape; **f. geométrica** geometric shape

formato *m.* format

foto *f.*, **fotografía** *f.* photograph, photography

fotografiar *v.* to photograph

fotográfico, -ca *adj.* photographic; **visor f.** *m.* viewer

fotógrafo, -fa *m.f.* photographer

franja *f.* fringe

fresco *m.* fresco

fundición *f.* (procedimiento) casting, blend

fundido, -da *adj.* melted, cast; **pieza f.** *f.* (objeto) casting

fundir *v.* to cast, blend

G

gama *f.* spectrum

geométrico, -ca *adj.* geometric

gis *m.* chalk

goma de pegar *f.* glue

grabado *m.* photographic print, etching, engraving

grabar *v.* to engrave

guardapolvo *m.* smock

H

historietas *f.pl.* comics, comic book, comic strip

hojalata *f.* (metal) tin

horizontal *adj.* horizontal

horizonte *m.* horizon

horno *m.* (cerámica) kiln

I

iluminar *v.* to highlight

ilusión *f.* illusion; **i. óptica** optical illusion

imagen *f.* image, picture

impresión *f.* (tipografía) printing; **i. fotográfica** print

imprimir *v.* to print

intensidad *f.* intensity

L

lápiz *m.* pencil; **l. de color** colored pencil

lienzo *m.* canvas

losa *f.* slab

M

madera *f.* wood

mano *f.* (pintura) wash

máscara *f.* mask

material de arte *f.* art material

matiz *m.* shading, hue

matizar *v.* to shade, tint

medida disminuida *f.* diminishing size

medio, -dia *adj.* medium

metal *m.* metal

mezcla *f.* blend, mix, collage

mezclar *v.* to mix, blend

miniatura *f.* (pintura) miniature; **esbozo en m.** *m.* thumbnail sketch

monocromático, -ca *adj.* monochromatic

mosaico *m.* mosaic

mural *m.* mural

muralista *m.f.* muralist

museo *m.* museum

N

naturaleza muerta *f.* still life

O

obra de arte *f.* artwork
ojeto de arte *m.* artifact
óleo *m.* oil, oil paint

P

paisaje *m.* landscape; **p. marino** seascape; **p. urbano** cityscape
paleta *f.* (de pintor) palette
papel *m.* paper; **p. de construcción** construction paper, drawing paper; **p. de Manila** Manila paper; **p. encerado** wax paper; **p. maché** papier mâché
parafina *f.* paraffin wax
paralelo, -la *adj.* parallel
patrón *m.* pattern; **p. aleatorio** random pattern; **p. estructurado** ordered pattern
pegar *v.* to glue
película *f.* (photographic) film
perspectiva *f.* perspective; **p. aérea** aerial perspective
piedra *f.* stone
pincel *m.* brush
pintar *v.* to paint
pintor, -ra *m.f.* painter
pintura *f.* paint, painting; **caja de pinturas** *f.* paintbox; **p. al óleo** oil paint; **p. al temple** tempera paint; **p. mural** mural; **p. al pastel** *pl.* pastels
plástico *m.* plastic
plegado, -da *adj.* folded

plegar *v.* to fold
pliegue *m.* fold
portafolio *m.* portfolio
primer plano *m.* foreground
profundidad *f.* depth
proporción *f.* proportion

R

realismo *m.* realism
realista *adj.* realistic
reducción dimensional *f.* diminishing size
representativo, -va *adj.* representational; **no r.** nonrepresentational
resaltar *v.* to highlight
resalte *m.* highlight
retratista *m.f.* portrait painter, portrait photographer
retrato *m.* portrait

S

serigrafía *f.* silk-screen painting; **hacer s.** *v.* to silk-screen
simbolizar *v.* to symbolize
símbolo *m.* symbol
simetría *f.* symmetry
simétrico, -ca *adj.* symmetrical
sombra *f.* shadow; **contorno de s.** *m.* shadow edge
sombreado *m.* shading
superponer *v.* to overlap

T

tamaño *m.* size
tebeos *m.pl.* comics, comic book, comic strip
técnica de brocha seca *f.* dry-brush

BELLAS ARTES

373

tejer *v.* to weave
tejido *m.* weaving, cloth, fabric
tejedor, -ora *m.f.* weaver
tejedura *f.* (action) weaving
telar *m.* loom
teñido anudado *m.* tie-dye
teñir *v.* to dye
terracota *f.* terra cotta
textura *f.* texture
tijeras *f.pl.* scissors
tinta *f.* ink, dye, dyeing
tinte *m.* dyeing, tinting
tinto, -ta *adj.* dyed
tipografía *f.* typography
tiras cómicas *f.pl.* comics, comic book, comic strip
tiza *f.* chalk; **escribir con t.** *v.* to chalk
tonalidad *f.* (en color) hue

toque de luz *m.* highlight
traslapar *v.* to overlap
trípode *m.* tripod

U
ubicación *f.* placement

V
vertical *adj.* vertical
vidriado, -da *adj.* glazed
vidriado *m.* glaze
vidriar *v.* to glaze
vidrio *m.* glass
visor fotográfico *m.* viewer

Y
yesero, -ra *m.f.* plasterer
yeso *m.* plaster
yesoso, -sa *adj.* chalky

COLORES

aguamarina *f.* aquamarine
amarillo, -lla *adj.* yellow
amarillo *m.* yellow
anaranjado, -da *adj.* orange
anaranjado *m.* orange
añil *adj. & m.* indigo
azul *adj. & m.* blue; **a. marino** navy blue
blanco, -ca *adj.* white
blanco *m.* white
caoba *f.* mahogany
cián *adj. & m.* cyan
ciruela *adj. & f.* plum
cobrizo, -za *adj.* copper
color carne *m.* flesh color; **c. cobri-**

zo copper; **c. dorado** golden; **c. vino tinto, c. borgoña** burgundy
colorado, -da *adj.* red
colorado *m.* red
dorado, -da *adj.* golden
escarlata *adj. & m.* scarlet
granate *adj. & m.* maroon, crimson
gris *adj. & m.* gray
lavanda *adj. & f.* lavender
magenta *adj. & f.* magenta
marrón *adj. & m.* brown; **m. claro** light brown, tan; **m. oscuro** dark brown
morado, -da *adj.* purple
morado *m.* purple

• •

negro, -gra *adj.* black
negro *m.* black
plata *f.* silver
plateado *adj.* silver
púrpura *adj. & m.* purple
rojo, -ja *adj. & m.* red
rosa *adj. & m.* pink, rose

rosado, -da *adj.* pink
salmón *adj. & m.* salmon
sepia *adj. & m.* sepia
turquesa *adj. & m.* turquoise
violeta *adj. & m.* violet
verde *adj. & m..* green; **v. azulado** teal; **v. esmeralda** emerald

FORMAS

arqueado, -da *adj.* curved, bent
bidimensional *adj.* two-dimensional
cilíndrico, -ca *adj.* cylindrical
cilindro *m.* cylinder
circular *adj.* circular
círculo *m.* circle
cónico, -ca *adj.* conical
cono *m.* cone
cruzado, -da *adj.* intersecting
cuadrado, -da *adj.* square
cuadrado *m.,* **cuadro** *m.* square
cúbico, -ca *adj.* cubic
cubo *m.* cube
curva *f.* curve
curvo, -va *adj.* curved, bent
diagonal *adj. & f.* diagonal
esfera *f.* sphere
esférico, -ca *adj.* spherical
hexagonal *adj.* hexagonal
hexágono *m.* hexagon
intersecado, -da *adj.* intersecting
línea *f.* line; **l. de contorno** contour line; **l. recta** straight line; **l. con-**

vergentes *pl.* converging lines; **l. intersecadas** intersecting lines
lineal *adj.* linear
octagonal *adj.* octagonal
octágono, octógono *m.* octagon
ondeado, -da *adj.* wavy
pentagonal *adj.* pentagonal
pentágono *m.* pentagon
piramidal *adj.* piramidal
pirámide *f.* pyramid
punteado, -da *adj.* dotted
puntillo *m.* small dot
punto *m.* dot
rectangular *adj.* rectangular
rectángulo *m.* rectangle
recto, -ta *adj.* straight
triangular *adj.* triangular
triángulo *m.* triangle
tridimensional *adj.* three-dimensional
unidimensional *adj.* one-dimensional
zigzag *m.* zigzag
zigzaguear *v.* to zigzag

BELLAS ARTES

TECNOLOGÍA

A

acceder *v.* to access

acceso *m.* access; **a. a Internet** Internet access; **a. compartido** shared access

acecho *m.* lurking

actualización *f.* update

actualizado, -da *adj.* updated

actualizar *v.* to update, upgrade

adjuntar *v.* (email) to attach

agregar *v.* to add; **a. impresora** to add printer; **a. programa** to add program

ajuste de línea *m.* word wrap

alfombrilla *f.*, **almohadilla** *f.* mouse pad

alimentación *f.* supply, feed; **a. de papel** paper feed; **fuente de a.** *f.*, **suministro de a.** *m.* power supply

alinear *v.* to align

almacenamiento *m.* storage

almacenar *v.* to store

alta *adj.* high; **a. definición** *f.*, **a. resolución** *f.* high resolution; **a. velocidad** *f.* high speed

amplitud de banda *f.*, **ancho de banda** *m.* bandwidth

antiintrusos *m.* firewall

antivirus *adj. & m.* antivirus

apagado, -da *adj.* power off

aplicación *f.* application, software; **a. espía** spyware; **a. gratuita** shareware; **a. maligna** malware

apoyo *m.* backup

archivo *m.* file, archive; **a. adjunto** attached file; **a. compromido** compressed file; **a. de almacenamiento** storage archive

archivos *m.pl.* files; **borrado de a.** *m.*, **eliminación de a.** *f.* file deletion; **conversión de a.** *f.* file conversion; **servidor de a.** *m.* file server; **transferencia de a.** *f.* file transfer

arrastrar *v.* to drag; **a. y pegar** to drag and drop

arroba *f.* at sign (@)

ASCII *m.* ASCII

asunto *m.* (email) subject

atasco en el suministro de papel *m.* paper jam

auntenticación *f.* authentication

B

bajar *v.* to download

banda ancha *f.* broadband

bandeja *f.* box; **b. de correos enviados** sent box; **b. de entrada** inbox; **b. de salida** outbox

barra *f.* bar; **b. de desplazamiento** scroll bar; **b. de herramientas** toolbar; **b. de menú** menu bar; **b. inversa, b. invertida** backslash (\); **b. oblicua** slash (/)

base de datos *f.* database

batería *f.* battery

blog *m.* blog

bloquear *v.* to crash

bloqueo *m.* crash

borrado de archivos *m.* file deletion

borrar *v.* to delete, erase

botón *m.* button; **b. del ratón** mouse button; **b. para avanzar** forward button; **b. para regresar** back button

buscador *m.* search engine

buscar *v.* to search

búsqueda *f.* search; **motor de b., servidor de b.** *m.* search engine

buzón de correo *m.* mailbox

byte *m.* byte

C

caballo de Troya *m.* Trojan horse

cable *m.* cable

cámara web *f.* webcam

carga eléctrica estática *f.* static electricity charge

cargar *v.* to upload

carpeta *f.* folder; **nombre de la c.** *m.* folder name

cartucho *m.* cartridge

casilla *f.* box; **marcar la c., seleccionar la c.** *v.* to check the box

CD-ROM *m.* CD-ROM

cibercafé *m.* Internet cafe

ciberespacio *m.* cyberspace

cibernauta *m.f.* surfer

clave *f.* password

clic *m.* click; **hacer c.** *v.* to click

codificación *f.* encryption

codificado, -da *adj.;* **cifrado, -da** *adj.* encrypted

codificar *v.,* **cifrar** *v.* to encrypt

compatible *adj.* compatible

compresión *f.* compression

comprimir *v.* to zip

computación *f.* computing; **c. en la nube** cloud computing

computadora *f.,* **computador** *m.* computer; **aprendizaje por c.** *m.* computer-based learning; **chip de c.** *m.* computer chip; **c. portátil** laptop computer

conectado, -da *adj.* online

conectar *v.* to connect

conexión *f.* connection; **c. de redes** networking

congelamiento *m.* crash

congelar *v.* to crash

contrabarra *f.* backslash (\)

contraseña *f.* password

controlador de dispositivo *m.* (aplicación) driver

conversión de archivos *f.* file conversion

convertir *v.* to convert

TECNOLOGÍA

cookies *f.pl.* cookies

copia de seguridad *f.* backup; **hacer una c. de s.** *v.* to back up

copiar *v.* to copy

cortafuegos *m.* firewall

cortar y pegar *v.* to cut and paste

correo *m.* mail; **buzón de c.** *m.* mailbox; **c. caracol** snail mail; **c. electrónico** email; **c. basura** junk mail, spam; **c. cifrado, c. codificado** encrypted email; **c. de voz** voice mail; **enviar un c. electrónico** *v.* to email; **revisar el c. electrónico** check email

correr *v.* (aplicación) to run

corriente *f.* power; **fallo de c.** *m.* power failure

cuenta de usuario *f.* user account

cursiva *adj. & f.* italic

cursor *m.* cursor

CH

charla *f.*, **chateo** *m.* chat; **sala de c.** *f.* chat room

charlar, chatear *v.* to chat; **c. en tiempo real** to chat in real time

D

dañado, -da *adj.* corrupted

datos *m.pl.* data; **base de d.** *f.* database

defecto *m.* bug

descarga *f.* download

descargar *v.* to download

desconectado, -da *adj.* offline

desinstalar *v.* to uninstall

destinatario *m.* email recipient

diagnóstico, -ca *adj.* diagnostic

diagnóstico *m.* diagnosis; **programa de d.** *m.* diagnostic program

digital *adj.* digital; **firma d.** *f.* digital signature

dirección *f.* address; **d. de correo electrónico** email address; **d. de Web** web page address; **d. Web** U.R.L.; **libreta de d.** *f.pl.* address book

directorio *m.* directory

disco *m.*, **disquete** *m.* disk; **d. de inicio** boot disk; **d. de respaldo** backup disk; **d. de sistema** system disk; **d. de seguridad** backup disk; **d. duro** hard disk, hard drive; **d. flexible** floppy disk; **lector de d.** *m.*, **unidad de d.** *f.* disk drive

diseño de página *m.* page layout

dispositivo *m.* device; **d. físico** hardware; **d. periférico** peripheral device; **d. portátil de memoria** flash drive, memory stick

disquetera *f.* disk drive

documento *m.* document

dominio *m.* domain; **d. público** public domain

E

ejecutar *v.* (aplicación) to run

elementos eliminados *m.pl.* (email) deleted items

eliminar *v.* to remove; **e. elemento** to remove item; **e. programa** to remove program

eliminación de archivos *f.* file deletion

●●●

email *m.* email

en línea *adj.* online

encendido, -da *adj.* power on

encriptación *f.* encryption

enchufar y usar *m. & v.* plug and play

energía *f.* power

enlace *m.* link

error *m.* error; **e. lógico** bug

escanear *v.* to scan

escáner *m.* scanner

escoger *v.* to select

escritorio *m.* (ordenador) desktop

etiqueta de Internet *f.* netiquette

explorador de Web *m.* browser

exportar *v.* to export

extensión *f.* extension

externo, -na *adj.* external; **memoria e.** *f.* external memory

F

fallo *m.* bug; **f. de alimentación, f. de corriente** power failure

favorito *m.* (Web) bookmark

fax *m.*, **facsímil** *m.* fax; **aparato de f.** *m.*, **equipo de f.** *m.* fax machine; **enviar un f.** *v.* to fax, send a fax

fichero *m.* file

firma digital *f.* digital signature

fondo *m.* background

formatear *v.* to format

formato *m.* format; **f. de fuente, f. de letra** (negrita o itálicas) type format

formulario *m.* form

fotocopia *f.* photocopy

fotocopiadora *f.* photocopier

fotocopiar *v.* to photocopy

fuente *f.* font

fuera de servicio *adj.* (enlace) out of service, dead, nonfunctioning

G

gigahertz *m.* gigahertz

grabación *f.* recording; **g. digital** digital recording

grabadora *f.* recorder

grabar *v.* to record

gráficos *m.pl.* graphics

grupo de noticias *m.* newsgroup

guardar *v.* (documento) to save

gusano *m.* worm

H

hacker *m.f.* hacker

hertz *m.* hertz

hipervínculo *m.*, **hiperenlace** *m.* hyperlink

hoja de cálculo *f.* spreadsheet

I

ícono *m.* icon; **í. de cerradura** (en un sitio Web seguro) padlock

imagen *f.* image

importar *v.* to import

impresora *f.* printer; **controlador de i.** *m.* printer driver; **i. de chorro de tinta** inkjet printer; **i. láser** laser printer

imprimir *v.* to print

inalámbrico, -ca *adj.* wireless; **señal i.** *f.* wireless signal; **red i.** *f.* wireless network

incorporado, -da *adj.* built-in

insertar *v.* to insert

TECNOLOGÍA

instalar *v.* to install
interface *f.* interfaz
Internet *m.* Internet
interno, -na *adj.* internal
I.S.P. *m.* Internet service provider
itálicas *f.pl.* italics

K

kilobyte *m.* kilobyte

L

LAN *f.* (red de área local) LAN
L.C.D. *f.* L.C.D.
lector de disco *m.* disk drive
libreta de direcciones *f.* address book
listserv *m.* listserv
lurker *m.f.* lurker
lurking *m.* lurking

M

marcador *m.,* **marcapáginas** *m.* bookmark
marcos *m.pl.* (página Web) frames
maximizar *v.* to maximize
megabyte *m.* megabyte
megahertz *m.* megahertz
memoria *f.* memory; **m. externa** external memory; **m. extraible, m. removible** flash drive, memory stick; **m. virtual** virtual memory
mensaje *m.* message; **encabezado de m.** *m.* message heading; **m. adjunto, m. anexo** email attachment; **m. instantáneo** instant messaging (I.M.); **m. saliente** out-

going message
mensaje de texto *m.* text message, texting; **enviar un m. de t., mandar un m. de t.** *v.* to text, to send a text; **redactar un m. de t.** *v.* to compose a text
menú *m.* menu; **barra de m.** memory bar *f.;* **m. contextual, m. desplegable** pop-up menu, drop-down list
microprocesador *m.* computer chip
miniatura de una imagen *f.* thumbnail
minimizar *v.* to minimize
módem *m.* modem
monitor *m.* monitor; **m. de color** color monitor
monocromo, -ma *adj.;* **monocromático, -ca** *adj.* monochrome
multimedia *adj. & f.* multimedia
multitarea *f.* multitasking
muro de fuegos *m.* firewall

N

navegador *m.* browser
navegar *v.* to navigate, surf
negrita *f.* (tipo) bold, boldface
nombre *m.* name; **n. de la carpeta** folder name; **n. de usuario** user name; **n. del archivo** filename

O

oculto, -ta *adj.* hidden
opción por defecto, opción predeterminada *f.* default
ordenador *m.* computer; **o. portátil** laptop computer

TECNOLOGÍA

P

página *f.* page; **diseño de p.** *m.* page layout; **p. raíz, p. inicial, p. principal** home page; **p. principal** main page; **p. Web** Web page

palabra clave *f.* keyword

panel de control *m.* control panel

pantalla *f.* screen, desktop; **p. digital interactiva** smart board; **protector de p.** *m.* screensaver

papel *m.* paper; **atasco en el suministro de p.** *m.* paper jam

papelera de reciclaje *f.* recycling bin

paquete de programas *m.* applications package

participante silencioso (-sa) *m.f.* lurker

pegar *v.* to paste

pestaña *f.* tab

pila *f.* battery

pirata informático (-ca) *m.f.* hacker

piratería informática *f.* hacking

pizarra digital interactiva *f.* smart board

plantilla *f.* template

portal *m.* portal

portapapeles *m.* clipboard

preferencias *f.pl.* preferences

preguntas frecuentes *f.pl.* frequently asked questions (F.A.Q.)

presionar *v.* to click

previa en miniatura *f.* thumbnail preview

privacidad *f.* privacy

procesador *m.* processor; **p. de texto** word processor

procesamiento de texto *m.* word processing

programa *m.* software, program; **p. de diagnóstico** diagnostic program; **p. espía** spyware; **p. gratuito** shareware; **p. maligno** malware

programar *v.* to program

proveedor de servicios Internet *m.* Internet service provider (I.S.P.)

puerto *m.* port; **p. de serie** serial port; **p. U.S.B.** U.S.B. port

pulsar *v.* to click; **p. una tecla** to press a key

punto com *m.* dot com

Q

quemador *m.* burner

R

RAM *f.* RAM

ratón *m.* mouse

rebotar *v.* (email) to bounce back

rebote *m.* bounce

recuperar *v.* to recover, undelete; **r. la base de datos** to retrieve database

red *f.* network; **r. social** social network

Red *f.* Internet; **R. informática mundial** World Wide Web

redactar *v.* to compose

reemplazar *v.* to replace

reemplazo *m.* replacement

regresar *v.* to go back

rehacer *v.* to redo

reiniciar *v.* to reboot

remoto, -ta *adj.* remote

reparar *v.* to repair

TECNOLOGÍA

respaldo *m.* backup; **disco de r.** *m.* backup disk

responder *v.* to reply; **r. a todos** to reply to all

restaurar *v.* to undelete, restore

S

sala de charla, sala de discusión *f.* chat room

salir *v.* to quit

salvar *v.* to save (documento)

seguro, -ra *adj.* secure

seleccionar *v.* to select

servidor *m.* server; **s. de archivos** file server; **s. de listas** listserv; **s. seguro, s. protegido** secure server

sistema *m.* system; **s. operativo** operating system

sitio Web *m.* Web site; **s. Web seguro** secure Web site

spam *m.* spam

subcarpeta *f.* subfolder

subir *v.* to upload

submenú *m.* submenu

suscribirse *v.* to subscribe

T

tablero de mando *m.* control panel

tableta *f.,* **tablet** *m.* tablet

tabulación *f.* tabbing

tabular *v.* to tabulate

tarjeta *f.* card; **t. madre** motherboard

tecla *f.* key

teclado *m.* keyboard

teléfono celular, teléfono móvil *m.* cell phone

texto *m.* text; **redactar un t.** *v.* to compose a text

tinta *f.* ink

tipografía *f.* typeface

tipo de letra *m.* font, typeface

transferencia *f.* transfer; **de t. continua** *adj.* streaming; **t. de ficheros, t. de archivos** *f.* file transfer

troyano *m.* Trojan horse

U

U.C.P. *m.* C.P.U.

U.R.L. *f.* U.R.L.

unidad de disco *f.* disk drive

usuario *m.* user; **cuenta de u.** *f.* user account; **nombre de u.** *m.* user name

V

ventana *f.* window; **v. emergente** pop-up window

video *m.* video; **cinta de v.** *f.* videotape; **v. clip** *m.* video clip; **v. llamada** *f.* video call

VRAM *m.* VRAM

videocámara *f.* camcorder

videoconferencia *f.* videoconferencing

videojuego *m.* video game

vínculo *m.* link

virtual *adj.* virtual

virus *m.* virus

W

web *f.* Web

Wi-Fi *m.* Wi-Fi

VIDA ESCOLAR

Fiestas y Celebraciones

• •

AÑO NUEVO *m.* New Year

aclamaciones *f.pl.* cheers

brindis *m.* toast

buenos propósitos *m.pl.* resolution

confeti *m.* confetti

cuenta regresiva *f.* countdown

cuetes *m.pl.* fireworks

champaña *m.* champagne

Día de año nuevo *m.* New Year's Day

¡feliz año nuevo! *m.* Happy New Year!

filo de la medianoche *m.* stroke of midnight

fuegos artificiales *m.pl.* fireworks

serpentina *f.* streamer

Víspera de año nuevo *f.* New Year's Eve

CUMPLEAÑOS *m.* birthday

anfitriones *m.pl.* hosts

dulces dieciséis *m.pl.* Sweet Sixteen

fiesta party *f.;* **f. de cumpleaños** birthday party; **f. de quince** fifteenth birthday celebration; **f. sorpresa** surprise party

globos *m.pl.* balloons

invitaciones *f.pl.* invitations

invitados *m.pl.* guests

juegos *m.pl.* games

notas de agradecimiento *f.pl.* thank you notes

pastel de cumpleaños *m.* birthday cake

pedir un deseo *v.* to make a wish

quinceañera *f.* fifteenth birthday celebration

regalo de cumpleaños *m.* birthday present

tarta de cumpleaños *f.* birthday cake

DÍA DE ACCIÓN DE GRACIAS *f.* Thanksgiving

agradecido (-da) por *adj.* thankful for

arándano *m.* cranberry

batata *f.,* **boniato** *m.* yam

dar las gracias *v.* to say grace

elote *m.* corn on the cob

festividad de la cosecha *f.* harvest festival

gluglú *m.* (pavo) gobble

gluglutear *v.* to gobble

mazorca de maíz *f.* corn on the cob

nativo (-va) americano (-na) *m.f.* Native American

ñame *m.* yam

pastel de calabaza *m.* pumpkin pie

pavo *m.* turkey

peregrino *m.* pilgrim

relleno *m.* stuffing

salsa *f.* gravy

sobras *f.pl.* leftovers

tarta de calabaza *f.* pumpkin pie

DÍA DE LOS MUERTOS
m. Day of the Dead

altar *m.* altar

antepasado, -da *m.f.;* **ancestro** *m.* ancestor

calavera *f.,* **cráneo** *m.* skull; **c. de azucar** sugar skull

cementerio *m.* cemetery

cempasúchil *m.,* **caléndula** *f.* marigold

esqueleto *m.* skeleton

flor de muertos *f.* marigold

lápida *f.* tombstone

ofrendas *f.pl.* offerings

oración *f.* prayer

pantión *m.* cemetery

tumba *f.* grave

velas *f.pl.* candles

DÍA DE SAN PATRICIO
m. St. Patrick's Day

amuleto de buena suerte *m.* lucky charm

duende *m.* leprechaun

gaitas *f.pl.* bagpipes

Irlanda *f.* Ireland

irlandés, -esa *adj. & m.f.* Irish

olla de oro *f.* pot o' gold

piel de gallina *f.* goosebumps *pl.*

ponerse ropa de color verde *v.* to wear green

trébol *m.* shamrock; **t. de cuatro hojas** four-leaf clover

tres deseos *m.pl.* three wishes

JANUCÁ *f.* Chanukah

dreidel *m.* dreidel

guelt *m.* gelt

libertad religiosa *f.* religious freedom

Macabeos *m.pl.* Maccabees

menorá *f.,* **menora** *f.* menorah

sevivón *m.* dreidel

tortitas de papas *f.pl.* potato pancakes, latkes

vela *f.* candle; **v. auxiliar más alta** shamash

NAVIDAD *f.* Christmas

acebo *m.* holly

adornos *m.pl.* ornaments

aguinaldo *m.* Christmas music (Puerto Rico)

ángeles *m.pl.* angels

VIDA ESCOLAR

árbol de Navidad *m.* Christmas tree

bobadas *f.pl.* humbug

calceta de Navidad *f.,* **calcetín de Navidad** *m.* Christmas stocking

cascabeles *m.pl.* jingle bells

castaños *m.pl.* chestnuts

corona *f.* wreath

Día de Navidad *m.* Christmas Day; **D. de Reyes** Three Kings Day

elfos *m.* elves

espíritu navideño *m.* Christmas spirit

estrella de Belén *f.* Star of Bethlehem

flor de nochebuena *f.* poinsettia

Jack Frío *m.* Jack Frost

José *m.* Joseph

Las Posadas *f.pl.* Latino celebration of the Nativity

leño de Navidad *m.* Yule log

misa del gallo *f.* Midnight Mass

muérdago *m.* mistletoe

muñeco de nieve *m.* snowman

natividad *f.* nativity

Navidad *f.* Noel

Niño Jesús, el *m.* Baby Jesus

Noche de Reyes *f.* Twelfth Night

Nochebuena *f.* Christmas Eve

Padre Invierno *m.* Jack Frost

Papá Noel *m.* Santa Claus

parranda *f.* Christmas caroling (Puerto Rico)

pastorela *f.* nativity

pastores *m.pl.* shepherds

pesebre *m.* manger

ponche de huevo *m.* eggnog

ramo *m.* wreath

regalo de Navidad, regalo navideño *m.* Christmas present

renos *m.pl.* reindeer

rompope *m.* eggnog

San Nicolás *m.* St. Nick

tonterías *f.pl.* humbug

tres reyes magos *m.pl.* three wise men

trineo *m.* sleigh

tronco de Navidad *m.* Yule log

villancico *m.* Christmas carol

Virgen María, la *f.* Virgin Mary

NOCHE DE BRUJAS *f.*
Halloween

bruja *f.* witch

brujo *m.* wizard

calabaza *f.* pumpkin; **c. iluminada** jack-o'-lantern

caldero *m.* caldron

casa embrujada *f.* haunted house

demonio necrófago *m.* ghoul

diablo *m.* devil

disfraz *m.* costume

duende *m.* goblin

encanto *m.* spell

escoba voladora *f.* flying broomstick

espeluznante *adj.,* **escalofriante** *adj.* spooky

espíritu maligno *m.* ghoul

fantasma *m.* ghost

gato negro *m.* black cat

hechicero *m.* wizard

hechizar *v.* to cast a spell

hechizo *m.* spell

hombre lobo *m.,* **licántropo** *m.*

VIDA ESCOLAR

VIDA ESCOLAR

werewolf
mago *m.* wizard
máscara *f.* mask
momia *f.* mummy
monstruo *m.* monster
murciélago *m.* bat
películas de terror *f.pl.* scary movies
telaraña *f.* cobweb
truco o trato *m.* trick or treat
vampiro *m.* vampire
zombi *m.f.* zombie

OTRAS FIESTAS *f.pl.*
Other Holidays

Año Nuevo Chino *m.* Chinese New Year
Cinco de Mayo *m.* Fifth of May
Día de César Chávez *m.* Cesar Chavez Holiday; **D. de Colón** Columbus Day; **D. de Expiación** Yom Kipur; **D. de Independencia** Fourth of July; **D. de la Independencia de México** Mexican Independence Day; **D. de la**
Madre Mother's Day; **D. de la Raza** Columbus Day; **D. de los Caídos** Memorial Day; **D. de los Enamorados** Valentine's Day; **D. de los Presidentes** Presidents' Day; **D. de los Veteranos** Veterans Day; **D. de San Valentín** Valentine's Day; **D. del Padre** Father's Day; **D. del Trabajo** Labor Day; **D. Internacional de los Pueblos Indígenas** Indigenous Peoples' Day
El Grito de Lares *m.* Lares Rebellion
Iom Kipur *m.* Yom Kipur
Kwanzaa *f.* Kwanzaa
Natalicio de Lincoln *m.* Lincoln's Birthday; **N. de Martin Luther King** Martin Luther King's Birthday; **N. de Pulaski** Pulaski's Birthday; **N. de Washington** Washington's Birthday
Pascua *f.* Easter
Primero de Mayo *m.* May Day
Ramadán *m.* Ramadan

Rutinas y Actividades de la Escuela

A
alumno, -na *m.f.;* **ayudante** *m.f.* student aide
alzar la mano *v.* to raise your hand
anuario *m.* yearbook; **venta del a.** *f.* yearbook sale
asamblea *f.* assembly; **a. de pre-**
mios awards assembly; **horario de a.** *m.* assembly schedule
asistencia *f.* attendance
Asociación de Padres y Maestros *f.* Parent Teacher Association (P.T.A.)
auditorio *m.* auditorium
ausencia *f.* absence

B

baile de graduación *m.* senior prom; **b. escolar** school dance

banda de marcha *f.* marching band

bocadillo *m.* snack

boleta de calificaciones *f.* report card

boletín informativo *m.* newsletter

boleto de almuerzo *m.* lunch ticket

C

cafetería *f.* lunchroom

calificaciones *f.pl.* (puntuaciones) grades

campana *f.,* **campanilla** *f.* bell

casa abierta *f.* open house

centros de actividades *m.pl.* activity centers

ceremonia de graduación *f.* graduation ceremony

certificado de nacimiento *m.* birth certificate

club de ajedrez *m.* chess club; **c. de ciencias** science club; **c. de drama, c. de teatro** drama club; **c. de tecnología** technology club

Comité de Padres Bilingües *m.* Bilingual Parent Committee

concurso de talentos *m.* talent show

conferencia con los padres *f.* parent conference

consejero, -ra *m.f.* guidance counselor

Consejo de la Escuela *m.* School Site Council

consejo estudiantil *m.* student council

D

día de campo *m.* field day; **d. de fotografía** picture day; **d. para la formación del profesorado** teacher in-service day

director, -ora *m.f.* principal; **oficina del (de la) d.** *f.* principal's office

E

elecciones del gobierno estudiantil *f.pl.* student government elections

equipo de debate *m.* debate team

escuela de verano *f.* summer school

estudiantado *m.* student body

evaluaciones estatales *f.pl.* state achievement tests

exámen *m.* exam; **e. final** final exam; **e. parcial, e. de medio periodo** midterm exam

F

feria de ciencias *f.* science fair; **f. del libro** book fair

formulario de matrícula *m.* enrollment form

G

grado *m.* (nivel) grade

graduación *f.* graduation

grupo asesor estudiantil *m.* student advisory group

guardián, -ana *m.f.* guardian

VIDA ESCOLAR

VIDA ESCOLAR

H

hora de la siesta *f.* naptime; **h. del cuento** story time

horario de asamblea *m.* assembly schedule; **h. de día corto** short-ened-day schedule; **h. escolar** bell schedule

I

inscripción *f.* registration, enrollment

J

junta del consejo escolar *f.* school board meeting

juramento a la bandera *m.* pledge of allegiance

L

lavado de manos *m.* hand-washing

lavarse las manos *v.* to wash your hands

lectura en voz alta *f.* read-aloud; **l. silenciosa, l. en silencio** silent reading

leer en voz alta *v.* to read aloud

levantar la mano *v.* to raise your hand

lista de honor *f.* honor roll

M

mal tiempo *m.* inclement weather

matrícula *f.* registration

merienda *f.* snack

mochila *f.* backpack

mostrar y contar *v.* to show and tell

N

Noche de Familias *f.* Family Night

normas escolares *f.pl.* school rules

notas *f.pl.* (puntuaciones) grades

P

pase de pasillo *m.* hall pass

permiso *m.* permission; **hoja de p.** *f.* permission slip

periódico estudiantil *m.* student newspaper

pizarra *f.,* **pizarrón** *m.* blackboard, chalkboard; **p. blanca, p. blanco** white board

plan de estudios *m.,* **programa de estudios** *m.* curriculum

ponerse en fila *v.* to line up

primer semestre *m.* first semester

programa de recuperación *m.* remedial program

R

recreo *m.* recess

regreso al hogar *m.* homecoming

reunirse en grupos *v.* to form groups, gather in groups

rincón de lectura *m.* reading corner

S

salón principal *m.* homeroom

segundo semestre *m.* second semester

semana de espíritu escolar *f.* spirit week

simulacro de desastre *m.* disaster drill; **s. de incendio** fire drill

T

tablero blanco *m.* white board
tarea *f.* homework
tarjeta de informe *f.* report card
tiempo de cuentos *m.* story time; **t. de limpieza** cleanup time
toma de apuntes, toma de notas *f.* notetaking
tomar apuntes, tomar notas *v.* to take notes
torneo de geografía *m.* geography bee; **t. de ortografía** spelling bee

trabajar en parejas *v.* to work in pairs
tutor, -ra *m.f.* guardian
tutoría tutoring *f.;* **t. después de clases** after-school tutoring; **t. entre iguales** peer tutoring

V

vacaciones *f.pl.* holidays; **v. de invierno** winter vacation; **v. de primavera** spring break; **v. de verano** summer vacation

Excursiones y Transporte

A

acompañante *m.f.* chaperon
acuario *m.* aquarium
asientos asignados *m.pl.* assigned seats
asistir a una función *v.* to attend a performance
autobus *m.* bus; **a. escolar** school bus; **a. público** public bus; **parada del a.** *f.* bus stop; **pase gratis de a.** *m.* free bus pass; **rutas del a. escolar** *f.pl.* school bus routes
autorización *f.* permission slip

B

biblioteca pública *f.* public library
boletos de admisión *m.pl.* admission tickets
bolsa de almuerzo *f.* bag lunch

C

camioneta *f.* van
centro de tercera edad *m.* senior citizen's center
cinturón de seguridad *m.* seat belt
compañero, -ra *m.f.* buddy
concierto de música *m.* music concert
conducta en el autobús *f.* conduct on the bus
credencial de estudiante *f.,* **carnet de estudiante** *f.* student identification card
cumplir con todas las normas de seguridad *v.* to abide by all safety rules

CH

chaperón, -na *m.f.* chaperon

VIDA ESCOLAR

D

de la noche a la mañana *adv.*
overnight

E

entradas *f.pl.* admission tickets
espectáculo de danza *m.* dance
concert

F

fondo para gastos imprevistos *m.*
money for incidentals

G

granja *f.* farm
guagua *f.* bus

H

hora de llegada *f.* arrival time; **h.**
de salida departure time

J

jardín botánico *m.* botanical garden

L

lugar de entrega *m.* drop-off point;
l. de recogida pick-up location

M

mareo *m.* motion sickness
museo *m.* museum; **m. antropo-**
lógico anthropology museum; **m.**
de arte art museum; **m. de cien-**
cias science museum; **m. de his-**
toria natural museum of natural
history; **piezas de m.** *f.pl.* museum exhibits

O

objetos perdidos y encontrados
m.pl. lost and found
observatorio *m.* observatory

P

parada del autobús escolar *f.* bus
stop
pareja *f.* partner
parque *m.* park; **p. de atracciones**
amusement park
pase gratis de autobús *m.* free bus
pass
paso de peatones *m.* crosswalk
permiso firmado *m.* permission
slip
pernoctación *f.* overnight stay
planetario *m.* planetarium
punto de desembarque *m.* drop-
off point

R

rutas del autobús escolar *f.pl.*
school bus routes

T

tarifa del autobús *f.* bus fare
tarjeta de identificación del estu-
diante *f.* student identification
card
teatro para niños, teatro infantil
m. children's theater
transporte *m.* transportation

Z

zoológico *m.* zoo

Biblioteca de la Escuela

A
apoyalibros *m.pl.* bookends
atrasado, -da *adj.* overdue
audífonos *m.pl.* headphones
audiolibro *m.* audio book
autor *m.* author

B
bibliografía *f.* bibliography
biblioteca *m.* library; **carnet de b.** *m.* library card; **horario de la b.** *m.* library hours *pl.*
bibliotecaria *f.* librarian
buscar en el catálogo *v.* to search the catalog
búsqueda en el catálogo *f.* catalog search; **b. por palabra clave** keyword search

C
carrito de libros *m.,* **cesta de libros** *f.* book cart
catálogo *m.* catalog; **c. de fichas** card catalog; **c. en línea** online catalog; **número de c.** *m.* call number
ciencia ficción *f.* science fiction
código de barra *m.* bar code
cuarto de estudio *m.* study room
cubículo *m.* cubicle

D
diario *m.* journal

E
enciclopedia *f.* encyclopedia
encuadernación dura *f.* hardback
estantes *m.pl.,* **estanterías** *f.pl.* bookshelves

F
fecha *f.* date; **f. de propiedad literaria** copyright date; **f. de vencimiento, f. de caducidad** due date
ficción *adj. & f.* fiction
fichero *m.* card catalog
folletos *m.pl.* pamphlets
fotocopiadora *f.* photocopier

H
hoja de presentación *f.* title page
hojear *v.* to browse
horario de la biblioteca *m.* library hours *pl.*

I
ilustración *f.* illustration
ilustrador *m.* illustrator
impresiones artísticas *f.pl.* art prints
índice *m.* index
investigación *f.* research

L
laminador *m.* laminator
librero *m.* bookcase
libro *m.* book; **l. de tapa dura** hard-

VIDA ESCOLAR

back; **l. de tapa flexible, l. en rústica** paperback; **l. electrónico** e-book; **lomo del l.** *m.* book spine; **sobrecubierta del l.** *f.,* **forro del l.** *m.* book jacket
lomo *m.* (libro) spine

M

mapas *m.pl.* maps
marcador *m.* book mark
materiales de referencia, materiales de consulta *m.pl.* reference materials; **m. digitales** digital materials

N

no ficción *adj. & f.* nonfiction
novelas para jóvenes, novelas juveniles *f.pl.* young adult novels
número de catálogo *m.* call number

O

orden alfabético *m.* alphabetical order

P

palabra clave *f.* keyword
periódico *m.* newspaper
publicación periódica *f.* periodical

R

revista *f.* magazine, journal

S

sacar libros *v.* to check out books
sala de estudio *f.* study room
señalador *m.* book mark
sistema decimal de Dewey *m.* Dewey decimal system
sobrecubierta del libro *f.* book jacket
soportalibros *m.pl.,* **sujetalibros** *m.pl.* bookends
sujeto *m.* subject

T

tarjeta de la biblioteca *f.* library card
título *m.* title; **página de t.** *f.* title page

Actividades de Recreo y Deportes

A

abdominales *m.pl.* sit-ups
aeróbico *m.* aerobics
agachar la cabeza *v.* to duck
alternarse *v.* to take turns
anotar *v.,* **apuntar** *v.* to score
árbitro *m.* referee

arenero *m.* sandbox
atletismo *m.* athletics
atrapar *v.* to catch

B

balancín *m.* teeter-totter, seesaw
balón prisionero *m.* dodgeball

baloncesto *m.* basketball
banco *m.* bench
barras de mono *f.pl.* monkey bars
bate *m.* bat
béisbol *m.* baseball
bloquear *v.* to block
botar *v.* to bounce
boxeo *m.* boxing

C

caja de arena *f.* sandbox
calistenia *f.* calisthenics *pl.*
campeonato *m.* championship
campeones *m.pl.* champions
cancha *f.* court
carrera *f.* race, (béisbol) run; **c. de
   relevos** relay race
casillero *m.* locker
clavado *m.* dive
columpiarse *v.* to swing
columpio *m.* swing
comba *f.,* **cuerda de saltar** *f.* jump
   rope
compañeros, -ras *m.f.pl.* teammates
competencia *f.* competition
correr *v.* to run; **c. a toda velocidad**
   to sprint
cuenta *f.* score

CH

chutar *v.* to shoot

D

dar a la pelota *v.* to swing at the ball
deporte de contacto *m.* contact
   sport
deportividad *f.* sportsmanship

deslizarse *v.* to slide
dominadas *f.pl.* chin-ups
driblar *v.* dribble

E

ejercicio *m.* exercise; **e. anaeróbico**
   anaerobic exercise; **e. cardiovascular** cardiovascular exercise
eliminación *f.* out
eliminado, -da *adj.* out
elongación *f.* stretching
empatar *v.* to tie
empate *m.* (juego) tie
engañar *v.* to cheat
engaño *m.* cheating
entrenador, -ora *m.f.* coach
entrenar *v.* to coach
equipo *m.* team
escalar *v.* to climb
escondite *m.* hide-and-seek
espíritu deportivo *m.* sportsmanship
espiro *m.* tetherball
esprintar *v.* to sprint
esquivar *v.* to dodge
estirar *v.* to stretch

F

falta *f.* foul
flexiones *f.pl.* push-ups
fuera *adv.* out; **f. de los límites** out
   of bounds
fútbol *m.* soccer; **f. americano** football

G

gimnasio *m.* gymnasium

VIDA ESCOLAR

VIDA ESCOLAR

gimnástica *f.,* **gimnasia** *f.* gymnastics

girar *v.* to spin

gol *m.* goal

golpear *v.* to hit

J

juego *m.* game; **j. de cuatro cuadros** four-square; **j. de los encantados** freeze tag

jugadores, -ras *m.f.pl.* players

jugar *v.* to play

K

kickbol *m.* kickball

L

lanzar *v.* to throw

levantamiento de pesas *m.* weight lifting

lucha *f.* wrestling

M

marcador *m.* scoreboard

marcar *v.* to score

N

nadar *v.* to swim

natación *f.* swimming

O

Olimpiadas Especiales *f.pl.* Special Olympics

P

parada de manos *f.* handstand

partido *m.* match

pasar *v.* to pass

patear *v.* to kick

patio de recreo *m.* playground

pega *f.* (juego) tag

pegar *v.* to hit

pelota *f.* ball

pídola *f.* leapfrog

pista de baloncesto *f.* basketball court; **p. de tenis** tennis court

pruebas de atletismo *f.pl.* track and field events

puntaje *m.* score

R

rayuela *f.* hopscotch

rebotar *v.* to bounce

rebote *m.* rebound

red *f.* net

regatear *v.* to dribble

reglas *f.pl.* rules

resbaladero *m.* slide

resbalar *v.* to slide

resultado *m.* score

rivalidad *f.* competition

S

saltar *v.* to jump

salto *m.* jump; **s. de paloma** handspring; **s. mortal** somersault

softbol *m.* softball

subcampeón, -na *m.f.* runner-up

subibaja *m.* teeter-totter, seesaw

subir *v.* to climb

substitución *f.* substitution

T

tanteador *m.* scorekeeper

taquilla *f.* locker
tejo *m.* hopscotch
tenis *m.* tennis
tetherball *m.* tetherball
tiempo muerto *m.* time out; **solicitar un t. m.** *v.* to call a time out
tirar *v.* to shoot, throw
tobogán *m.* slide
tomar partido *v.* to pick sides; **t. un descanso** to take a time out
torcer *v.*, **torcerse** *v.* to twist
trampa *f.* cheating; **hacer t.** *v.* to

cheat
trepar *v.* to climb
turnarse *v.* to take turns

V

vestuario *m.*, **vestidores** *m.pl.* locker room
voleibol *m.* volleyball
voltear *v.* to turn
voltereta *f.* somersault; **v. sobre manos** handspring

Salud Estudiantil

A

absceso *m.* abscess
abuso sexual *m.* sexual abuse
acidez *f.*, **ardor de estómago** *m.* heartburn
adicción *f.* addiction
agotamiento *m.* exhaustion
alergia *f.* allergy
amigdalitis *f.* tonsillitis
ampolla *f.* blister
anemia *f.* anemia
anomalía congénita *f.* birth defect
anorexia *f.* anorexia
anquilostoma *m.* hookworm
ansiedad *f.* anxiety
anteojos *m.pl.* glasses
antihigiénico, -ca *adj.* unsanitary
aparato auditivo *m.* hearing aid
apendicitis *f.* appendicitis

arañazo *m.* scratch
asma *f.* asthma
astilla *f.* sliver, splinter

B

bajón de azúcar *m.* low blood sugar, hypoglycemia
bienestar físico *m.* wellness; **b. infantil** child welfare
bizco, -ca *adj.* cross-eyed
bronquitis *m.* bronchitis
bulimia *f.* bulimia

C

calambres *m.pl.* cramps
calentura *f.* fever
cáncer *m.* cancer
cansancio *m.* fatigue
casa de acogida *f.* foster home
caso grave *m.* severe case

catarro *m.* cold; **coger un c.** *v.* to catch cold

cavidad *f.* cavity

cepillado dental *m.* tooth-brushing

cicatriz *f.* scar

coágulo *m.* blood clot

cojear *v.* to limp

cojera *f.* limp

comezón *f.* itch

complicaciones *f.pl.* complications

compresa *f.* sanitary napkin

concusión *f.,* **conmoción cerebral** *f.* concussion

condones *m.pl.* condoms

confidencialidad *f.* confidentiality

congelación *f.* frostbite

conjuntivitis *f.* conjunctivitis, pink-eye

contagioso, -sa *adj.* contagious

contusión *f.* bruise

convulsiones *f.pl.* seizures, convulsions

cortadura *f.* cut

cosquilleo *m.* tingling sensation

costra *f.* scab

crónico, -ca *adj.* chronic; **condición c.** *f.* chronic condition; **enfermedad c.** *f.* chronic illness

cuchillada *f.* gash

cuerpo extraño *m.* foreign body

CH

chequeo de salud *m.* check-up

chichón *m.* knot on the head

chocar contra *v.* to bump against

choque *m.* shock

D

daltonismo *m.* color blindness

daño *m.* injury; **hacer d.** *v.* to hurt

defecto de nacimiento *m.* birth defect

depresión *f.* depression

deprimido, -da *adj.* depressed

desmayado, -da *adj.* unconscious

desmayarse *v.* to faint

desnutrido, -da *adj.* malnourished

diabetes *m.* diabetes

diarrea *f.* diarrhea

dieta *f.* diet

digestión *f.* digestion

discapacidad *f.* disability; **d. física** physical disability; **d. temporal** temporary disability

discapacitado, -da *adj.* disabled

dislexia *f.* dyslexia

doler *v.* to hurt

dolor *m.* pain; **d. abdominal** abdominal pain; **d. agudo** acute pain; **d. de cabeza** headache; **d. de espalda** backache; **d. de estómago** stomach ache; **d. de garganta** sore throat; **d. de los muelas** toothache; **d. de oído** earache

dolorido, -da *adj.* sore

dosis *m.* dose

drogas *f.pl.* (ilegal) drugs; **estar bajo la influencia de d.** *v.* to be under the influence of drugs

E

embarazada *adj.* pregnant

encías *f.pl.* gums

enfermedad *f.* disease, illness; **e. contagiosa, e. transmissible** communicable disease; **e. crónica** chronic illness; **e. venérea** venereal disease; **propagación de la e.** *f.* spread of disease

enfermera de la escuela *f.* school nurse

enjuague bucal *m.* mouthwash

entumecimiento *m.* numbness

epidemia *f.* epidemic

epilepsia *f.* epilepsy

erupción de la piel *f.* rash

escalofríos *m.pl.* chills

escoliosis *f.* scoliosis

esguince *m.* sprain

espasmo *m.* spasm

estevado, -da *adj.* bowlegged

estornudo *m.* sneeze

estreñimiento *m.* constipation

estrés *m.* stress

evacuación intestinal *f.* bowel movement

examen médico *m.* physical examination

expedientes médicos *m.pl.* medical records

F

falta de aliento *adj.* short of breath, breathless

faringitis estreptocócica *f.* strep throat

fatiga ocular *f.* eyestrain

fiebre *f.* fever; **f. del heno** hay fever; **f. tifoidea** typhoid fever

flatulencia *f.* flatulence

fractura *f.* fracture; **f. de pierna** broken leg

frenillos *m.pl.* braces

furúnculo *m.* boil

G

gafas *f.pl.* glasses

gases *m.pl.* flatulence

glándulas inflamadas *f.pl.* enlarged glands

golpe *m.* bump

grano *m.* pimple; **g. enterrado** boil

gripe *f.*, **gripa** *f.* flu, influenza

H

halitosis *f.* halitosis, bad breath

hematoma *m.* bruise

hemorragia *f.* hemorrhage, bleeding

hepatitis *f.* hepatitis

herida *f.* injury, wound; **h. profunda** gash; **h. superficial** flesh wound

hernia *f.* hernia

herpes *m.* herpes

hiedra venenosa *f.* poison ivy

hilo dental *m.* dental floss

hinchado, -da *adj.* swollen

hinchazón *f.* swelling

hipertensión arterial *f.* high blood pressure

hipoglucemia *f.* low blood sugar, hypoglycemia

historia clínica *f.*, **historial médico** *m.* health history, medical record

hormigueo *m.* tingling sensation

hueso *m.* bone; **h. roto, h. fracturado** broken bone

VIDA ESCOLAR

VIDA ESCOLAR

I

inapetencia *f.* lack of appetite
incomodidad *f.* discomfort
inconsciente *adj.* unconscious
indigestión *f.* indigestion
infección *f.* infection
inflamación *f.* inflammation
influenza *f.* flu, influenza
inmunización *f.* immunization
insalubre *adj.* unsanitary
insensibilidad *f.* numbness
insolación *f.* sunstroke
intoxicación alimentaria *f.* food poisoning
irritación *f.* irritation
irritado, -da *adj.* sore

L

laringitis *f.* laryngitis
lastimar *v.* to hurt oneself
latir *v.* to throb
lentes *m.pl.* glasses; **l. de contacto** contact lenses
lesión *f.* lesion, injury
lombrices intestinales *f.pl.* intestinal worms
lunar *m.* birthmark, mole

LL

llaga *f.* sore; **ll. en la piel** skin sore

M

mal aliento *m.* bad breath, halitosis
malnutrido, -da *adj.* malnourished
mareado, -da *adj.* dizzy
mareo *m.* dizziness
medicación *f.* medication

medicina *f.* medicine
médico, -ca *adj.* medical
médico, -ca *m.f.* doctor
membrana timpánica *f.* eardrum, timpanic membrane
menstruación *f.* menstruation
migraña *f.* migraine
miope *adj.* nearsighted
miopía *f.* nearsightedness
moqueo *m.* runny nose
mordedura de serpiente *f.* snakebite
mordisco *m.* bite
moretón *m.* bruise

N

nariz mocosa *f.* runny nose
náusea *f.*, **náuseas** *f.pl.* nausea
neumonía *f.* pneumonia

O

obeso, -sa *adj.* obese
oído *m.* ear; **o. interno** inner ear
oreja *f.* outer ear
orina *f.* urine
orinar *v.* to urinate
orzuelo *m.* sty

P

pabellón auditivo *m.* outer ear
pálido, -da *adj.* pale
palpitar *v.* to throb
paperas *f.pl.* mumps
párpado *m.* eyelid
periodo, periodo menstrual *m.* menstrual period; **p. de incubación** incubation period

● ●

picada *f.,* **picadura** *f.* (insecto) bite, sting; **p. de abeja** bee sting; **p. de avispa** wasp sting

picazón *f.* itch

pie *m.* foot; **p. de atleta** athlete's foot; **p. zambo, p. equinovaro** club foot

pierna quebrada, pierna rota *f.* broken leg

píldoras *f.pl.* pills; **p. anticonceptivas** birth control pills

piojos *m.pl.* head lice

presión arterial *f.* blood pressure; **p. alta** high blood pressure

problemas respiratorios *m.pl.* breathing difficulties

procedimientos de seguridad *m.pl.* safety procedures

pulmonía *f.* pneumonia

pulso *m.* pulse; **tomarse el p.** *v.* to take your pulse

pus *m.* pus

Q

quebradura *f.* fracture

quemadura *f.* burn; **q. del sol** sunburn

quiste *m.* cyst

R

rascar *v.* to scratch

rasguño *m.* scratch

recaída *f.* relapse

reconocimiento médico *m.* checkup

regla, la *f.* menstrual period

remisión a un especialista *f.* referral to a specialist

resfriado *m.* cold; **pescar un r.** *v.* to catch cold

restricciones físicas *f.pl.* physical restrictions

ronchas *f.pl.* hives, swelling

ronquera *f.* hoarseness

rubéola *f.* rubella, German measles

ruptura *f.* rupture, hernia

S

sangramiento *m.* bleeding

sangrante *adj.* bleeding

sano, -na *adj.;* **saludable** *adj.* healthy

sarampión *m.* measles

sarpullido *m.* rash

secreción nasal *f.* runny nose

SIDA *m.* AIDS

síndrome de Down *m.* Down's Syndrome

síntomas *f.pl.* symptoms

sobredosis *f.* overdose

sobrepeso *adj. & m.* overweight

soñoliento, -ta *adj.* drowsy

soplo cardíaco *m.* heart murmur

sudoroso, -sa *adj.* sweaty

suicidio *m.* suicide

T

tarjeta de información médica *f.* medical information card

tartamudear *v.* to stutter, stammer

tartamudeo *m.* stuttering

tartamudo, -da *m.f.* stutterer

temperatura *f.* temperature

tensión arterial *f.* blood pressure

VIDA ESCOLAR

VIDA ESCOLAR

tétano *m.* tetanus

tímpano *m.* eardrum

tiña *f.* ringworm

toalla femenina *f.* sanitary napkin

tomar por vía oral, tomar oral-mente *v.* to take orally

torcedura *f.* sprain

tos *f.* cough; **t. ferina** whooping cough

tratamiento médico *m.* medical treatment

trauma *m.* trauma

tumor *m.* tumor

U

úlcera *f.* sore; **ú. en la piel** skin sore

urticaria *f.* hives

V

vacuna *f.* vaccine; **formulario de exención de vacunas** *m.* vaccine exemption form

vacunación *f.* vaccination

vacunar *v.* to vaccinate

varicela *f.* chicken pox

verdugones *m.pl.* welts

vértigo *m.* dizziness

verruga *f.* wart, mole

V.I.H. *m.* H.I.V.

viruela *f.* smallpox

virus *m.* virus

vista fatigada *f.* eyestrain

vomitar *v.* to vomit

Necesidades Especiales

A

acomodaciones *f.pl.* accommodations

acoso *m.* bullying

Acta para la Educación de Individuos con Discapacidades *f.* Individuals with Disabilities Education Act (I.D.E.A.); **A. para los Norteamericanos con Discapacidades** Americans with Disabilities Act (A.D.A.)

alojamientos *m.pl.* accommodations

ambiente menos restrictivo *m.* least restrictive environment

apoyos positivos de la conducta *m.pl.* positive behavioral supports

apropiado, -da *adj.* appropriate

aptitud *f.* aptitude

arrebato *m.,* **arranque** *m.* outburst

asesoramiento *m.* counseling

audiencia *f.* hearing; **a. del proceso legal debido** due process hearing; **a. imparcial** impartial hearing

autocontrol *m.* self-control

autodisciplina *f.* self-discipline

C

cambios de humor *m.pl.* mood swings

capacidad *f.* capacity; **c. de atención** attention span

ceguera *f.* blindness

ciego, -ga *adj.* blind

clases particulares *f.pl.* tutoring

cognitivamente atrasado (-da) *adj.* cognitively delayed

cognitivo, -va *adj.* cognitive

colocación *f.* placement

consejero (-ra) escolar *m.f.* school counselor

consentimiento *m.* consent

coordinador (-ora) del caso *m.f.* case manager

creatividad *f.* creativity

custodia *f.* guardianship

D

debilidad *f.* weakness

defensor, -ra *m.f.* advocate

deformidad *f.* deformity

desatención *f.* inattention

destreza *f.* dexterity

discapacidad *f.* disability; **d. del desarrollo** developmental disability; **d. en el aprendizaje** learning disability (L.D.); **d. intelectual** intellectual disability; **d. múltiples** *pl.* multiple disabilities

discapacitado, -da *adj.* handicapped; **d. intelectual educable** educable mentally handicapped (E.M.H.)

discriminación auditiva *f.* auditory discrimination

diseño universal *m.* universal design

dotado (-da) y talentoso (-sa) *adj.* gifted and talented

E

edad *f.* age; **e. cronológica** chronological age; **e. mental** mental age; **equivalente a la e.** *adj.* age equivalent

educación especial *f.* special education

elegibilidad *f.* eligibility

equipo del I.E.P. *m.* IEP team

evaluación *f.* assessment, evaluation; **e. independiente** independent evaluation

examen de selección *m.* screening test

expectativas de nivel de grado *f.pl.* grade-level expectations

explosión de cólera *f.* outburst

F

falta de atención *f.* inattention

fortaleza *f.,* **fuerza** *f.* strength

funcionamiento motor y sensorial *m.* motor sensory function

G

garantías procesales *f.pl.* procedural safeguards

H

habilidades motrices finas *f.pl.* fine motor skills; **h. m. gruesas** gross motor skills

hiperactividad *f.* hyperactivity

VIDA ESCOLAR

VIDA ESCOLAR

I

impedido, -da *adj.* handicapped

impedimento visual *m.* visual impairment; **i. auditivo** hearing impairment; **i. ortopédico** orthopedic impairment

impropio, -pia *adj.;* **inadecuado, -da** *adj.* inappropriate

incapacidad *f.* disability

inclusión *f.* inclusion

inglés como segunda idioma *m.* English as a Second Language

inhabilidad *f.* disability

intervención *f.* intervention; **i. temprana** early intervention

intimidación *f.* bullying

L

lectura de los labios *f.* lip reading

lenguaje *m.* language; **l. expresivo** expressive language; **l. receptivo** receptive language

Lenguaje Americano de Señas *m.* American Sign Language (A.S.L.)

lesión cerebral traumática *f.* traumatic brain injury

logopedia *f.* speech therapy

M

modificaciones *f.pl.* modifications

monitoreo *m.* monitoring; **m. del progreso** progress monitoring

motricidad fina *f.* fine motor skills; **m. gruesa** gross motor skills

multisensorial *adj.* multisensory

muy creativo (-va) *adj.* highly creative

N

neurológico, -ca *adj.* neurological

neurosis *f.* neurosis

P

parálisis cerebral *f.* cerebral palsy

paraprofesional *m.f.* paraprofessional

período de atención *m.* attention span

Programa de Educación Individualizada *m.* Individualized Education Program (I.E.P.)

promoción social *f.* social promotion

psicológico, -ca *adj.* psychological

psicólogo, -ga *m.f.* psychologist

R

reevaluación *f.* reassessment

remisión *f.* referral

Respuesta a la Intervención *f.* Response to Intervention (R.T.I.)

retraso del desarrollo *m.* developmental delay

revisión anual *f.* annual review

revocación del consentimiento *f.* revocation of consent

S

salón autocontenido *m.* self-contained classroom

seguimiento *m.* progress monitoring

servicios *m.pl.* services; **s. de consejería** counseling services; **s. de intérprete** interpreter services; **s.**

de orientación y movilidad orientation and mobility services

sicológico, -ca *adj.* psychological

sicólogo, -ga *m.f.* psychologist

síndrome *m.* syndrome; **s. de alcoholismo fetal** fetal alcohol syndrome; **s. de Asperger** Asperger's syndrome

sordera *f.* deafness

sordo, -da *adj.* deaf

sordoceguera *f.* deaf-blindness

T

tecnología de apoyo *f.* assistive technology

terapia *f.* therapy; **t. del habla** speech therapy; **t. física** physical therapy (P.T.); **t. ocupacional** occupational therapy

trastorno *m.* disorder; **t. de la conducta** behavior disorder; **t. del espectro del autismo** autism spectrum disorder; **t. del habla** speech impairment; **t. del lenguaje** language impairment; **t. emocional** emotional disturbance; **t. por déficit de atención** attention deficit disorder (A.D.D.); **t. por déficit de atención e hiperactividad** attention deficit hyperactivity disorder (A.D.H.D.); **t. visual** visual impairments

tutela *f.* guardianship

tutoría *f.* tutoring

Conducta y Disciplina

A

absentismo escolar *m.* truancy

acosar *v.* to bully

acoso *m.* harassment

acusar *v.* to charge

advertencia *f.* warning

amenazar *v.* to threaten

apelar *v.* to appeal

arma *f.* weapon

arrestar *v.* to arrest

arresto *m.* arrest

asaltar *v.* to assault

asalto *m.* assault

atestación *f.* testimony

audiencia *f.* hearing

ausencias *f.pl.* absences; **a. excesivas** excessive absences; **a. sin excusa** unexcused absences

B

burlar *v.* to taunt

C

carga de la prueba *f.* burden of proof

cargo *m.* charge

castigar *v.* to punish

VIDA ESCOLAR

castigo *m.* punishment, penalty
cómplice *m.f.* accomplice
comportamiento violento *m.* violent behavior
confesión *f.* confession
confiscar *v.* to confiscate
contestar con insolencia *v.* to talk back
contradecir *v.* to contradict
copiar *v.* to cheat
copión, -na *m.f.* cheater
cortaplumas *m.* pocketknife
custodia *f.* custody

D

declaración *f.* testimony
delito *m.* wrongdoing
desconfianza *f.* suspicion
destrozar *v.* to vandalize
detención *f.* arrest, detention; **d. después de clases** after-school detention
disciplina progresiva *f.* progressive discipline

E

entrar ilegalmente *v.* to trespass
escupir *v.* to spit
evidencia *f.* evidence
expulsión *f.* expulsion

F

falsificación *f.* forgery
fumar *m.* smoking
fumar *v.* to smoke

G

grafiti *m.pl.* graffiti
grosería *f.* obscenity, vulgarity

I

indecencia *f.* obscenity
infracción *f.* infraction, wrongdoing
insubordinación *f.* insubordination
insultante *adj.* insulting
intimidador, -ra *m.f.* bully
intimidar *v.* to bully
invadir *v.* to trespass

J

juego rudo *m.* horseplay

L

libertad condicional *f.* probation

M

mala conducta *f.* misconduct
matón, -na *m.f.* bully
mentiroso, -sa *m.f.* liar

N

narcótico *m.* narcotic
navaja *f.* pocketknife

O

obscenidad *f.* obscenity
ofensivo, -va *adj.* insulting

P

parafernalia de drogas *f.* drug paraphernalia
payasadas *f.pl.* horseplay

• •

pelea a puñetazos *f.* fistfight

peleonero, -na *m.f.* bully

pena *f.* penalty

permiso de los padres *m.* parental permission

perturbador *m.* troublemaker

política de tolerencia cero *f.* zero tolerance policy

prueba *f.* evidence

R

registro *m.* search

renuncia de derechos *f.* waiver of rights

replicar *v.* to talk back

retirarse de la escuela *v.* to withdraw from school

revoltoso, -sa *adj.* rowdy

robar *v.* to steal

robo *m.* theft

S

sanción *f.* penalty

seguridad *f.* safety, security

separarse de la escuela *v.* to withdraw from school

signos de pandilla *m.pl.,* **señales de pandillas** *f.pl.* gang signs

sospecha *f.* suspicion

sospechoso, -sa *m.f.* suspect

suspensión *f.* suspension

T

tardanza *f.* tardiness

tatuaje *m.* tattoo

testigo *m.* witness

trampa *f.* cheating; **hacer t.** *v.* to cheat

tramposo, -sa *m.f.* cheater

transferir *v.* to transfer

traspasar *v.* to trespass

V

víctima *m.f.* victim

violación *f.* violation, infraction

vulgaridad *f.* vulgarity

VIDA ESCOLAR

405

About the Editors

SHARON ADELMAN REYES, PH.D., has worked in education for more than thirty years as a teacher, principal, school district administrator, curriculum specialist, researcher, and university professor with extensive experience in bilingual and E.S.L. classrooms. She is author of *Engage the Creative Arts: A Framework for Sheltering and Scaffolding Instruction for English Language Learners* and coauthor of *Diary of a Bilingual School; Teaching in Two Languages: A Guide for K–12 Bilingual Educators;* and *Constructivist Strategies for Teaching English Language Learners.* Currently she serves as Program Director of DIVERSITYLEARNINGK12.

SALVADOR GABALDON, M.A., Director of Culturally Responsive Pedagogy for the Tucson Unified School District, specializes in E.S.L. and bilingual program development, language proficiency assessment, and multicultural education. He formerly taught high school English in Los Angeles and served as English Department Chair at Pueblo High School in Tucson. He recently coauthored "Legacy of Memory: The Debate over Ethnic Studies in Arizona Public Schools," in *Aztlán: A Journal of Chicano Studies.*

MSc. JOSÉ SEVERO MOREJÓN, Professor of English at La Universidad de Ciencias Pedagógicas "Rafael María de Mendive" in Pinar del Río, Cuba, prepares future teachers of English. In his country, he has been influential in popularizing the Interactive Approach (also known as the Communicative Approach) in language teaching and in the humanities generally. He is also co-scriptwriter of *Rainbow,* a program in the *Navegante* software series developed for the teaching of English in secondary schools throughout Cuba.

Suggestions?

Living languages are constantly evolving. In compiling this glossary, we aimed to feature the most common forms of Spanish and English now in popular usage. But *La Palabra Justa* is far from *la última palabra.* Given the rapidity of linguistic change, we expect to update this volume frequently. And we would appreciate your help. If you spot errors that need correcting or additional terms or translations that should be added, please email us at:

glossary@diversitylearningk12.com

Also Available from DiversityLearningK12 ...

DIARY OF A
BILINGUAL SCHOOL

Sharon Adelman Reyes
& James Crawford

© 2012 • 136 pp • 6" x 9"
ISBN: 978-0-9847317-0-1
Paperback: $19.95 • Kindle: $4.99
info@diversitylearningk12.com

"A must read for parents and teachers who value bilingualism, biculturalism, and positive identity construction for their children. Highly recommended."
— *Choice*

"Refreshing and inspiring ... If you are interested in learning how educators and parents can promote language acquisition, creating inventors who think creatively and (gasp!) even achieve excellent results on academic tests, this is the book for you."
— *Creative Educator*

DUAL IMMERSION, a popular new way to cultivate bilingualism, is capturing the attention of parents and educators alike. By bringing together children from diverse backgrounds to learn each other's languages in a natural setting, it has proved far more effective at cultivating fluency than traditional approaches.

But how do these programs actually work? What goes on in dual immersion classrooms? And what is it that makes them so effective?

Diary of a Bilingual School answers these questions with a unique mix of narratives and analysis. Depicting a year in the life of a 2nd grade classroom, it demonstrates what can happen when the instruction is bilingual and the curriculum is constructivist.

The book focuses on Chicago's Inter-American Magnet School, one of the nation's most acclaimed dual immersion programs, where children thrive in an environment that unlocks their intellectual curiosity and enthusiasm for learning. Simultaneously, without conscious effort, they become proficient in two languages and at home in a culture that differs from their own.

For those who want to discover the benefits of dual immersion for their children or for their students—or who want to learn more about child-centered approaches to teaching—*Diary of a Bilingual School* is a must.

ENGAGE
The Creative Arts

*A Framework for
Sheltering and Scaffolding Instruction
for English Language Learners*

BY
SHARON ADELMAN REYES

© 2013 • 152 pp • 8½" x 11"
$26.95
ISBN: 978-0-9847317-3-2
info@diversitylearningk12.com

Also Available from DiversityLearningK12 ...

"With **Engage the Creative Arts,** we are entering a new era in language instruction. This book vastly expands the options for providing second language students with what they really need: input that is both comprehensible and highly interesting, so interesting that students forget it is in another language. It is sure to make teaching second languages not only much more pleasant than current approaches, but also much more effective."

— *Stephen Krashen, Professor Emeritus, University of Southern California*

MEETING THE NEEDS OF ENGLISH LANGUAGE LEARNERS is one of the biggest challenges facing American schools today. Practical classroom strategies are essential. But it is also critical for educators to understand the rationale behind them: why a technique or methodology is working or not working for their students. **Engage the Creative Arts** is designed to build that understanding while also stimulating teachers' imagination to help them invent new strategies of their own.

The book introduces the **ENGAGE Framework for Sheltering and Scaffolding Language the Natural Way,** an approach developed by Sharon Adelman Reyes based on more than thirty years of experience working with English language learners. It emphasizes methodologies that are grounded in a constructivist educational philosophy and a comprehensive theory of language acquisition. Rather than prescriptive, step-by-step recipes for instruction, it features strategies that are open-ended, creative, and best of all, engaging for students.

Engage the Creative Arts is full of hands-on, ready-to-use activities in dramatic arts, creative writing, music and rhythm, dance and movement, and visual arts, along with ideas for developing many more. But the ENGAGE Framework can be applied to any academic content area. And the strategies in this book are designed for all teachers who work with second language learners, whether in bilingual, English as a second language, dual immersion, heritage language, or world language classrooms.

About DiversityLearningK12

Specializing in bilingual, E.S.L., and multicultural education, DiversityLearningK12 is a consulting group that provides professional development, keynote presentations, program design, educational publishing, and related services. For more information, please visit us at www.diversitylearningk12.com or email us at info@diversitylearningk12.com.